On the Front Lines of the Cold War:

Documents on the Intelligence War in Berlin, 1946 to 1961

Edited by Donald P. Steury

Center *for the* Study *of* Intelligence
Washington, DC 20505

CIA History Staff
1999

Contents

IV: Alltagsgeschichte: Day to Day in the Intelligence War   229

The editor of this volume has been given free access to official documents. He alone is responsible for the statements made and the views expressed.

Photo credit: The photo used at the start of Section V: The Berlin Tunnel and on the lower right of the back cover courtesy of W. Durie, Riehlstrasse 18, 14057 Berlin, Germany. Photo may not be reproduced without express written consent of the photographer.

Preface

In the summer of 1945 the Allied powers—the United States, Great Britain, France, and the Soviet Union—began what was to be a temporary, joint occupation of the city of Berlin. Despite an optimistic beginning, by 1948 Cold War pressures had created two separate cities, East Berlin and West Berlin. In 1948 the Soviet Union blockaded Berlin, cutting off deliveries of coal, food, and supplies. The Soviets declared the Western powers no longer had any rights in the administration of the city. The Western Allies responded with the Berlin airlift, in which Allied air crews flew 4,000 tons of supplies a day into the city. In May 1949 the blockade came to an end as the Soviets permitted the Western Allies to resupply Berlin by land. Berlin, however, was to remain a divided city with two governments until the end of the Cold War.

The divided city became a distinctive feature of the harsh political land-scape in post-World War II Europe. For the next forty-four years, Berlin played an enduring symbolic, and at times very real, Cold War role. The city, especially during the crucial early years, stood literally on the front lines of the Cold War. It was the recurrent focus of East-West confrontation. The division of Berlin also made it a focal point for high-level intelligence operations, espionage, exchanges of spies, and general international con-frontation.

In November 1958 a second Berlin crisis flared when Premier Nikita Khrushchev announced that the Soviet Union intended to turn over its responsibilities in Berlin to the East German government. Although Khrushchev did not carry out this threat, tensions remained high for several years. With East Germans fleeing to the West in record numbers in August 1961, the government of East Germany sealed the border by building the Berlin Wall. On 27 October 1961 U.S. and Soviet tanks faced off at Check-point Charlie in the center of Berlin. In retrospect, the construction of the wall marked the end of the sharpest confrontations in the city.

Berlin continued, however, as a potential flash point in the Cold War until the collapse of the Soviet Union and the reunification of Germany in 1991. During all of this time, an intelligence war raged in the city. Especially in the early period, 1945-1961, both sides mounted major intelligence opera-tions and sought intelligence advantages in Berlin.

The end of the Cold War has produced a window of opportunity for studying the intelligence dimensions of Berlin's role during this crisis period. The release of limited but significant documentary materials from both sides of the Iron Curtain now makes a scholarly discussion of intelligence activities in Berlin possible. The documents compiled in this volume by CIA historian Donald Steury add clarification to this intense conflict. Dr. Steury selected his material carefully to illustrate as fully as possible US intelligence activities in the city. The documents cover various aspects of the intelligence war, from operational field intelligence memoranda to National Intelligence Estimates produced in Washington. Taken together, they represent a detailed picture of a side of the Cold War long withheld from the general public. Dr. Steury also offers an interpretative introduction and editorial notes on the documents to guide the reader and to place the materials in their proper historical context.

Although much material remains classified, this release brings to light a substantial part of the intelligence story in Berlin during the early Cold War. The CIA's Center for the Study of Intelligence offers this collection as a first step to a fuller understanding of this complex and dangerous time.

Gerald K. Haines
Chief Historian
Center for the Study of Intelligence
Central Intelligence Agency
June 1999

Introduction

"When I go to sleep at night, I try not to think about Berlin."

—*Dean Rusk, ca. 1961*

For nearly 50 years the German city of Berlin was the living symbol of the Cold War. The setting for innumerable films and novels about spies and Cold War espionage, Berlin was, in truth, at the heart of the intelligence war between the United States and the Soviet bloc. For the United States and its Allies, Berlin was a base for strategic intelligence collection that provided unequaled access to Soviet-controlled territory. For the Soviet Union and the captive nations of the Warsaw Pact, the presence of Western intelligence services in occupied Berlin was a constant security threat, but also an opportunity to observe their opponents in action, and possibly to penetrate their operations. Perhaps nowhere else did the Soviet and Western intelligence services confront each other so directly, or so continuously. It thus seems appropriate to refer to this situation as an "Intelligence War"; not because the conflict between the opposing services regularly erupted into organized violence, but because it was a sustained, direct confrontation that otherwise had many of the characteristics of a war.

The genesis of this unique situation lay in the agreements reached by the victorious Allies at the end of World War II. Plans calling for the joint occupation both of Germany and of Berlin, its capital, had been agreed to by the Allied powers in November 1944. Thus, even though it was the Red Army that engulfed Berlin in the spring of 1945, the Western Allies were able to claim a stake in the city. To this the Soviets acceded, but only after the Allied Supreme Commander, Gen. Dwight D. Eisenhower, agreed to withdraw American troops from Czechoslovakia. Berlin nonetheless remained surrounded by Soviet-controlled territory, with the Allies dependent upon their reluctant ally for access to the city.

These arrangements were formalized on 5 June 1945, in the course of a meeting between Allied representatives held in Berlin itself. "Greater Berlin" was divided into three occupation "sectors," duplicating on a much smaller scale the division of prewar Germany into three occupation zones. British and American forces assumed control over the western half of the city, while the Soviet Union occupied the eastern half. At Anglo-American insistence, a fourth occupation sector was created in the northwestern part of the city, to be under French jurisdiction. Each of the occupying powers appointed a Commandant for their individual sector. Administrative control in the city as a whole was vested in an "Inter-Allied Governing Authority," made up of the four Commandants, each of whom served in rotation as the Chief Commandant. For some reason, this was known as the Berlin *Kommandatura*, a Russian word sometimes anglicized to Commandatura. Berlin was simultaneously to become the seat of the Allied Control Council, responsible for the military government of occupied Germany.[1]

In 1948 the Soviets walked out of first the Allied Control Council and then the Berlin *Kommandatura*, thereby unilaterally nullifying the arrangements made for the administration of Berlin. The arrangements nonetheless persisted as the basis for the Allied occupation of the Western half of the city until the end of the Cold War, even though both halves of Berlin had become self-governing in 1948 and West Berlin had become a Federal German *Land* in 1950. East Berlin was declared the capital of the Communist-controlled German Democratic Republic (*Deutsche Demokratische Republik*) in 1949.

Surprisingly, given Berlin's position deep inside the Soviet occupation zone, until 1972 there was no formal agreement guaranteeing the Western Allies continuous ground access to the city. This became profoundly important beginning in 1948, when the Soviets severed the road and rail routes leading from the American and British occupation zones into Berlin. Fortunately, concerns about air safety in November 1945 had led to a four-power agreement establishing air corridors linking Berlin to Hamburg, Hanover, and Frankfurt. Although the Western Allies subsequently demonstrated that they could supply Berlin by air, the lack of guaranteed ground access remained a weak point in the occupation of West Berlin.

The US intelligence presence in Berlin began in July 1945 with the Western military occupation and lasted for the duration of the Cold War. First to arrive were intelligence officers of the Office of Strategic Services (OSS), who awoke on 1 October 1945 to find themselves employed by the new Strategic Services Unit (SSU), itself assimilated piecemeal by the Central Intelligence Group (CIG) in 1946. CIG was replaced in 1947 by the newly created Central Intelligence Agency (CIA). Although just about every element of the Agency had some kind of stake in Berlin, the clandestine services were those principally interested in the city. For the early CIA, these were the Office of Special Operations (OSO), responsible for the collection of secret intelligence, and the Office of Policy Coordination (OPC), the Agency's covert action arm.[2] In August 1952 OSO and OPC merged to

---

[1] For the relevant documents, see US Department of State, *Documents on Germany, 1944-1985* (Washington, DC: 1971).

[2] Michael Warner, ed., *The CIA Under Harry Truman* (Washington, DC: Center for the Study of Intelligence, 1994), pp. xvi, xx-xxi.

become the Directorate of Plans (DDP).[3] The analytical arm of the CIG and early CIA was the Office of Reports and Estimates (ORE), which produced short-term, newspaper-like, current reporting and longer range, more predictive, intelligence "Estimates."[4] In 1950, newly appointed Director of Central Intelligence Walter Bedell Smith broke ORE into three offices: current reporting was now produced by the Office of Current Intelligence (OCI), with longer range, estimative analysis the responsibility of the Office of National Estimates (ONE). A new Office of Research and Reports (ORR) initially concentrated on the Soviet economy—a gradually expanding mandate that eventually included strategic intelligence on the Soviet military.

For the early Cold War period at least, "Berlin Operations Base" may be said to have been one of the most active and productive postings for CIA intelligence officers in Europe. Its first Chief of Base was Allen W. Dulles. Richard Helms succeeded Dulles in October 1945. Following in the shoes of these two future Directors of Central Intelligence were some of the most successful intelligence officers in the Agency—most of whom must remain anonymous even today. CIA Berlin was never an independent entity, however, but always was subordinate to the Senior Agency Representative in Germany.[5] Moreover, the CIA mission in Berlin was never more than a very small part of the much larger Allied presence.

Across the city, in their compound in the Karlshorst district of Berlin, the Soviet intelligence services—in their various guises—moved in about the same time as their Western counterparts. Their mission always was dramatically different from that of the CIA and the Western intelligence services, however. Whereas for the Western Allies, Berlin was and would remain an important strategic intelligence base, the city provided no equivalent advantages for the Soviet services. The main foreign intelligence target for the Soviets was the US military presence in Western Europe, a target the Soviets shared with their East German counterpart in the Normannenstraße, the *Hauptverwaltung Aufklärung* (HVA) of the *Ministerium für Staatssicherheit* (MfS, or Stasi). Nevertheless, both sides used Berlin as an arena in which they could challenge the intelligence services of the opposing side. Moreover, the high level of intelligence activity in Berlin meant that counterintelligence problems always assumed a high priority, sometimes even overshadowing the more important "positive" mission of intelligence col-

---

[3] William M. Leary, ed., *The Central Intelligence Agency: History and Documents* (Tuscaloosa, AL: University of Alabama Press, 1984), p. 50. In 1973 the DDP was renamed the Directorate for Operations (Leary, p. 97).

[4] Leary, p. 26. For a discussion of what an Estimate is, see pp. viii-ix, below.

[5] See Document I-7.

lection.[6] It was partly because of Berlin's value as an intelligence base for America and its allies that the East German government eventually sealed off the western half of the city in 1961—a move that severely inhibited Allied intelligence operations there without incurring a similar disadvantage for the Eastern Bloc services.

What follows is a sampling of CIA intelligence documents dealing with Cold War Berlin from the beginning of the Allied occupation in the summer of 1945 until the construction of the Berlin Wall in 1961. This might be regarded as the classical period of the intelligence war in Berlin, when the relatively unrestricted access permitted between the eastern and western halves of the city facilitated the intelligence operations of both sides. It was during this period that Berlin earned its reputation as a "den of espionage," a reputation that at least partly lived up to the romantic image created over the years by novelists and screenwriters.

In general, the documents included here may be divided into three broad categories:

- Internal memoranda concerning the conduct of operations or the establishment and maintenance of an American intelligence presence in Berlin.

- Intelligence reporting from the field on specific topics. These run the gamut from raw intelligence reports from the field to more finished products ultimately intended for dissemination to intelligence analysts and other recipients. In general, this kind of reporting would not be seen by policymakers until it had been subjected to some level of analysis and editing in Washington.

- Finished intelligence produced in Washington, DC, and intended for distribution to a widespread audience in the intelligence and policymaking communities. Included in this category are current intelligence reports, which keep policymakers and intelligence officers up to date on events as they happen, and National Intelligence Estimates[7] concerning Berlin.

National Intelligence Estimates, or NIEs, are at the pinnacle of the American intelligence process and represent the agreed position of the agencies responsible for producing intelligence on a given topic. They are designed to provide policymakers with regular, detailed analyses of diverse aspects of

---

[6] In the parlance of the 1940s, "positive" intelligence referred to collection of information on the other side's intentions and capabilities. "Negative" or (less often) "passive" intelligence referred to counter-intelligence activities.

[7] Strictly speaking, National Intelligence Estimates (NIEs) did not appear until 1951. However, we include in this category estimative reporting written by the Office of Reports and Estimates between 1947 and 1951.

the world situation, including the policy objectives and likely actions of other nations and their military capabilities and potential. Although predictive in format, they frequently devote much space to weighing the merits of often conflicting pieces of evidence. Special National Intelligence Estimates (SNIEs) are shorter, more ad hoc analyses written when a more rapid response is needed. Both NIEs and SNIEs are coordinated throughout the Intelligence Community and released only on approval by a standing intelligence advisory board committee, chaired by the Director of Central Intelligence (DCI) and made up of his deputy, the DDCI, and the heads of the departmental intelligence organizations in the military and the Department of State.[8]

Also included in the category of finished intelligence are Intelligence Memoranda issued on the authority of the Director of Central Intelligence (DCI) in his capacity as head of the CIA and the President's chief intelligence adviser. Unlike NIEs and SNIEs, these were not coordinated with the rest of the Intelligence Community, and thus frequently took stronger positions than would an NIE on the same topic.

A problem in selecting the documents for this volume derived from the sheer volume of the material. Precisely because it was so important as a base for collecting intelligence, Berlin figured one way or another in most of the intelligence operations mounted in Europe during the first two decades of the Cold War, but often only tangentially. For example, both the Pyotr Popov and Oleg Penkovsky cases—among the most successful of CIA's operations against the Soviet Union—touched upon the Berlin question, but both were focused elsewhere and neither could be said to be tightly interwoven into the fabric of Berlin's Cold War history.[9] To keep the size of this volume manageable, only those documents focused on Berlin were selected.

---

[8] The name of the this body has changed over the years. In 1946-47, it was the Intelligence Advisory Board (IAB); from 1947 to 1958 it was the Intelligence Advisory Committee (IAC). It was called the United States Intelligence Board (USIB) until 1976. Since that time it has been known as the National Foreign Intelligence Board (NFIB).

[9] Popov operated briefly in Berlin, but was most active in Vienna. Penkovsky was active primarily inside the Soviet General Staff in Moscow and provided only a limited amount of intelligence material on Berlin, but it was very important and arrived at critical moments in the Berlin Crisis of 1958-61 (reproduced as Docs. VII-5 and VII-11, below). Fortunately, splendid studies already exist on these important subjects. On Popov, see William Hood, *Mole: The True Story of the First Russian Intelligence Officer Recruited by the CIA* (New York and London: W.W. Norton, 1982). See also the cogent article by John L. Hart, "Pyotr Semyonovich Popov: The Tribulations of Faith," *Intelligence and National Security* (1997). On Penkovsky, see Jerrold L. Schecter and Peter S. Deriabin, *The Spy Who Saved the World* (New York: Charles Scribner's Sons, 1992). See also Oleg Penkovsky, *The Penkovsky Papers* (Garden City NY: Doubleday and Co., 1965).

Sadly, although the documentary record is voluminous, it is also in many respects incomplete for much of the period covered by this volume, so that a full accounting of many important events or periods in Berlin's Cold War history simply is not possible from CIA records alone.[10] Continuing security considerations have made it impossible to include many other important records. Some of those that have been reproduced have been redacted to conceal individual identities, or to protect still-sensitive sources and methods. Otherwise, the documents have been reproduced in their original state, without alteration or abridgment. This means that some of them are difficult to read, even though we have used the most legible copy available. The reader is further cautioned that some of the documents retain marginalia or handwritten comments that may have been added by researchers long after the fact. The historicity or accuracy of these additions cannot be guaranteed.

---

[10] A comprehensive collection of intelligence records dealing with Berlin nevertheless would demand at least a dozen volumes of this size.

I: The Opening of the Intelligence War

I: The Opening of the Intelligence War

The American and British forces that occupied their sector of Berlin on
4 July 1945 found a city that had been virtually destroyed. Germans everywhere were paying the price for the six years of aggressive war unleashed
by their government, but none more so than the citizens of Berlin. The
streets were filled with rubble: the destruction wrought by Allied bombers
over the winter of 1943-44 had been furthered by the relentless advance of
the Soviet Army in March and April 1945.[1] Berliners themselves were still
reeling from the orgy of pillage, rapine, and murder that had followed the
Soviet occupation. Soviet soldiers careened through streets in lend-lease
jeeps in search of violence, booty, and liquor. Other Soviet detachments,
sent off in pursuit of "reparations," stripped whole industrial districts and
sections of the countryside. Kidnappings and sudden, often inexplicable,
arrests were regular occurrences. As a result, Berliners often hailed as sav-
iors the first American soldiers entering Berlin to take over the Western half
of the city, yet the delineation of occupation zones and the regularization of
Allied control mechanisms that occurred over the summer at first could
only dampen the prevailing atmosphere of chaos, deprivation, and rampant
violence.[2] The inevitable friction between the Berlin population and the
occupying powers further eroded whatever initial enthusiasm Berliners may
have had for the Americans. Not until the Berlin Airlift did some Berliners
begin to see the Western occupying forces in a different light.

Late in 1945 the Soviets reined in their marauding troops, but they continued to exhibit a mixture of arrogance and brutality that made them detested
as conquerors and lived on to undermine the credibility of the collaboration-
ist East German regime.[3] In Berlin, as perhaps nowhere else in Germany,
the initial violence of the Soviet occupation permanently shaped popular
attitudes toward the occupation forces. Over the next fifty years, Berliners
might chafe at the presence of the Western Allies, but the contrast to the
arrival of the Soviet forces in 1945 was never forgotten.

The contrast between the attitudes of the occupying powers marked the
beginning of Berlin's role as a metaphor for the Cold War division of
Europe as a whole. West Berlin itself became a haven for the stream of refugees that poured across the intracity sector boundaries until the Wall went

---

[1] The effects of one air raid are reported in Document I-1.

[2] Thomas Parrish, *Berlin in the Balance, 1945-1949: The Blockade, the Airlift, the First
Major Crisis of the Cold War.* (Reading, MA: Addison-Wesley, 1998), p. 52.

[3] An analysis of the Soviet occupation may be found in Norman M. Naimark, *The Russians
in Germany: A History of the Soviet Zone of Occupation, 1945-1949* (Cambridge and
London: Harvard University Press, 1995).

up in 1961. All this only enhanced Berlin's value as a symbol of the United States' determination to maintain a presence on the Continent of Europe. Not incidentally, Berlin's status as an outpost deep inside Soviet-occupied territory and a gateway to and from East Germany made it immensely valuable as an intelligence base. As the lines were drawn in the postwar confrontation that ushered in the Cold War, these symbolic, political, and strategic considerations emerged as factors of permanent importance to US policy toward Berlin, Germany, and Europe.

Among the first Americans to enter Berlin was a detachment of soldiers and civilians assigned to the Office of Strategic Services (OSS), America's newest intelligence agency. Their presence was transitory: most would soon be demobilized and were looking forward to seeing their homes and families again, while the OSS itself would soon be gone. As a wartime agency, its raison d'être evaporated with the capitulation of Japan on 14 August 1945. On 1 October the agency itself was dissolved and most of its component parts absorbed by the War Department as the Strategic Services Unit (SSU).[4]

The creation of a postwar civilian intelligence presence in Berlin thus fell mainly to the representatives of the newly constituted SSU. Some had wartime intelligence experience, but many did not. None of them had the kind of background that would prepare them for what they were to face over the next few years in Berlin: as civilian intelligence officers they would quickly discover that the SSU was not a popular organization with other government agencies. The very idea of an intelligence service was anathema to most Americans, who equated it with the sinister dealings they identified with a police state. Furthermore, the Department of State and the military intelligence services who had resisted the OSS now resented what they regarded as an intrusion into their own spheres of operation. Since it was the military who ran Berlin—with the advice of the State Department—the SSU personnel assigned there found that they had to learn their new trade while they were establishing a niche in the military power structure.

It was far from clear what function the SSU would have in peacetime. Intelligence collection priorities were uncertain in the fluid situation that prevailed in the period immediately after the German surrender. Opinion was divided in the OSS (and later the SSU) between those, like Allen Dulles (Chief of the OSS Mission in Bern during the war), who were concerned about postwar problems dealing with the Soviet Union and others,

---

[4] SSU comprised the Secret Intelligence (SI) Branch—responsible for intelligence collection and the Counterintelligence Branch (X-2). The Research and Analysis Branch of the OSS (R&A) was transferred to the State Department's short-lived Interim Research and Intelligence Service.

exemplified by William Casey in Paris, who were more interested in working against the latent centers of financial and industrial power that still existed in even a defeated Germany.[5] This level of uncertainty is reflected in the fact that, although Berlin would soon be of pivotal importance for the collection of intelligence against the Soviet Union, there was not even a Russian-speaking intelligence officer present there until 1947.[6] Moreover, many American military officers felt that they could deal equitably with their Soviet counterparts in Germany and viewed the presence of an independent, American intelligence organization as symptomatic of the kind of political interference they saw being imposed upon the Soviet military from Moscow.[7] Equally important, the US Military Governor in Germany, Gen. Lucius D. Clay, was determined to maintain good relations with his Soviet counterpart, Marshal Georgiy K. Zhukov, and discouraged any activities that he thought might be detrimental to good relations with the Soviet Union.[8]

Ironically, SSU Berlin's problem of finding a place for itself in the military power structure soon eased considerably because of the actions of the Soviet Union. Zhukov was recalled early in 1946 and replaced by the hard-line Marshal Vassiliy D. Sokolovsky. The Soviets subsequently did everything possible to isolate the Allied garrison in Berlin and cut off any access to potential sources of information within the Eastern bloc.[9] American commanders and diplomats in Berlin soon found it necessary to rely on intelligence sources for even the most basic information on Soviet intentions or conditions inside East Germany. Although Clay apparently would have preferred to keep it at arm's length, he found himself increasingly dependent upon his SSU detachment for information. SSU Berlin frequently had to scramble to keep up with what was a rapidly changing situation, but in the process, established the administrative structures and lines of communication that would be in place for the next 50 years.

---

[5] Stuart E. Eizenstat, et al., *US Efforts to Recover and Restore Gold and Other Assets Stolen or Hidden by Germany During World War II* (Washington, DC: Department of State, 1997), pp. 39, 41.

[6] David E. Murphy, Sergei Kondrashev, and George Bailey, *Battleground Berlin,* (New Haven, CT: Yale University Press, 1997), p. 20.

[7] Jean Edward Smith, *Lucius D. Clay: An American Life* (New York: Holt, 1990), pp. 261-62; Robert Murphy, *Diplomat Among Warriors* (New York: Pyramid, 1964), p. 290.

[8] Document I-2, *Report on Berlin Operations Base, 8 April 1948.*

[9] David E. Murphy, et al., p. 11.

I-1: Damage to Berlin, 16 December 1943 (No MORI No.).
The transcript of a telephone call from OSS London to Washington, this document has been included to give some indication of the level of damage sustained by Berlin over the course of World War II.

Over the winter of 1943-44, the Royal Air Force's Bomber Command staged an all-out nighttime offensive against Berlin. For much of this period, Bomber Command's night attacks were supplemented by daylight raids carried out by the US 8th Air Force. This recounts the damage inflicted by the end of 1943, at the height of the offensive. Berlin continued to be bombed until it was occupied by Soviet troops at the end of the war. The intense street-fighting between the advancing Soviet forces and the German defenders only inflicted more damage. Eventually the rubble from all this damage was collected in a huge pile in the Grunewald Park, to become the Teufelsberg.

I-2: Report on Berlin Operations Base, 8 April 1948 (MORI No. 144185).
This excerpt from a much larger document chronicles the history of the SSU Detachment in Berlin from January 1946 until the end of 1947, a period in which many of the mechanisms for the collection and dissemination of intelligence were implemented.

The War Department's Strategic Services Unit (SSU) comprised the foreign intelligence and counterintelligence branches of the defunct OSS. In the spring of 1946, the War Department ceded the SSU to the newly created Central Intelligence Group (CIG), which incorporated its overseas operations into the Office of Special Operations that October.

The National Defense Act of 1947 transformed the CIG into the Central Intelligence Agency. OSO was the CIA office responsible for the clandestine collection of intelligence from human sources before 1953. A covert action organization as such did not exist in CIA until the establishment of the Office for Policy Coordination (OPC) on 1 September 1948 (although OSO undertook some covert actions in early 1948).

I-3: Intelligence Disseminations of War Department Detachment, APO 403; 24 October 1946 (MORI No. 145819).

I-4: Targets of German Mission, 10 January 1947 (MORI No. 144270).

I-5: Points for [DCI Vandenberg's] Discussion with General Clay, 16 January 1947 (MORI No. 144271).

I-6: Utilization of the Mass of Soviet Refugees, 19 April 1948 (MORI No. 144243).

I-7: Instructions [for Gen. Lucien K. Truscott], 9 March 1951 (MORI No. 144287).

I-8: Minutes of a Staff Conference in Munich, 26 October 1951 (MORI No. 144289).

Although the role to be played by SSU Berlin (and its successors) was essentially defined by the end of 1947, problems of definition and coordination persisted. These documents lay out some of the parameters defining the CIA's role in Germany. They reflect some of the bureaucratic difficulties the Agency had in establishing itself, as well as the problems experienced in formulating a postwar intelligence policy, given the prevailing tensions and uncertainties.

I-9: SMERSH Department of the Soviet Central Kommandatura, Berlin—Luisenstraße, 19 December 1946 (MORI No. 46629).

I-10: Reorganization of the RIS [Russian Intelligence Services] in Germany, 11 September 1947 (MORI No. 144169).

I-11: Memorandum [concerning Gen. Leonid A. Malinin] for the Director, Central Intelligence, ca. 9 December 1947 (MORI No. 144117).

At the end of World War II, the Soviet intelligence and security services began one of their recurrent periods of reorganization and change. This persisted until 1954, when what we know as the KGB finally emerged.

In April 1943, the Soviet intelligence service, the NKGB (People's Commissariat for State Security) had been made independent of the NKVD (Peoples Commissariat for Internal Affairs). In March 1946, both were raised to the status of ministries to become, respectively, the MVD (Ministry for Internal Affairs) and the MGB (Ministry for State Security). However, in October 1947 the foreign intelligence directorate of the MGB was combined with Soviet military intelligence (GRU) to form the independent Committee of Information (KI). This persisted until the summer of 1948, when the GRU was recreated as a separate agency under the control of the military. In November 1951, KI was reabsorbed by the MGB. On Stalin's death in March 1953, the MGB became part of the MVD, under the control of Lavrenty Beria. In March 1954 the MGB was removed from the control of the MVD and placed under the direct control of the Council Ministers and downgraded to a Committee, becoming the KGB.[10]

The dramatically named SMERSH (a contraction of the phrase, "*Smert Shpionam!*"—Death to Spies!) was an independent organization formed by Stalin out of counterintelligence elements of the NKVD in April 1943 and placed under his direct control. Theoretically responsible for counterintelligence operations, SMERSH in fact was Stalin's tool for eliminating "subversion" and collaboration in territories recaptured from the Nazis. After the war, it was primarily engaged in interrogating and executing returning Soviet prisoners of war.[11]

American intelligence officers confronting the shifting labyrinth of Soviet security services for the first time at the end of World War II had difficulty in keeping track of all this. The Soviet Union was still a mystery to most Americans, and Soviet specialists were virtually nonexistent. The following documents describe early US efforts to understand the organization of the Soviet intelligence services. Interestingly, Document I-11 describes a dinner meeting with Maj. Gen. Leonid A. Malinin, identified as "Deputy to Marshal Sokolovsky." Actually, Malinin was the KI *Rezident* (local head of operations) in Berlin and as such responsible for the collection of all foreign intelligence for the Soviets, a fact unknown in the West until after the Cold War was over.[12]

---

[10] Details of the organizational metamorphoses of the KGB may be found in Christopher Andrew and Oleg Gordievsky, *KGB: The Inside Story* (New York: Harper Collins, 1990), *passim.*

[11] Andrew and Gordievsky, pp. 342-343.

[12] Murphy, et al., pp. 411-414.

F-85-0886 12-16-43

<u>Phone Call</u>

<u>GERMANY</u>   December 16, 1943

(1). Here is a summary of ~~the most detailed~~ report I ~~have jet seen~~ on the bombing damage done to Berlin. The Wilhelmstrasse government quarter is not fully destroyed, as the press reported, but practically every house has some damage in this area. The Foreign Office, the Propaganda Ministry and in the special office of Ribbentrop at Wilhelmstrasse 65 work is being carried on only in the cellar and on the first floors. The British Embassy has been burnt. The Luftfahrtministerium and the Gestapo headquarters in Prinz Albrecht-strasse had some hits, but on the whole remained intact. Under den Linden suffered heavily. The French Embassy and the Speer Ministry have been made entirely unusable by fire and water. The nearby administration building of

2-150

7

GERMANY - 2

[handwritten: Esplanade-all windows, ?]

the I.G. Farben has been heavily damaged. The
Russian Embassy, the Ministry of Culture. the
Hotel Bristol, ~~the Ministry of the Interior,~~ *[handwritten: Hotel Kaiserhof]*
the Hotel Victoria, ~~the Commerzbank and the~~
~~Diskontogesellschaft~~ (David ~~Isaac Samuel~~ King
~~Olga Nora~~ Tommy Olga George ~~Edward Samuel~~
~~Edward Louis Louis Samuel~~ Charlie Henry Albert
~~Frank Tommy~~) ~~and~~ the palace of Kaiser Wilhelm
the First, the Prussian State Library, the
University, the State Opera House have all been
heavily damaged and many of them entirely burnt
out. In the Behrenstrasse (Bertram Edward Henry
Robert Edward Nora) the Dresdner Bank, the
Deutsche Bank, the *[handwritten: Commerz bank]* Metropol theater and the
Papal Nunciature have been heavily damaged.
In the Leipzigerstrasse from the Leipzigerplatz
to Dönhoffplatz (David Olga Nora Henry Olga
Frank Frank) was largely burnt out, including
Wertheims (William Edward Robert Tommy Henry
Edward Issac Mary). The Tietz (Tommy Isaac

GERMANY - 3

Edward Tommy zebra) establishment, however,
did not suffer. On the Alexanderplatz the
electricity works is out of order. The SS
Kaserne on the Alexanderstrasse has been burnt
out. The old Reichstag building also received
incendiary bombs, and this time not placed
there by Goering, but the building still stands.
The freight station on the Lehrter (Louis Edward
Henry Robert Tommy Edward Robert) Bahnhof
(Bertram Albert Henry Nora Henry Olga Frank)
was entirely destroyed and the well-known
bakery von Wittler (William Isaac Tommy Tommy
Louis Edward Robert) was very heavily damaged
and the entire supply of flour burned. This
bakery supplied almost half of Berlin with
bread. The Hotel Eden and the nearby theater
were destroyed. The Bahnhof Zoo had many hits
and also the flak (Frank R Louis Albert King)
tower in the Zoo was hit, but not destroyed.

GERMANY - 4

The Potsdamerbahnhof has collapsed. The
Anhalter- (Albert Nora Henry Albert Louis Tommy
Edward Robert) Bahnhof is still standing, but
the tracks have been torn to pieces. The
Stettiner-Bahnhof has partly collapsed. The
Friedrichstrasse Bahnhof has been put in
commission again for transit traffic. However
at the date of the report persons going to the
west take their trains in Potsdam and those to
the east in the Bahnhof Ostkreuz (Olga Samuel
Tommy King Robert Edward uncle zebra). para

In the workers quarters there was great
damage and entire housing quarters were destroyed. According to the report the number killed
is around 35,000, the number of homeless is
over a million. para

It is difficult to describe the reaction
of the population. The people are so busy
trying to take care of themselves that they

GERMANY - 5

have not had time to draw conclusions. The
Nazi leaders are busy spreading among the
population such phrases as quote English
cannibals unquote, requote British air pirates
unquote, but my informant does not think this
propaganda has had much effect and some of the
people were even heard saying it would have been
much better if we had never started anything.
para

Of course the list of factories hit is
also long and will be sent separately.

MORI Document ID:> 144185:144185

10

1/17

O F F I C I A L   D I S P A T C H

VIA: Air Pouch

No. B-226

8 April 1948

TO : Chief, Foreign Branch M (EYES ONLY)

FROM : Chief of Station, Karlsruhe, Germany

SUBJECT: Transmittal of Report on Berlin Operations Base

1. Transmitted herewith is Report on Berlin Operations Base, January 1946 to March 1948. The report is submitted in two copies with the master ditto. One has been sent to Karlsruhe headquarters, two are retained here.

2. A word of explanation is necessary concerning the origin and development of this report. It was begun originally as a Chief, Berlin Operations Base, Progress Report for 1947. It soon became apparent that it was impossible to discuss 1947 without going into the background of the preceding year, for which no overall report had been submitted. Inevitably the preparation of the report stretched out over the first three months of 1948. In the meantime, the situation was changed by the proposal that I be transferred from Berlin Base. With this possibility in view, my concept changed from that of a mere progress report, to an overall statement designed to help and guide my successor. From this concept emerged the thought that the same report might be of general interest to Headquarters, and it was with this in mind that it was finally written.

3. I do not know whether the report as finally presented requires any general circulation in your office or other parts of OSO. For that reason I have sent it Kapok, leaving it up to you to decide how far it should be shown. I am aware that some very frank statements are made about American officials and agencies, and for that reason you may wish to keep it closely restricted, or you may decide to break it up and circulate individual sections, suppressing others. In any case, I have no pride of authorship in the document.

/s/ [Dana Durand]

Chief, BOB

5-47

SECRET

PART I

INTRODUCTION

The basic element in the history of the Berlin Operations Base during 1946 and 1947 has been the maintenance of continuity as a unified Detachment, in what may be described as a semi-overt status. In this respect, no fundamental changes were made in the situation which had existed since the end of 1945. Throughout the two years of my regime, there have indeed been numerous occasions on which the advisability of maintaining this status has been questioned. Sometimes the question was raised by Heidelberg, sometimes by ourselves, but each time the answer was the same: the operational, administrative, and liaison advantages of a compact unified Base outweigh the security advantages of dispersal and deep cover. As long as our primary mission remains the servicing of the Theater Commander and other local customers, as opposed to the secondary mission of establishing a long range, permanent, truly clandestine coverage, the Army will have to know who we are and how to deal with us. Externally, the administrative and liaison connections which have been built up elaborately over two years are a precious asset which we are reluctant to liquidate. Internally, the cooperation between the Branches, the intimate connection between the case officers and the executive heads, the convenience of our building with its admirable facilities, all these have seemed to outweigh perfectionist conceptions of segregation and deep cover.

We have, in other words, maintained a middle course. We have avoided the "cordon sanitaire" ▆▆▆▆▆▆▆▆▆▆▆▆▆▆▆▆▆▆▆▆▆▆▆▆▆ but we have also kept a substantial measure of anonymity. It is, of course, impossible to be sure that our security measures have been sufficient to divert the attention of the opposition completely. In a position such as ours, one does well to remember the Greek moral "Count no man happy (read unblown) until he is dead!" Nevertheless, we feel some confidence that our security position is radically different from that of the overt agencies, S-2 Berlin Command, CIC, and the Intelligence Office of Military Government in Berlin (OMGBS). All their executive and staff personnel are known and have become Soviet EEI's. Perhaps our personnel may also figure on those EEI's, but so far no case of major significance has come to our notice. Some 10 British and American agencies which would be in a position to report any major security break affecting us have provided at least negative confirmation of our practical anonymity.

Security-wise, our semi-overt status has caused us some unhappy moments. The most alarming flurry was that brought about by the Associated Press dispatch on the so-called underground railway,

SECRET

- 2 -

alleged to have spirited Mikolajczyk out of Poland. The unfortunate reference to "a War Department detachment" sent us into a prolonged tailspin, from which we gradually emerged, clinging to the hope that the difference between "a" and "the" WDD may have escaped the attention of unfriendly eyes. At any rate, we did the best we could to lock the barn door; we found out the identity of the culprit and got the matter into IG channels. We were able to derive at least a vindictive satisfaction from the fact that the indiscreet OMGUS official was abruptly returned to the States. We have never been able to ascertain whether the other offender, i.e. the AP correspondent, felt any remorse for his unethical release of false information, damaging to American security, or whether any deterrent effect was achieved.

This incident remains the only one of which we are cognizant affecting the security of our Detachment as a whole. The resulting decision to change the name of the Detachment would have been inevitable in any case, since the passing of the War Department has made our designation a rather conspicuous anachronism. We look forward in the spring of 1948 to a carefully planned change of name and cover, carried out by an officer specially designated by Heidelberg to explore all the manifold administrative complexities which such a move entails. We hope for once to have a thoroughly cogitated and relatively foolproof approach to a problem which in the past no one has ever confronted with sufficient thoroughness.

The other principal blow to our security through indiscretions by the press was the publication by Joseph Alsop of the substance of one of our secret reports entitled "Speech by Sokolovsky". We have never fully got to the bottom of this leak, partly because it has seemed inexpedient to press too hard. It seems almost certain that this report was shown to Alsop on instructions of the highest State Department authority in Berlin. Whether this action was, as one important official put it, "a deliberate leak" based on orders from Washington, we have not attempted to find out, but we have let it be known at the highest level concerned that our agency does not recognize the existence of any authority competent to release our classified material for publication without prior clearance.

In connection with Detachment security, we have made repeated efforts to develop outside cover positions for individual staff members. From the outset, however, we have been greatly frustrated by an obstacle which for the time being seems insurmountable, viz. the refusal of General Clay to permit the use of Military Government cover for clandestine operations. During the first half of 1947 we made a number of tentative approaches to the problem. With the full approval of the OMGUS personnel Officer, the Theater Director of Intelligence, and even the Chief of Staff, Brig. Gen. Charles

MORI Document ID:> 144185:144185

SECRET

- 3 -

Gailey, we actually installed Henry Hecksner, Chief SC, in the Public Safety Branch of OMGUS, under an alias. However, as the result of an unfortunate ~~incident~~ and the Chief of Public Relations, Heckshert excellent arrangements were so badly disturbed that w were forced to withdraw him to the haven of our own Detachment. Since this incident raised the general principle to the level of the OMGUS Chief of Staff, we felt it advisable to push it to the final echelon, and clear up once for all the somewhat unknown quantity of General Clay's policy. The occasion could not have been more favorable for a strong presentation of our request, Brig. Gen. E. K. Wright personally presenting it on our behalf. General Clay's answer was a polite but unequivocal "No". He explained that his lofty concept of the integrity of the Military Government function ruled out altogether the practice of dissimulation and under- cover activity. He was quite willing to extend the use of military or any other related cover available in the theater, but under no circumstances that of Military Government. We of course assured him we would comply.

This ruling puts us at a great disadvantage ~~in~~ ~~the~~ However, it has not put us completely out of business. Within OMGUS there exist facilities which are not strictly those of Military Government, notably within the ad- ministrative and logistic headquarters known as Berlin Command. Berlin Command is not ruled out by General Clay's decision, and we have already found at least one admirable niche in the Provost Marshal's office for George Belic. We feel that other places will be available as the need occurs, and we have been able to count on excellent cooperation from the commanding officer down.

Establishment of cover on a group basis, which would be re- quired in the case of a dispersal of the Detachment, does not yet seem feasible. It was hoped that the proposed transfer of control from Army to State Department in July 1948 would open new cover possibilities, but the cancellation of the transfer set back those hopes indefinitely.

With the maintenance of our Detachment identity, unity, security, and cover has gone the retention of our physical prop- erty, especially our office building at 19 Foehrenweg. In the late summer of 1947 we were subjected to a rather serious attack, directed by the Chief of Staff of OMGUS, Brig. Gen. Charles Gailey, but actually inspired by General Clay himself. Since his accession to the Theater Command in March of this year, General Clay has repeatedly given evidence of the military man's (and engineer's!) fondness for tidying things up. He has showed

SECRET

SECRET

- 4 -

a predilection for consolidating the numerous scattered flags
and colored pins which dot the installation map in the S-4
office of Berlin Command. At times, indeed, this drive has had
unfortunate results, as in the case of General Clay's personal
order to pull all outlying MP detachments into a single central
barracks. The effect of this order, as pointed out to him in
advance by all the American law-enforcement and intelligence
agencies, has been to denude of police protection the highly
exposed areas bordering the Russian Sector, and to invite abductions and other Russian forays into our sector. General Clay
admitted that he was taking a "calculated risk".

General Clay's order to consolidate all minor headquarters
hit CIC, S-2, and ourselves at the same time, creating much
consternation. CIC faced the threat of GI regimentation in
barracks and the loss of its large billet and office compound.
S-2 was confronted with the disadvantageous prospect of sharing
a modest and completely public wing of Headquarters Command with
the other S's. And we were invited to give up our building and
move into the OMGUS area where it would be difficult, if not impossible, to operate our own motor pool, and maintain physical
security. As a result the three agencies made a common front,
and after some hesitation the Theater Director of Intelligence,
Major General Robert Walsh, went to bat successfully for all. In
our case, we invited a personal inspection by General Gailey,
and succeeded in convincing him that our building was not only
ideal for our purposes, but was much too desirable a property to
turn back to the German economy. We were greatly helped, I might
add, by the intervention of General Wright, whose visit to Berlin
coincided with the crisis.

I should also add that we did not make the fight to retain
the building, merely out of inertia and reluctance to be disturbed.
We examined carefully the alternatives which, besides dispersal,
included the choice of two buildings within the OMGUS compound,
more or less comparable in size to our own. We weighed the
security advantages of a change of location and found them wanting
against the equally obvious security risks of the physical move
and the inevitable setback to the continuity of our intelligence
production.

Perhaps the most important development of 1947 affecting the
Base as a whole was the reversal of the personnel attrition which
had taken place in 1946. When I arrived in January 1946, the
strength of the Detachment was about 27 Americans, including
enlisted men and secretaries. Shortly thereafter we were invited
to submit a personnel estimate, based on an optimum T-O for a
self-contained operating and reporting Base. We arrived at the

SECRET

SECRET

- 5 -

figure of 41 or 42 as the minimum for a fully rounded operation. However, the next few months marked a falling away from rather than an approach toward this goal. At the lowest point, which was reached in the summer of 1946, the entire strength of the detachment was 23 persons, civilian and military. However the tide turned, and gradually during the past year we have moved nearer and nearer to our T-O. As of the present writing our actual strength is 35 civilians, 5 EM. New recruits were sent out from the States and routine transfers were made from other parts of the Station. However, the greatest accession of strength occurred in the summer of 1947 through the dissolution of the Intelligence Branch at Heidelberg, and the transfer of its personnel to field bases.

The gain in personnel has been even greater in quality than in quantity. Washington recruiting, though limited in numbers, has produced an outstanding group of 6 young case officers, admirably suited to permanent careers in the organization. The breakup of Intelligence Branch gave us a new head for each of our operating branches ▮▮▮▮▮▮▮▮▮▮▮▮ bringing to us the full benefit of their desk experience at the level of an intermediate headquarters. All in all, we may thank both Washington and Heidelberg for a generous and wise allocation of personnel to what we naturally consider the all important level of direct intelligence production.

A word should be said concerning problems of morale. Despite ups and downs I believe that the curve has mounted steadily during the past year and that the morale of the personnel at this Base has never been better than it is today. Mutual confidence between Heidelberg and Berlin obtains on every level. Our case officers have recovered from the dismay brought on by our security losses. As indicated below, the administrative picture, especially transportation, has improved, bringing relief from the chaos and disorganization inherited from the break up of the wartime organization. And finally, and not least, the influx of dependents has stabilized the personal lives of a considerable percentage of our staff, and brought an element of maturity and dignity as an example to the rest. The situation is indeed by no means perfect. There are still instances of immaturity, emotional unbalance and social inbreeding within our little community, but these are being treated with tact or firmness, as the case demands, and gradually eliminated. We have entered 1948 with a spirited yet disciplined staff, in the true sense an elite group.

SECRET

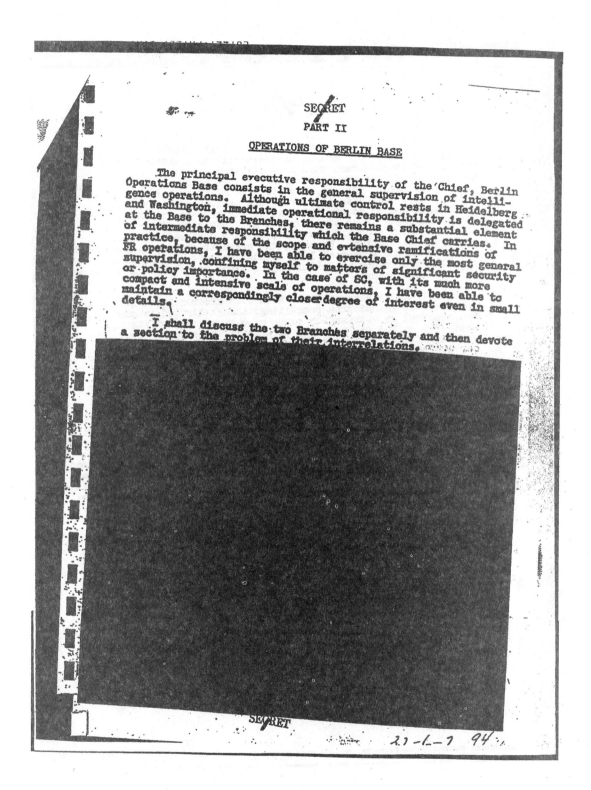

SECRET

PART II

OPERATIONS OF BERLIN BASE

The principal executive responsibility of the Chief, Berlin Operations Base consists in the general supervision of intelligence operations. Although ultimate control rests in Heidelberg and Washington, immediate operational responsibility is delegated at the Base to the Branches, there remains a substantial element of intermediate responsibility which the Base Chief carries. In practice, because of the scope and extensive ramifications of FR operations, I have been able to exercise only the most general supervision, confining myself to matters of significant security or policy importance. In the case of SC, with its much more compact and intensive scale of operations, I have been able to maintain a correspondingly closer degree of interest even in small details.

I shall discuss the two Branches separately and then devote a section to the problem of their interrelations.

SECRET

27-L-7 94

SECRET

- 7 -

The trend of FR intelligence production, as measured in number of reports, may be indicated by a few simple statistics. During the first eight months of 1946, the output of raw and disseminated reports rose from some 300 per month to an average of 500 and a peak of more than 700. With the reorganization of SSU into WDD on 20 October 1946, the present report series began with MGB-1 -- and almost a year to the day later the Berlin Base logged MGB-5000. (These included nearly three hundred SC reports.) In August 1947 a total of 525 reports was logged and forwarded, but a deliberate and vigorous effort to reduce the flow of useless or mediocre material brought the figure down to 213 by October and has kept it in that neighborhood ever since. Both case officers and reports officers were instructed to apply much more rigorous screening standards than before, so that we could concentrate on improving our output and free reports officers all along the line from a clogging weight of paper.

The statistics above are in themselves not particularly enlightening except as they indicate a phase of quantitative expansion, followed by one of contraction. In order to illustrate the real significance of this development, and comment briefly on the trends in scope and quality of FR coverage, I shall review in broad terms the historical development of FR operations since the establishment of the Berlin Base.

1. The development of the FR Branch of the Berlin Operations Base during the past two and a half years may be said to sum up the transition from the wartime operation of OSS/SI to the beginnings of the permanent long range organization of the post war era. This development has gone through four phases: a) July 1945 to February 1946, the attempt to convert the relics of wartime SI to the purposes of the occupation period; b) March to September 1946, concentration on military intelligence and the development of new chains, especially for extensive area coverage; c) October 1946 to June 1947, gradual shift to intensive coverage of fewer and more highly selected targets, beginning of liquidation of chains, and other security losses; and d) July 1947 to date, reconstruction and tightening of the FR agent system with a view to long range production.

a. July 1945 - February 1946. As was inevitable, the immediate postwar phase in Berlin was marked by the carry over of substantial parts of the wartime SI Branch. The Chief of the German Mission, Mr. Allan Dulles, brought with him from Switzerland a considerable group of high-level Germans, the so-called Crown Jewels, who had been recruited during the war. ▮▮▮▮▮▮▮▮▮▮▮▮▮▮▮▮▮▮▮▮▮▮▮▮▮▮▮▮▮▮▮▮▮▮▮▮▮ But however impressive on paper, the Crown Jewel program in practice proved unsuited to the

SECRET

19

prevailing situation. Most of the individual members naturally made haste to get back to their personal affairs, law, politics, journalism, business. Even had they been interested in continuing to work for OSS, there was little that they could contribute in the way of clandestine intelligence. The chief concern of many was to capitalize on the credit they had earned by their services during the war, and in some cases their exaggerated notions led to embarrassing and painful incidents -- for example, in the long drawn out termination of our relations with ▆▆▆▆▆▆. Today three Crown Jewels remain on our books in Berlin, including ▆▆▆▆▆ and our only remaining concern with him is to fulfill at long last our ancient promise to get him to the States.

The principal reason for the collapse of the postwar Crown Jewel program lay, however, in the disintegration of the OSS itself. After Mr. Dulles returned to the States in October 1945, a series of commanding officers and executives passed in rapid succession through the Berlin Detachment. Redeployment was swift, and in a few months the strength of the Detachment fell more than fifty per cent. SI Branch suffered heavily from this personnel attrition. Moreover it was split up into a number of separate operating units (Peter, David, etc.), physically isolated and with no control by the Berlin Chief -- control being exerted (if at all) by Wiesbaden. In large part, it is the memory of this atomistic and undisciplined era which has deterred us from undertaking a new program of dispersal.

During this period the presence of Mr. Dulles -- and for some time after his actual departure, the impact of his personal prestige -- enabled the Detachment to operate on a very high echelon. Intelligence reports were delivered personally to General Clay and Ambassador Murphy, and direct access to the "presence" was frequent. This was undoubtedly gratifying, but in the long run it produced unfortunate results for which we are still paying. The fact seems to be that SI production in the last quarter of 1945 was actually of low quality, and the effort to sell it directly to General Clay had the boomerang effect of giving him a low opinion of the organization. Indeed, he showed an indifferent if not hostile attitude to intelligence in general, during 1946 and 1947; an attitude which applied primarily to the G-2 agencies, but in part also to ourselves. Much of our effort during the past two years has been aimed at counteracting this negative view by steadily improving the quality of our service for Theater customers, so that the merits of our positive intelligence speak for themselves without special salesmanship. There is reason to believe that we are beginning to succeed.

Two other shortcomings were apparent in the SI production of this early period. In the first place, too much attention was paid to rumors, high level gossip, political chitchat. Lengthy

SECRET

- 9 -

reports from highly placed agents were purveyed as intelligence, whereas in many cases they represented mere axe-grinding or *Jammerberichte*. It is not surprising that material of this type soon elicited a negative reaction for the principal customers.

The second defect resulted from a mistaken judgment of target priorities. During this period an unduly large share of our attention was given to Poland and New Poland. This area was naturally a major target, but effective coverage was (and has remained) impracticable. We were never successful at re-cruiting agents who combined professional intelligence skills with the necessary knowledge of the area, courage to run the great risks, and dependability. Those whom we did recruit were motivated by overweening personal interests: business in Upper Silesia, undiscriminating agitation against the Oder-Neisse frontier, or smuggling and the black market. Further, this concentration on Polish-held areas distracted attention from our target of primary interest, viz. the Soviet Zone.

b. **March-September 1946.** This initial phase of post-war positive operations came to an end during the first two months of my regime. I do not take any credit for the transition, since it was largely directed from higher headquarters. *RICHARD HELMS* who had been the last chief of the Berlin Base prior to my arrival, was now in charge of the responsible desk in Washington bringing to headquarters his direct operating experience. Wiesbaden and later Heidelberg had shaken down the swollen wartime growth and set up the strongly staffed intermediate SI organiza-tion which culminated in the so-called Intelligence Branch. My own role in the conduct of SI operations was distinctly limited during this entire phase by the Heidelberg policy of strong inter-mediate control. Most of my attention was accordingly devoted to establishing liaisons and to coping with the inherited administra-tive disorder of the Base, leaving positive operations more or less to themselves.

The basic event of this second phase was the an-nouncement of the Grail Program in June 1946, which had been an-ticipated by an urgent shift to military targets for G-2 USFET (General Sibert) in March 1946. First Frankfurt requested, and then Washington required, that we elevate military intelligence, - especially Order of Battle of the Soviet armed forces, to the highest priority, at no matter what cost to our other operations. The effect on our positive operations was of course sweeping; in some respects it was disastrous. It was obvious that SI opera-tions had to be greatly expanded, and with great speed. The only way to do this was to build up large agent chains, reaching out and covering the Soviet Zone throughout its length and breadth.

SECRET

- 10 -

SI Branch embarked on this expansion with great vigor and enthusiasm. Under the guidance of the energetic but methodical Henry SUTTON, its operations office became a center of intense activity. Chains thrust out like rapidly forming crystal fingers. Reports flowed in and new briefs were issued, the great majority written by SUTTON himself, in response to the ever increasing impact of the Grails. It was a dynamic and exciting period as report numbers mounted and sub-agent chain numbers steadily proliferated.

In retrospect it is easy to criticize this free and easy period, but at the time everyone -- our customers, Heidelberg, Washington -- was immensely pleased and kept on demanding more. There was a certain gratification in being able to pinpoint a target anywhere in the Russian Zone, and dispatch an agent to cover it almost at a moment's notice. Perhaps the classic operation of this type was the surveillance of a large cache of uranium salts at Ludwigslust, which we carried out for the Manhattan Engineering District. We could put a man into the warehouse almost at will, and from afar we watched with satisfaction the elimination of the dangerous salts by their use in tanning white leather!

Although the production of military intelligence enjoyed top priority at this time, it did not preclude a vigorous expansion of our political and economic coverage. It was during this period that Peter Sichel, then Chief of the branch and SUTTON, developed clandestine intelligence reporting on the Soviet zone to the point of routine, and established the basic penetrations into the Central Administrations in Berlin which constitute the staple of FR Branch today. Although taken in detail this type of production was less spectacular than the Grail work, in the aggregate it has produced a more lasting impression. By the beginning of 1947 FR economic and political coverage was clearly established as the best produced by any intelligence agency in Berlin. Our prestige with ODI, OMGUS, reached a high peak from which it has never declined. So great was ODI's confidence in our Soviet Zone coverage that the Chief, Colonel Rodes, requested us to set up what amounted to a clandestine organization of resident intelligence agents, comparable to the overt intelligence officers of Military Government in the American Zone. The project, of course, was unfeasible, but it indicates the extent to which standing coverage through agent networks had come to be taken for granted.

c. **October 1946 - June 1947.** The transition to the third phase of positive production was gradual. Even at the height of the second phase there were misgivings, both in Berlin and in Heidelberg, that chains were being pushed beyond the danger

MORI Document ID:> 144185:144185

- 11 -

point. The old Vetting Desk of X-2 had broken down under the load of new recruitments, and the Agent Control Branch which had been set up under SI Steering was attempting to shoulder the responsibility for checking background and security. The Intelligence Branch was divided between the desire to continue the wave of expanding production and fear of the eventual consequences of the boom. My own position also was beginning to change. In October 1946 the Chief of Mission, Crosby Lewis, officially instructed me to assume a part of the supervisory responsibility for FR operations, which hitherto had been fairly closely held by SI Steering. I was glad to accept, and indeed had solicited this extension of my responsibility, but to a certain extent danger symptoms had already emerged which it was too late for me to check. Moreover an element of tension had developed between Berlin and Heidelberg in which personality factors were at times a grave source of friction rehension. In response to the Washington directives, SUTTON had driven the expansion phase of our program with all the energy and zeal of his powerful character. By the fall of 1946 he was, so to speak, caught in his own momentum. The pressure of chann ... . 's to and reports from more than 250 agents was such that SUTTON could hardly think any longer in terms of cutting down. The system was moving fast, if not hectically.

It would be a mistake to think that FR Branch in Berlin ... lost the faculty of self criticism. It is true that Mr. SUTTON appeared at times to lay himself open to the charge made by Mr. Lewis of being an "intelligence broker". NEVER THE less one must remember two things. In the first place SUTTON who has a strong strain of military discipline in his nature, was acting on his interpretation of higher orders. On the other hand, even at the height of his campaign to produce at all costs, he never lost sight of long range objectives, and indeed defined them more clearly and thoughtfully than almost anyone else in those days when the future of SSU was so tenuous. His fertile imagination and powerful intellect were repeatedly brought to bear on the long range problem, and produced ▮▮▮▮▮▮▮▮▮▮▮▮▮▮▮s much of our most stimulating thought on the subject. Thus it was not from an excess of "boyish enthusiasm" on the part of its directing personnel that FR Berlin eventually found itself in serious difficulties.

The bill for overexpansion was presented at the end of 1946, and we have been paying it in instalments ever since. The arrest of a large part of the ▮▮▮▮▮ chain in the last two weeks of December 1946 established a pattern which with many variations was followed in 1947 by the compromise of the ▮▮▮▮▮▮▮▮▮▮▮▮ chains, and in March 1948 the ▮▮▮▮ chain. Generally a single weak link was detected by Russian counter intelligence: sometimes by chance, perhaps as the result of a routine pick up for blackmarket or other charges, and sometimes through an agent gone sour and bought over. Only rarely if ever does the initial break seem to have come from a deliberate penetration.

Usually the Russians avoided direct action until they had learned almost all the details of the chain's makeup. Sometimes we were even able to follow their progress through attempts at kidnaping, luring agents into the Russian Sector or Zone, and arrests which were followed by attempts to double the agents and their subsequent release to work against us. Accordingly we were sometimes given advance warning and were able to save some of the wreckage; this was especially true in the case of the ██████ complex. But once the Russians had a sizeable group of men within their grasp they were usually able to make effective concerted swoops. As we learned to our cost, the time margin was extremely small; once the trap was sprung, it was usually too late for us to rescue the more remote agents. We have since learned something of the cost to the agents themselves; sentences of five to twenty five years in Siberia, misery and even destitution among the families left behind.

All these losses have been fully described in reports by the case officers concerned. The classic document of this type is ██████████ comprehensive study of the blowing of ████████████ tracing its causes back to the very origin of the chain and the operational handicaps in terms of physical facilities and security protection which characterized the Grail expansion. As a clear historical resume of an important characteristic case it should constitute a valuable training document. We may also mention ████████ memoranda on the ██████ complex and ████████ on ████████ not only as demonstrations of the conscientiousness and energy with which FR case officers have faced their baptism of fire, but also as products of FR's steadily increasing effort to achieve full and candid reporting on its operations. We have been gratified at the understanding reaction of higher headquarters to these reports.

Several lessons have emerged from this third period of our operations: 1) Operation of complex agent chains is risky and in the long run unprofitable. It is only worthwhile in a fluid tactical situation, where expense, measured in terms of human life, must be disregarded. 2) Chain operations, though achieving the wide coverage necessary in a tactical situation, yield on the whole low level and ephemeral results. 3) It is difficult, if not impossible, to accomplish hermetical compartmentalization within chains, when the physical location of the sub-agents allows the case officer no contact with them. Paper segregation of sub-agents

SECRET

- 13 -

seldom works out in practice, especially when physical facilities for housing and meeting are severely limited. 4) Operation through cutouts, though admirable in theory, does not work out in practice under the conditions so far prevailing in Germany. 5) No amount of coaching is likely to develop a real security consciousness in a German agent unless he has already had some taste of professional conspiratorial experience. 7) Cutting down a chain automatically brings forth additional security weaknesses. Dismissed agents either go sour or attempt to get recruited by another agency, or drift into black market and other illegal activities where they eventually expose themselves. There is no such thing as pruning or consolidating a chain with safety. When it has to be cut down, it had better be liquidated altogether -- and even then we and the dismissed agents remain in almost as much danger as ever. Many of our casualties were agents whom we had dropped many months before they were captured, and they in turn implicated other dropped agents and some who were still active.

The ultimate moral, and it is a painful one, seems to be that any successful productive operation must eventually be paid for by an even greater outlay of effort in disposal and liquidation. For that reason, perhaps the most important outside development of 1947 affecting FR operations was the organization of the disposal unit at Heidelberg. Their responsibility is a heavy one, for they have to suffer dismal headaches long after the shouting and the tumult have died away.

d. July 1947 to date. The transition from the third to the fourth phase of FR operations was gradual, but was well under way by 1 July 1947, when a major shift of personnel took place. Both SUTTON and SICHEL had arranged to return permanently to the States, and ▓▓▓▓▓▓▓▓▓ arrived in Heidelberg to become the new chief of the Branch. But Mr SICHEL who had been chief since the fall of 1945, at that time changed his long-standing plan to enter his family business, and magnanimously agreed to remain as FR Operations Officer in SUTTON'S place. Naturally his decision was more than welcome, not only to ▓▓▓▓▓▓ and myself, but to the case officers he had trained and to all others who knew how much of Berlin's success in positive intelligence was due to his unceasing energy, skill, and aggressive imagination.

This change in personnel was in part a result of an important reorganization carried out at Heidelberg. In the spring of 1947 it was decided to dissolve the Intelligence Branch at Headquarters and assign most of its staff personnel to the Operations Bases. The change, of course, greatly strengthened

SECRET

SECRET

- 14 -

the staffing of the bases, but in addition it bestowed upon them a much broader measure of operating autonomy than they had hither-to enjoyed. Although the Chief of Station has continued to main-tain full files of agent operations and exercise overall super-vision, he has in effect delegated all the detailed supervisory functions of the Intelligence Branch, retaining only the general policy control and the supervision of financial and supply account-ing in Headquarters.

In terms of organization and operations, Berlin's most important benefit from the dissolution of IB was the trans-fer to our own office of Agent Control. Not that the agent control function had been neglected by IB; on the contrary, first ███████████████ and later ███████████████████████ had carried it out with admirable thoroughness and objectivity. The Agent Review prepared by ███████████████ in the spring of 1947 was a masterpiece of analysis and criticism. Although at the time, there was some resistance to the sweeping house-cleaning which ███████████ recommended, in retrospect all of us will agree that it marked the beginning of a new era in FR Berlin. The wholesale dismantling of chains and liquidation of non-productive, marginal, and insecure agents eventually (and sometimes with the help of the RIS) followed ███████████ blueprint fairly closely, though here and there certain points of overemphasis have had to be corrected.

███████████'s agent review was the swan song of out-side agent control. The transfer of the function to Berlin was accompanied by two other new developments which made genuine and effective agent control possible for the first time:

1. ███████████████████████ came from IB to set up and maintain Agent Control in Berlin. During the past eight months ███████████ achievement has been truly monumental. The whole system of FR agent files has been revised and filled out so that it is now far more comprehensive, complete, and rational than ever before. Service records have been prepared for the hundred-odd agents who have been dropped. By daily contact with the case officers ███████████ has instilled a new sense of disci-pline into their preparation of operational reports, which in turn has reacted favorably on their whole technical approach, especially in matters of security and completeness of personal information on the agents. The typical agent dossier is now clearly organized, with summary and detailed statements of personal background, record of contacts, supplies issued, reports received, etc.

SECRET

MORI Document ID:> 144185:144185

SECRET
- 15 -

2.   The monthly progress reports by the case officers
have also helped to keep Heidelberg and Washington far better
informed on the exact status and scope of Berlin operations than
had ever been possible before. At first the reports, which were
initiated on instructions from Heidelberg, were written by the
overburdened case officers under dismayed protest. Gradually,
however, they have been accepted as an essential part of the
case officer's duty, invaluable not only to higher headquarters
but to the executive staff of the Base, and indeed to the case
officer himself.

A further systematization of our work resulted
from the reduction of agent operations to project form in July 1947.
Although this task seemed at first a mere bureaucratic nuisance,
we finally came to welcome the additional insight it gave us and
other headquarters into the whole FR picture. The first weeks of
████████'s tenure were profitably, if hectically, spent in comb-
ing the files, talking with the case officers, and condensing the
facts about each agent into a compact project summary. We were
gratified by the favorable reception and wholesale approval by
Heidelberg and Washington; we thought that the job had perhaps
been done once and for all, and that for future accounting periods
a statement of change or no change would be sufficient. When it
came time to restate our projects as of 1 January 1948, however,
████████ felt that so much had changed, and so much else needed
to be amplified and clarified, that mere revision would not suffice. Therefore his second project statements, almost without
exception, represented completely new formulations, fuller and
more realistic in general, especially with regard to costs and
eventual disposal problems. We have begun to face the eventuality of a currency reform, and have called attention to the
inevitable rise in hard cash and supply costs which it will bring
into our hitherto phenomenally economical mode of operation.

Another basic achievement of ████████'s regime has
been the reorganization of the Reports Board and its procedure.
The dissolution of the Intelligence Branch bestowed upon us a
greatly increased responsibility in reporting, but a gain of only
one person ████████████████ soon to return to the States). ████
████'s office was given entire responsibility for the handling
of FR intelligence reports from the moment they leave the case
officers until they are put into the pouches, by-passing the
screening which they used to receive in the Operations office at
a cost sometimes of considerable delay and duplication of effort.
One result of our increased local responsibility, especially for
screening out mediocre or useless material at the earliest possibl
stage, has been a speed-up in reports handling all along the line.

SECRET

- 16 -

Summing up the past two years' development in positive intelligence coverage, certain achievements and certain failures stand out. Broadly speaking our political coverage has remained at about the level it began to reach with our reports on the Hermes-CDU crisis of December 1945: all but exhaustive on the CDU, as much as necessary on the LDP, much less on the SPD ▓▓▓, and fragmentary but occasionally good on the SED and its ancillaries. The increasing coverage by other agencies and by the press has tended more and more to duplicate our own, and, because of the unique political situation in Berlin, the classic distinctions between clandestine and overt political intelligence, between straight news and behind-the-scenes information, between truth and deception, have broken down completely. Our present function in the political field has therefore become uncertain and confused, and we have tended to neglect current spot coverage in favor of long range penetration. In the case of one important target, the CDU, we had occasion at the end of 1947 to point out to our local customers (some of them amateur rivals in the matter) that the party was so redundantly covered by a variety of agencies that we were forced to protect our long-range interests by withdrawing from the spot-news field. In the main, however, we have supplied a steady stream of information on party politics, with a fair trickle on the political maneuvers of the Russians.

In the economic field our coverage has shown solid progress. Our long statistical reports based largely on documents purloined from the Central Administrations now constitute the bread-and-butter output of the Base. We are rifling the confidential files of the Reichsbahndirektion and the Derutra trucking network systematically, and our disseminations on freight shipments recall staple issues of SI during the war. It is in the field of Russian Zone manufactures, quotas, allocations, shipments, and accounting that we have provided our best and fullest information on Soviet aims and actions. The ▓▓▓▓▓▓ chain alone would suffice to give us a near monopoly of this field among Berlin agencies.

Finally we may point to the increasingly thorough coverage of scientific and technological developments as perhaps the most creative expansion of FR production. ▓ SICHEL'S keen eye for intelligence opportunities has been nowhere more penetrating, and several case officers (particularly ▓▓▓▓▓▓▓▓▓ have developed considerable flair in exploiting new leads. We have been greatly encouraged in this effort by the support of Washington, which has promptly answered briefing requests and has given us a sense of the value of our material. We have also been gratified by the occasional impact which we have been able to make on OMGUS, notably in the ▓▓▓▓▓▓ affair, which largely as a

SECRET

- 17 -

result of a strictly clandestine intelligence initiative by
Mr. Sichel has carried through to the successful prosecution
of the case against directors and engineers of the Askania
plant.

On the debit side of FR production we must place
our disappointingly small headway with ████████, where our penetrations are proceeding very slowly; and the almost complete lack
of Russian and other non-German sources. FR has developed no
important Russian case, defection or penetration, since its
temporary and limited participation in ████████ It is only
fair to point out that FR has been handicapped by lack of personnel specifically qualified to handle Russian cases. Moreover, it
is inevitable that SC Branch should have taken the lead in this
field, since automatically all Russian cases in their initial
stage must be handled as suspect penetrations. I shall return to
this question below, but I wish to emphasize at this point the
importance of assigning Russian-speaking case officers to FR as
well as to SC Branch.

Though there have been tenuous and inconclusive lead
into Yugoslav groups, and occasional scraps on the alleged recruitment of various nationals for fighting in the Balkans, FR's
non-German production has been uniformly meager. Our withdrawal
from the Polish operation, mentioned above, was an acknowledgment
that with our present type of staff and recruiting possibilities,
and under the conditions now prevailing in Poland and New Poland,
penetration from Berlin was ineffectual and unprofitable.

In concluding this highly generalized survey of
FR Branch, I should like to emphasize what seems to me its most
tangible and enduring achievement, viz. the training of intelligence officers. The case officers and the executive staff of
the Branch, not to mention SC and myself, have profited enormously
from the past two years' experience in positive operations. The
self-criticism inspired by the Agent Review, the self-discipline
and restraint which were required to meet and cope with our
security problems, the extension of our sphere of experience with
the contraction of our target areas--all these are grounds for
sober satisfaction. In my opinion the FR Branch in Berlin can
view the prospect of the future with confidence and optimism.

SECRET

SECRET

- 18 -

B. SC Branch

[redacted]

There have been no fundamental structural changes in the organization of the SC Branch since its activation. Naturally there have been the inevitable changes in personnel. The most important of these changes occurred in June of 1947; with the dissolution of IB in Heidelberg. [HECKsHER] was transferred to Berlin replacing [TOM POLGAR] as chief of the branch.

The intelligence production of the SC Branch has been relatively steady throughout 1946 - 1947, though the number of reports has constantly decreased. This was due to several factors: a) elimination of reporting on certain topics, such as former GIS members, Nazis in hiding, low-level RIS operations, etc.; b) elimination of operations reports unless the contents had direct bearing on intelligence; c) higher standards of reporting required from case officer. From a technical point of view, the only change in reporting technique occurred with the introduction of BSC Ops reports in late 1946; otherwise the standard RIR of old x-2 days was preserved with minor changes. Numerically, our reports were divided as follows:

	1946	1947
RIR	647	254
BSC Ops	10	193
Total	657	447

In operations as in personnel there has been both continuity and change. Our principal targets have been confirmed and priorities assigned by Washington directives. Our shifts in operational

SECRET

30

SECRET

- 19 -

emphasis were in part a response to directives, in part the natural outgrowth of the changes in personnel and the lessons of experience.

The primary SC target remained in 1947 as in 1946 the Russian Intelligence Service. But the method of approach has undergone a marked change. 1946 may be described as the period of endeavor through the classic method of the double agent, working on the tactical level. 1947 brought about a gradual disillusionment with this method, and a shift of emphasis to defection and straight penetration.

This disillusionment has grown out of a candid re-examination of our two principal endeavors in the double agent field, the ████████ case and the case of SAVOY which later was taken over by ████ alias ███████████. In both our effort had been to turn agents back against the Russian case officer and headquarters which had given them either counter-intelligence penetration or kidnaping assignments in the U. S. Sector. We hoped by doubling the agents to obtain the following: a) the identity and personal description of all Russian officers directly handling the agent; b) the location and order of battle of the controlling office; c) general knowledge of Russian methods at least in Berlin; d) security protection for FR operations; e) an "intoxication" of the Russian case officer, through which we might eventually be able to force him to work for us; f) a channel for passing deception material of either positive or counter intelligence importance if that should be required at a later date. The practical result of the ████████████████████████] and lesser cases has led us to the reluctant conclusion that our tactical double agent program has not rewarded our expenditure of effort. We are not sure, however, whether this generalization from our own experience in Berlin can be expanded to other situations, here or elsewhere.

The principal reason why our double agent work has fallen short of expectations seems to lie in an underestimate of Russian security and an overestimate of their ambition. In the case of ████████████████] it is our belief that our handling was sound, and that Major SKURIN is still not aware that his agents have been doubled. Nevertheless, he evaded the trap we carefully laid in April 1947 in the hope of forcing him to continue working for the Russians but under our control. As far as we can determine, the fact that he did not fall was not owing to any fault in our arrangements, but to an instinctive wariness, plus a last minute reversion to the sensible decision not to try a coup de main in the French Sector. Indeed, if we may generalize from SKURIN's general operational methods, Russian case officers are fully experienced in all the tricks of agent handling: neutral meeting points, aliases, red herrings, keeping the agent in blinders so

SECRET

SECRET
- 30 -

far as concerns the location of headquarters and identity of other agents or staff personnel. Moreover, we seriously doubt whether the Russians are in the habit of promoting their agents, i.e. shifting them to bigger and better assignments as a reward or recognition of successful performance. In other words there seems little likelihood that the successful cultivation of a double, even with the most promising build up material on our side will ever lead him into broader fields. Instead the prospect is one of diminishing returns in fairly tightly closed areas.

The meagerness of reward in our double agent operations has been emphasized by contrast with the fruitfulness of defection cases. The two principal counterespionage defections of 1947 (SAILOR and KRAVCHENKO) were neither one the achievement of SC Germany though the former was debriefed by GEORGE BELL and though we participated as equal partners with CIC in debriefing the latter. In any case, they illustrate the point that a single defector can, with a minimum of effort on our part, provide in-comparably better and more abundant CE information than any double agent whom we have yet been able to groom.

We may add that our experience in Berlin has been confirmed by the British, so far as we are able to estimate from their production. Our principal opposite number cultivated with great skill and persistence a promising double operation during a period of eight months. At the end, the order of battle on the RIS which he obtained covered only half a page. But in the meantime through a series of carefully encouraged low level defections (interpreters and secretaries) the same officer had paved the way for interro-gations covering in great detail all the principal RIS head-quarters in Berlin and the Soviet Sector, with names and descrip-tions of hundreds of staff and agent personnel. At least in this stage of our approach to RIS, the defection method seems over-whelmingly more profitable than the double agent.

It is of course true that the defection approach has its drawbacks. Defections are nearly always spontaneous and unpredict-able. It is difficult to get word of an impending defection, of one who is wavering or who has already made up his mind but does not know what steps to take. In other words it is a method based less on systematic effort than on patiently waiting for windfalls. It is not a method which, over a long period of time, will produce vigorous counterespionage officers and an efficient organization.

In addition to these two approaches: intensive cultivation of individual double agents and patiently extending a net for potential defectors, a third type of activity is open, viz. they systematic development of auxiliary CE coverages. In our opinion this third approach has proved the most profitable during the

SECRET

SECRET

- 21 -

past year, though we do not maintain that it will always continue to be.

The principal objectives of au-iliary CE operations in Berlin have been the penetration of the German police, the Soviet and Soviet-licensed press services, and the collection of background information on overt Soviet officials at the Allied Control Authority level (Project ███████).

The police coverage, indeed, may almost be regarded as a basic rather than as an au-iliary operation. In the early stages of the operation, which was initiated by ███████ in April 1946, our primary concern was our own defence. The Russian as the result of their e-clusive position in Berlin from April to July 1945, had established a strong hold on the police service of the entire city. This hold, or at least a powerful influence, was maintained for some time after the arrival of the other three powers, among other reasons because of Soviet occupancy of the central Polizeipraesidium in Linienstrasse. There was serious danger that they might continue to e-ercise police control in the three western sectors, thereby not only impairing our sovereignty but also greatly handicapping our intelligence activities. Fortunately this hold was broken by vigorous British and American action in the Kommandatura. Throughout the critical stage in la 1946, SC was in close touch with American Public Safety official and can claim credit for providing confidential reports on Russi and Communist machinations, which greatly strengthened the Ameri counteroffensive. It is no e-aggeration to say that the service we rendered Public Safety at that critical stage has been reward many times over in the material support and valuable leads they have given us (e.g. the initial tip on the British defection of Tokayev).

With the victory of American Public Safety, our interest in direct penetration of the police diminished. But in the meanwhi a new, and potentially more significant target arose, the Centra Administration of the Interior in Wilhelmsruhe. The penetration of that agency, when it was still in cadre stage, was accomplish by ███████ and his basic report on the CAI was the first ma: impact of an SC dissemination on the higher echelons of Military Government. Our coverage has continued to be fruitful. We have kept a sharp eye on any signs of a latent political police withi the CAI, and are confident that we will be among the first to de and penetrate any such insidious agency.

Thus while it cannot be said that our police and CAI covera; has yielded us much information of strictly CE nature, we can feel satisfied that it has kept us in position to spring upon a

SECRET

SECRET

- 22 -

covert German law enforcement agencies which the Russians may set up with the hopes of gaining a stranglehold on a future German central government.

In the second field of auxiliary coverage -- the Soviet and Soviet-licensed press services -- the counterespionage yield has admittedly been small, but something has been gained. By recasting the ████████/operation, ████████████ with relatively small outlay of time and energy, has accomplished a very thorough penetration of the two principal Russian controlled news agencies, ADN and SNB. Through operation ███████████ we hoped to extend our penetration beyond the German fringe, into the inner sanctum of Russian press and propaganda. SC interest in this group of operations was greatly stimulated by a report from London that Soviet Intelligence was using the facilities of the press services for the transmission of espionage reports and directives in western Europe. So far, we have not been able to confirm this report; but our instinct tells us that the "total espionage" principle, under which the Russians operate, makes it highly probable that they have not overlooked this convenient communications channel. Moreover, having scrutinized the activities of the Soviet journalists, both in the American and the British Zones, we have obtained conclusive proof that journalism and espionage for the Russians are complementary functions. Through ████████ we obtained our first glimpse of the cloak and dagger activities of Russian correspondents on their tours of the American Zone. ████████████████████████████████

██

████████████ Ironically, it was ████████ who called our attention to the fact that Amzon CIC had also entered the field, and was creating havoc by an excess of zeal -- obvious shadowing, rifling the baggage of the Russian correspondents, etc. We brought the matter to the attention of General Walsh, who instructed CIC in no uncertain terms that the correspondents were to be treated with the respect due "honored visitors".

Our third effort, Project ████████ started rather casually, as an effort to build up background personality information on Russian officials who appeared on the quadripartite level. The arrival of] *BELIC* , gave impetus and direction to this program, and we soon realized that ████████ afforded an excellent lead into echelons where promising defections or penetrations might be developed. In order to regularize our project, we concluded two working agreements. We arranged with Ambassador Murphy to have personality and background reports on Russian ACA personnel submitted by the Chief of Liaison and Protocol directly to Mr. *BELIC* SC thus was in a position to distribute this type of

SECRET

SECRET

- 23 -

information both to the State Department and the Army. At the same time, we concluded an agreement with General Walsh, whereby BELIC would have a monopoly of operations on the ACA level, while S-2 would handle the lower echelon of the Allied Kommandatura, information being exchanged on both. Both these agreements have been carried out satisfactorily. ▓▓▓▓ has produced a substantial sheaf of solid, if unspectacular, personality information. It has contributed to the build-up of BELIC and Hecksher as unofficial collaborators of the Political Advisor's Office, and has given us the kudos and the entree which enabled us to mount the ▓▓▓▓ operation.

To sump up the significance of these auxiliary CE operations, we feel that the following accomplishments may be recorded: a) support of American interests by penetration of sensitive Russian-controlled agencies; b) picking up numerous by-products of positive FR type information; c) delimiting and plotting areas of potential subversive Russian activity; d) establishing channels for receiving defection leads; e) confirming the habit and practice of CE briefing as an integral part of the approach to any positive intelligence target.

SC Branch enters 1948 with the conviction that its combination of approaches will pay off abundantly. After a rather dull beginning ▓▓▓▓ operation took on the aspect of a classical delayed defection with interim penetration. Although ▓▓▓▓'s target, the MVD, is no longer the heart of the RIS in Germany, it still is a part of the basic organism, and an important one. The ▓▓▓▓ operation, if it can be continued, has carried us into the highest echelon ▓▓▓▓ where intelligence, deception, and policy converge in a single (or perhaps dual) personality. A large point of uncertainty still lies in the question whether the classical double agent operation, typified in the ▓▓▓▓ case, can also be made to pay off. We have our doubts, but wish to give it further trial.

C. Interrelation of the Branches

The fundamental question of the future is the closer integration of FR and SC Branch. Whether they should be formally merged at all levels is of course a question for Washington to decide. At our level, we have done a great deal of thinking and experimenting, and have reached a few tentative conclusions. I shall attempt to synthesize what I hope would be a minimum of agreement among ourselves in Berlin.

The basic difference between counter and positive espionage seems to be irreducible, as far as product in concerned. For that reason, no unified system of reporting or filing seems feasible. On the other hand the operational approach and method, though

SECRET

MORI Document ID:> 144185:144185

- 24 -

distinct, tend to converge. There can be no doubt, in my mind, that every career intelligence officer should be equally grounded in both fields. Training techniques must be developed, both theoretical and practical, which are independent of branch distinctions. Eventually, the individual case officer may specialize in one or other of the two directions, but he must always keep up his skill in both.

It is no criticism of FR Branch to say that some of its short-comings in Berlin have been owing to the fact that none of its officers went through the wartime or postwar X-2 discipline. Moreover the high pressure of their work during the past two years has made it impossible for them to achieve any degree of self-training in the counter field. The nearest to an exception was ▓▓▓▓▓▓ B. ▓▓▓▓, who took the occasion of the blowing of the ▓▓▓▓ ▓▓chains, to embark on what might be called an FR counter program of his own. ▓▓▓▓▓▓▓ assembled several survivors of the blown chain, trained and organized them into a sort of surveillance and strong arm squad to assist him in protecting the other remnants and tracing down the source of the original blow. Although this was an interesting experiment, and yielded certain tangible results it was not in the long run a practicable venture for FR.

Two principal fields have emerged in which cooperation between the two Branches is essential, viz. ▓▓▓▓▓▓ and ▓▓▓▓▓▓▓▓ and the ▓▓▓▓▓▓▓▓▓▓▓ Considerable progress has been made in each project.

The ▓▓▓▓▓ Desk at Heidelberg has now been in existence for more than a year, and for the past six months it has had a representative in Berlin, ▓▓▓▓▓▓▓▓▓▓▓▓▓▓ Since ▓▓▓▓▓▓▓ is primarily an FR case officer, he has been able to devote only a fraction of his time to specifically ▓▓▓▓▓ work. He has maintained a close liaison with the Political Advisor's Office (Mr. Brewster Morris) and the Political Section of CIC (Mr. Gutman). Since the former is non-operational and the latter has achieved only a limited and dubious penetration of the SED, the total yield through this liaison has been small. Our own failure to initiate profitable penetrations is not to be blamed solely on the FR Branch, since ▓▓▓▓▓▓ by its very nature, is equally a concern of SC. The heads of both branches have agreed to work closely on all cases, and to place the highest priority for 1948 on getting results in this field. We plan in the near future to hold conferences with the head of the ▓▓▓▓▓▓Desk and other members of Heidelberg Operational Base, and to set down a sharply focused list of specific targets which will be immediately assigned to individual case officers. We shall no longer be content with the leisurely, long range approach of working likely young candidates up through the Party schools and hierarchy ▓▓▓▓▓▓▓▓▓▓▓▓▓▓▓▓▓▓▓▓.

MORI Document ID:> 144185:144185

SECRET

- 25 -

The problem of covering the SPD as a joint target has been
dramatized by a number of recent developments. The affair of the
notorious Protocol M, on which this Base reported in considerable
detail, carried us into a field in which we had hitherto had only
glimpses. Although it has been clearly established that the document itself was a forgery, it has not yet been determined what the
motives were, both in its concoction and in its rapid distribution
in SPD circles. Through our penetration of [   ]
Protocol M our attention was directed to [   ]

[   ] the so-called OSTSEKRETARIAT of the SPD. This clandestine
agency, which is run from the immediate entourage of the SPD
Party leader, Dr. Schumacher, includes elements of espionage,
black propaganda, and potential sabotage. It is achieving
increasingly large dimensions and now claims to have over 2000
agents or informants. Various British and American agencies have
latched onto it with varying measures of partial support, but the
institution seems to emerge as something which may be beyond the
power of occupying allies to control.

To conclude this discussion, I believe that Berlin Base could
operate under either a continued separation or a merger of the
Branches. In spite of the process of concentration and self-
criticism, we shall have to continue an extensive program of
straightforward, bread and butter coverage, for our customers in
the Theater and at home. We shall need a strong panel of case
officers specializing in "straight" methods, and a sizeable
reporting staff to screen, edit, and disseminate their reports.
On the SC side we shall continue the specialized counterapproach
to our primary target, the Russian Intelligence Service. These
activities can be carried out within the present Branch structure,
provided steady pressure is exerted by the Chief of Base to
insure the cooperation of the two. We have already taken certain
internal steps to insure close working harmony. Cable traffic is
routed to both Branches, except in the case of Eyes Only. The
Base Chief's daily staff conference includes the two ranking
officers of each branch and the Executive Officer. Important
cases are discussed fully at these conferences, irrespective of
Branch. The reporting procedure is constantly checked to make

SECRET

- 26 -

sure that subject matter rather than branch origin is the
criterion of distribution.

If, on the other hand, Washington should decide to abolish
Branch distinction, we would be prepared to operate on a different
basis. A single operating Branch would be feasible at this Base,
though a new differentiation would undoubtedly be called for within
that Branch. Such a differentiation might be grounded in the
distinction between operations using German agents on the one
hand and non-German, specifically Russian, on the other. The
counter as opposed to the positive type of operations could be
broken down satisfactorily on such a basis, within the framework
of existing personnel. Thus the group of German agent specialists
would handle such cases as the SPD OSTSEKRETARIAT with an eye to
both their positive and counterintelligence content. Similarly,
the Russian group would handle straight RIS penetrations, such as
 together with positive information cases of the type of
The facilities of the present Reports Board could be
adapted to the needs of both groups.

In effect, the problem is fairly simple, and is susceptible
of two solutions. The current operating strength of the Berlin
Detachment is about 15 case officers. This is a large group to
be operated without an internal division. Whether the split
should be made on the traditional lines of counter and positive,
or on the lines of German and non-German, and whether it should
include specialized desks such as ███████ is a matter for
further discussion. In either case, the two Branches or groups
can and must be made to function as a single entity. In my
opinion, no matter what measures of dispersal may be adopted, the
continued unity of the Berlin Base should be preserved.

SECRET

- 27 -

PART XII

LIAISON RELATIONS OF BERLIN OPERATIONS BASE

The conduct of liaison at the Berlin Operations Base has constituted one of our major activities, second in importance only to the supervision of operations. I feel that the progress in our liaison has been one of our principal achievements during the past two years, and has contributed more than any other single factor to the stability and future prospects of our Base. We have tried to govern our liaison by the principle of developing our sphere of usefulness and our prestige, while maintaining the "passion for anonymity". In all cases, the basic liaison is the responsibility of the Chief of Base, but day to day working liaison is extensively delegated.

A. Executive Liaisons

Four major executive echelons of the European Command are housed in the Director's Building of OMGUS, with each of which we have occasion to maintain direct contact. The first and highest echelon is that of the Commander in Chief and Military Governor (CINCEUR), General Lucius D. Clay. It is only on rare occasions and in matters of the greatest moment that we have had direct contact with General Clay. In 1946 there were two such occasions. The first was in March when the General requested the Deputy Chief of Mission, ████████████ and myself to transfer administrative attachment of this Base to Berlin District. The second was in October when the Chief of Mission, Mr. Lewis, notified the General of the changeover from SSU to CIA and solicited a request to continue our services. This request was drafted for General Clay by ODI OMGUS and passed by us to Washington where it was accepted. In 1947 our only significant business with General Clay was on the occasion of the visit of Brig. General Edwin K. Wright, at which time our request for Military Government cover was presented and refused. We were also indirectly in contact with General Clay on the occasion of the London Conference of Foreign Ministers in December 1947.

The second echelon is that of the Deputy Military Governor who is the Commanding General, OMGUS. On the whole our contacts at this level are rare, our business being conducted chiefly through the Office of the Director of Intelligence (ODI, OMGUS, see below, III D). The present incumbent is Major General George P. Fays. Our introduction to General Fays took place on the occasion of the visit of Mr. DONALD GALLOWAY a November 1947. GALLOWAY represented the role of our Detachment to General Fays and solicited his support for our administrative needs. This impact was reinforced by the December crisis, when our information on Russian reparations policy changes was submitted to General Fays personally, on his instructions, at the same time that it was transmitted to London.

SECRET

32-6-2-'47

39

SECRET
- 28 -

It is difficult to say what has been the impact of our organization on these echelons. In the past General Clay has been regarded as hostile, or at least indifferent, to intelligence. But, we believe, this hostility has largely been confined to Theater agencies, going back to the bitter feuds between Frankfurt and Berlin in 1945 and early 1946. Toward our own organization, his attitude has been correct and courteous. As representing an independent Washington agency, we have been accorded freedom and material support. As an integral part of the Theater Command, we have been able to enjoy the confidence and respect of the Commander and his Director of Intelligence, without having to submit to the full measure of command control.

General Hays like General Clay also appears to be somewhat negative in his attitude toward intelligence. As Commanding General of the 10th Mountain Division in Italy, he harbored a considerable personal grudge against OSS for claiming, as he felt, undue credit for bringing about the Italian surrender. As General Hays puts it, the Germans surrendered not because of OSS but because of the victorious advance of the ground troops. General Hays fortunately has not allowed this attitude to prejudice his judgment of our agency which as Mr. Galloway explained to him, is not the OSS.

The third directing echelon, that of the OMGUS Chief of Staff, Brigadier General Charles Gailey, is the highest with which we deal on basic administrative and executive matters. General Gailey performs for General Clay and General Hays routine staff functions without which a large and complex headquarters speedily tends to disintegrate. Some of our principal encounters with the Chief of Staff have been mentioned elsewhere in this report, viz. approval and subsequent withdrawal of *decorners* (cover) in Public Safety, sporadic pressure to move out of our building, clearance of travel orders for Germans, etc. In all these matters we have had to face a certain degree of initial negativeness. In part General Gailey's antipathy toward "Cloak and Dagger" may have been motivated by the fact that he was formerly Chief of Public Relations, and as such was one of the principal proponent's of General Clay's famous "Goldfish Bowl" policy. In part, it may be a reflection of General Clay's real or imputed antipathy toward intelligence. My policy has been extremely cautious with General Gailey. I have personally invited him to inspect our motor pool and building, and have, I believe, convinced him that our logistic requirements are reasonable. I have emphasized the service which we render to CINCEUR and OMGUS as customers, and have made every effort to enhance our prestige in his eyes. The effort, I believe, has paid off. A single instance may illustrate our present good standing: when the American Overseas Airlines introduced a Commercial service, Berlin to Frankfurt, for Germans, General Gailey without solicitation on our part included us in the very limited group of agencies which were to enjoy Priority I, an invaluable privilege in carrying out agent movements.

SECRET

SECRET

The fourth component in the directing echelon is the Assistant
Deputy Military Governor, Brigadier General W. Fesketh. The function of General Hesketh is that of Commandant of the American
Sector of Berlin. As such, he is the American representative in
the quadripartite Berlin Kommandatura, and makes the highest level
political decisions affecting the City of Berlin. We have relatively little occasion to contact General Hesketh, since most of
our business affecting the American sector is conducted in the
Office of Military Government, Berlin Sector (see below III, G).
We did however negotiate with him in connection with the mounting
of Project ▮▮▮▮▮ and were received in a cordial and friendly
manner.

Other elements in the "front office" include the Office of
the Secretary General and the Office of the Staff Secretary.
Since we are not an integral part of OMGUS, we do not appear on
the routing of official cables and do not attend the weekly staff
meeting of the Military Governor. We do maintain informal personal
contacts through which we are informed of any correspondence or
cable traffic affecting our interests. We also obtain an unofficial account of the weekly staff meeting through the Office of
the Director of Intelligence. In this way, we keep ourselves
informed of the principal local developments without exposing ourselves by public appearance.

Another important section of headquarters is the Office of
Management Control, a sort of super planning and coordinating
agency for the command echelon. We maintain close contact through
Dr. David G. White, formerly of OSS R & A.

███████████████████████████████████████

Finally mention should be made of the battery of special
assistants and advisors in the Director's Building of OMGUS.
General Clay has at various times had special advisors on German
politics, who for the most part have been distinguished figures
from academic life. The most influential was Dr. Walter Dorn,
formerly of OSS, R & A, who served as special advisor on denazification until September 1947 when he returned to his professorship
at Western Reserve University. Another distinguished advisor was
Dr. Carl Friedrich, Professor of Government at Harvard University,
who was in Berlin on three occasions during 1947, twice to advise

SECRET

SECRET 70

General Clay on the establishment of civil liberties in Germany, and the third time as consultant for the House Foreign Affairs Committee. Dr. Friedrich will return at General Clay's personal request in April 1948. Both of these special advisors were personal friends and professional colleagues of mine. We frequently found them useful as a source of background information on OMGUS and German political developments. However, we were careful to avoid giving them the status of intelligence customers, which, particularly in the case of Dr. Dorn, they occasionally tried to establish.

In addition to these academic advisors, General Clay also established an office known as "The Special Advisor" which since the middle of 1947 has been filled by Mr. Anthony J. Panuch. Mr. Panuch is a professional organizer, trouble shooter and public relations man, whose chief concern has been as he puts it to "sell" the American Public on Military Government in Germany. Despite his undeniably great influence, we have felt that no useful purpose would serve by making ourselves known to Mr. Panuch.

B. **Director of Intelligence, European Command**

During 1947, Berlin Operations Base has been in constant direct contact with the Office of the Director of Intelligence, European Command. The accidents of jurisdiction have forced onto our lower echelon the burden of day to day contact with an echelon to which we have not been strictly opposite. We trust that we have acquitted ourselves of this responsibility to the satisfaction of our higher echelons.

The first act of General Clay, on taking over the command of the European Theater from General Mc Narney, was to transfer all policy-making echelons from Frankfurt to Berlin. In the case of Intelligence, this resulted in a compromise solution of the problem which had split the Theater ever since the establishment of the two major headquarters. The bulk of the old USFET G-2 remained in Frankfurt, and continued to direct all the principal operations, such as CIC, Civilian Censorship, and such specialized institutions as the Interrogation Center at Oberursel and ███████ The policy control of intelligence was moved to Berlin in the person of first Major General W. A. Burress and later Major General Robert Walsh (March 1947). A small staff, never more than four or five officers and a half dozen clerical and enlisted personnel, supported this office. Our contact in this office has always been directly with General Walsh. It has been governed by the simple lines of the USFET directive of January 1946 which established SSU as a special staff section of the Theater under the "general staff supervision" of what was then G-2.

General Walsh has frequently stated his policy of establishing clear jurisdiction, according to lines of competence, so as

SECRET

42

MORI Document ID:> 144185:144185

– 31 SECRET

to avoid conflict or duplication. In the case of the agencies
directly under his command (CIC and S-2 Berlin), he has consistently ordered them to cooperate with us wherever we were entitled
to the initiative (e.g. confirmation of the Koval cable, Project
▓▓▓▓ on the ACA level). In cases where the dominant operational
role obviously lay with one of his own agencies, he has kept me
personally informed, and requested us to cooperate as far as possible or at least avoid interference. An example of the latter was
the major alert of CIC beginning on Christmas Eve, 1947, and continuing with top priority until after the New Year, and on lower
priority to the present. This alert, which was in response to a
Washington order, involved the external surveillance of principle
Russian headquarters in Berlin, with a view to detecting signs of
any unusual activity. (The results of the alert were largely
negative).

Inevitably, with its small staff, the office of General Walsh
has not required a detailed intelligence liaison contact. All
intelligence reports of sufficient importance to pass over the
Theater Commander's desk are transmitted through that office, and
we may, so far as we desire, have access to them. General Walsh
has offered to show us regularly the daily Top Secret summary which
is prepared for General Clay and which contains a large amount of
ESD material. General Walsh has also been extremely frank and open
in his discussion of such matters as the position of ▓▓▓▓▓▓▓ his
relations with his British opposite numbers, etc.

C. Office of the Political Advisor

In terms of echelon, the Office of the Political Advisor should
be placed ahead of the office of the Theater Director of Intelligence. USPOLAD, during the two and a half years of its existence
has indeed had a somewhat anomalous position. In effect it has
been an epitome of OMGUS some 100 strong, parallelling its major
functional divisions but without its executive authority. It has
been the State Department's cadre for a future embassy, and as
such includes the staffs of economic, legal, financial, and political (and at one time under Col. Fohenthal, military) attaches.
It has consistently reported to the State Department through its
own independent channels, and has preserved the integrity of its
special mission.

On the other hand, its very presence as an OMGUS within OMGUS,
has in part been on sufferance. As General Clay once said, he put
up with these "political commissars" largely because "Bob Murphy
was such a swell fellow." POLAD, indeed, is Ambassador Murphy,
the political advisor, in the fullest sense, of the Military Governor of Germany. Those who have had a glimpse of the day to day
relationship of General Clay and Ambassador Murphy have no doubt
that it is a relation of friends and equals, and possibly of
incumbent and successor. But it is also a relation of two very

SECRET

43

different organizations, the Army and the State Department, the one in control, the other awaiting its turn. Inevitably, the effects of this purely passive function are noticeable in the atmosphere of the POLAD staff. A large number of its members are relatively junior regular Foreign Service officers, who normally would be components of an embassy or consular establishment. Here they are supernumeraries or sideliners, in an active and powerful functional headquarters, several thousand strong, which looks upon them primarily as a necessary evil. The effect of this sense of accessoriness cannot be overlooked in discussing our dealing with the Political Advisor's office.

Stated in our own terms, POLAD is our second major customer. It receives all our reports on the same level of distribution as ODI, OMGUS (see below, Section D). But that is where the similarity ends. Usually nothing happens to our reports on the working level in POLAD. We receive almost no evaluations; we do not see any summaries issuing from the office, in which our material is incorporated, except the Brewster Morris reports on ███████. Doubtless, some of it gets back to Washington, but presumably not everything, since POLAD assumes that the State Department will receive reports directly from our own headquarters. We maintain virtually no direct contact with the individual Branches of POLAD, especially the Economics and Political Branches. It is true that in 1946 we did maintain such contact, but that has gradually dwindled, as we mutually recognized its non-functional nature. In short, the working staff of POLAD as an intelligence customer is receptive but unresponsive.

When we turn, however, to the higher field of policy relations, the story is different. As I have already stated, Ambassador Murphy is a power behind the throne with some of the aspects of an heir apparent. Moreover, from our viewpoint, he is the most powerful completely friendly figure on our horizon. General Clay, to us as to all, is aloof and Olympian. With General Walsh we cannot completely ignore the presence of a competitive or at least divergent interest. With Ambassador Murphy, we suffer no such difficulties. He has been eminently approachable. Moreover, in Ambassador Murphy's own background lies an important era of cloak and dagger work, which bit him with the same virus as ourselves. To put it in a nutshell, he understands what we are doing and enjoys occasionally taking part in it himself. He is the highest level to which we in Berlin can turn for the sanction of such delicate operations as the evacuation of ███████ or the approach to ███

For day to day affairs, as I have said above, we have stopped turning to the intermediate and lower echelons, because of their remoteness from the actual conduct of affairs. There are two principal exceptions. First is the office of the Director of Political Affairs, which is the number two position in POLAD.

SECRET

- 33 -

Until October 1947, the incumbent of this office was Mr. Donald Heath, a career State Department official, who is now Minister to Bulgaria. Mr. Heath was one of our friendliest supporters, and gave us an important boost by approving in principle the attachment of WDD personnel [redacted] in the Theater. But, in general, his experience was somewhat along conventional State Department lines, and did not include any special indoctrination in clandestine intelligence work. Our one principal effort to interest Mr. Heath in this field was a visit by [redacted] then Deputy Chief of Mission, who offered Mr. Heath the benefit of our contacts with the SPD, as a channel for conveying unofficial points of view from the State Department to the Party leadership. Mr. Heath expressed appreciation of our offer, but felt that it lay beyond present POLAD scope, and preferred that we confine ourselves to the reporting of inside developments within the SPD, rather than the transmission of sub rosa policy hints. This was, of course, an understandable reticence on Mr. Heath's part, in view of the limited scope of POLAD initiative.

In October 1947 Mr. Heath was succeeded by Mr. James Riddleberger, formerly head of the Central European Division of the State Department, and a good friend of our organization. Mr. Riddleberger brought a more dynamic approach into POLAD, particularly in regard to intelligence matters. He has been fully conscious of the interrelation between intelligence and policy, and has welcomed and acted upon our suggestions. A good example of his receptiveness was his prompt and effective action on the request of Gordon Stewart that he meet Dr. Gerstenmaier, chief of the Evangelische Hilfswerk. Largely as a result of Stewart's initiative and Riddleberger's reception, Gerstenmaier became completely persona grata in OMGUS, and was able to secure most gratifying offers of political and financial support from OMGUS officials.

[redacted]

SECRET

SECRET
- 34 -

The principal functional desk of POLAD is the Political Branch. The chief of Branch, Mr. Warren Chase, has been uniformly cooperative and friendly. However, it has been our practice almost invariably to deal with his superiors, Ambassador Murphy and Mr. Riddleberger. We have working contacts with the members of Mr. Chase's staff, especially with Mr. Louis Wiesner who handles Labor matters; but because of certain inadequacies in both his intelligence experience and security we have maintained considerable detachment toward Mr. Wiesner, and have, indeed, tactfully suggested to both Ambassador Murphy and Mr. Riddleberger that a little supervision and training might be in order. Both fully agreed, and Mr. Riddleberger informed us that he intended to exercise a much closer control over the entire Political Branch than his predecessor Mr. Heath.

From our viewpoint, the most important contact in the Political Branch is Mr. Brewster Morris, who over the past two years has firmly established his position as the State Department's authority on Communist activities in Germany. Although the bulk of his reporting has been based on overt sources, its real merit derives from the clandestine material which he has received principally from us and the Political Section of CIC. Morris himself has no operational facilities, but he is in a position to contact and entertain German officials and members of the SED party. Through him we can plant and receive operational leads of great value. We

SECRET

SECRET

In the economic field, our liaison with POLAD is very slight. Although the present chief of the Economics Branch, Mr. W. C. Haraldson and his predecessor, Mr. Lloyd Steere, have both expressed interest in our economic reports, the fact remains that the interest has been largely platonic. This is inevitable, since the Economics Branch of POLAD in its present status is the epitome of frustration, vis a vis the huge and omnicompetent Economics Division of OMGUS.

We have had little occasion to maintain official contact with the American Consulate General. ████████████████████
██
████████████████████████████████████

On the counter intelligence side, we maintain contact with the security officer of POLAD, Mr. John Reager. However, the bulk of Mr. Reager's activity concerns State Department personnel and physical security, and therefore does not fall in the sphere of interest of SC Branch.

Somewhat more useful to us is the Exploitation of German Archives Branch. The chief of branch, Mr. Wendell Blancke, was formerly in the Embassy at Buenos Aires, and has remained a specialist in the Latin American field, which is of relatively little concern to us in Berlin. He does, however, control the unit which houses and exploits the captured archives of the German Foreign Office. Although these documents are primarily of historical interest, they occasionally yield bits of currently useful information. Our chief operational contact with Mr. Blancke occurred in connection with the ████████ operation. Mr. Blancke and Mr. Morris were the two State Department guests of Mr. Murphy on the occasion of the dinner ██████████ Mr. Blancke cooperated with Mr. ████ in drafting the official report of that memorable occasion.

We may summarize our experience with POLAD during 1946-47 by saying that we have lifted ourselves almost completely from the lower to the higher echelon. We have interested and we believe instructed them (and ourselves) in the problem of putting clandestine intelligence at the service of policy while maintaining effective security. We have converted a passive customer into an active co-worker, and enlisted, I believe, the support of what may eventually become the governing agency of the American occupation.

D. Office of the Director of Intelligence, OMGUS

By far the most active outside relationship of the Berlin Base is with the Office of the Director of Intelligence, OMGUS. In order to understand our present position with ODI, it may be worthwhile to review briefly the history of that office.

SECRET

In the early stages of OMGUS, <u>ODI was conceived and set up with the intention of making it the principal intelligence agency</u> of the occupation. It was originally to have been headed by Brig. Gen. T. E. Betts, and when the latter was incapacitated, it was still headed in 1945 by a general officer, Brig. Gen. Bryan Conrad. It had a generous T/O, and actually was staffed at the top with four or five full colonels. In the fall of 1945 an ambitious staff study was drafted, which would have made ODI fully operational, with a panel of some 150 American special intelligence agents in Berlin and the American Zone. This plan was, however, quickly shelved, and ODI was prohibited from undertaking any operations, a prohibition which is still in force. Meanwhile, under the vigorous leadership of Brig. Gen. Edwin Sibert, the G-2 Section of USFET blossomed into the principal intelligence agency of the European Theater, and took over virtually all of the operational functions, except those exercised by SSU and minor agencies such as ONI. Further inroads were made into both the functions and the prestige of ODI by the ambitious political intelligence program of the Information Control Division. As a result, ODI in the spring and summer of 1946 declined rapidly, both in staff strength and in prestige. In September, it came within an ace of extinction, or at least of being taken over by ICD. The turning point came in October with the appointment of the present Director, Col. P.P. Rodes. Col. Rodes revitalized the nearly defunct office, appointing as the head of its Analysis and Research Branch, and later as Deputy Chief, Mr. Lawrence de Neufville, a former member of X-2 Branch, OSS. Col. Rodes, recognizing the limitations imposed by the prohibition against direct operation, placed the full emphasis of his office on the analysis of intelligence reports produced by other agencies. By gradually strengthening Mr. de Neufville's staff, he has been able in the course of a year and a half to develop his basic publication, the <u>ODI Weekly Notes</u>, into a massive and comprehensive intelligence summary, averaging more than 50 closely packed pages a week. The old rivalry with Army Intelligence has been largely resolved, ODI receiving from ODDI, EUCOM, the bulk of the latter's research and analysis functions. This transfer of responsibility has eliminated a major point of duplication and competition in the Theater intelligence, and has resulted in the development of an efficient, well-informed equivalent of the old R & A Branch of OSS, meeting a need which had been felt by all the agencies of OMGUS ever since R & A had been dissolved in Europe. Under present arrangements, ODI now prepares all except the purely military sections of the weekly intelligence cable to the Office of the Director of Intelligence, Department of the Army. <u>The ODI Weekly Notes</u> have been officially commended by the Department of the Army as the most valuable single intelligence publication from the Theater.

Our relations with ODI have naturally been influenced by the pattern of its own development. At the time I took up this post in January 1946, ODI had at times appeared to have a certain super-

SECRET

- 37 -

visory role in our relations with OMGUS. Our own status was
still somewhat unclear. The publication of the basic directive of
30 January 1946, placing SSU under the general staff supervision
of G-2 USFET, reduced our relation with ODI to a simple one of
producer and consumer. From the viewpoint of the Berlin Base, this
was, however, the primary local relationship. As a result, we
were to a certain extent committed to what might be called the
Berlin side, in the rivalry between G-2 and ODI. We represented to
Heidelberg the desirability, while remaining neutral as between
Frankfurt and Berlin, of strenghthening ODI and placing it on a
parity with G-2 in all except military intelligence disseminations.
At the low point of ODI's prestige (in late summer 1946) our defens
was to a certain extent intepreted by Feidelberg as perhaps excessive partiality for a local customer. Fowever, as events have
shown, it was a sound policy, and has won us the firm friendship
and solid support of ODI in its present prosperity.

ODI remains, indeed, the second rather than the first echelon
of Theater Intelligence. Col. Rodes in theory is one of two deputies to General Walsh, and as such is on a parity with the head
of ODDI Col Robert Schow, though of course Col Rodes' organization is of a very much smaller scale. But Col. Rodes at least de
facto is only to a limited degree subject to the jurisdiction of
General Walsh. In practice his function as the chief intelligence
officer of OMGUS entitles him to direct access to the Deputy Military Governor, General Hays, and at least in OMGUS staff meetings
and through the ODI Weekly Notes, he speaks directly to General
Clay.

We may state our own policy and practice in Berlin as follows.
On all political and economic intelligence of a routine nature,
we distribute through channels to ODI and to POLAD and leave to them
the responsibility of further use of our material. On major matter
affecting Theater or Washington policy, we usually take the intelli
gence direct to General Walsh, and to Ambassador Murphy, if the
matter is of unusual political interest. If it requires the attention of General Clay, it is presented to him by whichever of these
two officials is more directly interested or competent. In practic
even on the most important matters (as the Koval reparations cable)
we keep either Col Rodes or Mr. de Neufville informed, but we
usually do not ask them to approach General Hays or General Clay
for us.

Although ODI's use of our material has generally been quite
satisfactory, we have recently been obliged to reconsider certain
aspects of our relationship. It has long been my personal conviction that the mushrooming of the ODI Weekly Notes has resulted in
a dilution of its content and an increase of security risk. The
Notes are classed Secret, and given what might be called a limited
distribution: 80 copies reproduced of which some 60 are actually
distributed to regular listed customers. There can be little ques-

SECRET

SECRET
- 38 -

tion that all the customers of the <u>ODI Notes</u> are, in terms of
their position and their theoretical security, entitled to be on
the list. There is, however, a very serious question, whether
each one is entitled in terms of his special field of interest,
to read all the various unrelated items which are included in
that variegated digest. To put it more bluntly, I have been somewhat disturbed by the journalistic tendency of ODI to include
something of interest to everybody. Inevitably, I think, this
leads to a weakness of security, which gives us some ground for
apprehension.

It is only fair to say that there has, to our knowledge, been
no instance in which our material has suffered in security through
publication in <u>ODI Notes</u>. There have, however, been two or three
scares, all of which proved groundless, but which have left us with
an increasing concern. Col Rodes has agreed to give our secret
material Top Secret classification whenever we ask, thereby excluding it from the <u>Notes</u> but we are naturally reluctant to adopt such
a strong measure, which would result in a perhaps excessive restriction on its use. My own suggestion has been to split the <u>Notes</u> into
two publications. The larger, which could be graded secret or even
confidential, would include semi-overt material bearing on the
American Zone and Trizonia. The other which would be classed Top
Secret, though still given approximately the present distribution,
would center chiefly on the Soviet and Polish Zones. Although I
have repeatedly made this suggestion to ODI, both Col. Rodes and
Mr. De Neufville express themselves as satisfied with the present
state of affairs. And, as I have said, I have been reluctant to
force the issue unless an actual security break can be proved.

With this exception, our relations with ODI have been completely
satisfactory. Col. Rodes has shown the highest deference to our
organization, and stated officially to General Wright that he regards us as the elite among the Berlin intelligence agencies. On
the two or three occasions when we have had to call on him for
support or intervention with the Deputy Military Governor or the
OMGUS Chief of Staff, he has taken our side vigorously. He has
expressed satisfaction with our product, and has always said that
he wishes there were more of it. On the other hand, when we have ha
to withdraw from a field of production, as in the case of the CDU,
he has respected our motives for doing so, while regretting the
loss to ODI.

With Mr. de Neufville our relations are extremely close. As
a result of his OSS background, Mr. de Neufville fully understands
all aspects of clandestine operation. Although ODI is non-operational, he is frequently able to exploit his overt status as a
sort of informal cut-out, thereby providing us with a major point
of cover in the otherwise prohibited area of OMGUS. It would be
impossible to do justice to the innumerable tips, leads, follow ups
and ideas which we owe to him. In addition he has been our most
valuable single source on OMGUS itself, providing us with regular

SECRET

SECRET
- 39 -

accounts of General Clay's weekly staff meeting, which because of
our position, we have not felt it was advisable to attend. He
also keeps us informed on inside developments which may affect our
position or our operations, for example the progress of the secret
negotiations on currency reform, etc.

We also maintain extensive day to day contacts with the working staff of ODI. The principal analysts visit and are visited by
members of our Reports Board, commenting on our submissions and
showing us reports from other intelligence agencies which we do
not ordinarily receive. Certain policy matters affecting the funct:
al divisions of OMGUS may be channeled to or from us by the Securit:
Branch, which was recently formed by merging Liaison Counter Intell-
gence and Censorship Sections (Chief Mr. Campbell). This more or
less catch-all office handles, among other things, the reports
from the Berlin Documents Center, which frequently give us leads to
newly uncovered documents, such as the RSFA anti-Comintern files.
We have also concluded a useful working arrangement with Mr. L.F.
Orr in Mr. Campbell's office for the sponsoring of requests to the
Combined Travel Board, which results in the complete elimination
of our agency from any written records.

E. **Office of the Naval Advisor, Intelligence Officer**

Although small in size, the Office of the Naval Advisor, in
terms of echelon, stands on a par with the Office of the Political
Advisor. It is headed by a Flag Officer, Rear Admiral R. E.
Schuirmann, who enjoys privileges of honor parallel to those of
General Clay (military guard at his personal billet, etc.). Its
principal overall functions are representation on quadripartite
naval discussions, and carrying out special missions for the Chief
of Naval Operations in Washington. Its two principal day to day
functions are the procurement of naval intelligence for ONI (Capt
A. F. Graubart) and the study of naval technological questions
(Capt J.S. Crenshaw).

Our relations with ONA from the beginning have been extremely
cordial. Admiral Schuirmann was formerly head of the ONI in Washington and is fully conscious of intelligence interests. Although
we seldom have occasion to deal directly with Admiral Schuirmann
we have the satisfaction of knowing that on occasions of great

SECRET

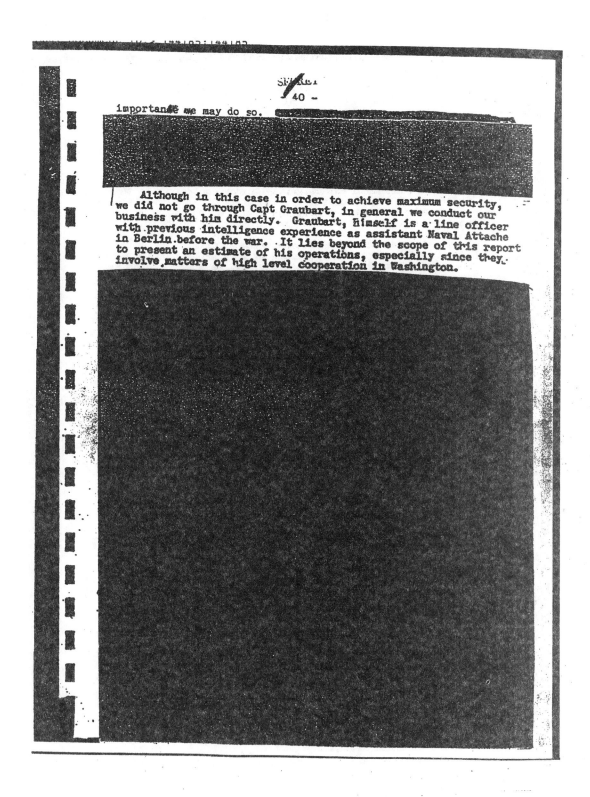

SECRET
- 40 -

importance we may do so.

Although in this case in order to achieve maximum security, we did not go through Capt Graubart, in general we conduct our business with him directly. Graubart, himself is a line officer with previous intelligence experience as assistant Naval Attache in Berlin before the war. It lies beyond the scope of this report to present an estimate of his operations, especially since they involve matters of high level cooperation in Washington.

Although we have declined to participate in several of Graubart's major projects, we have taken part or taken over altogether one or two limited individual operations. It must be said that the results have not been satisfactory. In the case of [redacted] we were finally obliged to turn him back, with thanks, allegedly on grounds that we were no longer interested in his targets, actually because he seemed more and more like a penetration agent. In the case of [redacted] whom Graubart runs directly, even to the extent of giving him a small room in the office of the Naval Advisor, we have repeatedly had to decline the offer of collaboration.

In spite of these relatively unsatisfactory experiences, I have not felt that it was wise to criticize Graubart directly, or to detach ourselves completely from operational contact. Graubart, in spite of a rather jaunty approach, is a shrewd and competent officer. He is completely relaxed in his personal attitude toward his official position, with the result that he is quite willing to expose himself, where others would shy away at the risks. Graubart is willing to exploit his overt position to draw the fire of Russian blasts against American intelligence, or to decoy potential defectors. In the defection field, he has had a certain measure of success. In general, however, when he has drawn a nibble, he has turned the case over to the British largely because he has been under the impression that they alone have the "facilities". I recently took occasion to disabuse Graubart of this notion, and to suggest that, within limits, we would be interested in examining his catches before he disposed of them to a non-American agency.

On the whole, though we have moments of apprehension over the free and easy character of Navy intelligence operations in Berlin, we make every effort to keep a warm and cordial relationship. And in the long run, it has paid off, and will continue to do so in even greater measure.

F. <u>S-2 Berlin Command and 970th CIC Detachment, Region VIII</u>

The principal operational liaison of the Berlin Base is with the two intelligence agencies of Berlin Command, S-2 and CIC. Strictly speaking, these are connected agencies, but the history and present status of their connection are rather complex. In the fall of 1947, by what amounted to a command decree of General Walsh, CIC was subordinated to S-2, thereby carrying out the wish of the Theater commander that all local CIC units be subordinate to local commands. But the situation remained in many ways unchanged, CIC Region VIII retaining its direct channel to the HQ of 970th CIC Detachment in EUCOM Frankfurt, and owing only a rather nominal obedience to S-2. This ambiguous relationship can be clarified further by an examination of the history and present status of each agency as a separate entity.

- 42 -

1. ~~I-2~~ Berlin Command.

The present S-2 is the lineal descendant of the original army intelligence agency in Berlin, which was known from July to November 1945 as G-2, 1st Airborne Army, and from then to October 1946 as G-2 Berlin District. Until September 1946 the head of this section was Lt. Col. William Heimlich. Heimlich, who was a former radio executive, has described one of his primary qualifications for intelligence work as consisting of a remarkable "joie de vivre". Unfortunately, it has not been our experience that that quality is an adequate substitute for discretion and security.

The first stage in our relations with G-2 Berlin District reached a crisis in the summer of 1946. As a result of a number of security lapses which came to our attention, we represented to Col. Quinn our serious misgivings about the extensive espionage work of that agency. These criticisms in turn were relayed to Brig. Gen. Edwin Sibert, and produced a result somewhat more drastic than we had anticipated. General Sibert in a letter to Col. Heimlich instructed the latter to cease all espionage operations the political and military fields directed against the Russian Zone since this was the province of SSU. There was a saving clau permitting Heimlich to coordinate his existing operations with u: and there was also a major joker in the failure to mention econo: espionage. Heimlich immediately consulted us, and we of course all initiative in bringing forth this bombshell, and assured his of our reluctance to see his activities impaired. Nevertheless, the handwriting was clearly visible on the wall, and Heimlich dr his own conclusions. In effect, he decided to retreat from his untenable empire, and to found a more modest one remote from di competition with SSU. This decision was perhaps encouraged by HQ shift which took place in October 1946, by which Berlin Dist from the status of an autonomous major command was brought under OMGUS as a subordinate agency known as Berlin Command. In the process, the reduction of echelon brought about the down grading of G-2 to an S-2, which it has remained ever since. Heimlich on hi own initiative was transferred to the position of deputy to the chief of the Civil Affairs Branch, Office of Military Government, Berlin Sector; there he continued to function as an intelligence officer until February 1948 when he became head of the radio statio in the American Sector (RIAS).

The past year and a half of our relations with S-2 Berlin Command have been a continuation of variations on the basic theme of the Heimlich era, polite non-cooperation, with a gradual reduction to the point of virtual elimination of the "non". There have been no less than four S-2s during that period: Lt. Col. John Merrill, Lt. Col. Wilbur Wilson, Col. G. W. Busbey, and Lt. Col. Harry Pretty. Each has imparted a slightly different personal character to S-2, without changing the basic setup. Col. Merrill delighted in playing a personal cloak and dagger role. It was he who originally recruited and operated ████████, our principal

SECRET

experiment in taking over an S-2 operation. The climax in our relation with Col. Merrill was reached in the affair of Lt. Jacques Saunder. Saunder was perhaps the most colorful operator in the gallery of motley figures in S-2, and certainly the most insecure. When it became evident that Saunder's ambitious ventures had gone beyond even the most generous margin of safety Berlin could tolerate, we made common cause with CIC in representing the danger to Col. Merrill. Merrill interpreted our action correctl, as an effort to handle dirty linen strictly within the Berlin commun ty, and took the necessary steps to get rid of Lt. Saunder.

Col. Merrill was succeeded in the summer of 1947 by Lt. Col. Wilson on an interim basis and then by Col. Busbey, formerly Provost Marshal, Berlin Command. Col. Busbey is a staunch cavalry officer, who had had no intelligence experience, but had made an excellent personal reputation among Berlin law enforcement and intelligence agencies, by his earnest efforts to bring about coopera tion and good will. His career in S-2, however, was brief, owing, among other circumstances, to the regrettable near scandal of Mr. Michael Tscherbinine. Tscherbinine, who subsequently achieved wide publicity through his role in the Prince Schoenaich-Carolath jewel case, attempted to interest us in what he claimed was a high class penetration of a dissident group within the Berlin MVD. Having been somewhat impressed with the initial lead which Tscherbinine had given us in the case of ███████ we followed his MVD lead in a conscientious and hopeful fashion, only to find that it ended squarely in the person of a pathological liar. Our presentation of the facts unfortunately led to the wrong action being taken; Col. Busbey was relieved as S-2 (though presumably on other grounds) while Tscherbinine still hovers as stormy petrel in Berlin.

With Col. Wilson who succeeded Col. Busbey, our relations were somewhat less dramatic, but even with him, we had at least one serious crisis. In the spring of 1947, the Russians arrested a group of CDU youth leaders, who were held for a long period and subsequently convicted of espionage for the Americans. Immediately after the first arrests, S-2 came across evidence which showed that one of the victims was an agent of ours, who in violation of all securi had some of our briefs and questionnaires in his apartment. Withou consulting us, Col. Wilson presented these facts in a highly derogatory and colored report to G-2 USFET. He neglected to mention, or perhaps did not know, that two of the arrestees were agent of S-2, who were guilty of at least equally great indiscretions. Col. Wilson's invidious action brought the whole matter to the attention of Col. Weirlich's office and even of ODI, creating a major display of dirty linen. We remonstrated with Col. Wilson, contrasting his action with our correct procedure in bringing the case of Lt Saunder directly to the attention of S-2. The results were salutary, and the remainder of Col. Wilson's stay in Berlin wa marked by generally friendly relations.

SECRET

SECRET

- 44 -

The fourth and current S-2, Lt. Col. Parry Pretty, has been the most satisfactory, from our viewpoint. Col. Pretty, like his predecessors, came to the job unencumbered by intelligence experience, but he has shown marked discretion and willingness to learn. In part his position has differed from that of his predecessors, in that he has been directly subjected to the day to day supervision of General Walsh. Fe has thus been the object of a greater degree of attention than any other subordinate agency of the Theater Intelligence. In addition, he has had thrust upon him, rather than seized, the jurisdictional control over CIC, which had in theory existed in 1945 under the regime of Col. Feimlich, but which had never been carried out de facto under Feimlich' successors.

Col. Pretty inherited a fairly large going concern, but one which was in dilapidated condition. At the time that G-2 was demoted to S-2 in Berlin, a paper T/O was established at considerable generosity, viz. 27 officers and some 80 enlisted men. To what extent this T/O has been met, we are unable to say with precision. In any case, S-2 has gradually lost most of its old stand-by officers, and has received replacements of junior and inexperienced regular Army officers, with which it is largely staffed today. As a result of this turnover, the productivity of S-2 has been lowered considerably.

The Berlin Base has not had a direct exchange of reports with S-2 since October 1946, when at the request of General Clay we agreed to use ODI as our intelligence channel within OMGUS. There have been occasional gestures of rapprochement initiated by S-2, and we have responded courteously, but without modifying the basic policy. As a result, we are not really in a position to assess the actual scope and value of the S-2 output. We do, however, see their work reflected in the same medium as our own, viz. the <u>ODI Weekly Notes</u>. From this we infer that they are reasonably productive in the economic field, which they continue to cultivate largely in virtue of the fact that it was not included in General Sibert's prohibition. They appear to be totally out of the political field, except for such work as is done by the Political Section of CIC (see below, para 2). We are quite unable to evaluate their work in the field of military intelligence, since that is all processed in Frankfurt. We have, indeed, been invited to maintain liaison with their Order of Battle specialist, but in view of our own slight interest in this subject, we have not made much of the contact.

In recent months our principal liaison with S-2 has been over the question of Russian defectors. The principal S-2 specialist, Capt A. Sogolow, approached us in the summer of 1947, with an offer to cooperate in the handling of Russian defection leads. His own semi-overt position exposed him to numerous propositions which it was beyond his capacity or that of S-2 to handle. For our part, we welcomed his offer to turn over promising leads, but insisted on two basic points: a) all such cases must be pre-

SECRET

SERET
- 4) -

sented to us at the earliest possible moment in their development; b) if we accept the case, we require complete turning over
to us, coupled with absolute subsequent security by S-2. This
general policy was also explained to Col. Pretty.

During the last months of 1947, Capt. Sogolow gave us a number of offers of defection leads. In the majority of cases we
were obliged to decline, sometimes for lack of facilities, sometimes for lack of interest or for doubts as to security. As a
result, Sogolow came to feel that we were indifferent to his
efforts, and we were repeatedly compelled to soothe his feelings;
and explain to Col. Pretty the real motives for our stand-offishnes
The proof that the cooperation was not totally empty came in the
case of ████ whom we received directly from Sogolow and cultivated into a promising penetration agent whose Order of Battle
information is now greatly appreciated by ODDI; EUCOM.

In any case the Sogolow era came to an end in January 1948, whe.
Major General Kotikov, Commandant of the Russian Sector, in a formal protest to the American Commandant, Brig Gen Hesketh, accused
the Americans of the "forcible" defection of a Russian captain.
Despite the fact that the bulk of Gen Kotikov's letter consisted
purely of shots in the dark, the case came to rest on Capt Sogolow'
doorstep. A high command decision was made - precisely on whose
initiative, General Walsh or General Hesketh, is not clear - and
Sogolow was flown out of Berlin to the States on a few hours notice

The departure of Sogolow has virtually eliminated S-2 from the
active cultivation of Russian defectors. Nevertheless, in a recent
conference on the subject, Col. Pretty has assured us that the
basic principle of cooperation still stands, and within the limits
of his personnel he will continue to make available leads which are
suitable to our mission and capabilities.

Other chapters in the cooperation of Berlin Base and S-2 have
already been mentioned, notably the London CFM crisis and the
agreement to divide the task of obtaining background information
on Soviet personnel at the ACA and Kommandatura levels. We might
also mention the completely amicable arrangement through which we
took over the services of ████ as an agent, while maintaining
intact his cover as an S-2 staff member. General Walsh and Col.
Pretty have been fully cooperative in this effort to retain the
services of a topnotch technical intelligence officer, who was
otherwise rendered ineligible by the application of the 10 year
citizenship rule. The entire setting up of this promising cover
arrangement has been characterized by stress on mutual advantage.

We shall strive to continue in this present vein of cordiality
and helpfulness. The pressure of empire building, of suspicion
and mistrust, seems to have died down in S-2, and, while it is too
early to speak of an entente cordiale, we have hopes that the two
principal American agencies in the clandestine field can be said
from now on to belong to the same team.

SE RET

57

- 46 -

2. CIC, Region VIII

The pattern of our relations with CIC in Berlin has been
distinctly more satisfactory than with S-2. Almost from the
beginning of my stay in Berlin, we established a harmonious
working relationship which has been mutually beneficial. It is
perhaps not unfair to point out that the cooperativeness of CIC
may have been favored by the fact that several key members of its
staff (unlike the regular Army personnel of S-2) have kept in
the back of their minds the prospect of future employment by CIA!

On the side of CIC the chief proponent of this policy of good
relations has been Major Joseph Stewart, until recently the head
of the detachment. In this he has been seconded by the most important member of his staff, Mr. Severin Wallach, head of the
Special Case Section. On our side not only myself but the two
chiefs of XC Branch [_HECKSHER AND TOM POLGAR_] and
SICKEL on behalf of FR, have assiduously cultivated the principal officers of CIC.

It would be impossible to give in detail a picture of the day
to day contacts between ourselves and CIC. Gradually these contacts have been extended from our Branch chiefs to include some
of the case officers. However, it must be admitted that this
practice of direct contact on the lowest working level has
occasionally produced some confusion, and by mutual consent, the
present tendency is to restore the liaison to the narrower basis
of the executive level.

From our viewpoint, the most important benefit of the CIC
liaison has been the enlistment of their executive facilities in
support of both our positive and counter operations. These have
ranged throughout the entire operational and technical field,
including surveillances, monitoring, protection of agents, forg-
ing of documents on occasion, and above all the conduct of vetting
and other investigations. On our part we have provided innumerable
leads to CIC as the by-product of our own operations. We have
also given them a sort of higher moral support during periods of
difficulty with the Theater Command and Director of Intelligence.
We have pointed out to General Walsh the importance of an autonomous CIC, exempt from onerous restrictions in regard to billeting,
uniform, and other military requirements. And above all we have
tried to emphasize the solidarity of interest between positive
secret intelligence and the protecting and supporting forces of counter intelligence.

As I have already indicated, CIC in Berlin has had a constant
uphill battle. It has always been torn between the pull of the
local G-2 or S-2 and the higher echelon of the 970th Detachment
at Frankfurt. It is only fair to say that this tension has frequently worked to the advantage of the local Detachment, enabling
it to play both ends against the middle. It is particularly note-

SERET

worthy that Stewart, with the rank of captain and then major, was able to sustain and defend a Detachment which elsewhere in the Theater would have been commanded by a Lieutenant Colonel or Colonel. This has been all the more remarkable as an achievement, because of the peculiarly exposed and vulnerable position of the Berlin Detachment. It is directly under the eye of the Theater Commander, and subject through his Director of Intelligence to both a more critical scrutiny and a more extensive set of demands than the regional detachments in the Zone. It is at the same time more open to the temptations of the black market and the corruption and seductions of metropolitan life. It is greatly to Major Stewart credit that, during the two years of his command, his detachment w without major scandal and was able to avoid the frequently severe strictures which General Clay has delivered against CIC in the Zone

The principal working contact with Berlin CIC is with the Special Case Branch, headed by Mr. Wallach. This Branch has varied somewhat in composition, but in general has comprised two main grou the Political and the Counter Espionage Sections. The Political Se tion is in fact almost exclusively concerned with penetration of the Communist Party and related organizations. Headed until recen by two former associates of Lt. Saunder – Mr. Manley and Mr. Gutman it has achieved a fair measure of success in penetrating the Berlin Communist-controlled SED party. Through our ▮▮▮▮▮▮ liaison [▮▮▮▮▮▮▮▮] we have had access to their results, and have been able to coordinate our own activities so as to avoid duplication. It should be stated, however, that both Manley and Gutman have inherited some of the careless and romantic traits of Lt. Saunder. They have on occasion fallen for major hoaxes. Indeed, it was largely through our warning that they escaped the greatest hoax of all, the notorious forgery of Protocol "M".

The Counter Espionage Section has, on the whole confined itsel to relatively low-grade cases, and has not, we believe, accomplish any major penetration of the RIS. It is only fair to say that they may have bigger things up their sleeve which they have kept from our eyes. For instance Mr. Wallach has hinted that he has been carrying out some ▮▮▮▮▮ operations, about which not even his immediate superiors have been informed. However that may be, we must agree that our close liaison with Mr. Wallach has paid off in the CE field: we need only mention the ▮▮▮▮▮▮ case, which came originally to CIC, but to which we were admitted on equal terms in the interrogation. Indeed, it was undoubtedly the brilliant approach of HECKSHER which enabled him and Mr. Wallach to work as a team, in extracting all ▮▮▮▮▮▮'s essential information in what was formally only a preliminary interrogation.

The most recent phase in our relations with CIC has marked per haps a slight recession from the uniformly high tide of cooperation which existed while Major Stewart was the commanding officer of the Berlin CIC. Stewart's successor, Major Claud Purkitt –

SERET

59

SECRET
- 48 -

formerly chief of the Regensburg CIC - was fully indoctrinated and has accepted both in principle and practice the tradition of close liaison with WDD and especially the SC Branch. The slight change in our relations was due to Purkitt's personality; while Stewart possessed maturity and intelligence experience and a quiet dignity far in excess of what one would expect of a man his age, Purkitt is impetuous, aggressive and relatively inexperienced in intelligence. His strongest point, and one which undoubtedly was considered before his appointment, is his tremendous personal energy and drive - qualities which are almost essential for the CO of a large CIC detachment operating under at least semi-combat conditions. It is only natural that Purkitt's interpretation of close liaison is different from Stewart's. Other factors complicate the situation: for one, a recent change of command in CIC at the EUCOM level. The new CO, as we understand, is not too favorably inclined toward our organization and has moved to restrict liaison except on the command level. This has not yet affected our local relationship materially; it may do so later.

Another factor affecting our relations with CIC at this time has been the planning for intelligence in the European Command after the transfer of authority (now cancelled) from the Department of the Army to the State Department, as of 1 July 1948. CIC, at both Berlin and EUCOM levels, has felt that it is fighting for its life. They think there is a good chance that the large intelligence-gathering organization built by CIC since the end of hostilities in Europe might be discarded altogether. Accordingly, CIC has been out to "sell" itself to the State Department. They have been particularly anxious to receive credit lines wherever possible, especially whenever their intelligence is disseminated locally. Since CIC conceives the WDD as its most dangerous current competitor it is understandable that their relations with us have been tainted lately with a certain suspicion. That those relations have nevertheless remained almost unchanged is largely due to the efforts of Mr. Wallach, who now heads all agent operations of the Berlin CIC. Mr. Wallach, whose contract with CIC was renewed after negotiations dragging over several months, is truly the moderating influence on Major Purkitt, and prevents the latter from carrying out certain hasty decisions in both liaison and operations. One example will illustrate: In February 1948 Major Purkitt assumed responsibility for all CIC outside liaison, both policy-making and operational. All other CIC personnel, including Mr. Wallach, were expressly forbidden to have liaison with other U.S. and Allied agencies. About one week of the new system proved conclusively to Purkitt that the job was too big for one man to handle and he was easily persuaded that Mr. Wallach should again be authorized to handle operational liaison. (We might add that Purkitt's original decision did not disturb us much, especially since Mr. Wallach assured us that liaison would continue de facto, if necessary on an entirely personal, after-office hours, basis.) On the whole, however, we welcomed the narrowing of the points of contact, since direct liaison on the lower levels had multiplied to the point of confusion.

SECRET

SECRET

To sum up, we believe that despite periodical ups and downs our relations with CIC will continue to be excellent, and we are confident that we can count in the future, as we have in the past, on the cooperation and basic good will of the Berlin CIC - which is undoubtedly today and probably will remain for some time the most important and largest operational intelligence organization in Berlin.

G. **Military Liaison Mission to the Soviet Zone of Occupation, Potsdam**

During the past year we have maintained an informal contact of quasi intelligence nature with the Military Liaison Mission to the Soviet Zone. This group of ten Army, Navy and Air officers, under the command of Brigadier General W. W. Fess, Jr. has headquarters and mess in Potsdam, though the members actually live in the American sector of Berlin. The Mission also maintains a small liaison office in the Armed Forces Building of OMGUS. The British and French have similar Missions at Potsdam, which in turn are parallelled by the Soviet Military Liaison Mission to the American Zone in Frankfurt.

The function of the Mission is to conduct liaison business of any kind between the American Theater Command and the Soviet Zone Command. This includes routine private transactions for American citizens, such as inquiries concerning American property in the Soviet Zone, etc. The actual volume of business is not very great, and the Mission in general has found that it is frequently obstructed, either wilfully or because of Soviet red tape or inefficiency.

It was apparent from the outset that the Liaison Mission would be expected to perform an intelligence function. Two former intelligence officials, Lt. Col. O. J. Pantuhoff and Captain P. Schneider were attached to the Mission with that purpose in mind. Col. Pantuhoff who is American born, is bilingual in Russian and English, and served as interpreter to President Roosevelt at Teheran and Yalta. In many ways he was admirably qualified to carry out intelligence observation as a side line to his liaison work. However, both Col. Pantuhoff and Capt. Schneider soon found themselves in difficulty with the Russians. Members of the Mission were theoretically at liberty to drive about the Soviet Zone, in uniform and in plainly marked American sedans. Actually their freedom of movement was seriously limited. Each trip had to be announced in advance, with a precise objective and itinerary, and the Russians frequently refused to grant clearance for areas of special interest (notably the uranium mine region of the Erzgebirge which was declared closed on grounds of "quarantine"). Pantuhoff and Schneider made repeated attempts to get at interesting targets, and as a result were frequently arrested and detained by local Russian commandants. Although they were always able to obtain

SECRET

SECRET

- 50 -

fairly prompt release by telephoning Potsdam, they gradually built up a record with the Russians which clearly marked them as conducting a form of espionage. The crisis occurred in January 1948, when on orders from General Fess, Pantuhoff attempted to gain entry to a factory which the Russians had barred. As a result, the Soviet commander declared Pantuhoff and Schneider persona non grata and asked for their recall.

From our viewpoint there was little to be gained by associating ourselves closely with this type of activity. Col Pantuhoff and General Fess have invited us to submit intelligence briefs, and to send a representative to the weekly staff meeting of the Mission in their Berlin headquarters. Although ████████ and others have attended these meetings fairly regularly, they have been increasingly impressed with the futility of the Mission, so far as intelligence is concerned. It is apparent that an American officer in uniform cannot conduct espionage on anything but the most obvious and uninteresting targets. Accordingly, after a few experimental briefs, we ceased to put any requests to the Mission. With the departure of Pantuhoff, our interest has dropped to zero, and we have discontinued the practice of attending their weekly meetings.

H. Office of Military Government, Berlin Sector Civil Affairs Branch

The Berlin Operations Base, in the liaisons described above, has occupied the position of an agency with a Theater-wide mission and scope. But we are also, inevitably, enmeshed in the narrower fabric of the city of Berlin, and specifically the American Sector. In this more restricted aspect of our work, we would normally direct our principal liaison to the Intelligence Office - if it existed - of the American Commandant in Berlin. Unfortunately, the one office which answers that description, has in fact, both through its jurisdictional ambiguity and the dubious cover position of its staff, been the one office which we take pains to avoid as much as possible.

As I mentioned above, the dissolution of the old G-2 Berlin District led to the establishment of a so-called intelligence office within the headquarters of the Berlin Commandant, Col. Frank Howley, specifically in the Civil Administration Branch under Mr. (formerly Colonel) L. Glaser. Under Mr. Glaser as Political Intelligence Officer was Mr. (formerly Colonel) William Heimlich, who also carried the title of Deputy Chief of Branch. When Heimlich left Berlin District, he took with him a small group of his former intelligence officers, notably Mr. F. Mathews and Mr. F.A. Dilger, whose Special Intelligence Reports have been the staple of Mr. Heimlich's production, both before and after the headquarters switch. Unfortunately, despite the merits of these officers, the very nature of their position has brought them, since the departure of Lt. Saunder, into the category of "best blown" intelligence officers in Berlin.

SECRET

SECRET

The basic fault of the Feimlich office lies deeper than mere
inherited insecurity. OKGBS, Col. Fowley's headquarters at 35
Grunewald Strasse, is the directing center of the American
occupation in Berlin. As such it is a workaday headquarters,
staffed by a rather pedestrian but vigorous group of extrovert
Army officers who run everything from motor pools to VD clinics.
The building is wide open, thronged by Germans, DP's, and allied
nationals with every conceivable errand. The headquarters is a
constant focus of publicity and inter-allied bickering in the
Berlin Kommandatura. Inevitably, clandestine operation from this
near madhouse is doomed to penetration and exposure.

Moreover, the Civil Administration Branch by its very nature
is incapable of housing a true intelligence office. The function
of Mr. Glaser is primarily to advise Col. Fowley on Berlin politics, and to provide him with the necessary ammunition to defend
American interests against the constant and shrewd attacks of the
Soviet Commandant, Major General Kotikov. It is clear that the
political information which Col. Fowley requires is primarily
overt. It seems therefore, to have been a basic mistake to have
attempted to house Mr. Feimlich's semi-covert operators in the
fully overt Civil Administration Branch. The best explanation
why such a step was taken, probably lies in the personal ambitions
of Mr. Feimlich. It is an open secret in OKGUS that Mr. Feimlich
hoped, through this cover in Civil Administration Branch, to
accomplish two things: a) to put himself in line for a decisive
role in Berlin politics, and b) to evade the jurisdiction of ODI,
OKGUS. Fe came fairly close to succeeding, but in fact, as it
turns out, actually failed in both objectives. It was no doubt
the realization of this failure which prompted him in February
1948 to accept a transfer, out of Civil Administration, into
Information Control Branch, where he now heads the radio station
in the American Sector (RIAS). In view of his extensive peacetime experience as a radio executive, this appears to be a good
solution of both his personal ambition and the dissatisfaction
which has been felt in OKGUS over his intelligence work.

The way is now open for the appointment of a new intelligence
officer, who would accept his full measure of responsibility
toward ODI, and function in parallel to the Land Intelligence
officers in the American Zone. This has long been the avowed
objective of Colonel Rodes, to bring Berlin into line with the
situation in the three American Laender, thereby enabling OKGUS
headquarters to draw directly on the political intelligence
produced under OKGBS. Whether this will lead to the establishment of a new and separate intelligence branch within OKGBS, or
whether it will continue, in the past, as a part of the Civil
Administration Branch under Mr. Glaser, remains to be seen, but
clearly the continuation of the status quo is undesirable.

SECRET

SECRET

- 52 -

In the light of this situation, it is easy to understand why our relations with Mr. Feimlich's office have been far from perfectly cordial. Mr. Feimlich has never forgotten the fact that General Sibert's letter of July 1946 deprived him of his principal franchise - running agents into the Russian Zone - in favor of SSU. We have never forgotten the fact that his office is staffed with German secretaries and has no possibility of maintaining internal security. We have indeed kept up a friendly personal contact with Mr. Mathews, and even accepted an occasional intelligence lead from him. However, even in such instances we have been forced to be exceedingly reserved, since there is abundant evidence that Feimlich's office is the classic point in Berlin for penetration feelers, not only from Soviet but from other allied intelligence agencies, and Mathews, by his own admission has been hit with devastating accuracy. Indeed, our caution now goes so far, that it can be said that we no longer are willing to accept any operational initiative which we know to have been associated in any way with Feimlich's office. Possibly under a new incumbent we may be able to relax our stand-offishness, but the fundamental difficulty will always remain, so long as overt and covert are completely intertwined, and the whole direction of intelligence is oriented toward a tactical political situation.

SECRET

I. Non-Intelligence Contacts

With the agencies described above, we have exhausted the roster of our major intelligence liaisons. There remain a large group of Berlin agencies, bordering upon or ancillary in function to clandestine intelligence, with whom we have close contact. These contacts cover every aspect of our operations and administration, and constitute a complex fabric which it is only possible to describe in very general terms.

1. Public Safety, OMGUS and OMGBS

Not strictly of an intelligence nature, but basic to the performance of our mission is our liaison with the Public Safety Branch of OMGUS and of OMGBS headquarters.

a. Public Safety Branch, OMGUS

As the senior headquarters in the Theater, Public Safety Branch OMGUS exercises general policy control in all matters affecting the German police and law enforcement agencies and denazification inspection, both in the American Zone and in Berlin, and participates on the quadripartite level in the ACA Public Safety Committee. It is a fairly compact office within the Internal Affairs and Communications Division.

OMGUS Public Safety with its subordinate echelons in the Laender owes its present distinctive pattern to the influence of Col. O.W. Wilson, who was chief of the Branch until the summer of 1947. Col. Wilson enjoys a wide reputation in the United States as the founder of what might be called the higher education of the professional policeman. As head of the graduate police school at the University of California, Col. Wilson established the concept

SECRET

of an elite corps; and trained according to this concept hundreds of officers who are now chiefs and senior officials of police forces throughout the country. He brought with him to Military Government his concept, which he himself embodies: the soft spoken, intellectual, gentlemanly type of police official, as opposed to the traditional "flat foot". Needless to say, this admirable discipline has been particularly effective in Germany, which has always had a highly trained, elite police bureaucracy. As a result, the German police in the American Zone and Sector of Berlin have displayed a respect for our Public Safety officialdom. which has not always been so apparent in other executive Branches of Military Government.

The cordial relations which Berlin Base established with Col. Wilson have continued under his successor, Mr. T. V. Fall, and his deputy Mr. J.L.McCraw. The full measure of their coopera- tion was demonstrated in the summer of 1947, when Mr. Fall granted the facilities of Public Safety cover to Mr. HENRY HECKSHER. Mr. H. was given a position as a special investigator. in the OMGUS office, under circumstances which allowed him com- plete operational latitude to perform his mission for the Berlin Base. Competent orders were procured, under ~~ ~~ working alias, and a desk and listed telephone were laid on. Unfortunately,

~~ ~~ As a result of General Clay's decisive veto on use of Military Government cover, we were obliged to withdraw Mr. HECKSHER from the office.

Despite this set back the close working contact has remained in effect.

b. <u>Public Safety Branch.-Office of Military Government Berlin Sector.</u>

With OMGBS our Public Safety ties are even closer than on the OMGUS level, amounting to a day to day working liaison of the

SECRET

66

SECRET
- 55 -

utmost value in support of our SC and FR operations. The original and still the basic contact has been with Mr. (formerly Major) Charles Bond, who was Chief until the spring of 1947 and is now deputy Chief of Branch, under Mr. Ray Ashworth. Bond is a professional police officer of long experience in the States. During the past two and a half years, he has built the police force in the American Sector of Berlin into a trustworthy and reasonably efficient organization, carrying out its mission, within the limit imposed by inadequate personnel and equipment, according to pre-war German standards. His greatest success has been in freeing the American Sector from the pernicious influence of the Soviet-controlled central Polizeipraesidium. Considering the strength of the prewar system of centralized police administration in Berlin, this has been a particularly difficult achievement. SC Branch, as I mentioned above, may claim considerable credit for strengthening Mr. Bond's hand, through its inside coverage of the police force.

The immediate benfits of this liaison are too numerous to catalogue. Hardly a week goes by without a visit to Mr. Ashworth or Mr. Bond, for the purpose of straightening out the affairs of an agent in trouble, securing police protection for our operations, or following up a lead of counter intelligence nature. Through Public Safety, we secured the full time services of a trained police detective to investigate the incidents of petty thievery in our motor pool and office premises. This experiment has paid off in the apprehension of a number of intruders, and in bringing to light points of weakness among our otherwise trustworthy German personnel. We are presently using the same detective to carry out vetting checks on all our indigenous personnel and to cast a protective eye over our billets and other official installations.

Finally, we may add, from these, our most trusted friends within OMGBS headquarters, we have obtained innumerable bits of inside information which enable us to keep on good terms with the other Branches of that rather tempermental headquarters. We have kept posted on affairs of vital concern to FR and SC, such as secret plans for raids and arrests carried out on a quadriparti level. Advance warning of such operations is of the utmost importance, especially to FR, since the Soviets have frequently tried to utilize quadripartite machinery to probe into the mysteries of American intelligence operations. On our side, we have done our best to strengthen the hand of Public Safety in its constant battle to curb abductions and other illegal Soviet incursions into our Sector. We have been able to use our ready access to the higher echelons of OMGUS to plead the cause of Public Safety in this matter, which, however explosive in nature, has generally failed to rouse a commensurate degree of interest on the Kommandatura and ACA echelons.

SECRET

SECRET

2. Information Control Division

Information Control Division, like Public Safety, is of interest to us on both the OMGUS and the OMGBS levels. Although by its charter it should be only indirectly concerned with clandestine operations as such, it has nevertheless figured prominently in the history of intelligence in Germany.

a. Information Control Division, OMGUS.

I have already alluded to the bitter struggle which took place in 1945 and 1946 between the Office of the Director of Intelligence and the Information Control Division. As I pointed out the pendulum reached full swing in September 1946 when ICD actually secured the approval of a staff study which would have brought ODI under at least the personal headship of the Chief of ICD, Brig. Gen. Mc Clure. Since then, the pendulum has swung nearly full in the opposite direction. The latest indications are that ICD will be withdrawn from the entire field of political intelligence which is presently being cultivated by its Research Branch under Dr. Robert C. Schmid (formerly OSS, R and A). In Bava indeed the Research Branch has already been merged with the Office of the Land Director of Intelligence, the chief of the former becoming head of the latter under the merger. It seems likely that similar mergers will take place in the other two Laender, to be followed eventually at the OMGUS level. Dr. Schmid is returning to the States in late Spring 1948, at which time his Branch will, in all probability be incorporated into ODI. Such a step would certainly clarify the situation in the field of political information and reduce a serious element of duplication.

To be sure the functions of ICD Research Branch are to some extent different from those of ODI. Research Branch is concerned primarily with the sampling of public opinion by an application of Gallup Poll methods. This type of work has an obvious bearing on the legitimate propaganda and educational functions of ICD, and there is consequently considerable pressure to retain at least the opinion polls within the Division. However, the basic weekly publication, Information Control Review, although based in large part on such samplings and on overt newspaper and periodical analysis, does in fact overlap to a considerable extent the political and sociological coverage of the ODI Weekly Notes. A clean-cut merger is obviously indicated.

The solution of this jurisdictional conflic is of only indirect concern to Berlin Operations Base. ICD has not attempted to extend its coverage into our principal target area, the Soviet Zone. Nevertheless, the consolidation and simplificatio of the political coverage which would result from such a merger, would react, I believe, beneficially to WDD Bases operating in the American Zone, and would reduce the incidence of potential friction with ourselves. In addition, it must be stated frankly, that the withdrawal of ICD will certainly not have an adverse effec

SECRET

- 57 -

on the security picture. ICD, by the nature of its function and by the quality of its personnel, has been notoriously insecure, dabbling beyond the edge of overt activity, and jeopardizing agencies legitimately chartered in the clandestine field. The loyalty of much of its foreign born personnel has been seriously questioned, and the need for a greater concentration of control and discipline is universally admitted. The most recent reaction to the presence of dubious elements in ICD has been the crisis over the radio station in the American Sector of Berlin, which culminated, as I mentioned above, in the transfer of Mr. Feimlich from Civil Administration Branch, OMGBS to RIAS.

Mention should be made of numerous incidental points of liaison with ICD, notably in the field of licensing periodicals and other means of publicity. We have not infrequently been requested by AEZON to promote with ICD the special interests of one of our agents or of a group or organization which we are interested in building up. In general, it has been our experience that these requests are dangerous. The insecurity of ICD makes it risky to display our interest in a publications project. Moreover, because of their sometimes prejudiced, sometimes reasonable lines of policy, it is extremely difficult to procure special favors from ICD without an effort incommensurate to the worth of the project. For that reason, we have not always been willing or able to undertake such intervention. Our credit with the present division chief Col. G. E. Textor is excellent, but we feel it wise policy to husband it for matters of vital concern and to keep minor requests to the minimum.

One principal point of potential contact with ICD lies in the field of propaganda, black or white. Here, again, extreme caution is indicated. It is well known that when General Clay announced the launching of an anti-communist propaganda drive in October 1947, Information Control immediately seized the ball and started running for a touchdown. It was halfway down the field when the referee's whistle was vigorously blown by ODI, POLAD, and CAD all at once, who pointed out that the ball had not even been put into play. Since then, ICD has been moving somewhat more cooperatively with the line of scrimmage, but there is always danger that it will try another runaway. At any rate, from our viewpoint, it is a team mate to be kept altogether under circumspection.

Our policy remains, as it has been since October 1946, no direct dissemination to ICD, OMGUS, and only a minimum of working contact.

b. <u>ICD, Berlin Sector</u>

The Information Control Branch of OMGBS is subject, in our mind, to the same weaknesses as its OMGUS parent, namely

SECRET

SECRET

- 58 -

insecurity and lack of discretion in intelligence matters. Nevertheless we have permitted ourselves a slightly closer working contact, both because it has been expedient and because there have been one or two individuals in whom we have had real confidence. This confidence applies chiefly to the former chief Mr. F. N. Leonard (now with OMGF), and the present deputy chief, Mr. M. Josselson. We have felt reasonably safe in turning to these officials for such incidental matters as checks on journalistic personnel, procurement of correspondent status for our agents, occasional straightening out of licensing problems and other minor favors. Mr. Josselson in addition has given us a number of valuable intelligence leads. It is to him that we owe the FH agent POHTOM. He is particularly useful because of his knowledge of Russian, and his close liaison contacts with his allied opposite numbers.

But unquestionably our most valuable contact in ICD Berlin is with Mr. Enno Hobbing, editor of the Berlin edition of the American-licensed newspaper, *Die Neue Zeitung*. Mr. Hobbing, who was one of my most talented students at Harvard, has had a brilliant career both in journalism and intelligence. Unlike many others of similar background, he has not allowed the former to drive out the latter. Because he is a Military Government official, and therefore not subject to the pressure of the commercial by-line, he is able to submerge his journalistic impulses in the interest of a clandestine operation. He, more than any other MG official of our acquaintance, presents the ideal qualifications for directing and carrying out propaganda work, whether of the white or black type. As the lines of such a campaign begin to emerge, we are convinced that our best opportunity to contribute, without loss of security, would be through further intensification of our present close working arrangement with Mr. Hobbing.

3. <u>Provost Marshal, Berlin Command</u>.

Essential to any conduct of intelligence and counter intelligence operations in an occupied area is a satisfactory working relationship with the non-indigenous law enforcement agencies. It has always been a cardinal point of our policy to be on good terms with the Provost Marshal and the Criminal Investigation Division. Unlike CIC, these are agencies from which we request considerable support and assistance, without being able to offer much in return. Good will with them, therefore, is more a function of personal respect than of mutual benefits.

During the past two years there have been two Provost Marshals of Berlin Command, both cavalry officers and admirable gentlemen. I have already mentioned Col. G. ... Busbey, who served a brief period as S-2 after more than a year as Provost Marshal. Col Busbey was by instinct a rough and ready diplomat in the field of law enforcement. He always displayed the utmost courtesy toward our organization, and granted any reasonable operational

SECRET

SECRET
- 59 -

requests. His successor Col. Falck, ████████████████████
████████████████ , has been even more friendly and cooperative.

The high point of our relations with the Provost Marshal
was reached when Col. Falck agreed to our use of his office as
cover : *GEORGE BELK*   . Because of *BELK'S* , knowledge of
Russian, it was essential that he have a post, sufficiently overt
to account for constant appearance in offices of every type, yet
sufficiently covert to permit the necessary security. This position was found in the Special Liaison Section, attached directly
to Col. Falck's office. In addition ████████████████████
it had the very mixed advantage of placing BELK in direct associa
tion with Mr. Michael Tscherbinine and the Soviet Liaison Section.
BELK has been able to make the most of this association, taking
unto himself potential CE leads which Tscherbinine uncovered,
while keeping at arm's length from the latter's notorious and
questionable associates. ████████████████████████

██
██
██

In administrative matters, as well as intelligence, our
Provost Marshal connection has been beneficial. We have been
able on the strength of our credit with Col. Falck to extract
ourselves successfully from difficult situations with the Military Police, such as are bound to arise in the conduct of delicate operations in a tightly patrolled area of occupation. We
have secured such important administrative favors as a completely
free hand in obtaining new license plates for blown automobiles.
In return we have, as I stated above, lent our moral support in
issues of vital concern to the Provost Marshal. Thus under the
regime of Col Busbey when General Clay ordered the pulling in of
outlying MP Detachments to a central barracks, we sent the
General a strong letter advising against this step. The fact that
General Clay overrode the protests of our agency and of several
others did not diminish the Provost Marshal's gratitude for our
effort.

4.   Criminal Investigation Division

CID in Berlin is a picturesque, hard-boiled outfit, contrasting sharply with the almost genteel atmosphere of Public
Safety. Owing only a nominal obedience to the Berlin Provost
Marshal, it has acted pretty much as a law unto itself, and has
carved its way into the lush lawlessness of Berlin with gusto and
abandon. Its chief, Mr. O.R. Carlucci, has worked himself
rapidly to a considerable eminence, enjoying in effect the status
of a sort of personal bodyguard and detective for General Clay.
His principal agent, Mr. M. A. Strauch is a well known and color-

SECRET

SECRET

- 60 -

ful figure, striking a mild degree of terror in the hot spots of Berlin.

The basic achievements of CID are not really impressive, though one must hasten to add that this is by no means their fault. In many of their principal efforts they have been frustrated, just short of bringing the criminal to justice. This was particularly apparent in the sad case of ▓▓▓▓▓▓▓▓ and ▓▓▓▓▓▓▓▓▓▓▓▓▓▓▓▓) who quite literally beat the rap on very heavy charges which CID had fully documented. This gross miscarriage of justice (which appears to have been engineered in Washington) so discouraged CID that they have subsequently confined themselves to such modest but sure publicity bringers as the Hohenzollern jewel case. They have made no real effort to enforce a high standard of integrity in matters of black marketing among OMGUS personnel, recognizing their limitations of manpower, and the lack of real interest in securing spectacular convictions. Even in the limited field of stolen American vehicles, they have found themselves obliged to turn over responsibility almost entirely to Public Safety and the German Police.

▓▓▓▓▓▓▓▓▓▓▓▓▓▓▓▓▓▓▓▓▓▓▓▓▓▓▓▓▓▓. We approached Mr. Carlucci, with the able assistance of Martin E. Sanford (Mr. Carlucci was a private detective in New Jersey where Mr. Sanford was a member of the State Police), and were able to insure the security of our organization's interests. Because of our general willingness to cooperate with the prosecution of the case, we won the confidence of CID, and have had no difficulty maintaining it subsequently.

CID is not much interested in intelligence as such, and possesses the virtue of complete security only in matters of vital concern to itself. We can always count on them to give us a reasonable degree of executive support, in such matters, for instance, as investigating black market activities of our agent or other German personnel. There is no question that our relationship with CID is of benefit to the organization. As an example we may point out that the original lead to SC's most important operation ▓▓▓▓▓ was obtained from the CID.

5. The Functional Divisions of OMGUS

In concluding the roster of our contacts with American agencies, a word should be said concerning the functional divisions of OMGUS. These divisions, now some 10 in number, are the basic executive organs of Military Government. They are patterned to correspond to the quadripartite structure of the Allied Control Authority, but the congruence is by no means absolute. The

SECRET

SECRET
- 61 -

divisions vary greatly in size and influence. By far the most powerful grouping are the Economics and related divisions (Transport, Finance, Manpower) which constitute the working arm of General Clay in the material rebuilding of Germany. The bulk of these divisions are moving to Frankfurt this spring, leaving only policy-making and advisory echelons to sit with the Theater Commander and the Deputy Military Governor.

Broadly speaking, we have eliminated direct contact with the functional divisions. Two years ago, we passed both disseminat and raw reports directly to Economics, to Transport, to Civil Administration and to Armed Forces Division as the subject matter required. In October 1946, when we concluded our agreement with General Clay, we undertook henceforth to use ODI as our basic channel to OMGUS, thereby concentrating the use of our material, eliminating our own distribution headaches, and tightening our security. We have adhered to this agreement, and none of our formal distribution goes to OMGUS except through ODI and FOLAD.

We have, however, maintained a considerable volume of direct contacts, partly on the basis of earlier connections. Thus when a case requires direct action, either of a policy or an executive nature we are not totally at a loss where to turn. The classic example of such direct action was the ████████ affair, in which we presented our inside information on the Askania Werke directly to the Industry Branch of the Economics Disivion. Only in this way, and by the assidious personal pressure of Mr. ████████, were we able to work up sufficient interest to lead to a thorough investigation resulting in the seizure of the plant and ultimate conviction of its directors. Had we been content to let this matter ride through ODI channels, it is doubtful whether any executive action would have been taken. This liaison with Industry Branch is further extended for day to day operational support of FR operations. Dr. Nordstrom, the Research Control officer of OMGUS, has provided us in the past with necessary background information for long range technical and scientific operations, and we believe that this liaison will prove invaluable in this important field in the future. His chief, Mr. (formerly Colonel) F. L. Mayer has been very helpful since initial contact was made with him by SICKEL in the ████████ case. He has passed on leads to us (one of them resulting in FR case ████████), and has provided valuable policy and background information for the prosecution of our operational program. One of the most valuable contributions from Mr. Mayer's office has been the intelligence passing through their hands as a by product of their day to day operations, which has often resulted in informatory cables from us to Washington.

Another instance of fruitful liaison is with the Finance Division. This liaison on one hand provides us with inside information on such important matters as the currency reform, and on the other hand furnishes occasional cover for specific jobs of case

SECRET

SECRET

- 62 -

officers. Two separate contacts are maintained in this division, both by ~~redacted~~, in the persons of ~~redacted~~ and ~~redacted~~ The former, by virtue of his position, ~~redacted~~, ~~redacted~~ has assisted us in many ways in our operations. ~~redacted~~ Both have provided investigative leads and details on personalities of interest to us, e.g., ~~redacted~~ s evaluation of ~~redacted~~ Contacts of this type are invaluable to preserve our anonymity in operational situations requiring a secure telephone number, a one time cut-out, a one time cover, etc.

Another reason for maintaining direct contact, here and there, is the importance of being able to locate and place our staff personnel and our agents under the cover of such agencies as the Joint Export-Import Agency, Bizonal Economic Council, eventually perhaps ERP, etc. It is only by personal acquaintance with a select and trusted group of the top echelons in the functional divisions that we can hope to achieve our ends. We must remain careful, however, not to allow such contacts to get us involved in affairs which are of no concern to our long term mission. We have repeatedly had to turn down requests or suggestions for special investigations on behalf of the functional divisions. It is only when, as in the ~~redacted~~ affair, a clandestine intelligence lead ends up in a clear call for executive action that we permit ourselves to deviate from the general rule - hands off OMGUS.

J. **Liaison With Allied Intelligence Services**

1. **British Intelligence.**

During 1947 our liaison with British Intelligence followed a pattern of continuing friendliness and cooperation, but with a steadily decreasing incidence of actual contact.

MORI Document ID:> 144185:144185

SECRET
- 63 -

SECRET

- 65 -

SECRET

SECRET

- 67 -

PART IV

ADMINISTRATION, BERLIN OPERATIONS BASE

A. General Remarks

During the past two years a very considerable part of my time and energy has been devoted to supervising the administration of the Berlin Operations Base. In part this absorption in administrative detail was beneficial, in that it brought me into direct contact with a great many individual problems of which, otherwise, I would have been imperfectly aware. On the whole, however, the fact that I did not have an executive officer during the bulk of 1946 and 1947 was unfortunate, since a fairly considerable part of my personal concentration on administrative matters was done at the expense of the supervision of operations and the conduct of liaison.

The question as to whether Berlin Base required an executive officer was discussed back and forth at intervals during the entire two years. For two months (October and November 1946) I was lent the services of ███████████. ███████████ greatly assisted me in straightening out a number of vital problems, notably the security of our building and the requisitioning of houses for agents. However, after the two months' trial, the Chief of Mission, Mr. Lewis, reached the conclusion that the problems of Berlin Base were not sufficient to warrant the assignment of a full time executive officer. I concurred in that decision at the time, though in retrospect I now see that it was unfortunate. I do not wish to complain in this matter, since it was my own desire not to tie up in executive work a competent officer who might otherwise be used for case work.

By the end of 1947, however, it became fully apparent to me and to the staff of this Base that an executive officer really was needed. We were losing our one remaining army officer (Capt. John Ives), and our administrative personnel (as I shall point out in more detail below) was completely swamped by its tasks. Accordingly, I requested the Chief of Station to authorize an executive officer. Since 1 January 1948 this position has been filled by one of the junior FR case officers, Mr. ███████████. The benefits of this new arrangement have been apparent. At least half of the minor administrative matters which were formerly laid before me, are now taken care of on a routine basis. ███████████ working with the administrative officer, ███████████ has introduced a new standard of efficiency, thereby greatly contributing to the improvement of morale at the Base. Moreover, he has been able to carry out his assignment on considerably less than a full time basis. It has been possible for him to continue part time case work, gaining experience in

SECRET

SECRET

- 68 -

both the executive and the operational aspects of intelligence.

In passing, I should like to make an observation based on the experience of the past two years. In my opinion it is essential that specially recruited and trained administrative officers should be made available for field bases. It is not sufficient to assign army or civilian personnel who are without intelligence background. We have had in Berlin since the end of 1945 four army officers, all of whom have been conscientious and hardworking, and reasonably efficient. But by the same token, all four have constituted personality problems, some of major proportions. The reason for this, as I see it, is that their limited and conventional experience in Army administration was quite inadequate background for the entirely different problems of our type of operation. As a result, there was a marked tendency to develop what might be described as "complexes" such as a feeling of inferiority and hostility toward case officers, jitters in the face of crises, lack of self-confidence and even certain paranoiac traits. In each of the four cases of which I speak, the officer frequently complained that he felt himself "out of his depth" or that he was a misfit in this type of organization. Despite constant encouragement and build-up on my part, all of them remained personnel headaches.

At present the situation is quite different. ▮▮▮▮▮▮▮ has been doing administrative work in support of intelligence for nearly three years (he was formerly with ODI, OMGUS). ▮▮▮▮▮▮▮ has had considerable intelligence training and experience, superimposed on a fairly extensive background in army administration. Both feel completely at home and happy in the hectic atmosphere of "flaps" and crises which is normal to a direct operating espionage unit. There is a complete understanding between case officers and administration, and personal friction is reduced to a minimum.

I am not attempting to elevate our experience at this base into a generalization, but I submit that it is well worth taking into consideration in personnel planning. Although the ideal can seldom be attained, it should be approximated: key administrative personnel who, if not by training, at least by temperament, are adapted to clandestine intelligence work.

In addition to our past difficulties with our administrative officers, we have to a considerable extent been handicapped by the inadequate staffing of the separate administrative functions. Our basic administrative T/O has been set at the figure of 9 persons, civilian and military. It is only as of the present writing that we have actually reached that strength. Our present staff comprises the administrative officer ▮▮▮▮▮▮▮ CAF-5),

SECRET

SECRET

- 69 -

the Registry clerk (⬛⬛⬛⬛⬛⬛⬛⬛⬛⬛ CAF-5), the motor sergeant
(Sgt. Harold Bartelt), the supply sergeant (S/Sgt. Tomlinson)
and his assistants (T-5 Davis and Sgt. Kilby), and the photographer (T-5 Smith). The administrative office has one secretary
⬛⬛⬛⬛⬛⬛ CAF-7). On 18 March⬛⬛⬛⬛⬛⬛⬛⬛⬛(CAF-5)
arrived in Berlin. He is assigned to services, but his duties
have not yet been fixed.

Even with our T-O filled, we are still operating on an absolute minimum basis. Considering the size of our detachment community (average strength 40 American members, with about twenty
dependents, thirty-five German employees, many with families)
and the magnitude of our operations (ranging from a maximum of
about 250 agents to a current figure of about 125), our administrative apparatus is strikingly modest. In part this is made
possible by the fact that some of the overhead administrative
functions are performed in Heidelberg (personnel records, supply
procurement, finance). However, the main basis for our economy
of personnel has been our success in obtaining building guards
from the Army (thereby freeing at least four T-O slots), and
running our motor pool with only one enlisted man who supervises
an average of 12 German mechanics and helpers, and himself does
much of the actual repair work, and emergency and operational
driving.

The same strictures apply to the quality of our enlisted personnel as were made in the case of our administrative officers.
During the past two years we have had in effect three complete
turnovers of enlisted men. Each group has had different characteristics. The first contingent were left-overs from the war,
who had been introduced to life in Berlin in the truly lush days.
They were on the whole a reasonably hard working lot, but it was
only after they were redeployed in the spring of 1946 that we
realized the full extent to which many of them had become involved
in various forms of corruption. The second crop of GI's was
the sorriest: very young, run-of-the-mill draftees for the most
part without any military experience or training, who adopted
the attitude of "conquerors" and were guilty of most of the faults
of the preceding group, without the merit of at least having
helped win the war. This group disappeared, with no regret on
our part, in the spring of 1947. The third and current contingent
of GI's include a number of re-enlistees, who consequently are at
least more mature than their predecessors and have some idea why
they are here. Moreover, a certain element of selection entered
into their recruitment, and one or two are young men of real promis
Others must be classed as "weak sisters" whom we hope to get rid
of as soon as replacements are in sight. We have on occasion been
tempted to dispose of certain individuals, even without visible
replacement, but we usually fall back on the principle of expedi-
ency: a body is a body, after all.

SECRET

Our extensive, and predominantly painful experience with unselected enlisted men has firmly convinced us that one carefully recruited and trained civilian clerk or administrative assistant is worth at least two of what "the cat brought in". If our T-O of 9 could be filled with a group of sound CAF-5 to 7 civilians, stateside trained, coupled with our present pair of responsible regular army sergeants for motor pool and supply work, I believe our efficiency would be doubled.

B. Administrative Relations with Berlin Command

The basic administrative support of the Berlin Base derives from Berlin Command, which is the administrative headquarters of OMGUS. During the past two years this support has been given generously: we have never been frustrated or disappointed in any vital respect. But this present excellent situation was not achieved without considerable effort. During the month of December 1945, the administrative relations of the Berlin Base with OMGUS had reached the point of disaster. On the morning of my arrival, 7 January 1946, I was confronted with the fact that the Director of Administrative Services, Brig. Gen. James Edmunds, had ordered the Military Police to impound the entire motor pool of the Detachment. Gen. Edmunds was motivated, as he frankly admitted, by the desire to appropriate our three Buicks which Mr. Dulles had purchased in Switzerland. Within two hours after my arrival, I secured the return of our motor pool, and convinced Gen. Edmunds that the Buicks were the inalienable property of SSU. The crisis was over, but Gen. Edmunds was hardly one to forgive and forget such a defeat.

In March 1946 Gen. Edmunds called to the attention of Gen. Clay the fact that our SSU detachment was an agency deriving material support from OMGUS, yet not strictly speaking under its command. On the strength of this representation, Gen. Clay requested that our unit drop all its administrative connections with OMGUS, and attach itself fully to Headquarters Berlin District. It will be recalled that, at that period, Berlin District was a separate major command, and was not under OMGUS. In October, when Berlin District was downgraded to a subordinate position under OMGUS, as Berlin Command, our attachment remained unchanged.

The present situation is therefore that Berlin Operations Base is attached for administrative support to Headquarters Berlin Command, and is thus a part of the general OMGUS complex. This arrangement was ratified orally by Gen. Clay in October 1946, at the time of the change from SSU to CIG. General Clay's personal assurance of continuing support was subsequently implemented by a number of written agreements with Berlin Command, which constitute the fabric of our logistic support. These agreements were

SECRET

- 71 -

concluded on various levels, chiefly through the S-4 of Berlin
Command (at that time Col. W. Hensey), with the approval of the
commanding officer (Col. R. A. Willard). Our present solid position is the product of : a) high level Washington directives,
notably the Top Secret War Department Order "Supplies and Equipment for CIG" of 24 October 1946 with supporting USFET and EUCOM
orders developed by Heidelberg and Frankfurt, which naturally
command immediate attention and respect from army administrators:
b) the expressed assurance of support and good will from General
Clay: c) the cooperative attitude of Col. Willard and his staff:
d) a multitude of working arrangements covering every aspect of
our administrative needs from the requisitioning of operational
liquor to the exclusion of our telephone numbers from the OMGUS
Directory. I shall allude to these in more detail under the
separate headings below.

It will readily be agreed that this complex tissue of administrative arrangement constitutes an extremely valuable asset.
It is understandable, I believe, that most of our thinking and
planning in regard to dispersal of the Base comes squarely up
against the reflection that our hard-won position should not be
put in jeopardy.

C. **The Administrative Office - Adjutant functions.**

Until the creation of an executive officer in January 1948,
the entire burden of administration rested on a single administrative officer, who, at least until the recruitment of ▮▮▮▮▮▮▮
in October 1947, had always been obliged to carry his manifold
burdens without the benefit of an administrative assistant. As I
said above, the four Army officers who acted as administrative
officers during 1946 and 1947 (▮▮▮▮▮▮▮▮▮▮▮▮▮▮▮▮▮▮▮▮▮▮▮▮▮▮▮▮▮▮) within the
varying limits of their personal capacities, performed their
duties with zeal and loyalty to the organization. The fact that
they were insufficiently staffed produced varying degrees of
frustration and discontent, but never led to a complete breakdown
of the administrative system.

1. **Travel.**

The primary adjutant function of the administrative officer has been the handling of travel orders. This function is,
however, somewhat limited in scope by the higher jurisdiction of
the Heidelberg Adjutant. When I arrived in Berlin, the administrative officer, ▮▮▮▮▮▮▮▮▮▮▮▮ was, at least de facto, exercising
real adjutant functions, notably issuing travel orders for personnel of the Base over his own signature. It soon became apparent that this practice was unauthorized, and we dropped it comple
At present, travel and leave orders for points within the Theater

SECRET

SECRET

I-2: *(Continued)*

- 72 -

are procured by our administrative officer from the Orders Branch of the Adjutant General, OMGUS. They are usually issued under Berlin Command heading. Duty travel from Berlin is cleared through Heidelberg, and if the travel is outside the Theater, the orders are issued either from Heidelberg or Frankfurt under EUCOM authority. Leave travel also requires Heidelberg approval, but the so-called Authorization to Travel can be issued here. All travel out of Berlin requires a Russian translation of the orders.

In addition to the travel of staff personnel, the administrative officer obtains orders for our agents. This was formerly a fairly substantial volume of business. It was not so great, however, as was claimed in the sensational Associated Press article which stated that "a War Department detachment" had been running an underground railway which was evacuating several hundred persons from Eastern Germany per year. It is true that the total number of orders issued at our request during the past two years has run into the hundreds, but of course only a very small percentage represented actual evacuations. The great majority were return trip orders, issued either for business connected with the agent's mission or as personal favors, such as facilitating convalescence from illness, settling an estate, or purely compassionate visits.

Despite the advantages to our operations of issuing American travel orders to our agents, we have in recent months greatly cut down on the practice. In part this cut has been the result of our increasing concern over the security risk involved in all forms of agent travel. But it has also been forced upon us, to a certain extent, by the stiffening of OMGUS policy. About six months ago a near crisis developed, when Marguerite Higgins, correspondent of the New York Herald Tribune, got wind of the clandestine evacuation by S-2 Berlin Command of a German national, who had fled the Russian Zone, allegedly in fear of his life. The operation was of quite low level and actually had no intelligence significance, but Miss Higgins thought she had the makings of a sensational story, comparable to her minor classic "I Interviewed Two Russian Spies". The publication of the story was headed off, but Gen. Gailey, Chief of Staff, OMGUS, issued instructions that all requests for travel orders for Germans must be personally screened and approved by himself. Gen. Gailey soon discovered that handling an average of thirty such requests a day was quite unfeasible, and delegated the responsibility to the Personnel Officer. The practical effects, as far as we were concerned, were nil. General Walsh gave what amounted to a blanket approval in advance to any requests we might make for orders involving return to Berlin, only stipulating that outright evacuation cases should be cleared with him. Even this proviso has not been insisted upon, and in practice we can

SECRET

84

SECRET

- 73 -

obtain orders for our agents without any difficulty. As I have said, however, we voluntarily keep our requests for agent travel to the minimum. We are not unduly concerned about the security of our requests within OMGUS. These are hand-processed to the head of the AG Travel Branch (Major J. B. Mallon), and are issued without passing through the hands of the German secretaries in his office. No copy of the request bearing the name of our organization is kept by the AG; we receive all copies of the orders from the mimeograph machine, and in effect there is no record of the affair in OMGUS.

Agent travel out of Berlin, in whatever form, presents serious security risks and technical difficulties. There are three possible methods, air, rail and highway.

Within the category of air travel, three different types exist. The first, and until recently the standard method of moving agents by air, has been the use of the regular European Air Transport Service planes. EATS carries both duty and paying passengers, and we can put agents and escorting officer on the plane in either category. The disadvantage of this system is that it involves sitting in the lobby of Tempelhof Airport, sometimes for many hours on consecutive days, waiting for the takeoff. Such delays inevitably make both the German civilian and his escort rather conspicuous, and constitute a serious security hazard. In addition the nerves of the agent may suffer considerably, especially if he has any reason to think he may be blown.

The second method is to lay on a special plane, or at least get permission to put our agent on an unscheduled flight, of which there are a considerable number from Tempelhof. This is undoubtedly the most secure method, since it is possible to drive directly to the runway and load the bodies without risk of observation from the terminal. Such flights require the clearance of General Walsh, which means that the operation must be explained to him in some detail. He has been cooperative in making arrangements with the Commanding Officer of Tempelhof, Col. W. H. Dorr. The actual technical details of handling have been developed through such cases as ███████████ to the point of routine, and the procedure as such is secure. There are certain drawbacks, however, in having to coordinate through General Walsh's office. Thus, in the recent evacuation of ███████ we concluded the necessary arrangements with General Walsh and Col. Dorr, only to find that S-2 Berlin Command also had a body (a Russian defector) to be evacuated at the same time. Since special flights are not a dime a dozen, General Walsh ordered Col. Pretty of S-2 to send his character and escort on the same plane as ours. This did not cause us any great distress, since ███████ was not particularly hot from the security viewpoint. Col. Pretty, however, was distinctly unhappy and protested in vain to General Walsh. The two operations went off

SECRET

- 74 -

simultaneously without incident, but it is obvious that in a highly sensitive operation such as ████████ it would have been impossible for us to agree on the sharing of the plane with another agency.

The third form of air travel is by commercial plane. American Overseas Airlines has recently introduced the practice of making available to German civilians empty seats on its Frankfurt-Berlin scheduled flights. The price is 110 RM, which is obviously within the reach of any German who wants to travel. Consequently there is an enormous waiting list, and a system of priorities has been introduced. As I mentioned above, Gen. Gailey has placed our agency in Priority I. The only other agencies enjoying this privilege in blanket form are S-2 Berlin Command, Public Safety OMGBS and the German Police in the American Sector. In cases where sufficient justification is present, the Joint Export Import Agency (JEIA) is authorized Priority I, but not on a blanket basis. We are not clear why CIC and CID do not enjoy this privilege. The advantages of this form of travel are obvious, being cheap and convenient. It can only be used, however, for routine cases involving interzonal passes rather than MG travel orders; it must be avoided where security factors occur. We have, during the six weeks since the system was initiated, used it at least a dozen times.

Until fairly recently, the principal method of agent travel has been by rail. The American duty train has one coach, intended primarily for Americans who do not have sleeping car reservations, but which may be used by German civilians traveling on MG orders. Theoretically such orders are restricted to bona fide employees of Military Government, but, in practice, we can obtain them for our agents merely by certifying that they are engaged on official business.

The principal drawback to the American train lies in the possibility that it may be subject to Russian control. Actually, during the past two years, there has been no instance of the Russians boarding the train and removing German passengers. However, during the past months a number of serious incidents have occurred with the British train. The Russians have demanded entry to the coaches carrying Germans, claiming, and rightly, that many of these were without interzonal travel passes. Interzonal passes are issued to Germans, nominally on the basis of quadripartite agreement, but actually unilaterally by any of the four occupying powers, who in turn delegate the authority to German Bürgermeisters. It has consistently been the American position that no interzonal pass is required by Germans using the duty train. In the American view the train is de jure American territory, and may not be boarded for executive action by the Russians, any more than they may legally enter our sector to make an arrest. The British, unfortunately, have not maintained this position. They have

SECRET
- 75 -

conceded the Russian claim that the duty train does not enjoy extra-
territorial status, and they now require German civilians to carry
interzonal passes which are subject to Russian check. This yield-
ing of the British has naturally weakened our own position, but
General Clay has continued to maintain a firm stand on the inviolability of the American train. In order to enforce his policy, two
MP's with submachine guns now travel on each of the coaches and
sleeping cars of the train. Orders have been issued to resist
Russian entry with force. If the Russians actually refuse to let
the train pass their frontier without inspection, the train comman-
is instructed to return the train to the point of departure -- Ber-
or Frankfurt. This display of toughness so far has had its effect
and the train has not been molested. But there may always be a fir
instance, and that thought lies in the background of General Clay'
and General Gailey's insistence on the strict control of German
civilian travel. It was undoubtedly the fact that the British had
played fast and loose with their train, moving literally hundreds
of agents and (from the Russian viewpoint) other questionable
characters, which brought about the showdown the Americans are trying to avoid.

The third method of travel -- by car -- involves a trip of abo
100 miles through the Russian Zone on the Autobahn between Berlin
Helmstedt. This journey, per se, presents no special risks in a
reliable car, but the vehicle and passengers are subject to Russia
control at the Helmstedt end. This control has always been perfun
tory, being carried out by quasi-literate Russian soldiers, who
make no effort to check the identity of the persons mentioned. It
glance at the Russian translation of the American travel orders bu
is easy and relatively safe to take Germans through the check poin
but it is advisable to have them wear American uniform. There is
of course, always the possibility of a sudden tightening of the
control, and in any case we would hesitate to take through any per
for whom the Russians might be looking, such as a Soviet defector
a prominent German politician. But for the average agent, whom we
no reason to believe to be blown, movement by car seems to be the
simplest and safest means.

I have dealt at some length with the problem of agent travel,
because it is a basic feature of our present operational procedure
If conditions should change markedly, through a tightening of the
situation in Berlin, we might be called on to evacuate compromised
agents in considerable numbers and at short notice. Since any suc
crisis would automatically produce a stiffening of Russian control
on the highway and probably the rail corridor, it is presumed that
the only feasible means of evacuation would be by air. Whether th
Russians would eventually harass or obstruct even this avenue, wou
be a function of the gravity of the situation itself.

SECRET

SECRET
- 76 -

2. Personnel functions.

The personnel functions of our administrative office are relatively minor. The basic personnel records are kept in Heidelberg — leave and pay data, 201 files, etc. Important matters such as change of station and transfer are taken up through Heidelberg to Washington by pouch or cable according to the degree of urgency. Civilian pay is disbursed by the Special Funds Office at Heidelberg, which pouches the funds and vouchers for each pay period. Since we no longer have an Army officer attached to this Base, it is necessary for an officer to come from Heidelberg to Berlin each month to pay our enlisted men. There is always sufficient other business to justify this trip by the Heidelberg adjutant or his representative and the system appears to be satisfactory.

D. Finance.

The financial responsibilities of the administrative office, though considerable, are not sufficient to warrant the assignment of a special funds officer. The financial reports are prepared jointly by the administrative and the executive officer, but are signed by the latter for the Chief of Base.

Broadly speaking our financial problems fall into two categori those involving payments in Reichsmarks and those which are met wi Military Payment Certificates, the dollar scrip of the American occupation personnel. We do indeed maintain a small account of American greenback dollars, and an inactive account in Russian roubles. We have virtually no occasion to use other foreign currencies, though we have recently raised with Heidelberg the question of maintaining a fund of Swiss francs for use as a basis of hard cash payments to agents in the event of currency reform. A small amount of British currency, the so-called BAFs, is require for trips into the British Zone, but this has usually been accumul unofficially by personal negotiation with our British opposite num who are always eager to obtain American scrip in order to make pur chases in the PX and clothing store. This exchange of currencies constitutes a small but significant item in operational good will.

Our official expenses, on instruction from Washington, are broken down into three categories, overhead, working and project funds. The dollar outlay in all three categories is relatively small, averaging during the past two years less than $500 per mont The largest single item under this category is the purchase of operational liquor. Occasional disbursements are made for direct purchases from the PX or the Army Exchange Service auto sales sec These are confined to such minor items as are urgently needed for agent operation or the repair of a vehicle which would be deadline

SECRET

SECRET
- 77 -

for a long period, if the part had to be procured by requisition through Ordnance or our own organization. Only three of our non-American agents are paid in dollar instruments.

Our expenditures in German currency range between 25,000 and 50,000 marks per month. At the official value of 10 cents per RM, this appears to be a fairly formidable sum. But, as is well known to Washington, the official value of the mark bears no relation to its actual purchasing power. Especially in the case of an agent, who frequently has to resort to the black market in order to survive the real purchasing power of the mark in Berlin is of the order of 1/2% to 2% of its nominal value. A pound of fat (margarine, lard, or tallow) at ration prices (one pound is approximately two months ration) costs 1.20 RM. At the black market rate it costs 220, and so on down the line. The black market value of commodities from the American PX is generally estimated on the flat basis of 350 RM to the dollar. Thus a Hershey bar is worth about 15 to 20 marks, which is the equivalent of two days' wages for a domestic servant or unskilled laborer. These elementary statistics are mentioned in order to throw into a more realistic perspective the accounting picture of our Reichsmark outlay.

Hovering in the background of all our financial arrangements with agents is the prospect of Währungsreform, reform of the German currency. Every German knows that economic recovery presupposes the establishment of a reasonably sound monetary system. The only question is when and how it will occur. The present trend toward splitting Germany into an eastern and a western grouping makes the actual realization of a monetary reform for all four zones seem somewhat problematical.

In any case Währungsreform, whether unitary or dual, will create a radically new set of conditions for our operations. We have attempted to plan for any contingency. We envisage the probability that our operations for some time to come would still be built primarily on payment in commodities: food, cigarettes, and supplies. But we will be able considerably to extend our control over agents by making up to them the losses which many will be bound to experience especially in the case of those who have substantial amounts of currency which they will be unable to convert without running into difficulties with the tax authorities. We also assume, as mentioned above, that a certain amount of hard currency, greenbacks or Swiss francs, will be a useful negotiable asset for an agent during the period between the currency reform and the relative stabilization of his earning power.

The mechanics of our financial accounting system are relatively simple. Payments are recorded on a simple voucher with receipts attached, and consolidated at the end of each month into the

SECRET

89

SECRET
- 78 -

appropriate category. Our reports are pouched to Heidelberg for consolidation in the overall Station account. In general our accounting seems to have been satisfactory to Heidelberg. Minor mistakes are usually the product of uncertainty as to the category in which a payment should be entered.

E. **Billeting and Agent Installations.**

Billeting is one of the most important responsibilities of the Administrative Office. It falls into two aspects, a) staff and b) agent billets.

a) **Staff billets.** The billeting of the American personnel of the Berlin Base is primarily a personal affair which can be handled directly with the OMGUS billeting office. Although there have been fluctuations in the real estate situation, in general there have always been enough quarters available to enable our staff to obtain accommodations appropriate to their rank or rating. However, in a number of instances we have found it advisable to classify the billets of bachelor case officers as operational installations. In such cases, the billeting office gives special treatment to our requests, making available small houses or apartments which would otherwise be earmarked for families. This preferential treatment, as indeed all services rendered to us by the billeting and real estate offices in OMGUS, are the result of basic agreements concluded with the S-4 of Berlin Command at various times during the past two years. These agreements have been implemented by good liaison/the part of our administrative officers, especially███████████. We have been at pains to assure Berlin Command that we will not abuse the right to requisition property for operational purposes, and that any request for change of quarters which is not motivated by bona fide security considerations will be submitted purely as a personal matter for routine disposition.

b) **Operational installations** fall into two categories. The bachelor case officer quarters are operational only in a limited sense. They may be used for entertaining of German contacts, primarily on a social basis. Occasionally, agents from out of town may be billeted for a short period in a case officer's quarters. This is done with careful consideration of security risks.

The second category of operational installations is the regular agent billet or holding area. The history of our agent housing in Berlin has been complex and at times rather painful. In the early days, with our overexpanded chain system, we maintained a number of large establishments, notably a 12-room house at 2 Promenadenstrasse and a 27-room villa on the Kleiner Wannsee ████████████. It was originally taken under the regime

SECRET

SECRET

- 79 -

of [~~Sutten~~] at a time when we had an ambitious project of training and holding a group of agents for work in the Polish Zone and Poland. When this project was abandoned, we continued to use ~~......~~ as an agent area. Because of its immense size and its isolation, we yielded to the temptation to house a considerable number of characters simultaneously. Despite the fact that the villa was admirably suited to internal compartmentalization, it was impossible with our inadequate American personnel to maintain strict segregation. As a result, the semi-permanent guests inevitably came to know a lot about each other, and even about the transients. When the security blows began to fall in the winter of 1946-47, it became apparent that our establishment was, if not actually blown, at least rendered untenable from the security viewpoint. We decided to give up ~~......~~ in the fall of 1947, and were luckily able to make a virtue of necessity by turning it over to CIC who needed just such a place as a special detention center. At about the same time we liquidated our other principal white elephant, No. 2 Promenadenstrasse, which had been set up in the fall of 1945 before my arrival. We were left with only one major agent house, 26 Ruhmeweg, which like the other two had served its usefulness, but which we have retained for temporary housing of blown agents.

Faced with an acute shortage of agent accommodations, we turned to the S-4 and Billeting Office with an appeal for a new type of property: small unpretentious houses or apartments, which could be kept up by a single German housekeeper, with or without the presence of a resident case officer or enlisted man. Berlin Command has been extremely cooperative in providing half a dozen such accommodations, stipulating only that we not compromise by an excess of clandestine activity, any billets which would be suitable for American families.

Only one other category of operational real estate remains to be mentioned, viz. permanent residences for agents in the American sector. This type is the hardest to procure. It must be realized that the real estate situation for Germans in Berlin, though less critical than in the American Zone, is nevertheless extremely tight (average 1.8 persons per room in the American Sector of Berlin). Accordingly, the possibility of setting up new living quarters for Germans through German channels on a routine basis is practically nil. Even if the agent is completely in order with his papers, he has virtually no hope of procuring an apartment through the Wohnungsamt in any of the five American Sector boroughs, unless he obtains a supporting order from American Military Government. Such an order will only be issued on behalf of an actual employee of MG, and, while we can readily procure it, we automatically expose the connection of our agent. Moreover, even if such an order is delivered to the Wohnungsamt, it is still not sufficient to guarantee the immediate availability of a suitable dwelling. Accordingly, we have frequently been forced to resort to the rather extreme measure of requisitioning under MG authority.

SECRET

- 80 -

This procedure is unsatisfactory. In the first place General Clay, as early as the fall of 1946, ordered the cessation of new requisitioning, and the turning back to the German economy of a substantial amount of property already requisitioned. By great effort, jointly between ourselves, Heidelberg, and Frankfurt, we were able to secure a high level authorization for requisitioning German property for operational purposes. The extent of this privilege was limited to ten separate dwellings. In actual fact, we have exercised our right in only five cases.

The upshot of our headaches with procurement of agent billets has been the adoption of a policy of putting the agent on his own. If his present position is not such that he can take care of himself, it is unlikely that he can ever become a useful agent with adequate security. Inevitably, this consideration has limited the scope of our recruitment, and occasionally compelled us to forego the services of an otherwise promising candidate. But it has also compelled us to be more realistic, and to assess an agent's prospects against his capacity to survive without artificial support in the existing German economy.

One result of this trend in our policy has been to turn our attention toward the outright purchase of real estate. Under prevailing conditions, with the powerful leverage of the inflated mark, it is possible to buy apartments, houses, and even business establishments at prices which we can readily afford to pay. The principal difficulty, of course, is setting up a cooperative and reliable German to hold the title, in such fashion that his purchase will appear to have been legal, without attracting undue attention from tax collectors, etc. To date, although we have examined a number of possibilities, we have not succeeded in actually mounting such a purchase. It will readily be seen that any transaction of this type will have to be associated with a degree of long range planning which the fluid situation in Berlin hardly encourages at the present moment.

Furniture also presents a headache to our administrative office. In the case of staff billets, the Army has usually been able to provide at least a decent minimum, which can be supplemented by a little enterprise on the part of the billet holder. But in the case of agent premises, furniture is extremely difficult to organize. Because of its immense black market value, furniture is also one of the last things an agent is willing to give up, if he is forced to leave Berlin. Nearly all our evacuation agreements are complicated by a housemoving proviso. Sometimes it is sufficient to move the furniture from another sector of Berlin into our own. But even this is hard to accomplish, as we have found out empirically; German or allied police are likely to turn up at embarrassing moments and question the transaction. If the agent is obliged to leave Berlin permanently, we frequently have to agree to ship his furniture and personal belongings to the

91

SECRET

- 81 -

American Zone, which may involve a 1000 or even a 1500 mile trip with a 2½ ton truck. Needless to say there always seems to be a discrepancy between what the agent claims he had and what actually arrives. Our long-suffering friends in the disposal unit at Heidelberg can testify to the intensity of these household woes.

F. Transportation

Motor transport is unquestionably the aspect of Berlin Base administration in which I have been forced to take the closest personal interest. It has always been my conviction that the efficiency of our intelligence production to a considerable extent has been a direct function of the efficiency of our transportation. I am glad to report a steady improvement in the latter which has certainly been paralleled by improvement in the former. I believe there is a real cause and effect relationship.

In January 1946, as I stated above, our motor pool narrowly escaped complete liquidation at the hands of OMGUS. With the exception of Mr. Dulles's three Buicks it was a sorry prize for General Edmunds. We had a fleet of about 10 beaten up wartime jeeps, half a dozen rattletrap Opels and Mercedes turned over to us as captured enemy equipment, an exotic and unreliable Tatra and some trucks.

During the first half of 1946, this dismal situation still further deteriorated, and with it the morale of our dwindling group of case officers. I first realized clearly in the Fall that my primary administrative obligation was to reverse this trend by building up our motor pool. By direct negotiation I succeeded in obtaining from the Chief of Ordnance, Berlin District, twelve salvaged sedans which the Army admitted it was unable to repair. These were of very diverse quality ranging from an excellent Buick, which only lacked a clutch throw out bearing, to moderately useful Opels and Mercedes. All twelve of these vehicles were towed to our motor pool and the painful process of rehabilitation was begun. Although in some cases the process took as much as six months, with parts being scrounged or hand made in obscure German garages or imported from Belgium or Switzerland, eventually all twelve sedans were brought into running condition. Seven are still serving us, for better or worse, today.

Although the acquisition of these 12 sedans marked the turning point in the history of our transportation, we still were faced with an actue shortage of vehicles. Because of the difficulty of repairs, and the bitter cold of the winter of 1946-47, as many as 50% of our vehicles would be deadlined at a given moment.

SECRET

- 82 -

Sedans were no longer available from the Army. The only prospect of immediate relief was to procure some Volkswagens. After securing approval from Heidelberg and Washington, in October 1946 I placed a request with our British friends in 7 CCU for an allocation of thirty "bumble bees". Despite the cooperativeness of our liaison contacts, the entire transaction became enveloped in a mass of red tape. After several months delay, the matter was finally carried through Brigadier Howard and Major General Lethbridge of Intelligence Division, CCG to the Director of the Economics Subcommission, Sir Cecil Weir, who personally authorized the allocation. From that point on, American red tape succeeded British but Heidelberg and Frankfurt successfully surmounted all obstacles created by USFET Ordnance, G-4, and Army Exchange Service. The thirty vehicles were delivered in a mass operation in early spring 1947, 10 being driven straight from the factory to Berlin. The arrival of the 10 Volkswagens on top of the 12 Ordnance sedans marked the final liberation of Berlin Base from the "struggle buggy" era. It now became possible to assign each case officer and executive member of the staff a closed vehicle, and to maintain a minimum reserve for periodic checks, deadlining and dispatch

The third turning point in the history of our transportation was the arrival in late summer of the first of the new American sedans, ordered by Washington. One by one these shiny vehicles have filtered in, and as of the present writing we have a total of 12 new American vehicles. We have gradually been able to shuffle off our worst pieces of junk, but we still find it necessary to retain a few substandard vehicles in order to meet all our operational, dispatch, visitors, and reserve requirements. We hope by this summer that every active member of the staff will have a permanently assigned reliable American sedan.

In order to service and maintain our vehicles with maximum efficiency we have found it necessary to keep a staff of German mechanics and helpers, averaging about 10 to 12. It is quite impractical to carry out repairs through Ordnance facilities, which are hopelessly swamped: they themselves have encouraged us to do third echelon work, which officially is prohibited for small motor pools in Berlin. Ordnance has been cooperative in issuing such parts as are available, making only the stipulation that we avoid stockpiling. Army Exchange Service maintains minimum facilities for servicing the thousand odd civilian vehicles in Berlin, but they are so inadequately staffed and stocked with parts that we can derive only slight support from them. Basically, we remain as we have been during the past two years—on our own. Our motor sergeant and his principal mechanics have developed a veritable network of German contacts who provide anything...at a price! Since the price is usually measured in terms of cigarettes or Lebensmittel, we are able to keep the wheels rolling for almost nothing. For example, a complete factory quality paint job worth $100 in the States costs an average of one Ten-in-One package or fifteen packs of cigarettes.

SECRET

- 83 -

Maintenance of a fully developed motor pool presents certain obvious drawbacks, chiefly from the security viewpoint, and we have frequently deliberated on the advisability of liquidating it. But the prospect of throwing fifteen active case officers and a bus administrative and executive staff completely "on the town", has always led us to cherish the status quo.

The question has occasionally been raised from Washington why we have laid such extraordinary emphasis and expended so much effort on transportation. No person who has been in Berlin ever raises this question. I can best put the situation in a few simple comparisons. The City of Berlin is almost four times the size of the District of Columbia. This area is inhabited to the city limits. The American Sector is as big as the City of Washington. It is possible to drive in a straight line in thickly settled areas for a distance almost as great as from Washington to Baltimore. In effect, Berlin is probably areawise the largest city in the world. Our business knows no sector limits.

The other side of the picture is the fact that for all practical purposes there is no alternative to motor transportation. The common carrier system has been restored, but the service is so poor that it cannot be used efficiently by American personnel, entirely apart from security or prestige considerations. There is a rudimentary bus service (six lines) between key American installations, which does not, however, connect with the other sectors. There is no commercial taxi service, and the handful of dilapidated German taxis operated under MG sponsorship are unobtainable because of the civilian demand. In short, without a car the conduct of our type of business is impossible. We are glad that this basic proposition has been recognized and Washington has undertaken to provide us with new and sound vehicle sufficient to our needs.

G. Registry.

An important administrative change coeval with the dissolution of Intelligence Branch in Heidelberg in June 1947 was the dispersal of Registry personnel and responsibilities. For the first time Berlin acquired a full fledged Registry of its own, and the services of a trained, conscientious registrar, Mr. ████████. Pouches had been prepared in the Adjutant's office, which was already overworked a dozen ways: such tasks as logging, indexing records, distribution of incoming pouches, internal routing of cables and memoranda, maintenance of Top Secret Control and maintenance of files had been scattered among several offices and performed in the catch-as-catch-can manner necessitated by personnel shortage. Now, however, ████████ has gathered all these and other functions into a smooth-running central Registry which has greatly improved the efficiency of this Base. One indication of the size of the job is that since he arrived the incoming and outgoing correspondence has numbered four thousand pieces and the cables more than two thousand.

SECRET

SECRET
- 84 -

H. Communications

Communications is perhaps the only administrative field in which we have never had any headaches. The high standard of efficiency and security which the Communications Branch of OSS developed during the war has been maintained, so far as we can judge, without impairment. Our present Chief Code Clerk, Mr. ▓▓▓▓▓▓▓ is a good example of this efficiency.

The cable traffic of the Berlin Base has varied considerably, but it has generally fallen slightly above the normal capacity of a single communications clerk. There have been peak loads when the code clerk was swamped, but we have fortunately had a few trained substitutes among the regular office personnel to step into the breach. The heaviest volume of traffic was reached in December 1947 with a total of 26,000 groups. This is almost double the amount which is considered normal for a single code clerk. Traffic has declined slightly since that peak, but still averages at least 50% more than a single clerk should handle. We hesitated, however, to ask for the outright assignment of a second clerk until we were absolutely sure that it was necessary. It was finally agreed in March 1948 to send a second clerk ▓▓▓▓▓▓▓▓▓▓▓▓▓▓▓ on an experimental basis.

The most important innovation in our message center was the installation in January 1948 of a teleprint connection with the OMGUS Signal Center, which provides direct relay of the encoded messages to and from our office. This put an end to the time consuming system of picking up the messages by courier, and insured that priority messages will be handled without delay.

Until the arrival of ▓▓▓▓▓▓▓▓▓ and ▓▓▓▓▓▓▓▓▓ we had had only girls as code clerks, a series of six or seven rotated to Berlin from Heidelberg. I wish to take this occasion to commend them all, for their efficiency, their patience under conditions of strain and for their friendly and cheerful participation in the life of our little community. Orchids to Commo!

I. Secret Section.

Berlin Base operates a Secret Section on a part time basis. During 1946 we embarked on a rather ambitious program of document reproduction, in support of our clandestine operations. We did this because the time factor in most cases ruled out processing documents through to Washington, and Heidelberg had not at that time reconstructed the liquidated C&D Section of the wartime OSS.

Unfortunately this document program ran into difficulties in the winter of 1946-47. Our principal German contact, the Zander Printing Company, was compromised in the blowing of the Cakewalk-Calesa-Calf chains. Moreover a number of security jolts had

SECRET

SECRET

- 85 -

convinced us that it was dangerous to equip our agents with forged papers beyond absolute necessity. It was not that our forgeries were incompetent. The danger lay rather in the fact that many other people were in the business, on a strictly money-making, as opposed to an intelligence basis. Consequently it was quite normal for the Soviet or German police to apprehend Germans with false Reisemarken, etc. Even though our agents might not incur special risks in such routine pick ups, there was always the danger that the investigation of a forged documents case might lead to the discovery of espionage activity.

We were further deterred from continuing in the documents business by the visit of Col. Leers. Col. Leers was chiefly concerned with the reorganization of the Secret Section in Heidelberg, to serve the purpose of an intermediate processing point between the field bases and Washington. He did, however, devote some attention to our own products. As a result of his critical scrutiny, we became aware of the fact that our efforts had frequently been clumsy or amateurish. We realized that, with the tightening of controls, we would only jeopardize our own and our agents' security by continuing to equip them with papers which would not stand rigid tests.

At present our activities in this field are greatly restricted. We have indeed one useful resource in cases of emergency, viz. CIC. Berlin CIC has the services of a really expert forger (formerly with the Abwehr I.G.), whom they are willing to make available for us on special occasions. Actually, we have taken advantage of this offer only *once*. For obvious security reasons, we prefer not to entrust our commissions to an outside agency, no matter how cooperative.

Our Secret Section functions are at present carried out by an FR Case Officer, ███████████████. ███████ in addition to document work, handles special equipment, secret inks, etc. It must be confessed that we have not been fully satisfied with the support he has received in these matters. We have been disappointed over delays in filling our requests. I also recommend greater liberality in supplying secret inks and special devices to the field. I realize that security considerations are paramount, but some risks must be assumed if we are not to sacrifice profitable current operations.

The greatest positive contribution of the Secret Section in Berlin has been the steady stream of documents, as well as document and operational intelligence which has been diligently and ably collected and passed on by ███████████. Indeed, we have fully realized that any future large scale reactivation of the Secret Section for day to day operational problems will necessitate the collection of documents and document intelligence in the intervening time. ███████████ has shown an outstanding aptitude in this field, and it is largely due to his diligence and conscientiousness that this has not been handled perfunctorily, as a secondary duty. An outstanding contribution in this field has been the

SECRET

LH-5

- 86 -

excellent working arrangement with the Reichsdruckerei, the
official German printing office. This working arrangement, originally set up by ░ ░ SIC+F. ░ ░ through ░ ░ ░ ░ ░ ░ is now
handled by ░ ░ ░ ░ ░ ░ ░ It has resulted in our procuring a copy
of every document of identity printed by the Reichsdruckerei.
We have been able with their assistance to obtain any type of
document paper which the Secret Section in Washington might need.
This has even resulted in the Reichsdruckerei offering their
very extensive dyeing facilities to duplicate paper samples.

A certain amount of special communications material is also
on hand. We have three different types of sound recorders, with
microphones and wire. We do not, however, have any competent
technician to install them, and therefore we have to call on
Heidelberg for support. It is possible that we can arrange to
have a technician trained for us, in the person either of our
photographer or our communications clerk.

We have at present a satisfactory listening and recording
arrangement in the house of the SC Branch chief, which has been
used effectively on several occasions. FR Branch has a similar
installation in one of its agent houses. We can also, if necessa
mount a recording machine in certain rooms of our office building
On the whole, however, as in Secret Section matters, we have been
insufficiently supported by higher headquarters in the training
of both staff and enlisted personnel. We hope that this defect
will be remedied. We also recognize that in part the fault has
been our own: it is a hard decision to detach a valuable case
officer for the considerable period of time necessary to give him
expert training.

J. Photographic Laboratory.

The photographic laboratory has been a vital part of the
Berlin Operations Base technical setup. As a result of our clandestine operations, we receive a substantial volume of reports
which have to be microfilmed or photostated for transmission to
Heidelberg and Washington. This work frequently has to be carrie
out on a rush basis, especially where the documents have been
purloined at night and must be returned by morning.

Our laboratory equipment is installed in a sizable room in
the attic of our building. The conversion of the attic to the
purposes of a dark room, constituted a major operation which could
only be carried out by resorting to the open German market for
lumber, insulation, black cloth and paper, etc. A large part
of the equipment was inherited from our predecessor organizations
some was procured from Washington, a small amount locally from
the Army, and individual items were purchased on the indigenous
market with inflated marks or cigarettes.

SECRET

- 87 -

Our photo laboratory was inspected by Col. Joseph Leers in the summer of 1947. Col. Leers made many important recommendations for the improvement of our service, both as to equipment and operating methods. So far as possible, these recommendations have been carried out. It still remains difficult to secure an adequate supply of materials within the Theater, especially enlarging paper, and we have not found that requisitions from Washington arrive very promptly.

Our Chief problem, however, has been personnel. During the past two years we have had to rely entirely on enlisted men, for the most part untrained in photographic technique at the time of their recruitment. Training has been carried out by Communications Branch at Heidelberg, and furthered, locally, as far as possible, after the transfer to Berlin. Nevertheless, none of our photograph technicians to date has been really satisfactory. As of the present writing, we have for the first time under recruitment a fully trained Army photographer. With his transfer, we shall finally enter an era of technically satisfactory photo work. As it has been in the past, our enlisted photographers have had to be closely supervised by a staff officer on any really important work. Fortunately, ████████████ takes a personal interest in photography, and has willingly devoted a considerable part of his spare time to developing the laboratory, training the photographers and supervising important assignments.

In addition to a microfilm camera, we have German photostatic equipment and enlargers, a Speed Graphic with accessories, German dryers and other special pieces of equipment procured locally. There is need for a new 35 mm enlarger, preferably of American manufacture.

K. Security.

It is altogether appropriate to conclude this lengthy survey of the Berlin Operations Base with a discussion of security. Volumes could be written on this subject, which has been our most constant and ever present concern.

Security falls into two broad categories, a) operational, and b) administrative, viz. security of installations, correspondence, and personnel. I have devoted considerable discussion to the former in treating the operations of FR and SC Branches. The only point that needs to be stressed here is the fact that the lack of an assigned security officer during the bulk of 1946 and 1947 was a great drawback to the operational Branches. This lack coupled with the removal of security functions from SC Branch was in large measure the cause for the material aspects of the major chain blows.

SECRET

SECRET

- 88 -

Administrative security was also badly neglected. During the period prior to the appointment of the present security officer, ▓▓▓▓▓▓▓▓▓▓ efforts were made from time to time to designate a particular case officer as being responsible for physical security, but the press of other duties, usually resulted in his neglecting the security responsibility. Two exceptions have already been noted: ▓▓▓▓▓▓▓▓ during his brief period as Executive Officer in 1946 prepared certain basic studies on the compartmentalization of our building with a view to segregating the German help. ▓▓▓▓▓▓▓ who also served as part time security officer for a few months in the fall of 1946 concluded the basic agreement with S-4 Berlin Command by which we obtained military and German Industrial Police guards for the inside and outside of the building. These were important achievements, but they were static, and did not meet the needs of a dynamic security defense.

It was in response to our lack of effective measures in both operational and administrative security that ▓▓▓▓▓▓▓ was assigned his present functions. In order to insure maximum effectiveness it was decided to make him directly responsible to the Base Chief. Actually he works closely with, but not under the Executive Office the two constituting a team for coordination of security and administrative matters of all types.

▓▓▓▓▓▓▓ first achievement was clearing up a rather unsatisfactory situation in our indigenous personnel office. We had long suspected the head of this office of being heavily involved in black market operations, and possibly connected with thefts of a number of our vehicles. The latter suspicion has not been confirmed, and we now feel that we were simply victims of outside operators, like hundreds of others in Berlin. The black market involvements were, however, established beyond doubt through ▓▓▓▓▓▓▓ investigation, and the offender was summarily dismissed with a strong threat of court action if he molested us in any way.

With the elimination of this sore spot, a major moral danger to our enlisted personnel and an ultimate security threat was removed. We were still painfully aware of the existence of a certain amount of petty thievery, chiefly in the motor pool. It is a regrettable but admitted fact in Berlin, that a certain amount of pilfering will always exist, so long as the indigenous personnel and their families live under the prevailing economic conditions. Motor pools are particularly vulnerable: portable items such as tools and cans of gasoline have a high value on the black market, and short of riveting them down, there is no way to keep them from disappearing. However, our security officer has made a determined and successful effort to reduce the amount of

SECRET

SECRET

- 89 -

loss through theft. Recognizing that only an inside German detective could cope with the problem, we obtained from Public Safety the loan of one of their most trusted and experienced Kriminalpolizei operatives. He was installed under cover of a driver for FR Branch, and contacted the security officer only after hours and outside the office premises. The report which this detective submitted at the end of two months indicated the following points. a) With the dismissal of our head of indigenous employees, the principal source of corruption was eliminated. Only one dishonest employee remains, who unfortunately has made himself nearly indispensable by his mastery of the art of scrounging parts for our cars. With great regret we have decided to get rid of him, too. b) The morale and attitude of the German mechanics and maintenance personnel on the whole are good. They, of course, realize that they are working for a secret organization, and have a pretty shrewd idea what it is all about. But they appear to have a real pride in their situation, and a considerable loyalty which has been strengthened by a generous and friendly treatment on our part (we have made small handouts about once every two months, a pack of cigarettes, a pound of lard and some PX items to each). Police file checks and background investigations have not brought to light any cases of security interest, so far. The danger of petty thievery in the motor pool is greater from outside than from within. This detective and (ironically) the dishonest mechanic referred to above, have captured several prowlers who escaped the vigilance of the German Industrial Police guard patroling the enclosure.

In addition to this type of direct protective work, our detective has also conducted background investigations of other employees including the servants in our operational installations, and, as far as practicable, in our staff billets. The latter, of course, are not direct employees of this Base, but are obtained from the Berlin Command Labor Office on a routine basis. While there is little security danger from that source, we are including them on our investigation program.

The security of our American personnel is largely a matter of maintaining a decent minimum of cover in the OMGUS community. On the whole we have had few unfortunate experiences in this respect. The existence and name of our Detachment are not classified information as such. Our personal mail is addressed to War Department Detachment, OMGUS APO 742. Inevitably the identity of the Detachment is known to a considerable number of German employees in OMGUS and Berlin Command, such as clerks in the Post Office and the commercial telegraph offices, in the various OMGUS clubs, etc. But the neutrality of the name and the normal behavior of our personnel are sufficient to allay latent curiosity. In casual ancial contacts with American personnel, our staff generally employs a minimum of cover subterfuge. Since it would be pointless to pretend to work with such agencies as POLAD or any of the functional divisions, we usually simply say that we are connected with the Office of the Director of Intelligence. If

SECRET

I-2: *(Continued)*

the questioner is connected with ODI he will already know who we are; if not, the answer is sufficient to satisfy.

We have had a very few moments of embarrassment from former OSS personnel, some of whom have casually turned up and made embarrassing remarks in public. There was one particularly bad case in 1946 of a disgruntled secretary, who had been dismissed from OSS on security grounds, and who took a vindictive delight in heckling some of our staff in the presence of outsiders. The situation became so critical that we had taken steps to persuade the Theater Commander to have her removed. Fortunately the problem was solved by her marrying and returning to the States.

By and large, our staff have preserved a high degree of anonymity. None of our billet telephones are listed and our names do not appear on published lists. This anonymity does not prevent the staff, and especially those with dependents, from enjoying normal social lives and blending inconspicuously with the large American community. I have never believed it wise to discourage normal social intercourse, not only with Americans but with selected Germans. Too much seclusion is bad for morale, and ultimately for security itself.

Our greatest security preoccupation has naturally been with our office building. Here we started with a great advantage in the very layout of the building and grounds. Our premises at 19 Foehrenweg were selected in July 1945 by Mr. Allan Dulles, at a time when the pick of the real estate was available. His choice could not have been better. The building is located on a one block long dead-end street, surrounded by a heavily wooded park of about four acres with high and strong metal fences. There is no house opposite our street entrance, nor indeed anywhere within 150 feet. In winter, when the shrubs are bare of leaves, our motor pool is indeed visible from a main and heavily travelled highway, a fact which we have had occasion to regret, since it attracted the unfavorable attention of General Clay and the OMGUS Chief of Staff. However, by systematically planting a curtain of evergreen shrubs, we have achieved a fair degree of privacy on that side, also.

The building itself is extremely solid of construction. Originally designed as a sort of rest home for high ranking German army officers, it is said to have served during the war as a personal headquarters for Field Marshal Keitel. At any rate, it was equipped with a special air raid shelter with gas decontamination equipment and a tunnel escape. There are massive steel doors at each level, and the windows which are accessible from the ground are furnished with heavy steel bars. The less accessible windows are also reinforced with strong solid steel shutters which lock from the inside. A highly professional and determined prowler could gain entry only under the most exceptional circumstances, and even this possibility has been virtually eliminated by an outside system of lights and a roving German guard.

SECRET

- 91 -

-in
Even/the improbable event of gaining entry to the building,
the intruder would be confronted with the fact that all our
classified material is locked in heavy American combination lock
filing cabinets. Moreover the American military guard at the
front entrance makes an hourly patrol of the inside of the
building. As a final precaution we have adopted the practice
of having several of our enlisted personnel sleep inside the
building. Of late we have been obliged to reduce the number,
partly because we have had to billet EM in some of our agent
houses, and partly because with the increase of our staff we
have had to take some of the billet rooms as office space.
At present it is our policy to billet three enlisted men in
the building, and the number may presently be reduced to two.
It is believed that this, with the presence of the military
and the German civilian guard, is sufficient to protect the
building against all but an onslaught in force. Even that
very remote contingency has been considered, and we have had
our building put on the beat of the roving MP patrol which cir-
culates through the OMGUS area hourly at night.

All our staff have been alerted to constant sensitivity in
regard to building security. As a result there have been a
number of incidents in which staff personnel have personally
arrested suspicious loiterers outside the building. One rather
comic instance occurred in 1946 when the Chief of SC Branch was
photographed by a German civilian on the street outside the
building. Our officer noticed that the civilian was accompanied
by an American captain who was sitting near by in a jeep. He
noted the number of the jeep, and later ascertained that it
belonged to the head of the Signals Photo Unit at Berlin District.
The civilian was being given a little training in candid photography, and, of all places, the captain happened to select our
building! Needless to say the film was recovered and destroyed.

We have frequently had our building checked for possible
microphones or telephone taps. The only serious danger, in our
opinion, would come from an outside tap mounted at a central
telephone exchange. We have frequently asked Army Signals for
their opinion as to our vulnerability and have received uniformly
reassuring answers. Although the telephone system has now been
restored to the German Reichspost, the administration is carried
out on a sector, rather than a city-wide basis. It is believed
that it would be difficult, if not impossible, for any of the
other three allies to operate a successful monitoring service
into the exchanges of the American sector without our becoming
aware.

SECRET

SECRET

- 92 -

Although we are thus relatively complacent about danger through the local telephones, we naturally practice all the normal forms of telephone security, avoid discussing confidential matters even within the strictly military exchange, and resort to double talk, use of first names, etc. The most serious danger comes from the long distance phone, which passes by land line through the Russian Zone. Although the relay stations on this line are manned by American soldiers, it must be assumed that the line can be and probably is tapped. The principal defense, apart from rigid security, is the fact that some thousand calls a day are made between Berlin and Frankfurt. It seems logical to believe that our small volume of traffic (average of two calls a day) would be lost in such a volume. In any case, we play it safe and relay all sensitive business by cable.

To sum up, our attitude toward security is one of constant watchfulness. We strive continually for greater protection without allowing it to become an inhibiting factor. With a detachment and operation of our size, there is danger of becoming muscle bound by an excess of precaution. The ideal toward which we aim has never been achieved to the full, but we have learned to relax while remaining alert.

SECRET

SECRET : 12   FSRO-706-a

OFFICE OF MILITARY GOVERNMENT FOR GERMANY (US)
Office of the Deputy Military Governor
APO 742

#1-a

Date 3/9/94

CIG-A 10.05

SUBJECT: Intelligence Disseminations of War Department
HRP 94-1 Detachment, APO 403

TO : Chief of Mission
      War Department Detachment

1. Reference is made to your letter, above subject, dated 20 October 1946.

2. Your predecessor detachment has been an importance contributor of intelligence required by the Office of Military Government for Germany (US), especially that concerning the other occupied zones. Such information is extremely useful to us in the formulation and execution of U. S. Military Government policy and in negotiations on a quadripartite basis. Until there is a free exchange of information among all four of the occupying powers, I shall continue to need such information and such other help and assistance as you can render me through my Director of Intelligence.

3. Specifically this office is interested in securing all available data which you may obtain on political, economic, and sociological developments in the other zones of occupied Germany, as well as in its peripheral countries such as New Poland, Poland, Czechoslovakia, Hungary and Austria, where conditions have a bearing on Germany and the Military Government of Germany. To assist you in assessing our interests I have had my Director of Intelligence prepare a detailed list of subjects which are of special import to Military Government. Because of the consolidation of the U.S. Army Headquarters, Berlin District, with this office, certain matters of purely Military Intelligence of concern to the Assistant Chief of Staff, G-2, Berlin Troop Command, have also been included in these requirements in a separate paragraph. The present list has been purposely prepared along somewhat general lines since any information on these subjects is of use. From time to time I am likely to require special reports on specific subjects of concern to Military Government; all such requirements will be submitted to you through my Director of Intelligence as individual requests.

4. It is my desire that the Office of the Director of Intelligence of this Headquarters handle the distribution of all intelligence reports to any interest echelons of Military Government. This method of handling dissemination should enhance the security of the information received from your detachment.

2 Incls:
    Incl 1 - letter CG, BD, Sub-
        missions from WD Detachment
    Incl 2 - list of subjects of
        Intelligence Requirements

/s/   Lucius D. Clay
      LUCIUS D. CLAY
Lieutenant General, U. S. Army
    Deputy Military Governor

HISTORICAL DOCUMENT

Destroy only with consent
  of the Historical Staff

Downgraded per XAAZ-32702,
12 July 74, 100-2-85

SECRET

Name:
Date:

CONFIDENTIAL

This document has been
approved for release through
the HISTORICAL REVIEW PROGRAM of 10 January 1947
the Central Intelligence Agency.

"CIG-A-10.05"

Date 3/9/94

MEMORANDUM

NRP   94-1

DOCUMENT NO. 002
NO CHANGE IN CLASS. ☐
☐ DECLASSIFIED
CLASS. CHANGED TO: TS-S Ⓔ 2010
NEXT REVIEW DATE: _____
AUTH: HR 70-7
DATE 1/25/80 REVIEWER: _____

SUBJECT: Targets of German Mission

From : Richard Helms

Herewith is a list of basic targets which are being covered currently by the German Mission. This list of targets highlights the commitments we have had to USFET, OMGUS, and POLAD in Germany.

✓ 1. OB Information

    A. OB information on Russian Army in Occupied Germany.
    B. OB information on Russian and Polish armies in Poland.
    C. OB information on Polish and Russian armies in Polish
       Occupied Germany.
    D. OB information on Russian Army in Baltic States and
       the Mother Country.
    E. Same information as (A-D) above on installations, posts,
       training camps, etc.

2. Political

    A. Clandestine coverage of three major political parties
       and trade unions in Russian Zone of Germany, including
       secret directives, connections with Russian, British,
       and other governments, financial aid, aims, and their
       general place in the long-range political plans of the
       Soviet Union.
  ✓ B. Coverage of political parties and political life of the
       Polish Occupied Zone of Germany.
  ✓ C. Coverage of political parties, trade unions, etc., in
       Poland.
  ✓ D. Coverage of political life, Communist Party policy and
       its implementation in the satellite countries and Russia.
    E. Coverage of land administrations in the Russian Zone of
       Germany, as well as in the Polish Zone of Germany, Poland,
       the Baltic States, and Russia to determine the extent and
       details of behind-the-scenes political direction and planning.
    F. Political indoctrination of the Russian and Polish armies.

HISTORICAL DOCUMENT

Destroy only
of the

CONFIDENTIAL

Form:
Date:

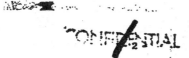

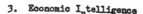

CONFIDENTIAL

3. Economic Intelligence

  ✓ A. Dismantling of factories in the Russian Zone of Germany, Polish Zone of Germany, the Baltic States, and Poland by the Russians.

     B. Dismantling in the Polish Zone of Germany by the Poles.

     C. Over-all industrial production of the Russian Controlled Economy.

     D. Over-all industrial production in Poland.

  ✓ E. Details of Germany production with delivery schedules to Russian and Germany Economy.

  ✓ F. Production of coal, iron, and other minerals in the Russian Controlled Economy, with delivery figures and etails.

     G. Coverage of over-all economic planning by Russian controlled German administration, Polish administration, and Russian administration in the Russian Zone of Germany, Polish Zone of Germany, Poland, the Baltic States, and Russian proper.

  ✓ H. Details on road and rail networks, and inland waterways in the Russian and Polish Zone of Germany, Poland, the Baltic States, and Russia proper, as well as extent of available transportation, extent of the use of same, and details on goods and personnel transported.

  ✓ I. Information installations and capacities of the Baltic ports.

4. Scientific Information

     A. Nuclear physics, coverage of raw material needed for research and production, as well as installations, laboratories, personnel, etc., participating in research or contemplated production in the Russian Controlled Economy.

     B. Research on supersonic devices, rockets, jet propulsion, and other special devices or weapons. Details on personnel, extent of research, extent of intended or actual production and purpose of same.

     C. Information on research on biological warfare, as well as full coverage of personnel, laboratories, installations and actual production.

CONFIDENTIAL

CONFIDENTIAL

This document has been approved for release through the HISTORICAL REVIEW PROGRAM of the Central Intelligence Agency.

Date 3/9/94

MEMORANDUM FOR GENERAL VANDENBERG

HRP 94-1

Subject: Points for discussion with General Clay.

16 January 1947

DOCUMENT NO. 003
NO CHANGE IN CLASS. ☐
☐ DECLASSIFIED
CLASS. CHANGED TO: TS S ☒
NEXT REVIEW DATE: 1990
AUTH: HR 70-2
DATE 3/25/80 REVIEWER: 061769

Up to the present time our missions in Central Europe have been devoting a major part of their operational energy to the procurement of tactical intelligence for the benefit of USFET, USFA, OMGUS and POLAD. The nature of the information which is currently being received is indicated in the attached memorandum of targets from Mr. Helms. Also attached is a letter from General Clay describing in detailed terms the type of information with which he would like to be supplied on a continuing basis.

In view of the mission of the Office of Special Operations "the conduct * * * of all organized Federal espionage and counter-espionage outside the United States and its possessions for the collection of foreign intelligence information required for the national security", it appears highly desirable to reorient our field operations toward a long-range strategic objective rather than toward the short-range tactical type of intelligence procurement. In order to regroup and realign our field operators and operations toward the proper objective, it will be necessary to reduce our local commitments to General Clay as well as other local customers. Specifically this will involve an elimination of, or at best a reduction in, concentration upon those subjects in Mr. Helms' list which are checked. The major elimination involves cessation of collection of OB material which requires a widely distributed operational effort and commitment of personnel not germane to our primary mission.

It is fully realized that we cannot entirely eliminate operations on those targets which are of importance to General Clay if he feels that information on them can be obtained in no other way. It appears essential, therefore, that you discuss this matter with General Clay with a view, (a) to explaining to him our long-range mission, and (b) to securing his reaction to the elimination of tactical intelligence operations now employing the major energies of our field units.

General Clay's personal familiarity with our work is probably largely limited to the operations of the Berlin Unit. With this in mind, it may seem desirable to go into considerable detail concerning the extent of our operations and our general commitment to supply the intelligence needs of major customers in Washington as opposed to the limited commitment to field representations of those major customers.

You may also believe it desirable to introduce personally to General Clay the representative of the German Mission. This would be par-

HISTORICAL DOCUMENT

Destroy only with consent of the Historical Staff

CONFIDENTIAL

Name: _____
Date: 15 March, 1965

Spec. Ops.

CONFIDENTIAL

icularly appropriate since a new chief of mission is being appointed in the person of Mr. Gordon Stewart. Mr. Stewart has been in Germany over an extended period and is completely familiar with both the potentialities and actualities of our operations in the area concerned.

DONALD H. GALLOWAY
Assistant Director
Special Operations

Attachments

CONFIDENTIAL

WORI Document ID: 144343-144343

Folder 9 Box 498
Job 81-00815R
Copy 4 of 7 copies
Page 1 of 2 pages

I6

514

TOP SECRET

ER- 428

1 This document has been
approved for release through
the HISTORICAL REVIEW PROGRAM of
the Central Intelligence Agency.

Date 12/9/94

HRP 94-1

MEMORANDUM FOR: EXECUTIVE SECRETARY
NATIONAL SECURITY COUNCIL

SUBJECT: Utilization of the Mass of Soviet Refugees.

Reference: NSCIC 373, 17 March 1948, Utilization of Refugees from
the Soviet Union in U.S. National Interest, Recommendation
6, as required of CIA.

PROBLEM:

Whether the mass of refugees from the Soviet world, now in free
Europe and Asia can be effectively utilized to further U. S. interests
in the current struggle with the USSR and whatever may eventuate therefrom.

ANALYSIS:

1. During the past three years, CIA (and its predecessors) has
systematically explored the potential intelligence value of the numerous
anti-Communist and anti-Soviet groups in Central and Eastern Europe.
Contacts have been developed with the leading groups of the mass of Soviet
emigres, e.g., Ukrainian, Georgian, Balts and White Russians. Although
these contacts were established primarily for purposes of procuring intelligence on Eastern Europe and the USSR, sufficient overall information on
these groups has been inevitably gathered to permit a sound evaluation of
their possible value to the U.S. Government for purposes of propaganda,
sabotage and anti-Communist political activity.

2. On the basis of experience and careful analysis CIA has found
the following characteristics in every group in the mass of Soviet emigres.

   a. These groups are highly unstable and undependable, split
   by personal rivalries and ideological differences, and
   primarily concerned with developing a secure position for
   themselves in the Western world.

   b. They have been completely unable to provide intelligence of
   real value since they are rarely able to tap useful sources
   of information within the USSR, and generally concentrate
   on producing highly biased propaganda materials in place of
   objective intelligence.

   c. They are almost exclusively interested in obtaining maximum
   support (usually from the U.S.) for their own propaganda
   activities and insist upon the provision of substantial
   financial, communications, propaganda, movement and personal
   assistance in return for vague and unrealistic promises of
   future service.

TOP SECRET

RECORD COPY

- 482

d. They immediately capitalize upon any assistance which they receive to advertise the fact of official (U.S.) support to their colleagues and to other governments in order to advance their own personal or organizational interests.

These groups are a primary target for the Soviet MGB and satellite security services for purposes of political penetration and counterespionage. CIA has sufficient evidence to indicate that many of these groups have been successfully penetrated by Soviet and satellite security services.

CONCLUSIONS:

RECOMMENDATIONS:

2. It is suggested that for purposes of refugees from the Soviet world, a systematic index should be developed by the State Department, or other appropriately located government agencies concerned, of all those refugees who possess qualifications which will make them of use in the event of war. In addition, it would be useful if there would be recorded in a single place the residences and occupations (and changes therein) of all available Soviet refugees.

3. Screening must include the object of isolating persons who are suitable for direct use if intelligence purposes as distinct from merely furnishing miscellaneous information.

/s/

R. H. HILLENKOETTER
REAR ADMIRAL, USN
DIRECTOR OF CENTRAL INTELLIGENCE

TOP SECRET

MORI Document ID: 144207-144207

DRAFT

CONFIDENTIAL

9 March This document has been
approved for release through
the HISTORICAL REVIEW PROGRAM of
the Central Intelligence Agency.

MEMORANDUM FOR: Lt. Gen. Lucian K. Truscott

SUBJECT: Instructions

Date 3/9/94

HRP   94-1

1. You will proceed to Germany and take station as senior Central
Intelligence Agency representative in Germany. Your general responsibilities are as follows:

a. You will be the senior Central Intelligence Agency
representative in the area, representing the Agency as a whole.
You will supervise all Central Intelligence Agency activities
carried on in Germany. Such supervision will normally be
exercised through insuring the coordination of all activities
and the cooperation of all elements of the Central Intelligence
Agency in your area. You are authorized to direct the deferment
of action on any Central Intelligence Agency project or operation
in your area until the matter has been reviewed and decided by
the Director of Central Intelligence.

b. You will keep the activities and personnel of OSO and OPC
separate from each other to the extent required by security and
necessary to preserve the effectiveness of the two staffs. You
will keep the activities and personnel of OSO and OPC separate
from the activities and personnel of all other Central Intelligence
Agency offices.

c. You will review administrative and support facilities and
determine the extent to which efficiencies may be effected by
consolidation or by other means.

d. You will review and supervise all budgets and will
supervise the expenditure of all Central Intelligence Agency
funds in your area.

e. You will supervise all Central Intelligence Agency
personnel actions in your area.

DOCUMENT NO.   008
NO CHANGE IN CLASS ☐
☐ DECLASSIFIED
CLASS. CHANGED TO: TS s ☉ 1990.
NEXT REVIEW DATE: _____
AUTH: HR 70-2
DATE: 3/13/80 REVIEWER: 061108

CONFIDENTIAL

CONFIDENTIAL
- 2 -

2. In addition to supervising the normal Central Intelligence Agency liaison functions, you will personally discharge, or personally delegate under your responsibility, such other duties as may be designated hereafter by the Director of Central Intelligence. It is considered desirable that steps be taken to coordinate the intelligence functions of CIA with the other U/S/A. intelligence agencies operating in Germany, and to effect a coordination of the agencies among themselves so as to avoid duplication of activities and to see that there is adequate coverage of the entire intelligence field. The CIA is charged, under the law, to make recommendations with respect to the coordination of the intelligence activities of the government relating to the national security. It is suggested, however, that in lieu of CIA's presenting this matter of coordination of intelligence in Germany to the ▮▮▮▮, you endeavor to work out such coordination among the various agencies in Germany by mutual agreement. It is suggested that you arrange, if possible, for periodic meetings of the respective intelligence agencies for this purpose; and that you advise the Director of the progress you may have made and your recommendations if any action is required or desirable here in Washington. As you know, through the IAC, I am directly in touch with the heads of the respective intelligence agencies of State and in the Defense Establishment, and I am, therefore, in a position to take up on a continuing basis any problems which you may find in Germany which require discussion here in Washington.

NSC

3. The following provisions apply to Central Intelligence Agency communications from or to your area:

a. All such communications, both cable and dispatch, to and from your area, including those between Assistant Directors and their field representatives, will be accessible to you to the extent and in the manner in which you desire.

b. All such communications will conform to the appropriate Central Intelligence Agency communication or pouch procedure.

c. Any such communication which contains particularly sensitive matter should indicate that it should be referred to the Office of the Director of Central Intelligence or the Deputy Director (Plans), in addition to any other indication of destination. You should likewise indicate any communication which you particularly wish the Director of Central Intelligence or the Deputy Director (Plans) to see.

CONFIDENTIAL

MORI Document ID: 144387-144387

CONFIDENTIAL

- 3 -

4. Your status in Germany will be that of Special ~~Assistant to~~ Consultant
the U.S. High Commissioner. Where necessary, you will state but will
not publicize your connection with the overt activities of the
Central Intelligence Agency. You will disclaim association with the
covert activities of the Central Intelligence Agency, except to the
following:

a. Responsible United States, British, French, and German
officials on a need-to-know basis.

b. Central Intelligence Agency personnel on a need-to-know
basis.

WALTER B. SMITH
Director

United States

CONFIDENTIAL

CENTRAL INTELLIGENCE GROUP
WASHINGTON, D.C.
December 19, 1946

Soviet Intelligence

Filed: 740.00119 Control
(Germany)/12-1946

R

N00001

REFER D CIA

COUNTRY: GERMANY (RUSSIAN ZONE)

SUBJECT: SMERSH Department of the Soviet Central
             Kommandatura, Berlin - Luisenstrasse

DATE OF
INFO: CURRENT

EVALUATION: B -2

The following information comes from a well-situated source who is
reliable and well-trained:

1. There are three staff sections "attached" to the office of Major
General KOTIKOV, Military Commandant of the Central Kommandatura on
Luisenstrasse, but only nominally under his command. These sections
are not to be confused with those offices directly commanded by KOTIKOV
and his staff. The three sections are:

     a. Office of the Prosecuting Attorney

     b. Military Court

     c. A so-called SMERSH Department

The above three sections are under the supervision of Brigadier Gen.
KART, but take orders from and report directly to their superiors at
SMA Karlshorst, while Gen. KART is only kept informed of their activities.

2. The SMERSH Department of the Soviet Central Kommandatura in Luisenstrasse is commanded by Colonel KOLINIK, who has about fifty officers
under him. Its function is the close surveillance of all personnel in
Berlin; Soviet, Allied and German civilians, especially in regard to their
contacts with Soviet military personnel. It is also concerned with the
"political integrity" of Soviet officers and keeps close check on the
activities of all Soviet personnel. At least one of the officers in
each department of KOTIKOV's Central Kommandatura is working for this
SMERSH Department at the same time; hence all are in the same building.
It is not known whether all officers in the SMERSH Department play a dual
role. NOTE: According to source, this SMERSH Department comes under
the jurisdiction of the MGB (Ministry of State Security), through
Karlshorst. Here again we find the term SMERSH used in a purely functional sense as indicating counter-intelligence, whereas we are dealing
probably with an echelon of the MGU, otherwise known as the Third
Administration of the MGU.

3. In addition to the SMERSH Department of the Office of the Military
Commandant, there is a so-called SMERSH Group in Luisenstrasse under the
command of Major SPIRENKO. This group consists of about four officers.
Its

9111/0 -1

⑤

117

-2-

Its particular job is the checking and surveying of all Soviet personnel at the Soviet Central Kommandatura.

4. General SIDEEV's Department, on the other hand, is MVD (Ministry of Internal Affairs) and entirely independent of the Office of the Military Commandant of the Central Kommandatura, even though they occupy the same building. SIDEEV is directly responsible to Colonel General SEROV and is more concerned with Public Safety and CI activities.

911176-2

2/35

FROM   :   Information Control, OSO.

COUNTRY   :   Germany (Russian Zone).

SUBJECT   :   Reorganization of the RIS in Germany.

DATE OF
INFORMATION: Current.

EVALUATION :   F-2.

The following information, based on the interrogation of a
defected interpreter from an MGB Operational Sector Headquarters
in Germany, is believed to be correct and has been partially
substantiated. Previous information on the suspected reorganization of the Russian intelligence service in Germany had been
fragmentarily reported by a number of sources. A lucid and
consecutive compilation, however, was not possible without the
additional and strategic information of this source. A series
of reports on the structure and key personnel of the Russian
intelligence service in the Russian Zone of Germany, and
specifically in the Province of Brandenburg, will be disseminated,
of which this is the first:

1.   The reorganization of the Russian intelligence service
in Germany, which began in September 1946, was completed in
November of that year. A uniform system of intelligence echelons,
under the exclusive jurisdiction of the MGB (Ministry of State
Security), entailing the liquidation of the old MVD (Ministry
for Internal Affairs) system, was accomplished. The reorganization was coincidental with the departure from Germany of
Colonel General SEROV and the appointment of his successor,
Lieutenant General KOVALCHUK.

NOTE: Whether the Russian intelligence service in its
pre-October 1946 form was essentially an NKVD organization,
is still a contentious question. Source states that in
preparation for the Potsdam Conference in September 1945,
approximately two thousand NKVD operatives were brought
from Soviet Russia to Germany. They were addressed by
Colonel General SEROV in Babelsberg, who was accompanied
by a number of ranking NKVD officers slated to become heads
of the newly established Operational Sectors. SEROV told
the group that they were responsible for all necessary
security precautions for the Conference and that their
task did not end with the Conference, but that most of
them would be retained in Germany.

- 2 -

2.   The basic structure of the old Russian intelligence
service remained, with the Operativni Sektor at the top level
(provincial), the Operativni Okrug at the district level, and
the Oper Grupa at the Kreis level, as the lowest echelon.
Source states that this organizational set-up, as well as the
functional sections of the Operational Sector as given in paragraph 3, is the same for the other five Operational Sectors in
the Russian Zone: Berlin, Land Saxony, Saxony-Anhalt, Thuringia
and Mecklenburg/Vorpommern.

NOTE: It can be assumed, however, that regional variations
are in effect. The organizational and functional plan of
MGB Operational Sector BRANDENBURG, for example, would not
necessarily apply to MGB Operational Sector BERLIN, which
is the only city in the Russian Zone set up in itself as
an Operational Sector.

3.   The MGB Operational Sector is divided into the following functional offices. Source is not able to explain the
difference between the two named categories, section and subsection, nor the obvious inconsistency of an alphabetical
denotation for one sub-section while using numbers for the rest:

Sub-Section A: An independent sub-section maintaining all
operational files of the Sector, except informant files. All
case files, as well as informant card indices, are kept by this
office. The latter contain the agent's personal description,
code-name, and assigned field of activity. No files can be
removed and special permission is required to gain access to
the card indices.

Sub-Section I: An independent sub-section for the collection
of positive intelligence. This is accomplished by maintaining
a net of informants in the American, British, and French Zones
and sectors and by sending agents on missions into those Zones
and sectors. The following information is gathered: OB of
American, British, and French troops in Germany; political,
economic and technical intelligence; public opinion; situation
in DP Camps; activities of foreign intelligence services.

NOTE: This section evolved, according to source, from
NVD Section IV, sub-section I, which was formerly charged
with positive intelligence.

Section II: This section conducts counter-intelligence operations. At least in the Operational Sector BRANDENBURG, this
Section has two branches, one dealing with U. S. espionage, the
other, with British and French espionage. It also engages in
offensive operations, sending agents into the American, French,
and British Zones on counter-intelligence missions.

NOTE: This section evolved, according to source, from

- 3 -

MVD Section IV, sub-section II, which was formerly charged with counter-intelligence. Agents of MVD Section IV could be sent on both positive and counter-intelligence missions. Under the MGB system, the chiefs of Sub-Section I and Section II are authorized to send agents only on missions germane to the basic functions of their respective sections.

Section III: This section covers, through informant nets, administrative agencies in the Soviet Zone of Germany. Informants are planted in every branch of the German Administration, in political parties, churches, schools, and cultural organizations.

NOTE: Under the MVD system, according to source, MVD sections I, II, and III represented functional divisions of the Operational Sector, each of which dealt with a specific phase of German public life: denazification, political parties, churches, etc. Under the MGB system, these sections were consolidated into Section III, which has been known to dispatch agents into the western zones, to corroborate facts brought to light in the course of investigations.

Sub-Section IV: An independent office for locating persons wanted by the Russian intelligence service. It maintains a number of German leg-men and makes extensive use of German police facilities.

Section V: This section maintains a net of informants within the Soviet Military Administration of Germany. Informants are placed in every Kommandatura, and in other administrative offices. Source considers it possible that this section also has its informants in military units.

Section VI: This is the investigative and interrogation section. Source was employed in such a section from November 1946 to June 1947. The section is charged with the investigation of all arrestees and performs interrogations on the basis of briefs submitted by other sections, particularly Sub-Section I and Section II. It is not authorized to engage in agent operations, but can brief and debrief agents of either Sub-Section I or Section II, with proper authorization, on the elements of information in which Section VI is interested.

Finance Section: This section maintains the payrolls of officers, enlisted men and civilian interpreters. It also distributes confidential funds at the request of section chiefs.

Kader Section: The personnel section of the Operational Sector, maintaining all personnel files of officers, enlisted men, and civilians.

4. Overall command is under the direction of Lt. General KOVALCHUK, whom source identifies as chief of the MGB in Germany. KOVALCHUK has a complete staff with functional staff-sections corresponding to those of the MGB Operational Sectors. Source

121

- 4 -

is uncertain whether such a staff existed under Colonel General
SEROV.

    a.   A central investigative group, similar to Section VI
of the Operational Sector, entrusted with investigative activity
covering the whole of Soviet-occupied Germany. Its offices are
located in POTSDAM, under Colonel CHIZENKOV.

    b.   A section, similar to Section III of the Operative
Sector, entrusted with surveillance of German public life in all
its aspects. This section is under the command of Colonel CHESTA-
KOVICE.

    c.   A central disbursing agency, similar to the Finance
Section of the Operational Sector, which manages finances of all
MGB installations in Germany. Its offices are presumably located
in BERLIN.

    d.   Source is unable to identify staff-sections correspon-
ding to Sections and Sub-Sections I, II, IV, and V of an MGB
Operational Sector; he is, however, convinced that such exist.

Source is not informed about command channels between Lt. General
KOVALCHUK's staff and the MGB Operational Sectors. He considers
it likely that the same system applies which is known to exist
between MGB Operational Sectors and MGB Operational Districts
under their command. Command channels of the Operational Sectors
reveal that the Sector has jurisdiction over its Operational
District (Okrug) offices, which correspond roughly to Regierungs-
bezirke. The CO of a sector can give orders directly to the CO
of an Okrug, as well as to the section chiefs within that Okrug.
Staff officers and section-chiefs on the provincial level of the
Sector can also give direct orders to their corresponding section-
chiefs on the district level. Similarly, the CO and section-chiefs
of the District office level have authority to issue direct orders
to the Oper Grupi, which are under the District's jurisdiction.
The close integration existing between the functional sections
of an MGB Operational Sector and parallel functional sections in
its Okrug offices, source illustrates by the fact that Okrug section-
chiefs report once a month directly to their counterpart section-
chief on the provincial level. Only after this has been done,
do they submit a report to their own Okrug commanding officer.
Thus a double chain of command is stressed with two parallel lines
of authority, one through the commanding officers on each level,
and the other through the functional section offices and section-
chiefs on each level. The second can evidently override the
authority of the CO's of the various level installations.

JPB:eda
11 September 1947.
Source: RSC-782, 792, 794.
TO: State, War, Navy.

SECRET CONTROL

CONFIDENTIAL

Return To
OSO

MEMORANDUM FOR THE DIRECTOR, CENTRAL INTELLIGENCE

app 3/5

After considerable exploratory effort, George Belic, a
staff member of our Berlin station ~~arranged~~ arranged to have himself and Major
General Leonid A. Malinin, Deputy to Marshal Sokolovsky, invited
to a dinner given on 9 December 1947 by a member of the OMGUS
Press Section. After dinner Belic and Malinin separated from
the other guests and talked from 1930 hours to 0300 hours —
Malinin consumed three water-glasses of vodka and five water-
glasses of undiluted American whiskey in the course of the conversation. The freedom with which Malinin discussed various political topics of significant interest, ranging from the current
Soviet name-calling propaganda campaign to the general strike in
France and the approaching devaluation of the ruble, encouraged
Belic to arrange another dinner-party at which Malinin suggested
he would be pleased to have Ambassador Murphy present.

On 16 January 1948 Ambassador Murphy, at the suggestion
of Mr. Durand, Chief of our Berlin station, gave a dinner-party
attended by General Malinin, Belic (interpreting), Mr. Durand,
and two members of the Polad staff. Malinin made the following
statements in the course of the evening's discussions:

    a. He depreciated attempts to settle outstanding
international issues at London-type conferences,
agreeing with Ambassador Murphy that the publicity
attending such conferences was prejudicial to understanding. He strongly urged a meeting of Truman and
Stalin to delineate "spheres of interest" stating that
he appreciated U.S. public opinion would resent the
choice of a meeting place within the Soviet orbit but
that he was sure the Politburo would veto Stalin's
travel to the Western hemisphere in view of his age and
the delicate state of his health. He stated the
Politburo might sanction a meeting at Stockholm.

    b. He agreed with Ambassador Murphy that the current
propaganda warfare has reached a dangerous pass and should
be called off. He believed that basic differences
are ideological and unlikely to lead to war, but that
the ideological conflict may last "for centuries".

CONFIDENTIAL

CONFIDENTIAL

c. He denied the possibility of a rift within the Politburo, pointing out that once the majority reaches a policy decision, the decision is accepted without dissidence. The four members who are "above criticism" are Stalin, Molotov, Beria, Zdhanov.

d. He characterized as American propaganda the alleged existence of a Paulus army, but conceded that Soviet charges on the militaristic character of the industrial police (in the Western Zones of Germany) may be unfounded.

e. He considered a quadripartite currency reform understanding possible on the basis that the currency be printed in Berlin and in Leipzig and both printing establishments made 4-power enclaves.

Malinin offered the following items of information on Stalin, Molotov, and Beria:

a. Stalin has had three serious attacks (of a nature not specified) within the past year.

b. Molotov is certain to succeed Stalin if the latter "should retire from active life within the next few months".

c. Beria has been only nominally concerned with NKVD affairs during the last seven years. During the war he was in charge of the Army supply system and is now in charge of heavy industries. Recurrent rumors of his visits to Germany are entirely unfounded: in view of his prominence such visits would have become known to many.

Malinin indicated that, although social contacts between Soviet and U.S. officials were strongly frowned upon by the Politburo, he and Sokolovsky share the conviction that many controversial Control Council issues are susceptible of settlement "sitting around the table drinking cocktails. Obviously if you and I agree, the British and French will not object afterwards." He declared to Belic his willingness to arrange further informal meetings, but requested that future invitations be extended to him privately and not through official channels since further official contact with Ambassador Murphy might result in his recall to Moscow.

Our Berlin station is in a position to continue informal contacts with Malinin, and if called upon, to initiate exploratory contacts in Marshal Sokolovsky's direction.

CONFIDENTIAL

II: The March Crisis and the Berlin Airlift

II: The March Crisis and the Berlin Airlift

1947 was a year of confrontation. In July the Soviets rejected the aid offered through the Marshall Plan and forced other Eastern Bloc countries to do the same in an effort to counter the growing American influence in Europe. In September, the Communist International was apparently reborn as the COMINFORM. At the end of the year the growing stalemate in the round-robin Conferences of Foreign Ministers (CFM) climaxed with a complete breakdown in London.

These ominous developments prompted equally dire warnings from within the US intelligence establishment. On 22 December a CIA Intelligence Memorandum warned President Truman that the Soviets would try, through obstructionism and harassment, to force the Western Allies out of Berlin.[1] On 26 and 30 December CIA's analysis was seconded by similar missives from the State Department in Washington, followed by a cable from the Ambassador to Moscow, Lt. Gen. Walter Bedell Smith.[2]

In Berlin itself, the political atmosphere grew more frigid with the replacement of the Soviet Military Governor, Marshal Georgiy Zhukov, by the hardline Marshal Vassily Sokolovsky in March 1946. The US Military Governor in Germany, Gen. Lucius D. Clay, had hoped to work cooperatively with his Soviet counterparts, but in October he began to worry about the exposed position of the US garrison in Berlin as the Soviets stepped up security for military exercises inside the eastern zone.[3] Rumors began to circulate that dependents would soon be sent home. The Allied garrison in Berlin became increasingly jittery over the winter.[4] In January 1948 the Soviets began to interfere with trains to Berlin from the western zones, and on the 20th of January Marshal Sokolovsky abruptly rejected Clay's proposals for currency reform within occupied Germany. The situation worsened over February when the Czech Communist Party overthrew the coalition government in Prague, even as the Allies were discussing plans for a new Western German state. Shuttling back and forth to London, Clay felt increasingly uneasy, and finally, on 5 March, Clay cabled his concerns to the Joint Chiefs of Staff in Washington:

> *For many months, based on logical analysis, I have felt and held that war was unlikely for at least ten years. Within the last few weeks, I have felt a subtle change in Soviet attitude which I*

---

[1] This memorandum is appended to Document II-2.
[2] U.S. Department of State, *Foreign Relations of the United States, 1947; Vol. II:* Council of Foreign Ministers; Germany and Austria (Washington, DC: Government Printing Office, 1972), pp. 905-908.
[3] William R. Harris, "The March Crisis of 1948, Act I," *Studies in Intelligence* (1966), p. 3.
[4] See Document II-1.

*cannot define but which now gives me a feeling that it may come
with dramatic suddenness. I cannot support this change in my
own thinking with any data or outward evidence in relationships
other than to describe it as a feeling of a new tenseness in every
Soviet individual with whom we have official relations. I am
unable to submit any official report in the absence of supporting
data but my feeling is real. You may advise the Chief of Staff of
this for whatever it may be worth if you feel it advisable.* [5]

Although Clay later denied that he had intended his carefully worded telegram to be a war-warning,[6] it was interpreted as such by the Pentagon. At
the behest of JCS Chairman Omar N. Bradley, the Intelligence Advisory
Committee ordered an ad hoc committee chaired by CIA's Office of Reports
and Estimates to draft an Intelligence Memorandum for the President judging the likelihood that the confrontation in Central Europe would escalate
into war.[7] The committee quickly became mired in bureaucratic rivalries.
Army and Air Force representatives feared that passage of the defense budget then being debated in Congress might hang on what was said about
Soviet intentions in Europe. Seemingly at particular risk was the Army's
proposal for universal military training. The Office of Naval Intelligence,
by contrast, remained conservative in its estimates and resisted saying anything that suggested war might break out in 1948. Consensus was, to say the
least, elusive. Although—after an initial period of alarm—no one on the
committee was willing to say that war was likely, the military representatives refused to say that it was unlikely.

Finally, on 16 March DCI Roscoe Hillenkoetter demanded straight answers
from the committee to three questions, to be given to the President that
morning:

> *(1) Will the Soviets deliberately provoke war in the next 30 days?*
> *(2) In the next 60 days?*
> *(3) In 1948?*

After some further hedging, the committee answered the first two questions
in the negative and deferred the answer to the third, to be dealt with by ORE
in an Estimate. A rider was attached to the memorandum dealing with the
Army's concerns for the defense budget still before Congress.[8] DCI
Hillenkoetter took advantage of the opportunity to append yet another

---

[5] Harris, p. 7.
[6] Lucius D. Clay, *Decision in Germany* (Garden City, NY: Doubleday and Company, 1950),
p. 354.
[7] Harris, p. 10.
[8] *Ibid.*, pp. 20-21.

memorandum reminding President Truman that CIA had analyzed Soviet intentions in these same terms on 22 December.[9] The promised follow-on Estimate, ORE 22-48, *The Possibility of Direct Soviet Action During 1948*, was published on 2 April.[10] In it—and in two similar estimates that followed over 1948-49—ORE discounted the possibility that the Soviet Union would deliberately initiate a war in the immediate future. However, ORE did underline the likelihood that the Soviet Union would apply increased political pressure to the US position in Europe, and warned that, in an atmosphere of increasing tension, the chances that war might break out by accident would increase.[11]

In Germany, Washington's alarm over Clay's 5 March telegram came as something of a surprise. On 12 March a quick poll of intelligence officers attached to the various commands in Germany produced a near-consensus that the Soviets were not ready for war[12]—only Clay's G-2, Maj. Gen. Robert L. Walsh, disagreed. While this was going on, the Soviets moved some 20,000 troops into frontal areas from within the Eastern bloc, along with an additional 12,000 MVD (internal security) troops from the Soviet Union. On 19 March a planned Communist takeover in Helsinki failed when the Finnish Minister of the Interior, Yrjo Leino, himself a Communist, alerted the Finnish army.[13] The next day Sokolovsky and the entire Soviet delegation walked out of the Allied Control Council in Berlin. This was followed by two weeks of exercises involving Soviet ground forces and police units inside East Germany. At the same time, the Soviets staged a series of carefully orchestrated incidents near the intra-German border, including the kidnapping and interrogation of German civilians, apparently with the intent of convincing Allied observers that the Soviets were preparing to take some undefined military action.[14]

In the time that had passed between the first Soviet provocations and the staged military incidents at the end of March, the Western Allies had the opportunity to consider possible Soviet actions in detail. As might be expected, the onset of large-scale Soviet military exercises triggered an alert in the Western zones, but by the time the Soviets began staging incidents along the intra-German border the debate over the Soviets' intentions for the near future was over. When, on 30 March, Sokolovsky's deputy formally notified his Western counterparts that, effective midnight, 31 March, all Allied traffic through the Soviet zone would be forced to submit to

---

[9] See Document II-2.
[10] See Document II-3.
[11] See Documents II-4 and II-5.
[12] David E. Murphy, Sergei Kondrashev, and George Bailey, *Battleground Berlin*, (New Haven, CT: Yale University Press, 1997), p. 54.
[13] Harris, p. 10.
[14] *Ibid.*, p. 13.

inspection, both General Clay and his superiors in Washington knew that they faced a political challenge to the US presence in Berlin—not the threat of war.[15]

From the intelligence standpoint, the chief effect of the March crisis was to provide a precedent by which future Soviet actions could be judged. In effect, Stalin had telegraphed his punches, so that, by the onset of the Berlin blockade that June, Western analysts had a better understanding of just how far he was willing to go. Under these circumstances, the outcome of the June crisis was pretty much a foregone conclusion—assuming that Western resolve remained intact.

Stalin hoped, of course, that by challenging the Allied position in Berlin, he would be attacking the Western coalition at its weakest point. Anticipating a postwar crisis in capitalist system, Stalin believed that Berlin was the point where, if he pushed hard enough, he would cause the Western Alliance to come apart at the seams.[16]

In pursuit of this goal, Soviet harassment of Allied military trains to Berlin continued over April and May, all but halting passenger traffic, although food shipments continued. On 5 April a Soviet Yak-9 fighter harassing a British airliner inadvertently collided with it, killing all on board both aircraft. Simultaneously, the Soviet Berlin Commandant, Gen. Alexander Kotikov, launched a blatant campaign to hamstring the *Kommandatura*. The scale of Soviet provocations increased until 16 June, when Kotikov denounced the American Commandant, Col. Frank Howley, for leaving his deputy to represent him in a meeting of the *Kommandatura* and walked out himself, thus abrogating the last vestiges of the quadripartite administration of Berlin.[17] Over 18-20 June the Soviets blocked the Western powers' plans for the introduction of a reformed currency into Berlin. On 19 June they finally halted all rail traffic into the city, and on 23 June they halted road and barge traffic and cut off the supply of electricity to West Berlin.[18] The Soviet blockade of Berlin had begun. On 26 June the first Allied transports began to airlift supplies into Berlin.

---

[15] *Ibid.*, p. 25.

[16] Vladislav Zubok and Constantine Pleshakov, *Inside the Kremlin's Cold War: From Stalin to Khrushchev* (Cambridge, MA: Harvard University Press, 1996), pp. 48-49.

[17] Frank Howley, *Berlin Command* (New York: G.P. Putnam's Sons, 1950), pp. 181-82.

[18] The Soviet effort to cut off West Berlin's electrical supply was only partially effective. Because the electrical net for the city of Berlin had been designed for a unified city (and not, of course, for one broken into two hostile halves) the Soviets found it impossible to completely cut off West Berlin's electrical supply without also severing their own. William Stivers, "The Incomplete Blockade: Soviet Zone Supply of West Berlin, 1948-49," *Diplomatic History* (1997), p. 586.

The Berlin blockade illustrated just how poorly Stalin was being served by his intelligence services. Soviet planning for the blockade was superficial at best: the Soviets apparently never anticipated that the West might hold out,[19] while no one in the Kremlin seems to have realized how much the eastern zone itself was economically dependent on the West.[20] Moreover, there is evidence that Soviet intelligence officers feared to bring bad news to Stalin and "cooked the books" in their reporting about the effectiveness of the blockade and Allied airlift.[21] Had they not done so, the Soviet blockade might never have gone on as long as did, despite its manifest failure.

By contrast, the record shows that US reporting accurately gauged Soviet intentions both before and during the crisis. In Washington, ORE persisted in its belief that Stalin would not deliberately push the Berlin confrontation to war.[22] Meanwhile, CIA intelligence officers provided insights into the strengths and weaknesses in Soviet planning[23] and were able to provide some of the first indications of cracks in Soviet resolve.[24] Policymakers in Washington were also kept apprised of the situation in Berlin through a stream of reporting on Soviet intentions and operations.[25]

II-1: Memorandum for the Chairman, Joint Chiefs of Staff, General of the Army Omar Bradley, 31 July 1947 (MORI No. 144273).
Tensions were running high in the summer of 1947, as reflected in this extract from a routine status report prepared in Berlin. The writer of the report would not have used such candor in referring to his military compatriots, were the report intended for other than internal consumption. It is interesting that the branch chief in Washington, future DCI Richard Helms, felt the report to be important enough that it be shared with JCS Chief Bradley without altering the language.

II-2: Memorandum for the President, 16 March 1948 (MORI No. 9259).
DCI Hillenkoetter's memorandum brought the curtain down on the March 1948 "war scare." Because General Clay's so-called "war warning" emanated from outside normal intelligence channels, Hillenkoetter apparently

---

[19] Murphy, et al., p. 57.
[20] The Allied airlift was able to meet Berlin's basic requirements for food and fuel, but the continued functioning of the city's economy depended on interchange with the eastern zone. This continued illegally under the blockade. Stivers, "The Incomplete Blockade...," *passim.*
[21] Murphy, pp. 62-63, 64-65.
[22] See Documents II-3 – II-6. See also Woodrow J. Kuhns, ed. *Assessing the Soviet Threat: The Early Cold War Years* (Washington, DC: Center for the Study of Intelligence, 1997), Docs. 67, 85, 145.
[23] See Document II-8.
[24] See Documents II-17 and II-18.
[25] See Documents II-9 – II-16.

felt that CIA's credibility was at stake. He thus appended a CIA memorandum from the previous December evaluating the situation and forecasting Soviet moves. That CIA was still a very young agency is reflected in the use of recycled Central Intelligence Group (CIG) stationery.

II-3: ORE 22-48: Possibility of Direct Soviet Military Action During 1948, 2 April 1948.

II-4: ORE 22-48, Addendum: Possibility of Direct Soviet Military Action During 1948-49, 16 September 1948.

II-5: ORE 46-49: The Possibility of Direct Soviet Military Action During 1949, 3 May 1949.

One of the most valuable functions played by the Intelligence Community during the crisis of 1948-49 was to provide policymakers with perspective on the changing situation in Berlin and Germany. In these three Estimates, the Office of Reports and Estimates (ORE) used assessments of Soviet capabilities to discount the possibility of Soviet military action in 1948 and 1949. Reporting of this kind helped policymakers understand Soviet actions in Berlin in context with broader Soviet intentions. Throughout this period, however, ORE was handicapped by a consistent lack of reliable information on Soviet intentions and capabilities, a deficiency clearly reflected in these Estimates. Interesting, too, is the fact that all these Estimates warn of the likelihood that war might break out inadvertently, should tensions continue to run high—a reminder that the memories of Sarajevo and the outbreak of World War I lingered in the minds of high-level officials on both sides.

II-6: ORE 29-48: Possible Program of Future Soviet Moves in Germany, 28 April 1948.

In the aftermath of the March crisis, ORE attempted to forecast possible Soviet moves in Germany. Although the Estimate raises the possibility of a blockade, the emphasis throughout is on the projected establishment of a Soviet-backed East German Communist regime.

II-7: Memorandum for the President, 9 June 1948 (MORI No. 9260).

Although the lines of confrontation certainly were being drawn, in June 1948 the situation in Germany remained fluid. This memorandum, prepared just before the Soviets severed land links between the eastern zone and the west, discusses likely Soviet reactions to the proposed merger of the three western zones of occupied Germany. It serves as a reminder of just how new—and unprecedented—the Cold War was in 1948. The governments here discussed as being established "provisionally" were to last nearly half a century.

II-8: ORE 41-48: Effect of Soviet Restrictions on the US Position in Berlin, 14 June 1948.

But a few days before the onset of the Berlin blockade (20 June), ORE considered the impact of Soviet efforts to restrict US military rail traffic to and from Berlin. Already Berlin's value as a base for the collection of strategic intelligence inside Soviet-dominated Europe is being emphasized.

II-9: CIA Memorandum for the Secretary of Defense, Subject: Situation in Berlin, 28 June 1948 (MORI No. 144438).

II-10: CIA Memorandum for the Secretary of Defense, Subject: Current Situation in Berlin, 30 June 1948 (MORI No. 145210).

II-11: CIA Memorandum for the President: Russian Directive Indicating Soviets Intend to Incorporate Berlin into the Soviet Zone, 30 June 1948 (MORI No. 97992).

II-12: Intelligence Report (IR): Russian Unilateral Dismissal and Appointment of Berlin Police Officials, 15 July 1948 (MORI No. 145211).

The four intelligence reports above demonstrate Soviet confidence that the blockade would bring an end to the quadripartite regime in Berlin. The reports of Soviet planning to assume full control of Berlin (Documents. II-9, II-11, II-12) reveal a thoroughness in operational matters that contrasts sharply with the more strategic failure to consider the effect the blockade would have on the East German economy. Document II-10 shows how the Soviets depended on German food supplies, even as they were taking actions that would throttle the East German economy. The documents also suggest that the Soviets never expected West Berlin to hold out for nearly a year.

II-13: CIA 7-48: Review of the World Situation, 14 July 1948 (MORI No. 8840).

The dramatic success of the Berlin airlift has tended to obscure just how perilous a situation Berlin was in the summer of 1948. As this CIA report shows, there were real doubts about the Allies' ability to maintain themselves in Berlin. Moreover, with both the Western and Eastern alliances in flux, more than the Allied position in central Europe was at stake. As the confrontation dragged on, each side's freedom of action gradually diminished.

II-14: Memorandum for the President on the Situation in Berlin, 10 December 1948 (MORI No. 145213).

II-15: IR: Soviet Measures to Further Tighten the Sector Blockade in Berlin, 30 December 1948 (MORI No. 145214).

II-16: Soviet Plans to Control the Western Sectors of Berlin, 6 January 1949 (MORI No. 145215).
The Allied capability to supply West Berlin with needed food and fuel was strained to the utmost in the frigid North European winter. Apparently believing that they could bring the confrontation to a decisive conclusion, the Soviets prepared to isolate West Berlin from the eastern half of the city and to abrogate what remained of the quadripartite governing arrangements. Once again, a Soviet intelligence failure is revealed in their ignorance of the economic interdependence of the city as a whole. Soviet efforts to halt economic intercourse between East and West Berlin failed, while the winter brought only a redoubling of Western supply efforts.

II-17: IR: SED Preparations for Illegal Work in West Berlin, 7 March 1949 (MORI No. 145217).

II-18: IR: Progress of the SED Membership Purge, 7 March 1949 (MORI No. 145218).
By the spring of 1949 a change in mood was evident in the East German Communist leadership, if not in Moscow. Having apparently reconciled themselves to the failure of the blockade to drive the Western powers out of Berlin, the SED prepared itself for long-term subversive activity in the western half of the city and began a purge of its leadership cadres.

II-19: CIA 5-49: Review of the World Situation, 17 May 1949 (MORI No. 8872).
With the blockade at an end, Western optimism is shown in the hope that the Soviets would be willing to negotiate a solution to the "German question." In fact, a solution already had been found: in the division of Germany into two separate states. Probably neither side recognized at this point just how enduring this solution was to be.

CONFIDENTIAL

31 July 1947

This document has been
approved for release through
the HISTORICAL REVIEW PROGRAM of
the Central Intelligence Agency.

Date 3/9/94

HRP 94-1

TO: ADSO

VIA: COPS

FROM: FBM

In connection with the briefing of General Bradley, I
thought that the attached extract from an informal report
made by the Chief of our Berlin Detachment would be of
interest to him in giving a behind-the-scenes picture of a
state of mind which exists in Berlin. Clearly, this report
was made for internal consumption only.

Richard Helms

Attachment

DOCUMENT NO. 014
NO CHANGE IN CLASS. ☒
DECLASSIFIED
CLASS. CHANGED TO: TS S C
NEXT REVIEW DATE: 1990
DATE 3/25/80 REVIEWER: 061169

<u>EXTRACT</u>

The month of June marked a new and severe crisis in the "Battle of Berlin". The City Assembly of Berlin by a vote of 87 to 17, elected Ernst Reuter as Oberbürgermeister, replacing Ostrowski who resigned after a vote of no-confidence in the Assembly. The Russians at the Berlin Kommandatura level refused to approve Reuter's election, and the matter has been referred to the Allied Control Council, where presumably the same Russian veto will be met. The constitutional issues, the statements of Allied officials, the maneuvering of the Berlin parties are adequately covered in news dispatches and intelligence reports. (In this connection attention is called to the article in ODI Weekly Summary, No. 59.)

The extent of the American setback in the Battle of Berlin was reflected in a recent press conference of the Assistant Deputy Military Governor, Brigadier General Ryan. Some 70 or 80 American correspondents "ganged up" on General Ryan in an extremely vigorous fashion, criticizing severely the American role in the quadripartite government of Berlin. When General Ryan pointed out the record of some 900 Kommandatura agreements, the New York Times representative acidly inquired whether this represented 900 American concessions. Colonel Howley, head of Military Government, Berlin Sector, challenged the proposition that the U. S. is losing the Battle of Berlin, and rather rashly suggested a poll of opinion among the correspondents. A show of hands was immediately called for, and every correspondent in the room and a number of officials, including Colonel Howley's chief political officer, voted that the battle was being lost.

Although it is true that there is a tendency of Americans in Berlin to magnify the significance of local developments, the unanimity of this pessimistic verdict is certainly sobering. One of the most disturbing features of the present state of mind, is the recurrence of what has been called the "invasion of Zehlendorf jitters". It may be recalled that exactly one year ago there occurred a near panic in American military command, touched off by a combination of wild rumors and apparently responsible intelligence reports to the effect that Russians were planning a sort of Pearl Harbor coup in Berlin, as a prelude to over-running western Europe. Elaborate and in some respects rather farcical plans were drawn up to evacuate women and children by air from Tempelhof, while defending American installations to the bitter end. Inevitably the precautionary measures called the attention of the German public to the scare, causing acute demoralization and loss of confidence in American occupation.

It is perhaps merely a seasonal phenomenon that the same atmosphere again prevails. High ranking Army officers speak seriously of the

-2.- CONFIDENTIAL

"Asiatic cunning" of the Soviets prompting a surprise attack. More thoughtful conjecture centers on the effect of the transfer of the bizonal economic headquarters to Frankfurt, and the prospect of a hardening East-West division in Germany, which would make our position in Berlin untenable. A Major General of EUCOM has expressed his private opinion that the effort of holding out in Berlin may be costing us more than it is worth. So far, indeed, General Clay has made it fully apparent that he entertains no thoughts of a withdrawal from Berlin, but firmly intends to stay on, as he put it, "to the bitter end". General Clay's repeated public assurances have helped to calm German fears, but each new set-back of quadripartite relations, whether reflected on the level of the failure of the Paris Conference, or of the Berlin City Assembly, touches off the rumor chain again.

MORI Document ID:> 9259:9259

NLT 77-79

CENTRAL INTELLIGENCE GROUP AGENCY
2430 E STREET NW.
WASHINGTON 25, D. C.

16 March 1948

MEMORANDUM FOR THE PRESIDENT

The Central Intelligence Agency and the intelligence organizations of the Departments of State, War, Navy and Air Force agree that if the Congress passes a universal military training act and/or a selective service act these measures, taken singly or together, will not of themselves cause the USSR to resort to military action within the next 60 days.

R. H. Hillenkoetter
Rear Admiral, USN
Director of Central Intelligence

Declassified by 058375
date 29 MAR 1978

MORI Document ID:> 9259:9259

TOP SECRET   ER 354

CENTRAL INTELLIGENCE AGENCY
WASHINGTON 25, D. C.

16 March 1948

MEMORANDUM FOR THE PRESIDENT

The Central Intelligence Agency and the intelligence organizations of the Departments of State, War, Navy and Air Force have reassessed Soviet intentions for the next sixty days and concur in the following conclusions with respect to the possibility of Soviet military action:

a. An examination of all pertinent available information has produced no reliable evidence that the USSR intends to resort to military action within the next sixty days.

b. The weight of logic, as well as evidence, also leads to the conclusion that the USSR will not resort to military action within the next sixty days.

c. There is, nevertheless, the ever present possibility that some miscalculation or incident may result in military movements toward areas, at present unoccupied by the USSR.

R. H. Hillenkoetter
Rear Admiral, USN
Director of Central Intelligence

Declassified by 058375
date 2 9 MAR 1978

TOP SECRET

137

MORI Document ID:> 9259:9259

~~SECRET~~   ER 8564

CENTRAL INTELLIGENCE AGENCY
WASHINGTON 25, D.C.

16 March 1948

MEMORANDUM FOR THE PRESIDENT

Under date of 22 December 1947, CIA reported that there was a possibility of steps being taken in Berlin by the Soviet authorities to force the other occupying powers to remove from Berlin. Delay in the formation of a separate Eastern German Government and in Soviet attempts to force the Western Powers from Berlin has probably been caused in large measure by the firm attitude of US officials in Berlin. While no further reports have been received indicating that the USSR has decided to force the Western Powers from Berlin, the recent US, UK, France, Benelux discussions in London concerning the formation of a West German State to be included in a Western European Union invite some form of Soviet response stronger than the mere protests received so far.

Soviet response will be timed to follow overt allied implementation of the London decisions, and will consist of the announcement of plans, such as a plebiscite, for an Eastern Zone "all-German state", claiming to represent the whole German people. Announcement of such plans would be followed by an intensified Soviet campaign to oust the Western Powers from Berlin. The most urgent dangers are: (1) "incidents" arising from the presence in Berlin of young, undisciplined troops; (2) aggravation of the situation by such German malcontents as want an East-West war; (3) any tendency towards war hysteria or lack of firmness and patience on the part of US officials in Berlin.

R. H. Hillenkoetter
Rear Admiral, USN
Director of Central Intelligence

Encl:
Copy, Memo for President,
12/22/47

Declassified by ___058375___
date ___2 0 MAR 1978___

~~SECRET~~

MORI Document ID:> 9259:9259

~~SECRET~~

22 December 1947

MEMORANDUM FOR THE PRESIDENT

The breakdown of the CFM in London may cause the USSR to undertake a program of intensified obstructionism and calculated insult in an effort to force the US and the other Western Powers to withdraw from Berlin all representatives except a small Allied Control Authority group. The implementation of such a program could create a situation of great tension which might lead to armed clashes between Soviet personnel and that of the other occupying powers.

The failure of the CFM to reach agreement on any question and the CFM's subsequent indefinite adjournment will result in an accelerated consolidation of eastern Germany. The USSR will attempt to incorporate thoroughly the economic system of its Zone into the Soviet economy and to orient the political system still more closely to the Soviet ideology. Soviet authorities will encounter difficulties in accomplishing both objectives because of the presence of US officials and troops in Berlin.

The presence there of this personnel hinders the ruthless and forcible communization of all eastern Germany, helps to sustain non-Communist opposition, and demonstrates that the US does not intend to abandon or partition the country. Berlin, of course, could hardly serve as the capital of an eastern German state, should the USSR eventually establish one, so long as the Western Powers maintain troops in the city. The Kremlin is aware of this situation.

The Kremlin is aware, also, that the present quadripartite occupation of Berlin furnishes the US with an excellent listening post and a base of operations for intelligence activities in the Eastern Zone as well as providing political refugees from Soviet areas with a convenient haven. Masters of propaganda themselves, the Soviet authorities are highly sensitive to the great propaganda value of the continued presence of US and the other Western Power forces and the guarantees they provide of relative political freedom for the residents of the city.

~~SECRET~~

Declassified by 058375
date 29 MAR 1978

MORI Document ID:> 9259:9259

~~SECRET~~

- 2 -

The USSR, consequently, cannot expect the US and the other Western Powers to evacuate the city voluntarily. The USSR, therefore, will probably use every means short of armed force to compel these powers to leave the city.

These devices may include additional obstruction to transport and travel to and within the city, "failure" of services such as electric supply, reduction of that part of the food supply which comes from the Soviet Zone, flagrant violations of Kommandatura agreements, instigation of unrest among Germans in the US sector, disregard of the elected municipal government, a deliberately intensified campaign of insult or personal injury to US personnel, and terrorization of their German employees.

The degree of danger inherent in such a campaign will depend on the accuracy with which Soviet authorities gauge US determination to remain and the state of discipline of US officials and troops. Overly enthusiastic resort to insults or personal violence by Soviet troops or Communists could well create "incidents", street fights, brawls, and other public disturbances which, in turn, might well lead to high-level repercussions of the gravest character. Only the greatest determination and tact on both sides could prevent a serious incident from deteriorating beyond control of the Berlin authorities. Even if Soviet estimates of limits to US patience are accurate, the situation could and probably would be aggravated by the activities of German malcontents, who for one reason or another, seek to bring about an open East-West conflict.

The Kremlin will probably defer its maximum effort to force Western Power evacuation of Berlin until it has fully calculated the risks and considered the problem in the light of Soviet strategy elsewhere. Nevertheless, in view of probable irresponsible action by local Soviet officials, the day-to-day developments in the immediate future will test the firmness, patience, and discipline of all US personnel in Berlin.

R. H. HILLENKOETTER
Rear Admiral, USN
Director of Central Intelligence

~~SECRET~~

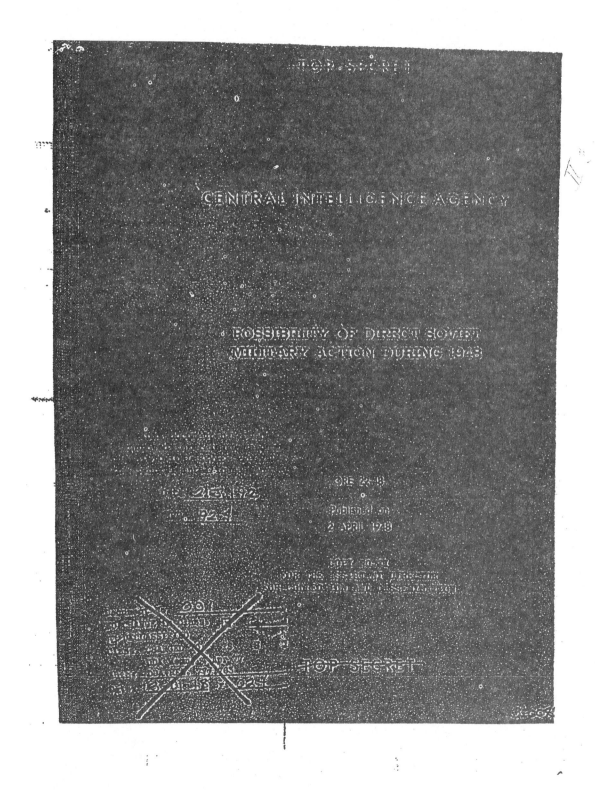

TOP SECRET

CENTRAL INTELLIGENCE AGENCY

POSSIBILITY OF DIRECT SOVIET
MILITARY ACTION DURING 1948

ORE 22-48

Published on
2 APRIL 1948

TOP SECRET

ORE 22-48 TOP SECRET

POSSIBILITY OF DIRECT SOVIET MILITARY ACTION DURING 1948
Report by a Joint Ad Hoc Committee *

THE PROBLEM

1. We have been directed to estimate the likelihood of a Soviet resort to direct military action during 1948.

DISCUSSION

2. Our conclusions are based on considerations discussed in the Enclosure.

CONCLUSIONS

3. The preponderance of available evidence and of considerations derived from the "logic of the situation" supports the conclusion that the USSR will not resort to direct military action during 1948.

4. However, in view of the combat readiness and disposition of the Soviet armed forces and the strategic advantage which the USSR might impute to the occupation of Western Europe and the Near East, the possibility must be recognized that the USSR might resort to direct military action in 1948, particularly if the Kremlin should interpret some US move, or series of moves, as indicating an intention to attack the USSR or its satellites.

---

* This estimate was prepared by a joint ad hoc committee representing CIA and the intelligence agencies of the Department of State, the Army, the Navy, and the Air Force. The date of the estimate is 30 March 1948.

1

TOP SECRET

ENCLOSURE

DISCUSSION

1. The Soviet military forces are estimated to have the current capability of overrunning all of Western Europe and the Near East to Cairo within a short period of time.

2. Soviet military forces along the frontiers of Western Europe and the Near East are estimated to be combat ready and generally so disposed that they could launch an immediate offensive.

3. Since the end of the war Soviet Ground Forces have been reorganized to provide a substantial increase in mobility, more effective firepower, and improved leadership on all levels. The mobilization system permits tripling of strength within 30 days. The air forces have been provided with a substantial number of jet aircraft and several regiments of long-range bombers and are now organized into fifteen air armies, as compared with seventeen at the end of the war. An extensive air defense system has been developed along the Eastern and Western frontiers, employing an increasing number of jet interceptors and an effective radar system deployed in depth. There is evidence of increased emphasis on the development and production of long-range high-speed submarines. Soviet industrial production has continued to emphasize military rather than civilian requirements.

4. By exploiting the postwar political and economic instability in Europe and the rest of the world along traditional Marxist lines, Soviet leaders have already obtained very substantial results. The exploitation of such unstable conditions is the cheapest and safest method by which Soviet leaders can obtain their objectives.

5. Certain basic factual data can be produced to help determine whether or not Soviet leaders would stand to gain or lose by exercising their current military capability of overrunning Western Europe and part of the Near East. Many factors bearing upon this problem, however, would still have to be determined on the basis of estimate and logic rather than upon factual evidence. (This problem is under detailed study.)

6. The determination at this time of whether or not Soviet leaders intend to employ their military capability rests, in the last analysis, essentially upon logic rather than upon evidence. We have no access to the thinking or decisions of the Kremlin and little contact with lower echelons of Soviet officialdom. Such evidence as is currently coming to hand, however, suggests that Soviet leaders do not presently intend to exercise their military capability of overrunning Western Europe and part of the Near East. Since the Czechoslovakian coup there have been some reports suggesting that Soviet leaders may intend shortly to resort to military action but these have been from unevaluated sources and can logically be interpreted as attempts by Soviet or anti-Soviet elements to exploit for their own purposes the fear psychosis prevalent throughout Europe as a result of the timing and rapidity of the Czech coup.

7. The intelligence agencies have generally taken the position that the USSR, in spite of its current military capabilities, would not commit itself to a course of action

2

leading to war until, in the opinion of Soviet leaders, its economic potential had become adequate for a global war and until it possessed a reasonable stock of atomic bombs. It has also been assumed in some quarters that if, prior to the realization of the above objectives, the USSR were faced with impending stability in Europe, it would temporarily abandon its expansionist policy, consolidate its gains, and await the opportunity to promote and exploit new conditions of instability as they might develop in the future.

8. The positions taken in 7 above require a careful reappraisal, particularly in the light of recent US policy statements and other measures against Communist expansion.

CONSIDERATIONS WHICH MIGHT INDUCE THE SOVIET LEADERS TO RESORT TO MILITARY ACTION, IN THE ORDER OF THEIR IMPORTANCE:

9. Soviet leaders may become convinced that the US actually has intentions of military aggression within the near future. In view of the well known suspicions inherent in the minds of Soviet leaders, and the isolation of most of these leaders from the west, it is possible that the Politburo might come to this conclusion.

10. Even if Soviet leaders did not expect imminent US aggression, they might estimate that an ultimate military clash with the US was inevitable and that, in view of current Soviet capabilities for overrunning Western Europe and the Near East, it would be to the USSR's advantage to strike at these areas in 1948. Soviet leaders may estimate that their military superiority relative to the Western Powers is now at its maximum. The USSR is faced with the prospect of (1) US rearmament and presumably the rearmament by the US of the Western European Powers now joined in a military alliance and (2) increasing US production of atomic bombs and longer range aircraft which will increase US capabilities for covering strategic Soviet targets.

11. Soviet leaders might estimate that if they overran Europe and part of the Near East they would vastly improve their military security and might obtain either a military stalemate or a negotiated peace based on the following considerations:

   a. That Soviet acquisition of Western Europe and the Near East might make it too difficult, or at least too costly, for the US to attempt an invasion of these areas by ground forces. The situation would differ greatly from that obtaining in World Wars I and II. In those wars the US had beachheads on the continent or in England and the Soviet Union was an ally or a neutral in the rear of Germany. In this case the US would be faced with the manpower and space of most of the Eurasian land mass.

   b. That domination of the channel coast would enable them to neutralize the UK.

   c. That under these circumstances:

      (1) the US public might not support the continuation of the war even if the military so desired, and

      (2) the US in any event would be restricted to an air war and naval blockade, which, although capable of inflicting substantial damage on the Soviet and European economies, would not be able to dislodge the USSR from its newly won position.

3

d. That the denial to the Western Powers of Near Eastern oil would seriously impair their war potential.

12. The Soviet leaders might believe that, in spite of the currently impoverished condition of Western European economy and the vast difficulties inherent in the organization, control, and assimilation of this area, the quickest and easiest way to remedy the economic deficiencies of the USSR would be to seize the industrial capacity, the technical skills, and the scientific resources of Western Europe.

13. Soviet leaders might estimate that the European recovery program will succeed in stabilizing Europe for a protracted period and thereby deny them the possibility of gaining control of Western Europe through revolutionary and subversive methods.

CONSIDERATIONS WHICH MIGHT RESTRAIN SOVIET LEADERS FROM RESORTING TO DIRECT MILITARY ACTION DURING 1948, IN THE ORDER OF THEIR IMPORTANCE:

14. The ultimate effectiveness of the European recovery program in stabilizing the economic situation in Western Europe is still far from assured, particularly in the light of Communist capabilities for disruption in Italy and France. The opportunities for further Soviet gains through the exploitation of economic, political, and social instability, while recently diminished, are by no means exhausted.

15. Soviet leaders have been in the past habitually cautious and deliberate, and, consequently, might be reluctant voluntarily to incur the risks inherent in a major war.

16. The occupation of Europe and the Near East would impose serious problems on Soviet leaders and expose them to grave risks.

a. The maintenance of military and police forces adequate to protect the defensive position gained by the occupation of most of Western Europe and the Near East would place a serious strain on both the economic resources and manpower reserve of the Soviet Union. Assuming that war with the US continues following the conquest of Western Europe and the Near East, the hostile populations of these areas and the satellites would form an enormous subversive element that would become particularly dangerous with the approach of US forces.

b. In addition to the problem of physical security, the control and assimilation of the economies of Western Europe and the exploitation of the resources of the Near East would impose a tremendous strain upon Soviet administrative organs and personnel resources, even with the help of well organized local Communist parties in some areas.

c. Soviet personnel would be exposed to the standard of living and political ideas of Western Europe. Following World War II, the Soviet leaders have had a serious problem of reindoctrinating not only the returned soldiers but the entire Soviet population. The exigencies of war, entirely apart from the possibility of any alien contamination, appear to undermine Soviet ideology and discipline.

17. The basic economic deficiencies of the USSR in terms of requirements for global war against the US:

4

TOP SECRET

    a. The USSR suffered enormous physical damage in World War II and has probably not regained production levels of 1940 in all basic industries.

    b. Capacity is inadequate in a number of vital fields, including transportation, communications, and in the production of steel, oil, and machine tools.

    c. In order to exploit the European economic potential, the USSR would have to supply raw materials and food to an already impoverished European continent cut off from the resources of the Western Hemisphere and other parts of the world outside the Soviet Union and her sphere of influence.

18. Soviet leaders may anticipate that, in spite of the European recovery program, the Marxist prediction that the capitalist world will collapse of its own accord will be fulfilled, following the economic dislocation of Word War II.

19. The US has a growing stock of atomic bombs. Soviet leaders may not regard this weapon as a decisive factor, and may have considerable confidence in the USSR's defensive capabilities against atomic attack; they probably recognize, however, that atomic warfare can inflict vast destruction and loss of life on the USSR.

20. The Soviet population is definitely war-weary and has long been promised an improvement in its standard of living. While the Russians traditionally unite to repel foreign invaders, Soviet leaders might question whether, under present circumstances, they could risk the possibility of a protracted global war.

21. The politicians in the Politburo have always been suspicious of the military. War would again bring the military to the fore and might constitute a real or imagined threat to the Party leaders.

TOP SECRET

5

FOR THE ASSISTANT DIRECTOR
FOR REPORTS AND ESTIMATES
CIA

21363

POSSIBILITY OF DIRECT SOVIET MILITARY ACTION DURING 1948-49

ORE 22-48 (Addendum)

CENTRAL INTELLIGENCE AGENCY

31004

DISSEMINATION NOTICE

1. This copy of this publication is for the information and use of the recipient designated on the front cover and of individuals under the jurisdiction of the recipient's office who require the information for the performance of their official duties. Further dissemination elsewhere in the department to other offices which require the information for the performance of official duties may be authorized by the following:

    a. Special Assistant to the Secretary of State for Research and Intelligence, for the Department of State

    b. Director of Intelligence, GS, USA, for the Department of the Army

    c. Chief, Naval Intelligence, for the Department of the Navy

    d. Director of Intelligence, USAF, for the Department of the Air Force

    e. Director of Security and Intelligence, AEC, for the Atomic Energy Commission

    f. Deputy Director for Intelligence, Joint Staff, for the Joint Staff

    g. Assistant Director for Collection and Dissemination, CIA, for any other Department or Agency

2. This copy may be either retained or destroyed by burning in accordance with applicable security regulations, or returned to the Central Intelligence Agency by arrangement with the Office of Collection and Dissemination, CIA.

DISTRIBUTION:
Office of the President
National Security Council
National Security Resources Board
Department of State
Office of Secretary of Defense
Department of the Army
Department of the Navy
Department of the Air Force
State-Army-Navy-Air Force Coordinating Committee
Joint Chiefs of Staff
Atomic Energy Commission
Research and Development Board

ORE 22-48 (Addendum)   ~~TOP SECRET~~

POSSIBILITY OF DIRECT SOVIET MILITARY ACTION DURING 1948-49
Report of Ad Hoc Committee [1] Reviewing the Conclusions on ORE 22-48

THE PROBLEM

1. We have been directed to estimate if the events of the past six months have increased or decreased the likelihood of a Soviet resort to military action during 1948-49.

BASIS FOR ESTIMATE [2]

2. Available intelligence bearing on the stated problem is too meager to support a conclusion that the USSR either will or will not resort to deliberate military action during 1948-49.

DISCUSSION

3. Our conclusions are based on considerations discussed in the Enclosure.

CONCLUSIONS

4. We do not believe that the events of the past six months have made deliberate Soviet military action a probability during 1948-49. They have, however, added some weight to the factors that might induce the USSR to resort to such action. It is considered, therefore, that the possibility of a resort to deliberate military action has been slightly increased.

5. However, the developments of the past six months which constitute setbacks to the Soviet international position have had the effect of adding to the pressure on the USSR. This pressure increases the possibility of the USSR resorting to diplomatic ventures which, while not constituting acts of war or even envisaging the likelihood of war, will involve an increased risk of miscalculations that could lead to war.

---

[1] This estimate was prepared by a joint ad hoc committee representing CIA and the intelligence agencies of the Departments of State, the Army, the Navy, and the Air Force. The date of the estimate is 27 August 1948.

[2] The Office of Naval Intelligence concurs generally in the discussion, as contained in the Enclosure.

However, ONI feels that the "Basis for Estimate" as stated is not valid. Evidence of Soviet intentions is meager, but such intelligence as is available does not indicate a resort to deliberate military action. If the position is taken that the intelligence available cannot support conclusions one way or the other, any conclusions drawn from such a basis of estimate are of doubtful value for U. S. planning.

Therefore, ONI feels that the conclusions stated in ORE 22-48, as modified by ONI comment, are still valid. ONI concurs, however, that the events of the past six months have increased slightly the possibility of military action through miscalculation as stated in paragraph 5 of subject report, and would include under miscalculation the possibility that minor military incidents might expand into uncontrolled conflict.

1   ~~TOP SECRET~~

ENCLOSURE

DISCUSSION

1. Reference is made to ORE 22-48. In general, and except for such modifications as follow, it is considered that the discussion and conclusions thereof are still valid and are, particularly in respect to the economic and political factors involved, still generally applicable to the immediate future.

EVENTS WITHIN THE SOVIET ORBIT WHICH MIGHT INDUCE A USSR RESORT TO EARLY MILITARY ACTION

2. In the USSR itself, we find no reliable evidence of military, economic, or political developments of sufficient importance to warrant any revision of our previous conclusions.

3. In the Eastern European Satellites, signs of nationalist sentiment, of mass peasant antagonism to Communist agrarian policies, and of dissension in Communist ranks, have suggested the growth of wavering loyalties and resistance to central direction from USSR. The defection of Tito and the Yugoslav Communist Party is our most striking evidence for the existence of an unstable situation. There is no doubt that this situation has caused concern in the Kremlin. While the USSR might consider the use of force to correct this situation, and general war might result, we think such a decision unlikely unless the Soviet leaders believe that the issue has reached a point where it seriously threatens their control of the Soviet orbit. At such a time the risk of war might seem preferable to the risk of losing control. There is no reliable evidence, however, that this point has been reached.

EVENTS IN WESTERN EUROPE WHICH MIGHT INDUCE A USSR RESORT TO EARLY MILITARY ACTION

4. The following events in Western Europe may have brought about some change in Soviet strategic thinking:

  a. The positive effort of the US to recreate economic and political stability through the European Recovery Program (ERP).

  b. The increasing firmness of the Western Powers toward Soviet-Communist expansion, with the growth of military solidarity among Western European nations.

  c. The initial steps to establish a Western German Government.

  d. The failure of Communist tactics in Western Europe.

5. In ORE 22-48, we stated that "the opportunities for further Soviet gains through the exploitation of economic, political and social instability, while recently diminished, are by no means exhausted." These opportunities probably appear to Soviet analysts to be still further limited in Western Europe. While it can be argued that an increasing reduction of opportunity may be an inducement to early Soviet military action, it is

2

possible that the events noted above have added to the strain on the Communist political control of Eastern Europe and therefore contributed to the weaknesses discussed in paras. 2-3 above. It is considered that the USSR, although confronted with resistance to Communist expansion in Europe, is still capable of exploiting existing political and economic instability, and is therefore more likely to continue to employ these means than to accept the risk of direct military action in the immediate future. Although Europe will remain the major objective, strategic areas elsewhere are also available for profitable exploitation.

EVENTS IN THE UNITED STATES WHICH MIGHT INDUCE A USSR RESORT TO EARLY MILITARY ACTION

6. Since Soviet leaders view, and Communist Parties are indoctrinated to regard the US as the chief bulwark of capitalism, and hence the major antagonist of the USSR, the strategy and tactics of the Kremlin are probably strongly influenced by an analysis of US capabilities and intentions.

7. Until recently, it has been supposed that Soviet planners were assuming a severe economic crisis in the US by the end of 1948, and that from this would follow a progressive weakening of US power potential. In turn, the political and economic recovery of Western Europe would be inhibited. It now appears possible that this assumption is being revised, and that Soviet planners now assume that US economy will continue productive and prosperous so long as it enjoys the export markets provided by the European Recovery Program.

8. It appears probable that Soviet leaders will be forced to admit a miscalculation of factors in US domestic politics which they earlier considered favorable. Neither the isolationists, the pacifists, nor the Wallace "Progressives" have seriously undermined popular support of a firm US diplomatic line or of adequate US defense proposals. Opinion with respect to US foreign policy has not been fundamentally split along partisan lines. Never before, in peacetime, has US opinion been so uniform on a question of foreign policy.

9. In ORE 22-48, we stated that "Soviet leaders may have become convinced that the US actually has intentions of military aggression in the near future." Recent events may have somewhat strengthened Soviet conviction in this respect. The passage of a peacetime Draft Act, the continued development of atomic weapons, the general acceptance of increased military appropriations, the establishment of US bases within range of targets in the USSR, the activities of US naval forces in the Mediterranean, and the movement to Europe of US strategic airforce units are instances in point. We think it unlikely, however, that these events have actually led Soviet leaders to the conclusion that positive US aggression must be soon expected. It is considered that they are more probably taken to mean that the ultimate conflict with the capitalist system will be resolved by force rather than by the methods of "cold war." While the danger of an early Soviet military move, made in calculated anticipation of this ultimate conflict may be slightly increased by these circumstances, we do not estimate that such a move has become a probability.

3

10. Soviet analysts, examining these evidences of US intentions, might conclude that they can no longer assume the early disintegration of the capitalist world, and that US military potential, now low, will steadily improve and will ultimately be accompanied by an improvement in the military potential of Western Europe. This might, in turn, suggest looking to military action for the achievement of their aims. However, since the usefulness of non-military methods has not yet been exhausted in Europe, and since there are other regions open to significant exploitation, we do not estimate that a USSR resort to deliberate military action has become a probability.

11. Several recent events—especially the Soviet blockade of Berlin—have served to increase the tension between the USSR and the US. With this heightened tension has come a corresponding increase in the possibility of a miscalculation which might result in general conflict.

4

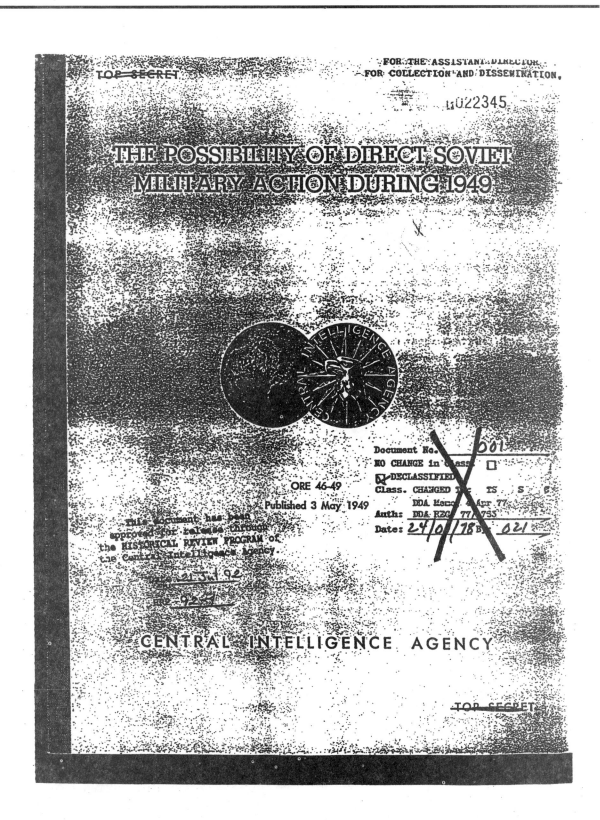

TOP SECRET

40022345

THE POSSIBILITY OF DIRECT SOVIET MILITARY ACTION DURING 1949

ORE 46-49

Published 3 May 1949

This document has been approved for release through the HISTORICAL REVIEW PROGRAM of the Central Intelligence Agency.

Date 21 Jul 92

HRP 92-7

Document No. 001

NO CHANGE in Class ☐

☒ DECLASSIFIED

Class. CHANGED TO TS S C

DDA Memo. 4 Apr 77

Auth: DDA REG 77/1753

Date: 24/01/78 By: 021

CENTRAL INTELLIGENCE AGENCY

TOP SECRET

ORE 46-49

THE POSSIBILITY OF DIRECT SOVIET MILITARY ACTION DURING 1949
Report of a Joint Ad Hoc Committee *

THE PROBLEM

1. We have been directed to estimate the likelihood of a Soviet resort to direct military action during 1949.

DISCUSSION

2. Our conclusions are based on considerations discussed in the Enclosure.

CONCLUSIONS

3. The USSR has an overwhelming preponderance of immediately available military power on the Eurasian continent and a consequent capability of resorting to direct military action at any time. The principal deterrent to such action is the superior war-making potential of the United States.

4. There is no conclusive factual evidence of Soviet preparation for direct military aggression during 1949.

5. A deliberate Soviet resort to direct military action against the West during 1949 is improbable. Moreover, the USSR is likely to exercise some care to avoid an unintended outbreak of hostilities with the United States.

6. As part of its efforts to counteract the Atlantic Pact and US military aid program, however, the USSR will seek to intensify and exploit the universal fear of a new war. In this it will pay special attention to Scandinavia, Yugoslavia, and Iran. It is unlikely, however, to resort to even localized direct military action.

7. The fact remains that international tension has increased during 1948. It will probably increase further during 1949. In these circumstances, the danger of an unintended outbreak of hostilities through miscalculation on either side must be considered to have increased.**

---

* This estimate was prepared by a Joint Ad Hoc Committee composed of designated representatives of the CIA and of the intelligence organizations of the Departments of State, the Army, the Navy, and the Air Force. It has been concurred in by the Directors of those agencies, except as indicated in the footnote below. The date of the estimate is 21 April 1949.

** The Director of Intelligence, Department of the Army, believes that the last sentence of paragraph 7 implies a greater possibility of war in 1949 than, in fact, exists; and that it should read "In these circumstances, the small but continuing danger of an unintended outbreak of hostilities through miscalculation on either side must be considered."

1

ENCLOSURE

1. As of 30 March 1948, we estimated that the preponderance of available evidence and of considerations derived from the "logic of the situation" supported the conclusion that the USSR would not resort to direct military action during 1948. Our present task is to prepare a corresponding estimate with respect to the possibility of Soviet military action during 1949.

2. The USSR continues to enjoy an overwhelming preponderance of immediately available military power on the Eurasian continent. During the past year it has maintained, and possibly accelerated, its efforts to enhance its military capabilities through both the intensive development of basic war industries and the qualitative improvement of its military forces. There has recently been a significant increase in Soviet troop strength in Germany through the arrival of recruits from the 1928 class. It is not yet apparent whether this increase is temporary or permanent. In general, however, Soviet military preparations appear to be precautionary or long-term. There is no factual evidence of Soviet preparation for aggressive military action during 1949.

3. In the absence of conclusive factual evidence, our estimate must depend on our appreciation of the fundamental objectives and strategy of the USSR. This appreciation, set forth in ORE 60-48, ORE 41-49, and elsewhere, need not be repeated here at length. The pertinent conclusion is that the USSR would be unlikely to resort to direct military action unless convinced that a military attack by the West on the USSR was in active preparation and impossible to forestall by non-military means.

4. Our estimate of 30 March 1948 (ORE 22-48) has been borne out by the event. We may be permitted, then, to assume that the situation as it existed a year ago was not such as would cause the USSR to resort to direct military action. Consequently we limit our present consideration to developments since that date which might cause the USSR to resort to such action. These developments are:

   a. An increasingly evident US determination to resist further Soviet encroachment in Europe, the Mediterranean, and the Near East, and to encourage, organize, and support local resistance in those areas. In the context of Soviet thought, this development must appear to be essentially hostile and preparatory to eventual US aggression, though not indicative of immediate attack. The USSR is particularly sensitive to the extension of US influence from Western Europe and the Mediterranean into Scandinavia on the one hand, the Balkans and Iran on the other.

   b. A gradual increase in the will and ability of Western Europe to resist Soviet political aggression, and a corresponding decline in Communist political and revolutionary capabilities in that area.

   c. Increasing rigidity in the partition of Germany and the development of an extremely taut situation at Berlin; in particular, the success of the airlift in defeating the blockade as a means of coercion with respect to Berlin, progress toward the establishment of Western Germany as a political and economic entity within the Western European community, and deterioration of the Soviet position in Eastern Germany and in Germany as a whole.

2

d. The persistence of individualism and nationalism in Eastern Europe, despite further forcible consolidation of the Soviet position in that area (excepting Yugoslavia).

e. Tito's successful defiance of the Kremlin, a matter of greatest significance in the development of international Communism and Soviet hegemony.

f. Failure of the situation in the Near and Middle East to develop as advantageously, from the Soviet point of view, as might have been expected, and the current trend toward adjustment and stabilization in the internal conflicts within that region.

Communist successes in China and prospects in Southeast Asia are matters manifestly unlikely to cause the USSR to resort to direct military action.

5. The rulers of the USSR are presumably realistic enough to perceive that these developments do not constitute a danger of immediate attack. They will appreciate, however, that the opportunity for Soviet expansion westward by non-military means has ended for the time being, and they will be apprehensive lest a continuation of the present trend result eventually in a corresponding stabilization of the situation in the Near East, a further deterioration of the Soviet position in Eastern Europe, and an ultimate danger of US attack upon the USSR. In these circumstances the USSR must give serious consideration to the advisability of resort to preventive war while it still enjoys a preponderance of immediately available military power on the Eurasian continent.

6. The deterrents to such a decision are the realization that it would precipitate an immediate decisive conflict with the United States, a present lack of adequate defense against atomic attack and of means for a decisive military attack on the United States, respect for the present general superiority of US war industrial potential in terms of a long struggle, and reasonable hope of improving the position of the USSR in these respects with the passage of time. Philosophically prepared to take the long view in the absence of an immediate threat and confident that future crises of capitalism will produce new opportunities for Soviet aggrandizement by non-military means, the Kremlin would have reason to avoid a premature showdown while assiduously developing its capabilities for eventual defense or aggression.

7. On balance we conclude that the USSR is unlikely to resort to preventive war during 1949 at least. Its most probable course of action will be to continue its preparations for eventual war while seeking to arrest or retard the indicated adverse trend of developments (para. 4) by political and psychological countereffects in forms currently familiar. In following this course the USSR will seek to intensify and exploit the universal fear of a new war. It will pay special attention to Scandinavia, Yugoslavia, and Iran. It is unlikely, however, to resort to even localized direct military action, except possibly with respect to Finland and Yugoslavia. In any such action taken, it will probably exercise care to avoid direct collision with the United States.

8. US and Soviet forces are in actual contact only in Germany and Austria. The fact that in the course of a year of acute tension the USSR has carefully avoided any action there calculated to precipitate armed hostilities establishes a presumption that the USSR would not resort to direct military action merely to break the deadlock at Berlin or to secure a satisfactory solution of the German problem. On the contrary, present indications are that the USSR may soon discard coercion, as repre-

3

sented by the blockade of Berlin, for the time being, in order to seek a more satisfactory situation through political negotiation.

9. The vulnerability of Finland to Soviet pressure and the gravity with which the USSR views Norwegian adherence to the Atlantic Pact requires specific consideration of that case. Threatening gestures toward Finland and Scandinavia might be expected to discourage any possible Finnish hope of rescue from the West, to confirm Swedish adherence to neutrality, and to inhibit Norwegian implementation of the Pact. A Soviet military occupation of Finland, however, might have exactly the opposite effect, driving Sweden into the arms of the West and stimulating Norwegian demands for direct military support. For these reasons, increasing intimidation is to be expected, but direct military action is unlikely.

10. Similarly, threatening Soviet gestures might be more effective than direct action in inhibiting Yugoslav rapprochement with the West. Basically, however, the continuing existence of the Tito regime is intolerable from the Soviet point of view and real efforts to liquidate it must be expected. Any attempt to do so by force of arms would probably take the form of insurrection within Yugoslavia with covert Satellite support, as in the case of Greece. Direct Soviet military intervention would be unlikely unless it became the only means of preventing the military alignment of Yugoslavia with the West. Even in that case, Soviet intervention would not be intended to precipitate a general war and could do so only if the West chose to take armed counteraction.

11. Soviet sensitivity with respect to Iran requires specific consideration of that situation also. In terms of the internal factors involved, the situation in Iran is more stable than it was a year ago. There has been, however, an intensification of Soviet pressure upon Iran and there remain opportunities for indirect Soviet intervention through indigenous "liberation" movements, as with respect to Azerbaijan and the Kurdish tribes. The immediate Soviet purpose appears to be to prevent Iranian adherence to a Near Eastern pact analogous to the Atlantic Pact and acceptance of substantial US military aid. Although the USSR has been at some pains to build up a legalistic basis for direct intervention with reference to the Treaty of 1921, this appears to be part of the war of nerves. Direct Soviet military action in Iran during 1949 is considered unlikely.

12. Accepting our estimate of Soviet intentions, the fact remains that international tension has increased during 1948 and will probably increase further during 1949. Both sides are actively preparing for eventual war. In these circumstances there is increasing danger of an undesired outbreak of hostilities through miscalculation by either side. Such miscalculation could occur in underestimating the determination of the opposing side or in exaggerating its aggressive intentions. Both miscalculations would be present in a situation in which one side took a position from which it could not withdraw in the face of an unexpectedly alarmed and forceful reaction on the part of the other.

4

SECRET

CENTRAL INTELLIGENCE AGENCY

POSSIBLE PROGRAM OF FUTURE
SOVIET MOVES IN GERMANY

ORE 29-48

Published
28 April 1948

SECRET

320019

ORE 29-48 SECRET

POSSIBLE PROGRAM OF FUTURE SOVIET MOVES IN GERMANY
SUMMARY

1. The following discussion covers a program that might be resorted to by the USSR in Germany in an effort to cause the Western Powers to leave Berlin, to consolidate the Soviet hold over Eastern Germany, and to extend Soviet influence into Western Germany. Until recently this review of possible Soviet intentions was considered purely speculative and the program one that would be attempted only after the USSR had concluded that Soviet interference with the Allied efforts in Western Germany could not be effected by legal international means or through local Communist subversion. The timing of the individual stages of the program would probably be conditioned upon the timing and success of Western Power action.

2. The recent Soviet walkout from the Allied Control Council and Soviet efforts to impede transportation to and from Berlin indicate that this program may already be under way, and, that while risk of war may be involved, the plan possibly can be effected without military violence.

3. It is believed, therefore, that recent Western Power action may have caused the USSR to decide that:

    a. hope no longer remains for interfering through quadripartite means with the production of Western Germany upon which the success of the European Recovery Program substantially depends;

    b. the Soviet Zone must be placed under permanent control of a well organized German group, loyal to the USSR, and supported by police state measures;

    c. the Peoples' Congress should be the instrument for the formation of such a provisional German Government;

    d. in order to prevent Allied interference with this process of political consolidation, the Allied Control Council should be abolished, or permanently boycotted, and the Western Powers forced out of Berlin;

    e. the new German "Government" should be acknowledged, at a propitious time, as the official administration for Eastern Germany, with propaganda pretensions to authority over all of Germany;

    f. the Soviet Army should remain as the "protector" of the new Reich pending creation of a new German Army, by agreement with this government; and

    g. in an effort to undermine the Western Power program Western Germany should be pressed, by all possible methods, to "rejoin" the Reich.

Note: The information in this report is as of 2 April 1948.
    The intelligence organizations of the Departments of State, Army, Navy, and the Air Force have concurred in this report.

1

SECRET

POSSIBLE PROGRAM OF FUTURE SOVIET MOVES IN GERMANY

1. With the conclusion of the London tripartite talks and the decision to consider Western Germany in the ERP planning, the Kremlin may have decided that little hope remains for the USSR to interfere with US/UK Zone production.

Three events: the results of the Soviet-sponsored Peoples' Congress, the abrupt departure of the Soviet delegation from the Allied Control Council (ACC) meeting of 20 March, and the subsequent Soviet efforts to impede both freight and passenger traffic between Berlin and the West indicate that at least the first steps in the outline of possible Soviet action may no longer be entirely in the realm of speculation.

2. CIA has believed and continues to believe that the USSR might encourage the Peoples' Congress to organize a future "national" administration and establish a *de facto* Government for the Eastern Zone while propagandistically claiming to speak for all the country. The Peoples' Congress partially confirmed this opinion when it convened on 17 March, advocated the early establishment of a Government to replace the ACC, and evidenced its pretensions to speak for the German people.

3. CIA has believed and continues to believe also that in preparation for the new "government", the USSR would attempt to discredit the ACC. While the abrupt termination of the Control Council meeting of 20 March has not yet been extended to a permanent Soviet withdrawal from the Council, Soviet officials have charged that the Western Powers, by unilateral action, have already made the work of the Council worthless.

4. The presence of the Western Powers in Berlin adds to the difficulty of establishing a Soviet puppet government in Eastern Germany, because of the "opposition" that operates from the sanctuary of the Western Powers' sections of the city. The USSR would consequently desire to effect a Western Power evacuation of Berlin as expeditiously as possible. The Soviet attempt to impede transport threatens to render untenable the position of a sizeable Allied group isolated over a hundred miles from the Western area, and, additionally, to cut off the industrial contribution of the US and UK sectors of Berlin from the Bizonal economic structure.

5. Should the Peoples' Congress, in fact, set up a "government" of the Soviet Zone, and lay claim to "represent" all of Germany, the Soviet Military Administration might accord it local recognition as the established German administration and give propaganda-credence to its pretensions to govern all of the Zones. The USSR and its satellites might then be expected to enter into provisional political and economic agreements directly with this "government", laying the foundation for eventual formal recognition at such time as the USSR considers it feasible to press the puppet government's claim to German sovereignty.

2

6.   A Soviet-sponsored provisional government which would, in all probability, control the Soviet sector of Berlin, might attempt by constant propaganda and possibly by direct interference in the public utilities affecting the Western sectors to obtain the withdrawal from Berlin of Western representation in the event that any still remained. The USSR could support this program with further concrete action similar to the transport block and declare the dissolution of the ACC, seeking to place the onus for its failure on the West.

7.   If, at any time, the Soviet Union decided that the new government of Eastern Germany is sufficiently loyal or adequately controlled by the USSR to be a trusted satellite, that further Soviet interference in Western Germany through quadripartite means is hopeless, and that the Western Powers are susceptible of blame for the partition of Germany, the USSR might officially recognize the Eastern German government, and by agreement continue the "protection" of the Red Army while developing a German Army and perfecting the police system. Both the USSR and the Eastern German "state" would then launch a campaign for German unity and independence designed to win sufficient German converts in the Western Zones to reduce materially German cooperation in the West and to attempt to undermine the program of the Western Powers.

8.   Although each of these successive steps involves the risk of war in the event of miscalculation of Western resistance or of unforeseen circumstances, each move on the program could be implemented without the application of military force if adroitly made as merely a retaliatory measure necessitated by unilateral Western Power action, and if pressed only at opportune moments.

3

(14)

CENTRAL INTELLIGENCE AGENCY
WASHINGTON 25, D. C.

9 June 1948

MEMORANDUM FOR THE PRESIDENT

The unification by the US, the UK, and France of their zones of Germany under a provisional government and the internationalization of the Ruhr under the control of the western powers presumably will be interpreted by the Kremlin as potential barriers to the basic Soviet objective of preventing the economic recovery of European countries outside the Soviet sphere.

As yet no conclusive evidence has come to light that the Kremlin believes the reorganization or unification of the western zones can . successfully accomplished or will materially assist the European recovery program. In view of the complexities inherent in the establi... ment of a provisional government under the London agreements, the USSR is likely to delay any counter-moves until the Kremlin is convinced tha... the western German organization is becoming a threat to Soviet foreign policy. In determining its course, the USSR will take careful note of: (1) the difficulties to be overcome by the US, the UK, and France in furnishing the new regime with proper political guidance and adequate and timely economic assistance; and (2) the extent of German cooperatio... or non-cooperation, particularly in the Ruhr.

The Kremlin's immediate reaction to the trizonal merger, there... will probably be an intensification of present Soviet activities in Germany rather than an abrupt change in either attitude or course of action. The USSR may be expected to continue its hindrance of western powers in Berlin and elsewhere in Germany by means short of military fo... It will further consolidate Communist control of the eastern zone in or... to obtain a "loyal" and "democratic" area, which can eventually be decl... a "free German" state or used to Sovietize a unified Germany. The USSR may be expected also to step up its propaganda efforts to discredit the western powers in German eyes as the disrupters and despoilers of Germa... and to depict the Soviet Union as the champion of a unified Germany.

If the trizonal merger appears successful and promises to re- habilitate western Germany as well as contribute to the European recover... program, the Kremlin will probably be impelled to alter its present tact... Exclusive of a resort to military force, the Kremlin can logically pursu... one of two courses: (1) ostensibly abandon its recalcitrant attitude an... make an attractive offer to form a unified German Government under quadr... partitite control (in order to slow the progress of German recovery); or (2) retaliate by establishing an eastern German state.

Declassified by 058375
date 29 MAR 19

- 2 -

The Kremlin will probably resort to the course outlined in (1) and make a vigorous effort to persuade the western powers that the USSR is sincere in its promises of cooperation. The Soviet Union is likely to make a serious endeavor to join its zone to the western zones under a single government, unless western terms for Soviet participation in a new quadripartite structure are prohibitive. If the Kremlin concludes that it cannot make the concessions demanded by the western powers, the USSR will likely adopt course (2) and announce the establishment of a new state in eastern Germany with propaganda pretensions of being the only legally-constituted German Republic and the representative government of all Germans.

R. H. HILLENKOETTER
Rear Admiral, USN
Director of Central Intelligence

ESTIMATE OF SOVIET REACTION IN GERMANY TO UNIFICATION
OF THE THREE WESTERN ZONES

APPENDICES A & B

A - Discussion of possible Soviet course (1)

Any suggestion by the USSR that it join the western powers in the quadripartite control of a unified German government would be made with the full realization on both sides that past Soviet obduracy, chiefly in the matter of economic unification, had exhausted the patience of the US, the UK, and France, and had led directly to the present tripartite action. The USSR will realize, too, that the western powers would be extremely reluctant to abandon their program for the western zones either to please the Soviet Union or to take part again in fruitless discussions in an impotent Allied Control Council or elsewhere. It is probable, therefore, that any Soviet overture would be carefully worded to give the impression that the USSR had abandoned its previous intransigent attitude, and sincerely believed its own propaganda for German unity. The overture would seriously urge the western powers to consider an overall political and economic unification of Germany under a German government with a minimum of overt occupation power control.

Because the primary Soviet purpose in making such a suggestion would be to delay German and hence western European recovery by discussions and other typical Soviet delaying tactics, the USSR would be prepared to offer important tactical concessions in the form of the German administration to be established. Under almost any circumstances, the USSR could be sure that the merger of the Soviet Zone in any form of a unified Germany would assure the existence of a Communist-controlled bloc which could be relied upon to delay and block economic recovery throughout the country. Under these conditions, the USSR might also offer, largely for German domestic consumption, to reduce or drop some Soviet reparations claims, or even possibly to consider substantial reductions in the occupation forces after a "democratic" state had been firmly established.

If the western powers should permit the USSR to join in a quadripartite zonal merger without first having absolute and therefore practically impossible clarification of Soviet intentions, the USSR, either directly or through its German representatives, would work actively to defeat western plans

Declassified by 069315
date 2 9 MAR 1978

TOP SECRET

by such actions as: (1) demanding a Soviet voice in the control of the Ruhr; (2) proposing that all political organizations not now permitted in various areas be recognized on a quadripartite basis; (3) urging similar recognition of the Communist-dominated Free German Trade Union League in order to facilitate future Soviet control of a unified labor movement, particularly in the Ruhr; and (4) supporting rightist as well as leftist political elements in the west in order to add strength to the Soviet-controlled bloc.

B - Discussion of possible Soviet course (2)

The present high degree of Soviet control over the eastern zone of Germany would greatly facilitate the conversion of that area into a Satellite state, if the Kremlin decides to retaliate by setting up a provisional government in eastern Germany. No serious opposition could arise within the zone to the appointment, under the pretense of popular elections, of Soviet candidates to the leading positions in the new state. The creation of such a state, however, would give the USSR no immediate benefits beyond those now received from the same area. Long-range benefits would be dependent upon the acceptance by opportunistic Germans of transparent Soviet propaganda designed to depict the Soviet-sponsored state as a restoration of the Reich. The USSR would attempt to undermine the tripartite German state by urging the western Germans to rejoin the Reich. Except for the questionable value of such propaganda, the USSR would have at its disposal only strikes and sabotage with which to interfere with the economic and political recovery of western Germany.

A Satellite state, in short, would promise the USSR neither additional economic nor political benefits of any magnitude, and would fall short of the immediate objective of blocking the western power program. Such a state would guarantee continued zonal autonomy and allow the western powers to continue their independent course without serious Soviet interference.

- 2 -

TOP SECRET

CENTRAL INTELLIGENCE AGENCY

EFFECT OF SOVIET RESTRICTIONS ON
THE US POSITION IN BERLIN

ORE 41-48

Published on
28 JUNE 1948

ORE 41-48

EFFECT OF SOVIET RESTRICTIONS ON THE US POSITION IN BERLIN

SUMMARY

Contrary to many published reports, the chief detrimental effect on the US of the Soviet restrictive measures imposed in Berlin, since the walkout of the USSR from the Allied Control Council, has not been interference with transportation and supply but curtailment of certain US activities having to do for the most part with intelligence, propaganda, and operations of the quadripartite Kommandatura.

Concurrently with attempted inspection of US military rail traffic, the Soviets both tightened their "security" measures and manifested greater intransigence in all city affairs. As a result: (a) the general usefulness of Berlin as center of an intelligence network has been impaired, while in particular, access to Soviet deserters and anti-Communist Germans has been made more difficult; (b) since friendly Germans cannot move freely to and from the Soviet Zone or within the city, the US cannot as before, support anti-Communism within the Soviet Zone; (c) US propaganda cannot be freely disseminated except by radio; (d) commodities manufactured in Berlin cannot be shipped to the Western zones; and (e) the ACC and the Kommandatura have, at least temporarily, lost their usefulness in keeping up German hope of unity, revealing coming Soviet moves, and easing US-Soviet tension below the governmental level.

Note: The information in this report is as of 1 June 1948.

    The intelligence organizations of the Departments of State, Army, and the Navy have concurred in this report; the Air Intelligence Division, Air Intelligence Directorate, Department of the Air Force, concurs with those portions which pertain to air intelligence.

1

EFFECT OF SOVIET RESTRICTIONS ON THE US POSITION IN BERLIN

Imperative as it is for the US to remain in Berlin, its mere physical presence there does not insure continuance of all the strategic benefits that might be derived therefrom, and this strategic position has, in fact, been undermined already by unpublicized Soviet action, taken for the most part in general security and local political matters. The hindrances imposed by the USSR during the past several weeks on transportation to and from Berlin have not seriously interfered with the logistic position of the US but rather with its strategic position.

Continued US occupation of Berlin requires supply from the west of food and such other necessities as coal for both the US personnel and the German population of the US sector of the city. Incoming barge transport, carrying the bulk of food for the western sectors of the city, reportedly is unchanged and continues adequate, notwithstanding stoppages of short duration on British transport through the Soviet Zone. Inbound military and civilian rail freight, hauling the necessary coal and other supplies, continues to move as before, except that the civilian freight routes have been somewhat restricted.

The present transport situation is the result of Soviet efforts to extend the right of civilian rail traffic inspection, which the USSR has always exercised, to Western Power military traffic. Civilian passenger traffic apparently continues unchanged, but military passenger traffic does not function because of Western Power refusal to accede to Soviet demands for the right of personal inspection. Incoming road transport continues normal except for slight difficulties in routing; as yet, the USSR has not attempted seriously to restrict Western Power air transportation. The transportation situation, as outlined above, indicates that the necessities for the German population and for the US personnel in Berlin are still being supplied.

The US strategic position in Berlin, as contrasted with its logistic position, has been impaired both by the Soviet transportation restrictions and, more particularly, by other Soviet measures taken concurrently with the imposition of logistic hindrances. These comparatively unpublicized measures, which soon followed the walkout of the USSR from the Allied Control Council, have involved: general tightening of Soviet "security" measures throughout the Soviet Zone; greatly increased police controls in and around Berlin; and Soviet efforts to block the operations of both the Allied Kommandatura and the non-Communist city government. As a result the following material benefits to the US arising from the presence of US officials and troops in Berlin have been reduced or eliminated:

(1) The value of Berlin as a center of an intelligence net covering the city itself, the Soviet Zone of Germany, the eastern satellites, and the USSR has been threatened.

(2) The value of Berlin as a sanctuary and transfer point for anti-Communist refugees or Soviet Army deserters has been reduced, in that: (a) heightened Soviet security precautions make access to the western sectors of Berlin from the adjacent

2

Soviet Zone increasingly difficult; (b) Soviet travel restrictions on westbound passenger rail traffic have curtailed the means of evacuation of refugees and deserters, who must now be limited to relatively high-level personnel warranting air transport.

(3) Except for the capacity of the Berlin radio of the US sector, the value of Berlin as point for the dissemination of Western propaganda through the Soviet Zone has been, and despite new Soviet assurances is expected to be, curtailed by Soviet interference with the dissemination of Western publications and impediments to the issuance of any German pro-Western material in the Soviet Zone.

(4) The security and transport regulations have limited the value of Berlin as a base from which the US can support anti-Communism in the Soviet Zone. Western Zone Germans can no longer easily enter or leave the Soviet Zone, while tightened police controls have reduced the capabilities and the freedom of movement of anti-Communist elements already within the Zone.

(5) The Soviet-imposed demands for inspection of all westbound freight have prevented the shipment of Berlin manufactures that contribute to the finished production of the Western Zones and eliminated almost all commerce between Berlin and the west.

(6) Although the Allied Control Council remains in the city to embarrass the USSR as a symbol of quadripartite agreement in Germany, its functional impotence and failure to meet since the USSR abruptly terminated the 20 March session has: (a) diminished remaining German hope of implementing the Potsdam method of unifying Germany politically and economically; (b) eliminated a sounding board for the revelation of future Soviet moves; and (c) eliminated a useful safety valve for easing US-USSR tension below the governmental level.

The USSR still has at its disposal further means for harassing the US and making the latter's position in Berlin more difficult. These means include: imposition of unilateral traffic regulations on inbound food and freight shipments, attempted enforcement of unilateral regulations on the flight of Western Power aircraft over the Soviet Zone, complete repudiation of quadripartite Kommandatura jurisdiction over the Soviet sector of the city and the incorporation of that sector into the Soviet Zone, and, finally, increased efforts to create unrest among the civil population of the Western sectors of the city.

Strategic losses such as the damage to US propaganda machinery, to intelligence operations and to the use of the US sector as a sanctuary for refugees from the Soviet system, cannot be completely retrieved except by the removal of all the Soviet-imposed restrictions and impediments referred to above. Though the US could recapture a degree of the strategic initiative by intensified clandestine intelligence operations, such action could do nothing to remedy the unfortunate situation in which recent Soviet hindrances have placed the anti-Communist Berlin city government or to relieve the tension brought by increased Soviet intransigence in the quadripartite Kommandatura.

3

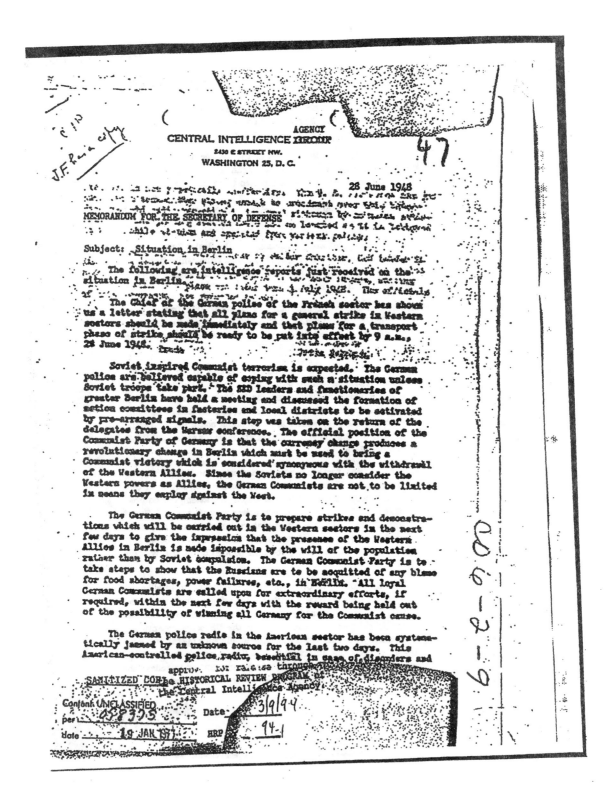

CENTRAL INTELLIGENCE AGENCY
2430 E STREET NW.
WASHINGTON 25, D. C.

47

28 June 1948

MEMORANDUM FOR THE SECRETARY OF DEFENSE

Subject: Situation in Berlin

The following are intelligence reports just received on the situation in Berlin.

The Chief of the German police of the French sector has shown us a letter stating that all plans for a general strike in Western sectors should be made immediately and that plans for a transport phase of strike should be ready to be put into effect by 9 a.m., 2t June 1948.

Soviet inspired Communist terrorism is expected. The German police are believed capable of coping with such a situation unless Soviet troops take part. The SED leaders and functionaries of greater Berlin have held a meeting and discussed the formation of action committees in factories and local districts to be activated by pre-arranged signals. This step was taken on the return of the delegates from the Warsaw conference. The official position of the Communist Party of Germany is that the currency change produces a revolutionary change in Berlin which must be used to bring a Communist victory which is considered synonymous with the withdrawal of the Western Allies. Since the Soviets no longer consider the Western powers as Allies, the German Communists are not to be limited in means they employ against the West.

The German Communist Party is to prepare strikes and demonstrations which will be carried out in the Western sectors in the next few days to give the impression that the presence of the Western Allies in Berlin is made impossible by the will of the population rather than by Soviet compulsion. The German Communist Party is to take steps to show that the Russians are to be acquitted of any blame for food shortages, power failures, etc., in Berlin. All loyal German Communists are called upon for extraordinary efforts, if required, within the next few days with the reward being held out of the possibility of winning all Germany for the Communist cause.

The German police radio in the American sector has been systematically jammed by an unknown source for the last two days. This American-controlled police radio, essential in case of disorders and

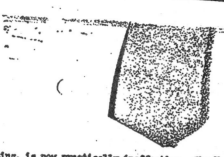

rioting, is now practically ineffective. The U. S. Air Force has just supplied a transmitter strong enough to broadcast over this interference, and radio reception is improved although by no means satisfactory. The jamming station could not be located as it is believed it is a mobile station and operated from various points.

A report from a source ~~[redacted]~~ indicates that a German government will be announced in the near future, stating that this will take place not later than 3 July 1948. The officials of this government are reported to be:

Prime Minister   Otto Pieck
Foreign Minister   Otto Grotewohl
Interior   Kris Reschke
Trade   Fritz Soppman

Dissemination of the above items has already been made to the State Department and the Armed Services.

R. H. HILLENKOETTER
Rear Admiral, USN
Director of Central Intelligence

-2-

This document has been
approved for release through
the HISTORICAL REVIEW PROGRAM of
the Central Intelligence Agency.

CENTRAL INTELLIGENCE GROUP AGENCY

2430 E STREET NW.
WASHINGTON 25, D. C.

30 June 1948

MEMORANDUM FOR THE SECRETARY OF DEFENSE

Subject: Current Situation in Berlin

Information has been received that a conference was held in
Karlshorst on 28 June 1948 between Russian officials, headed by
Marshal Sokolovsky, and German members of the German Industrial committee. Sokolovsky opened the conference by asking the German indus-
trialists what influence on the Eastern Zone of Germany would exist
because of the blockades from the Western Zone.

A German representative stated that being cut off from the West
meant a complete stoppage of production in sugar refineries for lack
of 50,000 meters of steel piping on order in the Western Zones; it
almost meant a complete closing down of canneries since the entire
raw material was received from the West; and a certain discontinuance
of the Baltic fishing fleet within a short time because of lack of
machinery parts. Sokolovsky evidenced a great consternation at this
statement, replying that the Russians had been led to believe the
East could be independent of the West. The German member then stated
that the heavy industries, particularly the steel mills in Hennigsdorf,
could not produce without the West and that other heavy industries in
the Eastern Zone would be equally affected. The Russians appeared
greatly shocked, and a Russian General, in charge of trade and supply,
said, "We had no idea of this situation; Russia is suffering from
heavy droughts and is counting on German food supplies this year.
Food supplies must be maintained, come what may. If we had known this,
we would not have gone so far."

During the meeting Sokolovsky stated that three possibilities were
available:

a. Start a war.

b. Lift travel restrictions on Berlin.

c. Leave entire Berlin to West, giving them the rail line.

After the meeting Tulpanov, who was also present, said that war was
impossible due to bad harvest prospects and that lifting travel restrictions would make the Russians lose face. The third possibility was that
the West would have to feed all of Berlin and would have more on their
hands than they bargained for. He stated that 2,000 tons of food would

Declassified by 058375
18 JAN 1977
18 JAN 1977

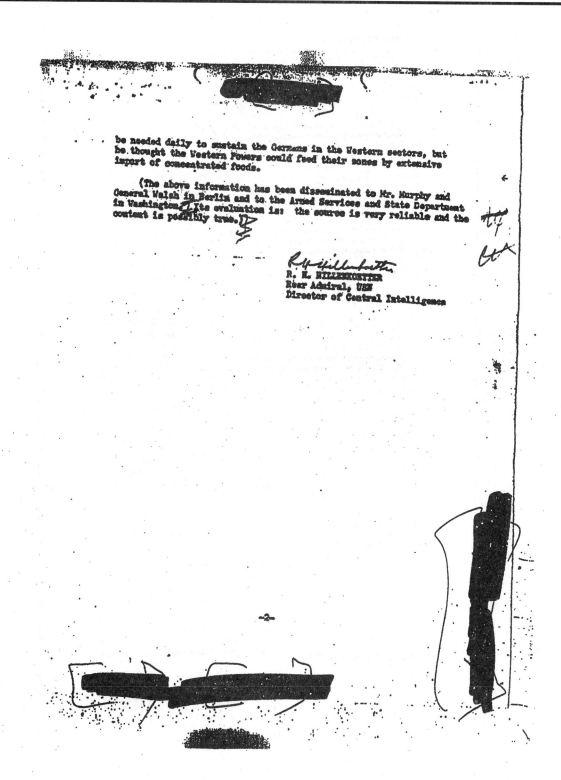

be needed daily to sustain the Germans in the Western sectors, but he thought the Western Powers could feed their zones by extensive import of concentrated foods.

(The above information has been disseminated to Mr. Murphy and General Walsh in Berlin and to the Armed Services and State Department in Washington. Its evaluation is: the source is very reliable and the content is possibly true.)

R. H. HILLENKOETTER
Rear Admiral, USN
Director of Central Intelligence

-2-

173

NLt 85-43

5

⑱

Washington ... Security Council

CENTRAL INTELLIGENCE AGENCY

~~SECRET~~

IR 0103

30 June 1948

MEMORANDUM FOR THE PRESIDENT

Subject: Russian Directive Indicating Soviets intend to Incorporate Berlin into the Soviet Zone

On 23 June 1948, the justice administration of the Soviet Zone issued a directive on the judicial measures to be taken in connection with currency reform. Addressed to the Ministry of Justice, Soviet Zone Laender, the Landgericht, and the Kammergericht in Berlin (both located in the Western Sectors), the directive treats Berlin as a part of the Soviet Zone. A copy of the directive is in the possession of the Central Intelligence Agency.

The above directive was discussed on 26 June 1948 among the justice and police officials of the Soviet Zone. When the Chief of Police of the legal section stated that the directive cannot be enforced because of the geographical location of the courts in Western Berlin, former President Wagner of the Interior Administration stated that this was of no consequence since detailed instructions for enforcement will not be ready for three weeks, by which time the Western Allies will have evacuated Berlin. This view was seconded by President Malzhaimer of the justice administration.

Field Comment: The above information is an indication that the Soviets mean business in the present crisis. Having gone this far, it is difficult to see how they could back down without a maximum loss of face even in their own camp.

(The above information has been disseminated to Mr. Murphy in Berlin and to the Armed Services and State Department in Washington.)

R. H. HILLENKOETTER
Rear Admiral, USN
Director of Central Intelligence

03854

APPROVED FOR RELEASE

cc - Admiral Souers, NSC

~~SECRET~~

18

CENTRAL INTELLIGENCE AGENCY

INFORMATION REPORT

REPORT NO.

3/16

COUNTRY   Germany (Russian Zone)

SUBJECT   Russian Unilateral Dismissal and
Appointment of Berlin Police Officials

DATE DISTR. 15 July 1948

NO. OF PAGES

PLACE
ACQUIRED   Germany, Berlin

NO. OF ENCLS.
(LISTED BELOW)

DATE OF INFO   14 July 1948

SUPPLEMENT TO
REPORT NO.

GRADING OF SOURCE						COLLECTOR'S PRELIMINARY GRADING OF CONTENT					
COMPLETELY RELIABLE	USUALLY RELIABLE	FAIRLY RELIABLE	NOT USUALLY RELIABLE	NOT RELIABLE	CANNOT BE JUDGED	CONFIRMED BY OTHER SOURCES	PROBABLY TRUE	POSSIBLY TRUE	DOUBTFUL	PROBABLY FALSE	CANNOT BE JUDGED
A.	B. X	C.	D.	E.	F.	1.	2. X	3.	4.	5.	6.

THIS IS UNEVALUATED INFORMATION FOR THE RESEARCH
USE OF TRAINED INTELLIGENCE ANALYSTS

SOURCE   A well-informed, reliable source.

Lt. Colonel Kotyshev, Internal Affairs Section, SMA, instructed Police
President Markgraf on 14 July 1948 to dismiss immediately, because of
their provocative attitude toward the SMA, the Chief of the
Schutzpolizei Hans Kanig (now on leave), Dahler, Chief of the Riot
Squads (now on leave), and Hagendorf, Chief of the Präsidialabteilung.
Kotyshev also ordered the appointments of Wagner and Eckemayer to
succeed Kanig and Hagendorf, respectively.

(Field Comment: The Soviet move involves the dismissal and appointment of "city-wide officials" subject only to Quadripartite action.
This is considered the worst provocation to date on the city level,
especially in view of Colonel Kalinin's statement when the Komendatura
was dissolved that the Soviets will "continue to respect Quadripartite
agreements".)

This document has been
approved for release through
the HISTORICAL REVIEW PROGRAM of
the Central Intelligence Agency.

Date 3/9/94

HRP   94/

BY CABLE

DATE		NAVY		NSRB	DISTRIBUTION					
STATE	X		X							
ARMY	X	AIR	X							

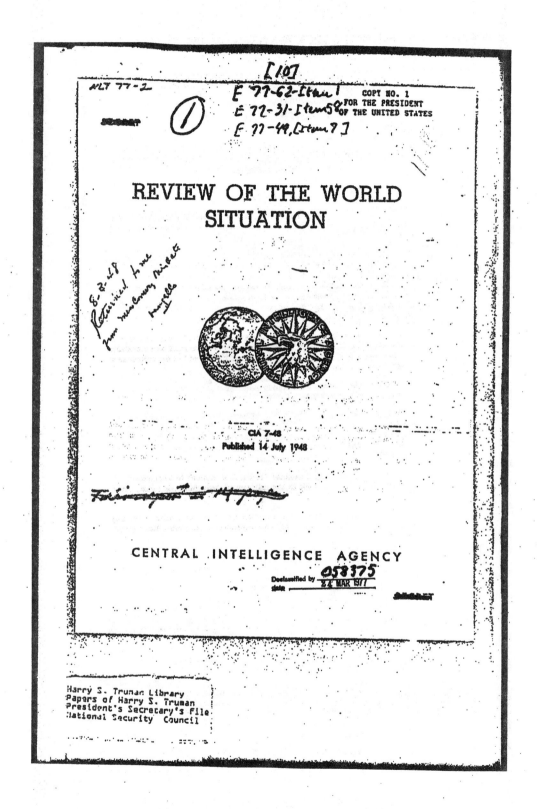

REVIEW OF THE WORLD SITUATION AS IT RELATES TO THE SECURITY OF THE UNITED STATES

SUMMARY

1. The primary purpose of the Soviet blockade of Berlin is to compel the Western Powers to reopen quadripartite negotiation with respect to Germany as a whole (infra., para. 1).

2. The breach between Tito and the Kremlin brings into the open the latent conflict between international Communist discipline and national interest which has been inherent in the situation since the expansion of Communist control beyond the historical frontiers of Russia and puts in question the ability of Russian-controlled Communism to retain power indefinitely beyond those frontiers. For the short term, at least, it seems probable that Tito will succeed in making good his assertion of Yugoslav independence (infra., paras. 2 and 3).

3. Tito's contumacy will probably cause a widespread and disruptive purge of Communist ranks which will complete the elimination of Communism as a formidable political movement in Western Europe, but perfect the remnant of the faithful as a disciplined fifth column (infra., para. 3).

4. The favorable general trend toward world economic recovery continued during the second quarter (Appendix).

5. Unless the Arabs can force political concessions from the Jews during the next two months, logistical difficulties may compel them to withdraw their armies from Palestine. Under continuing guerrilla attack, however, and in political and economic isolation from neighboring states, Israel would remain dependent on the support of an outside Power or Powers (infra., para. 11).

6. Prevailing conditions throughout the Far East continue to be adverse to US strategic interests and favorable to the extension of Soviet influence (infra., paras. 13-17).

7. Latin America is approaching a political and institutional crisis which may seriously affect its ability to afford valuable cooperation to the United States (infra., para. 18).

SECRET

REVIEW OF THE WORLD SITUATION AS IT RELATES TO THE SECURITY OF THE UNITED STATES

GENERAL

1. SOVIET PURPOSES IN GERMANY.

The Soviet blockade of Berlin is consistent with the desire to negotiate indicated in CIA 6-48. The Soviet purpose in any negotiations, however, would be offensive rather than defensive or conciliatory.

The blockade of Berlin is designed, in the first instance, to compel the Western Powers to reopen quadripartite negotiations with respect to Germany as a whole and to render them acquiescent to Soviet terms. At no more cost than the relaxation of this pressure for the time being and perhaps minor concessions on such matters as reparations, the USSR would hope to gain an effective voice in the control of Western Germany and especially of the Ruhr. By this means it could prevent the consolidation of a West German state aligned with the West and could gain an opportunity to bring about an eventual eastward orientation of Germany as a whole. The corresponding broader consequences would be to reduce the contribution of the Ruhr to the recovery of Western Europe, to gain a share in Ruhr production for the USSR and its satellites, and to prevent or retard the consolidation of a Western European community antagonistic toward the USSR.

If the Western Powers refuse to negotiate, however, or to accept in negotiation the USSR's terms, the current blockade of Berlin will have so weakened the Western position there as to hasten the day when the USSR would expect it to become untenable. Denied quadripartite agreement on Germany as a whole, in all probability the USSR would intensify its presently coercive blockade into a decisive effort, by all means short of armed force, to compel the Western Powers to withdraw from Berlin, would establish there a "national" German government, and would employ every means of political warfare and subversion to prevent the consolidation of a West German state and to bring about an eventual unification of Germany by accession of the West to the Soviet-controlled East.

2. THE BREACH BETWEEN TITO AND THE KREMLIN.

The breach between Tito and the Kremlin is the most significant development in international Communism in twenty years. It brings into the open the latent conflict between international Communist discipline and national sentiment which has been inherent in the situation since the expansion of Communist control beyond the historical frontiers of Russia and puts in question the ability of Russian-controlled Communism to retain power indefinitely beyond those frontiers.

SECRET

1

The essential complaint against Tito is that he pursued his own political interest and the national interest of Yugoslavia rather than the objectives of the Kremlin and that he remained defiantly impenitent when called upon to confess his error and mend his ways. The principal issue was probably his persistent advocacy of a Balkan federation, which could cloak Yugoslav imperialism and could result in the creation of a power capable of asserting its independence of the USSR in the international balance of power. An incidental aspect of this tendency was his disposition to exploit the situation in Greece to Yugoslav advantage and Communist disadvantage.

The Kremlin's decision to call Tito to account appears to have been taken in February, when he failed to practice self-criticism and abasement with respect to Balkan federation, as did Dimitrov of Bulgaria. Tito's formal indictment occurred in March and was generally known throughout the higher echelons of the Communist Party in Eastern Europe. The conflict became public, however, only on Tito's refusal to leave the safety of his own country to attend the June meeting of the Cominform.

The open scandal has been most untimely from the point of view of Molotov and his diplomatic interests, suggesting a conflict of purposes, if not of personalities, between him and Zhdanov, the guardian of ideological purity and party discipline. The Kremlin may have been so ill informed as to suppose that Tito would not dare to refuse the awful summons to Canossa. In any case, it was compelled to invoke open sanctions against his contumacy, lest that demoralize the remaining satellites in Eastern Europe. The event is evidence that excommunication and interdict were the only sanctions available to the Kremlin in this case.

The Yugoslav Communist Party is unique (except for the Chinese) in that it is of local development and self-contained. It is rooted in the Yugoslav Partisan movement, which was genuinely patriotic in its appeal, for all its Communist leadership. Such outside support as the Partisans had came not from the USSR, but from the West. The Partisans could readily be led again to defend Yugoslavia from foreign domination.

The Kremlin cannot brook Tito's recalcitrance, but neither can it immediately overcome him, in view of the loyalty of the Yugoslav Party, Police, and Army to him personally. Even if Tito were to be assassinated, that act would make him a martyr to Yugoslav independence and would stimulate rather than subdue Yugoslav resistance to Soviet domination. Economic sanctions would have only indirect effect, and might force Yugoslavia into closer economic and political relations with the West. Armed invasion would provoke a frenzy of patriotic resistance, would afford greater opportunities to the Western Powers, and would involve unacceptable risk of a general war. Only by long term penetration and subversion can the Kremlin get at Tito, yet each passing day of his impunity damages its prestige in Eastern Europe.

Tito, for his part, cannot immediately turn to the West without rendering his position vulnerable. He must demonstrate his loyalty to Communism and protest his innocence of heresy. Inexorably, however, the logic of his position will force him into association with the West as a factor in the balance of power, however Communistic his domestic policy. The greater the pressure exerted on him by the Kremlin, the more rapid this transition will be.

3. **INTERNATIONAL COMMUNIST DISCIPLINE.**

The Kremlin is quite capable of exploiting the sentiment of nationalism for its own purposes, as currently in Southeast Asia (para. 16). In both theory and practice, however, it cannot permit either individualism or nationalism to impair the absolute obedience of local Party leaders to its own dictates. A conflict between such rigid discipline and local judgment is implicit in the character of International Communism. Apart from any latent patriotism, it may appear in a national leader's presumption of better understanding of the national temperament or of the local situation. This disciplinary problem is currently rendered the more acute by the fact Communists now man the governments of half a dozen supposedly sovereign national states.

Within the Soviet Union the conflicting requirements of particular nationalisms and monolithic Soviet unity are reconciled by loose federation in the governmental structure and tight control through the parallel party organization. A similar device would serve to reconcile the nominal independence of Poland, for example, with the absolute domination of the Kremlin, so that Poland's "independence" would be no greater than that of the Ukraine, but the effectiveness of the system would depend upon absolute party discipline.

The Tito affair has exposed the Cominform as no mere information bureau, but, as supposed, the successor of the Comintern as the device for Kremlin control of foreign Communist parties and the governments of "independent" states where Communists are in power. Also made starkly plain is the Kremlin's subordination of every national interest and consideration to its own absolute power. This revelation should preclude the further political association of any patriot with international Communism and so reduce the Communist parties of Europe to those militants who have irrevocably transferred their entire allegiance to the Kremlin.

This tendency had been apparent in the French Communist Party since the establishment of the Cominform, but the process is as yet by no means completed. The Italian Communists avoided the forfeiture of national character and as recently as April could command 8,000,000 votes, but in June they too adopted the strict Cominform line, no doubt prepared to accept the logical consequences.

In Eastern Europe considerable latent nationalism persists even among Communists, especially in Poland and Czechoslovakia. Ironically, the vehemence of the Albanian and Bulgarian denunciations of Tito is attributable as much to individualistic and nationalistic fear of Tito's ambition and Yugoslav imperialism as to Communist discipline.

Tito's example could prove infectious in the non-Russian Communist world and cause a schism comparable only to that between Trotsky and Stalin. In any event, the apprehensions of the Cominform will probably produce a widespread and disruptive party purge. This process will probably complete the elimination of Communism as a

3

SECRET

formidable political movement in Western Europe, but at the same time it will render the faithful remnant more effective as a disciplined fifth column.

The Chinese Communist Party is guilty of most counts in the indictment of Tito, but nothing is likely to be said about that.

4. THE ECONOMIC TREND.

The favorable general trend toward world economic recovery continued during the second quarter (see Appendix, p. 10).

PARTICULAR SITUATIONS IN EUROPE

5. THE UNITED KINGDOM.

The most serious postwar crisis has found the British Government resolute in policy and strongly supported by the British people. Fears that war weariness and economic weakness might induce a mood of appeasement in the face of Soviet menace have been disproved.

The United Kingdom's international balance-of-payments position remains critical, however, despite a marked increase in industrial production, a record volume of exports, a restriction of imports to approximately four-fifths of the prewar level, and the prospect of substantial ECA assistance. It seems clear that, even with ECA support, the drain on dollar and gold reserves will continue through 1948.

6. FRANCE.

The National Assembly, in approving the Six-Power Agreement on Germany by a narrow margin, "admonished" the Government to seek more extensive international control of the Ruhr, to avoid the reconstitution of an authoritarian and centralized Reich, and to endeavor to obtain quadripartite agreement with respect to Germany. Although the Government's adherence to the existing Agreement is unqualified, it will presumably heed the Assembly's "admonitions" in its attitude during the further development of the situation in Germany.

The Assembly's action on the Six-Power Agreement coincided with an outbreak of violence as security forces broke up a sit-down strike in the rubber plants of Clermont-Ferrand. The strike, in support of wage demands, was part of a Communist plan to keep France in a ferment of local economic strikes while avoiding another general test of strength with the Government until Communist control of labor had been re-established. Local militants, however, seized the occasion to instigate disorder at Clermont-Ferrand and to call sympathy strikes throughout France, and the Party was compelled to support them. This attempt to exploit the situation was defeated, however, by the aloofness of non-Communist labor and the decisive action of the Government's security forces: within a few days the strike wave had subsided. The Communists, reverting to their previous strategy, are unlikely again to challenge the Government until the "social climate" improves.

SECRET

4

These labor troubles, however, point up the wage-price dilemma confronting the Schuman Government. The non-Communist unions, at the risk of losing members to the CGT, have withheld wage demands in order to support the Government's effort to reduce prices. Retail prices, however, are rising again and are already back at the high reached in February. The non-Communist unions are thus compelled to demand a return to price control and to consider demands for wage increases. The Government's position is rendered the more difficult by the fact that DeGaulle, in an effort to win labor support, has now seized upon this issue and instructed his labor cells to take the lead in wage demands. Some upward adjustment of wages would appear to be politically imperative, but satisfaction of the workers' demands would launch another round of inflation equally dangerous to the Schuman Government.

7. ITALY.

Like their French comrades, the Italian Communists are seeking to reassert their leadership of labor by exploiting legitimate economic grievances, with particular reference to inadequate pay and increasing unemployment. Their latest device, a series of token general strikes in successive industries, has met with success because of the inability of non-Communist labor leaders to oppose them on these issues.

The Socialist Party Congress rejected Nenni's leadership, the Popular Front as an electoral device, and resistance to the European recovery program, but these concessions to rank-and-file sentiment were offset by lack of progress toward reunion with the moderate Socialists and a resolution in favor of continued collaboration with the Communists. Although the situation within the Party is fluid, developments probably depending on factional opportunism, continued indirect Communist control of the Party apparatus may be suspected.

Meanwhile the Government has taken no constructive action to allay labor discontent, and appears unlikely to do so before the impending adjournment of Parliament. Its inactivity with respect to promised reforms has caused concern among its Socialist and Republican members. The policy of the Government may be to rely on ECA allocations to ameliorate economic conditions in Italy, basic reforms being opposed by powerful industrial and ecclesiastical influences. Such a policy would play into the hand of the Communists.

8. GERMANY.

The Western German attitude toward the Six-Power Agreement remains unenthusiastic (CIA 6-48). Both major parties, the Social Democrats and Christian Democrats, argue that the people are more concerned with economic than with constitutional problems and hold that nothing more than a basic administrative statute could be formulated in present circumstances. In keeping with this attitude, the representatives of the eleven Western laender have agreed to the proposed establishment of a central administration at Frankfurt, but have requested that the words "constitution" and "government" not be used with reference to it.

5

SECRET

The initial effects of currency reform in the Western Zones have been generally good. The ultimate effect will depend largely on increased production of consumers goods before goods hoarded hitherto have been sold off. In contrast, Soviet currency reform appears to have been hasty and slipshod. Despite the precariousness of the situation in Berlin, Western marks are at a premium there over Soviet marks.

The German population in the Western sectors of Berlin continues to be strongly anti-Soviet in attitude. Its faith in the Western Powers has been strengthened by their evident determination and the scale on which supplies are being flown in. These Germans will generally remain steadfast in this attitude unless their will is sapped by starvation or by conviction that Soviet occupation is inevitable.

The British embargo on shipments into the Soviet Zone has had a damaging effect on the economy of that area and has correspondingly enhanced the bargaining position of the Western Powers with respect to the blockade of Berlin.

9. YUGOSLAVIA (see also para. 2).

Even before Tito's break with the Cominform, the Yugoslav economy was in difficult straits (CIA 6-48), largely because of the inability of the USSR to deliver capital goods, and Tito had shown anxiety to obtain from the West the economic support which the East could not provide. In present circumstances, and in view of the "technical difficulties" which have already arisen with respect to Danubian shipping and Rumanian oil, Tito will be all the more anxious to develop trade with the West. His economic need, however, is balanced by political necessity to avoid the charge that he has sold out to Wall Street, so that great delicacy is required in this matter.

THE NEAR AND MIDDLE EAST

10. GREECE.

The resistance met by the Greek Army in the critical operation of its summer campaign indicates that the guerrillas are not yet ready to abandon their cause as hopeless.

Markos, already apprehensive of Yugoslav designs on Greek territory, has no choice but to adhere to the Cominform in its quarrel with Tito. He will presumably receive the continued support of the Cominform, Albania and Bulgaria. Supplies stockpiled for him in those countries are sufficient to keep him in business for some time, if he can avoid defeat in the field.

11. PALESTINE.

Since 15 May the Jews and Arabs have experienced four weeks of bitter hostilities and four weeks of uneasy truce, without any weakening of either Jewish determination to establish a sovereign state or Arab determination to prevent it. The period of hostilities led to a military stalemate. The period of truce was advantageous to the Jews. The Arabs have now refused to accept an extension of the truce unless their proposals for a political settlement (a unified Palestine with restrictions on Jewish immigration) are accepted as the only basis for further negotiation.

SECRET

6

In the resumption of hostilities the Jews will probably seek to consolidate their control of the coastal strip and of Galilee and to gain complete control of Jerusalem. The Arab main effort will presumably be to reimpose their blockade of Jerusalem. The success of the Arabs is doubtful in view of their acute shortage of ammunition.

Unless the Arabs can force political concessions from the Jews within the next two months, logistical difficulties will probably compel them to withdraw their armies from Palestine. However, they can be expected to support guerrilla operations there indefinitely. Arab raids, non-recognition, and economic sanctions will isolate and harrass Israel, impose upon it a heavy burden of defensive precautions, and stifle its economy. Israel will thus remain entirely dependent on the goodwill and support of some outside Power or Powers.

12. THE MIDDLE EAST.

The new Hajir Government in Iran gives promise of a resolute policy toward the USSR and even of some internal reform. Hajir's success will depend largely on the continued support of Qavam against the bitter opposition of anti-court and radical elements.

The potentially explosive Kashmir and Hyderabad disputes remain unsolved, but the danger of armed conflict between India and Pakistan appears not to be immediate.

THE FAR EAST

13. GENERAL.

Prevailing conditions throughout the Far East continue to be adverse to US strategic interests and favorable to the extension of Soviet influence. Fear and suspicion of US efforts to bring about the industrial rehabilitation of Japan are widespread. Uncertainty as to the continuance of US support for the newly elected government in South Korea and the rapid deterioration of the situation in China are both damaging to US prestige and influence. Southeast Asia has recently been the scene of intensive Soviet and Communist activity apparently intended to deny to the Western Powers the strategic materials produced in that area.

14. KOREA.

The "National Assembly" in Seoul will probably establish a professedly national government for Korea on 15 August. The North Korean radio has threatened that, in this event, a national government, including South Korean representation, will be established in the North, and that this government will demand the withdrawal of all foreign troops.

In keeping with previous estimates, the Soviet strategy foreshadowed in this propaganda is to delay until US responsibility for the division of Korea is "proved" by the inauguration of a separate South Korean regime and then to establish the proposed Korean People's Republic in the North, with membership from both sections of the

7

SECRET

country, which the government at Seoul would lack. At the request of the People's Republic, Soviet troops would be withdrawn. At the September session of the UN General Assembly the USSR would then demand that the People's Republic, rather than the government at Seoul, be recognized as truly national, and that US as well as Soviet forces be required to withdraw from Korea.

15. CHINA.

Within the past month the prestige and authority of the National Government have sunk to a new low marked by the sudden fall of Kaifeng and the spectacular decline in the value of the Chinese dollar.

The National Government has no program for arresting the continuing deterioration of the situation. Despite increasing criticism, Chiang Kai-sek continues to rely on personal adherents, including many of proved incompetence. In default of effective national leadership, provincial authorities tend increasingly to shift for themselves on a regional basis. This tendency, involving conservation of local military and economic resources, hastens the disintegration of the national effort.

Continuation of the existing trend in China will inevitably result in chaos, from which will emerge either general Communist domination or a new period of regional war-lordism.

16. SOUTHEAST ASIA.

The extent of Soviet penetration in Southeast Asia (CIA 6-48) has been rendered more apparent by the outbreak of violence in Malaya, where local Communists (predominantly Chinese) are conducting a campaign of destruction and terrorism against the operation of rubber estates and tin mines. A major British effort will be required to safeguard the continued production of these strategic materials.

At the same time, the endurance of Vietnam as the principal stronghold of Communist influence in Southeast Asia is underscored by the ineffectualness of the French-sponsored Xuan regime and the ambiguity of French policy toward it.

By supporting native nationalism throughout Southeast Asia the USSR is not only undermining Western political domination of that area and spreading Communist influence there, but is gaining a capability to deny the strategic resources of the region to the Western Powers.

17. THE PHILIPPINES.

The grant of a general amnesty to the Hukbalahap and the seating of its Communist leader, Luis Taruc, in Congress may result in solving the Philippine Government's most vexatious internal problem, if the Huks actually surrender their arms, as required, and the Government actually carries out promised agrarian reforms. This reversal of the policy of the late President, however, is a further manifestation of an increasingly nationalistic (anti-US) trend in Philippine politics. Taruc, as a Com-

SECRET

8

SECRET

munist, opposes US influence under color of ardent nationalism and in effect has imposed his own terms on the Government as a precondition of his acceptance of amnesty.

LATIN AMERICA

18. GENERAL.

It is becoming increasingly evident that Latin America is approaching a political and institutional crisis which may seriously affect its ability to afford valuable cooperation to the United States. Stability in the region has been shaken by the impact of rising import prices on raw material economies, by the disappearance of many of the former bases of political power, and by the ability of the extreme right and the extreme left to exploit the growing power of labor. Merely palliative measures, such as repression of Communist parties, are unlikely to cure the underlying unrest, or to create a new broad basis of political power, or noticeably to diminish the capabilities of subversive elements to exploit the disturbed situation. Continuing tension between international alignments in the Caribbean, internal struggles for power in Panama, Ecuador, and Peru, instability in Bolivia, and the long-continued inability of the President of Chile to govern without extraordinary powers are symptoms of the general condition of affairs. Even Argentina, a few months ago seemingly stable and prosperous because of advantages seized in a sellers' market, must now, with the disappearance of these temporary advantages, consider increasingly authoritarian measures to augment production and may, failing substantial US aid through ECA purchases or otherwise, yield to nationalistic pressure for non-cooperation with the United States. Generally increasing pressure for US aid is merely additional evidence that Latin American leaders cannot find within themselves or their countries the means to restore stability and achieve real authority for their governments.

SECRET

9

APPENDIX

DEVELOPMENT OF THE WORLD ECONOMIC SITUATION DURING THE SECOND QUARTER OF 1948

GENERAL

World economic recovery, as measured by industrial output and international trade, continued its upward trend during the second quarter. Increase in the availability of consumer goods, however, is still restricted in many industrial countries by the imperative need for reconstruction of war-damaged-facilities and modernization of industry. Prices of most internationally traded primary commodities remained firm; the price of wheat, however, declined about 5 percent, while prices of several metals, notably tin and lead, increased. Work stoppages attributable to strikes and labor unrest were comparatively few during the quarter, but Communist-instigated labor disturbances remain a serious threat to production in parts of Western Europe and Southeast Asia.

STEEL AND NONFERROUS METALS

Steel production expanded at an accelerated rate in several of the major industrial countries. The United Kingdom, still lacking hoped-for quantities of scrap from Germany as well as high-grade imported iron ores, reached a rate, at least temporarily, of 15.5 million metric tons per year. France was producing steel at a rate of 7.7 million metric tons annually, which rate was above expectations. In the Bizone of Germany steel was being produced at an annual rate of about 4.25 million metric tons, somewhat below previous estimates of probable productive capacity. This short-fall may be corrected yet this year if more high-grade iron ore is obtained from foreign sources and an adequate share of domestic scrap and coal are allocated for this purpose. In the United States, steel output was set back temporarily in the spring owing to the coal strike; at that time production declined to about 70 percent of capacity, but by mid-year it had reached an annual rate of 82 million metric tons, equal to the wartime maximum. World-wide requirements for steel, however, continue to exceed availabilities. Supplies of chrome, nickel, and other alloy steels and steel-alloying metals, although not plentiful, are in general meeting minimum requirements.

Nonferrous metals continued in short world supply as demand was maintained at a high level. This world shortage may grow more acute during the second half of 1948, although some Western European countries will obtain larger supplies under European recovery program than were available to them during the first half of the year. With demand running persistently ahead of production, prices of lead, tin, aluminum, and antimony increased during the second quarter. With a continuation of the

10

SECRET

tight supply, nonferrous metal prices may be expected to hold firm throughout the remainder of the year.

The production of lead and zinc is increasing in Canada, Mexico, Australia, and the United States, although Mexico had a marked set-back in the early spring owing to labor strikes which have since been settled. In Australia any increase in the availability of mine production will depend on improvement in transportation facilities.

Copper production in Canada, Chile, and the United States is increasing, but there is little change in Northern Rhodesia and the Belgian Congo.

Mine production of tin in Malaya and the Netherlands East Indies is larger as a consequence of rehabilitation of the mines, but local authority in Malaya is presently being threatened by terrorist activities which are in large part Communist-inspired and directed. There is also some improvement in Bolivian tin production whereas the rate of production in the Belgian Congo and Nigeria has not changed materially.

The antimony shortage is becoming more serious. Bolivian output is increasing, but production in China is only a fraction of normal. Mexican production was impeded by labor difficulties in the spring of the year and by the wide discrepancy between the price paid for ores from small producers and the world price for the metal.

Aluminum production has been hampered by shortages of soda ash and electric power in Europe and by floods and shortages of electric power in the United States. There were, however, substantial increases in output in Canada and Norway. Supplies of secondary aluminum accumulated from war scrap in European countries and the United States are virtually exhausted. Bauxite production has increased much faster than aluminum; consequently, there were no shortages of that raw material except where in a few instances transportation was a temporary bottleneck.

COAL AND PETROLEUM

Compared with the same period last year, output of coal was larger in the principal coal producing countries, except the United States, where about 48 million tons of coal were lost through strikes. The smaller volume of coal mined in this country did not appreciably interfere, however, with meeting the requirements of Western Europe, in view of the rising output of coal in the United Kingdom, Germany, Poland, and France. Moreover, increased production in Europe reduced the tonnages required from the United States, thereby releasing dollar exchange for other purposes. Aside from some shortage of coking coal, European output plus imports was generally sufficient to meet requirements, although transportation was at times inadequate to move coal out of Germany and Poland to importing countries.

World production of petroleum, except in a few areas, notably the Satellite States of Eastern Europe and recently Iraq, has been running well ahead of last year. Production was adequate to meet mounting requirements in the United States and elsewhere in the world except in some parts of Europe, the Middle East and Far East, where inadequate refining and transportation facilities have caused shortages of refined products.

SECRET

11

SECRET

RUBBER

World production of crude and synthetic rubber is now ample to meet demands for current consumption. Synthetic rubber production in Canada, the Soviet Zone of Germany, and the United States has declined in recent months compared with the corresponding period a year ago and will be substantially less for the year as a whole than for 1947; synthetic rubber production in Western Germany ended on 1 July. The large output of the USSR, however, is expected to increase moderately in 1948.

Communist-instigated disturbances in Malaya, which produces about half the world's supply of crude rubber, may, if continued, seriously curtail rubber production in that area. In such eventuality United States operating and standby capacity for synthetic rubber would be ample to offset a substantial decline in receipts of Malayan rubber.

Increasingly large Soviet purchases of Malayan rubber at premium prices and with provision for special packaging indicate stockpiling of that commodity by the USSR.

CHEMICALS AND FERTILIZERS

The world-wide shortage in many chemicals, including nitrogenous fertilizers, continues. Scarcity of alkalies, coal-tar crudes, nitrogenous fertilizers, and other basic chemicals will not be alleviated for a year or more, but improvement may be expected as coal supplies increase and new or rehabilitated production facilities become available.

The alkali shortage has limited production of rayon, glass, aluminum, and many industrial chemicals. Recent increased production of alkalies in Western Europe has been due principally to rehabilitation of war-damaged plants and increased supplies of coal. No new major production facilities are expected to come into operation in that area for a year or two. Over half of the German production is in the Western Zones, where several important plants were severely damaged by bombing. In the USSR a large part of productive capacity of alkalies was destroyed during the war and will not be fully restored until 1950 or later. Output of the Eastern European Satellites has not regained the prewar level. In the United States, increased capacity recently completed is still insufficient to meet both the domestic demand and the export demand, the latter mainly from Latin America and Southeast Asia.

The shortage of coal-tar crudes, which are used mainly by the plastics, dye, and synthetic organic chemicals industries, is directly related to the rate of operation of by-product coke ovens, which in turn are dependent on adequate supplies of coking coal. In Western Europe the improved coal situation, which had previously limited operations, made possible an increase in output of these products. Further rehabilitation of plants and a few new installations, together with adequate supplies of coal, should materially alleviate the shortage of crudes in that area before the year-end. In the USSR the large number of by-product coke ovens destroyed during the war are in process of restoration, but reconstruction work will not be completed until 1950 or later; consequently the shortage of coal-tar crudes in that country is acute. In the

SECRET

12

United States the second quarter coal strike resulted in a substantial reduction in output of coal-tar crudes, the domestic and export demands for which show little sign of abating.

Chile, the United States, the United Kingdom, and Belgium continue as the world's largest postwar exporters of chemical nitrogen, although the United States is on a net import basis. The more than doubled output of the last three-named countries since 1937 has not been sufficient to compensate for production losses in other former major producing countries. Germany, once the largest producer and exporter of synthetic nitrogen, now depends partly on imports because of war-damaged or dismantled plants and restriction of production by the occupying powers. Japan, formerly the second largest producer of the synthetic product, now depends on imports to a much greater degree than formerly. Rehabilitation of plants in the Netherlands, France, Italy, and Poland, and operation of German plants at greater capacity, together with more plentiful supplies of coal, will reduce the nitrogen shortage in the current fertilizer year. The USSR, although exporting small quantities of nitrogen to neighboring states and India, is increasing as rapidly as possible its chemical nitrogen industry, a large part of which was destroyed during the war.

FOOD

The per capita supply of staple foods in Europe, Asia, and certain other areas remained abnormally low. This was especially true of cereals, meat, and fats. The situation was alleviated somewhat, however, by larger exports of grain from the United States than had been anticipated and by an exceptionally mild winter and early spring in Europe, which increased significantly the production of dairy products and vegetables.

The acreage planted to food crops to be harvested in 1948 showed a substantial increase over plantings in previous postwar years. In general, temperatures and rainfall have been favorable to the early growth and development of crops, particularly in North America and Europe, thus indicating a 1948 food harvest almost equal to prewar harvests.

WORLD TRADE

World trade continued to increase during the second quarter of the year, although trade and exchange controls were almost everywhere maintained. Increases in production of goods for export, in combination with a ready world market, contributed largely to the continued world trade expansion.

Trade among the Western European countries, however, is currently impeded by serious payments problems, which in turn reflect the economic vacuum left by Germany and the inability of the United Kingdom to assume its prewar role in European trade. Although European countries have made substantial gains in reviving their export trade, it is estimated that their current volume of exports is only about two-thirds that of 1937. The volume of European imports, on the other hand, approaches or surpasses that of the immediate prewar years. The United Kingdom, however, is a notable

13

SECRET

exception in both cases. The exchange and transfer problems thus generated have been heightened further by rising price levels. Western European exports, though lagging below prewar, have increased moderately since a year ago. Eastern European countries are exporting little more than half their prewar volume.

Exports from the United States fell well below the level for the corresponding months of 1947 primarily as a consequence of the world shortage of expendable gold and dollars. Nevertheless, on a quantum basis United States exports during the first half of the 1948 were at a rate about double that of the prewar years. United States imports, on the other hand, though increasing in volume moderately over the level of 1946-47, were only slightly above prewar. Consequently, the dollar gap between United States imports and exports continued to be large and contributed cumulatively to monetary and exchange problems abroad. In 1946 and 1947, the United States had a net export balance of roughly 5 to 10 billion dollars respectively; in 1948 its export balance was at an annual rate of about 6 billion dollars.

* * *

The progress toward economic recovery observed in this summary of developments during the second quarter of 1948 is encouraging. It must be strongly emphasized, however, that the attainment throughout the world of conditions of economic well-being, even approximating those prevailing before the war, will require still higher levels of production in many countries and a larger volume and better balance in world trade than at present.

SECRET

14

DISSEMINATION NOTICE

1. This review has not been coordinated with the intelligence organizations of the Departments of State, Army, Navy, and Air Force, though information copies were circulated on 14 July. The information herein is as of 12 July 1948.

2. This copy of this publication is for the information and use of the recipient designated on the front cover and of individuals under the jurisdiction of the recipient's office who require the information for the performance of their official duties. Further dissemination elsewhere in the department to other offices which require the information for the performance of official duties may be authorized by the following:

    a. Special Assistant to the Secretary of State for Research and Intelligence, for the Department of State

    b. Director of Intelligence, GS, USA, for the Department of the Army

    c. Chief, Naval Intelligence, for the Department of the Navy

    d. Director of Intelligence, USAF, for the Department of the Air Force

    e. Director of Security and Intelligence, AEC, for the Atomic Energy Commission

    f. Deputy Director for Intelligence, Joint Staff, for the Joint Staff

    g. Assistant Director for Collection and Dissemination, CIA, for any other Department or Agency

3. This copy may be either retained or destroyed by burning in accordance with applicable security regulations, or returned to the Central Intelligence Agency by arrangement with the Office of Collection and Dissemination, CIA.

WARNING

This document contains information affecting the national defense of the United States within the meaning of the Espionage Act, 50 U.S.C., 31 and 32, as amended. Its transmission or the revelation of its contents in any manner to an unauthorized person is prohibited by law.

DISTRIBUTION

The President
Secretary of State
Chief of Staff to Commander in Chief
Secretary of Defense
Secretary of the Army
Secretary of the Navy
Secretary of the Air Force
Executive Secretary, National Security Council
Chairman, National Security Resources Board
Chief of Staff, US Army
Chief of Naval Operations
Chief of Staff, US Air Force
Joint Chiefs of Staff
Atomic Energy Commission

~~TOP SECRET~~

(96)

CENTRAL INTELLIGENCE AGENCY
WASHINGTON 25, D. C.

10 December 1948

MEMORANDUM FOR THE PRESIDENT

The recent action of the USSR in recognizing an
east Berlin government is representative of the shift which
has taken place in the Kremlin's estimate concerning its
capabilities in the Berlin dispute. Originally, it appeared
that the Soviet blockade of Berlin was designed primarily to
gain western power concessions regarding western Germany
and secondarily to force the US, the UK, and France to evacuate
Berlin. The refusal of the western powers to negotiate under
duress has apparently convinced the Kremlin that its chance
of gaining the primary objective is remote. Soviet strategy
is now concentrating upon the secondary objective, with a view
to forcing the West either to evacuate the city or to negotiate
on terms which will make the western position in Berlin ineffective and eventually untenable.

Stringent blockade   In pursuit of this objective, the USSR
                       may now impose a more stringent blockade
of the western sectors of Berlin. The USSR can cite the recent
"illegal" elections in the western sectors, or the possible
introduction of the western mark as the sole legal currency
in the western sectors, as an excuse to throw a cordon around
the western area and thus enforce a blockade much more effective
than the present one. The successful sealing-off of the
western sectors of the city, combined with the establishment
of the east Berlin government, would seriously damage both
the political and the economic position of the western powers
in Berlin.

Political effects   In the political realm, the effect of this
                      double action would be to: (1) destroy
all pretense that Berlin is a unified city, thereby making UN
agreements on overall Berlin affairs all but impossible to
implement; (2) hamper the administration of Berlin's western
sectors by cutting off the operation of public utilities and
services on a city-wide basis; (3) dispirit pro-western elements in both the east and west sectors; (4) diminish Berlin's
accessibility as a political sanctuary for anti-Communist Germans and Soviet deserters; and (5) reduce the capabilities of
the western powers for supporting anti-Communist factions in
the Soviet zone.

~~TOP SECRET~~

Declassified by letter from NARA
date ___

TOP SECRET

Economic effects. The economic effects of this action would
be to: (1) drastically reduce commerce
between the east and west sectors, which now permits the
blockaded Berliners to maintain a minimum business activity,
thereby making it necessary to considerably expand the airlift;
(2) increase physical hardship and curtail business activity
through the probable stoppage of public utilities now supplied
from the Soviet sector of the city; (3) cut off thousands of
Berliners who live in one sector and work in the other from
free movement to and from their work; and (4) force the western
powers to make the western mark practically the sole currency
for their sectors of Berlin in order to support the trade formerly conducted in eastern marks and to overcome the currency
shortage.

Soviet position. The intensification of the Soviet blockade
of Berlin, combined with the establishment
of the Soviet sector government, will considerably bolster the
bargaining position of the USSR. In response to future UN
recommendations, the USSR may insist, as a condition to further
negotiations, either that UN action is applicable only to the
western sectors of Berlin or that the Soviet-controlled regime
of eastern Berlin must be recognized as the sole legal government for the city. More likely to seem an appealing solution
to the neutral nations in the UN, however, would be a claim
by the USSR that the Soviet-dominated administration of eastern
Berlin must be merged into any Berlin government. Acceptance
of this claim would permit the USSR to regain an indirect control over key positions in the western city government, leading
to a probable future assumption of complete administrative
power. Such control would enable the USSR ultimately to realize
its objectives in the Berlin dispute.

R. H. HILLENKOETTER
Rear Admiral, USN
Director of Central Intelligence

- 2 -

TOP SECRET

PLACE
ACQUIRED Germany, Berlin

DATE OF INFO. 10-28 December 1948

This document is hereby regraded to CONFIDENTIAL in accordance with the letter of 16 October 1978 from the Director of Central Intelligence to the Archivist of the United States.
Next Review Date: 2008

NO. OF ENCLS.

43721

SUPPLEMENT TO
REPORT NO.

GRADING OF SOURCE						COLLECTOR'S PRELIMINARY GRADING OF CONTENT					
COMPLETELY RELIABLE	USUALLY RELIABLE	FAIRLY RELIABLE	NOT USUALLY RELIABLE	NOT RELIABLE	CANNOT BE JUDGED	CONFIRMED BY OTHER SOURCES	PROBABLY TRUE	POSSIBLY TRUE	DOUBTFUL	PROBABLY FALSE	CANNOT BE JUDGED
A.	B. X	C.	D.	E.	F.	1.	2.	3. X			

This document has been approved for release through the HISTORICAL REVIEW PROGRAM of the Central Intelligence Agency.

THIS IS UNEVALUATED INFORMATION

Date. 3/1/94

HRP 94-1

SOURCE

1. The head of the Kriminal Direktion of the East Berlin Police stated on
28 December 1948 that the complete sealing of Soviet Sector streets leading
into the western sectors is to be carried out soon. With the exception
of a few main thoroughfares, the streets will be closed with wooden barriers.
Traffic through the streets remaining open will be closely checked by foot
patrols. Vehicles attempting to pass from the Soviet Sector to the western
sectors without a proper police permit are to be summarily confiscated.
(Source Comment: Police officials are aware that it is impossible to hermetically
seal the sector boundaries. It is assumed that the Soviets want to show
their strength by the control of motor traffic and add further discomforts
to life in Berlin.)

2. The following measures are being taken to increase sector boundary controls:

a. Paul Markgraf stated at a meeting of his staff on 10 December 1948 that
the auxiliary police (Wachpolizei) would be absorbed into the uniformed
police (Schutzpolizei).

b. The duties of the auxiliary police are to be taken over by civilian guards.

c. On 21 December according to the Markgraf Kriminal Direktion, the sector
boundary patrols were increased by 1000 men. Police dogs were to be used.

d. According to a less reliable sub-source, 2000 Land Saxony paramilitary police
garrisoned in Berlin-Friedrichshagen are to be absorbed into the Soviet
Sector police on 28 December.

(Field Comment: There are 1300 auxiliary police in the Soviet Sector. If the
above figures are correct, this means that the uniformed police of the Soviet
Sector have been strengthened by 3300.)

3. Increased control of U-Bahn and S-Bahn passengers at the sector boundaries
began on 26 December. Police are under instructions to confiscate all packages
larger than brief cases. There is no legal basis for such confiscation.
Markgraf was instructed by the Central Komendatura to issue a police proclama-
tion justifying the action. The police met with scattered resistance from
outraged passengers. Railroad personnel showed passive resistance and in
many cases, gave passengers warning or concealed parcels. As a result
police assigned to this duty are being strengthened.

GAI instructions to the Markgraf Police Presidium, until 1 March 1949.
Such persons, meanwhile, are allowed to proceed as before if they are
not transporting merchandise. (Field Comment: See also SO-19233
on Brandenburg Police measures to tighten the blockade.)

SECRET 2

196

DATE OF INFO. 6 January 1949   HRP 94-1

SUPPLEMENT TO
REPORT NO.

GRADING OF SOURCE						COLLECTOR'S PRELIMINARY GRADING OF CONTENT					
COMPLETELY RELIABLE	USUALLY RELIABLE	FAIRLY RELIABLE	NOT USUALLY RELIABLE	NOT RELIABLE	CANNOT BE JUDGED	CONFIRMED BY OTHER SOURCES	PROBABLY TRUE	POSSIBLY TRUE	DOUBTFUL	PROBABLY FALSE	CANNOT BE JUDGED
A.	B.	C.	D.	E.	F. X	1.	2.	3. X 4.		5.	6.

THIS IS UNEVALUATED INFORMATION

SOURCE

1. In an informal discussion, the informant, whose duties include the ideological and military-technical training of Soviet Sector police officers, expressed his conviction that in the foreseeable future the western sectors of Berlin will come under the influence of the German Economic Commission or of the staff now constituting that agency. The informant based this conclusion on the instructions which he receives in connection with his work of training the "activist" elements in the Markgraf police. This training includes weapons training for street fighting, with emphasis on local conditions in Greater Berlin, and political and ideological indoctrination and training.

2. According to the official instructions, ideological indoctrination should include discussion of the following two possibilities regarding the future of Berlin:

    a. At a given time the Soviet occupation power will transfer all authority in the Soviet Zone and Greater Berlin to a government formed primarily on the basis of what is now known as the German Economic Commission. At the same time the bulk of the Soviet armed forces now in Germany will retire, leaving only a few key locations occupied. Subsequently, the Western Allies will be prevailed upon to take similar measures at least in Berlin and possibly in Western Germany. It will then become the task of the Berlin police forces to insure that the western sectors recognize the political authority of the Soviet Zone government.

    If the above described possibility cannot be realized, it is still expected that under clandestine SED leadership, riots and disorders will be organised in the western sectors of Berlin. The disorders will be organised on a large enough scale to justify the "legal" Police President Markgraf's ordering reliable Soviet Sector police into the western sectors to restore order. It is hoped that the outcome will be a "fait accompli" which will eventually lead an incorporation of the western sectors into the Soviet Zone. To carry out this plan, the Soviet Sector police force is being systematically reinforced by reliable and loyal Soviet Zone policemen, and several closed formations of Soviet Zone police are being deployed around the west sector boundaries.

CONFIDENTIAL

CLASSIFICATION SECRET

STATE	X	NAVY		NSRD		DISTRIBUTION				
ARMY		AIR	X	FBI						

SECRET

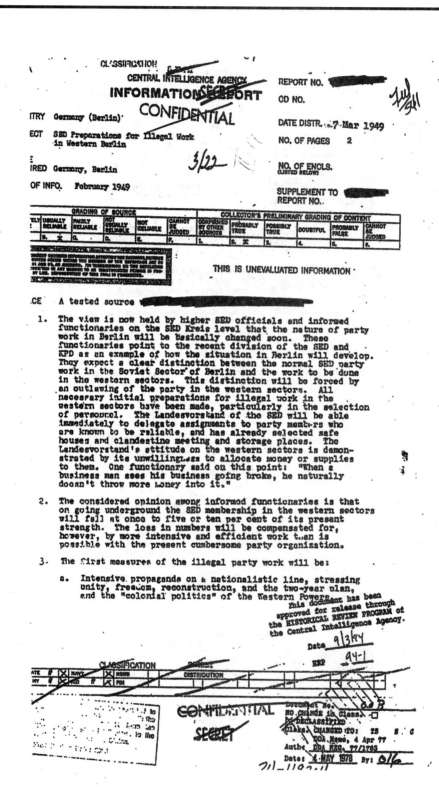

CLASSIFICATION

CENTRAL INTELLIGENCE AGENCY

INFORMATION REPORT

~~SECRET~~

CONFIDENTIAL

REPORT NO.

CD NO.

ITRY Germany (Berlin)

ECT SED Preparations for Illegal Work
in Western Berlin

IRED Germany, Berlin

OF INFO. February 1949

DATE DISTR. 7 Mar 1949

NO. OF PAGES 2

NO. OF ENCLS.
(LISTED BELOW)

SUPPLEMENT TO
REPORT NO.

	GRADING OF SOURCE					COLLECTOR'S PRELIMINARY GRADING OF CONTENT					
TLY	USUALLY RELIABLE	FAIRLY RELIABLE	NOT USUALLY RELIABLE	NOT RELIABLE	CANNOT BE JUDGED	CONFIRMED BY OTHER SOURCES	PROBABLY TRUE	POSSIBLY TRUE	DOUBTFUL	PROBABLY FALSE	CANNOT BE JUDGED
B.	X C.		D.		E.	F.	1.	2. X	3.	4.	5.	6.

THIS IS UNEVALUATED INFORMATION

CE A tested source

1. The view is now held by higher SED officials and informed
functionaries on the SED Kreis level that the nature of party
work in Berlin will be basically changed soon. These
functionaries point to the recent division of the SED and
KPD as an example of how the situation in Berlin will develop.
They expect a clear distinction between the normal SED party
work in the Soviet Sector of Berlin and the work to be done
in the western sectors. This distinction will be forced by
an outlawing of the party in the western sectors. All
necessary initial preparations for illegal work in the
western sectors have been made, particularly in the selection
of personnel. The Landesvorstand of the SED will be able
immediately to delegate assignments to party members who
are known to be reliable, and has already selected safe
houses and clandestine meeting and storage places. The
Landesvorstand's attitude on the western sectors is demonstrated by its unwillingness to allocate money or supplies
to them. One functionary said on this point: "When a
business man sees his business going broke, he naturally
doesn't throw more money into it."

2. The considered opinion among informed functionaries is that
on going underground the SED membership in the western sectors
will fall at once to five or ten per cent of its present
strength. The loss in numbers will be compensated for,
however, by more intensive and efficient work than is
possible with the present cumbersome party organization.

3. The first measures of the illegal party work will be:

a. Intensive propaganda on a nationalistic line, stressing
unity, freedom, reconstruction, and the two-year plan,
and the "colonial politics" of the Western Powers.

This document has been
approved for release through
the HISTORICAL REVIEW PROGRAM of
the Central Intelligence Agency.

Date 9/3/44

HRP 94-1

CLASSIFICATION

ATE X NAVY NSRB DISTRIBUTION
MY AIR FBI

CONFIDENTIAL
SECRET

CENTRAL INTELLIGENCE AGENCY

- 2 -

b. Intensification of party work in western sector
industries, particularly in those factories which
have had to curtail production and in the Siemens
plants.

c. Penetration of the bourgeois parties, especially
the SPD, and mass organisations (UGO, VVN, Sozialhilfe)
in the western sectors.

d. Rebuilding the Rotfrontkämpferbund outside the party
and the organization and training of small "goon
squads". At present only the organization of these
groups has been decided on; specific assignments
and work for them will be determined later.

e. All supplies, equipment, files, and other party
property which can be spared are being moved to
storage points in the Soviet Sector.

III·13

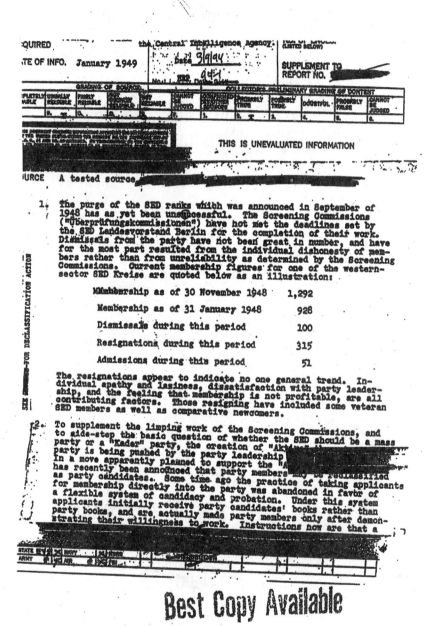

QUIRED

TE OF INFO.   January 1949   Date 3/9/94

SUPPLEMENT TO REPORT NO.

the Central Intelligence Agency.

SOURCE   A tested source

1. The purge of the SED ranks which was announced in September of 1948 has as yet been unsuccessful. The Screening Commissions ("Überprüfungskommissionen") have not met the deadlines set by the SED Landesvorstand Berlin for the completion of their work. Dismissals from the party have not been great in number, and have for the most part resulted from the individual dishonesty of members rather than from unreliability as determined by the Screening Commissions. Current membership figures for one of the western-sector SED Kreise are quoted below as an illustration:

Membership as of 30 November 1948   1,292

Membership as of 31 January 1948   928

Dismissals during this period   100

Resignations during this period   315

Admissions during this period   51

The resignations appear to indicate no one general trend. Individual apathy and laziness, dissatisfaction with party leadership, and the feeling that membership is not profitable, are all contributing factors. Those resigning have included some veteran SED members as well as comparative newcomers.

2. To supplement the limping work of the Screening Commissions, and to side-step the basic question of whether the SED should be a mass party or a "Kader" party, the creation of "Aktive" party is being pushed by the party leadership In a move apparently planned to support the "A has recently been announced that party members may be reclassified as party candidates. Some time ago the practice of taking applicants for membership directly into the party was abandoned in favor of a flexible system of candidacy and probation. Under this system applicants initially receive party candidates' books rather than party books, and are actually made party members only after demon-strating their willingness to work. Instructions now are that a

STATE   NAVY
ARMY   AIR

dues and, at least, the passive allegiance of the inactive
masses in the party.

Document No. __005
NO CHANGE in Class. ☐
☒ DECLASSIFIED
Class. CHANGED TO: TS S C
DDA Memo, 4 Apr 77
Auth: DDA REG. 27/1263
Date: 4 MAY 1978 By: 016

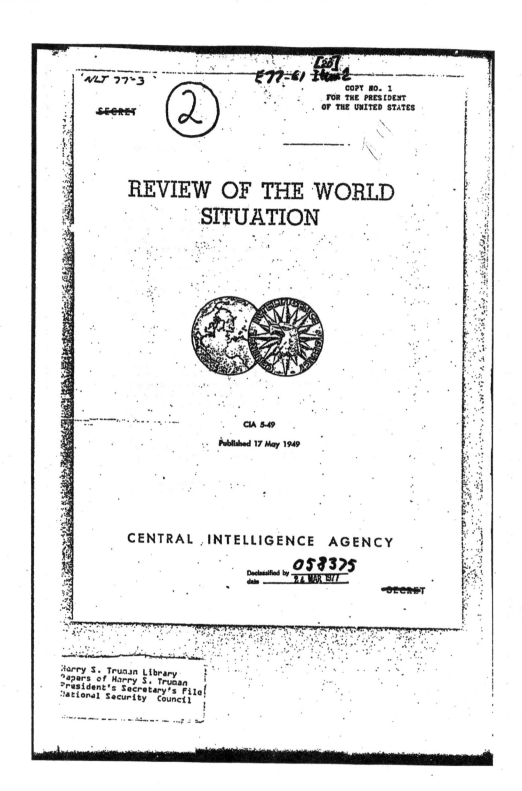

REVIEW OF THE WORLD SITUATION AS IT RELATES TO THE SECURITY OF THE UNITED STATES

SUMMARY

1. The context of power relations in which the USSR has lifted the Berlin blockade and secured Western agreement to reconvene the CFM is such as to suggest that the USSR may intend to seek some sort of agreement. There is no evidence that necessity obliges the USSR to seek agreement. There are, however, elements in the situation to justify thinking that the USSR may desire agreement in order to pursue its long-term objectives by other methods.

Analysis finds two basic alternative courses before the USSR. The first is to enter negotiations solely in order to attempt to delay and confuse Western policy. The second is to enter negotiations with the intention of reaching an agreement that would:

   a. At the minimum, remove Germany as a "bone of contention," while permitting the East-West struggle for the German potential to go on more slowly and through other channels.

   b. At the maximum reach a *détente* with the West in Europe, in order to permit the fuller exploitation of opportunities elsewhere—especially in the Far East.

The first would be essentially a continuation of tactics that have already reached a point of diminishing returns. The second would constitute, not a change in fundamental objectives, but a genuine shift in the emphasis, timing, and direction of approach.

No firm conclusion can yet be drawn about a Soviet choice between these basic alternatives; but it is expected that the course of the negotiations will permit a judgment to be made. The logic of the situation suggests that the second alternative is the more likely to be developed.

2. There have been no significant changes in trends in the Far East, the Near East, or Latin America that require examination in relation to US security. Certain selected events, however, have been noted: (a) India remains a member of the Commonwealth; (b) the Greek guerrillas make peace proposals; and (c) Zaim's *coup* in Syria revives Arab disunity.

Note: This review has not been coordinated with the intelligence organizations of the Departments of State, Army, Navy, and the Air Force. The information herein is as of 13 May 1949.

1

SECRET

REVIEW OF THE WORLD SITUATION AS IT RELATES TO THE SECURITY OF THE UNITED STATES

1. GERMANY: BLOCKADE AND NEGOTIATIONS.

The situation created by the lifting of the Berlin blockade and by the agreement to reopen Four-Power negotiations on Germany is here examined in a broader context than that provided by the detailed issues that have accumulated around the German problem in the course of three and a half years. At least three such broader contexts can be identified. First, the global power relations and the respective power potentials of the US (and the West) and the USSR (and the East). Second, the over-all situation in Europe and its capacity to effect changes in the relative position and potentials of the West and the East. Third, the long-term importance, to both West and East, of controlling—or neutralizing—the potential of Central Europe (Germany and Austria).

Broad Contexts Examined

CIA 4-49, drawing up a balance sheet of the relative security positions of the US and the USSR, estimated that the global situation had slightly changed in favor of the US, primarily because of an improved position in Europe. It was further estimated, however, that the position in the Far East was definitely less favorable to the US. These estimates came at the end of a year in which the first phase of ERP was completed, a North Atlantic Defense Pact was negotiated, a military aid program was contemplated by the US, and Soviet plans for the consolidation and control of its orbit began to run into difficulties. During the same year, Chinese Communist forces brought about the collapse of Chiang Kai-shek's regime, and anti-colonial nationalist trends in Southeast Asia grew into serious political, economic and security problems.

At the start of this period, roughly December 1947, when the CFM (Conference of Foreign-Ministers) in London broke down, the over-all picture was very different. Western Europe was then susceptible to an expansion of Communist influence. The moderate governments of France and Italy, in view of economic instability, industrial disorganization, and limited resources, seemed to have little more than an even chance of survival. Smaller states, though politically more sound, obviously sought neutral positions in a developing "cold war." The condition of the national economy of the UK left much to be desired in any calculation of a power balance. Western Germany still seemed likely to collapse economically in spite of heavy US subsidies. In the Far East, on the other hand, the Chinese Communists showed few signs of the knockout power they were to develop. Nationalist movements in Southeast Asia were still describable as the work of disaffected groups rather than as potent political trends.

In the context of 1947, the USSR, with very little evidence of an active US determination to restore Western Europe, had small interest in the maintenance of Four-Power harmony in Germany. Soviet policy for Europe as a whole and for Germany in particular called for little in the way of tactics except the obstruction of Western efforts to keep a bad situation from getting worse. Obstructionism and a readiness to exploit its

SECRET

2

consequences, working on an apparently well-defined drift toward political, economic and social confusion, might be presumed to be leading to Soviet hegemony in Europe.

However, a Western reaction to the state of affairs in Europe gradually developed under US stimulation; and, in addition, the long-anticipated economic crisis in the US did not appear. The strength of the reaction can be traced through the linked stages of ERP, the recession of Communist power in France and Italy, the reorganization of Western Germany, the growing integration of Western economic policy, the negotiation of the Atlantic Pact, plans for the rehabilitation of the military power of Western Europe, and the intention of establishing a West German federal government.

Initiative in the comprehensive competition for the potential of Western Europe was in danger of passing to the US. Soviet counter-measures began to be taken. The Satellite states were forced to refuse to participate in ERP. Communist-directed strikes, aimed at undermining the schedules for economic reconstruction, were initiated. A propaganda campaign against US "dollar diplomacy" was fully developed. These measures not only failed, but, by stimulating the West to increased efforts, actually began to create problems for the USSR within its own orbit.

While it is not likely that the USSR ever considered that the communization of Eastern Europe would be a pushover, it probably did not anticipate the difficulties that arose in 1948. When the Satellite states were cut off from participating in ERP, contrasts developed between the speed of economic reconstruction in the West and the slowness with which the communized economies of the Satellites were able to produce tangible benefits. Efforts to improve the situation by increasing Soviet controls and reorienting Satellite economies led to tensions which developed into nationalist deviations from the Cominform line.

The natural consequence of the breakdown of the CFM was a *de facto* partitioning of Germany. The West developed plans which would permit the ultimate integration of the Western Zones with a Western European system. The USSR developed plans which would permit the ultimate incorporation of the Eastern Zone in the Soviet orbit. As these plans developed, they began to produce a situation unfavorable to the Soviet interest. The USSR attempted to force a return to the *status quo ante* of unworkable Four-Power control. Pressure tactics were employed which finally resulted in the Berlin Blockade and the Air Lift. These actions completed the stalemate of US-USSR relations in Germany.

An essential factor in the situation was not, however, neutralized by this stalemate. An immense industrial and manpower potential still existed in Germany. The contest for the control of this potential underlay all the tactics, strategy, and tensions of US-USSR relations in Europe. The *de facto* partitioning of Germany primarily worked to bring this essential factor into sharper focus. The issue of ultimate control was more openly contested by political, economic, and psychological means. Short of actually using overwhelming force, however, the USSR now appeared to hold the weaker cards. Efforts to bring pressure to bear on the West, and the devices by which a firmer grip was taken on the Eastern Zone, perceptibly pushed the German people toward the West, if only as the lesser of two evils. Simultaneously, the success of the West in reviving the Western Zones acted as a supplementary pull. Finally, the Berlin Blockade

3

SECRET

and the Air Lift became, in German eyes, a test case of East-West strength. The test has now been interpreted—again by German feeling—as a victory for the West.

A direct consequence of the manner in which the contest for Central Europe developed has been the restoration of Germany to the strategic position it had previously occupied—that of an enormous potential lying between two power clusters, each of which seeks to attach this potential to itself, or alternatively to prevent its attachment to the other. The potential consequently becomes free to organize itself in its own interests. Germany has become a significant party to the problem of controlling German potential. While Germany obviously cannot at present take full advantage of being once more in this favorable position, opinion and policy in the states bordering Germany are hypersensitive to the possibilities inherent in it.*

There is little room for doubting that the cumulative effects of these developments was to oblige the USSR to reappraise the situation, and to look back to the period of an unpartitioned Germany as having been more favorable to Soviet interests and to regard the CFM as a useful device for projecting Soviet influence. This is the frame of reference for the Soviet decision which made it both possible and necessary for the West to undertake negotiations once more.

Soviet Timing

It is considered that the Soviet decision arises more from choice than from necessity. While signs have appeared that restrictions on Western exports to the Soviet sphere were retarding plans for the economic development of the entire Bloc, there is no evidence which indicates an approaching crisis. While it is true that the Western counter-blockade of the Eastern Zone of Germany has aggravated deficiencies in the economy of that Zone, there is no evidence which suggests that anything more than a gradual economic retrogression was resulting. These difficulties are far from constituting the sort of pressures that might force the USSR to seek an accommodation with the West in order to reduce them at all costs.

On the political side, the USSR has lost ground in Germany in twelve months. Its efforts to organize a rump government for the Eastern Zone have led to nothing very convincing. Related efforts to organize para-military police cadres have been equally behind schedule. The facade of a People's State that has been made ready does not appear to represent an effective and reliable counterweight to the political advances of the West or a check on the adverse effects of Soviet methods on German opinion generally. Yet, in the political field too, no immediately compelling pressures can be observed. The most that can be noted is that the substantial progress made by the West in reactivating German potential has generated a trend which, in the long run, could be contrary to the Soviet interest.

The over-all situation in Europe, however, throws some light on the decision. By and large the West was beginning to restore the balance of power in continental Europe.

---

* This is as true for Poland and Czechoslovakia in the East as for France and the Benelux countries in the West. Its existence somewhat checks both the US and the USSR in developing courses of action which the logic of their power relations might suggest as desirable.

SECRET

4

SECRET

In consequence, attention was increasingly being focused on Central Europe as the one unsettled item in the balance. The previously satisfactory stalemate which the USSR had created in this area could not be indefinitely maintained in the new circumstances that were developing.

It is, accordingly, judged that the USSR, still free to choose its time, called for a revival of Four-Power negotiations before the moment at which it was estimated the West might be irretrievably committed to the positive course on which it was started. It is noted, in this connection, that the Soviet proposals were initiated after it was clear that the Western Powers were determined to set up a West German state but before that determination had been converted into fact. It is further noted that a propaganda campaign, the "peace offensive," was well under way before the proposals were made. This campaign, though designed to counter the Atlantic Pact, could be used also to keep the West from evading negotiations on Germany by setting too high a price. Western public opinion, though skeptical of Soviet motives, was still susceptible to the notion that peace was desirable and might be found in accommodation. Currently, the "peace offensive" is being used in an effort to cancel any loss of prestige involved in the lifting of the Berlin Blockade.

The Soviet decision, especially since it was accompanied by a willingness to retreat from formerly held positions, suggests the existence of a new reading of the existing power situation. Some further progress can be made by analyzing the positions that the West has taken and from which it asserts it will not be moved, and by considering the alternative possible courses of action open to the USSR.

The Position of the West

With the abandonment of Four-Power controls in Germany, Western policy has been concerned with three objectives. These are:

1. To defeat the assumed Soviet objective of communizing Central Europe and opening the way to USSR hegemony.

2. To fit the German potential into the developing system of Western European states, while guarding against an ultimately superior German influence in that system.

3. To reactivate Germany politically and economically.

The steps taken to realize these objectives, taken in spite of the difficulties of securing adequate Allied agreement concerning them, have put the West into positions in Germany where concessions with respect to details can scarcely be made without endangering purposes that have been vigorously pursued over a considerable period of time.

It is, therefore, assumed that a West German state will be firmed up, that the USSR will not be permitted a voice in the Ruhr authority, that the level of German industry in the Western State will be unilaterally set by the Allied Powers, that reparations will not be given serious consideration and that the political machinery established for the West German state will be so designed as to prevent the Communists from gaining control by pseudo-parliamentary devices.

It is further assumed that the USSR, as far as the present negotiations are concerned, is under no significant illusion about the difficulty of attempting to break these

SECRET

5

positions down.* This assumption leads to the possible alternative courses of action that may underlie the recent Soviet decision to seek to negotiate with the West.

Soviet Alternative Courses

Two obvious alternative courses of action are here listed and discussed. Each could be considered in several variant forms; but the discussion is confined to the basic pattern.

1. The USSR might enter the CFM simply with the intention of delaying the implementation of an already clearly indicated Western policy. No intent to reach agreement need exist, and concessions made in order to reconvene the CFM could be rescinded without essential prejudice to the general positions already established in a divided Germany.

This course of action would represent little more than the tail-end of a long-standing policy; namely, to prevent the consolidation of Western Germany and the reactivation of the potential of Western Germany as adjuncts of the power of the West.

The hopes of the USSR in this course may not yet be exhausted in spite of its plainly diminishing returns. Soviet proposals, designed to appeal to German desires for the withdrawal of occupation forces, a unified centrally governed state, and a peace treaty, might be made as one more effort to sow confusion in German political feeling and retard the progress of the West Germans toward a viable state long enough to throw Allied plans out of gear and to permit Allied differences sharply to develop.

However, it is estimated that the US (and the West) position has been firmly enough agreed and developed to check this conventional Soviet line. It is further estimated that the USSR appreciates the changed situation in Europe and is aware that its chances are slim of being permitted to engage in a long, devious, and inconclusive negotiation for no purpose but to confuse and delay. The possibility that Soviet policy is not fluid and still clings to established interpretations and methods must, however, be recognized.

2. The USSR might enter the CFM with the intention of reaching, as a minimum, an agreement that would remove Germany as a "bone of contention," while permitting the struggle for the ultimate control of German potential to proceed at other levels and by other channels; or, as a maximum, a *détente* with the West that would, by reducing tensions in Europe, permit a more concentrated exploitation of the opportunities that have apparently opened elsewhere in the world—especially in the Far East.

This course of action would imply that Soviet tactics to date have been written off as having failed to produce their intended results. It would further imply a decision to shift policy to the longer term and to seek its objectives by slower methods—the infiltration of Communist influence into the operations of a unified German state, and flank attacks on the power potential of Europe by way of the Near, Middle, and Far East.

The USSR, if preparing the ground for a policy shift of this order, might well make extensive concessions on existing issues; estimating that these issues would not be as

---

* The ability of the US, however, to maintain its over-all position throughout a negotiation is only as good as its ability concurrently to carry on persuasive talks with its Western Allies. Known and suspected differences are, therefore, continually open to probing and exploitation by the USSR, which is comparatively free from similar limitations.

6

SECRET

significant to long-term strategy as they have been to short-term tactics. This course of action, however, would have certain essential requirements. The USSR would have to seek to gain an economic *quid pro quo* that would permit a more rapid rate of industrialization. The USSR would have to feel certain that it could guard its Eastern European Satellites against Western democratic infiltration. The USSR would also have to seek a German state that it could hope to keep from firm alignment with the West, and a German Government in which the Communist Party could reasonably hope later to operate effectively.

A considerable degree of accommodation could be made before these limits were reached, and calculated risks might well be taken in the expectation that what was given away in the short-term could be taken back in the longer. The danger of a rapid restoration of Western European potential in consequence of a comprehensive *détente*, might presumably be balanced in Soviet calculations by the following considerations: (a) that the rate at which Soviet potential was being developed could be increased; (b) that the "inherent contradictions" of capitalist economy would ultimately reduce the effectiveness of the potential that Western Europe was recreating; and (c) that the fundamental balance of power in the world was being slowly altered in the Soviet favor by an effective development of Soviet policy in Asia.

This course of action would imply—not a change of fundamental Soviet objectives—but a genuine shift in the emphasis, direction, and timing of the Soviet approach to these objectives. Essentially it would suggest that a conclusion had been reached that the short-term opportunities in Europe were for the moment being exhausted but that the long-term opportunities in Asia were becoming ripe for the picking.

If this course should be developed, it will probably be combined with the appeals to German opinion noted earlier. In this connection, however, these appeals would be designed to force the West to outbid the USSR for German support rather than to address itself directly to Soviet proposals. The intent would be to secure a form of German State and political machinery more satisfactory to the USSR by putting the West under the necessity of accommodating itself to German feeling. The Western position, admirably fitted to come out ahead in a negotiation where agreement is not being sought, can only with difficulty be adjusted to meet the type of problem presented by a negotiation in which agreement is intended. The West would find it hard to refuse agreement, if concessions to its present position were freely made, even though it had clearly identified the Soviet purposes for wishing agreement. The pressure of Western public opinion to accept the immediate practical comforts of an agreement on Germany or a genuine *détente* in Europe might complicate negotiations for the West. Support could not easily be developed for dealing effectively with security problems remotely developing in Asia or concealed in the apparent confusions of domestic German politics.*

---

* It is noted that this introduces the probability of German opinion becoming a target of competitive bids for the future alignment of a German state. This would bring the question of French security decisively into the councils of the West and weaken the capacity of the West to engage effectively in such a competition.

SECRET

7

SECRET

Conclusions

There is no evidence available at present to justify a firm conclusion with respect to a basic Soviet choice between these alternatives. It is to be expected, however, that the negotiations themselves will gradually permit a judgment to be made. Possible clues may be found in the actual worth of the concessions proposed and in the speed with which the USSR permits the negotiation to move toward tangible agreements.

It is considered that the tactics applicable to the first alternative may be used as an initial device for probing Western intentions and testing their firmness. It is also possible, if the Western price for agreement is so high as to spoil a calculated risk, that the adoption of the first alternative may be forced by default.

But, in the absence of special pressures within the Soviet system forcing the USSR to seek agreement, the logic of the situation suggests that the USSR is choosing to seek agreement, and that the second alternative is the one more likely to be developed.

In the context of the global power situation, the real issue before the CFM is not the settlement of Germany, but the long-term control of German power. If the CFM is able to avoid the real issue, it may arrive at patched-up, temporary solutions for the secondary problems. However, none of the parties to the negotiations, including the unrepresented Germans, will overlook the long-term question of who is going to control German potential and thus hold the balance of power in Europe. Agreement on Germany, or a *détente* in Europe primarily means that time is being taken to build up strength and to maneuver for positions elsewhere.

2. THE FAR EAST.

There have been no significant changes in the general trend in the Far East. The problems that have been created for US security are continuing to expand under the impact of numerous detailed events; but there has been no definite speeding up of admittedly unfavorable developments.

At two points only have signs begun to appear to suggest that more favorable positions might be developed in the course of time. One of these, India, is discussed in para. 3 below. The other is Indonesia, where the Dutch and Republicans have reached preliminary agreements on the restoration of the Republican administration and on issuance of a cease-fire order. Prospects for an eventual settlement appear to be better at this time than they have during the past year.

In China, the methodical Communist conquest of the Yangtze Valley is proceeding. Shanghai, though it can presumably be occupied whenever desired, will probably be left as it is for the time being. Trouble is to be expected as food and other shortages develop in the isolated city; but this will add little to the basic US problem. The Nationalist ranks continue to fall apart. Chiang Kai-shek is concentrating his efforts on strengthening Taiwan as his last retreat. Li Tsung-jen is trying to obtain recognition of his supreme authority in the crumbling National Government while at the same time preparing to fall back to his native province of Kwangsi. Autonomous

SECRET

8

SECRET

movements are under way in the southwest and northwest provinces. The most pressing current problem for the US and other foreign powers is that of deciding the nature of their future diplomatic and commercial relations with the new regime which the Communists will certainly establish within the next few months. With respect to Hong Kong the UK has expressed its determination to defend that Crown Colony and has recently dispatched reinforcements.

The French military position in Indochina has become increasingly tenuous because of intensified guerrilla activity, particularly in the Sino-Tonkinese border region. Meanwhile continued French political control in Indochina is dependent upon former Emperor Bao Dai's ability to rally non-Communist elements to a new government and even more on the ability of the French Government to make liberal enough concessions to attract these elements. In Siam, political tension is mounting again. After making full allowance for the fact that the Siamese Government tries to capitalize on Western fears of Communism in order to get military and economic aid, it is evident that Chinese Communist successes are now genuinely regarded in Siam as a growing threat to Siamese security. The situation in Burma remains as anarchic as before. While the number and intensity of terrorist incidents in Malaya have declined during the last few months, Britain's security problem remains serious and there is no reason for long-range optimism.

3. UK-COMMONWEALTH-INDIA.

The basis for a more realistic pattern of relations between the West and Asiatic nationalism has been provided by the recent Commonwealth Conference. The basis of cooperation devised by the Conference very properly ignored logic and precision in order to adjust the useful tradition of Commonwealth association to present political and strategic realities. It is of considerable importance in establishing a global balance of power that India is enabled to continue a member of the Commonwealth while remaining free to pursue its aspirations as a republic.

The linking of India with states, some of which are involved in supporting the US interest in Western Europe and others concerned in the US interest in the Far East, is of considerable value to US security. India, as the major coherent center of power at present existing in Asia, can on this basis come into working conjunction with the potential of the West.

The atmosphere of good will in which the basis of cooperation was worked out is an immediately valuable fact. Complementary interests were apparently so clearly understood that other considerations became irrelevant. The Indian interest in keeping Western military and industrial potential and technical competence related to the problem of realizing Indian aspirations was realistically balanced by the US-UK interest in having in Asia a locally powerful supporter speaking with a native voice. The development of these complementary interests into firm political, economic, and strategic cooperation obviously calls for time and tact; but the present situation should gradually add up to an improved security position for the US on, at least, the South Asiatic littoral.

SECRET

9

4. NEAR EAST.

The general situation in the Near East has undergone no significant change. Such events as deserve notice are of local concern and, for the present, have little or no relation to the larger and more pressing security issues now before the US.

The only possible exception to be noted is the bid for peace negotiations which the Greek guerrillas have made to President Evatt of the UN General Assembly. This may be designed to reinforce the over-all Soviet "peace offensive," and, if so, may be part of a broad adjustment to the situation analyzed in para. 1 above. On the other hand, there has never been a complete lull in guerrilla peace propaganda since the start of the year. At this moment, however, the guerrilla peace proposals may hit world opinion, much of which is ill-informed about the situation in Greece, with some effect. Certainly, the approach to Evatt was a smart move. He has displayed a tendency to rush towards opportunities to be a "Balkan Conciliator," in spite of lacking an adequate background; and he may be pulled into discussions which would by-pass the Greek Government with serious consequences for Greek morale and for the position of the West in Greece. The present proposal has been accompanied by a new major guerrilla offensive, by preparation for further activity, and by strenuous efforts to strengthen the Communist underground and to increase activities in the trade unions.

Turkey is still busy adjusting itself to its exclusion from the Atlantic Pact. The Foreign Minister has been in the US to discuss Turkey's security problems. He has been given reassurances of a firm US interest but no commitments that the US would enter a contractual security arrangement with Turkey. Requests for additional financial aid were channelled to ECA by way of OEEC. Opposition elements in Turkey will undoubtedly stress that the government has failed in its attempt to get a firm US commitment. However, the critics have nothing better to propose. The Foreign Minister proposes to visit Bevin in London on his way back to Turkey. It is possible that he may suggest some revisions of the Anglo-French-Turkish Treaty of 1939, which can be construed as a sort of security link for Turkey, by way of the UK and France, with the North Atlantic Treaty states.

The relations of Israel and the Arab states remain essentially stalemated in their armistice form. Israel's claims are being more cold-bloodedly examined by the Western world, even though Israel has become a member of the UN. The Arabs, largely as a result of the inter-Arab reactions to Zaim's coup in Syria, have lost all clarity of policy toward the Palestine issue.

Zaim's coup has had repercussions throughout the Arab world. The first reaction was alarm at the spectacle of a constitutional government being overthrown by force. When, however, the Syrian people accepted Zaim, although without enthusiasm, the leaders of other states began to vie with each other for his support. Iraq and Trans-Jordan have tried to draw him into the Greater Syria camp. Egypt and Saudi Arabia have tried to persuade him to resist these Hashemite blandishments. The old problem of the balance of power among the Arab states came out of the cupboard in which the Arab League had shut it up. A rash of visits, counter-visits, notes, consultations, and conversations broke out. Zaim finally emerged with recognitions from Egypt,

10

Saudi Arabia, and Lebanon; repudiated the Greater Syrian project; and declared his support of the Arab League. By this time, the Arab world was becoming alarmed at its own disunity, remembering that a peace with Israel was still to be achieved. Consequently, "discussions" have begun between Egypt and Transjordan to try to find some common ground again. In short, Arab relations are very much running in their normal channels.

As a footnote to this, neither Israel nor the Arab states appear to have much faith in one another's peaceful intentions. All are attempting to strengthen their military forces; but the Arab states also seem to have an eye fixed on inter-Arab animosities as they think of military equipment.

There have been some indications of a temporary let-up in Soviet pressure on Iran, coincidental with the departure of the Soviet Ambassador for consultation—an event that has produced a crop of rumors. Iranian leaders, although not immediately apprehensive of the Soviet menace, are calling for aid from the US in quantities comparable with that being given to Turkey. There is no indication that the attitude toward the USSR will be reversed.

5. LATIN AMERICA.

The Latin American states are watching with interest the developments following the lifting of the Berlin blockade. None of these states have illusions regarding the long-term motives of the USSR, but they hope that any relief in the tension between the US and the USSR may permit the US to pay more attention to the problems of the Western Hemisphere. Within the Hemisphere, inter-American antagonisms have been reduced. The quarrel between Peru and Colombia over the case of Haya no longer is critical; Uruguay's threat to prefer charges before the UN against Venezuela regarding the treatment of political prisoners is unlikely to materialize; and the potentially troublesome Havana meeting on Dependent Territories was conducted with reasonable restraint. The most serious and perhaps the most pressing situation in the area is that of Argentina where domestic economic problems, dropping world prices, and government bungling could very well have adverse effects upon that country's political stability.

11

III: June 1953

III: June 1953

Stalin's death in March 1953 raised expectations everywhere that the new Soviet leadership would relax its grip on Eastern Europe. As the first actions of the new leadership proved these hopes to be false, popular revolts broke out in East Germany, Poland, and Hungary. All were swiftly and brutally put down, either by the indigenous Communist regime or by Soviet Bloc troops brought in for the purpose.

The Berlin uprising of 16-17 June 1953 was the first of these protests. It began with an orderly march in protest of newly increased work quotas involving an estimated 5,000 workers at noon on the sixteenth. This ended about three hours later, but protests resumed early the next day with some 17,000 people in the streets, a figure that may eventually have risen to anywhere from 30,000 to 50,000 to several hundred thousand by noon. Traffic came to a halt and the demonstration turned violent; thousands of people swarmed through the Potsdammer Platz to the Lustgarten Platz, tearing down Communist flags and overturning kiosks. But East German and Soviet troops with tanks and armored cars had quietly moved into East Berlin the previous night. Early on the afternoon of the seventeenth they drove into the crowds, firing automatic weapons and small arms. At 2:20 PM the East German government declared a state of emergency; the revolt was quickly crushed. Like after-shocks following a major earthquake, strikes, demonstrations and isolated "incidents" continued to occur throughout the DDR over the next few weeks, but with the crackdown on 17 June the Communist regime demonstrated that, even if it had little popular support, it was nevertheless firmly in control.

The Berlin uprising was a spontaneous action that took American intelligence officers by surprise. Although the United States had waged an active propaganda campaign that encouraged dissatisfaction with the Communist regime, it had not worked directly to foster open rebellion and had no mechanism in place to exploit the situation when it arose. US authorities in Berlin thus had no alternative but to adopt an attitude of strict neutrality.[1] Many East Germans nonetheless expected the United States to intervene. These expectations persisted, unintentionally fueled by a US-sponsored food-distribution program that began on 1 July and lasted until the East Berlin government put an end to it in August.[2]

---

[1] On the US response to the Berlin uprising in general, see Christian Ostermann, "The United States, the East German Uprising of 1953 and the Limits of Rollback," *Cold War International History Project Working Paper, No. 11* (Washington, DC: Woodrow Wilson International Center for Scholars, 1994).

[2] *Ibid.*, pp. 25-31.

The Berlin uprising effectively ended the limited political plurality hitherto tolerated by the East German regime. More than 6,000 people were arrested. A statewide purge eliminated dissidents both in the official party, the SED (*Sozialistische Einheits Partei Deutschland*), and in the state-tolerated "opposition" parties. Ironically, the principal effect of the uprising was to further consolidate the existing power structure in the DDR: East Germany's President Walter Ulbricht used the revolt as an excuse to eliminate rival factions within the SED, while measures were taken to ensure that the security apparatus would not be caught napping again.[3]

III-1: NIE 81: Probable Soviet Courses of Action with Respect to Germany Through Mid-1954, 22 May 1953.

III-2: SE-47: Probable Effect of Recent Developments in Eastern Germany on Soviet Policy with Respect to Germany, 24 July 1953.
These two Estimates weigh the importance of the DDR to the Soviet bloc before and after the Berlin uprising and predict Soviet actions to stabilize control of the East German state. Of note is the special concern accorded the Federal Republic of Germany in Soviet planning.

III-3: Comment on the East Berlin Uprising, 17 June 1953 (MORI No. 144301).
This the first full report of the uprising to be disseminated in Washington.

III-4: Closing of Berlin Borders, 18 June 1953 (MORI No. 144211).
The powder-keg atmosphere that remained on 18 June is reflected in this terse report of security measures taken along the inter-Berlin border.

---

[3] Mary Fulbrook, *Anatomy of a Dictatorship: Inside the GDR, 1949-1989* (Oxford: Oxford University Press, 1995), pp. 185-187.

NATIONAL INTELLIGENCE ESTIMATE

PROBABLE SOVIET COURSES OF ACTION WITH
RESPECT TO GERMANY THROUGH MID 1954

NIE-81

(Published 22 May 1953)

(Supersedes NIE-53 and NIE-57/1)

CENTRAL INTELLIGENCE AGENCY

PROBABLE SOVIET COURSES OF ACTION WITH RESPECT TO GERMANY, THROUGH MID–1954

THE PROBLEM

To estimate probable Soviet courses of action with respect to Germany, through mid-1954.

ESTIMATE

1. We believe that current Soviet "peace" tactics do not indicate any change in the ultimate Kremlin objective with respect to Germany, which is to bring the entire country under Soviet control. The Kremlin must recognize, however, that it is not in a position to advance directly toward this ultimate objective by political action because of the hostility of the overwhelming majority of Germans to Communism. It must also recognize that an attempt to impose Communist control over all Germany by force would result in general war.

2. We believe that through the period of this estimate the Kremlin will seek by political warfare to prevent or at least to retard the Western program for West German rearmament and the integration of West Germany with the West. The Soviet leaders will probably continue to believe that there is a good chance of thwarting the Western program through a political warfare campaign which plays upon Western European fear of German rearmament and upon German desire for unity. Even if the EDC is ratified and West German rearmament begins, the Kremlin will probably believe that the implementation of the EDC agreements and the rearming of West Germany will proceed slowly, and that there will continue to be opportunities to thwart the Western program. In any case, it is unlikely that by mid-1954 the re-

armament of West Germany will have advanced to a point at which the Soviet leaders would regard West Germany as a serious military threat.

3. The Kremlin in its political warfare directed against West Germany will seek to encourage defeatism and neutralism by emphasizing Soviet military might and determination, while at the same time it will use "peace" tactics to counter rearmament sentiment. Soviet propaganda will appeal to German nationalism by exploiting anti-American themes and by seeking to aggravate Franco-German differences. Trade offers and the lure of former German markets in Eastern Europe and mainland China will be dangled before West German businessmen.

4. As part of its "peace" tactics, the Kremlin may during the period of this estimate make proposals for the establishment of a united, independent, and neutralized Germany on the basis of free all-German elections and the withdrawal of all occupation forces from Germany. However, we believe that such proposals would contain conditions which the Kremlin would intend to be unacceptable to the West, or that the Kremlin would intend to prevent the implementation of agreements embodying these proposals.

5. We believe that during the period of this estimate, the Kremlin will not give up or

1

weaken its control over East Germany even to prevent West German integration with the West or West German rearmament. So long as it retains East Germany, the Kremlin will remain in a position to use East Germany as a lever in negotiations with the West and to prevent German unification on terms unfavorable to the ultimate extension of Soviet control to all Germany. Furthermore, so long as Soviet troops occupy East Germany the USSR will retain a valuable base for either offensive or defensive military operations and for attempts to intimidate the West. Finally, East Germany has great economic and technological importance for the Bloc. For instance, we estimate that East Germany contributes about 40 percent of the Bloc's total production of uranium ores and concentrates. It is unlikely that the Kremlin will surrender the great advantages which it derives from its control over East Germany in return for the establishment of a united and neutral Germany which it might hope subsequently to subvert. The Kremlin almost certainly fears that, even if a united Germany were not only neutralized but disarmed, it would eventually rearm and turn against the USSR.

6. We believe, therefore, that the Kremlin will retain and consolidate its hold on East Germany and will seek to increase East German economic and military power. The Soviet program will be tantamount to making East Germany into a full-fledged Satellite with security measures as rigorous, and isolation of the population almost as complete as in the other Satellite states. However, the Kremlin probably believes that the formal integration of East Germany into the Soviet Bloc as a "People's Democracy" would be likely to hasten the rearmament of West Germany and its integration with the West and to turn the pressure for German unity against the USSR. Therefore, the Kremlin will probably continue to make concessions to the needs of the propaganda campaign for all-German unity by preserving a multi-party facade in East Germany and by allowing some non-governmental groups to maintain tenuous connections with West Germany. On the other hand, if the Soviet "peace" tactics are abandoned and the EDC agreements are ratified, the Kremlin

may conclude a separate peace treaty and an alliance with East Germany and incorporate it into the Bloc as a "People's Democracy."

7. The Kremlin probably estimates that the maintenance of Soviet control in East Germany is dependent upon the presence of Soviet forces in East Germany. However, the Kremlin may estimate that it could greatly increase the effectiveness of its political warfare campaign by removing some of its overt control mechanisms from East Germany, including some of its military forces. The Kremlin might expect that such moves would give the impression of Soviet willingness to withdraw entirely from East Germany, thus intensifying German hopes for unification and the expectations in Western Europe, particularly in France, for a satisfactory settlement of the German problem.

8. It is even conceivable that at some stage the Soviet leaders might withdraw all Soviet forces from East Germany, if they were convinced that such a step would lead to the withdrawal of all US forces from Europe and would create conditions favorable to the imposition of Soviet control over all of Germany. This is only a remote possibility, at least for the period of this estimate, but we believe it cannot be excluded entirely.

9. Despite the recent lessening of Soviet pressure on West Berlin, we believe that the Kremlin objective of forcing the withdrawal of the Western Powers from West Berlin remains unchanged. So long as the Kremlin continues its "peace" tactics, it will probably not undertake new harassing measures against West Berlin. However, preparations for sealing off West Berlin from East Germany and East Berlin have been substantially completed. If the "peace" tactics are abandoned, West Berlin will probably be isolated from adjacent Soviet-controlled territory. The likelihood of interference with communications between West Berlin and West Germany, possibly including a surface blockade of West Berlin, will increase substantially if the EDC agreements are ratified. However, we believe that the Kremlin will carefully assess Western reaction to the various forms of pressure employed, and that

3

the Kremlin is unlikely to adopt courses of action which, in its estimation, would involve grave risk of general war.

10. In conclusion, there can be no doubt that the Kremlin regards West Germany as potentially the most powerful state in Western Europe, and as potentially the most danger-ous, both to the realization of Soviet aggressive plans and to the security of the Bloc. During the period of this estimate, the Kremlin is likely to believe that the German situation is not yet dangerous and that there remain opportunities for influencing developments in Germany by political warfare.

SECRET
SECURITY INFORMATION

SPECIAL ESTIMATE

PROBABLE EFFECT OF RECENT DEVELOPMENTS IN EASTERN GERMANY ON SOVIET POLICY WITH RESPECT TO GERMANY

SE–47

Approved 21 July 1953

Published 24 July, 1953

The Intelligence Advisory Committee concurred in this estimate on 21 July 1953. The FBI abstained, the subject being outside of its jurisdiction.

The following member organizations of the Intelligence Advisory Committee participated with the Central Intelligence Agency in the preparation of this estimate: The intelligence organizations of the Departments of State, the Army, the Navy, the Air Force, and the Joint Staff.

CENTRAL INTELLIGENCE AGENCY

SECRET

PROBABLE EFFECT OF RECENT DEVELOPMENTS IN EASTERN GERMANY ON SOVIET POLICY WITH RESPECT TO GERMANY

THE PROBLEM

To estimate the probable effect of recent developments in Eastern Germany on Soviet policy with respect to Germany.

ESTIMATE

RECENT DEVELOPMENTS IN EAST GERMANY

1. *The Recent Communist Reforms in East Germany.* In late May 1953 the USSR appointed a civilian to the post of High Commissioner of the Eastern zone of Germany, thereby implying a deëmphasis of Soviet military control over that area. On 10 June the Communist authorities in East Germany proposed a series of measures involving major modifications and, in some cases, even reversals of past Communist programs. The government subsequently announced that it would halt the collective farm program at its present level; restore confiscated property and full civil rights to East German refugees who returned; make state bank credits available to private businessmen; provide a general amnesty for prisoners guilty of minor economic offenses; and issue ration cards to some 250,000 East Germans who had recently been deprived of them. On the same day the East German Government and Protestant Church leaders jointly announced that they had resolved most of their outstanding conflicts.

2. Soviet recognition that the accelerated pace of East German satellization had produced serious popular dissatisfaction almost certainly was a factor in bringing about the adoption of these measures. Though the Communists realized that these measures would retard their basic program of communization, they may have felt that the establishment of substantial armed forces and the rapid pace of industrialization were causing dangerous strains in the East German economy. It is also likely that they expected to encourage West German belief that early unification is feasible. They may have hoped thus to obstruct West German rearming and integration with Western Europe and to help bring about the defeat of Adenauer in the forthcoming West German elections.

3. *The Disorders in Mid-June.* A small demonstration took place in East Berlin on 16 June and expanded on the following day into strikes and riots there and throughout the Soviet zone. The Soviet authorities declared martial law and proceeded to put down the disorders, relying almost exclusively on the use of Soviet troops. The USSR began to withdraw these troops on 24 June, when order was apparently restored. However, there are reports of continuing outbreaks, and some Soviet troops remain in the affected areas.

4. At this time the full significance of these disorders is difficult to assess. At least:

1

2

a. The disorders demonstrated the intensity of East German resentment against the regime and the willingness of the East German people to undertake active resistance despite the extended period of Communist control.

b. The extent of the disorders appears to have been wholly unexpected by the East German authorities. The decision to employ primarily Soviet forces to quell the disorders indicated Soviet distrust of the East German police, military, and security forces.

c. The disorders themselves, and the fact that Soviet troops were required to maintain the authority of the East German Government, have further discredited that government in the eyes of the East German people. More significantly, the government has lost standing with the Soviet leadership.

d. The disorders have probably convinced the USSR that Soviet control over East Germany can be assured only by maintaining Soviet troops in the area.

e. The disorders have further encouraged German hopes for unification and considerably increased West German demands on the Adenauer government for greater readiness to explore possibilities for unification even at the expense of progress toward rearmament and European integration.

f. A workers' revolt against the authorities of a "workers state" is in itself a setback for worldwide Communist propaganda.

THE EFFECTS OF THESE DEVELOPMENTS ON SOVIET POLICY IN EAST GERMANY

5. The riots have not so far resulted in a reversal of the June concessions. In fact, the Communist authorities in East Germany have not only announced that these measures will be carried through, but that they will be amplified. For example, a decrease has been promised in the allocation of resources to heavy industry and the East German army (KVP) in favor of an increased supply of food and consumer goods. We believe that the Communists will attempt to implement these economic concessions within their economic capabilities. We estimate, however,

that they are unlikely to carry out any economic or other measures that would endanger their control over East Germany.[1]

6. We believe that within the next several months the Soviet authorities will probably reconstitute the East German Government and purge the East German Communist Party (SED). Although the USSR would achieve a propaganda advantage in both East and West Germany by including more non-Communist representatives in the East German Government, there are few, if any, political leaders left in East Germany who are not well-known Communist collaborators. Hence, we believe that the USSR will build a new East German Government around a purged SED. Non-SED parties may be encouraged to take a more independent line, to assume some superficial aspects of a "loyal opposition," and to attempt to develop ties with West German political parties.

7. In restoring order and maintaining control over East Germany the Soviets are faced by a dilemma. Additional concessions and admissions of error may convince the people in East Germany and in other parts of the Soviet Bloc that their plight can be relieved by active resistance. If, on the other hand, the Kremlin withdraws all concessions and exacts submission by a regime of force and terror, it must reverse its newly adopted "soft" policy and jeopardize its chance to influence West Germans. We believe that the Kremlin will probably attempt to continue this "soft" policy in East Germany, although it will employ force as necessary to maintain order.

SOVIET APPROACH TO GERMAN UNIFICATION

8. The Soviet approach to German unification will be determined within a larger framework than that of recent developments in East Germany alone. However, the USSR will not ignore the renewed upsurge of unification sentiment which has appeared in both East and West Germany. The USSR will

---

[1] See footnote of the Deputy Director for Intelligence, The Joint Staff, to the first sentence of paragraph 9, page 3.

probably agree to a Four Power conference, though not necessarily to the proposals contained in the Western notes of 15 July. It will probably regard such a conference as an appropriate forum in which to exploit the unification sentiment in Germany in an effort to delay West German rearmament and integration with the West. In such a meeting the USSR might propose several plausible but unacceptable schemes of German unification, involving, for example, various methods of holding "free" elections which would not in fact be free, or a German unification on the Austrian pattern, with continued military occupation. The USSR might even advance proposals unsatisfactory to itself, but which it would expect the Western Powers to reject, hoping to derive propaganda advantages from the fact of Western rejection. Despite these and other possibilities, the USSR would probably consider that the basic alternatives before it in such a negotiation reduce to two:

a. To agree to the creation of a unified and neutral Germany on the basis of free elections and the withdrawal of all foreign troops from Germany, which would mean the relinquishment of Soviet control in East Germany; or

b. To negotiate for unification, but with no intention of agreeing to any solution that would involve the relinquishment of Soviet control over East Germany.

9. We estimate that the USSR is unlikely to adopt the first alternative.[2] However, recent developments in the Soviet Union and elsewhere in the Bloc suggest the possibility of some change in Soviet policy. The Kremlin might come to the conclusion that a solution of the German problem could no longer be postponed, and yet could not be achieved without losing control of East Germany. It might even see some compensating advantages in the first alternative. For instance,

an agreement on a unified, neutralized Germany would eliminate the potential German contribution to Western military strength. In addition, the USSR might estimate that such an agreement would relax present East-West tension and thus abort the Western impetus for rearmament and weaken the cohesion of the NATO Powers. Moreover, the USSR might believe that if Western troops were withdrawn from West Germany, the stationing of US troops elsewhere in Western Europe would create dissension between the US and its allies.

10. We believe that the second of these alternatives is far more likely.[2] So long as Soviet troops occupy East Germany, the USSR will retain a valuable base for either offensive or defensive military operations and for attempts to intimidate the West. So long as the Kremlin retains control over East Germany, it remains in a position to use East Germany as a lever in negotiations with the West and to prevent any unification of Germany which would prejudice its ultimate objectives in Germany. East Germany has great economic and technological importance for the Soviet Bloc. The Kremlin almost certainly fears that a united Germany would eventually rearm and turn against the USSR. It is, therefore, unlikely that the Kremlin will surrender the great advantages which it derives from its control over East Germany in return for the establishment of a united and neutral Germany which it might hope, at best, eventually to subvert. Furthermore, the Kremlin probably estimates that weakening or relinquishing its control over East Germany would have adverse political and psychological effects on the remainder of the Soviet Bloc. In conclusion, therefore, as indicated in NIE-81,[3] we believe it unlikely that the USSR will agree to any solution of the German problem that involves the surrender of Soviet control over East Germany.

---

[2] The Deputy Director for Intelligence, The Joint Staff, believes that the first alternative is more likely.

[3] NIE-81, "Probable Soviet Courses of Action with Respect to Germany, through Mid-1954," published 22 May 1953.

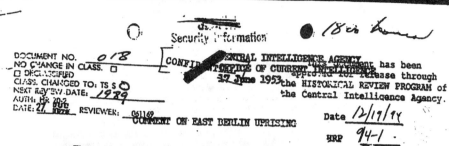

Security Information

CENTRAL INTELLIGENCE AGENCY
OFFICE OF CURRENT INTELLIGENCE
17 June 1953

This document has been approved for release through the HISTORICAL REVIEW PROGRAM of the Central Intelligence Agency.

Date 12/19/94
HRP 94-1

COMMENT ON EAST BERLIN UPRISING

The uprising of tens of thousands of East Berliners on 16 and 17 June, which had to be quelled by Soviet troops, is an unprecedented demonstration of hostility to a Communist regime. In West Germany, the uprising has increased demands for German unification, but East German Premier Grotewohl says the riots will make unity more difficult. The uprising will also have serious consequences for the Soviet "peace campaign" throughout the world.

The rioting apparently commenced with a small controlled demonstration of some 5,000 people, about noon on 16 June, against the recently decreed 10 percent increase in work norms. It is likely, though unproved, that this was planned to enable the government to yield on the question without losing face.

About 2 P.M., however, a cabinet minister addressing the crowd was pushed aside by a worker who shoted, "What you have declared here is of no interest to us. We want to be free. Our demonstration is not against norms .... This is a people's revolt." The demonstration dispersed about an hour later with threats of a general strike. American observers mingled freely with the small remaining groups, in which party workers seemed to be trying to argue down demonstrators complaining against food shortages and lack of freedom. During the evening there was sporadic violence.

At 8 P.M., Premier Grotewohl and Communist Party Chief Ulbricht addressed a closed meeting of the Berlin party members calling for a rallying of the people around the party and promising "further far-reaching measures" to correct the past mistakes.

At 4:30 A.M. on Wednesday, a West Berlin Police unit observed 12 Russian tanks approaching the US Sector border in the areas of Gross Zeithen. At 5 A.M. an advance unit of 20 Russian tanks were observed passing Adlershof in East Berlin in the direction of the center of East Berlin.

By 8:30 A.M. there were 17,000 marchers in East Berlin. Soviet soldiers wearing battle dress and in troop carriers were located in various sections to reinforce the police, but at this time there was no intervention on their part.

Security Information

In the course of the morning struggle, nearly 2,000 persons came into the West sectors of Berlin, but remained quiet. By 11 A.M. some of the Berlin elevated railway traffic had been halted; a complete cessation of both elevated railway and subway traffic was subsequently reported.

Later, up to 30,000 demonstrators on the Potsdamer Platz overturned kiosks and police shelters, and tore down Communist flags and posters. Smoke columns were reportedly seen rising from the East German government's main office building, and Peoples' Police inside finally opened fire on the crowd, wounding some. Fire hoses failed to disperse the crowd.

In the Lustgarten Platz, where the demonstrators planned to converge eventually, Soviet tanks took up stations and German reenforcements from the Saxony area were called for. Increasing numbers of the Peoples' Police were reported defecting to the West.

The West German Post Office reported that the East German postal and telecommunications workers struck and that Peoples' Police had taken over the communications. From noon on, the demonstrators were reported to be uncontrollable; the violence being accompanied by shouts of "Ivan go home."

Press estimates of the size of the mobs vary from 50,000 to several hundred thousand.

Shortly after noon actual firing was heard from West Berlin. One report stated that 15 Soviet medium tanks, 20 armored cars, and 30 truckloads of machinegunners had been concentrated on the 50,000-man mob storming the government headquarters. Tanks drove into the mob here. Both Soviet and East German forces used small arms fire to scatter the mobs. Forty wounded were brought to one West Berlin hospital alone, after being hit by bullets or clubbed.

At 2:20 P.M., the East Berlin radio announced a state of emergency in the Soviet Sector, banned all demonstrations, rallies, and gatherings of more than three persons, proclaimed a curfew from 8 P.M. to 4 A.M., and declared violaters punishable according to martial law.

It is believed that by the most serious local disturbances had been brought under control when this announcement was made.

All other broadcasts by the East German radio minimized the uprising. At 4 A.M. on 17 June it referred blandly to an SED meeting the previous evening at which Ulbricht had said that the party should listen more carefully to the criticisms of the working people, and Grotewohl had promised measures to increase the standard of living. Forty-five minutes later it announced in a similar brief, that Ulbricht had promised to increase the supply of consumers goods.

At 6 A.M. the radio stated that the demonstrations of the previous day had been only local, incited by provocateurs from West Berlin. At 10:30 it announced that the majority of the workers in Berlin had resumed work. At 1:35 P.M. a Grotewohl statement announced that the 28 May decree for the raising of work norms by June 30 had been abolished.

Shortly after, at 2:20 P.M., came the broadcast declaring a state of emergency and 15 minutes later the entire East German network went on the air again with the appeal that provocations and grave disturbances in the Democratic sector of Berlin would only make the establishment of German unity more difficult. The government asked the population to help restore order and create conditions for normal and peaceful work; and also to apprehend the provocateurs and turn them over to the police.

At 5:33 P.M., in ostensible capitualtion to the demands of the workers, the radio announced that "the decisions of the Politburo of the SED and of the government assured the prompt fulfillment of your justified demands." The regular program was interrupted about an hour later for a similar appeal to the people to maintain order. Western provocateurs were again blamed for the disturbances.

Actually, the only known formal encouragement from West Germans came at 5 on 17 June, when the leader of the West Berlin German Trade Union Federation, using the facilities of the American Radio in Berlin, requested the East Berlin population to support the day's demonstrations. He stated that he could not give them instruction, but only advice. He spoke of the justification of their demands for tolerable work norms, prompt payment of wages, and a reduced cost of living.

Latest press reports state that the entire Soviet Zone railroad network is on strike, and that rioting and strikes have broken out also in Dresden, Halle, Chemnitz, Zwickau, and a large number of other industrial centers.

The rioting, coming hard on the heels of the East German Government's 9 June campaign of conciliation, has left the regime in a dilemma.

To quiet popular clamor Deputy Premier Ulbricht has already ordered an increase of consumer goods production. Steps will probably be taken also to improve working conditions and adjust wages.

But the regime was defeated in its effort to bow gracefully to the demands of workers, and instead has given the appearance of weakness. This could encourage the populace to even greater resistance. Hence the government, for its own security, may have to reverse that part of its 9 June program calling for freer movement of the populace. Severe reprisals have already been ordered for the "provocateurs," and this move runs directly contrary to the "peace offensive."

- 3 -

CENTRAL INTELLIGENCE AGENCY

NFORMATION REPORT

SECURITY INFORMATION

COUNTRY	Germany (Berlin)	REPORT NO.	
SUBJECT	Closing of Berlin Borders	DATE DISTR.	18 June 1953
		NO. OF PAGES	1
DATE OF INFO.	18 June 1953	REQUIREMENT NO.	RD
PLACE ACQUIRED Germany, Berlin		REFERENCES	

BY CABLE

THE SOURCE EVALUATIONS IN THIS REPORT ARE DEFINITIVE.
THE APPRAISAL OF CONTENT IS TENTATIVE.
(FOR KEY SEE REVERSE)

SOURCE: ▆▆▆▆▆▆▆▆▆▆▆▆ Appraisal of Content: 3.

THE FOLLOWING REPORT WAS PREVIOUSLY DISTRIBUTED AS PRELIMINARY DISSEMINATION NUMBER ▆▆▆▆▆
PD-170

1. Since about 9:00 in the morning of 18 June, East German police, both regular police and members of the KVP, supported by Russian soldiers with tanks, have barred all the entrances into the Eastern sector of Berlin from West Berlin. No one has been allowed to cross, not even persons holding East German identification papers who were attempting to return to East Berlin. Civilians (presumably belonging to the SSD) with machine guns are firing at individuals who try to cross the line without permission.

2. This is the most complete isolation of West Berlin from the Russian zone that has yet been enforced.

3. The Glienicke Bridge leading from the American sector to Potsdam is still open.

IV: *Alltagsgeschichte*: Day to Day in the Intelligence War

IV: *Alltagsgeschichte*: Day to Day in the Intelligence War

The high level of intelligence activity in Cold War Berlin meant that each side was subjected to constant scrutiny by the other. This not only applied to the kind of so-called "positive" intelligence that might be collected in Berlin—the details of the Western military garrisons, for example, or orders of battle for Soviet military units stationed in East Germany—but also information collected for counterintelligence purposes. Precisely because Berlin was so important as a base for Western intelligence, effective Allied counterintelligence was a vital prerequisite to the collection of the strategic intelligence that was its raison d'être. The following documents represent a much larger body of material collected on the Soviet and East German intelligence and security services in Berlin. They presumably would be matched by an equivalent or larger corpus of intelligence reporting collected by the Soviet bloc services on the Western intelligence presence in Berlin.

IV-1: Current Intelligence Weekly Summary (CIWS): The Soviet Establishment in Karlshorst Compound in East Berlin, 7 May 1959 (MORI No. 145728).

This document describes the principal KGB facility in Berlin at the height of the Cold War. The size of the Soviet establishment and the degree to which it was designed to be self-contained contrasts sharply with the Allied presence in West Berlin, where American officers lived in much closer daily contact with the local population.

IV-2: The KGB in East Germany, April 1970 (MORI No. 144336).

Although dating from 1970, this report provides details of life in the KGB *Rezidentura* that probably would be more-or-less equally valid throughout the Cold War. Seemingly trivial details of the kind included in this report often were invaluable for operational purposes.

IV-3: Soviet Intelligence and Security: Lt. Gen. Pitovranov, 23 July 1958 (MORI No. 145209).

Appointed KGB Berlin *Rezident* in the summer of 1953, Lt. Gen. Yevgeny Petrovich Pitovranov was brought in to "fix things" following the death of Stalin and the uprising of June 1953. He served in Berlin until 1958, when he was replaced by Gen. Aleksandr Mikhailovich Korotkov, a Berlin veteran.[1] This brief bio on Pitovranov gives an indication of the goldfish-bowl-like environment in which many intelligence officers in Berlin lived, despite the aura of secrecy shrouding their profession.

---

[1] David E. Murphy, Sergei Kondrashev, and George Bailey, *Battleground Berlin*, (New Haven, CT: Yale University Press, 1997), pp. 285-86.

IV-4: Activities of Gen. Ivan A. Serov in Poland, 8 November 1958 (MORI No. 144168).

SMERSH Chief in Soviet-occupied Germany, General Serov arrived with advancing Red Army in the summer of 1945 and left late in 1947, apparently the victim of political machinations in Moscow.[2] In 1940-41, during the first Soviet occupation of the Baltic states, Serov had been responsible for the deportation of some 134,000 "class enemies" to slave labor camps.[3] A confidant of Nikita Khrushchev, in 1953 Serov engineered the overthrow of Stalin's Internal Security Chief, Lavrenty Beria. In 1954, Serov was made the first chairman of the newly created KGB.[4]

IV-5: IR: Organization of the Soviet Intelligence Organs, 24 February 1955 (MORI No. 144214).

This report provides an overview of the changes in Soviet intelligence that occurred near the end of Stalin's life and during the brief period that Lavrenty Beria was in complete control of Soviet intelligence. Note that, although the "Date of Info." given is December 1952-January 1954, the report was not issued until February 1955, by which time the MGB had been replaced by the KGB.[5]

In December 1952, Stalin created a Chief Directorate of Intelligence (*Glavnoye Razovodyvatolnoye Upravleniye*—the same name as Soviet military intelligence) over the MGB's First Directorate (Foreign Intelligence) and the Second Directorate (Counter Intelligence) in an effort to insure closer coordination between the two directorates. The change was recommended by Ye. P. Pitovranov, who had been Chief of the MGB's counter-intelligence directorate until his arrest in October 1951. He was released by Stalin in November 1952 and made Chief of the First Directorate (Foreign Intelligence). This arrangement lasted only until Stalin's death and Beria's reorganization of the Soviet intelligence establishment in March 1953. Pitovranov was sent to Berlin as head of the Karlshorst *apparat* soon after the June 1953 uprising.[6]

IV-6: HVA Meeting Chaired by [Markus] Wolf, 2 February 1953 (MORI No. 145205).

---

[2] Murphy, et al., pp. 31-32.
[3] Georg von Rauch, *The Baltic States: The Years of Independence, 1917-1940* (New York: St. Martin's Press, 1995), p. 228.
[4] Murphy, et al., pp. 154, 277, 289.
[5] See above, p. 119.
[6] These paragraphs are based on information contained in a letter to the author from David E. Murphy, 29 June 1999.

IV-7: HVA Meeting [Sondersitzung] Chaired by [Markus] Wolf, 7 March 1953 (MORI No. 145348).

Western intelligence officers in Germany had to be concerned not only with the Soviet KGB but also with East Germany's highly effective intelligence and security agency, the *Ministerium für Staatssicherheit*, also known as the MfS or Stasi. The branch of the Stasi responsible for the collection of foreign intelligence was the *Hauptverwaltung Aufklärung* (HVA, usually translated as the Main Administration for Foreign Intelligence), known until 1956 by a cover name, *Institut für Wirtschafts-Wissenschaftliche Forschung* (IWF, or Institute for Economic Research). For most of the Cold War the IWF/HVA was headed by the enigmatic Markus "Mischa" Wolf. Widely regarded as Moscow's man, Wolf was appointed to head the DDR's foreign intelligence service in late 1952—on the strength of his Soviet connections, according to the Stasi rumor mill.[7]

Document IV-6 is a transcript of a meeting of IWF Department (*Abteilung*) heads on 2 February 1953. In this, the first meeting he chaired as head of the IWF, Wolf ordered a formal distancing from the Central Committee of the East German Communist Party (SED, or *Sozialistische-Einheitspartei Deutschland*).

Document IV-7 describes a special meeting held on 7 March 1953, the day after Stalin's death was announced. Here the principal concern was that the West might somehow exploit the demise of the Soviet leader to mount an assault on the Soviet bloc. The agent reporting on this meeting describes an atmosphere of deep depression in IWF headquarters: "The women personnel appeared in black clothing and behaved as if their own mother had died. The men were similarly affected, but were less demonstrative."

IV-8: Pictures of Mischa Wolf, 9 April 1959 (MORI No. 145204).

IV-9: IR: Markus Johannes Wolf, 11 October 1973 (MORI No. 144083).

Markus Wolf, who became the head of the DDR's foreign intelligence service late in 1952, cloaked himself in anonymity. However, as this first document shows, by 1959 he had been singled out and identified in photographs taken during the 1946 Nürnberg trials. In fact, Western intelligence probably knew as much or more about Markus Wolf than it did about many Eastern Bloc senior intelligence officers, as the second document included here, a brief biography, would suggest. The report is, nonetheless, inaccurate in some of its details. According to Wolf's memoirs, he began work for the IWF when he was recalled to Berlin in August 1951, not in 1952.[8] Wolf

---

[7] Murphy, et al., p. 138.
[8] Markus Wolf with Anne McElvoy, *Man Without A Face* (New York: Random House, 1997), p. 44.

does not mention "Department XV" in his memoirs, but recounts that the IWF was absorbed by the *Ministerium für Staatssicherheit* in 1953. In 1956 the IWF cover was dropped and the German foreign intelligence service became the *Hauptverwaltung Aufklärung* (HVA).[9]

Wolf was a highly effective intelligence chief and the HVA prospered under his leadership.

IV-10: IR: The Supply and Distribution of Foodstuffs, 3 December 1952 (MORI No. 145223).

IV-11: IR: 1. SED Proposal of Restrictions on Escape from East Germany/ 2. Plants Guards, 5 December 1952 (MORI No. 145224).

IV-12: IR: Establishment of Farm Cooperatives, 10 December 1952 (MORI No. 145225).

IV-13: IR: SED Directives on Refugees... 4 March 1953 (MORI No. 145227).

In the winter of 1952-53, even as Stalin was publicly holding up the prospect of German reunification, the East German regime proceeded with a program of ruthless Sovietization, as these intelligence reports show. At the same time, the DDR moved to tighten controls at the border in a vain effort to halt the flood of refugees. Reporting like this highlights the degree to which the East German regime depended upon diverse organs of control, deeply ramified into German society.[10] It also gives some idea of the difficulties faced by Western intelligence officers in penetrating a highly regimented, tightly controlled police state.

IV-14: Memorandum to the DDI; Subject: Soviet Interference with Berlin Rail Access, 24 November 1956 (MORI No. 6496).

Although the Soviets never again repeated their efforts to isolate Berlin from the outside world, they continued to interfere occasionally with Allied ground transportation. Each incident (such as the one described here) had potentially serious implications for the Allied garrison in Berlin, but Moscow did not allow such small-scale confrontations to escalate into a major crisis.

---

[9] Wolf, p. 46.

[10] On this, in detail, see Mary Fulbrook, *Anatomy of a Dictatorship: Inside the GDR, 1949-1989.* (Oxford: Oxford University Press, 1995).

CONFIDENTIAL

CURRENT INTELLIGENCE WEEKLY SUMMARY

7 May 1959

17/7

PART III

PATTERNS AND PERSPECTIVES

THE SOVIET ESTABLISHMENT IN KARLSHORST COMPOUND IN EAST BERLIN

The main symbol of the Soviet occupation of Berlin is the Kommandatura--the headquarters of the USSR's Berlin garrison--headed by Maj. Gen. Nikolai Feodorovich Zakharov in the 160-acre Karlshorst compound in East Berlin. Also located there are the headquarters of the Soviet state security organization (KGB), the KGB communications regiment, certain Soviet military intelligence (GRU) units, and housing for all major Soviet units stationed in East Berlin, including elements of the embassy and trade delegation. The Soviet Embassy itself is not in the compound but is located on Unterden Linden near the Brandenburg Gate. Responsibility for the over-all physical security of the compound is vested in the East German Ministry for State Security (MfS).

Kommandatura

The Kommandatura exercises all Soviet quadripartite responsibilities over Berlin and

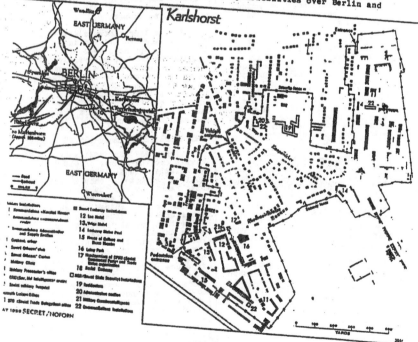

Karlshorst

SECRET/NOFORN

~~SECRET~~
CONFIDENTIAL

PART III

PATTERNS AND PERSPECTIVES

SECRET

CURRENT INTELLIGENCE WEEKLY SUMMARY

7 May 1959

access thereto, including control of the checkpoints at Babelsberg and Marienborn at the eastern and western ends of the autobahn. Its withdrawal from the city would therefore presumably indicate that the Soviet functions there were being transferred to the East Germans and might be the prelude to the legal incorporation of East Berlin into East Germany.

Soviet staff headquarters is located in the so-called Marshal House. Nearby are the Kommandatura communications center, administrative and supply offices of the garrison, and a field branch of the Soviet State Bank (Gosbank). A Military Prosecutor's Office is also attached to the Kommandatura. Outside the compound there is a Soviet officers' club; inside, there is a stadium, a swimming pool and gym facilities, and an officers' mess.

In addition, a military clinic under the general direction of the Central Military Hospital at Berlin-Oberschoeneweide provides medical care not only to Soviet troops but to members of the embassy and trade delegation. The Kommandatura also maintains a hotel, a bachelor officers' quarters, and an apartment building, and there is a hunt club for military and civilian personnel.

The group of Soviet military advisers to the East German People's Army residing in the compound has been in the process of dissolution in recent months, and most of these officers reportedly have returned to the USSR. Similarly, the group of Soviet Ministry of Interior (MVD) officers attached to the MfS is being disbanded.

Guard functions for military headquarters are furnished by the Soviet 133rd Independent Guard Battalion, which also provides guards for Spandau prison

and for maintaining control on the US-Soviet sector border.

In recent months Moscow has made various preparations which will permit the withdrawal of the Kommandatura with little or no further notice. It has, however, also taken steps to provide cover under which certain Soviet units—notably the KGB and GRU—could continue to function within the compound. Military units have not withdrawn, and construction in progress outside the city—such as the high-priority building project in the neighborhood of Bernau and Wandlitz—has not been specifically identified for the use of Kommandatura elements. On the other hand, the units have not yet received their 1959 funds for the maintenance of property and housing, and even the commanders reportedly do not know what to expect.

Soviet long-distance telephone exchange facilities in Karlshorst, operated by Soviet military personnel, reportedly are to be dismantled in the near future and removed to an unidentified location. There is some evidence that the Soviet Embassy expects to take over this function from the Kommandatura when the withdrawal occurs.

Soviet Military Intelligence

Since 1957 the USSR has sharply cut the number of GRU installations in Karlshorst, until at present the only major units remaining are the Agent Operations Section and what are believed to be combined elements of the Strategic Intelligence Residentura, naval intelligence, and an intelligence advisory group. GRU reportedly intends to move part of its staff to the headquarters of the Soviet Group of Forces in Germany (GSFG) in Wuensdorf but will leave as many operational personnel as possible under cover of the military attaché section of the Soviet Embassy.

SECRET

CURRENT INTELLIGENCE WEEKLY SUMMARY

7 May 1959

Embassy and Trade Delegation

The Soviet Embassy in East Berlin, while outside the compound, has several installations and extensive housing facilities inside. These include the Lux Hotel, used for VIP housing; the Volga Hotel; a motor pool; a house of culture, which supervises the Dram Theater; an amusement area in Letny Park; a film storage and distribution center; and a library. Headquarters of the Soviet Communist party and trade-union organizations, both embassy connected, are also located here. In addition, the embassy maintains an elementary and secondary school outside the compound and a kindergarten and vocational schools inside.

The trade delegation, like the embassy, has its main offices on Unter den Linden and, with the exception of the liaison office of the Wismuth uranium-mining company, only housing and support units are located within the Karlshorst compound. The liaison office's function is to assure swift and uninterrupted deliveries from the Wismuth mines to the USSR.

There is every indication that these civilian installations will remain in the compound, although certain changes may be made in physical arrangements. For example, the Volga Hotel reportedly was released to East German authorities on 1 March, but its restaurant still functions under embassy management. Furthermore, the Dram Theater has ordered an expensive new movie projector, suggesting that there is no intention of withdrawing. Finally, there have been reports that the trade delegation is to be merged with the embassy's economic section. The delegation's motor pool has already been consolidated with that of the embassy inside the compound.

KGB Rezidentura

KGB installations dot the Karlshorst compound. The four-story Rezidentura—the former St. Antonius Hospital—houses all the elements necessary for a self-contained intelligence unit. It is surrounded by a special fence and is under the surveillance of KGB-controlled Soviet guards. Subsidiary to this headquarters are various other KGB administrative and housing units, including a clinic, a hotel, and a motor pool.

KGB counterintelligence headquarters, located adjacent to the Military Prosecutor's Office, includes a section responsible for the loyalty and security of Soviet forces in the Berlin garrison. Certain KGB advisers attached to MfS headquarters also maintain offices there and live in the compound. KGB communications installations are believed to be housed at three points, one within the Kommandatura headquarters area, another on Ehrenfelsstrasse, and the third in the KGB administrative section on Frankestrasse.

There have been reports that the KGB will vacate the Rezidentura and move its headquarters and all administrative, technical, and communications sections out of Berlin to nearby areas. A German source recently stated that communications personnel had been moved out of the Frankestrasse unit to an unidentified location. Furniture from several housing units reportedly was recently removed on KGB trucks—in two instances to Bernau. This suggests that at least some KGB facilities may move to the Bernau-Wandlitz site.

In recent weeks, the KGB appears to have taken steps to place some of its services under cover. Effective 1 April

SECRET

CURRENT INTELLIGENCE WEEKLY SUMMARY

7 May 1959

the administrative section reportedly instructed German firms and public utilities to address bills to the Soviet Embassy but gave an address in the compound. During the first quarter of 1959, some 35 apartments were released by the KGB to the MfS. Since there was no indication that the Soviet families had moved out, it appears that some KGB personnel, at least, may continue under MfS cover.

Concurrently, in order to tighten security, the KGB offices have dismissed their German employees. Some of the work formerly done by Germans in the motor pool will be performed by Soviet personnel, and cleaning and janitoring responsibilities are to be carried out by Soviet rather than German women.

Security Precautions

Karlshorst compound is surrounded by a fence six feet high which was repaired last year at considerable expense; this fence is patrolled by well-armed MfS guards. At night these guards extend their patrols into the compound area, but they no longer are accompanied by dogs. The compound can be entered through either the main vehicle entrance on Waldow Allee or through certain other approved gates; a pass is required with a different document for the various categories of Soviet and East German personnel.

An intensive screening of all East German employees was begun last year, and in recent weeks Soviet authorities have been sharply reducing the number of German employees in the compound. Some individuals who had worked for Soviet authorities since 1945 have been dismissed, and a well-integrated system of MfS informers has been established among the remaining German employees. (SECRET NOFORN)

*   *   *

SECRET

DIRECTORATE OF
PLANS

Soviet Intelligence

THE KGB IN EAST GERMANY—
AN AGENT DEFECTOR SUMMARY OF
FACILITIES, TARGETS & TRADECRAFT

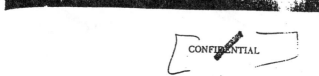

PART III. KGB FACILITIES IN EAST GERMANY (DDR)

SOVIET INSTALLATIONS AVAILABLE TO THE KGB

The Karlshorst Rezidentura

The Karlshorst *Rezidentura* is located in a building inside a compound which is bound by four streets: Bodenmaiser Weg, Zwieseler Strasse, Dewetallee and Arberstrasse. There are two entrances to the compound, one on Dewetallee, the other on Bodenmaiser Weg. One may drive into the area through Dewetallee and, from the south, through the entrance at the control point on the Rheinstrasse. This latter entrance is directly at the intersection of Rheinstrasse and Koepenicker Allee. The building itself is multi-storied and gives the appearance of a barracks or caserne. There are a number of high antenna masts on the roof, all connected to each other by cables; thus, the building is easily recognizable and the masts are visible from afar. (*Source Comment:* He has never entered the building and therefore can provide no description of the interior.) Before moving into the present *Rezidentura*, the KGB had offices in the large building located on the corner of Frankestrasse and Koepenicker Allee.

The regular office hours at the *Rezidentura* are from 0800-1300 hours, 1400-1600 hours. Evidently there is a rotating duty roster which all KGB case officers are subject to since each case officer serves periodically as Duty Officer and remains in the *Rezidentura* overnight. Even though a KGB officer works the evening before, he is in the office punctually in the morning. Source frequently called about 0800 hours and found his KGB contact already at work. An agent (such as Source) wishing to contact his case officer after hours does not call the Duty Officer at the *Rezidentura*, but contacts his case officer directly at the latter's home, no matter what the hour. (*Source Comment:* The Duty Officer's function is not to serve as a communication channel between the *Rezidentura* and the agents. The Duty Officer is probably in charge

of the physical security of the *Rezidentura*.) Every Monday morning, KGB case officers meet for their weekly political discussion. Party meetings take place on an irregular basis.

Many of the KGB case officers who were working in the Karlshorst *Rezidentura* had identity documents issued by the DDR Foreign Ministry which stated that the bearer was a member of the USSR Embassy in the DDR.

The Soviet Hospital in East Berlin

There is a Soviet hospital, used by both Soviet Embassy personnel and the KGB, which is located in the area bounded by Rummelsburgerstrasse, Hermann Duncker Strasse, and Am Walde. The hospital entrance, which is on Hermann Duncker Strasse, is guarded at all times by a Soviet soldier.

The Motor Pool in East Berlin

The motor pool and repair facilities for vehicles used by all Soviet installations in East Berlin, including the KGB, is located at the intersection of Rummelsburger Landstrasse and Grenzweg on the pre-war property of the *Allgemeine Elektrizitaets Gesellschaft* (AEG). Its official designation is "Motor Pool of the Soviet Embassy." The entrance, which is always guarded by an armed Soviet soldier, is on Grenzweg. There is a formal control point through which visitors must pass. Although Source never actually entered the motor pool, he did notice in passing that most of the cars are of Western manufacture. The majority are Volkswagens, but there are some Moskvich cars and a few Wartburgs. Source saw no Skodas. Soviet army mechanics work on the cars.

Vehicles used by the KGB bear regular East Berlin registrations which are issued by the MfS. Prior to the end of 1968, all Soviet vehicles were licensed through the Soviet Embassy. Toward the end of 1968, vehicles of all embassies in the DDR were issued red license plates to differentiate the

9

embassy vehicles from regular DDR cars. Thus in order to remain anonymous, the KGB had to change the system of registering their cars through the embassy.

Shopping Facilities in East Berlin

The Soviets do not have exclusive shopping facilities similar to some of the Western countries, which provide their personnel with goods in exchange for the respective Western currency. However, there is a store, stocking mainly Soviet goods, located in Andernacher Strasse where Soviets do shop. Anyone, including West Berliners, DDR citizens and members of the Allied military from West Berlin, may shop there. All the employees of the store are Soviet nationals and can speak only Russian.

Rest Homes in the DDR

Source was aware of the existence of only one KGB vacation facility—a house located on a lake near Neustrelitz. KGB case officers and families usually use vacation and recreation facilities which belong to the MfS. One such MfS house is located on a lake east of Berlin. Also, there is an MfS vacation house in Masserberg, Thuringia. Source never used any of these facilities.

KGB District Offices in the DDR

KGB District Offices are located in Soviet *Kommandatura* buildings. Each Soviet *Kommandatura* is well known in the headquarters town, and directions for finding it can be easily obtained by inquiring on the street. Each KGB District Office, depending upon the size of the district, contains from five to twenty KGB officers. While Source was not permitted entry to the Karlshorst *Rezidentura* building, he could walk directly into any KGB District Office. Although Source has not visited all of the District Offices, he has dealt with the KGB chief or other KGB officers of the following District Offices: Leipzig, Gera, Magdeburg, Neustrelitz, Frankfurt/Oder, Suhl, and Rostock. KGB District Chiefs maintain close contact with the Karlshorst *Rezidentura* and frequently travel to East Berlin. KGB case officers from Karlshorst also frequently visit KGB District Offices.

Source did not notice any radios or tape recorders in any of the KGB District Offices he visited. Neither did he see any Soviet females in these offices.

(1) *The District Office in Magdeburg:* This KGB District Office is located in the Soviet *Kommandatura*, a large building. There is a fence around the building and an armed Soviet soldier stands guard in an anteroom just inside the entrance. Source, who visited the Magdeburg District Office only once, in 1957, could not pinpoint the location of the KGB offices in the building because there were so many hallways and turns involved in getting to the KGB section. He saw only one room of the KGB section. A relatively small room, it contained a safe with a key lock, one desk, and a long conference table which was pushed against the desk in T-formation. He is certain that there were other KGB rooms in this building, since the KGB case officer he dealt with at the time would leave the room, walk a few paces, and, judging by the sound of opening and closing doors, enter another room.

(2) *The District Office in Gera:* The KGB office is located in the Soviet *Kommandatura*, a three-story building which is opposite (kitty-corner) to the railroad station. There was no guard posted outside the building. However, in an anteroom just inside the entrance to the building, there is a small guard room, with a glass window, where a visitor was required to report on entering the building. The KGB occupied several rooms on the top floor. Source saw only one room in the KGB section. The room was small. It contained a safe with a key lock, a desk, and a conference table which was pushed against the desk in T-formation. Source believed, but is not certain, that the door to this room was padded on the inside.

(3) *The District Office in Neustrelitz:* The KGB District Office in Neustrelitz is located in the Soviet *Kommandatura*, a three-story building. The building is surrounded by a brick wall. In one side of the wall, there is an iron gate through which cars may drive into a courtyard. The KGB office which Source visited was located on the second or third floor. The room was a very large one and contained a safe with a key lock, a desk, and large conference table which was pushed against the desk in T-formation.

10

(4) *The District Office in Suhl:* The Suhl KGB office is located in the Soviet *Kommandatura* building and is approximately a five-minute walk from the Suhl Railroad Station. Across the street from the *Kommandatura* is a small hill with a building which may be either a church or a government office. The *Kommandatura*, a two-story building, is about the size of a four-family house. It sits directly on the street and is surrounded by a metal fence. There is a yard which contains a front garden. There is no space inside the yard for automobiles, which must be parked on the street. The gate through the metal fence is always kept locked. Entrance is gained by ringing a bell. The visitor must then state his business to an armed Soviet soldier who comes to the gate. Source was never confronted with this situation, since he was always in the company of a KGB case officer who would take care of any explanations to the soldier.

Source was in only one room of the KGB section. This office was located on the top floor, on the right hand side as one faces the building from the street. The room contained two desks, a metal safe with a key lock, a table, and a picture of Lenin. There was a telephone in the room, telephone number unknown. However, the telephone number was an extension from the MfS District Office. The entrance door to the room was padded on the inside. Source believes that this one room housed the entire KGB District Office in Suhl. Source knew of two KGB officers there: a Colonel (name unknown) whose private residence was located in Suhl at Schmiedefeldstrasse 83, first floor left, and another officer known as Gennadiy.

TELEPHONE AND POSTAL SERVICES IN THE DDR

Telephone and Telegraph Communications

Only local calls can be made from the telephone booths located on the sidewalks in East Berlin.

Long-distance telephone calls can be made from all Post Offices in East Berlin. Each has a "Long-distance telephone section" from which one may place a long-distance call. Before placing the call, the caller must deposit DME 5 or DME 10 with the clerk as insurance that the caller will not disappear without paying the bill. The caller, after placing the deposit, gives the clerk the telephone number to be called and the city wherein it is lo-

cated. He then waits in the lobby of the Post Office until the clerk pages him and assigns him to a telephone booth. The booths are numbered and have doors to insure privacy. No identification documents are required to place a long-distance call. Telephone calls to most countries, including the United States but excluding West Germany, can be put through in less than ten minutes' time. Telephone calls to West Germany can take as long as five or six hours because there are so few lines available, and many calls are continuously placed between East and West Germany. The DDR Government refuses to install additional lines, thus the delay in telephone traffic. (*Source Comment:* In placing some long-distance calls, he would wait only a few minutes, then cancel the call, since any delay in completing the call might indicate the possibility that, either routinely or for some specific reason, the call was being monitored.)

Long-distance calls can also be placed from one's own home or from a public place, such as a hotel or restaurant. These latter have the facilities and permit the placing of calls, knowing the caller will remain to pay the costs.

Telegrams can be sent from Post Offices or by private telephone, in which case the cost of the telegram is charged to the telephone owner. No identification documents are required to send a telegram from the Post Office. While there is a section on the telegram which the sender has to fill in regarding the sender's name and address, one may use any name and address, or even no name and address, except that the latter would look suspicious.

Postal Services and Censorship

Postage stamps can be purchased at Post Offices, stationery stores, hotels, and newspaper stands. Registered letters can be sent only from a Post Office. No identity documents are needed to send registered letters. When registered letters are delivered to the addressee's home, no identity document need be shown to take possession of the letter, but the addressee must sign for it. If the addressee is not at home, the mailman leaves a slip of paper notifying the resident that there is some registered mail for him, whereupon he must go to the Post Office to pick it up. When picking up registered letters at the Post Office, the addressee

11

must show identity documents. Identity documents must also be shown when picking up money orders or packages at the Post Office.

Source had no information concerning routine censorship imposed on domestic mail within the DDR. International mail is censored on a spot-check basis. The exception to the aforementioned is mail addressed to or sent by individuals whose names are placed on a "Watchlist."

Post Office boxes can be rented by going to the postmaster's office, filling out a form requesting the rental of a Post Office box, and producing identity documents. No reason need be given for wanting to rent the box. The box rental is due and payable quarterly at one of the Post Office windows. No identity documents need be shown when paying the rental. The payer merely gives his box number and pays the fee.

LIAISON BETWEEN THE KGB AND THE MfS IN THE DDR

In 1953 Source's KGB case officer told him that the top echelon of the MfS knew of Source's employment as a full-time KGB agent in the DDR, presumably as Karl HAGER.

Source has little knowledge of the MfS since he never worked with the MfS on any operation. Only once was an MfS agent turned over to him by an MfS officer.

From the time of Source's arrival in the DDR in 1953 until the early 1960's, he noted that the KGB had appeared to have sufficient money at its disposal for conducting any type of intelligence operation. Additionally, the KGB received whatever operational support (e.g., name checks, documentation, backstopping, etc.) it required immediately from the MfS whenever that was considered necessary. During this period, it appeared to Source that the KGB pretty much ran things in the DDR as far as intelligence matters were concerned. In 1963, however, Source learned from three friends who were also full-time agents of the KGB that all of the KGB *Hauptamtlicher Mitarbeiter* in the DDR, with the exception of Source, were to be dismissed from the KGB. This was confirmed to Source by his KGB Section Chief. Source was told that he was too valuable to the KGB and thus would not be released. Those *Hauptamtlicher*

Mitarbeiter who were dropped by the KGB were picked up by the MfS, according to statements later made to Source by one of his subsequent KGB case officers and by a former *Hauptamtlicher Mitarbeiter*. As far as Source could determine, this mass dismissal of *Hauptamtlicher Mitarbeiter* was due to the probability that the KGB apparently no longer had sufficient funds for salaries. In this regard, Source believed that some of the KGB budget in the DDR was derived from occupation costs levied on the DDR (a treaty was apparently reached between the USSR and the DDR, reducing the latter's occupation payments). This loss of revenue to the Soviets in the DDR might have caused the dismissal of Source's colleagues. Source also noted that after 1963 the KGB was not nearly as generous with its gifts and bonuses as it had previously been. Another factor, in Source's opinion, was the growing feeling of independence and national sovereignty of the DDR. One of Source's KGB case officers and a KGB officer from one of the District Offices told Source independently, and at different times, that "now we are only guests here . . . we can only request things from the MfS, not demand." Additionally, a former *Hauptamtlicher Mitarbeiter* told Source in about 1967 that the MfS no longer did things the way the Soviets wanted.

It is a basic rule of the KGB in the DDR that the MfS should know as little as possible about KGB activities. This rule was repeatedly violated, as Source notes. Many of the leads he worked on came from the MfS, and considerable operational support was afforded by the MfS even in those cases where they did not supply the leads. Sometimes they helped Source make an initial contact. Additionally, the MfS is evidently aware of all the leads which are followed up by the KGB Liaison Officer to the MfS. (*Comment:* A Colonel LESSIN, first name unknown, is the KGB Liaison Officer who is called by the MfS border guards whenever persons of operational interest pass through the East/West Berlin border-crossing point.)

It is Source's opinion that the KGB and the MfS have agreed that operations in the DDR involving the American target are to be handled by the KGB. Source bases this opinion on the fact that all of the leads, either offered or supported by the MfS, invariably dealt with the American target. He does not know whether there is a similar agree-

12

ment whereby the West German target is handled solely by the MfS. He doubts that such an agreement exists since he knows that the West German target is also worked on by the KGB. He knows of no case involving a West German citizen that the KGB developed itself and then later exposed to the MfS or for which any operational support was requested from the MfS. Once the KGB had a unilateral operation going, it was kept unilateral. There were no restrictions or prohibitions whatsoever on the KGB in regard to its recruitment of DDR citizens. However, Source was emphatically convinced that the MfS, in turn, was not allowed to recruit or otherwise make any operational use of a Soviet citizen without the knowledge, consent and assistance of the KGB.

At the District-Office level of the KGB, liaison between the KGB and MfS personnel was usually on a very close and personal basis. For example, Source knows that the KGB Chief in Suhl and the KGB Chief in Neustrelitz often went hunting with their MfS counterparts. The KGB Chief in Neustrelitz once turned down Source's offer for lunch, saying that he felt he should go hunting with his MfS colleague to cement their rapport and relationship.

As stated above, KGB officers and families usually use vacation and recreation facilities which belong to the MfS. Apparently, since Source was told about it by his KGB case officers, neither the KGB nor the MfS had any qualms about mixing a large number of their staff officers and families at the vacation home in Masserberg, Thuringia. Source had no information regarding its administration, since he was never there, but he presumes that the MfS and KGB officers using the Masserberg facility went there under some kind of alias.

23 Jul 58

SOVIET INTELLIGENCE AND SECURITY

Lt Gen E. P. PITOVRANOV

<u>Source:</u>   A clandestine source of established authenticity

<u>Date of Information:</u>   May 1955 - April 1956

I. <u>INTRODUCTION</u>

   1.   This report, based on information available from this source
as of 22 Jul 58, is one of a series on senior military intelligence
and KGB officers in East Germany.

II. <u>BACKGROUND</u>

   2.   <u>Full Name:</u>   Evgenii ("Zhenya") Petrovich PITOVRANOV

        <u>Rank:</u>   Lieutenant General

        <u>Assignment:</u>   Chief KGB Residentura, BERLIN, and
concurrently, Senior Counsellor at the
Soviet Embassy, BERLIN.

        <u>Date of Birth:</u>   Estimated between 1910 - 1915.

        <u>Residence in USSR:</u> MOSCOW (Tel No K-4 1751)

   3.   <u>Wife:</u>   Elisaveta Vasil'evna PITOVRANOVA

        <u>Children:</u>   Daughter (first name possibly Gavrilova).
There were other children in the household
in BERLIN but it is not certain whether they
were PITOVRANOV's children or grandchildren
(see paras 6 and 7).

.../...

TOP SECRET

Other Relatives: PITOVRANO	Dr Natalya Vasil'ovna PETROVA, probably PITOVRANOV's sister-in-law. (This relationship was not conclusively established, but is based on her sharing the same patronymic with his wife, and a request by PITOVRANOV to his wife, after a family conversation, to "kiss Natalya and Mama for me"; on 11 Mar 56 PITOVRANOV booked a private telephone call to Dr PETROVA of the "First Surgical Section" of a hospital in MOSCOW, Tel No K-6 8974; (the only N.V. PETROVA listed in the 1954 edition of the MOSCOW Telephone Directory resided at 6, Shchuseva Ulitsa Tel No K-4 6696).
4. Education and Accent:	No information is available from source material on PITOVRANOV's educational background other than that he speaks as a well-educated man with a Great Russian (MOSCOW) accent.

III.   OTHER PERSONAL PARTICULARS

5.   Details of Family:

Mme PITOVRANOV's rather listless and apathetic manner during her telephone conversations gave the impression that she was either a sick person or one of negative personality. She seemed unable to raise any enthusiasm when appealed to by her husband on 20 Oct 55 to fly back from MOSCOW to BERLIN on the following day. She agreed only after much prompting, despite the fact that her younger children (or possibly grandchildren) appeared to be in Germany. (Her reaction may have arisen from the fact that she had just suffered the loss of her mother, Elisaveta Ivanovna (snu), who died on 17 Oct 55). PITOVRANOVA was noticeably apathetic, however, in a February 1956 discussion with a staff officer of Marshal A.A. GRECHKO (CinC, GSFG) on the question of certain domestic transactions for Mme GRECHKO.

6.   Mme PITOVRANOV was in MOSCOW again in December 1955 and flew back to BERLIN with her granddaughter on the 24th or 25th of that month. On 10 Jan 56 she flew again to MOSCOW, this time with her daughter, and possibly granddaughter, but was present in BERLIN on 23 Feb 56 when she attended the Red Army Day reception at the Soviet Embassy.

7.   An exact identification of the junior members of the family was not possible from the few passing references available in source material. PITOVRANOV once said, in answer to his wife's telephone enquiry from MOSCOW, that "the children are doing their lessons" and mentioned "Serosha" (Sergei) by name. Other references to a daughter and granddaughter, however, made in connection with bookings of plane flights, leave the question open as to whether they were in fact PITOVRANOV's children or grandchildren.

...../......

TOP SECRET

8. <u>Recreations</u>: Shooting, fishing, and tennis.

IV. <u>CHARACTER AND EFFICIENCY</u>

9.   There is evidence that PITOVRANOV was quick and incisive when making decisions and was esteemed as a man who backs up his subordinates. If it is assumed that the efficiency of his unit reflected his own capabilities, then on at least one occasion he was awarded a considerable compliment by a military intelligence colonel who had recourse to PITOVRANOV and his organization for help with an operation.

10.   Col M.G. BELOV (Chief of an element in BERLIN subordinate to the Intelligence Directorate, HQ, GSFG) approached the KGB Residentura for help and co-operation with some agent activities on 17 Dec 55. This involved calling on the chiefs of five departments and finally discussing the matter with PITOVRANOV. The results, as described by BELOV to Col VI.I. SMIRNOV and Lt Col Yu.P. BUIKOV (both of the Operations Department, Intelligence Directorate, HQ, GSFG), were that PITOVRANOV had "stated his decisions swiftly" and had said that he would "give the order immediately."

11.   Later, in reply to SMIRNOV's query as to the success of the operation, BELOV said that it had gone excellently - in fact, he had been told that it was "as quick as lightning" and nobody had noticed anything. PITOVRANOV's people had made all the security arrangements, as well as directing the affair, and had done it very well.

12.   A tribute to PITOVRANOV was paid by M.I. MARCHENKO (Deputy Chief, Department 2, KGB Residentura element, STEGMAR-SCHOENAU) while discussing pressure of work with a friend: he said that things were so hot it was "like sitting on a powder barrel," but it was very good working with PITOVRANOV as "he is a fighter and stands up for his people."

13.   Source has provided some indication of PITOVRANOV's standing with senior officers outside the KGB. In brief talks with Maj Gen MALYI (Chief, Frontier Control Directorate, HQ, GSFG) and Maj Gen P.V. VASHURA (Deputy Chief, Political Directorate, HQ, GSFG) it was clear that they both treated him with every respect. PITOVRANOV in his turn spoke quietly and politely but with noticeable firmness and authority.

14.   Maj Gen P.A. DIBROVA (Commandant, Soviet Garrison, BERLIN) was somewhat disdainful about PITOVRANOV's plan for hunting wild boar at night with the use of beaters and infra-red telescopic sights. DIBROVA commented to Lt Gen A.Ya. KALYAGIN (GSFG liaison with DDR), that PITOVRANOV was a fool to introduce a system which reflected on his hunting ability; he was also concerned over the danger of some of the local population getting killed in the process.

V. <u>MOVEMENTS AND OTHER ACTIVITIES</u>

15.   PITOVRANOV flew back from MOSCOW to Germany on or about 14 Aug 55. This was revealed in a conversation on 13 August with Maj Gen VASHURA who, having just returned from MOSCOW himself, advised PITOVRANOV to fly back with an aircraft which was available on the following day. The reasons for this visit to MOSCOW, and its duration,

...../....

- 4 -

are not known to source.

16.   There is evidence that PITOVRANOV paid a visit to STAHNSDORF between 23 and 27 Jan 56. Capt M.T. KOZYREV (KGB CI officer with 260 Independent Line Construction Battalion, then at STAHNSDORF) on 30 January tried to contact his superior officer, Col G.V. SHATALOV (Chief, KGB CI Department, in BERLIN). Failing to do so, he gave Lt Col V.M. SPIVAKOV (SHATALOV's deputy) the news that PITOVRANOV had come "here to me", but he did not know on what business. SPIVAKOV replied that KOZYREV, if invited by PITOVRANOV, was to go to the Residentura and tell him all he wanted to know. The purpose of PITOVRANOV's visit may have been to investigate personally the after-effects of the defection of Lt I.V. OVCHINNIKOV from the 28 Special Purpose Radio Regiment (HQ, STAHNSDORF; subordinate to the GSFG Intelligence Directorate); STAHNSDORF was also the location of a KGB Radio Intercept Station.

17.   On 28 Jan 56 PITOVRANOV flew to MOSCOW and on 6 February an aircraft was sent from East Germany to MOSCOW to bring him back. The take-off for the return journey was to be at PITOVRANOV's convenience. G.M. PUSHKIN (Soviet Ambassador to the DDR) wished to be given the place of landing in MOSCOW so that he could inform PITOVRANOV.

18.   On 12 Feb 56 he flew again to MOSCOW, this time in the company of Marshal GRECHKO and Ambassador PUSHKIN, presumably for the Twentieth Congress, CPSU. His date of return is not known to source, but his presence in BERLIN again was confirmed on 12 Mar 56.

19.   PITOVRANOV paid a visit to KARL-MARX-STADT (CHEMNITZ) on 11 or 12 Apr 56. This was stated by BEDIN (fnu; KGB advisor to the East German Ministry for State Security) when receiving instructions for submitting to PITOVRANOV a report on an industrial explosion.

VI.   FRIENDS AND CONTACTS

20.   In view of PITOVRANOV's status, those personalities who appear to have connections with him only as a result of working relationships have been included, as also those whose identity and therefore importance could not be defined by source.

B.S. ALEKSEIKO

21.   The wife of Boris Sergeevich ALEKSEIKO, (Head, 'Soviet Export Film' office, BERLIN) was able to supply the BERLIN home telephone number of the PITOVRANOV's at the request of Maj Gen G.K. TSINEV (Chief, KGB Third [CI] Directorate, POTSDAM).

S.T. ASTAVIN

22.   The "Sergei Timofeevich" who called on PITOVRANOV on 18 Oct 55 was probably Sergei Timofeevich ASTAVIN (Chief, Political Department, Soviet Embassy, BERLIN, who dealt with WISMUT affairs). On this occasion he went to the cinema with PITOVRANOV and the latter's deputy, Col M.N. GOLOVKOV, the wives of both then being in the USSR.

.../...

A.A. GRECHKO

23. The PITOVRANOV's relationship with Marshal Andrei Antonovich GRECHKO and Mme GRECHKO were friendly, as far as can be judged from source material, but there is no evidence that they extended beyond a sympathetic regard for each other in their appointed spheres. GRECHKO sent a telegram of congratulation to "Evgenii Petrovich" on the anniversary of the October Revolution, wishing him success in his activities "from the bottom of my heart", and Mme GRECHKO selected Mme PITOVRANOV as the most suitably prominent escort for her daughter at the Red Army Day reception in 1956. Mme GRECHKO was also concerned with Mme PITOVRANOV in transactions involving the selection of a watch for the former and the selling of skins or furs.

V.V. NARUDDINOV/NARUBINOV and Ya.S. NASRIDDINOVA

24. Viktor Vasil'evich NARUDDINOV was a deputy to the Supreme Soviet and First Secretary of the TASHKENT City Party Committee. He was member of a delegation of deputies to the Supreme Soviet which was touring the DDR in November/December 1955. On 4 December he was in KARL-MARX-STADT (CHEMNITZ) and telephoned his wife Yadgar Sadykovna NASRIDDINOVA from the Soviet Consulate. NASRIDDINOVA was in MOSCOW and had just attended a birthday party given by FURTSEVA (presumably E.A. FURTSEVA of the Central Committee). They discussed political matters in both the Russian and Turkman languages. NARUDDINOV also told his wife that "many of the comrades" who knew her sent their greetings, and mentioned PUSHKIN (see para 25), PITOVRANOV, KISELEV (u/i) and GUSEV (u/i, at KARL-MARX-STADT) in that order.

> Comment: Another source has confirmed that a Ya.S. NASRIDDINOVA was a member of the Central Committee elected at the 20th Party Congress in February 1956. Despite the discrepancy in names there is considerable evidence that the speakers were husband and wife.

G.M. PUSHKIN

25. PITOVRANOV's official position (Senior Counsellor) with the Soviet Embassy in East BERLIN appeared to involve some degree of active partnership with Ambassador Georgii Maksimovich PUSHKIN. Source was unable to determine PUSHKIN's exact position vis-a-vis PITOVRANOV, i.e., whether he played a role more significant than acting as a "front" for the latter.

PUZANOV (fnu)

26. On the orders of PITOVRANOV, a message was relayed on 7 or 8 Dec 55 to the Frontier Control Directorate, HQ, GSFG, on the subject of PUZANOV and his wife, who apparently had recently arrived in BERLIN. They were leaving BERLIN the next day via the same check point on route for BAD BRAMBACH (Bezirk KARL-MARX-STADT, on the borders of Czechoslovakia), and they would arrive at the

.../...

frontier at 1600 hours. They would be escorted by N.M. GALUSHIN (Chief of KGB Residentura Secretariat) and would call at LEIPZIG on the way.

P.V. VASHURA

27.   Some degree of familiarity was shown by Maj Gen Petr Vladimirovich VASHURA when, addressing PITOVRANOV by first name and patronymic, he explained why he had been unable to fulfil an arrangement to travel together with the latter on a return flight from MOSCOW to Germany (see also para 14). Since neither used the intimate form of speech and since VASHURA showed a marked deference to PITOVRANOV, this was, presumably, a friendly working relationship. (Subsequently, according to other sources, VASHURA was promoted to become Chief of the GSFG Political Directorate).

Antonina Pavlovna (snu)

28.   A lady of this name wished the news of the death of PITOVRANOV's mother-in-law to be passed to him by his deputy, Col GOLOVKOV, should he not already have heard from Mme PITOVRANOVA. This message was relayed to GOLOVKOV by his wife, who was in MOSCOW at that time.

Newspaper Editor

29.   On 14 Sep 55, PITOVRANOV booked a telephone call to "the editor of the newspaper TSINYA in RIGA." No information is available from source to identify the editor or to explain this action.

E N D

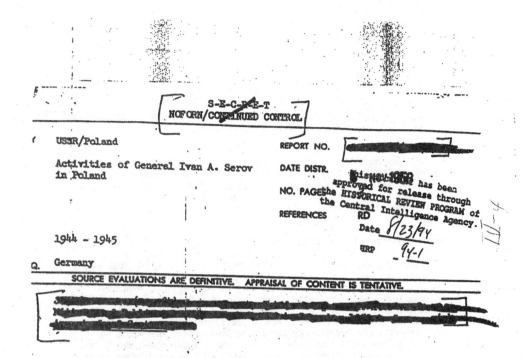

S-E-C-R-E-T
NOFORN/CONTINUED CONTROL

USSR/Poland

Activities of General Ivan A. Serov
in Poland

REPORT NO.

DATE DISTR.

NO. PAGES

REFERENCES   RD

1944 - 1945

Q.   Germany

SOURCE EVALUATIONS ARE DEFINITIVE.   APPRAISAL OF CONTENT IS TENTATIVE.

1. Source first met General /Ivan Aleksandrovich/ SEROV in the fall of
    1944 in Wolomin, Poland, where SEROV, who was then head of all
    Soviet SMERSH operational groups in Poland, had his headquarters.1
    SEROV was introduced to source as General IVANOV, and this is the
    only name source knows him to have used while in Poland. From
    other Soviets source learned soon after this meeting that IVANOV's
    true name was SEROV. Source has also positively identified
    photographs of SEROV as the man he knew under the name of IVANOV.
    Source does not know the name MALINOV and has never heard this name
    in connection with SEROV. Source states the following facts from
    very close personal association with SEROV during 1944-1945, and
    from information obtained from other Soviets attached to SMERSH,
    with whom source lived and worked during this period.

2. SEROV arrived in Poland with the advancing Red Army in 1944 as the
    head of SMERSH ("Death to Spies," Soviet Military Counter-Intelligence).
    His first headquarters were in Lublin, then these were transferred to
    Wolomin, then - about early 1945 - to the Warsaw suburb of Praga on
    Sieradzka Street. About May 1945, sometime after the fall of Berlin,
    when the headquarters of the Soviet Army were transferred to Germany,
    SEROV also transferred to Germany, and after that date had nothing
    more to do with Polish affairs and as far as source knows never
    returned to Poland.

3. Successors to SEROV as top Soviet security officer in Poland were
    the following generals, all of whom are believed to have been officers
    of the NKVD: /Nikolay Nikolayevich/ SELIVANOVSKIY (1945 - for unknown
    period), DAVIDOV (unknown period up to ca. 1951-1952), Nikolay Kuzmich
    KOVALCHUK (ca. 1951 to 1953), and LALIN (from ca. 1953 for an unknown

S-E-C-R-E-T
NOFORN/CONTINUED CONTROL

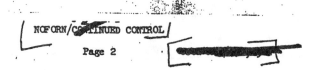

period). During SEROV's tenure of office as chief of SMERSH in Poland (1944-1945), one of his subordinates was a General MELNIKOV, also personally known to source. Source at no time has heard the name MALINOV, or of anyone else, other than the above named generals, who was the chief Soviet security officer in Poland.

4. During SEROV's stay in Poland he was exceedingly active in all security matters. He personally planned, directed, and was informed of all security cases of significance. No operations were run, or prominent individuals arrested, without his knowledge and approval, and, according to source, "all security actions were under his personal supervision and personal care." SEROV was responsible for counterespionage in Poland, and personally saw all interesting documents and reports, personally attended portions of most interesting interrogations, etc. According to source, he personally had his hand in almost every case, and knew most details of everything that was being done in counterespionage in Poland. He had the overall direction of all operations against the AK (Home Army, non-Communist underground), the SN (Peasant Party), etc. He devised the plan for the arrest of Wincenty WITOS, leader of the Peasant Party. He personally recruited many agents, including Boleslaw PIASECKI, now chairman of the PAX organization of proregime Catholics; BIENKOWSKI, AK leader who was later in the Polish Parliament; Tadeusz REK, who was Vice Minister of Justice in 1953; one unidentified agent with the pseudonym ATAMAN; and an unidentified woman from Lublin who had been active there in the AK and who identified to him all AK personnel in that area.

5. SEROV was unusually energetic and worked very long hours. He often woke source in the middle of the night to arrest a particular individual of interest to him in an investigation. He also took one of source's agents, a woman, GRUBER (fnu), born ca. 1918-1919, with him to Germany when he left to use her in operations there. An insight into SEROV's operational mentality can be had from the following incident. Source first met SEROV at a meeting which had been arranged in Wolomin in order that SEROV express his views regarding the future of a certain case. The case was that of the AK leader of the Warsaw district, Colonel "ALEKSANDER", who had been arrested by the MO (Citizens Militia), and whom the leader of the MO for the Warsaw district, Grzegorz KORCZINSKI - today head of Polish Military Intelligence (Q-II) - wanted to liquidate on the spot. SEROV rejected this proposal, and ordered the case taken over by the Soviets, pointing out to KORCZINSKI that "ALEKSANDER" could and should be made to talk, thereby being much more useful in the CE investigation than if he were dead.

6. Source believes that SEROV was unquestionably the motivating force behind the arrest of the 16 Polish underground leaders in 1945 who revealed themselves to the Soviets after being

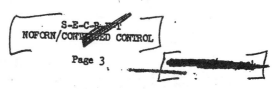

S-E-C-R-E-T
NOFORN/CONTINUED CONTROL

Page 3

located at Pruszkow under the command of the Soviet officer
PIMONOV. These and all other SMESH units were directly
responsible to SEROV. Most or all of these units were
involved in operations against the AK in their area, and
there was close coordination of these operations from
Wolomin, i.e., by SEROV. PIMONOV somehow got in touch with
an underground general and offered him and others safe
conduct if he and others would reveal themselves. This was
obviously done with SEROV's knowledge and approval, since
nothing of this magnitude was ever done without his approval.
The underground leaders were then arrested by PIMONOV and his
men. SEROV probably planned this betrayal himself, but the
operation was actually carried out by his subordinate PIMONOV.

7. Source knows nothing further about SEROV's activities. He has
very great respect for him, considering him extremely intelligent, a very hard worker, with great experience and knowledge
in the field of intelligence work, capable of making decisions
whenever necessary and not afraid to accept responsibility.
Source states that SEROV was not only highly respected by his
subordinates for his ability, but was very well liked for his
human treatment of subordinates - knowing, for example, when
they had earned a rest from the intense pace of operations at
that time, and showing appreciation when work was well done.
Source believes that SEROV must have had a high protector in
Moscow becaue of his complete self-confidence and willingness
to assume responsibility in the direction of these CE operations.
Source believes that he is probably also a completely convinced
Communist.

1. <u>Headquarters Comment:</u> It is believed that SEROV was not merely
head of SMERSH in Poland but had wider responsibilities for
intelligence and counterintelligence activities in Poland.

CENTRAL INTELLIGENCE AGENCY

43

INFORMATION REPORT

9/58

[SECRET]

This material contains information affecting the National Defense of the United States within the meaning of the Espionage Laws, Title 18, U.S.C. Secs. 793 and 794, the transmission or revelation of which in any manner to an unauthorized person is prohibited by law.

COUNTRY	USSR	REPORT NO.	CS
SUBJECT	Organization of the Soviet Intelligence Organs	DATE DISTR.	FEB 24 1955
		NO. OF PAGES	9
DATE OF INFO.	December 1952	REQUIREMENT NO.	RD
PLACE ACQUIRED	Germany	REFERENCES	

This document has been approved for release through the HISTORICAL REVIEW PROGRAM of the Central Intelligence Agency.

Date 10/21/94

THE SOURCE EVALUATIONS IN THIS REPORT ARE DEFINITIVE.
THE APPRAISAL OF CONTENT IS TENTATIVE.
(FOR KEY SEE REVERSE)

SOURCE: Reliable source (B) with access to this information. Appraisal of Content: 3.

The Chief Intelligence Directorate (GRU) of the MGB.

1. The Chief Intelligence Directorate (Glavnoye Razvedyvatelnoye Upravleniye) of the MGB was created by a directive of the Council of Ministers, USSR, in December 1952. The directive was signed by Stalin. (Lieutenant General) Sergey Ivanovich Koltsov was appointed as Chief of the GRU, MGB, which was composed of two directorates: the First Directorate (Intelligence) and the Second Directorate (Counterintelligence).

The First or Intelligence Directorate (Razvedyvatelnoye Upravleniye) carried on active intelligence and counterintelligence work abroad. The directing body of the First Directorate was:

a. Chief – (Major General) Yevgeniy Petrovich Pitovranov.

b. Deputy Chief – (Lieutenant General) Petr Vasilyevich Fedotov.

c. Deputy Chief – (Colonel) Aleksandr Mikhaylovich Sakharovskiy.

d. (Colonel) /Andrey Makarovich/ Otroshchenko – Although Otroshchenko, as a former Deputy Chief of the First Chief Directorate of the MGB, for pay and prestige purposes held the title of Deputy Chief of the Intelligence Directorate, he was actually a section chief, possibly for Near East affairs. Otroshchenko is 45 to 47 years old. He is of average height (170 cm) and weighs approximately 90 kg. His build is heavy and he has a large paunch. He has a dark complexion, dark eyes, and thin dark hair, which he wears brushed straight back. He has a round, puffy face and a large bulky nose. He speaks in a husky voice and has a slow, ponderous walk. He has been with the Soviet security services for at least 15 years, almost always in important positions. Until 1951 he had been a member of the Advisory Board (Kollegiya) of the Committee of Information (KI) and a deputy chairman of the KI for the Near East.

SECRET

STATE		ARMY	X	NAVY	X	AIR	X	FBI	X	AEC				

(Washington distribution indicated by "X"; field distribution by "#".)

-2-

3. The Intelligence Directorate was composed of the following sections:

   a. American Section or Section of the Principal Enemy (Otdel Glavnovo Protivnika). This was the First Section and was responsible for the United States, including Alaska, and all of Latin America, but not Canada.

   b. English (Second) Section - England, its colonies, and the members of the Commonwealth, except Australia, India, and Pakistan.

   c. Austro-German (Third) Section - Germany and Austria. As the section was originally organized, (Colonel) Georgiy Stepanovich Yevdokimenko was Chief of Section. Yevdokimenko, born in 1915, had worked in Baden to late 1949 or early 1950, was an advisor in Hungary in 1950, and in 1950-51 was deputy chief of the Khabarovsk Kray RID. (Colonel) Mikhail Nikolayevich Shostakov was Deputy Chief for Germany, and (Lieutenant Colonel) Leonid Yemelyanovich Siemaniak was Deputy Chief for Austria. Siemaniak had worked in Austria until 1952. He had had experience in diversion and partisan activities. During the war he had trained saboteurs and partisans and had made jumps himself behind the German lines in Kiev and Mogilev. He is about 40 years old and an engineer by profession. He is married and has one child. Yevdokimenko was later transferred to be a Deputy chief of the Advisors' Section and Shostakov was sent to Rumania. Gorskiy (fnu) became Deputy Chief for Germany and, in effect, acting chief of the section.

   d. European (Fourth) Section - France, Benelux, Italy, Greece, Switzerland, Yugoslavia. (Colonel) Ivan Ivanovich Agayants was section chief and (Colonel) Voyabel (fnu) was his deputy.

   e. Scandinavian Section - Denmark, Norway, Finland, Sweden. (Colonel) Tarasov (fnu) was section chief.

   f. Near East Section - Iran, Turkey, Afghanistan, Egypt, Israel, Syria, Lebanon, Ethiopia. The chief of the section was (Colonel) Yelisoyov.

   g. Asian Section - India, Pakistan, the countries of the Indo-Chinese peninsula, Indonesia.

   h. Far East Section - Japan, South Korea, China, Philippines, Hong Kong, Australia.

   i. Counterintelligence (Ninth) Section (Kontrrazvedyvatelnyy Otdel) - The section chief was (Colonel) Sergey Mikhaylovich Fedoseyev.

   j. Advisors' Section (Sovetnicheskiy Otdel) - Bulgaria, Albania, Rumania, Hungary, Czechoslovakia, Poland, China, North Korea, Mongolia. The section chief was (Colonel) Sergey Nikolayevich Kartashov and his deputy was Colonel Chestneyshiy.

   k. "KR" Section - Soviet colonies abroad. The section chief was Colonel Kashevnikov.

   l. "E" - Emigration (Emigratsiya) Section. The section chief was (Lieutenant Colonel) (name). (name) is 40 to 42 years old. He is short and has a normal build except for a small paunch. His hair is dirty blond and he has light eyebrows and lashes. His complexion is light. He does not wear glasses.

   m. Deep Cover Section (Otdel Nelegalov) - The section chief was (Colonel) Aleksandr Mikhaylovich Korotkov.

   n. Scientific-Technical Intelligence Section (Otdel Nauchnoy-Tekhnicheskoy Razvedki) - The section chief was Colonel Krasilnikov.

   o. Cipher Section

   p. Operational Registry and Archives (Operativnyy Uchet i Arkhiv) or 16th Section - Section Chief, (Colonel) Polyakov (fnu). Colonel Polyakov has been with the security services for more than 25 years and in June 1953 was sent to China as

SECRET

253

-3-

an IWD advisor.

q. Personnel Section (Otdel Kadrov) - The section chief was Colonel Boris Petrovich Sorogin.

r. Secretariat - The section chief was (Lieutenant Colonel) Fedor Yakovlovich Gubarenko.

s. Finance Section - The section chief was (Colonel) Tarakanovskiy.

t. Foreign Language Courses - This unit was not formally a section, although in size it approximated one. The unit was headed by a major who knew four or five languages. He was about 50 years old, was tall, and tried to create the impression that his linguistic accomplishments were more than they were in fact. The major had a large staff of instructors under him, as well as a regular administrative staff. At the beginning of each training year, in the fall, various sections of the directorate submitted to the language training unit the names of persons selected for language training. The language unit then organized small groups of two, three, or four persons. Each group met three times a week for two hours each session. Since the working day was from 1130 to 2400 and the language groups met from 0900 to 1100 or 1000 to 1200, alternatively, part of the instruction was on the student's own time and part on government time. Some groups met from 2000 to 2200. Those taking language training were not excused from their normal duties. Language instruction was usually provided for officers who would need the language in their work. In the case of a transfer from one geographical area to another, however, an officer would be permitted to complete a course already begun in a language even though he might no longer need to know it.

4. The Second (Counterintelligence) Directorate was responsible for counterintelligence in the foreign embassies and other foreign installations located within the USSR. Among the personnel were:

a. Chief - (Lieutenant General) V.S. Ryasnoy. In early March 1953, Ryasnoy became chief of the GRU, MID. Ryasnoy is a Great Russian, about 50 years old. He is 163 cm tall, stout (weighing about 70 kg), and has a noticeable paunch. He has a pale, round face, a long nose, brown hair and yellow (sic; possibly hazel) eyes. He is a heavy smoker.

b. Deputy Chief - (Colonel) Gribanov, who later became chief of the Second Directorate of the GRU.

c. Chief of the American Section - (Colonel) Kozlov. His deputy was (Lieutenant Colonel) Gorbatenko.

d. Chief of the German (Fifth) Section - (Major) Perfilyev. This section was responsible for operations against the DDR and its representatives in the Soviet Union.

5. When the MGB and the MVD were merged in March 1953, the Chief Intelligence Directorate of the MGB ceased to exist. The First (Intelligence) Directorate of the GRU became the Second Chief Directorate of the MVD, and the Second (Counterintelligence) Directorate of the GRU became the First Chief Directorate of the MVD.

6. Legend to Organizational Chart of the Second Chief Directorate of the MVD after March 1953 (see page 6):

(1) Chief of the Second Chief Directorate - (Nachalnik Vtorogo Glavnogo Upravleniya, MVD, SSSR).

The Second Chief Directorate was composed of the following sub-divisions:

(2) The Secretariat - (Lieutenant Colonel) Gubarenko was chief. This section served

IV-5: *(Continued)*

-4-

the needs of SCD personnel in both the top and the working echelons. Specifically, it was responsible for the checking and registry of secret and top secret documents of the SCD, the operation of the typing pool, the providing of stenographic help, the receipt and dispatch of diplomatic mail, and the handling of incoming correspondence and its distribution to the appropriate sections. Within the secretariat there was also a Housekeeping (Khozyaystvennoye) Subsection which was charged with the custody of living quarters of the employees of the SCD while on duty abroad. Members of the secretariat also might be given various non-operational tasks by the chief of the directorate or his deputies. In addition, the chief of the secretariat kept the duty officer roster and appointed operational and staff duty officers for nights, non-working days, and holidays.

The following were operational sections performing regular intelligence functions:

(3) First Section - American Section.

(4) Second Section - Great Britain, its colonies, and the Commonwealth.

(5) Third Section - Intelligence and counterintelligence in Germany and Austria.

(6) Fourth Section - Continental Europe and Scandinavia, except Germany, Austria, and the satellites. Colonel Taymbal was chief of this section. Taymbal was approximately 40 years old, was short, and had red hair.

(7) Fifth Section - Emigration. This section was responsible for placing agents within emigre groups.

(8) Sixth Section - Near and Far East, except China, North Korea, and Mongolia. The chief was Lieutenant Colonel Vertiporokh.

(9) Seventh Section - The Advisors' Section. Helped and exercised control over the state security organs of the European satellites, China, North Korea, and Mongolia. The chief was Colonel Aleksandr Mikhaylovich Sakharovskiy, with Colonel Chesnoyshiy as deputy.

(10) Scientific and Technical Intelligence Section. The section chief was Kvasnikov (fnu).

(11) Ninth Section - The Illegal Section (Otdel Nelegalov) - A section for the selection, preparation, and dispatching of deep cover agents for deep cover work abroad.

(12) Tenth Section - Delegations and Merchant Seamen. The chief was Colonel Siberin. This section handled the agents within Soviet delegations sent abroad and also directed the agents on Soviet merchant ships sailing to foreign ports. The network covered all vessels sailing abroad, and agents would be, as a rule, under cover as members of the crew. There was a regulation which stipulated that, when members of the merchant marine were abroad, they could go ashore alone and must go in groups of not less than three persons. While there would not necessarily be an MVD man in the group, agents were alerted to keep an eye on shore parties. If one member of the group should break away, even for a few hours, he immediately would become suspect and would not get a second chance either to go ashore or to sail abroad again. For three persons to go ashore and get drunk together was not considered a serious offense. When a ship was bound for a foreign port, the resident of that country was notified by telegram from the Second Chief Directorate as to the date of the ship's arrival.

(13) Information Section (number of section not known) - The chief of the section was Colonel Novoselov. Novoselov had been Chief of the Directorate of Information under the NKVD. In 1951, this directorate was known as the Fifth Directorate. When the KGB was established it became the Information Section and continued as a section under the Second Chief Directorate of the MVD. All intelligence information from abroad was forwarded to this section, where it was processed, put in report form or summarized, and then forwarded to the appropriate ministries or other government agencies which would be interested in

255

it, if it warranted being so spent.

The following were so-called non-operational sections:

(14) Code Section (Shifrovalnyy Otdel) - This section was actually subordinate to the chief of the Second Chief Directorate; but, at the same time, organisationally, it was also under the chief of the Eighth Directorate ("D" on the chart) i.e., the Code Directorate. Physically, it was located next to the offices of the Second Chief Directorate, while the Eighth Directorate was located in a suburb of Moscow. The chief of this section, while nominally subordinate to the chief of the Eighth Directorate, was not allowed to show to the latter, or to other workers in the Eighth Directorate, any of the code messages he received for the Second Chief Directorate.

(15) Operational Registry and Archives Sektor (Sektor Operativnogo Ucheta I Arkhiva - Registry of active and of former agent personnel composed of foreign nationals working abroad, registry of deep cover agents (nelegalov) and of prospective agents being considered for or actually in the process of recruitment, custody of operational and personal agent files. This Sektor was also subordinate to both the chief of the Second Chief Directorate and the chief of the First Special Section, MVD, USSR ("C" on the chart). The official designation of this unit was "Fifth Sektor of the First Special Section, MVD, USSR." Its chief was (Colonel) Andreyev.

(16) Finance and Disbursing Sektor (Finansovo-Valyutnyy Sektor) - The section chief was Colonel Kurakhovskiy. This unit also had a dual subordination: to the chief of the Second Chief Directorate and to the chief of the Finance Section, MVD, USSR ("D" on the chart).

(17) Personnel Section - Also subordinate to both the chief of the Second Chief Directorate and to the chief of the Personnel Directorate, MVD, USSR ("E" on the chart).

(18) Courses of Foreign Languages - The instructors in this unit gave language instruction to the members of the Second Chief Directorate only. However, in academic matters, methodology, and guidance in the use of text books and training aids, they were subordinate to the chief of the Department of Foreign Languages of the Higher School of the MVD, USSR ("F" on the chart), at the present time called the Law Institute (Yuridicheskiy Institut).

(19) The Party Committee (Partkom) - The Party Committee was not formally subordinated to the chief of the Second Chief Directorate. It was directly under the Party Committee, MVD, USSR ("A" on the chart). However, it was responsible for a joint, consultative effort (with the chief of the Second Chief Directorate) directed toward the improvement of Second Chief Directorate work in general.

(20) Komsomol Committee - Supervised the Komsomol work in the directorate. However, since there were comparatively few members of the Komsomol in the directorate, and these were almost exclusively from among the ancillary and support personnel, the secretary of this committee performed these duties in addition to his other normal work and not on a full-time basis.

256

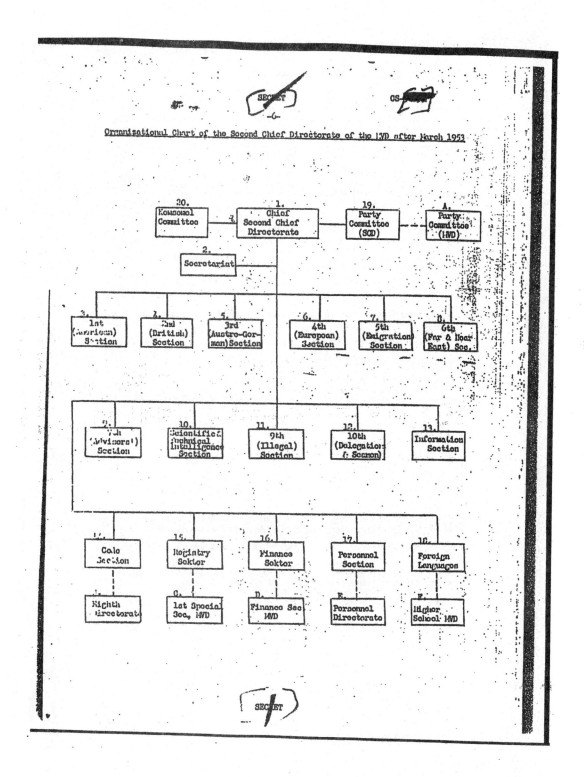

Organizational Chart of the Second Chief Directorate of the MVD after March 1953

Proposed Reorganization of the Second Chief Directorate

7. Approximately in the middle, or the beginning, of August 1953, Panyushkin called a meeting of all chiefs of sections and the secretaries of the Party Bureaus of the Second Chief Directorate. The agenda of the meeting required that all of those present put forth their proposals on the subject of how to improve the organization of the work of the Directorate. Each one was requested to submit his own proposals on how to revamp the structure of the directorate for greater effectiveness. This question was posed on the grounds that Beriya, during his tenure as Minister (MVD), disrupted the work of the Second Chief Directorate, unnecessarily discharged a large number of Second Chief Directorate employees, and put through a completely faulty reorganization of the Directorate.

8. The following is a list of specific proposals presented during the described meeting:

   a. The American Section was to be made into two separate sections, i.e. one section to work against the United States only, and the other to work against Latin America.

   b. The British Section was to be left without a change, except that Australia was to be transferred to the Far East Section.

   c. The Austro-German Section was to remain as it was, but to be strengthened by the addition of four or five more workers.

   d. With regard to the European Section, a proposal was made to break it up into three sections, i.e.:

      1) France, Belgium, the Netherlands, and Luxembourg;

      2) Finland, Norway, Sweden, and Denmark;

      3) Italy, Greece, and Yugoslavia;

   e. The Emigration Section was to remain as it was, but with an addition of five or seven more employees.

   f. With regard to the Sixth (Near and Far East) Section, there was a proposal to break it up into three separate sections, namely:

      1) Iran, Turkey, Syria, Lebanon, and Egypt;

      2) Afghanistan, Pakistan, and India;

      3) The Far East Section, to include Japan, the Phillipines, Australia, New Zealand, and Indo-China;

   g. No changes were proposed with regard to the Advisers' Section, except that the chief of section asked for an increase in his T/O of five or six people.

   h. No changes were proposed with regard to the Scientific and Technical Intelligence Section.

   i. There were two major proposals with regard to the Deep Cover Section. One proposal was to make the section into a Deep Cover Directorate, within the Second Chief Directorate, to comprise three sections, which would be charged with all deep cover activities. The second proposal had in view the creation of three independent sections, as follows:

      1) A section charged with the selection and training of agents for deep cover work.

SECRET

2) A section charged with the legalization aspects of deep cover work, to include the documentation of agents and their dispatch or infiltration into the foreign countries for deep cover work.

3) A section charged with the actual running of deep cover operations and the maintenance of contact with deep cover agents.

j. No changes were proposed with regard to the 10th (Delegation) Section.

k. With regard to the Information Section, it was proposed that it be considerably enlarged and that the Translators' Sektor be removed from its jurisdiction, since the direction of the work of translators required entirely too much time and effort on the section's part.

l. The next question raised at the meeting dealt with the proposal to return to Second Chief Directorate organizational control the subdivisions removed from the direct control of the former First Chief Directorate. Specifically:

1) The Code Section - It was proposed that it be returned to full Second Chief Directorate control.

2) Registry and Archives Sektor - The proposal called for its return to full Second Chief Directorate control and again raising it to a section.

3) Finance and Disbursing Sektor - It was proposed to return it to full Second Chief Directorate control as a section.

m. No objections were raised with regard to the dual subordination of the Personnel Section (to the Second Chief Directorate and to the Personnel Directorate, MVD).

n. No changes were proposed with regard to the status of the Foreign Languages Courses.

The measures listed above were not put into effect as of February 1954, i.e. before the Committee for State Security (KGB) was established. However, while probably not all of the proposals were finally adopted and implemented, it is fairly certain that some of them were carried out, especially those referring to the break-up of the European and the Near/Far East Sections. Such measures were necessary since the sections had grown too unwieldy to be run efficiently.

The First Chief Directorate of the MVD after March 1953

The First Chief Directorate was a CE directorate which was responsible for all foreigners within the Soviet Union. Its specific responsibilities were as follows:

a. Counterespionage work against all foreign diplomatic installations and all foreigners legally in the Soviet Union. This work was handled by sections which were broken down by country as in the Second Chief Directorate.

b. Apprehension of all foreign agents dispatched into the Soviet Union. This work was handled by the 11th Section, known as the Section for the Search of Para-chutists (Otdel po Rozysku Parashyutistov).

c. Operational direction of the cases of all foreign agents apprehended in the Soviet Union. This may have been part of the work of the 11th Section or there may have been a special section just for this purpose.

The work of the 11th Section was a continuation of the work of the old wartime Fourth (Partisan) Directorate. This section inherited the Partisan Directorate's agents but it probably was much smaller now than it was during the war. The 11th Section may have had a small group in each oblast and kray MVD directorate.

The First Chief Directorate did not maintain personnel abroad. The only circumstance under which a First Chief Directorate case officer might have gone abroad would have been operational necessity. For example, if a case officer of the American Section of the First Chief Directorate became friendly with an American in the Embassy and the American returned to Washington, this case officer might have been transferred to

-9-

Washington if the MVD thought that a continuation of the friendship might have valuable results. However, under such circumstances the case officer would have been temporarily transferred to the Second Chief Directorate and the case would have become a Second Chief Directorate case. Source knew of no foreign operations in which First Chief Directorate personnel have actually participated.

6/35

2 Feb 53

(Der Tagesordnungspunkt 1 hatte besonders die Arbeit im allgemeinen, Kaderfragen
und organisatorische Fragen zum Inhalt).

Zeit der Sitzung:
Die Sitzung begann 10'30 und endete etwa 15'30 Uhr.

Zu Tagesordnungspunkt 1 und 2 :

Der Leiter des IWF, Micha Wolf, eroeffnete die Dienstbesprechung und fuehrte aus:
Die Arbeitsplaene fuer das I. Quartal 1953 habe er nicht restlos termingemaess
erhalten. Einen Teil der erhaltenen Plaene habe er zurueck geben muessen, da sie
formell waren. Ueberhaupt sei der groesste Teil der Plaene des Hauses formell. Die
Arbeitsplaene muesste operative Plaene sein und alles beinhalten. Ferner muessten
verstehen, alle Kraefte unserer Abteilung richtig zu mobilisieren.
Viele Mitarbeiter des Hauses wuerden bei ihren taeglichen Arbeiten sich verzettel
und die Massnahmen zur Erreichung der gesteckten Ziele ganz vergessen/ bezw. auss
acht lassen.
Aeusserst wichtig in unserer Arbeit sei der Aufbau der Residenturen. Bei der
Suche und Auswahl der Residenten wuerde man nur die Ausbildung sehen. Die Voraussetzungen fuer eine Einschleussung und Eignung fuer eine Spionagearbeit wuerden
viele Mitarbeiter bei ihrer Auswahl ganz vergessen. Erst wenn die Ausbildung lauf
kaeme man dahinter, dass die Einschleusung Schwierigkeiten bereite und der gesetzt
Termin nicht eingehalten werden koenne.
Bei ausgebildeten und eingeschleusten Residenten soll man nicht den Fehler macher
diese sich 8 Wochenlang legalisieren lassen. Die eingeschleusten Residenten soller
sofo ausser ihrer Legalisierung sofort anfangen allmaehlich zu arbeiten. Bei der
Organisierung von Residenturen soll man sich nicht zu sehr auf die Bereitstellung
von Quellen durch die Zentrale verlassen. Es sei der Fehler gemacht worden, dass be
der Ausbildung der Residenten gesagt wurde, die erforderlichen Quellen wuerde die
Zentrale bereitstellen. Dies sei in Zukunft zu unterlassen. Die Residenten sollen i
der Suche nach Quellen selbst aktiv sein. Selbstverstaendlich muessten wir von der
Zentrale aus auch nach Quellen umsehen, um sie zu einem bestimmten Zeitpunkt einer
Residentur anzuschliessen. Grundsatz sei aber, dass sich die Residenten selbst he
muessten.
Die Arbeit der Abteilungen und der Mitarbeiter muesse systematischer gestaltet we
das heisst, dassdas zu bearbeitende Objekt studiert werden muss. Dies sei Vorausset
in der Schaffung von Anhaltspunkten fuer die Werbung von Quellen, wie z.B. in den
Ministerien der Bonner - Regierung.
Z.Zt. besitze das IWF wenig politsche Nachrichten und fast keine oekonomische Nach
richten. Die wenigen Nachrichten, die uns z.Zt. zur Verfuegung stehen reichen nicht,
um unsere Regierung und Fuehrung ausreichend zu informieren. Wolf betonte deshalb
nochmals, dass die Herrausarbeitung von Schwerpunkten in unseren Arbeitsplaenen
aeusserst notwendig sei. Er betonte ferner, dass bei der Durchfuehrung der Arbeit b
einem Teil der Mitarbeiter eine Impotenz bestuende.
Um in Zukunft schneller und besser vorwaerts zu kommen, bezw. den Sicherheitsfaktor
staerker walten zu lassen, sei folgendes notwendig:
a) Konkrete Arbeitsplaene, einschliesslich gut durchdachter Legenden, dies ist die
Grundlage unserer Arbeit. Die gemachten Fehler der Vergangenheit zeigten dies
eindeutig.
(Ich moechte hierbei an folgende Vorkommnisse erinnern: Fall Planert/-I. Abteilun
Verhaftung eines Beauftragten der 2. Abteilung durch die VP an der Grenze, Beschi
ung eines Grenzkuriers der 2. Abteilung durch die Grenzpolizei der DDR, das Hoch
gehen der Agenten der I. HA im vergangenem Jahr, der Fall Weis -1. Abteilung, die E
[illegible] ei[illegible] Saimon u.a.
b)Die Partei -SED- ist bei unserer Arbeit aus dem Spiel zu lassen [redacted]

(Page 2 missing from the original document)

Der Grundpfeiler ist unsere Zuverlaessigkeit. Im Unterschied... diese bei kapitalistischen haben sich unter anderen auch... des ZK der SED, illegitim und ... bei vorkommnissen hinfuer ... ungeeignet ... viele Mitarbeiter reisten auf Kosten des ZK der SED als Legende, obwohl Walter Ullrich streng verboten hat, dass wir die Partei fuer unsere Arbeit nutzen, bezw. die Organe der Partei betreten. Nur einer sehr geringen Anzahl ...-Mitarbeiter standen ZK-Ausweise ... hinzu fuegen, dass 1952 ca.12 - 15 Mitarbeiter ZK-Ausweise besassen. Ende Maerz 1953 wurde hiermit radikal Schluss gemacht.

c) Alle geworbenen Agenten, Residenten, Kuriere, Ablagestellen, Treffwohnungen, Deckadressen usw. muessen aeusserts gewissenhaft und genau ueberprueft werden. Nicht nur eine aeusserliche Beberpruefung durchfuehren, so ... tief in das Innere eindringen. Verwandtschaft, Umgebung, Frau und Kinder besonders, der Verkehr usw. muessten sehr gewissenhaft abgeklaert werden. Wenn wir alles sehr gewissenhaft durchfuehren, so koennten wir gewiss sein, dass wir sehr wenig Rueckschlaege erleben wuerden. Rueckschlaege sei ueberwiegend die Ursache leichtsinniger Arbeit.

d) Die Verantwortung fuer die Arbeit traegt den Hauptabteilungsleiter sowie der Abteilungsleiter. Wolf fuegte hier hinzu, dass ... verschiedener Abteilungsleiter dass die Verantwortung fuer die Arbeit bei der Leitung liege ... sei. Verantwortlich ist in erster Linie der Abteilungsleiter und dann erst die Leitung. Ebenfalls traegt jeder Mitarbeiter fuer eigenmaechtige Arbeit die Verantwortung. Die Mitarbeiter muessen so erzogen werden, dass Zuverlaessigkeit in allen dienstlichen und privaten Angelegenheiten aeusserste ... Grundsatz ist.

e) Ausnutzung aller sich ergebenden Moeglichkeiten fuer unsere Nachrichtenarbeit. Wolf ging hierbei hauptsaechlich auf die Ausarbeitung guter Legenden ein. Eine gute Legende muesse alle objektiven und subjektiven Moeglichkeiten beinhalten. z.B. nicht nur reine Lebenslegende sondern auch Fragen wie Verhaftung, Befragung, politische Auseinandersetzungen usw. Hierher gehoert auch das Verhalten bei Beruehrung mit westlichen Agenten, z.B. in der Abwehr, in der Zusammenarbeit mit Agenten der westlichen Parteien usw...

f) Werbung von Quellen durch die Residenten ... Wie bereits zum Ausdruck gebracht, sollen die Residenten sich nach Moeglichkeit an der Suche nach Quellen stark beteiligen. Wenn der Resident nach Westdeutschland eingeschleust wird und in der DDR der SED angehoert ... Werbung von Agenten nicht durchfuehren. Alle uebrigen Residenten die bereits eingesetzt sowie in Westdeutschland geworbenen, koennen nach Bestaetigung durch die Zentrale von Fall zu Fall Werbungen durchfuehren. Eingeschleuste SED-Residenten haben nur mit angewiesenen Quellen zu arbeiten.

g) Die Anleitung der Mitarbeiter durch die Abteilungsleiter ... Das Benehmen der Hauptabteilungsleiter und Abteilungsleiter gegenueber den Mitarbeitern muss korrekt und diszipliniert sein. Es darf sich kein Kumpelt hin entwickeln. Die Mitarbeiter muessen untereinander und auch vor dem Abteilungsleiter Achtung haben. Alle Vorhaben und Arbeiten muessen mit den Mitarbeitern durch die Abteilungsleiter gruendlich besprochen werden. Die Abteilungsleiter sind fuer die Arbeit und fuer die Sicherheit ganz und gar verantwortlich. Letzteres nicht nur fuer die Arbeit in der Abteilung, sondern auch fuer die Mitarbeiter. Es muss in der Abteilung eine schoepferische Arbeit entwickelt werden.

Die Punkte a - g stellten Ergaenzungen zu den bereits bekannten Methoden der SED dar.
Micha Wolf fuhr sodann in seinen Ausfuehrungen wie folgt fort:

In unserer Arbeit sollen wir in der Abklaerung von Personen [illegible], sowie auch in der Abklaerung von Objekten ruhig Auskunftsbueros und Detektivbueros in Anspruch nehmen. Derartige Einrichtungen koennen uns in vielen Dingen helfen. Die eigentliche Spionagearbeit muss sehr gruendlich vorbereitet sein. Alles muss gruend lich studiert werden. Jeder Mitarbeiter muss auf seinem Gebiet legale und halblegal Nachrichten [illegible] ausnuetzen und systematisch sammeln.
Wolf bat sodann alle Hauptabteilungsleiter und Abteilungsleiter nochmals der IV. HA westliche Urkunden usw aus Westdeutschland zu ueberlassen. Das ganze IWF wuerd [illegible] ja davon [illegible].
Ganz besonders schaerfte er allen Hauptabteilungsleitern und Abteilungsleitern die Erziehung der Mitarbeiter ein. Diese sollen keine Nebensaechliche Arbeit machen, sondern sie muessen zuegig mit der Arbeit vertraut gemacht werden. Wenn dies unsere Mitarbeiter feststellen, so werden sie sich doppelt anstrengen.
Nach diesen Ausfuehrungen ging Wolf auf die Arbeit der einzelnen Hauptabteilungen [illegible] Abteilungen ueber. Er sagte:

I. Hauptabteilung.

Die I./HA sei sehr im Rueckstand. Die Schwierigkeiten seien der Leitung des IWF bekannt. Man hoffe jedoch, dass das kein Dauerzustand bleibt. Der erlittene Rueckschlag muesse doch nun bald ueberwunden sein. In der Erfuellung des Arbeitsplanes im I. Quartal 1953 sehe er – Wolf – z.Zt. sehr schwarz, da hierfuer viele Voraussetzungen fehlen, und wir schliesslich schon Ende Februar schreiben.
Henschke gab hierauf folgende Erklaerung ab:
Die Schwierigkeiten mit der seine Hauptabteilung z.Zt. zu ringen habe sind der Lei[illegible] bekannt. Ebenfalls kennt die Leitung die Kadersorgen der Hauptabteilung. (Hier mein[illegible] Henschke, dass er keine richtigen Mitarbeiter besitze, es fehlen die geistigen Voraussetzungen.) Er hoffe jedoch, dass er die Schwierigkeiten in baelde ueberwunde[illegible] habe. Die Arbeitsplanerfuellung bereite ihm ohne Zweifel Schwierigkeiten, dennoch h[illegible] er, seinen Arbeitsplan einigermassen zu erfuellen. Henschke fuehrte ferner aus, dass [illegible] sich von den Arbeitsbesprechungen auch einen Erfahrungsaustausch erhoffe, wie z.B. ueber die Organisierung von Grenzuebergaengen, Legalisierung von Residenten in We[illegible] deutschland usw. Er habe den Eindruck, dass jeder Hauptabteilungsleiter und Abteil ungsleiter ueber gesammelte Erfahrungen sich ausschweigt. Diese Methode sei doch Unsinn. Der eine Mitarbeiter habe hier, der andere dort grosse Erfahrungen. Derartig[illegible] Erfahrungen muesse man doch fuer alle [illegible]. Er kaeme z.B. in seiner Hauptabte[illegible] ung nicht mit seinen Grenzuebergaengen voran. Seine Abteilungen haben diesbezuegli[illegible] viele Schwierigkeiten. Es sei ihm jedoch bekannt, dass die II. HA auf diesem Gebiete gute Erfolge zu verzeichnen habe. Wenn dies der Fall ist, so soll doch die II. HA [illegible] ~~Erfolge~~ Erfahrungen austauschen. Die I. HA koenne vielleicht auf einem anderen Gebi[illegible] helfen.
Wolf erwiderte hierauf, dass man sich hierueber noch in der Leitung unterhalten m[illegible] Man muss die Konspiration beruecksichtigen. Ebenfalls muesse man diese Frage noch [illegible] den Beratern besprechen.

II. Hauptabteilung.

Die II. HA wuerde voraussichtlich als einzige HA ihren Plan fuer das I. Quartal 19[illegible] erfuellen. Es muesste jedoch hinzugefueg t werden, das Zsinda (HA.-Leiter der II. [illegible]) seinen Arbeitsplan erst Anfang Februar eingereicht habe. Erst haette Zsinda eine[illegible] Telegramm – Plan eingereicht, ~~und~~ den er zurueck bekam, und dann haette er mehrma[illegible] ermahnt werden muessen bis der Plan tatsaechlich vorgelegt wurde. Zsinda muesse [illegible] fuer die Zukunft merken, Termin sei Termin und damit Befehl. Sonst muesse er – Wol[illegible] jedoch zum Ausdruck brin gen, dass die II. HA sehr fleissig gearbeitet habe und wi[illegible] schon gesagt, als einzige Hauptabteilung bezw. Abteilung ihren Plan erfuellen wird. Zur II. HA sei ferner zu sagen, dass sie bei ihrer Arbeit nicht das Objekt ausser Acht lassen soll. Die Arbeit muesse planmaessiger gestaltet werden. Bei der II. HA scheint es so zu sein, dass alles was anfaellt genommen wird. Dies sei zwar augenb lich richtig, muesse aber unbeding t geaendert werden, es koenne sich [illegible] unsystematische Arbeit entwickeln. Ebenfalls muessten in der II. HA bestimmte spor[illegible]

Zuege wegfallen (...) da an als
ausserordentlich (...) Zainde aus den Sachen (...) Zusammenarbeit (...) Wolf koennte
Wolf, dass wir das Objekt Bernstein - Thornolle - sehr gut und gruendlich bearbeit
moechten, da hier eine sehr, sehr gute Sache aufgebaut werden koennte.

1.Abteilung

Ueber die Arbeit der 1.Abteilung aeusserte sich Wolf sehr wenig. Die 1.Abteilung
wurde im Februar noch von dem Genossen Felix vertreten unter direkter Anleitung
Micha Wolf. Wolf machte lediglich die Bemerkung, dass er ueber den Stand der Arbe
unterrichtet sei. Er muelltagnoch etwas vor sich hin vor die zu entnehmen war, das
die Arbeit in der 1.Abteilung nur kleine Erfolge zu verzeichnen habe, und es war
lich auch nicht so mit der Arbeit voran geht, als man sich das vorgestellt hatte.
(Ich moechte hier hinzufuegen, dass die 1.Abteilung Anfang (...) einen neuen Abt
ungsleiter vom Ministerium fuer Staatssicherheit bekommen hat.)

2.Abteilung

Wolf brachte zum Ausdruck, dass die 2.Abteilung am schwierigsten zu ueberwachen s
in ihrer Arbeit. Die Abteilung haette in letzter Zeit einige operative Fehler gem
was in Zukunft wegfallen muesse. Die Abteilung sei jetzt 1:1 (2 Operative Mitarbe
und eine Sekretaerin) besetzt und muesse doch in ihrer Arbeit (...) Wolf
meinte ferner, dass er die Schwierigkeit der Wissenschaftlichen und technischen
Spionagearbeit keinesfalls verkenne, aber die Arbeit muesse (...) und er ka
genug Moeglichkeit (...) auf diesem Gebiet sowie (...) Stellen insbesondt
land Sowjetunion (...)
Der Abteilungsleiter der 2.Abteilung, Heinrich Weihberg, (...) hierauf folgend
Die Leitung wisse ganz genau wie schwierig die Arbeit seiner Abteilung ist. Er ha
zwar 3 Mitarbeiter, aber nur einer von diesen drei Mitarbeitern und zwar Willi
Neumann, sei ein wirklicher operativer Kraft. Ueber Kollegen (...) aeusserte er
sich nicht besonders lobend. Besonders die negative Haltung zu Peter (...) erstim
mich. Weihberg fuehrte ferner aus, dass er in seiner Abteilung fuer die verschied
Gebiete der Wissenschaft Spezialkraefte benoetige. Mit seinen jetzigen Mitarbeiter
koenne er keinesfalls die gestellten Aufgaben loesen (...) sweier
operativen Aufgaben (...) und (...)
deinigen Abteilungen (...)
Er fuehrte als Beispiel die 1.Hauptabteilung an und (...) (das die) politische
Aufgaben von den Mitarbeitern auf Grund ihrer Schulung (...) gefordert (?)
In seiner Abteilung wuerden andere Voraussetzungen erwartet. Er bat deshalb die
Kaderabteilung dafuer zu sorgen, dass die Abteilung schnellstens eine Verstaerkung
von Wissenschaftlern und Technikern bekomme, um die gestellten Aufgaben (...)
einigermassen loesen zu koennen. Die Arbeitsplanerfuellung fuer das 1.Quartal sei
fuer die 2.Abteilung schwer, es wuerde aber alles daran gesetzt, um das Maximale an
Denkbaren zu erreichen. Der sowjetische Berater Bronski sei vollkommen ueber die
Lage in der Abteilung informiert. Auch diesen habe er gebeten, dass er sich bei Eug
dafuer einsetzen moege, dass die Abteilung die noetigen Mitarbeiter bekommen.
Micha Wolf sagte zu den Ausfuehrungen des Weihberg abschliessend folgendes:
Er verkenne keinesfalls die besondere Lage der 2.Abteilung. Es wuerde seitens der L
Leitung alles getan um aus der 2.Abteilung die gewuenschte Abteilung zu entwickeln
Die Abteilung muesse aber Verstaendnis dafuer haben, dass die Kaderabteilung des M
keine Kader backen koenne. - Betreffs Kaderfrage siehe 3.Abteilung.-

3.Abteilung - Kaderabteilung

Am schaerfsten griff Wolf die Kaderabteilung an. Der Hauptvorwurf bestand darin, da
die 3.Abteilung nicht organisieren koenne. Man verglich (...) vor, dass er auf K oder r
reite und sich nicht entscheiden wuerde. Ebenfalls wuerden sich die Hauptabteilun
sowie Abteilungen beschweren, dass sie Eingaben (...) ueberhaupt icht wuerd
bekommen. Gleichfalls seien die Mitarbeiter der 3.Abteilungen unzufrieden ueber
die Arbeitseinteilung und Vorbereitungen von (...) in das Gebiet der r (...) Aun
(...) ausgruefung. Der Arbeitsplan der 3.Abteilung sei unkonkret und nicht rich
durchdacht.

Vertraulich

Man machte Willi Woehl den Vorwurf, dass er zu buerokratisch sei. Woehl verteidigte sich damit, dass er zum Ausdruck brachte, die Mitarbeiter muessten die Verantwortung und Stellungnahme zu Kaderfragen usw. Waere. Woehl sah seine Arbeit, bei Kaderueberpruefungen, Nachbrichtigten seiner Verteidigung ferner an, dass die Betriebe, Verwaltungen und sonstige Institutionen nicht freiwillig ihre Kaderarbeit erfuellen und dadurch bei Kadersuche sich grosse Schwierigkeiten zeige. Wie schwierig ist geeignete Kader zu finden, koenne man sich kaum denken. Es sei ja alles schon abgegrast. Woehl bat in diesem Zusammenhang alle Hauptabteilungs- und Abteilungsleiter ebenfalls in der Kadersuche behilflich zu sein, denn und wuerden auch viele Kader taeglich durch die Finger gehen. Besonders bat er uns /////// geeignete Funker zu finden.

In der Kaderfrage ergriff sodann Zainia das Wort und erklaerte, dass die Kaderabteilung Verstaendnis fuer die Operativen Abteilungen haben muesse. Seine Hauptabteilung besaesse fuer 7 operative Mitarbeiter eine Sekretaerin. Bei einem derartigen Zustand muesse die Arbeit darunter leiden. Ebenfalls bekaeme er eingereichte Kadervorschlae an die Kaderabteilung ueberhaupt nicht zurueck. Entscheidungen wuerde die Kaderabteilung ueberhaupt nicht faellen. Die Abteilungen wollten doch vorallem wissen, wie sie sich in bestimmten Kaderfragen zu verhalten haben. Die Kaderabteilung muesse nun endlich dazu uebergehen, schnell Entscheidungen zu treffen. Wie sei doch den Hauptabteilungen und Abteilungen gleich, aber sie wuessten wenigsten woran sie sind. Wenn eine Entscheidung, infolge der Verantwortung, nicht gleich moeglich ist, so soll man doch wenigstens Zwischenbescheid geben.

Diesen Standpunkt teilte sodann auch Benschka.

Nach dieser Diskussion erhielt Woehl, vom Leiter des IWF den Auftrag, die Arbeitsweise in seiner Abteilung zu aendern. Ziel muss sein, schnellere Entscheidung in allen Kaderfragen.

4. Abteilung -Archiv-

Wolf machte alle HA und Abteilungsleiter darauf aufmerksam, dass die Aktenfuehrung in vielen Faellen noch zu wuenschen uebrig lasse. Dies kaeme auch fuer die Registrierung von Mitarbeitern //// in Frage. Ein Mangel bestuende auch in der Uebergabe von Akten an andere Mitarbeiter innerhalb der Hauptabteilungen und Abteilungen. Hie fehlte sehr oft die Umregistrierung sowie die Anfertigung des erforderlichen //// Protokolls. Kontrollen der Genossin Emmi Becker haetten dies fast ueberall gezeigt. Wolf erteilte hierauf Emmi Becker das Wort. Sie sagte:

Um fuer die Leitung und die Freunde -Russen- jederzeit einen Ueberblick zu haben, ist es einfach eine ausserst dringende Notwendigkeit, dass die operativen Mitarbei ihre Aktenfuehrung in Ordnung haben. Sie betonte ferner, dass sie in Zukunft des //// oefteren in den Abteilungen Kontrollen durchfuehren werde, um zu sehen, ob alles den Anordnungen entsprechend gemacht wird. Becker ging dann zu der Frage der Registrierung von Kadern mit operativer Interesse ueber. -Ich moechte erlaeutern, Hinsu hege dass es sich hierbei um Kader handelt, die fuer die Abteilungen von besonderer Interesse sind, aber noch ///// keine Werbungsabsichten bestehen.- Fuer derartige Kader sollen die Abteilungen eine sogenannte Hinweisakte fuehren. In dieser Hinweis akte soll auch die Registrierung erfolgen, also innerhalb der Hauptabteilung bei de Abteilungen sowie bei den selbstaendigen Abteilungen. Kader fuer die kein Interesse mehr besteht, sollen in das Archiv abgegeben werden. Das Archiv wird ebenfalls eine derartige Hinweisakte (Akten) fuehren ohne dabei eine Sperrkarte oder sonstige Kar karte anzulegen. Die Kader werden wie bei den Abteilungen innerhalb der Hinweisakt gefuehr t. Man sei noch bei der Ueberlegung, ob man fuer derartige immerhin wichtige Kader eine besondere Kartei anlegen soll. Die Freund e seien jedoch dagegen und vertreten den Standpunkt, entweder ist der Kader so wichtig, dass man mit ihm arbeit oder aber er ist ein Agent. In beiden Faellen muessten ja sowisso Sperrkarten angelegt werden. Die uebrigen Kader seien nicht so wichtig, dass man eine Kartei anlegt, selbst wenn sie einmal fuer das IWF von operativen Interesse waren. In der darauf folgenden Diskussion brachte vorallem Zainia zum Ausdruck, dass die Genossin Becker ihre Kontrollen abnehmen moechte, damit keine unnuetze Arbeitszeit f die Buerokratie verwendet wird. (Zainia war sehr gegen Emmi Becker eingestellt).

Micha Wolf bekraeftigte die Ausfuehrungen des Becker und machte darauf aufmerksam, dass ... in unseren Abteilungen noch auf dem Gebiet der ... gruendlich sein sollen. (XX)

...

Zu Tagesordnungspunkt 3 -Ansprache des sowjetischen Chefberaters Eugen-, ... eine eigene Dolmetscherin mit hatte, musste aber den Hauptabteilungs... als Dolmetscher fungieren ...

Eugen sagte:

Das IWF sei verantwortlich fuer die Parteifuehrung und die Staatsfuehrung der DDR und ... alle Vorgaenge politisch-oekonomisch, wissenschaftlich und technisch, militaerisch und abwehrmaessig ... Interesse- ... Natur in der westdeutschen Bundesrepublik ...

messe jedoch in Zukunft besser als in der Vergangenheit ausgenutzt werden. Alle un
denkbaren Moeglichkeiten muessen zum unsere Arbeit ausgenutzt werden. Wir, er n
damit uns Deutsche- koennen doch die deutschen Verhaeltnisse besser als sie. Wenn
ihnen moeglich ist in Indien, Sued-Amerika, USA bzw. reinzudringen, so wird es uns als
Deutsche doch moeglich sein in die Bundesrepublik einzudringen. Fuer die Hauptabtei
leiter und Abteilungsleiter darf nicht nur die Frage der Erziehung anderer Mitarbe
stehen, sondern es muss gleichzeitig die Arbeit durchorganisiert werden das ist
aeusserst wichtig. Die Genossen Zschinda und Rausche haben besonders betonnt, bei
offenen Diskussionen in den monatlichen Sitzungen die Konspiration verletzen. Die
Konspiration sei ausser Haus richtig, aber bei derartigen Sitzungen wie die im Ha
des IMF selbst, solle man die Konspiration nicht uebertreiben. Beim derartigen koenne
man in derartigen Besprechungen wie heute die Probleme die richtig erkannten Punkte
ruhig behandeln, man brauche ja nicht das Letzte in allen Teilen zu besprechen gros
Mangel im IMF bestuende darin, dass die Leitung selbst keine Aufgaben darstellt vor
nimmt. Nicht nur in den Arbeitsplaenen der Hauptabteilungen und Abteilungen muessen
Aufgaben und Schwerpunkte stehen, sondern die Leitung des IMF muss den Hauptabteilu
und Abteilungen bestimmte Aufgaben und Schwerpunkte stellen die Durchfuehrung der
Kontrolle von der Leitung ueber die Hauptabteilungsleiter und Abteilungsleiter bis
zu den Mitarbeitern muesse auch noch besser entwickelt werden. Die Frage der Kritik un
Schwach. Die Kritik und Selbstkritik muesse auch in IMF noch besser entwickelt werd
Erst durch eine gesunde Kritik und Selbstkritik koenne eine gesunde und eine
entwicklungsfaehige Nachrichtenarbeit. Wir sollten den Beschluss des ZK ueber
Entwicklung von Kritik und Selbstkritik nochmals durcharbeiten. abschloss. sein
Ausfuehrungen, indem er nochmals darauf aufmerksam machte, dass fuer alles Ginen. sets
muessten, die Parteifuehrung und die Staatsfuehrung mit den besten Moeglichkeiten zu
sehen, um eben eine richtige Politik zu betreiben. Unsere Arbeit wuerde nicht nur d
DDR" staerken sondern das gesamte Weltfriedenslager.

Zu Punkt 4 der Tagesordnung -Diskussion und Schlusswort-
Die Diskussion habe ich bereits in den Tagesordnungspunkten 1 und 2 eingebaut, sod
ich hierauf nicht noch einmal eingehen brauche. Nebensaechliche Diskussionen habe
ich weggelassen.
Micha Wolf brachte abschliessend zum Ausdruck, dass er hoffe, dass auch die heutige
Sitzung dazu beigetragen habe, die Arbeit in Zukunft zu verbessern und vor allem vor
zutreiben. Hauptaufgabe in den letzten Quartalswochen sei die Erfuellung des Arbei
planes. Alle Moeglichkeiten muessten restlos ausgenutzt werden um unsere Plaene zu
fuellen. Er stuende allen Hauptabteilungsleitern und Abteilungsleitern zur Verfueg
um sich zeigende Schwierigkeiten operativ und schnell zu ueberwinden zu helfe
Die Wachsamkeit legte er allen nochmals sehr nahe.

IV-7: "HVA Meeting [Sondersitzung] Chaired by [Markus] Wolf" 7 March 1953 (MORI: 145348).

[Because important parts of this document are nearly illegible in the original, the following transcription has been made. It duplicates the original insofar as is possible. Any spelling or grammatical errors in the original have been retained. Places in the original text that were totally illegible or questionable have been noted. A copy of the original document immediately follows this transcription.]

Niederschrift ueber die Sondersitzung aller IWF-Mitarbeiter an 7.3.53

Bevor ich auf die eigentliche Sitzung eingehe moechte ich die Vorgeschichte zu dieser Sitzung erlauetern. Wie bekannt, starb Stalin in der Nacht vom 5.3 bis zum 6.3.1953. Am 7.3.53 hatten alle zum Parteiactiv des IWF gehoerigen Mitarbeiter eine vertrauliche Sitzung ueber die Trauerfeierlichkeiten im IWF anlaesslich Stalins tot.
In diesen Tagen (6.3.53-10.3.53/ besonders am 6.3. am 7.3.53) war anlaesslich das weibliche Personal. Bereits am 6.3.53 erschienen das Weibervolk (!) in schwarzen Kleidung und benahm sich so, als wann die eigene Mutter gestorbern waere. Den groessten Teil des maennlichen personals benahm sich aehnlich, nur etwas sachlicher. Es herrschte eine allgemeine Niedergeschlagenheit.
Am 7.3.53 ereignete sich unabhaengig von der Trauerstimmung und der Vorbereitungen hierzu folgendes:
Etwa 14.45 Uhr—es war Sonnabend—lief durch das Baus der Leitungsbefehl dass allen operativen Mitarbeiter in IEF zu verbleiben haben es finde noch eine sehr wichtige Besprechung in Gegenwart allen sowjetischen Berater statt. Die Berater aus Karlshorst seien bereits auf dem Wege zum IWF.
Wir waren alle der Annahme, dass die Sitzung im Zusammenhang mit Stalins tot steht. Obwohl es 14.45 Uhr hiess, die Berater seien bereits unterwegs, trafen diese erst gegen 15.45 Uhr im IWF ein. Sie fuehrten eine Unterredung mit dem Leiter des IWF Micha Wolf, und etwa 16.00 Uhr begann dann die Sitzung.
Es waren anwesend:

Micha Wolf, Leiter des IWF.

I. Hauptabteilung

Hensche Herbert, Leiter der HA.I-
Schoenherr Alfred, Abteilungsleiter.
Gaila Kurt Mitarbeiter bei Schoenherr.
Wilzchek Franz,
Hartung Fritz Abteilungsleiter.
Brand Elfriede, Mitarbeiter bei Hartung.
Ein weiter Mitarbeiter von Hartung, Brillentraeger, Name bekannt.
Steinfuehrer Heinz Abteilungsleiter.
Jenicke Horst, Abteilungsleiter.
Jacob Otto Abteilungsleiter.
Eine weitere Anzahl von Mitarbeiter der I.HA die namentlich bekannt sind wie Siegfried Knobelsdorf, Mar Heim, Steinbock, usw.

II. Hauptabteilung

Zsinda Gustav, Leiter der HA. II.
Witzel Werner, Abteilungsleiter.
Alfred Runge, Mitarbeiter.
Herman Nebelung, Mitarbeiter,
Kr. Abteilungsleiter.
Kurt Dumke, Mitarbeiter.
Gerhard Eckert, Mitarbeiter.

III. Hauptabteilung

Gerhard Huebel, Mitarbeiter.
Freitag   Mitarbeiter.
Korb befand sich noch im Krankenhaus.

IV. Hauptabteilung

Hartwig Helmut, stellv. Hauptabteilungsleiter.

1. Abteilung

Felix   , stellv. Abteilungsleiter.
Karl Geake, Mitarbeiter.
Willi Otto, Mitarbeiter.
Klaus   , Mitarbeiter.
Karl Behrand, Mitarbeiter.

2. Abteilung

Heinrich Weihberg, Abteilungsleiter.
Willi Neumann, Mitarbeiter.
Gustav Kollega, Mitarbeiter.
Kurt Peter, Mitarbeiter.

3. Abteilung

Willi Woehl, Abteilungsleiter.
Peter Scheib, stellv.

4. Abteilung

Emmi Becker, Abteilungsleiter.

Die sowj. Berater.

Eugen, Chefberater
Dolmetscherin,
Berater I.HA.,
Berater II.HA., Margaschow,
Berater III.HA., Bronski,
Berater IV.HA,
Berater 1.Abteilung
Berater 2.Abteilung, Bronski,
Berater 3.Abteilung.

Zeitdauer der Sitzung.
Etwa 16.oo Uhr bus 16.30 Uhr.

Die Sitzung wurde geleitet von Micha Wolf. Wolf spach in der SU. nach Stalins tot.
Er fuehrte aus:

Die aussergewoehnliche Sitzung sei aus bestimmten Gruenden notwendig. Die operativen Mitarbeiter aller Hauptabteilungen und Abteilungen haben mit Hilfe ihrer Agenten ab sofort folgendes ~~festzustellen~~ in Westberlin und Westdeutschland festzustellen.

1.) Die Reaktion auf Stalin's tot.

2.) die Reaktion auf die Regierungsumbildung in der SU. nach Stalins tot.

3.) der wahre Grund des Abfluges der DDR Fluechtlinge mit alliierten Flugzeugen.
    aus Westberlin nach Westdeutschland

Micha Wolf gab hierzu folgende Erlaueterung:
Die Freunde[1] brauchen dringend die gewuenschten Nachrichten: Mit Hilfe unserer Agenten muss sofort eine Stossaktion eingeleitet werden. Die gewuenschten Nachrichten muessen aus Bonnen Regierungskreisen, Wirtschaftskreisen und aus Kreisen der westdeutschen Parteien kommen. Besonders soll versucht werden derartige Nachrichten aus Kreisen der Hohen Kommissare in Westdeutschland zu bekommen. Die Nachrichten zu 1) und 2) im detzigen Stadium eine politische Notwendigkeit. Es muessen alle Nachrichten ob positiv oder negativ gesammelt werden, wie z.B. erhofft man sich nach Stalins) tot eine Aenderung der innen- und Aussen- Poltik der SU; wie ist die Meinung zu Malenkow als neuen Regierungschef und seiner Regierung; wie ist die wahre Meinung zu Stalins tot, ist man froh oder bedauere man es wird den Westen, besonders Amerika, die Gelegenheit nuetzen und politische oder militaerische Provokationen sowie Massnahmen starten u.s.w.
Wolf ging sodann auf die Nachrichten zu 3) ein. Er fuehrte aus:
Die westdeutsche Regierung sowie der Reuter - Senat haben die Alliierten gebeten, fuer den Abtransport von der DDR Fluechtlingen [aus Westberlin] Militaerflugzeuge bereitzustellen. Ist nun diese Bereitstellung von Militaerflugzeugen durch die Alliierten und besonders durch die Amerikaner fuer den Fluechtlingsabflug aus Westberlin der wahre Grund oder steckt hier mehr dahinter. Es besteht die berechtige Annahme dass der Abflug von Fluechtlingen [mit Militaerflugzeugen] aus Westberlin nur eine Legende ist. Es sei deshalb notwendig ganz besonders auf diesem Gebiete eine sehr schnelle und systematische Spionagearbeit in Westberlin und in der Bundesrepublik zu betreiben. Diese Nachrichtenarbeit sei eine sehr, sehr eilige und sehr wichtige. Heute noch muessen alle unsere Agenten aufgesucht werden oder aber herangeholt werden, um ihnen die Auftraege, ganz besonders den Letzten , richtig zu erteilen. Die Freunde wuenschen dass sie schon morgen Sonntag die ersten Nachrichten von uns besitzten. Die obigen 3 Aufgaben und wiederum besonders die Letzte stellen in den naechsten Wochen neben unserer normalen Arbeit die Wichtigsten Schwerpunkte dar. Auch am morgigen Sonntage wird gearbeitet. Jeder Mitarbeiter hat das menschenmoeglichste zu leisten bezw. Einsatzbereitschaft zu zeigen um die uns uebertragenen Aufgaben bestens zu erfuellen. Wolf machte mehrmals darauf aufmerksam, dass die Aufgabe die wichtigste und entscheidenste ist. Die Aufgaben 1) und 2) koennen in der Nachrichtenarbeit von unseren Agenten gut als Diskussionsgrundlage mit westdeutschen Regierungsvertretern u.s.w. benutzt werden um gute Nachrichten fuer Schwerpunkt 3) zu erlangen.
In Zusammenhang mit den Fluechtlingstransporten mittels Militaerflugzeuge muss besonders der Flugplatz Tempelhof und die westdeutschen Flugplaetze beobachte werden ob die Maschinen leer nach Berlin fliegen oder aber Truppen und Kriegsgeraete nach Berlin transpotiern. Genaus Bezeichnung ~~der~~ etwaiger Ladungen mussen aus den Nachrichten ersichtlich sein.
Unsere Agenten, die nach Westdeutschland fahren, haben zusaetzlich folgende Aufgaben: Welche Truppenbewegungen der Alliierten vollziehen sich in Westdeutschland. Die Form der Truppenbewegungen, also, per Eisenbahn oder per Landstrasse u.s.w. Um welche Waffengattungen handelt es ~~dabei~~ sich dabei. Ebenfalls sollen Beobachter nach Kiel, Hamburg, Bremen u.s.w. geschickt werden [???] in den Haefen festzustellen welches Material geloescht wird bezw. welche Kriegsschiffe vor Anker liegen.

---

[1] The Soviets.

Bei legalen Reissen von Agenten, wie z.B. Minsiteriumsbeauftragten u.s.w. nach West~~deuts~~ deutschland, sollen diese in Regierungskreisen und Wirtschaftskreisen die Reaktion. auf die Ratifizierung der EVG Vertraege im Bundestag ermitteln.

Wolf Schloss mit den Worten, dass er hoffe dass wir die Wictigkeit des Auftrages erkennen und unseren ganzen Ehrgeiz einsetzen den erteilten Auftrag zu erfuellen.

Meine Bemerkung zu dieser maerkwuerdigen Sitzung:

Wir, noch die Russen hatten am Morgen des 7.3.53 eine Ahnung von einer derartigen Sitzung am Nachmittag. Die Berater waren erst am Vormittag—einige von ihnen selbst bis 14.oo Uhr—im IWF und wusste nichts von einer derartigen wichtigen Besprechung am Nachmittag. Ich selbst hatte bis Mittag mit dem sowjetischen Berater Margaschow eine Besprechung ueber den fall Engelhardt. Margaschow hatte nicht die geringste Ahnung von einer bevorstanden Sitzung. Diesen Eindruck hatte nicht nur ich von den Russen sindern es war die Meinung aller operativen Mitarbeiter. Die sowj. Nachrichtenzentrale in Karlshorst muss erst am Nachmittag selbst aus Moskau unterrichtet worden sein. Die ganze Art wie diese Sitzung stattfand zeigte mir dass selbst die Sowjets erstaunt waren. Ferner muss man bedenken dass ja schliesslich Volkstrauertag war.

Das es sich weniger um die Punkte 1) und 2) des Auftrages handelte, zeigte mir die im Anschluss an dieser Sitzung durchgefuehrte Abteilungsbesprechung bestens. Alle Abteilungen mussten im Anschluss an dieser gemeinsamen Sitzung eigens Besprechungen durchfuehren um einen Arbeitsplan fuer die Stossaktion zu erstellen, der bis Sonntag, den 8.3.53 der Leitung vorzulegen war. In meiner Abteilung nahm der Sowjetischer Berater Margaschow ~~teil~~ an dieser Besprechung auch teil. Ich entwickelte meinen Plan und liess mit Absicht den Punkt 3) etwas im Hintergrund. Sofort hakte Margaschow ein und brachte zum Ausdruck, dass dieser Punkt das Wichtigste sei. Besonder[s] hierauf solle man sich konzentrieren. Den ganzen Maerz hindurch bis zu meinem Abgang, spukte diese Flugzeugaktion als wichtigste Aufgabe im IWF und bei den Russen. (Siehe auch meiner Niederschrift ueber die Sitzung der Hauptabteilungsleiter und Abteilungsleiter vom 27.[3?].53).

Meine Erfahrungen und Erkenntnisse ueber die russische Methode zeigen mir eindeutig, dass auch der Flugzeugabschuss bei Boizenburg/Elbe—englische Maschine—und der Flugzeugabschuss an der tschechischen Grenze—amerikanische Maschine—im gleichen Zusammenhang mit der Aktion im IWF steht. Selbst die Besprechungen der alliierten Bevollmaechtigten mit den Russen ueber Fragen der Luftkorridore und Luftsicherung nach Berlin, die z.Zt. noch laufen, stehen im Zusammenhang mit dem o.a. Auftrag der Russen an die IWF-Mitarbeiter.

Abschliessen moechte ich noch hinzufuegen, dass alle Berichte in der o.a. Angelegenheit dreifach an ~~das~~ die IWF-Leitung einzureichen waren. In dieser Spionageaktion wurden von meiner Abteilung folgende Agenten eingesetzt:

Putzke Rudolf in Westberlin,

Todtmann, Vizepraesident den deutschen Notenbank, in seiner Taetigkeit.

Dewey, Charles, Direktor den deutschen Notenbank, in seiner Taetigkeit.

Renneisen, Hauptabteilungsleiter Valuta im Ministerium fuer Inner und ausser deutscher Handel, in seiner Taetigkeit und besonders ~~Doering~~ auf seiner Reise nach Westdeutschland.

Doering, Chefredakteur der Wirtschaft, in seiner Taetigkeit.

Kahn Siegbert, Deutsches Wirtschafts Institut, in seiner Taetigkeit.

Wieland [illegible] in ihrer Taetigkeit.

Thorndike, Andrew [DEFA?] in der Taetigkeit zur Fa. Opriba.

Saloman Generaldirektion Schiffahrt, in seiner Taetigkeit.

Die geworbenen Schiffer—Magdeburg nach Hamburg—von der DSU in Magdeburg

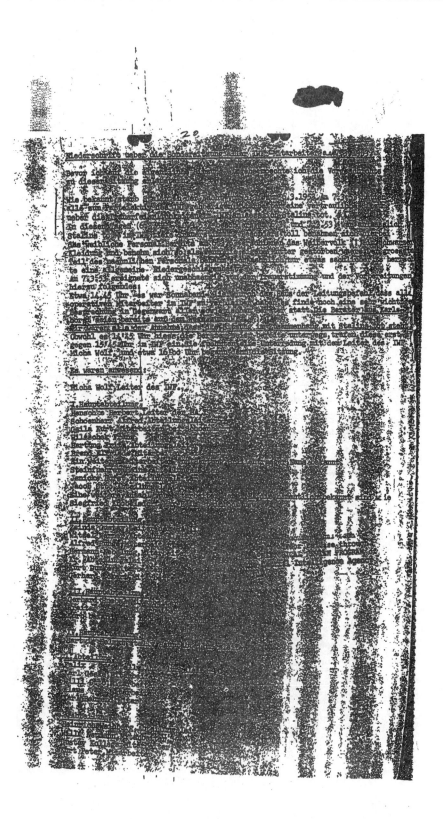

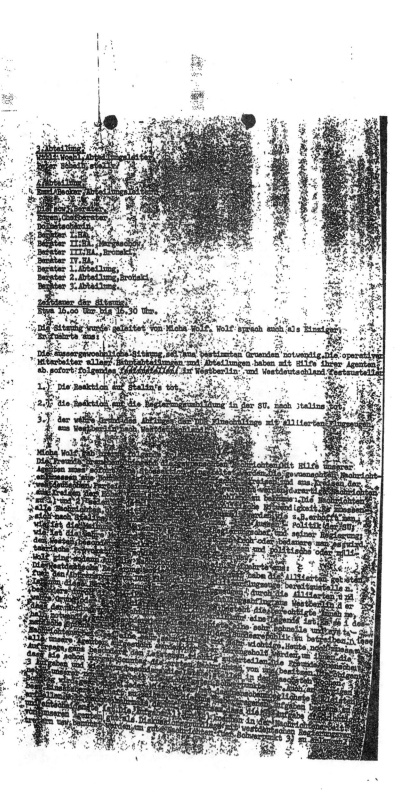

3. Abteilung:
Mühl,Wohl,Abteilungsleiter
Alter, Schain, stellv.

4. Abteilung:
Bunn, Becker, Abteilungsleiter

Die sow. Berater:
Eugen, Chefberater,
Dolmetschérin,
Berater I.HA.,
Berater II.HA., Margaschow,
Berater III.HA., Bronski,
Berater IV.HA.,
Berater 1.Abteilung,
Berater 2.Abteilung, Bronski,
Berater 3.Abteilung.

Zeitdauer der Sitzung:
Etwa 15.00 Uhr bis 16.30 Uhr.

Die Sitzung wurde geleitet von Micha Wolf. Wolf sprach auch als Einziger.
Er fuehrte aus:

Die aussergewoehnliche Sitzung sei aus bestimmten Gruenden notwendig. Die operativen
Mitarbeiter aller Hauptabteilungen und Abteilungen haben mit Hilfe ihrer Agenten
ab sofort folgendes *festzustellen* in Westberlin und Westdeutschland festzustellen:

1.) Die Reaktion auf Stalin's tot.

2.) die Reaktion auf die Regierungsumbildung in der SU. nach Stalins tot.

3.) der wahre Grund des Abfluges der DDR Fluechtlinge mit alliierten Flugzeugen
aus Westberlin nach Westdeutschland.

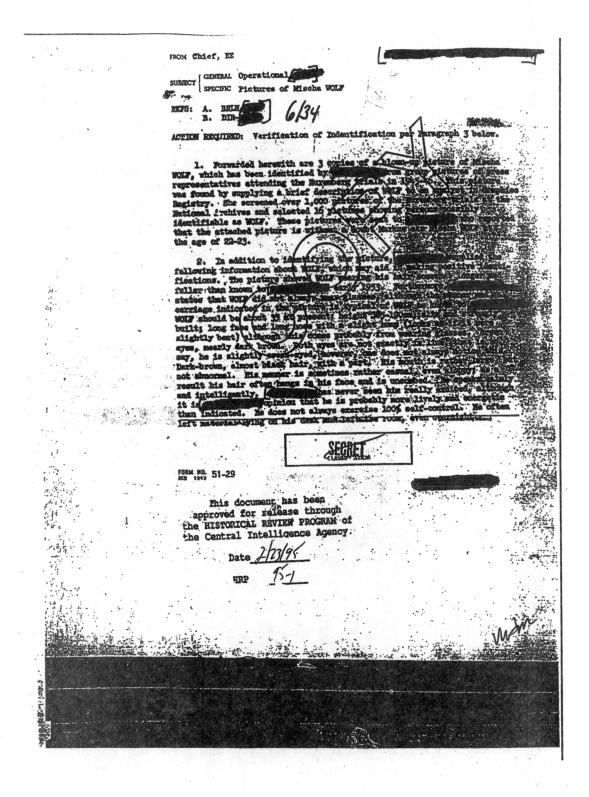

FROM Chief, EE

SUBJECT { GENERAL Operational

{ SPECIFIC Pictures of Mischa WOLF

REFS: A. BRIN

B. DIR-   6/34

ACTION REQUIRED: Verification of Identification per Paragraph 3 below.

1. Forwarded herewith are 3 copies of a blown-up picture of Mischa WOLF, which has been identified by representatives attending the Nuremberg Trials in was found by supplying a brief description of WOLF Registry. She screened over 1,000 pictures of National Archives and selected 16 pictures identifiable as WOLF. These pictures were that the attached picture is the age of 22-23.

2. In addition to identifying the picture following information about WOLF, which may aid fications. The picture shows WOLF wearing his fuller than known states that WOLF did carriage indicated in WOLF should be about 35 built; long face and slightly bent) although eyes, nearly dark brown say, he is slightly Dark-brown, almost black hair, with a part not abnormal. His manner is sometimes rather casual, even result his hair often hangs in his face and is unnoticed and intelligently. it is opinion that he is probably more lively and than indicated. He does not always exercise 100% self-control. He often left materials lying on his desk and in his room, even

┌─────────────────┐
│   SECRET   │
└─────────────────┘

FORM NO. 51-29

This document has been
approved for release through
the HISTORICAL REVIEW PROGRAM of
the Central Intelligence Agency.

Date 2/23/95

HRP 75-1

Robert KORB told ████████ once, before WOLF became head of the ███ that WOLF still had a great deal to learn, because he was too irresponsible. WOLF wears dark horn-rimmed glasses, and he was often seen by ███████ without glasses. In general, he makes a pleasant and intelligent impression. For example, there is no comparison between WOLF and ██████ ████████ believes also that he would not be brutal, but sensitive. ████████ told ████████ that as a result of the Nazi rise to power ██████ ████ his father and went to the Soviet Union, where he received his ████ and higher education. He is married and, according to ████████ must have a very nice wife to whom he was quite attached. She should have ████ two children. ████████ does not know whether he was married ████ or in the Soviet Union. According to comments which he made ████ did always enjoy his stay in the USSR. ████████ does not know ████ ████ but something appeared to be bothering him in this respect. (NOTE: His wife's mother was imprisoned for a long time in the Soviet Union in the 1930's). WOLF's facial make-up does not appear to be totally German. It could be that he is Jewish. This is particularly evident in his brown eyes and black-brown hair, as well as his nose and mouth.

In 1953 WOLF drove a small Soviet automobile, which was probably a 1952 model.

Anton ACKERMANN thought a great deal of WOLF and so did the Russians according to ████████ and BECKER told ████████. However ████ ████ ULBRICHT was not in favor of his appointment as head of the IWF ████████ and the Russians, however, were able to overrule ULBRICHT. He was known in the IWF as "Genosse Mischa".

3. In addition to the above picture and identifying data ████ ████████ ████ we are sending two sets of 4 pictures each of other persons according to ████████ are not WOLF, but also attended the Nuremberg trials. These may be used to bury WOLF's picture when testing ████████ ████████ for further identification of present and past activities of WOLF.

9 April 1957
2 - Attachments: 1. Picture of WOLF
2. 4 sets of other persons who attended Nuremberg trials. pictures of

Distribution:

SECRET   COPY

IV-9: IR: "Markus Johannes Wolf," 11 October 1973 (MORI: 144083).

[Because important parts of this document are nearly illegible in the original, the following transcription has been made. It duplicates the original insofar as is possible. Any spelling or grammatical errors in the original have been retained. Places in the original text that were totally illegible or questionable have been noted. A copy of the original document immediately follows this transcription.]

[Handwritten date] 11 Oct. 73

Markus Johannes WOLF

Chronology

19 January 1923. Markus Johannes WOLF was born in Hechingen, Wuerttemburg. His father was Dr. (of medicine) and author Friedrich WOLF, born 23 December 1888, died 5 October 1953 in Lehnitz, Oranienburg. Friedrich WOLF was a well-known communist and East Germany's first post-war ambassador to Poland. Markus' mother and Friedrich's second wife was Ilse, born 20 May 1893.

June 1933. Markus and his brother Konrad, and their father fled Germany to France. In November 1933 they moved to Switzerland.

March 1934. The father and sons arrive in the USSR.

1934-1942. Markus WOLF attended Karl Liebknecht school and a high school specializing in aeronautics. The latter school moved from Moscow to Alma Ata during the war. WOLF was a Komsomol member.

1942. He attended a Comintern school at [Kuschnarenkovo?]. One fellow student there was Wolfgang LEONHARD, author of Child of the Revolution (German title: Die Revolution entlaesst Ihre Kinder), London, Collins St. James Place, 1957. Also studying there were the sisters Emma and Ilse STENZER. Markus WOLF later married Emma STENZER. Wolf's alias at the school was "FOERSTER".

1942-1945. Markus WOLF worked in various places in the USSR primarily as a radio propagandist (Radio Moscow) against fascism. He also studied law. At some time during his Moscow period, WOLF met and fell in love with a German girl, Margrit KNIPPSCHILD, who disappeared in the USSR.

1944. WOLF married Emma, nee STENZER, in Moscow. She was born 21 October 1923 in Munich but, like her husband had become a Soviet citizen. Her mother was imprisoned in the USSR for a long time, but no further information is now available. Her father was a minor KPD functionary. He may well have been the Franz STENZER who appears in footnote 8, pp. 102-103 of Die KPD von 1933 bis 1945, Horst Duhnke, Klepenheuer U. Witsch Cologne, 1972. LEONHARD, cited above says (p. 467) that WOLF married ["]Emma STENZER, the blonde, blue-eyed girl from the Comintern school...who had reported my remarks to the school supervisor...." The STENZER girls, whose father was murdered by the Nazis used the cover name STERN at the Comintern school.

Late May 1945. WOLF and his wife arrived in Berlin. He appeared in the uniform of a Russian colonel and wore a uniform while traveling, although he usually wore civvies. They moved into an apartment at Bayernallee 44, Berlin Charlottenburg, in the American sector and near the communist-dominated Berliner Rundfunk (radio station). They lived at this address from 23 June1945 to 15 November 1949. They were Soviet citizens and hence were not subject to German registration laws. Neither did they need food ration cards.

19 November 1945. WOLF went to Nuremberg to serve as an assistant to Prosecutor General Roman Andreyevich RUDENKO, the chief Soviet prosecutor, and as a special reporter. He remained at Nuremberg or went there periodically until early 1946.

28 June 1946. The WOLF's first son was born in Berlin/Charlottenburg. They may have had two other children. The first son was named Michael.

Ca. 1946. LEONHARD (p. 467) wrote, "Upon my return [[to Germany]] I visited my former friend Mischa WOLF, whom I had known in the Comintern school. He was now commentator on foreign policy for the East Berlin radio and was using the name Michael STORM....Mischa, who had excellent relations with the highest Soviet officials, lived in a luxurious five-room apartment in Bayernallee...." By August 1947 WOLF also owned a fine villa near Lake Glienecke.

All manuscripts prepared for use by Berlin radio had to be countersigned by WOLF. He also edited all interviews.

April 1948. By this time, WOLF had become a member of the SED, the East German communist party. In April 1948 he traveled to Poland as a member of the first delegation of East German journalists to go there. In June 1948 he was in Prague, working as a reporter.

16 October 1949-1952. The East German government announced the appointment of Markus WOLF as first councillor (Erste Missionsrat) to the first East German mission in Moscow. His primary duties, however, were those of a cultural and press attaché. During this period he was also given basic training in intelligence. While Markus was in Moscow, his father Friedrich served as the chief of the first East German mission to Poland.

August 1951. Markus WOLF returned on a visit to Berlin to attend a conference of chiefs of DDR diplomatic missions.

1952. WOLF returned from Moscow and joined the Institut fuer Wirtschaftswissenschaftliche Forschung (IWF Institute for Economic and Scientific Research), a cover organization for East German (and hence Soviet) espionage. It had its headquarters in East Berlin at Klosterstr. 59. In late 1952, WOLF, not yet 30 years old, succeeded Anton ACKERMANN as chief of the IWF. ACKERMANN had had a nervous breakdown. Walter ULBRICHT opposed WOLF's appointment, but the Soviets rode down ULBRICHT's objections. WOLF worked closely with Gustav SZINDA in setting up Abteilung (Section) 1a, which had as its mission the penetration of the West German government, specifically including the police and the judiciary. At this time WOLF lived at Heinrich Mann Platz 16 (probably Pankow).

1953. An IWF official defected, and the IWF was disbanded. WOLF, by now a brigadier general, had become chief of Department XV of the MfS (Ministry of State Security). His mission was unchanged.

1957. By this date WOLF, still chief of Department XV, was also a deputy Minister of the MfS.

December 1958. WOLF participated in a conference in Moscow, attended by Soviets and Poles.

June 1960. By this time WOLF was the chief of the HVA (Hauptverwaltung A) of the MfS. The HVA is charged with conducting foreign intelligence. With a

Polish intelligence officer he discussed the organization of aid for Cuba. He also discussed, with UB staff members, operations against the Irish.

4

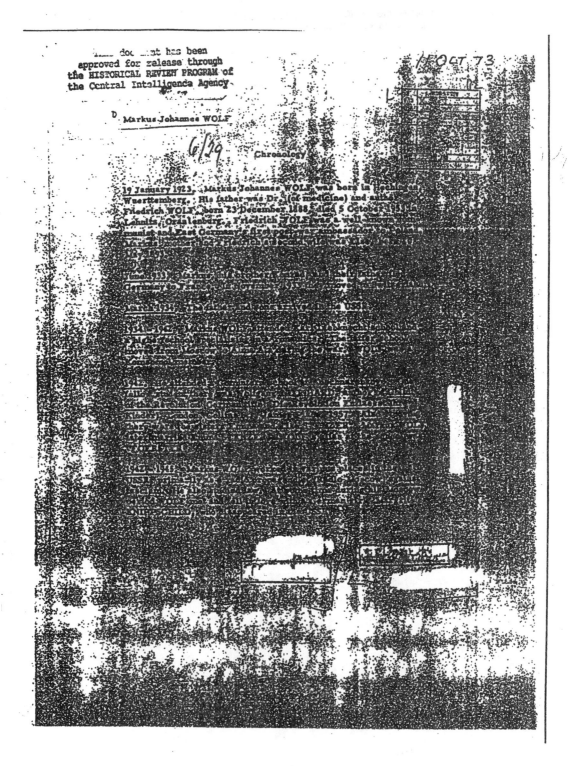

D. Markus Johannes WOLF

6/29   Chronology

19 January 1923. Markus Johannes WOLF was born in [illegible] Wuerttemberg. His father was Dr. (of medicine) and author Friedrich WOLF, born 23 December 1888 [illegible] 5 October [illegible]

1944. WOLF married Emma, nee STENZER, in Moscow. She was born on 21 October 1923 in Munich but, like her husband, had become a Soviet citizen. Her mother was imprisoned in the USSR for a long time, but no further information is now available. Her father was a minor KPD functionary. He may well have been the Franz STENZER who appears in footnote 5, pp. 102-103 of : KPJ von 1933 bis 1945, Horst Duhnke, Klepenheuer U. Witsch, Cologne, 1972. LEONHARD, cited above, says (p. 467) that WOLF married Emma STENZER, the blonde, blue-eyed girl from the Comintern school . . . who had reported my remarks to the school supervisor . . . :" The STENZER girls, whose father was murdered by the Nazis, used the cover name STERN at the Comintern school.

Late May 1945. WOLF and his wife arrived in Berlin. He appeared in the uniform of a Russian colonel and wore a uniform when traveling, although he usually wore civvies. They moved into an apartment at Bayernallee 44, Berlin/Charlottenburg, in the American sector and near the communist-dominated Berliner Rundfunk (radio station). They lived at this address from 23 June 1945 to 15 November 1949. They were Soviet citizens and hence were not subject to German registration laws. Neither did they need food ration cards.

19 November 1945. WOLF went to Nuremberg to serve as an assistant to Prosecutor General Roman Andreyevich RUDENKO, the chief Soviet prosecutor, and as a special reporter. He remained at Nuremberg or went there periodically until early 1946.

28 June 1946. The WOLF's first son was born in Berlin/Charlottenburg. They may have had two other children. The first son was named Michael.

Ca. 1946. LEONHARD (p. 467) wrote, "Upon my return /to Germany/ I visited my former friend Mischa WOLF, whom I had known in the Comintern school. He was now commentator on foreign policy for the East Berlin radio and was using the name Michael STORM . . . Mischa, who had excellent relations with the highest Soviet officials, lived in a luxurious five-room apartment in Bayernallee. . . ." By August 1947 WOLF also owned a fine villa near Lake Glienicke.

All manuscripts prepared for use by Radio Berlin had to be countersigned by WOLF. He also edited all interviews.

-2-

April 1948. By this time WOLF had become a member of the SED, the East German Communist Party. In April 1948 he travelled to Poland as a member of the first delegation of East German journalists to go there. In June 1948 he was in Prague, working as a reporter.

16 October 1949 - 1952. The East German government announced the appointment of Markus WOLF as first councillor (Erste Missionsrat) to the first East German mission in Moscow. His primary duties, however, were those of a cultural and press attache. During this period he was also given basic training in intelligence. While Markus was in Moscow, his father Friedrich served as the chief of the first East German mission to Poland.

August 1951. Markus WOLF returned on a visit to Berlin to attend a conference of chiefs of DDR diplomatic missions.

1952. WOLF returned from Moscow and joined the Institut fuer Wirtschaftswissenschaftliche Forschung (IWF, Institute for Economic and Scientific Research), a cover organization for East German (and hence Soviet) espionage. It had its headquarters in East Berlin at Klosterstr. 59. In late 1952 WOLF, not yet 30 years old, succeeded Anton ACKERMANN as chief of the IWF. ACKERMANN had had a nervous breakdown. Walter ULBRICHT opposed WOLF's appointment, but the Soviets rode down ULBRICHT's objections. WOLF worked closely with Gustav SZINDA in setting up Abteilung (Section) 1 a, which had as its mission the penetration of the West German government, specifically including the police and the judiciary. At this time WOLF lived at Heinrich Mann Platz 16 (probably Pankow).

1953. An IWF official defected, and the IWF was disbanded. WOLF, by now a brigadier general, became chief of Department XV of the MfS (Ministry of State Security). His mission was unchanged.

1957. By this date WOLF, still chief of Department XV, was also a deputy Minister of the MfS.

December 1958. WOLF participated in a conference in Moscow, attended by Soviets and Poles.

June 1960. By this time WOLF was the chief of the HVA (Haupt-verwaltung A) of the MfS. The HVA is charged with conducting foreign intelligence. With a Polish intelligence officer he discussed the organization of aid for Cuba. He also discussed, with UB staff members, operations against the Irish.

INTELLOFAX 21

CLASSIFICATION

CENTRAL INTELLIGENCE AGENCY

INFORMATION REPORT

REPORT NO. SC

CD NO.

COUNTRY   East Germany

SUBJECT   The Supply and Distribution of Foodstuffs

PLACE
ACQUIRED   Germany, Frankfurt

DATE OF
INFO.   Prior to May 1952

DATE DISTR.   3 December 1952

NO OF PAGES   8

NO. OF ENCLS   1 (33 pages)
(LISTED BELOW)

SUPPLEMENT TO
REPORT NO.

This document has been
approved for release through
HISTORICAL REVIEW PROGRAM of
the Central Intelligence Agency.

GRADING OF SOURCE						COLLECTOR'S PRELIMINARY GRADING OF CONTENT					
COMPLETELY RELIABLE	USUALLY RELIABLE	FAIRLY RELIABLE	NOT USUALLY RELIABLE	NOT RELIABLE	CANNOT BE JUDGED	CONFIRMED BY OTHER SOURCES	PROBABLY TRUE	POSSIBLY TRUE	DOUBTFUL	PROBABLY FALSE	CANNOT BE JUDGED
A.	B.	C.	D.	E.	F. X	1.	2.	3. X	4.	5.	6.

THIS IS UNEVALUATED INFORMATION

SOURCE   Untested, through a usually reliable channel.

1. The entire supply and distribution of foodstuffs for the DDR is directed by a central office, the Main Department for Provisioning (Hauptabteilung Versorgung), which is headed by Prof. Dr. Karl Ritter and is part of the State Planning Commission. The main department fixes the ration card amount and the special foodstuff allotments for the sundry consumer groups and is alone responsible for pertinent legislation. The executive organ for the main department is the Ministry for Trade and Supply. This ministry determines the distribution to the sundry states and Kreise according to the number of nationalized and private farms. The ministry also sees that quotas are fulfilled.

2. The State Secretariat for Control and Purchasing of Agricultural Products (Staatssekretariat für Erfassung und Aufkauf landwirtschaftlicher Erzeugnisse), headed by State Secretary Hermann Streit, to which the Unions of Nationalised Control and Purchasing Enterprises (Vereinigungen Volkseigener Erfassungs- und Aufkaufsbetriebe)(VVEAB) are subordinate, and the State Secretariat for the Food Industries (Staatssekretariat für Nahrungs- und Genussmittelindustrie), headed by State Secretary Rudolf Allrecht, which also is responsible for the most economical processing of agricultural products, are independent executive organs.

3. The DHZ Internal Reserve is responsible for the execution of orders issued by the DDR cabinet and by the SCC to build up the state reserves. The DHZ does not control the state reserve depot for foodstuffs but merely administers it.

4. The priority for the distribution of home-produced and imported foodstuffs is assigned as follows:

   a. Red Army in the Russian Zone (GSOV)

   b. State reserve

   c. Export and reparations

   d. Privileged circles (party and government functionaries, working intelligentsia)

CLASSIFICATION

STATE	X	NAVY		X	NSRB	DISTRIBUTION							
ARMY	X	AIR		X	FBI	ORR	ISI						

- 2 -

e. General population

5. The supplying of the distribution points is done in the following order:

a. the HQ

b. the "Konsum" (consumer cooperative)

c. private business

The wholesale trade is conducted by the DHZ Foodstuffs in accordance with directives of the Main Department for Provisioning of the State Planning Commission.

6. In spite of the strenuous efforts of and the large investment of money by the DDR government, the planned peacetime agricultural yield per hectare has not yet been reached. In 1951, 142,500,000 east marks were invested, of which 26,800,000 was spent for improvements and 38,400,000 for machine lending stations (MAS). The plan for 1952 calls for an investment of 184,300,000 east marks, of which 63,700,000 is for the construction of 15 machine lending stations. The machine lending stations are being expanded considerably. This is attributable to a dearth of draft animals and to the great strategic importance of the MAS.

7. The DDR balance sheet for supply and distribution in 1952 showing imports and home-grown foodstuffs is as follows. The amounts are in tons.

Product	Home-grown	Imported	Total 1951
Meat	582,600	79,500	662,100
Fish	84,200	62,000	146,200
Animal fats	48,700	36,200	84,900
Butter	76,600	32,300	108,900
Oil	54,200	16,200	70,400
Flour	1,246,100	346,000	1,592,100
Sugar	807,800		807,800
Potatoes	4,726,300	86,500	4,812,800

8. The following is the 1955 plan for foodstuffs in the DDR according to records of the State Planning Commission. The amounts are in thousands of tons.

Product	Production	Import	Total
Meat	924	26	950
Fish	212	74	286
Animal fats	245	-	245
Butter	100	28	128
Oil	88	17	105
Flour	1,900	-	1,900
Sugar	888	-	888
Potatoes	17,000	-	17,000

In 1951, foodstuffs were imported in part from the free world, but by 1953-1954 it is expected to import such items only from the East Bloc states.

9. The total supply of foodstuffs consists of inventories at the beginning of the year in processing plants; enterprises, and dealers' stocks, and also of production and imports. The distribution of the total supply is made in accordance with a priority schedule set up by the SCC economic planning commission in early 1949. Since the middle of 1951, this distribution of the state reserve (called the plan reserve in official terminology) has assumed greater importance.

- 3 -

The priority schedule is as follows:

a. Quota bearers (Kontingentträger)

b. Reparations

c. GSOV

d. Export

e. Plan reserve

f. Material reserve

C. Inventory 31 December 1951

10. In 1951, the foodstuffs were distributed to the "quota bearers" - that is, the DDR population, as follows. The amounts are in thousands of tons.

Meat	434.6
Fish	103.9
Animal fats	60.8
Butter	72.4
Oil	39.6
Flour	1,080.9
Sugar	423.9
Potatoes	3,413.2

True distribution figures cannot be arrived at from these amounts because the differentiation in the distribution to the population is too great. There are three groups supplied in the DDR; party and government functionaries the HO, the AG and VEB plant cafeterias, and the normal consuming section of the population. Moreover substitutes are supplied to the third category in place of the meat and fat rations found on the ration cards.

11. In 1951 the foodstuffs were exported and delivered as reparations as follows (The amounts are in thousands of tons):

Product	Export	Reparations	Total
Meat	3.8	-	3.8
Fish	2.4	-	2.4
Animal fats	-	-	-
Butter	-	-	-
Flour	62.4	-	62.4
Sugar	104.3	82.7	187.0
Potatoes	426.3	134.2	560.5

The amounts under sugar reparations were not sent to the USSR but were used by the Russians in barter dealings with the West. The potatoes delivered as exports and reparations were mostly seed potatoes or were used to make up for poor harvests (in this case Poland).

12. In 1951, the foodstuffs were delivered to the Russian army as follows. The amounts are in thousands of tons.

Meat	96.7
Fish	18.6
Animal fats	8.6
Butter	28.4
Oil	3.1
Flour	275.2
Sugar	76.4
Potatoes	604.5

- 4 -

13. If part of the foodstuffs delivered to the Russian army in the Russian Zone exceed the requirements of the several troop units, it is sold to regional Russian zone authorities, or sales cooperatives (Konsum and HO). Other foods or consumer goods are purchased with the proceeds. The deliveries to the GSOV are credited as occupation costs.

14. Material reserves in the Russian Zone refer to those foodstuffs which are stored for further processing. As of the end of 1951 the material reserves in the plants were on hand in the following amounts. The amounts are in thousands of tons.

Meat	22.5
Fish	-
Animal fats	2.4
Butter	-
Oil	7.4
Flour	46.2
Sugar	35.7
Potatoes	158.7 (mainly for processing into potato starches and dried potatoes)

15. The state reserve of foodstuffs, officially designated the plan reserve, is subordinate to the DDR cabinet and the LCG. Some state reserve depots are under the People's Police. The state reserves can only be used by permission of the DDR cabinet, the LCG, or the People's Police.

16. The can containers necessary for the storing of foodstuffs are given production priority. The iron industry must give priority to the rolling of the needed strips and sheets. The following allocation of the sheet for tin can production was made in 1951. The amounts are in tons.

State reserve	7,240
Reparations	1,950
Civilian requirement	1,080
Export	2,160
Total	12,430

A total production of 18,700 tons is planned for 1952.

SAG Thale/Harz, the VEB Kaltwalswerk Bad Salzungen, and the VEB Kaltwals-werk Oranienburg are producing the sheet for the most part.

17. In 1951, the following foodstuffs were stored in the state reserve. The amounts are in tons.

Meat	108.5
Fish	22.0
Animal fats	11.0
Butter	8.2
Oil	18.6
Flour	203.5
Sugar	115.0

In addition 8,500 tons of dried potatoes were stored.

IV-10: *(Continued)*

18. The following is a list of the principal state reserve storage depots.

Place	Product Stored	First Quarter 1952, Amounts in Tons	Maximum Capacity in Tons
Rostock-Marienehe	Fish, canned	4,250	6,700
Rostock-Bramo	Grain	18,700	40 -43,000
Sasquits-Lonoken	Fish, canned	8,700	11,300
Lauterbach on Rügen	Fish, canned	13,200	15 -16,000
Wurzen/Saxony	Flour	32,650	40,000
Friotschmuhle			
Oschatz/Saxony, right by Southern Railroad	Butter	1,760	4 - 5,000
line Wurzen-Riesa	Flour	19,7--	4 -21,000
Dresden, Harbor basin SSW	Meat	6,400	7 - 7,500
from Wettinerstr. railroad station	Fats	2,135	3,650
Magdeburg, Liebknechtstr.	Fats and oils	7,630	11 -13,000
Burg, northwest of the railroad station near the Ihlekanal	Butter and other Fats	2,840	4 - 6,000
Anklam/Mecklburg, Mutelusterstr.	Sugar	7,360	12,000
Velten/Brandenburg, Berlinerstrasse	Dried potatoes	8,500	
Gotha/Thuringia Perlstrasse	Oil and animal fats	4,520	6,300
Doehlen/Saxony Zuckerfabrikstr.	Sugar	21,600	25 -26,000
Chemnitz, Alt Chemnitzerstr.	Butter	3,725	5,800
Lina/Saxony	Meat	24,250	30 -32,000
Ascheraleben-Bhf. Nord	Meat	17,300	30,000
Riesa/Saxony	Oil and animal fats	15,200	19 -21,000
Rostock, Werftstr.	Butter	2,870	8,500
Dessau, August-Bebel-Strasse	Sugar	42,700	50,000
Genthin/Saxony-Anhalt	Sugar	20,360	26,400
Dresden-Stockyard	Meat	21,200	40 -45,000
Ostberlin, Sehala	Grain	14,200	20 -25,000
Osthafen, near the Warschauer Brücke			
Zwickau-Eckersbach	Meat	6,240	6,500 - 7,000
Leipzig-Wahren	Meat	8,530	11 -14,000
Ostberlin Slaughterhouse	Meat	7,200	9 -10,000
Erfurt-railroad station area	Meat	8,560	10 -11,000
Halle-Trotha	Meat	11,750	14,600
Alsleben/Saxony-Anhalt	Sugar	2,760	3,200
Grottewitz near Liebenwerda	Sugar	4,200	5 - 7,000
Halle, Raffinerie-strasse	Sugar	7,460	9 -11,000
Magdeburg-Sudenburg	Sugar	5,240	8 -10,000
Zeitz/Saxony-Anhalt	Sugar	2,830	10 -11,000
Rosita/Thuringia	Sugar	4,600	4,600

19. The following is a list of newly constructed cold storage plants.

Berlin, slaughterhouse — 2,300 ton capacity for meat

Frankfurt/Oder freight station area — 4,000 ton capacity for meat and fat

Dresden-Trachau — 3,150 ton capacity for butter, fats, meat, and eggs

- 6 -

Prenzlau at the corner of 109
and 198 streets

2,600 ton capacity for meat
and fats

These cold storage plants are for the use of the People's Police exclusively
and are managed by it.

20. The following are 1951 balance sheets for supply and distribution. The
amounts are in thousands of tons.

a. Supply of Meat

Inventory 1 January 1951		12.4
Production		582.6
Import from USSR	46.4	
elsewhere	33.1	79.5
		674.5

Distribution of Meat

Quota bearers	434.6	
Reparations	-	
GSOV	96.7	
Export	.3.8	
Plan reserve	108.5	
Material reserve	22.5	
Inventory 31 December 1951	8.4	
	674.5	

b. Supply of Fish

Inventory 1 January 1951		6.8
Production		84.2
Import from USSR	8.8	
elsewhere	53.2	62.0
		153.0

Distribution of Fish

Quota bearers	103.9	
Reparations	-	
GSOV	18.6	
Export	2.4	
Plan reserve	22.0	
Material reserve	-	
Inventory 31 December 1951	6.1	
	153.0	

c. Supply of Animal Fats

Inventory 1 January 1951		3.5
Production		48.7
Import from USSR	24.1	
elsewhere	12.1	36.2
		88.4

Distribution of Animal Fats

Quota bearers	60.8	
Reparations	-	
GSOV	8.6	
Export	-	
Plan reserve	11.0	
Material reserve	2.4	
Inventory 31 December 1951	5.6	
	88.4	

d. Supply of Butter

Inventory 1 January 1951		4.6
Production		76.6
Import from USSR	26.1	
elsewhere	6.2	32.3
		113.5

Distribution of Butter
Quota bearers	72.4
Reparations	-
GSOV	28.4
Export	-
Plan reserve	8.2
Material reserve	-
Inventory 31 December 1951	4.5
	113.5

e. Supply of Oil
Inventory 1 January 1951		5.1
Production		54.2
Import from USSR	12.7	
elsewhere	3.5	16.2
		75.5

Distribution of Oil
Quota bearers	39.6
Reparations	-
GSOV	311
Export	-
Plan reserve	18.6
Material reserve	7.4
Inventory 31 December 1951	6.8
	75.5

f. Supply of Flour
Inventory 1 January 1951		183.5
Production		1,246.1
Import from USSR	297.5	
elsewhere	48.5	346.0
		1,775.6

Distribution of Flour
Quota bearers	1,080.9
Reparations	-
GSOV	275.2
Export	62.4
Plan reserve	203.5
Material reserve	46.2
Inventory 31 December 1951	107.4
	1,775.6

g. Supply of Sugar
Inventory 1 January 1951	112.4
Production	807.8
Import	-
	920.2

Distribution of Sugar
Quota bearers	423.9
Reparations	82.7
GSOV	76.4
Export	104.3
Plan reserve	115.0
Material reserve	35.7
Inventory 31 December 1951	82.2
	920.2

h. Supply of Potatoes
Inventory 1 January 1951		107.5
Production		4,726.3
Import from USSR	-	
elsewhere	86.5	86.5
		4,920.3

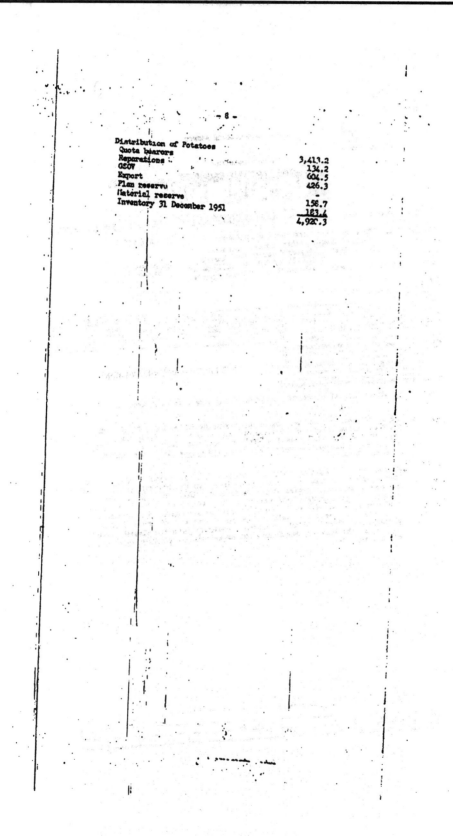

- 8 -

Distribution of Potatoes

Quota bearers	
Reparations	3,413.2
GSOV	134.2
Export	604.5
Plan reserve	426.3
Material reserve	-
Inventory 31 December 1951	156.7
	183.4
	4,920.3

...ELLUFAX 21

CLASSIFICATION

CENTRAL INTELLIGENCE AGENCY

SECURITY INFORMATION

INFORMATION REPORT

REFERENCE COPY
DO NOT CIRCULATE

REPORT NO. SC

CD NO.

COUNTRY East Germany

SUBJECT 1. SED Proposal of Restrictions on Escape from East Germany This document has been
2. Plants Guards approved for release through the HISTORICAL REVIEW PROGRAM of the Central Intelligence Agency.

DATE OF INFO. 1 to 27 September 1952

PLACE ACQUIRED Germany, Berlin

DATE DISTR. 5 December 1952

NO. OF PAGES 1

NO. OF ENCLS. (LISTED BELOW)

SUPPLEMENT TO REPORT NO.

GRADING OF SOURCE						COLLECTOR'S PRELIMINARY GRADING OF CONTENT					
COMPLETELY RELIABLE	USUALLY RELIABLE	FAIRLY RELIABLE	NOT USUALLY RELIABLE	NOT RELIABLE	CANNOT BE JUDGED	CONFIRMED BY OTHER SOURCES	PROBABLY TRUE	POSSIBLY TRUE	DOUBTFUL	PROBABLY FALSE	CANNOT BE JUDGED
A.	B.	C.	D.	E.	F. X	1.	2.	3. X	4.	5.	6.

THIS IS UNEVALUATED INFORMATION

SOURCE A minor official of the SED, most frequently employed as a courier.

1. At a 27 September 1952 meeting of the German Socialist Unity Party (SED), in East Berlin, a bill about the introduction of capital punishment for those who attempt to escape from East Germany, was discussed. This bill, if passed, will bear the name Republik-Flucht-Gesetz (law concerning flight from the Republic).

2. On 1 September 1952, two new guard organizations were established in all of East Germany. In cities, towns, and villages, an Objektschutz (plant guard) has been organized to guard plants, public buildings, etc., and in the country the Flurschutz (field guard) has been set up to guard agricultural equipment. Participation in the organizations is compulsory and there is no salary. In the plants, all personnel are organized, after the Soviet pattern, into "workers' defense forces", and must guard the plants day and night. In the country, the farmers are organized in a similar way by the village mayors.

CLASSIFICATION

STATE	X	NAVY	X	NSRB		DISTRIBUTION						
ARMY	X	AIR	X	FBI		ORR BY X						

CENTRAL INTELLIGENCE AGENCY

INFORMATION REPORT

REPORT NO. SO

CD NO.

COUNTRY   East Germany

SUBJECT   Establishment of Farm Cooperatives.

DATE DISTR.   10 December 1952

NO. OF PAGES   2

PLACE
ACQUIRED   Germany, Munich

NO. OF ENCLS.
(LISTED BELOW)

this document has been
approved for release through
the HISTORICAL REVIEW PROGRAM of
the Central Intelligence Agency.

DATE OF
INFO.   9 August 1952

SUPPLEMENT TO
REPORT NO.

	GRADING OF SOURCE					COLLECTOR'S PRELIMINARY GRADING OF CONTENT					
COMPLETELY RELIABLE	USUALLY RELIABLE	FAIRLY RELIABLE	NOT USUALLY RELIABLE	NOT RELIABLE	CANNOT BE JUDGED	CONFIRMED BY OTHER SOURCES	PROBABLY TRUE	POSSIBLY TRUE	DOUBTFUL	PROBABLY FALSE	CANNOT BE JUDGED
B.	C.	D.	E.		F. X	1.	2.	3. X	4.	5.	6.

THIS IS UNEVALUATED INFORMATION

REFERENCE COPY
DO NOT CIRCULATE

SOURCE   Untested.

1. At a conference of chief editors held in the office of the Central Committee
of the SED on 9 August 1952 Albert Schaefer, a member of the Agricultural
Department of the Central Committee, stated that more than 100 cooperative
farms had been established and that several hundred organizational committees
were working on the establishment of more such farms. Schaefer said that many
of the   people   still believe that there is a difference between these
cooperative farms and the collectivization of farming. This opinion must not
be attacked in the East German press. However, the party must be aware that this
opinion is erroneous and that the same development is now taking place in East
Germany that took place in the U.S.S.R. in 1927. According to Schaefer, the only
difference between conditions which existed in the U.S.S.R. in 1927 and those prevailing now in East Germany lies in the fact that farmland in the U.S.S.R. was
nationalized prior to collectivization whereas in Germany it will be nationalized
only in the normal course of the collectivization. In this connection Schaefer denounced Slansky who had stressed the national form of farm cooperatives which had
been organized in Czechoslovakia.

2. In addition, Schaefer made the following statements:
Meetings, which envisage the establishment of farm cooperatives, must be
approved by the Kreisamt, which will screen the members of the founding
committee. Access to these meetings will be only by invitation. In several
cases, expropriated farmers of large estates tried to become members of the
executive board of farm cooperatives. No farmers of large estates or innkeepers
must be admitted to meetings held in connection with the organization of farm
cooperatives even though they be members of the SED. All the members of farm
cooperatives will have the same standing. The wives of the farmers must also
acquire membership. There will be no hired farm hands in the cooperatives.
Former farm workers, who became cooperative farmers, ceased to be members of
the Union of Farm Workers within the FDGB. The former property of farmers, who
were expropriated in the border zone for political reasons, became state property.
Farm workers, who were put on these farms, had to turn over their property to the
farm cooperatives except for some livestock. Making workers previously employed
by farmers of large estates members of farm cooperatives represents political
progress and a set-back for capitalism in the country. On the other hand, farm

CLASSIFICATION

		NAVY		NSRB		DISTRIBUTION							
		AIR		FBI									

- 2 -

hands of nationalized estates must not become cooperative farmers, as this would mean a step in the wrong direction. The shortage of labor in the country must not be discussed in the press, as this is an argument put forth by the enemies of the working class. By a mechanisation of farming methods, it will become possible to release even more farm workers for industrial production.

3. HRD cadres will have to be formed in farm cooperatives. However, they should become active only after a certain stabilisation period. Committees of women are also to be organised. They should assume their activities without delay, as clergymen oppose the farm cooperatives from their pulpits and try to influence the farmers' wives especially.

CENTRAL INTELLIGENCE AGENCY

INFORMATION REPORT 7/13

SECURITY INFORMATION

COUNTRY	East Germany	REPORT NO.	CS
SUBJECT	SED. Direc...	DATE DISTR.	4 March 1953
		NO. OF PAGES	1
DATE OF INFO. 10 February 1953		REQUIREMENT NO.	RD
PLACE ACQUIRED Germany, Munich		REFERENCES	

BY CABLE

THE SOURCE EVALUATIONS IN THIS REPORT ARE DEFINITIVE.
THE APPRAISAL OF CONTENT IS TENTATIVE.
(FOR KEY SEE REVERSE)

SOURCE: Unidentified source (F); supposedly based on a copy of the directive.
Appraisal of Content: 3.

1. The Politbüro of the SED issued a directive to the East German press on 10 February 1953, giving the following instructions:

   a. Refugees fleeing from East Germany are to be described as "fugitives from the Republic (republikflüchtige)". Only in exceptional cases is the term "deserter (Ueberläufer)" to be applied.

   b. Propaganda for the return of the refugees is to be increased.

   c. Particular emphasis is to be placed on the danger facing young male refugees that upon their arrival in the West they may be shanghaied by the French Foreign Legion.

2. The directive declared that the fact that every such person returning to East Germany is immediately arrested and confined for a period varying from two weeks to three months must be kept quiet. This imprisonment is considered to be for "re-educational purposes", while allowing sufficient time for an investigation of the person's activities during his stay in the West. In case of acquittal, the confinement is to be regarded as a police punishment for failure to register the change of address with the local police.

STATE		ARMY		NAVY		AIR		FBI		AEC				
	x		x		x		x							

Note: Washington Distribution Indicated by "X"; Field Distribution by "#".

OCI No. 546?.56
Copy No.

CENTRAL INTELLIGENCE AGENCY
OFFICE OF CURRENT INTELLIGENCE
24 November 1956

250

TO : Deputy Director (Intelligence)

SUBJECT: Soviet Interference with Berlin Rail Access

The Soviet commander at the East German check point at Marienborn has informed the British that Soviet authorities intend to start exercising their "right" to board Allied trains running between Berlin and West Germany on the night of 25-26 November. Another threat to start boarding trains on the night of 23-24 November apparently was not carried out.

Colonel Kotsiuba, the Soviet acting commandant in Berlin, asserted on 22 November it would be necessary for Soviet authorities to board trains in order to inspect passengers' documentation. He also asserted the Soviet right to pass judgment on whether specific individuals should be authorized to travel under orders issued by Allied authorities. These are the two major points of Soviet-Allied disagreement.

Allied officials in Bonn decided on 24 November to send a further protest to Colonel Kotsiuba, stating that Allied train commanders would not permit Soviet authorities to board the trains. On 24 November the Allied ambassadors agreed that trains should turn back rather than permit Soviet authorities to board them or take off passengers.

Soviet authorities appear to be testing Allied reaction to pressure, and may impose further restrictions on surface travel if successful at this. They claim that persons have been traveling on military trains, and under military orders on the autobahn, who are unauthorized because they are not directly connected with the military garrison in Berlin, while the Allies claim the sole authority to decide who has such travel rights.

If the Soviet authorities do not yield and the Allies are forced to send trains back to prevent their being boarded, the Allies might find themselves maneuvered into becoming the victims of a self-imposed partial blockade of Berlin.

Dist: White (Colonel Goodpaster)
State Dept (Mr. Armstrong)
DCI   DDP   ADSI
DD?I ADNE
DDI   ADRR

CONFIDENTIAL

V: The Berlin Tunnel

V: The Berlin Tunnel

No single operation more typifies Berlin's importance as a strategic intelligence base than the construction of the Berlin Tunnel. Probably one of the most ambitious operations undertaken by the CIA in the 1950s, it succeeded despite the fact that the KGB knew about the operation even before construction of the tunnel began!

The genesis of the tunnel operation lay in Berlin's location in Europe and its prewar status as the capital of a militarily and economically dominant Germany. The largest city on the Continent, Berlin lay at the center of a vast network of transportation and communications lines that extended from Western France to deep into Soviet Russia and Eastern Europe. This was still true in the 1950s; Soviet telephone and telegraph communications between Moscow, Warsaw, and Bucharest were routed through Berlin, for example.[1] This became a factor of crucial importance beginning in 1951, when the Soviets began to shift from wireless communications to encrypted land lines for almost all military traffic.[2] Land lines existed in two forms: overhead lines strung from telephone poles and underground cables. Both carried encrypted messages as well as nonsecure voice communications.

CIA officers examining this situation in 1952 concluded that underground cables offered the more valuable target, since they were buried and hence not subject to constant visual surveillance. If a tap could be placed covertly, it would be likely to remain in place for some time. Thus was born the idea of tunneling into the Soviet sector of Berlin to tap into Soviet military communications. The concept was tested in the spring of 1953, when an agent in the East Berlin telephone exchange patched an East Berlin telephone line into West Berlin late one night to sample what might be obtained. Even after midnight the communications traffic was sufficiently valuable that CIA Headquarters decided to go ahead with the operation.[3]

During 1953, CIA continued to gather data and test the idea of tapping communications in East Berlin. By August 1953, detailed plans for the tunnel were completed and a proposal was drawn up for approval by DCI Allen Dulles. After much discussion, this was obtained on 20 January 1954.[4]

---

[1] G.J.A. O'Toole, *Encyclopædia of American Intelligence and Espionage: From the Revolutionary War to the Present* (New York: Facts on File, 1988), p. 66.
[2] David E. Murphy, Sergei Kondrashev, and George Bailey, *Battleground Berlin*, (New Haven, CT: Yale University Press, 1997), p. 208.
[3] *Ibid.*, pp. 208, 211-212.
[4] *Ibid.*, pp. 212-213, 219.

Having learned the location of the underground cables used by the Soviets from an agent inside the East Berlin post office, the Altglienicke district was selected as the best site for a cable tap.[5] Work began in February 1954, using the construction of an Air Force radar site and warehouse as a cover.[6] The tunnel itself was completed a year later, at the end of February 1955, and the taps were in place and operating shortly thereafter.[7]

Unfortunately, the whole operation was blown even before the DCI approved the project. On 22 October 1953, US intelligence officers briefed a British Secret Intelligence Service (SIS) audience that included KGB mole George Blake. Blake reported the existence of the tunnel project during his next meeting with his case officer, Sergei Kondrashev, in London the following December. However, a full report was not sent to Moscow until 12 February 1954.[8]

Although the KGB was aware of the potential importance of the tap, its first priority was to protect Blake.[9] Knowledge of the tunnel's existence was very closely held within the KGB—neither the GRU (Soviet military intelligence) nor the East German Stasi was informed. Rather than immediately shutting down the tunnel, the Soviets thus implemented a general tightening up of security procedures. A small team was formed to secretly locate the tap, which they did by late 1955. Early in 1956 the Soviets developed a plan whereby the tap would be "accidentally" discovered without putting Blake at risk. On the night of 21-22 April 1956, a special signal corps team began to dig.[10] By 0200 they had discovered the tap chamber. At 1230 the following day they opened a trapdoor leading from the tap chamber down a vertical shaft to the tunnel. By 1420 they had penetrated the tunnel in the full glare of a well-organized publicity coup.[11]

The digging operation had been seen from an observation post atop the warehouse in West Berlin and the tunnel evacuated long before the Soviets entered the tap chamber. A microphone was left in place to record what was going on.[12] The Soviet publicity coup backfired: rather than condemning the operation, the non-Soviet press hailed it as audacious and well-planned. Of course, at the time, no one knew the extent of Soviet foreknowledge.

Since KGB archives remain closed, we cannot be certain that the Soviets did not exploit their prior knowledge of the cable tap for their own

---

[5] *Ibid.*, p. 210.
[6] *Ibid.*, p. 219.
[7] *Ibid.*, p. 222.
[8] *Ibid.*, pp. 214-216.
[9] *Ibid.*, pp. 217-218.
[10] *Ibid.*, pp. 226-227.
[11] *Ibid.*, pp. 230-231.
[12] See Document V-5 for a transcript of the recording that was made.

purposes—to plant false information, for example. However, according to former DCI Richard Helms, the possibility that the Soviets used the tunnel for "disinformazia" (disinformation) was closely examined after Blake's exposure and arrest in 1961. Finally, it was concluded that the intelligence that had been collected was genuine.[13]

The sheer volume of the "take" from the tunnel operation would tend to support that conclusion. In all, about 40,000 hours of telephone conversations were recorded, along with 6,000,000 hours of teletype traffic.[14] Most of the useful information dealt with Soviet orders of battle and force dispositions—information that was invaluable in the days before reconnaissance satellites and other, more sophisticated means of collection became operational. Not until more than two years after the tunnel was exposed and shut down was the task of processing this immense volume of data completed.[15]

V-1: Field Project Outline, 16 September 1953 (MORI No. 144126).
This memorandum outlines the basic concept for the Berlin Tunnel project. It was prepared in August and September 1953.

V-2: Memorandum for COM Frankfurt from COB Berlin; Progress Report—28 August through 17 October 1954, 18 October 1954 (MORI No. 144129).
A memorandum documenting some of the problems encountered while excavation of the tunnel was in its early stages.

V-3: Memorandum for the Record, 29 November 1954 (MORI No. 144130).
This memorandum describes some of the security measures in place while the tunnel was in operation.

V-4: Clandestine Services History Program (CSHP) History: Soviet Discovery of the Berlin Tunnel, 15 August 1956 (MORI No. 144132).
The circumstances of the tunnel's discovery is described in this declassified history. As noted at the beginning of this document, it was prepared before the role played by KGB mole George Blake was uncovered. The description of the tunnel's actual discovery is accurate, however.

---

[13] Thomas Huntington, "The Berlin Spy Tunnel Affair," *Invention and Technology* (1995), p. 52.

[14] See Document V-7, below.

[15] G.J.A. O'Toole, *Encyclopædia of American Intelligence and Espionage: From the Revolutionary War to the Present* (New York: Facts on File, 1988), p. 67.

V-5: CSHP History: Soviet Discovery of the Berlin Tunnel, (Tape Transcript) Undated (MORI No. 145737).

The entry of the Soviet and East German security forces into the tunnel was monitored by specially concealed microphones. This is a transcript of the recording. Much of it is garbled. The English voices are those of US intelligence officers listening to the activity in the tunnel—their comments were accidentally recorded at the same time.

V-6: CSHP History of the Berlin Tunnel, G. Berlin Tunnel, Undated (MORI No. 144450).

V-7: CSHP History of the Berlin Tunnel, V. Production, [from the Berlin Tunnel Operation], Undated (MORI No. 144445).

V-8: CSHP History of the Berlin Tunnel: Appendix B. Recapitulation of the Intelligence Derived, Undated (MORI No. 145735).

These documents describe the importance of the Berlin Tunnel as a source of intelligence information. The volume and the quality of the information derived suggests that the tunnel was a valuable source despite having been compromised early in the planning process. Until the relevant Soviet records are made available to researchers a comprehensive evaluation of the project will not be not possible, however.

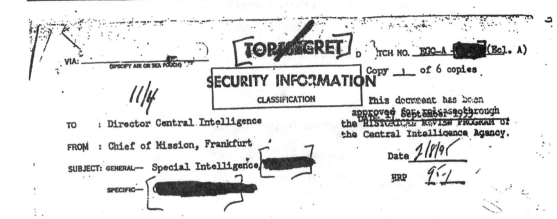

TOP SECRET

D TCH NO. EGO-A ▮▮▮▮ (Ecl. A)

Copy _1_ of 6 copies

SECURITY INFORMATION

CLASSIFICATION

This document has been approved for release through the HISTORICAL REVIEW PROGRAM of the Central Intelligence Agency.

Date _2/8/95_

HRP _95-1_

VIA: _____ (SPECIFY AIR OR SEA POUCH)

11/4

TO : Director Central Intelligence

FROM : Chief of Mission, Frankfurt

SUBJECT: GENERAL— Special Intelligence ▮▮▮▮

SPECIFIC— ▮▮▮▮▮▮▮▮▮▮

In accordance with our discussion of 28 August the attached field project outline has been prepared and is being forwarded for presentation to you through ▮▮▮▮▮▮ of Staff D.

I am of the opinion that the key to the success of this project is primarily a matter of maintaining the highest possible degree of security. For this reason I am most anxious to confine knowledge of the plan to an absolute minimum; in fact, it is my conviction that only those individuals who can make a specific contribution to the success of this operation should be made aware of its existence.

Considering the tremendous amount of time consuming work that lies ahead of us in this undertaking, it is of the utmost importance that we begin as soon as possible in order to be ready for the final phase which must necessarily be accomplished at the end of the summer of 1954.

LUCIAN B. TRUSCOTT

This document is part of an integrated file. If separated from the file it must be ▮▮▮▮ review.

Dist:
    Copies 1-3 - Wash

17 September 1953

FORM NO. 51-28 A
MAR. 1949

TOP SECRET
SECURITY INFORMATION
CLASSIFICATION

SECURITY INFORMATION

(Encl B)

FIELD PROJECT OUTLINE

This document has been approved for release through the HISTORICAL REVIEW PROGRAM of the Central Intelligence Agency.

Recommended by:

Approved by:

Cryptonym:

16 September 1953

Date 2/8/95

HRP 95-1

1. Pursuant to discussions of 28 August 1953 between COM Germany and the DCI, wherein it was agreed that the intelligence potential of the subject project justified its inherent risk and financial cost, the following outline and plan of action is submitted for approval and the implementation indicated.

2. It should be noted that this project will be developed jointly and exploit in accordance with existing formal agreements between ⬛⬛⬛⬛⬛⬛⬛⬛⬛ For security reasons resulting from the physical location of the project ⬛⬛⬛⬛ participation must be limited during the earlier phases of the operation.

3. In view of the absolute necessity for maintaining complete operational security, all aspects of this project must be handled separately ⬛⬛⬛⬛⬛ all intelligence matters will be communicated ⬛⬛⬛⬛⬛⬛⬛ separately handled ⬛⬛⬛⬛⬛⬛ separate and unique correspondence channels. Further, in consideration of the high intelligence potential of the operation and of the considerable risk involved, it is imperative that all other activities in this particular field, both existing and proposed, be kept under constant review to insure that no one of them adversely affects it.

4. The objective of this project is to collect covertly the Soviet intelligence known to be passing over certain underground telecommunication cables that are adjacent to and accessible from the U.S. Sector of Berlin. ⬛⬛⬛⬛⬛⬛⬛⬛⬛ From reliable technical information collected over a period of several years, it has been established that these cables carry Soviet Military, Security Service and Diplomatic telephone and telegraph traffic to and from various Soviet Headquarters in Germany and in certain instances between those Headquarters and Moscow. ⬛⬛⬛ Access to these cables however can be secured only through the construction of a subterranean passage approximately 1800 feet in length, one-half of which will be in Soviet Sector territory.

5. Although the technical and engineering difficulties of this undertaking cannot be minimized, they can for the most part be met with experience developed from similar operations conducted elsewhere. Confining knowledge of this operation in all its phases, however, is

This document is part of an integrated file. If separated from the file it must be subjected to individual systematic review.

TOP SECRET

GQTS 678

Copy 1 of 4 copies

SECURITY INFORMATION

Page 2

the greatest problem. In this respect and considering the location of the site of the operation, it is difficult to visualize an installation and activity of the size required being established at this remote spot. It is, nevertheless, reasonable and possible for the U.S. Forces in Berlin to construct a number of warehouses within the U.S. Sector. Although such constructions will attract attention, the fact remains that knowledge of what transpires within these buildings is a matter not beyond control. In actuality, therefore, the problem is not so much the establishment of a perfect cover, but more a matter of maintaining absolute internal security within a physically enclosed area housing the operation. To meet these operational, construction and security requirements, it is planned to have the U.S. Army activate a plan calling for the construction and maintenance of three warehouses located along the US/Soviet Sector and the US/Soviet Zone borders. These warehouses will for all intents and purposes constitute an emergency equipment dispersal system operated in connection with the security of U.S. Forces in Berlin. Each of these installations will be manned by a carefully hand-picked and screened detachment of 2 officers and 16 enlisted men who will be engaged in the handling of cargo shipments. Actually these detachments will be engaged in the construction of the subterranean passage and the handling of equipment and supplies related to this activity from the one installation which is adjacent to the target. The officers and men of these units who will be specially trained and thoroughly indoctrinated from the accomplishment of their missions and the maintenance of absolute security which must, from its inception, be divorced from all reference to the intelligence activity. (Control and security will be exercised in every instance through properly indoctrinated officers assigned to the units.)

6. Implementation of the above proposed action will be accomplished in four phases and as follows:

A). Initial stage: (1) Collaboration between the appropriate U.S./British engineers will be established for the purpose of preparing an engineering study and training plans. (2) In association with a C.G. USAREUR appointed staff officer, a plan calling for the establishment of an emergency equipment dispersal installation in Berlin will be drawn up. Based on this plan Berlin Military Post will establish a Post engineer project requiring the construction of the three warehouses. (3) Simultaneously and as a part of the above plan the officers and men required to man the warehouses will be recruited and assigned to a ~~newly activated and formally designated Army Service Unit which will~~ eventually be assigned to the Berlin Command.

B) Training stage: (1) During the construction of the required buildings in Berlin the recruited teams will be in training. This training will consist of normal military subjects including driving,

GQTS 678

SECURITY INFORMATION

Page 3

operation of power tools, tunnel construction, and above all development of personal security. (2) At the conclusion of this training, subject to the completion of the warehouses, the detachment will move into these installations and begin receiving and storing the equipment that will be required for the primary operation.

C) Construction phase: At the appropriate time the units established in the warehouse covering the target site will commence work on the passageway. During the course of this work personnel, equipment and spoil will be moved as required among the three installations. Upon completion of the passageway, ▬▬▬ specialists will begin work on the critical and hazardous task of constructing the tap chamber and opening of the cables. (The element of hazard is particularly acute due to the fact that the target cables lie only 28 inches from the surface of the earth.) After successfully opening the cables the taps will be led away through the passageway to the U.S. Sector into the recording unit. It is estimated that this construction will require nine months time. In any case the cable tapping can only be attempted during a long dry period (late summer 1954).

D) Operational phase: (1) Installation of terminal equipment, switch boards and recorders. (2) Selection and recording of target circuits. (3) Processing.

▬▬▬▬▬▬▬▬▬▬▬▬▬▬▬▬▬▬▬▬▬▬▬▬▬▬▬▬▬▬▬▬ this ▬▬▬▬▬▬▬▬▬▬▬▬▬▬▬▬▬▬▬▬▬▬▬▬▬▬▬▬▬▬▬▬ includes labor costs and an approximation of construction material and equipment costs. It does not include the cost of warehouse construction. It is not possible to schedule exact costs until final arrangements vis a vis U.S. Army support and procurement of construction materials and equipment have been made. In any case, special arrangements for funding this project will be made.

8. In view of the major degree of assistance and cooperation that will be required from USEUCOM, USAREUR and USCOB to fulfill the above plan, national intelligence level support to it will undoubtedly be required. In accordance with the aforementioned DCI/COM German discussion and immediately subsequent to DCI approval of this project, it is recommended that support be obtained in Washington at the highest level and that the Commanding Generals of the EUCOM, USAREUR and USCOB be informed of the project on an eyes only basis and their support to it requested. (See Tab C).

9. It will be necessary for Headquarters to provide the following support to this activity:

A) Full time assignment of a specially qualified engineer with experience in the construction of subterranean tunnels.

TOP SECRET

GQTS 6-78

V-1: *(Continued)*

Page 4

B) Establishment of technical equipment requirements.

C) Procurement and stockpiling of technical equipment in readiness for shipment as required in the field.

D) Organization and staffing of a unit to process the results obtained from the operation.

E) Procurement of special processing equipment for (D) above.

F) Preparation of specialized training material needed in conjunction with the operation.

This document is part of an integrated file. If separated from the file it must be subjected to individual systematic review.

GQTS 678

307

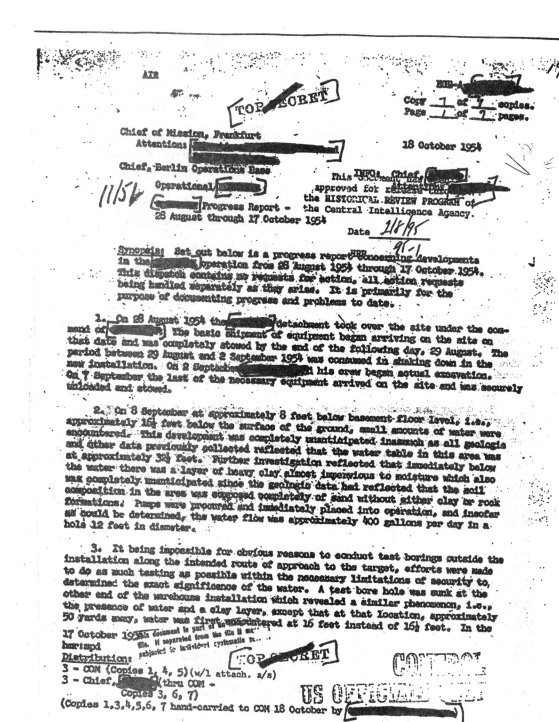

AIR

TOP SECRET

Copy 1 of 7 copies.
Page 1 of 7 pages.

Chief of Mission, Frankfurt
Attention: ▓▓▓▓▓▓▓▓▓▓▓▓▓▓

18 October 1954

Chief, Berlin Operations Base

Operational ▓▓▓▓▓

INFO: Chief ▓▓▓▓▓
Attention ▓▓▓▓▓

This document has been
approved for release through
the HISTORICAL REVIEW PROGRAM of
the Central Intelligence Agency.

Date 2/8/95

▓▓▓▓▓ Progress Report –
28 August through 17 October 1954

Synopsis: Set out below is a progress report concerning developments
in the ▓▓▓▓▓▓ operation from 28 August 1954 through 17 October 1954.
This dispatch contains no requests for action, all action requests
being handled separately as they arise. It is primarily for the
purpose of documenting progress and problems to date.

1. On 28 August 1954 the ▓▓▓▓▓ detachment took over the site under the command of ▓▓▓▓▓▓▓ The basic shipment of equipment began arriving on the site on
that date and was completely stowed by the end of the following day, 29 August. The
period between 29 August and 2 September 1954 was consumed in shaking down in the
new installation. On 2 September ▓▓▓▓▓▓▓▓▓ and his crew began actual excavation.
On 7 September the last of the necessary equipment arrived on the site and was securely
unloaded and stowed.

2. On 8 September at approximately 8 feet below basement floor level, i.e.,
approximately 16½ feet below the surface of the ground, small amounts of water were
encountered. This development was completely unanticipated, inasmuch as all geologic
and other data previously collected reflected that the water table in this area was
at approximately 32½ feet. Further investigation reflected that immediately below
the water there was a layer of heavy clay almost impervious to moisture which also
was completely unanticipated since the geologic data had reflected that the soil
composition in the area was composed completely of sand without either clay or rock
formations. Pumps were procured and immediately placed into operation, and insofar
as could be determined, the water flow was approximately 400 gallons per day in a
hole 12 feet in diameter.

3. It being impossible for obvious reasons to conduct test borings outside the
installation along the intended route of approach to the target, efforts were made
to do as much testing as possible within the necessary limitations of security to
determined the exact significance of the water. A test bore hole was sunk at the
other end of the warehouse installation which revealed a similar phenomenon, i.e.,
the presence of water and a clay layer, except that at that location, approximately
50 yards away, water was first encountered at 16 feet instead of 16½ feet. In the

17 October 1954
bsr:mpd

TOP SECRET

Distribution:
3 - COM (Copies 1, 4, 5)(w/1 attach. a/s)
3 - Chief, ▓▓▓▓▓ (thru COM -
Copies 3, 6, 7)
(Copies 1,3,4,5,6, 7 hand-carried to COM 18 October by ▓▓▓▓▓▓▓▓▓

308

TOP SECRET

17 October 1954

hole where the excavation was originally started and where water had been encountered at 16½ feet, test holes were bored down through the clay layer and a sump hole was sunk for approximately 8 feet additional depth for testing purposes. These test borings reflected that the clay stratum at that point was approximately 6 feet in thickness and that underneath it was located comparatively dry sand, indicating that the true water table was considerably below this point. An examination was made of the cesspool located approximately 50 feet beyond the far warehouse wall and the site of the original excavation, and it was determined that at that point water and the clay stratum apparently did not appear until a depth of approximately 22½ feet.

4. Insofar as it was possible securely to do so, a check was made of the location of water during the drilling of the well, which was completed during the construction period, approximately 30 - 40 yards northeast of the location where the original excavation was started by ███████. The record of the well drilling reflected that usable amounts of water were reached at approximately 33 feet. It will be recalled that in the immediate vicinity of the site are located a number of sand pits which on the basis of direct visual observation plus stereoscopic examination of aerial photographs had been estimated at 32 feet in depth. These pits which are in the immediate proximity of the site were again examined and determined to be dry to within a few inches of the bottom, despite recent heavy rains in the vicinity. To be absolutely positive of the depth of these pits, an altimeter was carried concealed to the bottom of one of them resulting in a reading of approximately 25 feet.

5. During this checking period from 8 until approximately 15 September 1954, the pumping of the water from the excavation continued steadily with only a very slight appreciable lessening of the water flow. While there was no indication thereof, the possibility was considered that since the outlet from the pumps was being piped into the cesspool system, the pumped out water could conceivably through some odd subterranean formation be flowing back into the excavation. Consequently, a quantity of phenothalein dye was procured and in alcohol solution mixed with the pumped out water. Tests over a period of several days clearly established that the pumped out water which had been mixed with phenothalein dye in solution was not flowing back into the excavation and therefore must have been draining off normally at cesspool level (22½ feet) or below.

6. On the basis of all of the above factors, the conclusion was reached that what had been encountered in the excavation was a perched water table caused by the presence of a clay lens approximately 6 feet thick but of unknown dimensions. It was considered probable also that this situation was aggravated by the fact that the summer of 1954 was an unusually rainy period in the area. While without test borings along the target line, which it is impossible to take, no one can be positive of this conclusion, it appears probable that the clay lens does not extend throughout the entire area. This was considered particularly probable in view of the depth of the adjacent sand pits, the fact that geologic data showed no extensive clay formation, and that the water and clay level in the concrete bottle of the cesspool, a short distance ahead of the original excavation, was approximately 6 feet deeper.

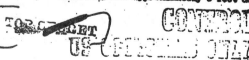

TOP SECRET

CONTROL
US OFFICIALS ONLY

Encountering a clay lens of limited proportions is not unusual, can seldom be predicted, and frequently cannot be forecast in a given area from available geologic data. The presence of clay lenses, particularly those not covering an extensive area, apparently occurs without rhyme or reason very much along the line of the old drillers' adage that "oil is where you find it." It is probable, however, that if clay strata exist under the entire area, the geologic data available would have given some indication thereof, which they did not. It was considered probable also that the clay lens slanted downwards beneath the surface in the direction of the target objective since it was approximately 6 inches higher at the back end of the warehouse and approximately 6 feet lower at the bottom of the concrete cesspool bottle.

7. The unanticipated discovery of water and the impervious clay lens underneath it raised a serious question as to exactly what construction approach should be used. As you will recall, we had originally intended to complete the construction with an overhead cover of approximately 9 feet; however, upon the initial examination of the site and upon determining from the first few feet of excavation that the sandy soil involved was extremely easy to work in, it was decided to drive considerably deeper and to operate with a cover of approximately 16 to 18 feet, which according to the water table level figures available to us would still have been several feet safely above the true water table. This was decided not only because of the ease with which the construction could proceed in the soil involved but also as an additional precaution to cut down the maximum amount of detectable noise. Approximately 8 to 9 feet of cover would still be possible above the 7 foot diameter tunnel as originally contemplated by driving the construction to the level where water was discovered unless the clay lens and the perched water table rise instead of drop, it being noted as set out above that every indication is that they would drop as the construction progressed. The other alternative is to cut through the clay lens, go underneath into the layer of sand above the true water table, and then drive the construction straight ahead. It is considered that two definite risks exist in this latter course, i.e., at some undetermined point in the future progress of the construction, a sharp drop out of the clay lens above the construction could cause a sufficient flow of water from the perched water table to raise a serious possibility of collapse; or, secondly, if by an chance, the clay lens continues to be present above the construction up to the point of reaching the target objective, it will be necessary to drive the construction and the terminal chamber up through the clay lens, which would cause serious construction problems, particularly if water still exists in a perched water table above the lens. A further complication results from the fact that careful survey of the proposed construction route from the site reflects that the terrain between the starting point of the excavation and the target point contains a definite dip estimated at between 5 and 6 feet over the approximately 1,500 foot target route. This dip or depression reaches its lowest point approximately halfway between the site and the target and rises gradually from that point to the target point.

8. On the basis of the above factors, the following conclusions were reached:

a. What had been encountered in the construction was a clay lens of limited but unknown dimensions approximately 6 feet in depth, sufficiently impervious to water to create a perched water table approximately 16 feet above the true water table.

TOP SECRET

17 October 1954

b. Below the clay lens there is present additional easily workable sand down to the true water table at approximately 32 feet.

c. On the basis of the test borings, the well data, the geologic data, and the water level in the cesspool concrete bottle, it is probable that the clay lens sinks gradually and perhaps drastically ahead of the original excavation and along the construction route and may, in fact, disappear altogether. In the absence of test borings, which it is impossible for security reasons to take, however, there is no absolute guarantee of this.

d. Initiating the construction by driving beneath the clay lens involves some risk of collapse or cave in if along the construction route a sudden drop off of the clay lens causes sufficient flow of water from the perched water table to saturate the surrounding sand.

e. If carefully done, construction can be effected along the top of the clay lens and the perched water table with sufficient cover that the project will not be detected through noise and will not run substantial risks of collapse or cave in. This was considered particularly advisable in view of the strong indications that the clay lens and the perched water table will sink as the construction progresses. The most serious drawback in driving the construction ahead on the top of the clay lens and the perched water table is the possibility that the clay lens will not sink or will rise again which would mean that when construction reaches a point midway between start and finish at the greatest depth of the terrain depression noted above, the construction would be operating with the benefit of only a few feet of cover which would compound the risk and make the noise factor an appreciable one.

f. At any point in the progress of the construction where the clay lens or the perched water table above it ceased dropping or appeared to rise, it would then be possible to cut through the clay lens and by use of well points, bore holes through the clay for drainage, etc., keep the tunnel dry and still continue progress at greater depth to afford adequate overhead cover without running any greater, if as great a risk of a sudden drop off and water flow as would be run if the construction were originally to begin below the clay lens.

9. On the basis of the above conclusions, it was tentatively decided that:

a. Construction should be commenced above the clay lens and should continue following the level of the clay lens and the perched water table toward the target and that if and as the perched water table and the clay lens dropped, the construction should drop along with them.

b. That at the point of reaching the depression midway between the starting point and the point of completion if the clay lens had not dropped sufficiently to afford the requisite overhead cover, the construction would then drive down through the clay lens taking maximum advantage of drainage pumps, well points, drainage borings through the clay lens, etc., to remove the water as a possible danger to the construction. (It should be noted that in the opinion of HALFWAY and his crew, this would be entirely possible and should involve no undue construction difficulties or risks.)

TOP SECRET

TOP SECRET

Page
17 October 1954

9. In view of the unanticipated discovery of water and the problem of overhead cover created thereby, extreme caution would be used to reduce noise and to key the construction to our visual observation of possible countermeasures to the maximum degree possible.

10. Upon the completion of all of the above steps and upon reaching the above conclusions, this matter was discussed in detail by ████████████████████ and ████████ with the ████ of ████████ who was requested to arrange for the immediate ███ to Berlin of the ████ consulting engineer, ████████████ for the purpose of having ████ examine the site and add his technical opinion to that of ████████ on the question of exactly how the construction should proceed. Unfortunately ████████ was not immediately available in view of other commitments, and one of his assistant engineers arrived in Berlin on 21 September to make a complete examination of the site and to discuss the attendant problems in detail with ████████████████ This ████ engineer after completing this assignment returned to London on 27 September 1954, and on the night of 4 October 1954 ████████ arrived in Berlin for a personal examination of the premises and discussions with ████████ These were completed by the afternoon of 6 October at which time a detailed discussion of the operation and particularly of the construction approach that should be used took place between ████████████████ and ████████ ████████ findings and his analysis of the engineering construction factors, together with this discussion, confirmed completely ████████ analysis and the original conclusions which had been reached, and at this meeting the following decisions were made:

a. Construction will proceed at the level immediately above the clay lens and the perched water table.

b. The excavation will be kept dry by continual pumping and as construction progresses, drainage holes will be bored through the clay lens and test borings regularly conducted to determine the exact depth of the clay lens and the perched water table.

c. The construction will follow the clay lens and the perched water table down as far as they recede, maintaining at all times a minimum overhead cover of 8 to 9 feet. If at any point in the progress of the construction the perched water table and clay lens rise or do not sink sufficiently to afford necessary cover, then the construction will drive into or through the clay lens in order that necessary cover will be possible.

d. The construction will be conducted with maximum caution to avoid detection through noise or through any unfortunate subsidence of the overhead soil.

e. Well point data is being procured and well points will be used to drain the soil ahead of the shield if it becomes necessary and advisable to do so.

11. As a result of these discussions, construction was recommenced on 11 October, and on 11 and 12 October the shield was emplaced and construction started at the level of approximately 16½ feet. The next several days up to 17 October were consumed in establishing the position of the shield and in driving the construction to and through the concrete foundation of the warehouse wall.

TOP SECRET

CONTROL

[TOP SECRET]

12. Attached is one copy of a drawing made by [REDACTED] of the construction site which shows in exaggerated profile the depression which reaches its deepest point approximately halfway between the start of the construction and the target objective and which shows other pertinent terrain factors, including the known clay level at various points. Only one copy of this is available, and if it is desired by COM to forward a copy of this to Headquarters, it is requested that copies be made by COM since it is not desired to duplicate this drawing here. No copy of this drawing is being retained in BOB files.

13. In connection with the progress of this operation, the following additional steps have been taken in connection with general operational security and related factors which are of sufficient interest to be briefly summarized:

a. Twenty-four hour observation was instituted beginning on the day the site was taken over of the target area of the entire area between the site and the target and all movements of personnel and vehicles, including Vopo patrols in the neighborhood. A daily log is being kept of all movements and developments in this connection, including a pedestrian and vehicle count of traffic along the road adjacent to the target site. [REDACTED] crew has been supplied with a pair of 12 x 60 Leitz night binoculars and with an infra-red binocular viewing kit. Through the use of this equipment excellent night observation is possible and except on nights when there is heavy fog, it is believed it will be impossible for substantial activity to take place in the target area without our being aware thereof. The log which is being maintained is being periodically reviewed to be certain that there is no gradual change in traffic or observation patterns. There has been no indication of the use of infra-red light against us for observation purposes.

b. A considerable amount of interest, curiosity, and observation of the installation has been noted on the part of Vopos, apparent civilians, and individuals believed to be Russians in civilian clothes, but the interest exhibited and the observation noted do not appear to be more intensive or any more unusual than would normally be expected in connection with an installation of this type located where it is.

c. We have every indication that the cover story used has been effective, not only from the exterior appearances of the installation but from what we have been able to gather concerning the reaction in the Berlin Command to the installation. In fact, the acceptance of the installation in the role paraded for it has, we believe, been even better than we had hoped.

d. A careful review has been made of the guard system, the security precautions, and the preliminary instructions as to what is to be done in case of emergency, and they appear to be excellent. [REDACTED] has been furnished with two Schmeisseranden for warning and guard purposes. Emergency two-way radio communications are in the process of being set up. In addition, we are supplying [REDACTED] with microphone installations to be concealed on the fence which, it is believed, may pick up Vopo conversations in the immediate vicinity. On 15 September the premises were completely

CONTROL
US OFFICIALS ONLY

EG&A
Page 7
17 October 1954

except for the presence of microphones, telephone taps, or other listening devices without detecting any indications of the presence of any such coverage. It is of interest to note that the three large diesel generators at the installation create such noise that it would be extremely difficult to install effective audio surveillance of any kind, and, in addition, create sufficient ground noise and vibrations to assist greatly in concealing construction noise.

&. Secure clandestine arrangements have been effected for contacts between ████████ and ████████ as necessary, and visits to the site by all individuals other than ████████ assigned crew have been kept to an absolute minimum. All such visits that have been made have been made by the individuals concerned traveling to and from the site in a closed three-quarter ton truck where they have been subjected to no outside observation whatever.

&. ████████ and his officers who as necessary proceed to downtown Berlin in civilian clothes have been issued short-barrelled 38 special revolvers for concealed carrying and through secure channels between COB and Heidelberg have been furnished permits therefor.

14. Considerable thought has been given to the problems involved in establishing a firm SOP for the action to be taken in the event of an unfortunate detection of this operation and the problems involved in the establishment, cover, and operation in Berlin of the proposed forward processing unit. These problems have been discussed in detail by ████████ with the ████████ and also with ████████ and C████████ ████████ POB. Specific recommendations concerning these two points will be made formally within the immediate future.

15. It is impossible to estimate with certainty the completion date of ████████ phase of this project. Such an estimate depends too completely upon future contingencies to be exact at this point; however, ████████ conservative estimate at the present time is that he should complete his phase of this project by approximately 22 January 1975 unless we encounter the remote possibility that the clay lens and the perched water table site instead of drop and do not disappear so that it is necessary to drive below them at or about the location where the depression midway between the site and target reaches its greatest depth. If that contingency does occur, the time for the completion of this phase of the project will be appreciably longer.

16. This is the first progress report that has been submitted on this operation since the occupation of the site on 28 August. Documentation of this operation is for obvious reasons being kept to the barest necessary minimum as previously discussed with ████████. It was felt, however, that in view developments and the necessary construction decisions resulting therefrom, a progress report in some detail should be submitted at this time.

W. K. HARVEY

314

V-3:

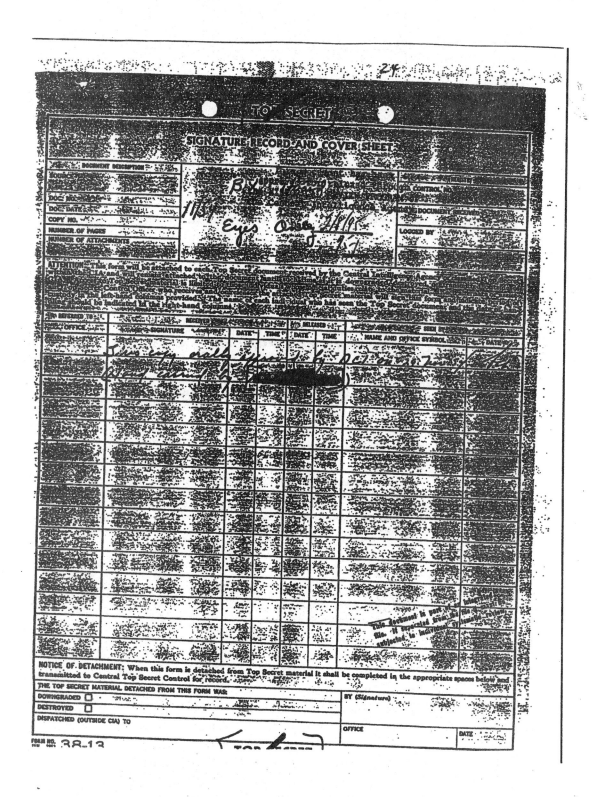

315

TOP SECRET

This document has been
approved for release through
the HISTORICAL REVIEW PROGRAM of
the Central Intelligence Agency.

29 November 1954

MEMORANDUM FOR THE RECORD

SUBJECT: ▓▓▓▓▓

Date 2/8/45

HRP 95-1

1. In order that there will be a complete and detailed record of the specific precautions, policies and courses of action authorized by the DCI in connection with the above project there is set out below a resume of the decisions reached and approved by the DCI at the conference held in his office on 18 November 1954 which was attended by the DCI, D/DCI, DD/P, C/OPS, ADCO, CFI, C/STD and ▓▓▓▓▓ W. K. HARVEY.

2. At all times during the construction phase and after the completion of this project, the target objective and the surrounding area will be kept under constant visual observation.

3. The following physical precautions will be taken within the tunnel and the site itself, each one being put in place as soon as the construction permits it to be safely and efficiently installed:

   a. On the near side of the pre-amp chamber a heavy steel door set in substantial concrete slabs will be emplaced with an adequate lock and bar on the inside and wired with an alarm system against tampering. This door will be locked at all times except when individuals are actually inside the pre-amp chamber. Telephone connections will be established between the pre-amp chamber and the site.

   b. An area forty feet long, ten feet on the near side of the demarcation line and thirty feet on the far side of the demarcation line will be mined as soon as the construction has progressed sufficiently to permit. It will be mined by using C-3 plastic in sealed garden hose threaded behind the liner plate in sufficient quantities that when exploded

TOP SECRET

-2-

it will collapse the tunnel without causing a major surface explosion. After mining, the necessary caps and fusing for arming this mined area will be fixed and secured in the immediate area but the mined area will not be armed except in case of emergency, and no effort will be made to lay in the explosives on a "push button" basis.

 c. The near end of the tunnel at the building line will be closed by a second steel, concrete emplaced door.

 d. The entrance to the shaft from the basement floor will be covered and concealed as well as possible.

 e. The ramp leading from the basement to the first floor of the warehouse will be covered and concealed as well as possible and equipped with a locked steel door.

 4. In the event enemy action is observed which could logically be construed as possibly leading to discovery of the project, i.e. at the target objective or between the target objective and the installation, the following steps will be taken:

 a. Simultaneously, and as rapidly as possible all personnel will be removed to the site and the Chief, BOB, will be immediately notified. Emergency two-way radio communications will be provided for this purpose in the event telephone service fails at any given time.

 b. If the enemy action observed is such that time permits, there will be immediate consultation between the Chief, BOB, and the Commanding Officer of the site as to further steps.

 c. If time permits, consideration will be given to removing as much of the equipment as possible.

 d. Coincident with the removal of the personnel, the steel doors will be appropriately secured and if discovery appears really imminent, the mined area will be armed and blown when it appears necessary to prevent entry or progress of enemy personnel through the tunnel.

TOP SECRET

-3-

e. Under no circumstances will the installation be precipitately abandoned.

f. In the event there is any imminent move against or attempt to gain entry to the installation, regardless of by whom or under what circumstances such occurs, the Commanding Officer of the installation will have orders to resist entry with all means at his disposal notifying Chief, BOB, and USCOB immediately.

g. In the event of discovery and any possible protest the official American reaction is to be flat, indignant denial ascribing any such protest to a baseless enemy provocation. Further possible policy and propaganda manuevering in such an event cannot be decided upon at this time.

5. With specific regard to Paragraph 4 above, the question of whether or not Ambassador Conant should be briefed was again brought up and reconsidered by the DCI. After considerable discussion and careful reconsideration it was the DCI's decision that Conant should not be briefed and that he did not desire to re-raise this issue with the highest policy levels with whom it had been previously discussed.

6. After discussion it was decided that the personnel for the forward processing unit would be covered by preparing and processing them in the States and sending them to Berlin in the normal manner as members of the 9539th TSU, Signal Corps, the present cover organization for the site. These personnel will at no point appear as KUBARK personnel.

Chief,

TOP SECRET

S E C R E T

41

11/71

APPENDIX A

NOTE: This assessment was prepared by the (_____)staff *Tunnel Project* Immediately after the discovery of the tunnel and is based on pertinent information available. At the time the report was prepared BLAKE's activities had not been surfaced.

15 August 1956

DISCOVERY BY THE SOVIETS OF ~~_____~~ *THE TUNNEL*

Analysis of all available evidence – traffic passing on the target cables, conversations recorded from a microphone installed in the tap chamber, and vital observations from the site – indicates that the Soviet discovery of ~~_____~~ *the Tunnel* was purely fortuitous and was not the result of a penetration of the ~~_____~~ agencies concerned, a security violation, or testing of the lines by the Soviets or East Germans. A description of the events leading to these conclusions is contained in this paper.

Following heavy rains in the Berlin area a number of telephone and telegraph cables were flooded and began to fault between Karlshorst and Mahlow on the night of 16 April 1956. The first major fault was discovered on cable FK 151 at Wassmannsdorf on 17 April. The fault was repaired by cutting the defective stretch of cable and replacing a 3000 meter length with a temporary replacement cable. Between 17 and 22

S E C R E T

(Page 2 missing from the original document)

continued. This general situation was noted by personnel at the site who checked the tap on the morning of 19 April and found it to be in good condition with no faults present. Berlin notified Headquarters of this fact on the evening of 20 April, noting, "available precautions taken including primary one of crossing fingers."

Throughout 20 April Soviet operators at Karlshorst, the Mahlow cable chamber, and Zossen/Wuensdorf checked FK 150 pairs carrying circuits serving high ranking officials and made switches where necessary or possible. Nothing was said concerning the testing being conducted to discover the faults or work being done by a Soviet labor force lent to the Germans to assist in digging up bad stretches of cable. On 21 April a Karlshorst technician told a colleague in Zossen/Wuensdorf the FK 150 had not yet been repaired and that another two days' work would probably be necessary to clear up the trouble. Testing and rerouting of circuits were stepped up during the evening of 21 April, and the Soviets showed considerable concern over the failure of the Moscow-GSFG Air Warning telegraph channel which had been transferred to FK 150 on 17 April. Lt. Colonel Vyunik, Chief of the GSFG Signal Center at Wuensdorf, telephoned Major Alpatov, Chief of the Karlshorst Signal Center, at his apartment to inform him of the failure of the Air Warning circuit. They agreed that communications had to be

established before morning and Alpatov left for his duty
station.

There is no significant information available on the
actual progress of the testing and repair program proper from
0300 hours on 20 April to 0050 hours on 22 April. On the basis
of available information, however, it seems probable that (a)
the testing program continued north until a fault was located
near the site and a decision was made to replace an entire
section of cable which embraced the tap site; or (b) the repeated faulting coupled with the age and physical condition of
FK 150 led the opposition to the conclusion that the only
effective remedy was to replace the cable, section by section,
and that this program was inaugurated somewhere south of our
site and continued northward until the tap was discovered.

At approximately 0050 hours on 22 April, 40 or 50 men
were seen on the east side of Schoenefelder Allee, deployed
along the entire area observable from our installation,
digging at three to five foot intervals over the location of
the cable and, incidentally, the tap chamber. At approximately
0200 hours the top of the tap chamber was discovered, and at
0210 Russian speech was heard from the microphone in the tap
chamber. The first fragments of speech indicated that the discovery of the tap chamber aroused no suspicion among those
present. A small hole was broken in the tap chamber roof

S E C R E T

permitting limited visual observation of the chamber, and a
Soviet captain [2] was brought to the spot. After some discussion all agreed that the discovery was a manhole covering a
repeater point, and the working crew began enlarging the hole
to gain access to the "repeater point."

While the working party was uncovering the tap chamber,
Major Alpatov and Lt. Colonel Vyunik discussed the communications situation in a rambling telephone conversation at
approximately 0230 hours. They indicated relief at the restoration of Air Warning Communications with Moscow, and Vyunik
went on to express suspicion about the continued trouble on
FK 150. In context it appears that this suspicion was
directed at the failure of the Germans to clear up the difficulties on FK 150 once and for all. In any event, Alpatov
clearly did not share his colleague's doubts. The general
tone of this conversation was relaxed and casual, completely
in keeping with the character of the two men, both of whom
we know well. The conversation appears to be a clear indication that, as of 0230 hours on 22 April, neither of these
responsible officers was aware of the existence of the tap.

---

[2] Presumably Captain Bartash, an engineer who later
received an unspecified award from Marshal Grechko for the
discovery of the tap.

5

S E C R E T

(S E C R E T)

Meanwhile back at the site the work of enlarging a hole
to give full access to the tap chamber continued. At approximately 0250 hours an unidentified Soviet Colonel arrived on
the scene, presumably in response to a request for guidance
by the working party. The Colonel did not appear to be a
signal officer since he took no active part in the investigation and remained on the scene only for a short time. Having
enlarged the hole in the tap chamber roof, the workers saw for
the first time the cables and the trap door on the floor of
the chamber. They assumed the trap door to be "some sort of
box" and had no suspicion of the true nature of the installation. At approximately 0300 hours barriers were erected to
keep inquisitive onlookers away from the excavation and it
was suggested that someone be sent to the Signal Directorate,
presumably to obtain relevant cable data. At the same time
the first German voice was heard, in conversation with a
German-speaking Russian. The German stated that two trucks
must have passed the spot without locating it. The Russian
answered that "Soviet troops are coming as well," and added
that they must wait "until morning" for the decision as to
what further work would be undertaken.

While these developments were taking place, Vyunik held
a telecon with the Air Warning Center in Moscow in which he
referred to the move of the GSFG Air Warning Center and

6

(S E C R E T)

(SE**/**R E T)

discussed, in detail, communication arrangements necessitated by this move. This revealing teleconference tends to support other evidence indicating that as of 0300 hours the true nature of the installation had still not been established.

The work of excavation continued, and fragments of conversation connected with it were picked up by the tap chamber microphone. A German-speaking Russian commented that "somebody has come from there and there are fewer workers there," suggesting that similar work was in progress at another point. The Russian gave instructions that nothing in the installation was to be touched. A German remarked that the chamber might be connected with sewage work and proposed that plans of the sewage system be obtained from the responsible authorities. The Russian answered that they already had this information and that the plans showed "that chamber" to be 120 meters away from this point. At about 0320 hours, when still more of the tap chamber was revealed and a better view of the interior obtained, those present began to speculate vaguely about its exact nature and the time of its construction. One of the Soviets, probably an officer, suggested that it might have been built during the war, possibly for "Vhe Che" (Russian abbreviation for "high frequency transmission," but used loosely to denote anything connected with secure communications.) Shortly after 0330 hours, the Soviets left the site by motor

.7

S E C R E T

vehicle, presumably to report their findings. For approximately one and one-half hours - from 0330 to 0500 - no sounds or voices were recorded.

At approximately 0415 hours Vyunik telephoned Alpatov's apartment in Karlshorst and asked Alpatov if he had spoken with General Dudakov, Chief Signal Officer, GSFG. Alpatov said that he had, that he was getting dressed, and that he would go to his signal center as soon as possible. Vyunik told Alpatov to telephone him at the GSFG frame room at Zossen/Wuensdorf, adding, "When we speak we must do so carefully. We know what the matter is, so we will speak carefully." This indicated clearly that by 0415 hours the GSFG Signal Directorate and General Dudakov, the Chief Signal Officer, had been informed of the discovery of the () chamber, viewed it with extreme suspicion, and planned to re-route circuits passing over the target cables. This coincides neatly with the departure from the tap site of the Soviets at 0330. At 0630 Vyunik telephoned Alpatov at the Karlshorst Signal Center and informed him that Lt. Colonel Zolochko, Deputy Chief of the Lines Department, GSFG, had left Wuensdorf at 0625 to go "there." Vyunik, in a resigned tone, then added that all that remained for him and Alpatov to do was to sit and wait.

In due course Lt. Colonel Zolochko arrived at the site, accompanied by an unnamed Colonel and Captain Bartash, the

8

S E C R E T

Commander of the working party. By this time the Soviets apparently had brought circuit diagrams to the site and were aware of the pair allocations on the affected cables. There was considerable discussion of the discovery, and one of the crew actually entered the chamber and made a superficial and inconclusive examination. Shortly afterwards the statement, "the cable is tapped," was made for the first time on the scene.

At about this time (0635 hours) Lt. Colonel Vyunik telephoned Major Alpatov and asked whether he had received the "task" and whether its meaning was clear. Alpatov replied that he had received and understood the assignment. Speaking in unusually vague terms, Vyunik instructed Alpatov to take over two low-frequency channels, presumably provided by the KGB signals organization. (These channels would provide telephone communications between Berlin and Wuensdorf via overhead line and would by-pass the tapped cables.) Vyunik added that they could continue necessary technical discussions on the new facilities.

Although teletype traffic continued until the tap wires were cut - at 1535 hours on Sunday afternoon - the last telephone call of any interest was placed sometime between 0800 and 0900 hours on 22 April, when an agitated General speaking from Marshal Grechko's apartment attempted to contact Colonel

9

S E C R E T

Kotsyuba, who was then acting for General Dibrova, Berlin
Commandant. Unable to locate Kotsyuba, the General talked to
Colonel Pomozanovskii, Chief of Staff of the Berlin Garrison,
stressing the urgency of his call. Pomozanovskii promised to
find Kotsyuba at once and get him to return the call. The
return call was not intercepted, but there appears to be no
doubt that Marshal Grechko had by this time been informed of
the discovery and wished to discuss it with Colonel Kotsyuba.
A few telephone calls were attempted after this, but the operators refused to place the calls, and in one case a Karlshorst
operator said, "I won't put you through to anyone. Don't ring,
that's all. I won't answer you any more. It's in the order."

Between 0700 and 0800 hours a number of additional Soviet
officers arrived at the excavation, including Colonel Gusev
of the KGB Signals Regiment. A Russian-speaking German was
heard to remark that a "commission" was expected, and a Soviet
officer said that they would await the arrival of this commission before making a decision as to what the next step would
be. In answer to a question as to whether anything should be
disconnected, the same officer stated that nothing should be
done beyond making motion pictures of the chamber. He added,
however, that the hole providing access to the chamber should
be enlarged and a detailed inspection should be carried out.
The general discussion continued, and the possibility of some

10

S E C R E T

form of explosive booby trap in the chamber was discussed at some length. There was widespread belief that the trap door, which in fact provided access to the tunnel proper, was a "box" or "battery box" possibly involving a booby trap. One of the Soviet officers, probably Zolochko, suggested that, after everything had been carefully noted and recorded, a grappling iron could be attached to the "box" in order to tear it away. "If there is no explosion," he said, "then we can calmly go ahead and deal with it."

Several individuals, presumably German cable splicers, agreed that the cables were fully tapped and discussed the method employed. They agreed that it must have been done in such a way as to render the tap undetectable by measurements, although one of them failed to understand why the actual cutting of the cables was not detected. He added that at that time "everyone must have been quite drunk." The Germans continued to speculate on the nature of the "box" and about the means of access to the tap chamber. One of them said, "They themselves must have some means of entering this place, but naturally it's highly improbable that they have constructed a passage for getting from here to there!"

Some of those present apparently believed that the tap was an old one and had been abandoned due to recent faults on the cable. During this discussion the microphone was twice noted, but was not recognized for what it was. In the first instance the speaker said, "That is not a microphone," and in the second it was described as "a black ball."

The general discussion continued, with speculation as to the nature of the "battery box" and with several comments that it should be possible to identify the tappers "from the make of the materials" and the techniques employed. While the Germans began work enlarging the hole around the tap chamber, the Soviets discussed in some detail the order in which technical experts and administrative representatives would carry out their inspection. The Soviets identified the lead-off cable as "not ours," indicating that after the inspection they planned to disconnect the lead-off cable and to "check how far it goes from here" – probably by means of electrical measurements. It is evident that at this time (approximately 1130 hours) the Soviets and Germans were still unaware of the existence of the tunnel, the means of access to the tap chamber, or those responsible for the tap.

At approximately 1145 hours one of the German crew was heard to exclaim, "The box is an entry to a shaft!"

From the tenor of the ensuing conversation it would seem that a small hole had been made near the still-intact trap door. The Germans debated the removal of the trap door, but continued to work at and around it despite the alternate

(S E / R E T)

suggestion that "we should open up the road opposite until
we reach the cable or the shaft." By approximately 1230
they had removed the hinges and entered the lower part of
the tap chamber. The padlock which secured the trap door from
below was examined and was identified as "of English origin."
Failing to open the door separating the tap chamber from the
equipment chamber, the Germans, after approximately twenty minutes, broke a hole through the wall and gained visual access
to the equipment chamber, which they described as "a long
passage." By 1300 they evidently had enlarged the access hole
and described "a completed installation - a telephone exchange..
..... An installation for listening in /Abhoeranlage7."

Additional motion pictures were made and frequent excla-
mations of wonder and admiration were heard. At 1420 a Soviet
Colonel, probably Zolochko; a person addressed as Nikolai
Ivanovich, probably Major Alpatov; and a Captain, presumably
Bartash, entered the chamber and discussed the method used
by the tappers in gaining access to the cables. Zolochko
evidently still believed that this was done "from above."
Conversations indicated that the joint Soviet-German commission, mentioned earlier, had already visited the site and
established the nature of the installation without going into
technical details.

13

(S E / R E T)

[S E C R E T]

Measurements of parts of the interior were then taken,
discussion of the installation became general, and the partici-
pants clearly indicated that the means of access and full implications of the operation were finally appreciated. Conversations
reflected that all present realized that the planning of the
tunnel approach to the cables must have necessitated a very
detailed study of relevant maps and plans. The stress to which
the roof of the chambers would be subjected and the necessity
of preparing the lead-off cables beforehand were mentioned,
and a German was heard to exclaim, "It must have cost a pretty
penny." A Russian-speaking German added, admiringly, "How
neatly and tidily they have done it." It was decided that
work on the tunnel must have been carried out during the day
when the sound of the street traffic would drown any noise,
whereas the actual tapping was done "during the night, between
one and two o'clock, when the traffic on the cables is slight."

One of the Germans rather indignantly exclaimed, "What a
filthy trick. And where you would least expect it." -- to
which another replied, "Unless one had seen it for oneself,
nobody would believe it."

Between 1515 and 1530 hours the tap wires were cut, and
at about 1545 the attention of the Germans began to concentrate
on the microphone itself. One of them assumed it to be an
"alarm device - probably a microphone," to give warning of

14

[S E C R E T]

approaching motor traffic, and added that it ought to be photographed. At 1550 hours work began on dismantling the microphone. Shortly afterward the microphone went dead and, after 11 months and 11 days, the operational phase of *THE TUNNEL*  was completed.

REEL 1 A   11/71

Reel starts with 8 minutes of noise, as of falling debris, pounding shoveling, intermingled with muffled voices and the sound of passing motor vehicles. This period is followed by approximately two hours of relative silence punctuated by the sound of passing traffic, occasional pounding and muffled voices.

* * * * * * * *

SOUND OF SOMEONE ENTERING/ GARBLED SPEACH, MUFFLED VOICES.

(6)   RUSSIAN

NOISE -- RUSSIANS LEAVE.

SOUND OF PASSING TRAFFIC: MUFFLED VOICES.

SOUND OF SOMEONE ENTERING. (10 MINUTES AFTER ABOVE)

GARBLED SPEACH: MUFFLED VOICES.

NOISE OF WORKMEN: GARBLED AND DISTORTED SPEACH. (RUSSIAN)

(5)   ((XG) DIE LAMPE DA RUNTER GEGEBEN (MG).)

SOUND OF HEAVY BREATHING: WHISTLING.

SEVERAL SENTENCES OF RUSSIAN

NA, SIEHSTE (MG)

SOUND OF WORKMEN.GARBLED SPEACH: NOISE.

RUSSIAN -- SEVERAL SENTENCES.

NOISE OF WORKMEN GARBLED SPEACH.

NOISE OF WORKING: SHOVELING. SOUND OF PASSING TRAFFIC, BARKING DOG.

SEVERAL MINUTES OF RELATIVE SILENCE.

SOUND OF ENTERING: MUFFLED VOICES. ('ABSTUETZ')('KABEL') ... UND DANN KABEL IST [2M]

GERMAN TECHNICIAN OR OFFICIAL: DAS KABEL GERT NACH DRUEBEN DURCH IN drunter DEN SCHACHT/***** EINFACH DIE KABEL *** UND HABEN *** [XM]

[XM] SECRET [LMJ]

SAG MAL WIE GEHT DENN DAS ~~EVAA~~ DA DURCH, JA?
(GARBLE) (WAR der?) schon ~~kommeny~~ so lang (hier durch?))?
(WORKMEN) SHOUTING DROWNS OUT PORTIONS OF CONVERSATION)

NICHT HIER ZU KOENNT
(XG) ** ~~DASS-ES-HIER-KEIN~~ (1M) UND DIE STRASSE (MG)

SEVERAL PERSON SPEAKING AT ONCE, INCLUDING WORKMEN, RUSSIANS,

AND GERMANS.

GERMAN OFFICIAL OR TECHNICAN EXPLAINING SETUP: "

DIESE LEITUNGTRAEGER (SEV. M) SIE HABEN (SEV.M) RUNTER (SEV.M)

[8M]
UND ES GEHT DANN RUNTER (SEV.M)(NUR ICH WEISS, DASS DIESE/GEHT)NICHT DURCH ∉ U

(SEV.M ES GEHT NOCH EINER NACH)(MG) (SHOUTING OF RUSSIANS AND WORKMEN

DROWNS OUT PASSAGES OF CONVERSATION.)

GARBLED AND MUFFLED SPEACH. SEVERAL PERSONS SPEAKING AT SAME

TIME IN BOTH RUSSIAN AND GERMAN.

(4/5)_____ RUSSIAN_____

GERMAN OFFICIAL, APPARENTLY SPEAKING TO WORK BOSS:
[1M]
"HABT IHR WAS DAGEGEN/WENN IK DIE GENOSSEN, ~~DIE GENOSSEN~~ ANFANGEN

HIER EIN BISSCHEN ZU UNTERSUCHEN? (MG)"

"ABSOLUT NICHTS!"

_____RUSSIAN_____

GERMAN OFFICIAL SPEAKING: "(MG) DA UNTEN (SEV.M) ABGESCHNITTEN (MG)

REST OF STATEMENT DROWNED OUT BY MIXED GERMAN AND RUSSIAN.

NOISE; SHOVELING, FALLING DEBRIS, ETC.

WHISTLING.

GARBLED AND DISTORTED SPEACH: APPARENTLY GERMAN WORKMEN.

SOUND OF MEN WORKING: SHOVELING, FALLING DEBRIS.

WORKMAN SPEAKING: ("FAENGT HIER IN (1M) AUF.")

SOUNDS, AS ABOVE, CONTINUE FOR ABOUT 10 MINUTES.
(RUSSIAN)
SILENCE, AS WORKMEN LEAVE. SOUND OF PASSING TRAFFIC, ROOSTER

SECRET

CROWING.

LAST 15-20 MINUTES OF REEL DEAD.

SECRET.

SECRET ①

2 B

WILLST DU MAL LANGSAM [XM] SCHALLSCHUT
JEH?
WAS?
SCHALLSCHUTTEN
(? SCHALLSCHUTEN?)   ER IST HIER DARUNTER
M.V. (LAUGHTER)
NOISE   ES MUSS JETZT HIER DINE, DINE
M.V.
HANSI
M.V.
(SCHALLSCHUTEN - SCHALLSCHUTEN?)   - Significant
- English
STATIC, MUFFLED VOICES

nearly 1200
when finally
broke through
wall next to
steel door

(XG) UND DENN (½=5 G) UND DENN ——— EINSCHUTEN ——— SCHALLSCHUTEN ———
M.V.
UND HIER IST EIN UNTERSCHACHT —— UND ——
HIER DURCH
NOISE: BELL.
(JA??)
JA Bitte
ALSO! JA! JETZ GET'S WEITER, JA? ES HAT (4=6 G) HIER EINMAL 'N APPARAT
C/M [hat sie denn]
JA Lich wollte sagen] wir haben ein anderen Apparat
ANGESCHLOSSEN.
(English Comment: ... other machinery
HAJA HIER BRAUCHT MHN [YM](.
NOISE. MUFFLED VOICES. COUGHING ("VERBINDUNG")
COUGHING
M.V.
SO'S GUT.
M.V.
(ENGLISH COMMENTS WALKED PAST —
NEVER EVEN FAZED HIM.

PICK AND SHOVEL NOISE
ABER, WARUM STEHT IHR NUR DA?
(XG — SCHAUFEL — XG

MUFFLED VOICES. NOISE
FAIRLY QUIET
M.V.
JA SS ES GEHT IMMER NOCH (1=G) DARUNTER, HA?
[YM] ALSO, GEBEN SIE MIR [YM] DARUNTER, JA?
M.V.
FALLING DEBRIS DEBRIS. PANTING

WER IST DENN DA? [XM] MUSS MAL NACH DER ANDEREN SEITE RUEBER.
JA, JA
GARBLE
NA, RUNTER, RUNTER!
(GARBLE)
NUN, RUEBER! WEITER!
SO WEITER
—[XM]
WASS IST DENN DASS? MANN MUSS SICH HIER JA RUNTER LASSEN, NICHT? (4-6 G)

NOISE. FAINT ENGLISH COMMENT. NOISE. MUFFLED VOICES
FAIRLY QUIET

RUNTER! (XG)

NOISE. FALLING DEBRIS. LAUGHING. MUFFLED VOICES.

RUSSIAN   SECRET

008632

②

ALSO, DAS BING ZEIGT GLEICH WIE ES DA WEITER GEHT.

EINER VON EUCH MUSS IMMER UNTEN BLEIBEN.

MUFFLED VOICES.

                    RUSSIAN

(XG) ~~IN DIE LUFT GESCH~~ (3 G) --- IN STUECKCHEN WEITER.

HANS! HANS!

DU SOLLST MAL EBEN EIN DAS TELEPHONE DURCH ZIEHEN --- STEHT, VON UNS.

WAT? HAENGT 'N MIT REIN (XG)
OBEN WEG
KURT!

[WAT?]

MUFFLED VOICES. NOISE.

JA! WILLST DU ANSETZEN DA UNTEN, JA?

JA!

JA, NUR DAS PASST NICHT.

KEINE PAUSE.

                    RUSSIAN

PAUSE. DIGGING

HAST DU DAS GESEHEN?

NEIN (XG)

LAUGHING.
HIER DURCH, HIER GEHT ES DURCH.
        RUSSIAN

(? (XG) DAS DAS DRECK DAVON WEGKOMMT. (M/G) ?)

NOISE.

SAGEN SIE (M/G)

WHISTLING.

WILLSTE ASSEN [GEHEN] ?
[XM]
NICHT MIT. DICHTER

③

(XG) [2M] AUSSEN GEHEN.   ~~SECRET~~

(3G) MAL RUNTER.
  [XM] ERST MAL 'RUNTER
(XG) RAUS ~~GEHEN (GL)~~ GEGEBEN.
(NOISE)
KOMMSTE DURCH? (XG)
(NOISE)
~~DONNERWETTER!~~ ~~GUCK DOCH~~ MAL DEN [BAU?] ~~BLOSS MAL HIN!~~
[XM] UNTER,
~~ES LAEUFT DA UNTER DER STRASSE.~~ — WIE HAMSE DAS JELEISST?

'S IST JA FANTASTISCH!

GEHT'S ~~NOCH~~ NICHT ?

JA! BITTE?
HALLO!
HALLO!
HALLO!

(G) MEISTEN (MG)

M. VOICES.

GEH . . . . . . DA HINTEN [1M]
~~HALLO! HALLO!~~ [XM] JA FANTASTISCH [3M] GEHT

JA!
[3M]
HIER
~~GIB MIR MAL 'NE GROSSE BRECHSTANGE MAL.~~
PASS MAL AUF, WIR BRAUCHEN 'NE BRECHSTANGE MAL

HALLO!

DIGGING. OTHER NOISES.

HALLO!

MUFFLED VOICES.

[? WER IST DENN DAS?]? ; HANS ?
~~(XG) HA?~~

HALLO!

    [XM]   JA'
HALLO! ~~GEBN SE MAL 'NE GROSSE BRECHSTANGE HER.~~

EINE ~~BRECHSTANGE~~X BRAUCHE NOCH MAL.

WA? ~~AUT ~~ ~~MAL WEG DAVON VON DER BURSCHENLINIE~~
WART E'MAL IK GEH MAL WEG [XM]
HA, HA.

(MG)   ~~SECRET~~

④

DIGGING.   ~~SF~~

(2G)

DIGGING. MUFFLED VOICES. COUGHING.

[DA ERSTICKT MAN.]

DIGGING.

(4G)

MUFFLED VOICES. BELL.
GEH MAL WEG

[? PASS OP! KRIEG'S ~~NIGHT~~ IN DE AUGEN. (MG) NICHT.?]

JA!

(MG)

JA. ——————— ZEUG DA!
DA HABEN'SE DA! DRIN [2M] EINE GANZE [2M].
~~DIGGING.~~ WART EIN MAL, WART EIN MAL
ES GEHT SCHON
VORSEHEN!

(MG)

_____ .IL

VORSEHEN! VORSEHEN!
GIB MIR MAL DAS DICKE HER
FALLING DEBRIS.

NA, DA KOMMT SIE SCHON RAUS.
(NOISE)
KOMMSTE?
SO, DU GEHST MAL 'RUNTER
AUGENBLICK!

HO, HO, HO

(MG)
HIER 'RUNTER
HIER ~~KOMMAL~~ 'RUNTER
[1M] HIER 'RUNTER
DIGGING. OTHER NOISES.

(XG)

DA MAL VORSTEHEN!
(M.V.) (ICH NEHM MIR GLEICH MIT?)
(ALSO, ZURÜCK MIT DAS DING.?) JA?   (NOISE) severnt
TA, TA, TA   ~~SF~~   minutes

(HIER BRAUCHEN WIR NICHT MACHEN?) ?

NEE, NEE, NEE
[XM] DIE DREI KABEL DA
(DIE SOLL IN DE SOLE.
:E,NEE,(IM) DIE SOLE, SOWIE DIE SOLE)

~~SECRET~~

IHR MACHT DENN HIER WEITER. (MG)

SO NICHT IN DE[ECKE?] (MG)
(GARBLE)   HIER, NICHT?
         ER IST
BLOSS NICHT SO DICHT DARUNTER / UNTER? (XG) NICHT DEN KABEL, NICHT?
JA, JA
JETZT IST DA NOCH -- [YM] DA IST ES SCHWARZ, SCHWARZ
JA, JA. -- DA IST NICHT EIN KABEL, NICHT? [XM]
WHISTLING.

ALSO GEHT ES DENN (MG)

COUGHING. DIGGING.

HIER IST ES NUN 2 METER, NICHT? Aaaa' ALSO UEBER'S JAHR. ZWEI
METER, NICHT?
       (GARBLE)   JA.
FUENF METER BIS UNTEN / HIER 2 METER HER (XG)
-- DREI METER --
NOISE, DIGGING.

ALSO BRAUCHES -- (3 G)
(NOISE)
(XG)

DAS GENUEGT (G) SO.

(XG)
(NOISE AND PANTING)
HOL ES MAL RAUS.

JA!

HO. (MG)

[?(XG) ES MUSS HIER (XG) ES JA LIEGEN (XG) HA! (XG) NEE (XG) ?]
WIR MUESSEN [HIER?] NOCH WEITER GEHEN
SO, JOST! (MG)
[XM] ANDERE MENSCH
       (GARBLE)(INCLUDING PHRASES:"AUFMAIMEN" AND " ZWEI ANDERHALB
SIE LASSEN SICH (MG)   METER HIN")
       (GARBLE) UNTEN
(?GUCK MAL?) WIE SICHER, MIT ZEMENT. (XG)   [?...]

MUFFLED VOICES.
(NOISE- POUNDING)   ES SIND DOCH DREI, ZWEI [IM] ZUS
ES IST HIER NOCH ANDERES HIER. (A) SIEHST DU DAS NICHT HIER?
        SIND
(GARBLE AND NOISE)("BRECHSTANGE")
(MG) NOCH GANZ WEG (MG)
(NOISE)
SAMMEL'S RAUS.

(?(XG) PICKE! (XG) ?)   ~~SECRET~~
    IN DER ECKE DA, BITTE

DER GANZE ,FERTIG
.(NOISE + GARBLE)

GEHEN SIE'S MAL AUS DER ERKE. (MG)
(NOISE + GARBLE)

~~ES MAL HIER SCHAUFELN, WEG~~!
[XM] JETZT MAL WEG SCHAUFEL (LM)

DIGGING. + NOISE
(GARBLE)

(?(XG) DAS WERKZEUG (XG)?)

~~NU, SIEHST DU MAL HIER. (XG)~~
[XM] GEHSTE NOCH EINMAL HIER
(NOISE + M.V. + GARBLE)

HIER WAS. ABER DAS NICHT. (XG)
D   HIER
HIER (NOISE + GARBLE)

(4G) ABER GROSS, JA?
M.V.
FALLING DEBRIS
VORSICHT! VORSICHT!
. (NOISE)

(3G) DAS (XG)
(NOISE)

VORSICHT!'
(NOISE)

DIE (3G)

(XG)

DIE (1G) DA WEG KOMMEN.
(NOISE)

DAS GEHT (4-6G)
(GARBLE + NOISE)

WILLSTE NICHT HOCH? WILLSTE NICHT HOCH?
(NOISE)
T   JETZT
? DA HINTER DAS (1G) HIER HINTER DE IGGE RAUS NEHMEN.
(M.V.)

(1G) RAUSNEHMEN!
(NOISE)(GARBLE)

HIER IS DE DRECK UNTER GEWESEN.   (XG)
[M]
DRECK! (GARBLE)("LEITER"E) /GIB MIR'S 'RUNTER
~~NICHT! DAS MUSS UNTER HER.~~ (XG)   JA!
[GARBLE; ~~DOCH HINTER~~
DRIN
HIER IST DIE LEITUNG DRUNTER.

HIER IST DIE ~~LEITUNG~~ ANGESCHLOSSEN. [V]
WO WELCHE LEITUNG ?
HIER. DIE, DIE
RUSSIAN.

[?HIER IST] DIE BRUECKUNG.   [DA KUMMT?] EIN ANDEREN
[XM] DIE BRUECKUNG [XM]   NEE, NEE , NICHT EIN ANDEREN
                                       GARBLE
~~GERMAN/RUSSIAN. MUFFLED.~~   DAS HABEN DIE GEMACHT
                                  [YM] LEITUNG
WHISTLING.   GARBLE
(GARBLE)
--- WAS DENN ...
~~DAS IST DIE VERBINDUNG.~~ (JA DAS IST UNS EGAL?)
GARBLE
~~NOCH MAL AUF?~~

342

~~CRET~~   4675   ⑦

(XG) SHOVELING.

(IM)! (*Probably* HENIE.)

WAS?!

(XG) DA IN DE ECKE.

M. V.

(XG) DA HINTER (XG)

DRUNTEN! DRUNTEN! DRUNTEN! (*POUNDING - POSSIBLY INSTRUCTIONS TO POUND LOWER*)

(GARBIS)(MORE POUNDING)

JETZT KOMM HER.

(XG) HIER IST DIE SCHRAUBE. HIER IST DIE SCHRAUBE. (SCHRAUBENZIEHER!?)

(GARBLE) ("ANGESCHRAUBT")

~~XXXXX 18, 18! HIER IST (XG) SCHRAUBE (XG) 18 und 18 UND 20.~~

(GARBLE)(SCHOENE AM)

DA DRÜBEN, DA DRÜBEN IST 'NE SCHRAUBE DRIN

~~ZWISCHEN DIE SCHRAUBEN.~~ ACHTZEHNER

(GARBLE)

~~GIBS DAS DING 19?~~ SEBHSZEHN ODER ACHTZEHN

(XM) ACHTZEHN " ZWANZIG

~~NEN MUFFLED VOICES.~~

~~HIER IST NOCH UNE SCHRAUBE DRIN, 18ER, 18ER, 18 UND 20.~~

~~AUF~~

NOISE (GARBLE)

NEF. HINTER HINTER STEHT ER. NEBEN DEN GERAET.

DER HAT (YM)

(ENGLISH COMMENT. FAINT.)

[HIER] IS WAT VOR.

(NOISE)

[DREH DIES MAL] LOS. (MG)(GARBLE)

DA SPRINGT EINE

ALSO DAS IST ES (YM)(breathing heavy)

HIER (3 G) WO DAS (??MAEDCHEN?) IST. (MG) GARBLE

(GARBLE)

NOISE

SCHAUFEL WEG!

       (YM) ist gar niet da

       (GARBLE)

       (YM) Schraube.

SCHRAUBE. (XG) SCHRAUBE (XG) GESCHRAUBT (XG) Naechst

       (Garble + NOISE)

       (POUNDING)

FABELHAFT! (XG)

       (YM)[holt mal?] den Hammer hin

HALT MAL AM ENDE FEST. (XG) DASS NICHT.   (GARBLE + POUNDING)

       WILLSTE WAS?

       (POUNDING)

SCHRAUBE HER!   (GARBLE + POUNDING)

       (GEH WEG MAL GEH MAL 'runter

WILLSTE IHN WAS?   (spoken rapidly)

       (YM) EINZAL (die das naeher

(XG)   sein?)

       (M.V. + POUNDING)

(XG) EINZELN (XG)   'N Bisschen. Das ist 'raus

(XG) BISCHEN (XG) SCHRAUBE (XG)   ~~SECRET~~

(GARBLE) +(POUNDING)

(MG) MUSSTE (MG)   ~~SECRET~~

KOMM MAL HER.

EENE HIER IS JE   (MG)
    (POUNDING)
DE ZEMENT DA (XG) DE ZEMENT DA   (SNEEZES)
    (POUNDING)
(MG) FEST DA (MG)

JUT!
    (M.V.)

[NA, JETZT WISSEN SE] WIE SE DA REIN KOMMEN, NEE?

[2M] NICHT RUNTER SCHMEISSEN! NICHT RUNTER SCHMEISSEN!
      WAS?
[2M] SCHMEISS SIS NICHT 'RUNTER, NICHT WAHR? [3M]
      NEE, NEE
      JA. (GARBLE)

SEHSTE HIER WAS?   geht los
                          wie?
                          geht's jn los.
WO?   [YM] sie mit
                          (XM] bis die eine 'raus ist.
NADDESSTE HIER NICHT RECHT.   [XM] hinter geht
                          (M.V.)
SAGEN SIE WIE, BITTE? (MG)   (Garble)
                          [XM][anderen Seite?] dreht sich nicht
WAT IS DENN LOS?   (MG)   Nee
                          (M.V.)
                          [2M] mit!
SEHSTE DASS ALLES RAUS IST. (MG)   kann schon liegen, kann schon liegen
                          geht da [Draht?) noch
WAT HAMSE?   (garble).
                          geht da drunter
(MG) MIT?   (garble) (word like "Proschin"?)
                          (Wollte Ihr nur?) eins ausnehmen?
(MG) DRUNTEN (MG) DARAN!! JUT!   Eins doch
                          [2M] 'raus kommen
(MG) MASCHINE (XG) MASCHINEN.   (garble)
                          eins
NUN, ALLES RAUS NEHMEN. RAUS NEHEEN.   (garble)
                          (pounding)
DAMIT SIE BESSEN REIN (XG)

POUNDING.

GARNISCHT.
    (GARBLE).
[XM] BESSER RIN UND RAUS KLETTERN.
    (GARBLE)

SIN JA SOWIESO ~~(MG)~~ (drei?) [XM]
    (garble)
    (YM) kriegst nur eins 'raus (schon schutten?)
    (Habt Ihr eins?) oder nicht mehr?
~~HIER DA NOCH DAS EINE.~~   ~~SECRET~~

344

⑨

PASS MAL OP.

(?LASS MAL DEN?)HANDSCHEINWERFER(SEHEN), DA LAEUFT MIR DIE SAEURE RAUS.
GARBLE
KURT, WALTER ! MAL HIN.
M.V.
COUGHING. (SCRAPING SOUNDS.)
(M.V.)
(GARBLE)
ACH, JO.
M.V.
ES GEHT DA WEITER RUNTER. *(Ach da sehen 'se mal hinter durch weiter.*
(XM)
ALLES STAHLBUERSTE! *(BELL)*
(FAINT ENGLISH COMMENT)
ENTERHEMNT

UN' DA HAM'SE SCHRAUBEN HINGEHOERT. (MG)
(traffic)
(GARBLE)
ICH BIN SPRACHLOS, MENSCH, ICH BIN SPRACHLOS.
(M.V.)
WAS? (MG)
(M.V.)
LYMD *runner gegangen*
WOHIN.
(GARBLE)
WER SIND DENN DIE SCHON DRIN?
(GARBLE)
MUFFLED VOICES.
[XM] die oder die.
... ... HUESSEN GEGANGEN.
WOHIN SIND DE RUSSEN GEGANGEN? *(M.V.)*

BITTE?
(M.V.)
UND DA MUESSEN WIR DIE (??STRUEPPEN??) DA SCHON JAHRELAND (MG)
(M.V.)

HIER IS WAT VOR.
(GARBLE)

JUT, JUT!
(GARBLE)

(XG) HIER (2G) APPARAT NOCH (MG)

(ENGLISH COMMENT. FAINT)

(XG) SOUNDS OF SHOVELING.
(M.V.)
UND HIER KOMMT ALLES [XM]
ALLES WEG
DAS SIE HIER JETZT (4-6 G) (MG) *[RAEUMEN?] [GARBLE] +[SHOVELING SOUND]*
GUT
(GARBLE)(WOHS "ZWEI MAN)
SOUND OF PASSING CARS. CLANKING OF SHOVELS. NEAR SILENCE.

APPROACHING VOICES.

7/ RUSSIANS

(ENGLISH COMMENT: ——GET A WORD NOW AND THEN. YES, SOUNDS LIKE
RUSSIAN. THEY'RE OUTSIDE THE HOLE NOW.) SECRET.

THERE'S A COV   SECRET   10

(THOSE RUSSIANS ARE GIVING INSTRUCTIONS ON WHAT TO DO WITH THE CABLES.

THEY'RE NOT TO CUT THEM YET.

(NO. HE'S ONLY A MAJOR)

(FAINT VOICE.

(THE COLONEL IS OUTSIDE THE HOLE. ___

COUGHING

(THERE ARE QUITE A NUMBER OF RUSSIANS THERE)

        RUSSIAN.

        WAS? (XM)   JA JA, JA , (GARBLE). DIE HABEN JA
A BIST DU DA? WILLSTE RUNTER? DA MAL RAUS. V(XO) DAT IS LOGISCH. ICK
 (GARBLE)(WORDS "KISTE" AND "SPRENGSTOFF")
HABE OK DAT (MG) VIELLEICHT (20) MIT SPRENGSTOFF HERREIN GETAN?
 SO EBEN GEDACHT DASS [RM] IHR SPRENGSTOFF [XM]
        RUSSIAN.
          GING DA DURCH!
JA, DIE KABEL IN (??LOGISCH??) DAS IS ALLES (MG)
 (M.V.) (GARBLE)   JA?(RUSSIAN?)/(M.V.)
 NA, DU BIST GANZ TIEF DRIN? WIR RECHTS, ALSO AN DEIN RUECKEN ZU.
          [M] dritte
DASS SIND KEINE (?DRUEPPERT)

(ENGLISH COMMENT: COME ON, SPEAK UP BOY!)

NOISES. SOUND OF STEPS, HAMMERING.

HIER MUSS (MG) JEMAND (DURCH')..
 (GARBLE)
(MG) IST DER OBERFUEHRER (MG) JEMAND HIER AUFTRITT (XM)
 (GARBLE)

(ENGLISH COMMENT: HE'S COMING IN. IT'S RUSSIAN AND GERMAN BOTH AT

THE SAME TIME.)
 (GARBLE)
JA! JA!

PAUSE.

7-8   RUSSIAN.

RUNTER?

NOISES   SECRET

(MG) DAS KABEL (MG) JA.

~~SECRET~~ [XM] ich weiss

(17)

(MO) GRUNDWASSER. (MO) UEBERBRUECKT, UEBERBRUECKT, NICHT WAR?/ UND DANN DURCH-

GESCHNITTEN (XG) UND DANN DIE (XG)

M.V. HIER

HIER IST JA PLATZ NOCH ZUM (??HAAR??)

[WIE]HAMSE HIER LUFT[UNTEN] ?

(ENGLISH COMMENT: VERY FAINT.

[~~HER HABSE~~ DEN KRAM. WAT KOST DAT NOCH ALLES!!]

oil ce...

(LAUGH)

8.   (RUSSIAN.)

SOUND OF TRUCK PASSING.

(RUSSIAN

(LM)   WEG DURCHGESCHNITTEN.

RUSSIAN.

DER UNTERGANG IST JA ZIEMLICH ENG.

LAUGH

JETZT GEHT'S RUNTER

WIEDER

VOICE OF OFFICIAL APPROACHING: ABER DAS KOENNTE DU NICHT ERLAUBEN,

WEIL SIE SAGEN DANN KRIEGEN SIE ZU SCHWERE — LAST! [DASS HABEN SIE]ABER

HIER.   GEKRIEGT HAT

ZIEMLICH STARK GEMACHT. [WAS SIE DA ZUM STUETZEN GEBRAUCHT, DASS/ ES

DA NICHT EINBRACH.

RUSSIAN.

HAT [XM]

M JA NE, [WAS IST]HIER RUM [WART HIER NICHT RUM.] (MO)

MIXED VOICES. (TRUCK APPROACHES)

GARBLE

((ENGLISH COMMENT: VERY FAINT.)   STECKEN DIE OBEN....

So! [ZM] HOCH GEHEN

JA, WAS WIR ALLES MACHEN DA (MO)   [GARBLE]

[XM] ALLES MACHEN, ALLES MACHEN

((ENGLISH COMMENT: VERY FAINT.)   (GARBLE)

RUSSIAN.

~~SOUND OF PASSING TRUCK.~~   (TRUCK APPARENTLY LEAVES)

RUSSIAN.

HIER IST (2G) RAUS/ DAS MACHT SICH BEQUEM (BETRIEBEN LASSEN?).

JA.   ~~SECRET~~

347

(wispering)

WISPERING: (HIER IST WASS. SEHEN, HIER ? (MG) ?)

WISPERING:

(HO, DA NICHT SCHNEIDEN. ?)

(ENGLISH COMMENT: A LITTLE LOUDER. SO I CAN HEAR) I DIDN'T HEAR THAT.

MIXED GERMAN AND RUSSIAN VOICES.

(ENGLISH COMMENT: VERY FAINT.)

RUSSIAN.

(ENGLISH COMMENT: THEY'RE NOT IN YET.
(GARBLE (XM)
(MG) HOEH ZU MACHEN, NICHT WAR? UEBERBRUECKEN, UEBERBRUECKT, JA (XG)
NEE, UEBERBRUECKEN, NICHT WAHR.
JA, ALSO JETZT GARBLE
STEHT DIE SACHE so (SEVERAL G) LASSEN SIE ALSO (HEUTE?) BIS [GARBLE
(GG) BIS ALSO ? (MG) [DAS HIER ?

IBEI 'NE SCHRAUBE IST.
(GARBLE)
DAS PASST HIER ALSO.

N GERADE AUF. DANN WIRD'S JA BALD
JA, JA, (SEVERAL G) DANN GEHT'S OFT. DIE MASCHINE IST ZENGEN

SCHON JANZ JUT. (MG)
M.V.
(ENGLISH COMMENT: HE'S RECOGNIZING THE (FADES OUT)
(BELL)
NEIN (3M)
JA, DAT [JEHT NIT. ?)

ICH BIN DER MEINUNG, MAN SOLLTE NOCH WARTEN MIT DEM, [DEM DRUEBEN (MG) ?

(ENGLISH COMMENT: I'M OF THE OPINION WE COULD MANAGE IT TODAY.

NOISE. SHORT SILENCE. NOISE AGAIN.

9: RUSSIAN.

IMMER NICHT?
NA, SO, SIE HABEN HIER GROSSE SCHULDEN, HA? (MG)
(M.V.)
DAS IST JA DAS SELBE VERFAHREN.
(GARBLE)
(ENGLISH COMMENT: VERY FAINT.
(QUIET)
(GARBLE)
[IM] SIE HABEN, SIE HABEN SEHR LANGE DAVON (MG)
M.V.

HIER IST UEBERBRUECKT, ALLES HAMSE, ALLES HAMSE GESCHNITTEN (GG)

SEHR, SEHR, SEHR, SEHR SAUBER.

WAHRSCHEINLICH . [YM]
WAS-MAN NUR ALLES NACHTS, ,NACHTS ——
[XM] NAINTS [YM]
.NACHTS SCHLIEFFEN WIR ALLE!

JA! LAUGHTER.
M.V.
(SIEHST DU DAS HIER?) [HABEN SIE NUR] NACHTS MIT DER BETRIEB GANZ, GANZ WIE

(??GEMAHLES??), JA? WENN [WENN SO ETWAS?] WAS, WAS ((??UHR??) IST

[BRAUCHEN?] SIE'S GEMACHT (MO)

WISPERING.
(RUSSIAN)
(ENGLISH COMMENT: . SOMETHING GOING ON.
(GARBLE\
LAUGHTER.
(M.V.)
HIER IST SO KNAP, JA?
SO KNAP
M.V
OR TRUCK IDLING
BACKGROUND NOISES. TRAFFIC, SCUFFLING. QUITE LOUD. QUITE QUIET AGAIN.

(ENGLISH COMMENT: . EAST (GERMAN?)

VOICES, TRAFFIC SOUNDS. DISTANT VOICES.
(NOISE)
[XM] VORSEHEN! DA (MO)

JA!

STEPS. VOICES.
.(NOISE)
HIERHER
WENN SIE BIS SO EIN (2G) DAS WAR ABGEDECKT (SEVERAL G) OB DAS EBEN
ALLES IST
(WAGNA NICHT?)?
VON HIER AUS ZU (2-0) XXXXXXXXXXXX DASS DAS DURCH/NIEDER(X) .]
[XM]
IST (DAS ABGESTELLT?
HABT?)

ABGESTELLT, JA.
(GARBLE)
JA, KOMMSTE HIER DENN DURCH?
M.V
[GEHT'S] DENN UNTER?
M.V.
[XM]
(MO) DIESEN (?STROM; STUNDE?) NEHM ICH DEN STROM WEG.
JA WIR HABEN ALSO
WIR (ANGEKRATZT, NICHT WAHR?), JA, ALSO [XM]
JA, ALSO, SIE HABEN LICHT ANGEHABT HIER. UND DEN SCHEINWERFER, IST-ER (MO)
(ENGLISH COMMENT)
(GARBLE) [XM] [XM] JA,
HIER IST UNGEFAEHR X METER TIEF MIT ALLEN KANALEN. /UND ZWAR, HIER GEHT'S JETZ
V BIS IST HIER IN
UNGEFAEHR 'NE BREITE VON 80CM MAL 40-50 CM EEN TIEFER SCHACHT. RINGS
(EI)

349

V-5: *(Continued)*

VER

HERUM MASSIV GEKLEIDET. UNGEFAEHR 4 - 5 - 6 METER VON DER ABRUNDUNG,

UNGEFAEHR 4-6 METER RUNTER.

(ENGLISH COMMENT: VERY FAINT.

NOISES. (HUMMING SOUND?)

DER GANG SELBST IST DANN HOEHER, JA?
           M.V.   BELL
TRAFFIC NOISES. ∧ DISTANT VOICES.
    (GARBLE)
IMMER WEITER, KOMM IMMER WEITER.

(ENGLISH COMMENT: VERY FAINT.:

(BELL RINGS(3 SEPARATE TIMES)

JA, WAS IST?
          M.V

NUN, DA MUSS MAL HEUCHMANN KOMMEN. - (GARBLE)
   XM   DAS   MAL   ES FINEN NACH DEN ANDEREN
[JA, DESHALB SPRECHT ES MAL MIT IHM AB, DASSM-MAN-MAL-EINMAL-(MG)
  (XM)   M.V.
(HUMMING SOUND. COUGHING.
      M.V.
- IST, IST-SCHRAEG-(MG)

DISTANT VOICES. WISPERING (GERMAN)

DAS-IST-UNSERE-WOHN-(MG)   SCHRAUBENDIENER
                                M.V
(XO)-

(ENGLISH-COMMENT: - VERY-FAINT.

STEPS, NOISE. LOUD NOISES.

WA? WAT?

(XO)

SOUND OF HEAVY BREATHING.

NA, HEINZ?

JA, KOMM-GEHN!
   HEAVY BREATHING
(WIE GEHT'S DANN? [YM] !)

350

16

SMALL NOISES.   SECRET

(ENGLISH COMMENT: THAT'S NUMBER ONE, EH?
                          M. V.
((MAYBE. ?) | JA JA :
                               | (M.V.)
((HE SAYS (MG) ?) | GAR NICHT IN ERSCHEINUNG
                                       MV
                   DASS DIE   "   IN   "   GETRETTEN
DA SIND WIR (2G) GANZ KURZ. [YM] RICHTIG SPRECHEN
                                   GARBLE
SOUND OF PASSING TRAFFIC.   [YM] GANZ KURZ

         M.V.
HIER IST DIE EINE.
         M.V.
(XG)

  [XM]————
MUSS-MAN-MAL ZURUECK WO ES RAUSKOMMT, [IM], NICHT WAHR ?

MUFFLED VOICES.

        [BITTE], DA   GENAU
(XG) RUNDSTUECK HABEN SIE HIER DIE SCHWARZE (XX) GEHABT. SIND SIE HIER
RANGEKOMMEN WAHRSCHEINLICH UND [XM]
AM (XX).   M.V. (GEHEN'SE 'REIN)
                   EING
[ACHTUNG, EINS UND ZWEI (XG)

NOISES. SOUND OF HEAVY BREATHING. LOUD NOISES. COUGHING.

JA! DA WIEDER.

MUFFLED VOICES.

10.   RUSSIAN

(ENGLISH COMMENT: VERY FAINT.
 (BELL)
MAN MUSS NICHT VERKEHRT RUMDREHEN.

(ENGLISH COMMENT: THERE IS SOMEBODY IN THERE NOW.

(THINK THEY MAY BE INSIDE?

      RUSSIAN.

(XG) HAT DAS VERKEHRS UMGEDREHT (XG) (GARBLE)

JA. BITTE?

HOEHR MAL ZU. IST DA VON I.I., JA?

AUGENBLICK MAL. HIER IST FEUERWEHR.   SECRET

351

V-5: *(Continued)*

1. NA, IST EGAL. PASS MAL AUF. IHR SOLLT MAL VON UNTEN AUS GEGEN DIE

DECKE KLOPFEN, DAMIT SIE OBEN BEIM (3-4 G) [UNTERSCHACHT?] [XM]. ~~PASST IHR MAL AUF~~, OB IHR DAS

KLOPFEN VON OBEN ~~HEERT~~ HOEHRT.

RICHTIG.

UND DANN SAGT MAL DURCH.

JA.

WEITER RECHTS, WEITER LINKS.

JA.

SO UNGEFAEHR., BLEIBT STAENDIG AM APPARAT AN. *(ES ... JEMAND)*

JA (2 G)

MUMBLING: REPEATING INSTRUCTIONS.

(ENGLISH COMMENT: VERY FAINT.

POUNDING. MUFFLED VOICES. SOUND OF TRAFFIC.

HAMSE SCHON (2-G) DAS HEISST (XG) [DER SCHWEIZER SO KURZ, JA?] *(MENELOGT?)*

HOLEN SIE MAL 'RUNTER.

VARIOUS NOISES.

HALLO!

JA!

(XG)

JA. *(JA)*

(GARBLE) — HIM[: DU DEN GANZE HER?]

BRAUCH -- BRAUCHEN WIR NUR

SOUND OF POUNDING.

~~NOCH HOEHR ICH IRGENDWAS.~~ HOERT IHR ETWAS (VOICE IN THE DISTANC

(XG)

~~ESKRIS~~ NICHTS ZU HOEHREN. *(ABSOLUT)*

NICHTS ZU HOEHREN.

NEIN.

JUT!

(17)

(ENGLISH COMMENT: VERY FAINT.

SE̶CRET̶

NICHTS ZU HOEHREN.

NOISES. MUFFLED VOICES.
[IM] ZIEMLICH TIEF, JA
JA, BIS HIER, HIER HOEHER.
(WIRD ES DENN?) HOEHER
UND DIE.RICHTUNG IST RICHTIG, JA?
JA

DIE RICHTUNG HIER.
JA

(XG)

TRAFFIC NOISES. HUMMING SOUND. DISTANT VOICE.

SOLA
(XG) [DIE HOEHE HINEIN?](XG)

E   [LM]
(XG) GEHT DANN RUNTER, NICHT RUNTER.

(XG)
HAUPTSAECHLICH [GLEICH GENAU]
[IM]
HIER, HIERVON, BITTE.

(ENGLISH COMMENT: VERY FAINT.

11.   RUSSIAN.
M.V.

SOUND OF POUNDING. DISTANT VOICES.
ALSO, DAS SIND DIE.
ES GEHT DURCH
JA (GARBLE)
(ENGLISH COMMENT: THROUGH. THROUGH.
UND EINMAL HIER ES GEHT SCHON DURCH ZWO METER, DAS
SIND JETZT ZWO METER FUEFZIG ...... UND NOCH EINMAL---
---- VIER METER FUENF ...... FUENF METER. (M.V.)
STELL DICH NICHT SO WEIT DARUEBER, WEIL DAS AUF DER HOEHE SITZT....
(XM)

(ENGLISH COMMENT: VERY FAINT.
(GARBLE) (ARBEITEN)
(IM) TECHNISCH GUCK DAS MAL. ACH SO IST DAS DENN.
[XM] NOCH MAL 'RUNTER
[IM]
NOCH-MAL.   [YM] NOCH EINMAL DARUNTER
NOCH EINMAL 'RUNTER
DIE-ARBEITET-NOCH.   (M.V.)
ALSO, WIR HABEN EINE [IM]

GUCK DER DA MAL HIN!
(GARBLE)

SO IDEAL DURCHGEBRINGEN. [IM]
M.V.

WO IST DAS DENN [ABGELASSEN?]

[HIER IST JA EINFACH DER KABEL [HINGELEGT.?]

(XG)

SE̶CRET̶

(GARBLE)

SO, WO KOMMT DENN, DAS JETZT?

DAS IST NOCH [VON UEBER.]
[3 M]
DAS IST WAS DENN UNTEN?

VON WESTEN (XO)
(GARBLE) (DRUEBEN IST WESTEN SCHON)
BELL RINGS.
M.V.

NA DER KABEL GEHT SO (MG)
GARBLE
DAS LETZTE
DAS IST DOCH UNSER KABEL HIER (2 G)
NA, JA.

HIER ABGEZAPFT.
(XN)

SCHOEN GEMACHT.
(GARBLE)

(XO) DISTANT VOICES.
[PASS 'N'MAL AUF!]
(ABGESEHEN?) [XM]
HIER HABEN HIER KABEL GELEGT. ICK HABE GESEHEN. SIE HABEN HIER GEGRABEN, FRISCH
GEGRABEN
(GARBLE)
DURCH GEGRABEN (XO) JA DIE. HABEN FRISCH GEGRABEN
HIER
D'RAN (GARBLE)
M.V.
WO DU GERADE VON DENKST. (2 G) WENN MAN DAS NICHT SELBST SIEHT, JA?

WUERDE MAN NIE GLAUBEN, DASS ES [GEHT?] [M].

DISTANT VOICES.
[DOCH! HAST RECHT?]
KOMME HIER
DA HINTER — WAS? HIER SIEHST DU GANZ DEUTLICH, SIEHST DU GANZ

DEUTLICH.

MUFFLED VOICES: RUSSIAN AND GERMAN TOGETHER.
[XM] WIR WISSEN JA GENAU WIE ... [XM]
M.V.
VON HIER, VON DER KANTE [GEHT ES.]

(XO) (GARBLE)

(XO) DIE ANDEREN VERBINDUNGEN.
M.V.

HALLO!
(PAUSE)

HIER WIRD GERUFEN?
HALLO M.V.
(ENGLISH COMMENT: VERY FAINT.
WASSER! WASSER! WASSER
M.V.
1. HALLO.
2. JA

1. (XO) GLEICH OB (XO)

ES GEHT NICHT GERADE AUS. ES WEICHT NACH DER (2G) XB UEBER.
(GARBLE)

ES WEICHT AB.

(XG)

NA, DA WIRD GESTOPPT. [DAS IST MIR] JA JANZ EJAILE.
DIESES, DIESES· M.V.
HIER DING DING HIER. DING D4.
[YM]....... VIER METER
ES SIND SCHON VIER METER.

[YM] FUENF METER.
"   "
[YM] DIESER, JA.

(XG)

[XM) MUSS MARU EHM
WIR WOLLEN MAL JENAU MESSEN.
·MUSS MAN GENAU MESSEN

(XG)
GANG JENAU . MESSEN
(GARBLE)
NOCH?

NOCH!

(XG)

IST DAS DIE WAND? SO!

HINTEN RUNTER.

VIER METER, JA. · · VORSICHTIG [IN]
FUENFUNDSIEBZIG
SIEBENUNDDREISIG·

VIERFUENFUNDSIEBZIG.

(XG)

ERST MAL MESSEN.

VIERFUENFUNDSIEBZIG!
(IM)!
JA, [YM] WAS DURCH
NA JA. HIER MAL RUNTER. ERST N MAL   VIERFUENFUND ZIEBZIG
(GARBLE)
MEMENT.
JA MOMENT MAL

JA, ICH KOMM DA MIT 'N KOMPAS.
(PAUSE)
SO!

SECRET (20)

MUFFLED VOICES.

(ENGLISH COMMENT:(M/G US GOVERNMENT PROPERTY M/G ?)
NAJA kuck mal... [YM] KIES KEIN MEHR
LIN[]
MUFFLED VOICES. POUNDING. HEAVY BREATHING. (KIES KEIN MEHR

HALLO, HALLO, HALLO

(3G)
[IM] MUESSEN ZURUECK
NOISES AND MUFFLED VOICES. DISTORTION IN TAPE. M.V. WITH
(LAUGHTER)   (I M)
[UM] 'RUNTER KOMMT?   Kommt
JA GEH MAL VOM LOCH WEG.   (GARBLE)

(ENGLISH COMMENT: THEY'RE ALL THE WAY DOWN.

(NO, NOT YET.

                    AUTO
WENN (?OTTS?) KOMMT (M/G)

MICROPHONE DISCOVERED AT THIS POINT. (TAPPING ON microphone)
Yes, but not recognized as, such DIESEN?
AH! DAS IST MOEGLICH.   Ja!
(M.V.)   ES GEHT HIER IMMER? HIER
                                  NA JA. [YM] DING ES PASST JA D'RAN
[2M] GEH MAL WEG!   ES IST NUN JETZT [DER ART DER) [YM]

    IST DAS EIN MIKROPHON?
    DAS IST WAHRSCHEINLICH
KOMM MAL RUNTER, [IM]

(ENGLISH COMMENT: THEY'RE NOT QUITE SURE OF IT.
              M.V.
GLAUBST DU?

SMALL BACKGROUND NOISES.

(ENGLISH COMMENT: I DON'T KNOW. NOTHING IN PARTICULAR. HUH? NO.

(THEY'VE FOUND THE MICROPHONE BUT ARE NOT SURE YET. THEY THINK

IT'S A MICROPHONE.

NOISES. POUNDING, TEARING SCRAPING.

(ENGLISH COMMENT: VERY FAINT.

MUFFLED VOICES.
  (GARBLED)
GLAUBST DU?

MOEGLICH.

SECRET

GARBLE (" ABSCHIESSEN)

SCHRAUBENZIEHER!

MOEGLICH, JA

(21)

(ENGLISH COMMENT: CAN'T UNDERSTAND THIS.

(THEY'RE CUTTING WIRE -- XXXX I THINK.

M.V.
RAUS, JA
(GARBLE)
ICH MUSS NAEMLICH 'RAUS
WAS DENN

(I THINK THEY'RE IN PROCESS OF CUTTING WIRE. LT. BECK IS IN THERE.
M.V.

(TURNED OFF, ISN'T IT.

VOICES. SOUND OF LAUGHTER.

(THEY'VE TURNED OFF ALL THEIR ~~sa.~~ [2M]

SMALL NOISES. · GARBLE

[WM] HIER IST
~~ES IST JA HIER~~ VIER METER FUENFZIG [XM] >

WIE GROSS BIST DU?

[XM] ICH BIN EINSECHSUNDSIEBZIG.
[3M]
UMDSIEBZIG ~~%~~-- 170 - ~~%~~ 420 UND NOCH MINDESTENS EIN METER ZUM RAHMEN DREI FUENFZIG DES FUENF METER [2M]
(ENGLISH COMMENT: CITING FIGURES IN ENGLISH

(ENGLISH COMMENT: THEY'RE CUTTING IT OFF.

[XM] FIVE SPRING KAPSUL MUFFLED VOICES
WO? HIER!
JA
(ENGLISH COMMENT: _____ SPRING CLIP.
ABER [XM] 'RAUS?
JA DA KANNST DU NAEMLICH [XM] WAHRSCHEINLICH
~~HOECHST WAHRSCHEINLICH~~

(ENGLISH COMMENT: VERY FAINT.

MUFFLED VOICES. (ENGLISH AND GERMAN)

JA, ICH WIRD SIE HIER INS LAPP ZIEHEN.
WART, EINMAL
JA
(IM) MAL WEG (GARBLE)
DAS IST OFFENE (I G)
M.V.

(ENGLISH COMMENT: VERY FAINT. THEY'RE CUTTING WIRE ....

DAS MIKROPHON (M/G)
M.V.
DOCH JA

SOUND OF FILING OR SCRAPING.

MUFFLED VOICES.

[SCHRAUBENZIEHER!]

(22)

(ENGLISH COMMNET: CAN HEAR WIRE CUTTERS.

SECRET

(YA, THEY'RE CUTTING THEM.

[xM] BITTE HIER (20)
(GARBLE)

ICH WILL'S HIER ABSCHNEIDEN. [xM]
[ENGLISH COMMENT: NEVER MIND, CUT THEM ALL.

ACH, IS/ IST ANGESCHRAUBT.
NEE, NEE DAS GARBLE ("BLOSS AUFGEZWICKT HIER")
MIKROLEONE = MUFFLED VOICES.

IST MOEGLICH.

MUFFLED VOICES. WHISTLING.
(NOISE RIGHT AT THE MICROPHONE)

EIN KLEINEN SCHRAUBENZIEHER MAL.

(M/G)

EIN KLEINEN SCHRAUBENZIEHER. MAL 'N GROSSEN.
GARBLE ("ABGEZWICKT")
(ENGISH COMMENT:)
MUFFLED VOICES. GARBLE)

(XG) DAS GEHT.
(GARBLE)
KOMM HER, KOMM HIER, (IM), HIER AWAT ANDERES

MAL SEHEN, [WAT IT IS.?]
GARBLE ("BISSCHEN WEITER?")
MUSS 'N GROSSEN SCHRAUBENZIEHER.
EIN GROSSEN "

ES GIBT HIER POTENZIAL.
GARBLE
(WIR WOLLTEN DAS, WIR WOLLTEN DAS NOCH FINDEN?)
DER IST ZU GROSS. 'N MITTLERE. GARBLE
HABE ICH NICHT
NICHT
(ENGLISH COMMENT: VERY FAINT. (GARBLE)

SMALL SOUNDS. BREATHING.
(pounding, whistling)
SEE SLIGHT NOISE
HAST 'N SCHRAUBENZIEHER MITGEBRACHT?
WIE?
HAST DU 'N " " "
kommt GLEICH.
(whistling)

TAPPING SOUND ON MIKE.

SO!

MUFFLED VOICES.
GARBLE
SECRET
(HIER GEHT ER.?)

SECRET   23

(MAL HIN.?)

MUFFLED VOICES.

GARBLE
WAS HAT MAN 'DRAN? WAS HAT
MAN 'DRAN? [YM]

DAS GEHT JA HIER RUEBER.
JA, JA JA, JA

(ENGLISH COMMENT: THEY'RE TAKING THE LAST ONE AWAY FROM US NOW.

(TRYING TO FIND OUT WHERE IT IS, TOO.
(GARBLE) ('SCHWEINEREI') } several seconds
(SOUND OF TOUCHING MIKE)
SOUND OF TRAFFIC.

WISPERING -- GERMAN.
HIER IST ENGE, HIER
DER GRMFEE LEUTNANT IST NOCH UNTEN
[.LM] JA
WAS IST DAS. SOLL DAS DAS DING SEIN?
NEIN, NEIN

JA — JA1

(ENGLISH COMMENT: VERY FAINT.

WAS IST DAS HIER?

WOLL' MAL SEHEU [IM]
[LM] MIKROPHON DRIN. HAMSE 'N ANDEREN SCHRAUBENZIEHER DA?
GARBLE
ER, DA ANSCHLIESSEN.   IST   DER   ANSCHLIESSNID [YM]

JA, ER IST DA DRIN
(SOUN OF something touching mike)

SOUND OF LAUGHTER. SMALL SOUNDS.

plein
DA IS 'N MIKRO DRIN.

(X/G)

(ENGLISH COMMENT: VERY FAINT.
MENSCHENSKIND !
M.V.
(XG) DAS IST EIGENTUEMLICHS, JA?
M.V.

AUCH DIE KAPSUL HIER. DAS IST [KM]
KEINE KAPSUL [IM] MEINEN SIE SO-
GAR, MEINEN SIE NUR SOGAR [YM]

SMALL SOUNDS.
ES KANN WAS ANDERES
M.V.
(XG) UNGEFAEHR   214 METER
SMALL SOUNOS
ER WILL
so! SOLL ICH DEN APPARAT MIT NEHMEN?
M.V. + SMALL SOUND

UEBER DA EINSTECKEN.

MUFFLED VOICES.

JA, WILL 'N ANDERS (1G)
SMALL SOUND
MUFFLED VOICES.

SECRET

359

MUSST DA NOCH SCHRAUBEN ZIEHEN?
JA
(GARBLE)("KLEINER")

SCHRAUBENZIEHER DER NICHT ZU GROSS IST
NEE, NEE, NEE
(GARBLE)

HALLO,   NEIN, DER IST ZU KLEIN KLEIN. [YM]
NOISE + M.V.

ENGLISH COMMENT: IT'S GONE JOHN!

app 3/9

9

G. **Berlin Tunnel**

Soviet discovery of a tunnel in the Altglien-icke section of East Berlin allegedly on 22 April 1956 put an end to a most imaginative CIA-MI-6 operation against the RIS. CIA and MI-6 personnel had tapped into the main telephone and telegraph lines of the Soviet forces between Moscow and Berlin and trunk lines between Berlin and major East German cities. The tunnel was about 500 yards long and was constructed from a position just inside the US sector in extreme south Berlin.

Mr. George Blake, the MI-6 officer and KGB agent, admitted at his investigation that he had informed his KGB principals of Allied planning for the tunnel in which he was a participant prior to his early 1955 departure for Berlin. Because of the worthwhile information developed from the operation on the Allied side, it is presumed that the Soviets were faced with either stopping a potentially harmful operation and losing a valuable penetration

- 207 -

SECRET

agent in Blake or else in protecting Blake and
risking unauthorized disclosure of classified information. They chose the latter course and allowed
it to run apparently unimpeded from May 1955 to April
1956 when a Soviet maintenance crew "found" the tunnel.

Analysis of the telephone traffic soon revealed that of the telephone lines tapped, 25 carried RIS conversations, mostly of the GRU and of
the RU units attached to various units of the Group
of Soviet Forces Germany (GSFC). The CI product
from the operation consisted primarily of the iden-
tifications of over 350 GRU and RU officers in East
Germany, another 300 KGB officers in East Germany
and the USSR, and GRU officers in the USSR. The
operation developed a total of about 2,000 names of
CI interest. The tap also had the effect of identifying Soviet intelligence units by number and location in East Germany.

FI/D initially was responsible for processing
the voice circuits containing RIS conversations. In
January 1958 the componet was formally
attached to SR/CI/ Research and Support (R&S) where

- 208 -

SECRET

reports on the RIS were issued and summaries were made of RIS information for the SR/CI/R&S files. The project was completed in late 1958.

Aside from the large number of RIS officers exposed as a result of the Tunnel operation there was also developed direct information on Soviet intelligence organizations. For example, lengthy collated reports were disseminated as a result of the Tunnel operation on: KGB radio intercept capabilities in the Berlin area; personnel of the GRU headquarters in Moscow; telephone numbers, addresses, and field post numbers of RIS units in East Germany; personnel and organization of the Potsdam headquarters of the KGB's Third (Counterintelligence in the Soviet Armed Forces) Directorate; and organization, cases, liaison, security, tradecraft, and administration of the Operations Department of the KGB's Directorate of Special Departments in Potsdam. There also was produced a collated study of the organization and personnel of the KGB headquarters; the organization and activities of the KGB advisors to the MfS Main Department I; personnel and location of GRU and GSFG RU communications units; and Soviet

– 209 –

SECRET

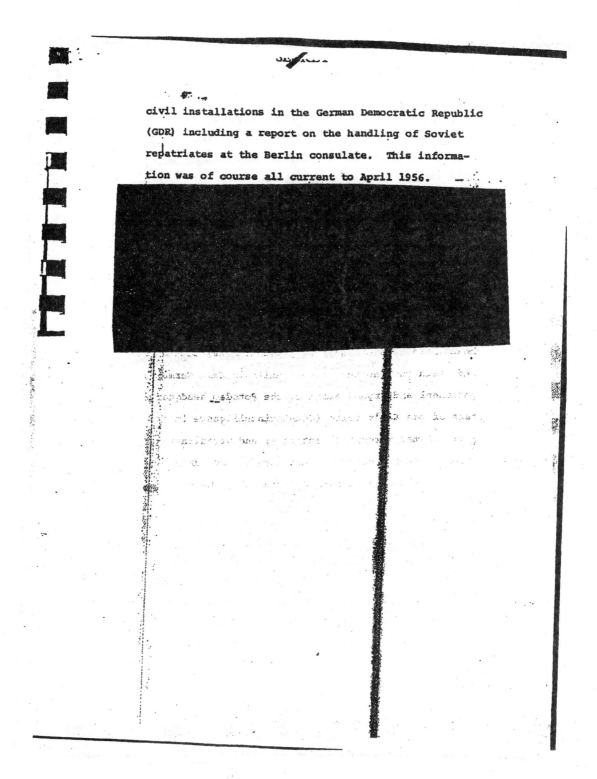

civil installations in the German Democratic Republic
(GDR) including a report on the handling of Soviet
repatriates at the Berlin consulate. This information was of course all current to April 1956.

app S⁵/t

SECRET

V. PRODUCTION

The following statistics may be of interest in evaluating the project:

a.   Three cables were tapped. They contained 273 metallic pairs capable of transmitting a total of approximately 1200 communications channels. The maximum number of channels in use at any one time approximated 500. On the average 28 telegraphic circuits and 121 voice circuits were recorded continuously. Approximately 50,000 reels of magnetic tape were used - some 25 tons.

b.   The (voice) processing center employed a peak number of 317 persons. Twenty thousand Soviet two-hour voice reels containing 368,000 conversations were fully transcribed. In addition, 13,500 German two-hour voice reels were received and 5,500 reels containing 75,000 conversations were processed. Seventeen thousand of these conversations were fully transcribed.

c.   The (teletype) center employed 350 people at its peak. Eighteen thousand six-hour Soviet teletype reels and 11,000 six-hour German teletype reels were completely transcribed. It should be borne in mind that many of these reels contained as many as 18 separate circuits, some of which utilized time-division multiplex to create additional circuits. The potential of any given six-hour teletype reel was approximately 216 hours of teletype messages. Both plain text and

25

SECRET

(SECRET)

encrypted traffic was received. The daily output was
about 4,000 feet of teletype messages. Printed in book
form, these messages would have filled a space ten feet
wide, 15 feet long, and eight feet high.

    d.   A small processing unit (two to four persons)
was maintained at the Berlin site to permit on-the-spot
monitoring of engineering circuits for the protection of
the project and scanning of the more productive circuits
for the "hot" intelligence. Daily reports of sufficient
value to warrant electrical transmission to Washington
and London were produced.

    e.   Processing of the backlogged material con-
tinued until 30 September 1958 and resulted in a total
of 1,750 reports plus 90,000 translated messages or
conversations.

    f.   The total cost of the project was $6,700,000.
The information from this material was disseminated in
a closely controlled system called  Appendix B
consists of a summary of the value of the material received
together with typical customer comments. Despite our knowledge of the fact that certain elements of the Soviet Government were aware of our plans to tap these cables, we have no
evidence that the Soviets attempted to feed us deception
material through this source.

26

(SECRET)

apps 5/4 (S E C R E T)

APPENDIX B.

RECAPITULATION OF THE INTELLIGENCE DERIVED

Set forth below are a recapitulation of intelligence
derived from the ~~tunnel~~ *tunnel* material and some typical consumer
comments.

GENERAL

The ▓▓▓▓ operation provided the United States and the
British with a unique source of current intelligence on the
Soviet Orbit of a kind and quality which had not been available since 1948. Responsible ▓▓▓▓▓▓▓▓▓▓▓ officials considered ▓▓▓▓▓▓ *the tunnel* during its productive phase, to be the
prime source of early warning concerning Soviet intentions in
Europe, if not world-wide. Following are examples of items
of intelligence for which ▓▓▓ *the tunnel* was either a unique or most
timely and reliable source.

POLITICAL

Throughout the life of source (11 May 1955 - 22 April
1956) we were kept currently informed of Soviet intentions in
Berlin; ▓▓▓ *the tunnel* provided the inside story of every "incident"
occurring in Berlin during the period - a story which was in

(S E C R E T)

(S E C R E T)

each case considerably at variance with accounts of the same
incident as reported by other sources. ~~The tunnel~~ showed that,
contrary to estimates by other sources, the Soviets at that
time did not intend to relinquish their prerogatives vis-a-
vis the other three occupying powers despite continually
increasing pressure from the East Germans to assert their sovereignty in East Berlin as well as in the rest of East Germany.
THE TUNNEL ~~provided~~ provided a clear picture of the unpreparedness, confusion,
and indecision among Soviet and East German officials whenever
an incident occurred in East Berlin involving citizens of one
of the Western powers.

The Soviet decision to implement the establishment of an
East German Army was disclosed by ~~The tunnel~~ in October 1955, in
time to notify our representatives at the Foreign Ministers
Conference in Geneva to that effect.

~~The tunnel~~ provided a detailed account of the Soviet program
for implementation of the decisions of the 20th Party Congress,
including measures to suppress unrest among Soviet nuclear
scientists resulting from a too-literal interpretation of the
new theory of collective leadership and the denigration of
Stalin.

The progress of Marshal Zhukov's attempt to curtail the
influence of the political officer in the Soviet Armed Forces
(which led to his subsequent downfall) was traced in ~~tunnel~~

2

(S E C R E T)

(S E C R E T)

material from the autumn of 1955 to mid-April 1956.

The tunnel provided considerable intelligence on the relationships between various key military and political figures of
the Soviet hierarchy and on relations between the Poles and
the Soviet military forces stationed in Poland.

MILITARY

General

a.   Reorganization of the Soviet Ministry of
Defense.

b.   Soviet plans to implement the Warsaw Pact by
increasing Soviet-Satellite military coordination.

c.   Implementation of the publicly announced
intention to reduce the strength of the Soviet Armed Forces.

d.   Identification of several thousand Soviet
officer personnel.

Air

a.   Development of an improved nuclear delivery
capability in the Soviet Air Army in East Germany.

b.   Re-equipment of the Soviet Air Army in East
Germany with new bombers and twin-jet interceptors
having an airborne radar capability.

c.   Doubling of the Soviet bomber strength in
Poland and the appearance there of a new fighter division.

3

(S E C R E T)

(S E C R E T)

    d.   Identification and location of approximately 100 Soviet Air Force installations in the USSR, East Germany, and Poland, including a number of key aircraft factories.

Ground Forces

    a.   Order of battle of Soviet ground forces within the USSR not previously identified or not located for several years by any other source.

    b.   Soviet training plans for the spring and early summer of 1956 in East Germany and Poland.

    c.   Identification of several thousand Soviet field post numbers (used by G-2 to produce Soviet order of battle intelligence).

Navy

    a.   Reduction in the status and personnel strength of the Soviet Naval Forces.

    b.   Organization and administrative procedures of the Headquarters of the Soviet Baltic Fleet and Soviet Naval Bases on the Baltic Coast.

SCIENTIFIC

Identification of several hundred personalities associated with the Soviet Atomic Energy (AE) Program.

Association of certain locations in the USSR with AE activities.

4

(S E C R E T)

(S E C R E T)

Organization and activities of Wismuth SDAG (mining uranium in the Aue area of East Germany).

OPERATIONAL

Organization, functions, and procedures of the Soviet Intelligence Services in East Germany; identification of several hundred Soviet Intelligence personalities in East Germany and Moscow.

5

(S E C R E T)

SECRET

6
SECRET

VI: The Berlin Crisis

VI: The Berlin Crisis

By the mid-1950s the Soviets' Berlin strategy had changed. Although the expulsion of the Western Allies from the city undoubtedly remained a goal, after the suppression of the Berlin uprising in 1953 the Soviets gradually moved to at least a general acceptance of the status quo in Central Europe. For the Soviet Premier, Nikita Khrushchev, in particular, the first priorities in Soviet German policy were the stabilization and legitimization of the Soviet-backed East German regime. Ironically, Khrushchev seems to have been primarily concerned that the rapid revitalization of West Germany would allow it to break free of American influence and pursue a conservative-led irredentist policy in Central and Eastern Europe. That the Bonn Republic might remain a pacific, democratic state seems to have been dismissed as an implausibility by the Kremlin. By the fall of 1958, the Soviet leadership had apparently convinced itself that Bonn was planning to displace Soviet influence in Eastern Europe by a strategy of far-reaching economic penetration. The possibility of West German military action was discounted but not precluded.[1]

Khrushchev thus acted to prop up the East German regime and dislodge Western forces from Berlin before the West German regime could grow too strong and independent. As a curtain raiser, the Soviets resumed regular interference with military trains to and from Berlin early in 1958. That November, Khrushchev issued a demand that the Western powers renounce their rights in Berlin in favor of the DDR. On the 27th of that month, he threatened to transfer unilaterally Soviet control of East Berlin and of the access routes to West Berlin to the DDR within the next six months, thereby putting an end to quadripartite control of the city and forcing the Western Allies to deal directly with the East German regime.

But the willingness of the US, Great Britain, and France to negotiate a solution to the Berlin problem seems to have convinced Khrushchev that it would be possible to persuade the West to abandon its support of what he perceived to be Bonn's aggressive designs toward Eastern Europe. In January 1959, Khrushchev sent clear signals that he would not go to war over Berlin, but would not be part of an agreement that included the Bonn government—which then had as its Chancellor the Christian Democrat Konrad Adenauer—as a signatory. Khrushchev's subsequent willingness to submit the whole German question to a meeting of Foreign Ministers suggests that, by the following March, displacement of the Western powers from Berlin

---

[1] Vladislav M. Zubok. "Khrushchev and the Berlin Crisis (1958-1962)," *Cold War International History Project* (Washington, DC: Woodrow Wilson International Center for Scholars, 1993), pp. 3-8.

had moved into second place in Soviet priorities behind a draft German peace treaty. But this new plan fizzled: none of the Western Allies would agree to abandon Bonn and Khrushchev himself decided to defer the question, first until his trip to the US to meet with President Eisenhower that Fall and then until the Four-Power summit scheduled for the following May. In the meantime, he counseled patience to the East Berlin regime, but continued to pressure the Western Allies into a final settlement by threatening to sign a separate Soviet–East German peace treaty.[2]

By the spring of 1960 it must have become apparent to Khrushchev that this strategy had not worked; that Western solidarity remained intact, and that a peace treaty and a solution of the Berlin question on terms agreeable to the Soviet Union was not in the offing. He thus used the 1 May shoot-down of Francis Gary Powers' U-2 spy plane as a pretext to kill the Paris summit, thereby avoiding being "outgunned and humiliated" on the Berlin question.[3] In doing so he also bought time to await possibly favorable changes in the Western leadership constellation: West German Chancellor Adenauer was faced with elections that September; President Eisenhower certainly was going to be replaced the following November. Replacement of one or both of these key figures might produce a political environment more favorable to a Soviet-backed peace treaty.[4] Or so it was possible for Khrushchev to hope.

The principal intelligence problem in this Berlin crisis was to understand Khrushchev's shifting motives and to gauge how far he would go—and in which direction. However, as was frequently the case in analysis of political events, the US Intelligence Community often had little more to go on than was reported in the open press. Under such circumstances, the CIA's role was primarily to serve as a clearinghouse for information brought in from every conceivable source. The value of the intelligence provided to policymakers thus generally derived more from the experience and expertise of the intelligence officers producing the reports than from their access to any special sources of information. In this situation, intelligence derived from clandestine sources frequently filled in important gaps, or contributed an added dimension that otherwise would not be present.

---

[2] Hope M. Harrison, "The Berlin Crisis and the Khrushchev-Ulbricht Summits in Moscow, 9 and 18 June 1959," *Cold War International History Project Bulletin* 11 (Winter 1998), p. 205.

[3] Sherman Kent, the Chairman of the Board of National Estimates from 1952-67, was present at the May 1960 Paris Summit to provide intelligence support to the US delegation. In 1972 he wrote up his impressions of the event in an article for the CIA's professional journal, *Studies in Intelligence*. This has been reproduced in Donald P. Steury, ed., *Sherman Kent and the Board of National Estimates* (Washington, DC: Center for the Study of Intelligence, 1994), pp. 157-172.

[4] Zubok, pp. 12-13.

As can be seen from the following documents, policymakers were provided with a broad spectrum of intelligence reporting. The most comprehensive, long-range analysis generally appeared in the periodic NIEs or Special National Intelligence Estimates (SNIEs). But, as these could seldom be written quickly enough to keep up with developments, it was necessary to backstop and update this analysis with daily and weekly reports. These in turn provided much of the information used by the Board of National Estimates to draft the NIEs. Policymakers and senior officials also were kept apprised of events through daily briefings and—less frequently—other kinds of communications that do necessarily appear in the historical record.

As the crisis developed over 1959, the status of the Soviet military presence in East Berlin was seen to be a key indicator of Soviet intentions. The KGB base in Karlshorst thus was closely monitored. Throughout the spring of 1959, there was much movement of Soviet personnel, but by the end of June it became obvious that, although the Soviets had delegated control of the sector crossings and access routes to the DDR, there would be no significant diminution in the Soviet presence in East Berlin.[5] This fact helped Western analysts gauge Khrushchev's threats of a separate peace and decide how best to respond. Actually, it is still far from clear whether Khrushchev had ever intended a Soviet pullout from East Berlin—but then had been dissuaded by Western persistence—or whether it had all been a sham all along.

VI-1: CIWS: USSR Threatens Western Position in Berlin, 13 November 1958 (MORI No. 45621).

A near-contemporaneous analysis of Khrushchev's actions, largely from open sources, this report supplements the publicly available information with additional material from diverse sources— such as an appraisal of East Germany's ability to provide trained air traffic controllers.

VI-2: CIWS: Internal Situation in East Germany, 11 December 1958 (MORI No. 45626).

Much like a newspaper, CIA often supplemented its daily reporting with longer, more in-depth analyses, such as this piece on the internal situation in the DDR that provides background on the situation in Berlin. Such reports generally reached a wider audience than if they were written in an NIE.

---

[5] David E. Murphy, Sergei Kondrashev, and George Bailey, *Battleground Berlin,* (New Haven, CT: Yale University Press, 1997), pp. 317-319.

VI-3: SNIE 100-13-58: Soviet Objectives in the Berlin Crisis, 23 December 1958.
In this, the first Estimate to appear on the 1958 Berlin crisis, the Board of National Estimates takes advantage of its relative "distancing" from events to summarize and analyze developments before projecting future Soviet actions.

VI-4: CIWS: The Berlin Situation, 15 January 1959 (MORI No. 144339).
This excerpt from the weekly summary reports on the Soviet peace proposal announced five days previously and places it in context with concurrent developments in Germany and elsewhere.

VI-5: Cable: Current Status Report Soviet Compound Karlshorst..., 16 January 1959 (MORI No. 144340).

VI-6: Cable: Current Status Report Soviet Intelligence Services East Germany, 21 January 1959 (MORI No. 144341).

VI-7: Cable: B[e]rl[i]n Sitrep, 11 February 1959 (MORI No. 144342).
These reports show the Soviets making preparations for a large-scale evacuation of military personnel from Berlin, but also provide evidence that the KGB intended to remain. These three documents represent raw intelligence reporting—a key source for both current intelligence reports and the longer range Estimates. Only in exceptional circumstances would a policymaker receive intelligence in this form.

VI-8: CIWS: Communist Tactics Against West Berlin, 5 February 1959 (MORI No. 28210).
With Khrushchev more-or-less quiescent on Berlin in February 1959, the Current Intelligence Weekly Summary took advantage of the opportunity to summarize Soviet tactics to date. Such reporting supported and anticipated NIEs and SNIEs then in production or scheduled to appear—almost as a kind of "interim Estimate" (see Document VI-11).

VI-9: CIWS: Flight of Refugees From East Germany, 12 February 1959 (MORI No. 45580).
The DDR's biggest problem—and a major factor in the Berlin crisis—was the steady hemorrhage of defectors to the West. CIA tracked East Germany's refugee problem and reported on it periodically.

VI-10: SNIE 100-2-59: Probable Soviet Courses of Action Regarding Berlin and Germany, 24 February 1959.

Written in response to a request from Secretary of State Christian Herter, this Estimate addresses a series of questions concerning probable Soviet actions concerning Berlin and likely responses to proposed US actions. Compare it with Document VI-9, above. Estimates are, of course, generally much longer than current intelligence reports, but also are far more predictive in format and general subject matter.

VI-11: CIWS: USSR Prepares To Vacate East Berlin, 5 March 1959 (MORI No. 45584).

With Khrushchev threatening to turn over to East Germany all Soviet rights in Berlin as well as control of the access routes to the western half of the city, the status of the Soviet garrison in Berlin was seen as a solid indicator of future Soviet actions. The Soviet presence in Karlshorst thus was closely monitored. Note the shift in the tone of this document as compared with Document VI-5, above.

VI-12: CIA Memorandum: Soviet and Other Reactions to Various Courses of Action in the Berlin Crisis, 27 March 1959 (MORI No. 14231).

Written solely for the President and his senior advisers, this CIA memorandum addresses issues similar to the SNIE prepared one month before (see Document VI-11), but discusses the possible outcomes of some of the more extreme courses of action that might be taken by the United States. It also refers specifically to the possibility that the Berlin crisis might escalate into an intercontinental nuclear exchange.

VI-13: IR: Soviet Official's Comments on the Berlin Situation, 6 April 1959 (MORI No. 144343).

The uncertainty prevailing in the Berlin crisis is reflected in this report from April 1959, which raises both the possibility of war and of Soviet measures short of war. Although this report gives the impression that the Soviets were about to pull their forces out of Berlin, CIA was unable to confirm this from other sources.[6] In fact, the Soviets did not withdraw from Karlshorst or East Berlin until the end of the Cold War.

---

[6] Murphy, et al., p. 317.

VI-14: CIWS: The Problem of Western Access to Berlin, 30 April 1959 (MORI No. 45593).

As the East Germans assumed control of access corridors into and out of Berlin, the possibility of another blockade loomed. This report reviews Western access rights and the implications of a determined Soviet/East German attempt to block access to Berlin.

VI-15: CIWS: Foreign Ministers' Talks, 21 May 1959 (MORI No. 145741).

Here the Current Intelligence Weekly Summary documented Soviet efforts to drive a wedge between the three Western Allies in the Foreign Ministers' talks then under way. These efforts proved to be fruitless: the Western Alliance held fast on Berlin.

VI-16: SNIE 100-7-59: Soviet Tactics on Berlin, 11 June 1959.

A nuanced analysis of Khrushchev's motives and a prognosis of his future moves from the summer of 1959.

VI-17: CIA Memorandum: U.S. Negotiating Position on Berlin, 1959-62, 13 July 1959 (MORI No. 11599).

With East and West well and truly deadlocked over Berlin, CIA sent forward a memorandum considering the impact that projected shifts in the balance of military power would have on the Berlin situation. The 1958 Berlin crisis introduced a new element into the confrontation in Central Europe: strategic nuclear weapons. Under Khrushchev's leadership, the Soviet military had extensively adopted nuclear weaponry and modernized and expanded its long-range naval and airstrike forces. The Soviet Union could now legitimately lay claim to world-power status. Although it would be some time before the Soviet nuclear capabilities even approached those of the United States, contemporary intelligence reporting shows how from 1958 onward US planners had constantly to reckon with the possibility that a crisis in Central Europe might escalate into an intercontinental nuclear exchange—however unlikely that eventuality might be at any given moment. There was, in addition, the menace of theater nuclear weapons (e.g., shorter range weapons for use in Europe), of which both sides had large and growing inventories. Nuclear weapons are not known to have ever been deployed in Berlin by either side, but the Soviet and Western intelligence personnel deployed there now faced each other under the deepening shadow of the nuclear arms race.

VI-18: CIWS: East German Pressure for Access Controls Appears Suspended, 27 August 1959 (MORI No. 45604).
Throughout the crisis, Khrushchev walked a narrow path between belligerency and outright confrontation. The difficulties in following his tacks and veers are seen in this report, which shows him restraining the East German government on the eve of his trip to the United States to meet with President Eisenhower.

VI-19: SNIE 100-5-60: The Soviet Attitude and Tactics on the Berlin Problem, 22 March 1960.

VI-20: CIWS: Khrushchev's Strategy on Berlin, 18 August 1960 (MORI No. 144106).
Over 1959-60, the US intelligence community continued to submit Khrushchev's Berlin tactics to periodic review. These two documents provide interesting counterpoints to each other—being written shortly before and after the May 1960 summit.

CONFIDENTIAL
~~SECRET~~

OCI NO. ~~0000/00~~
13 November 1958

CURRENT INTELLIGENCE WEEKLY SUMMARY

CENTRAL INTELLIGENCE AGENCY
OFFICE OF CURRENT INTELLIGENCE

CONFIDENTIAL

SECRET

CURRENT INTELLIGENCE WEEKLY SUMMARY

13 November 1958

THE WEEK IN BRIEF

PART I

OF IMMEDIATE INTEREST

USSR THREATENS WESTERN POSITION IN BERLIN . . . . Page 1

Khrushchev's threat on 10 November to "revise" the international status of Berlin presages a period of mounting tension in Germany during which the USSR will probably take steps to transfer to the East German regime Soviet authority in Berlin derived from quadripartite agreements. A new juridical basis for the presence of Soviet troops in East Germany would be established. These actions would be designed to force the West to deal with the Ulbricht regime in order to maintain Western access to Berlin. Bonn has hinted it might consider severing relations with Moscow if the USSR should abrogate the four-power agreement on Berlin.

. . . . Page 3

NR

SECRET

CONFIDENTIAL

CURRENT INTELLIGENCE WEEKLY SUMMARY

12 November 1958

PART I

OF IMMEDIATE INTEREST

USSR THREATENS WESTERN POSITION IN BERLIN

Khrushchev's threats on 10 November to "revise" the international status of Berlin presage a period of mounting tension in Germany. During this period the USSR will probably take a series of steps to transfer to the East German regime Soviet authority in Berlin derived from quadripartite agreements. A new juridical basis for the presence of Soviet troops in East Germany would be established.

Khrushchev declared that the Western powers, by violating the "Potsdam Agreement"—notably by sanctioning the remilitarization of West Germany—had forfeited their right to remain in West Berlin, and he indicated that the USSR would hand over its remaining functions to East Germany. He further declared that any attack on East Germany would be considered an attack on the USSR itself. He gave no indication, however, of how or when the USSR planned to hand over its functions. Soviet Foreign Minister Gromyko on 11 November said this would not happen immediately but would not be long delayed. Further, a Soviet Foreign Ministry official informed American Ambassador Thompson that German problems should be dealt with on a step-by-step basis.

The Soviet actions would be designed to enhance East German sovereignty, thus underlining the Soviet contention that there are two Germanies and, by invoking the threat of a blockade, to force the West to deal with the Ulbricht regime. A broader purpose may be to further increase world tension with a "western Quemoy" in order to strengthen bloc unity against the common enemy and to block West German attempts to establish normal relations with the East European countries, particularly Poland. Further, the

WEST GERMANY—BERLIN COMMUNICATION ROUTES

move is designed to undercut forthcoming West German proposals regarding a four-power conference on German reunification.

Moscow's move at this time will strengthen the hand of the Ulbricht regime against popular unrest stemming from the sudden

CONFIDENTIAL

OF IMMEDIATE INTEREST   Page 1 of 8

CURRENT INTELLIGENCE WEEKLY SUMMARY

13 November 1958

change in over-all policy from a "hard line" to one of concessions to certain elements of the populace. As a result of concessions to physicians, industrial workers were considering work slowdowns to pressure the regime into improving their own conditions.

Moreover, the flow of refugees to the West, although somewhat reduced, has continued. During October, more than 19,000 East Germans, including many intellectuals and technicians, fled to the West, approximately 75 percent through West Berlin. A sealing off of West Berlin would thus greatly diminish refugee losses.

In a press conference on 12 November, East German Premier Grotewohl, referring to the possibility of a withdrawal of Soviet troops from Germany, stated that he understood Khrushchev's speech raised such a possibility, "naturally" on the premise that the other powers took the same steps. This suggests that East German officials may depart for Moscow in the near future to negotiate a new agreement along these lines, perhaps after the forthcoming elections of 16 November, as reported by a fairly reliable source.

Moscow might transfer its membership in the Berlin Air

SECRET

CURRENT INTELLIGENCE WEEKLY SUMMARY

13 November 1958

Safety Center to the East Germans, thus confronting the West with a situation in which it would be required either to deal with East German officials or fly without guarantees of safety. However, the East Germans are not now believed to be in a position to exert effective control of flights in the corridor and they apparently do not possess the trained personnel to take over all the Soviet positions at this time.

West German officials believe that Khrushchev's speech is aimed at testing the firmness of the Western resolve to remain in Berlin and at exerting pressure on German public opinion to accept direct political talks with East Germany. French and British foreign affairs officials have strongly rejected any unilateral abrogation of the Potsdam Agreement, and the West German press chief on 12 November hinted that Bonn might consider severing its relations with Moscow if the USSR abrogated the four-power status of Berlin.

Increased harassment of West Berlin and Allied and West German access to it is now likely. Various measures to inhibit traffic on the lifeline to Berlin could be taken by the USSR or East Germany, and the East Germans could move to seal off West Berlin by imposing border restrictions and halting municipal transport. Although West Berlin municipal officials report that there is no indication of public disquiet in the city, they feel that acceptance of East German control over highway access to Berlin would be an "intolerable situation." British officials in Berlin, however, warn of the danger of a "self-imposed" blockade if the Western powers refuse to accept East German control over access to Berlin.

NR

SECRET

384

CONFIDENTIAL
~~SECRET~~

OCI NO. 5647/58

11 December 1958

CURRENT
INTELLIGENCE
WEEKLY
SUMMARY

CENTRAL INTELLIGENCE AGENCY
OFFICE OF CURRENT INTELLIGENCE

CONFIDENTIAL
~~SECRET~~

CURRENT INTELLIGENCE WEEKLY SUMMARY

11 December 1958

NR

PART III

PATTERNS AND PERSPECTIVES

The Berlin issue has been brought forward at a time when Walter Ulbricht has completed the consolidation of his control of the East German party and government. He has purged his opponents and obtained the strong backing of Khrushchev; but his regime faces grave problems, and only sustained Soviet support will keep him in power. Control of access to West Berlin would solve two of East Germany's major problems—the exodus of refugees to the West and the influx of anti-Communist influences.

vi

THE WEEK IN BRIEF

CURRENT INTELLIGENCE WEEKLY SUMMARY

11 December 1958

NR

* * *

THE INTERNAL SITUATION IN EAST GERMANY

The reintroduction of the Berlin issue in international politics comes at a time when party boss Walter Ulbricht has solidified his control of the East German regime.

The Purge and Its Causes

Between mid-October 1957 and February 1958, Ulbricht forced a reluctant party central committee to adopt a sweeping program to speed up socialization—a move probably coordinated with Khrushchev during his visit to East Germany in August 1957. Party elements headed by Karl Schirdewan, who had generally been regarded as Ulbricht's successor, strongly condemned the proposed measures as unrealistic and likely to lead to dangerous public unrest; they called instead for a pro-

gram tailored to the country's needs. Schirdewan himself apparently felt that a slower pace would facilitate eventual German reunification, since drastic socialization of East Germany would make union extremely difficult. Pragmatic economists like Fred Oelssner, Heinrich Rau, and Fritz Selbmann pointed to the economic disorganization they thought would result from Ulbricht's decentralization measures.

The decisive clash between Ulbricht and the Schirdewan faction came at the 35th party plenum in February 1958. In a searing attack, Erich Honecker, Ulbricht's hatchet man, charged Schirdewan and former State Security Minister Ernst Wollweber with "fractional" activities—a major Communist crime—as well as with softness toward

SEC̲̅R̲̅E̲̅T

PART III   PATTERNS AND PERSPECTIVES   Page 3 of 15

CURRENT INTELLIGENCE WEEKLY SUMMARY

11 December 1958

counterrevolutionaries and, in the case of Schirdewan, opposition to Ulbricht. Both were removed from the central committee. Former party theoreti-

ULBRICHT

cian Oelssner was accused of "opportunism" in agricultural policies and opposition to Ulbricht's decentralization proposals, and was dropped from the politburo. Schirdewan, Wollweber, "and others" were further charged with "revisionist views" and faulty ideological interpretations.

The purge was completed last July at the fifth party congress--attended by Khrushchev--when no fewer than 17 central committee members and 10 candidate members were eliminated. Both Oelssner and Selbmann fell at this time.

Other high-level functionaries who have at times wavered in their support of Ulbricht survived, at least temporarily. These included Rau, who was retained as a politburo member and deputy premier, and Premier Grotewohl, who went on "a rest cure of several weeks" in the USSR after the plenum--lending support to reports that his position was shaky.

Effect of Purge

The purge restored party "unity," but uncertainty and unrest were rampant throughout the party apparatus. Since Schirdewan had headed the party's personnel office, many functionaries were personally linked with him and fearful for their positions.

The elimination of Schirdewan and others who had had some measure of popular approval confirmed for East Germans, especially the intellectuals, that there was little hope for any real improvement in political conditions.

To replace the purgees, Ulbricht installed several new central committee secretaries, including Honecker and certain district party secretaries. Control of the party personnel organization was turned over to Berlin party boss Alfred Neumann, thus marking him as a man of increasing importance. Ulbricht's personal toady, Erich Mielke, had earlier replaced Wollweber in the Ministry of State Security.

HONECKER

Ulbricht then rammed through the party congress his political and economic program

388

CURRENT INTELLIGENCE WEEKLY SUMMARY

11 December 1958

keyed to overtaking West Germany in consumer-goods production and food consumption by 1961 and pushing ahead to complete the "building of socialism" by 1965. The implementation of economic decentralization actually was designed to give Ulbricht even closer control over all East German economic life, since the measure provided for greatly increased authority to the State Planning Commission, which is headed by Ulbricht's tool, Bruno Leuschner.

This far-reaching economic program was based on closer economic ties with the USSR. As a measure of Soviet economic aid, East Germany's annual payments for the maintenance of Soviet occupation forces, estimated at approximately $150,-000,000, were canceled effective 1 January 1959. Special targets for socialization were small businesses and agriculture, while the professional classes--notably doctors--were to be brought into state-controlled organizations.

Communist indoctrination was to be stepped up in schools through "polytechnical" education--i.e., combined physical labor and study obligatory for all students above the age of eleven. By 1960 all prospective university students were to have served for one year in a factory, in agriculture, or in the armed forces.

These measures were accompanied by intensified efforts to limit contacts with West Germany through curtailed travel and by more stringent police measures against defectors and those who aided them.

Consequences of Hard Course

The new program vastly increased smoldering popular discontent and seriously disrupted certain areas of the economy, notably retail trade. Regime promises were treated with derision. Essentially, however,

political oppression and severance of ties with the West constituted the main grievances.

According to a reliable Western correspondent who visited

LEUSCHNER

Leipzig in September, no one could complain of "really critical shortages of the main things people eat and wear," but Leipzigers were apprehensive in the face of advancing socialization. Small shopkeepers feared they would be wiped out in the next few months. The correspondent also noted that people referred to the 17 June 1953 uprising as if it had happened yesterday.

Even more than the "bourgeois remnants," East Germany's intellectuals--professional men, scientists, technicians, university professors, and students-- began to despair of a change for the better. Already hard hit by repression and increasingly barred from contact with West Germany and Western culture, intellectuals were subjected to unremitting demands for ideological subservience. In the universities, politically unreliable professors were dismissed and students were forced to take an oath to support the regime. Twenty-four Jena University students and young workers were secretly tried in early October for allegedly plotting against the regime and proposing reunification with West

CURRENT INTELLIGENCE WEEKLY SUMMARY

11 December 1958

Germany on the basis of free elections. A Jena University official who defected said these students became the "toast of the Soviet Zone." East Germans now knew the truth of Pasternak's description--"the feeling of the state closing in on individual privacy."

Oppression of the middle class and intellectuals led-- as the Schirdewan group had warned--to a mass exodus to the West. Professional men, scientists, and technicians whom the regime could ill afford to lose constituted an increasingly large proportion of the refugees. Many were party members. In the first nine months of 1958, more than 250 university professors and instructors, 2,393 schoolteachers, and many youths escaped. The loss of 813 doctors, approximately 8 percent of East Germany's total, left some areas temporarily without medical care. The flight of business executives, retailers, and artisans left dangerous gaps in the economy. Opposition in the higher levels of the party to Ulbricht's economic policies was mounting, reportedly centered as before among the pragmatic economists in the government, including the State Planning Commission. Reflecting such opinions, a fairly

reliable source reported that Heinrich Rau had warned Moscow that mass disaffection of farmers, workers, and intellectuals was building up.

Shift to Softer Party Line

By early September it apparently became clear even to Ulbricht that a drastic change in the party line was required to reduce popular unrest and stem the refugee flow. The new line was unveiled with an announcement of far-reaching concessions to doctors to permit private practice, do away with ideological qualifications, and permit travel to the West. To implement the new policies, two special politburo commissions were set up under Kurt Hager: one received sweeping powers to make "all possible" concessions to doctors; the second was to supervise school affairs.

In a move to stem the flight of small businessmen and artisans, Ulbricht himself announced a slowdown in the socialization of small business enterprises, giving notice that "in one or two years" such individuals would probably enter a socialized agency "voluntarily." Party activists and officials were

EMIGRATION FROM THE SOVIET ZONE AND THE SOVIET SECTOR OF BERLIN

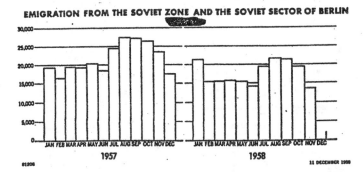

390

CURRENT INTELLIGENCE WEEKLY SUMMARY

11 December 1958

accused of arbitrarily raising work norms or being overzealous in carrying out party directives to collectivize independent farmers, and their co-

HAGER

ercive measures were stigmatized as "distortions" of party congress directives.

Although Ulbricht probably had discussed his modifications of the hard line with Khrushchev during his visit to the USSR in August, a delegation of ten high-level Soviet party functionaries was sent to East Germany in early September to survey the situation and to impress East Germans that the shift in policy had the Kremlin's blessing.

The further demotion of Fritz Selbmann at this time from his post as deputy premier and his removal from the staff of the party theoretical journal probably were meant as a warning to Ulbricht's party opponents not to misinterpret the shift to a softer line.

Pressure for More Concessions

Ulbricht's reversal immediately began to backfire.

Many people conceived the idea that the regime's difficulties could be exploited to gain concessions for themselves, particularly since the approaching elections made the regime somewhat more responsive to public opinion. The populace in general became more open in its criticism. An American officer during a tour talked with many East Germans who were "highly derisive and sarcastic" about the Russians and the East German regime. He noted that he had never before heard such bitter and outspoken criticism expressed so openly. Workers in the important Leuna works were openly cynical about the elections.

Responding to these pressures, the regime instituted further concessions to improve living conditions. On 3 November the politburo announced that more consumer goods would be available, demanded that private retailers receive adequate supplies, and sharply reproached government officials for permitting price increases.

As did the purge of the Schirdewan group, Ulbricht's maneuvers increased intraparty strains. Party officials found it difficult to adapt themselves to the new line.

The Berlin Gambit

Against this background, the introduction of the Berlin issue appears designed at least in part to strengthen the East German regime by emphasizing its "sovereignty" and eliminating West Berlin as a Western enclave in the bloc. Moscow's handling of the affair has played up Ulbricht's authority, and his adherents in the party are reported gloating over the adoption of "his" policies by Khrushchev.

SECRET

CURRENT INTELLIGENCE WEEKLY SUMMARY

11 December 1958

Ulbricht in the meantime appears to be taking even more decisive steps to tighten his control over the party organization. A source with connections on the East German party central committee reports that an internal screening of officials in the central party ap-

NEUMANN

paratus now is in progress. As a result, morale is said to be low among these employees, and tension and mutual distrust are rising daily.

Since Schirdewan's dismissal, no other party figure has emerged as a potential contender for power or even as heir apparent among the top party leadership. Of the possible successors, Hermann Matern and, more recently, Alfred Neumann appear to hold the edge; Moscow-trained Erich Honecker might in time aspire to the mantle.

The outlook for the East German people is gloomy. Ulbricht's recent concessions were purely tactical, and he has not basically retreated from

MATERN

his intention to impose Communism on the people. Recent developments, moreover, have made East Germany increasingly dependent on the USSR both politically and economically. If access to the West through West Berlin is cut off--the interzonal borders are already largely sealed--little hope of escape will remain for East Germans, who will be forced to make their peace with Ulbricht on his terms. Ulbricht and his party will still be faced with an essentially unstable internal situation-- one of such magnitude that the USSR knows it cannot safely withdraw its troops for a long time to come.

* * *

SECRET

SECRET

SOVIET OBJECTIVES IN THE BERLIN CRISIS

THE PROBLEM

To assess Soviet objectives and probable policy in the Berlin situation.

CONCLUSIONS

1. Moscow's move to raise the issue of Berlin at this time is probably not the result of any single development but stems from several converging factors; some of these bear on the shoring up of the Communist position in Eastern Europe, others on weakening the Allied position in Germany and in Western Europe generally. We view Moscow's move as another manifestation of the hardening tendency in Soviet foreign policy and of the Soviet's growing confidence in the general strength of the Bloc's position vis-a-vis the Western Powers.

2. We believe that the Soviet objectives in their move against Berlin include:

 a. To remove or reduce the disruptive influence which Berlin poses to the East German regime and thus to the consolidation of the Soviet order in Eastern Europe.

 b. To increase the international prestige of the German Democratic Republic (GDR) in order to strengthen the regime's internal position and to support the Soviet-GDR program to "reunify" Germany by confederation.

 c. To move the West toward acceptance of the USSR's version of the *status quo* in Eastern Europe.

 d. To foster discord among the NATO states, to reduce West German confidence in its allies, and to encourage Bonn to seek a separate deal with the USSR on the German problem.

 e. To bring about West Germany's withdrawal from NATO and to impose limitation on German armament, and particularly to prevent German acquisition of a nuclear capability.

 f. To maneuver the West into accepting Soviet proposals for an early summit meeting and perhaps to induce the US to enter bilateral top-level negotiations.

3. If the Soviets fail to make significant progress in possible negotiations with the Allies, they will sooner or later have to face up to the question of fulfilling their announced intention to turn over to East Germany their controls over access to West Berlin. Their decision will be greatly affected by the Soviet assessment of

SECRET

1

2

the degree of tension which had developed and particularly the firmness of the Western position at the time, and it is possible that the Soviet leaders might decide to back down under whatever smokescreen of explanation seems most expedient. However, we consider it more likely that the USSR would proceed with the turnover of controls to the East Germans. The Soviet leaders probably intend to be cautious and tactically flexible. We believe that they will try to direct Soviet and East German maneuvering in a manner which will avoid military conflict with the Western allies, while at the same time they will be prepared to take advantage of any signs of weakness on the part of the West, or of inclinations to compromise on major issues. Nevertheless, they have already committed themselves considerably, and we believe that the crisis may be severe, with considerable chance of miscalculation by one or both sides.

DISCUSSION

4. Moscow's move to raise the issue of Berlin at this time is probably not the result of any single development but stems from several converging factors; some of these bear on the shoring up of the Communist position in Eastern Europe, others on weakening the Allied position in Germany and in Western Europe generally. We view Moscow's move as another manifestation of the hardening tendency in Soviet foreign policy and of the Soviet's growing confidence in the general strength of the Bloc's position vis-a-vis the Western Powers. Khrushchev apparently genuinely believes that Soviet weapons advances and economic successes are shifting the world balance of power. The strength of this conviction, frequently expressed in recent Communist pronouncements, is evident from the firmness with which he has demanded that the issue of Berlin be reopened. Soviet leaders must be aware that there is virtually no point of controversy between East and West on which the West has so thoroughly committed itself, and that there can scarcely be a more dangerous international issue to push to the point of crisis.

5. We do not believe that the more assertive tone of Soviet foreign policy in general or the Soviet move on Berlin in particular indicate any greater Soviet willingness deliberately to risk general war. The Soviets have almost certainly not intended to give the crisis the character of a military showdown but have intended to develop it in political terms. Thus Moscow will seek to avoid placing itself in any position from which it must either back down completely or resort to military force. Nevertheless, Soviet prestige is already strongly committed on the Berlin issue: the Soviet Government has announced that it will turn over to the East Germans its functions in Berlin, including access controls. The Soviets have given public assurances of military support to East Germany in the event that the latter's "frontiers" are "violated" by the Allies. The Soviets may even believe that the West itself is less disposed to run substantial risk of war and that therefore the Western Alliance is more likely to give in to pressure.

PRINCIPAL SOVIET OBJECTIVES

6. We believe that the Soviet objectives in their move against Berlin include:

a. To remove or reduce the disruptive influence which Berlin poses to the East German regime and thus to the consolidation of the Soviet order in Eastern Europe.

b. To increase the international prestige of the German Democratic Republic (GDR) in order to strengthen the regime's internal position and to support the Soviet-GDR program to "reunify" Germany by confederation.

c. To move the West toward acceptance of the USSR's version of the *status quo* in Eastern Europe.

d. To foster discord among the NATO states, to reduce West German confidence in its allies, and to encourage Bonn to seek a separate deal with the USSR on the German problem.

e. To bring about West Germany's withdrawal from NATO and to impose limitation on German armament, and particularly to prevent German acquisition of a nuclear capability.

f. To maneuver the West into accepting Soviet proposals for an early summit meeting and perhaps to induce the US to enter bilateral top-level negotiations.

7. The first three of these objectives are concerned with shoring up the Communist position in Eastern Europe, a problem which has preoccupied the Soviets especially during the past few years. The political and economic stability of the GDR has been a troublesome problem, which has been pointed up in recent months by the flight of professional personnel through West Berlin. If the Western Powers could be persuaded to withdraw their forces from Berlin, the GDR authorities would be able to restrict the flow of refugees as well to reduce the political challenge which West Berlin has presented the GDR. Together with implicit Western recognition of East Germany, these developments would significantly reinforce the Soviet position in Eastern Europe by giving permanence and stability to the weakest and most exposed of the satellite regimes. Barring an Allied withdrawal, the Soviets hope to force the Allies into official dealings with East German authorities on the question of access to Berlin. They hope thus to strengthen the international prestige of East Germany, formalize the division of Germany (with adverse effects on the populations of both West and East Germany), and lay the foundation for further pressure on the Allies' presence in Berlin.

8. At the same time, and by the same measures, the Soviet leaders aim to undermine the Allied position in Western Europe. They probably believe that they can use a Berlin crisis to exploit latent differences among the Allies concerning the German problem in general, and the method of dealing with the GDR in particular. They hope to estrange the Federal Republic from its allies, since any Western accommodation with the GDR would convince large sections of German opinion that the West was retreating from the position it had hitherto taken on reunification. The Soviet leaders probably believe that any apparent failure of the Bonn Government to maintain close association with the Western great powers would undermine its domestic position, spread feelings of helplessness and isolation among the West German population, and lead to broader support for an attempt to explore the possibility of a separate deal with the USSR on the German problem. It is probably the Soviet view that if such tendencies became dominant in West Germany, the collapse of NATO and its defense structure would be in sight.

POSSIBLE COURSES OF SOVIET ACTION

9. The Soviets almost certainly did not expect Western acceptance of their 27 November proposal to make West Berlin a "free city." They probably foresee some form of negotiations with the allies before they turn over to the East Germans control over Western access to Berlin. However, it is possible that in certain eventualities, such as an outright Western refusal to enter into negotiations, the Soviets would take this step before the expiration of the six months' period stipulated in their note. At any stage of the crisis, of course, they may threaten to make such a move in order to put pressure on the Allies. But, on the whole, we believe it unlikely that they will actually make a precipitate move, regardless of initial Western responses.

10. The Soviets probably now anticipate a Western proposal to discuss Berlin within the context of the entire German problem. We do not think that such a proposal would be greeted with outright Soviet rejection but would probably be met with counteroffers designed to exploit any show of Allied indecision generated by the Berlin crisis.

4

11. At least initially, any such counteroffers would probably center around Soviet proposals for disengagement in Central Europe and/or for negotiations on a German peace treaty. These might be presented in the form of a Soviet package for a general European settlement which would include such proposals as a revised Rapacki Plan, the immediate conclusion of a German peace treaty as a step toward confederation of two German states, and an East-West nonaggression pact. The Soviets might make some conciliatory gestures in order to render their proposals more palatable.

12. In making such proposals, the Soviets would estimate that certain elements of European opinion would react favorably to those features of their proposals which provide for military disengagement — withdrawal of forces and banning of nuclear weapons from Central Europe. They would expect to appeal in particular to those Westerners who regard the presence of nuclear-equipped forces of both sides in Germany as a main cause of tension and war danger. They would hold out the prospect to the Social Democrats and neutralists in West Germany that further progress toward unification would be possible once acceptance of Soviet proposals had brought a general easing of the tensions which surround the German problem. By appeals of this kind to various elements of opinion in Europe, they would try to make it as difficult as possible for the Western European Powers to reject their proposals altogether.

13. We believe it likely that at some moment which the Soviets judge favorable they will again bring forward a dramatic proposal for a summit meeting on the whole array of issues which will have been raised. The moment chosen for this move would be one at which tensions were high over the prospect of a deadlock; and at which the Soviets might consider opinion in the West to be deeply divided over the next steps. In such a summit meeting the Soviets would try to bring the Western Powers to accept agreements which, while trumpeted as a great advance for peace, would in fact amount to acceptance of the main Soviet terms.

14. Whether or not a summit meeting develops, the Soviets, either to stimulate further negotiations on Germany as a whole or to overcome a deadlock, might at some stage attach new features to their "free city" proposals to make them more attractive to Western opinion. They may, for example, offer to include East Berlin in their proposal for a demilitarized "free city." They may also offer to place access to the city under formal UN guarantees, perhaps with UN observers present in the city and on access routes. Such offers would almost certainly still be conditional on the continuation of a Communist government in the Eastern sector, an end to the East German refugee flow through West Berlin, and a cessation of Allied "subversive" and intelligence activities in the city.

15. We thus believe that Soviet tactics will retain some flexibility, the better to take advantage of the situation as it develops. However, Soviet opposition to German reunification on any basis other than a confederation which preserved Communist East Germany will be in the background of all Soviet maneuvers. The Soviet leaders almost certainly do not contemplate relinquishing control over East Germany because of the threat such action would pose to their whole position in Eastern Europe, beginning with Poland.

16. If the Soviets fail to make significant progress in possible negotiations with the Allies, they will sooner or later have to face up to the question of fulfilling their announced intention to turn over to East Germany their controls over access to West Berlin. Their decision will be greatly affected by the Soviet assessment of the degree of tension which had developed and particularly the firmness of the Western position at the time, and it is possible that the Soviet leaders might decide to back down under whatever smokescreen of explanation seems most expedient. However, we consider it more likely that the USSR would proceed with the turnover of controls to the East Germans. The Soviet leaders probably intend to be cautious and tactically flexible. We believe that they will try to direct Soviet and East German maneuver-

5

ing in a manner which will avoid military conflict with the Western allies, while at the same time they will be prepared to take advantage of any signs of weakness on the part of the West, or of inclinations to compromise on major issues. Nevertheless, they have already committed themselves considerably, and we believe that the crisis may be severe, with considerable chance of miscalculation by one or both sides.

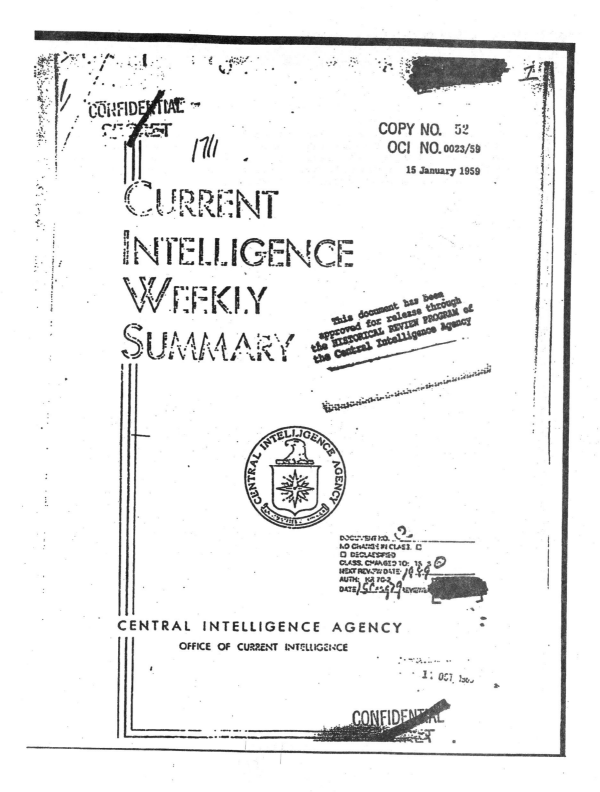

CONFIDENTIAL

COPY NO. 52
OCI NO. 0023/59

15 January 1959

CURRENT
INTELLIGENCE
WEEKLY
SUMMARY

This document has been approved for release through the HISTORICAL REVIEW PROGRAM of the Central Intelligence Agency

CENTRAL INTELLIGENCE AGENCY

OFFICE OF CURRENT INTELLIGENCE

CONFIDENTIAL

CURRENT INTELLIGENCE WEEKLY SUMMARY

15 January 1959

PART I

OF IMMEDIATE INTEREST

THE BERLIN SITUATION

Soviet Peace Proposal

The USSR's notes of 10 January to the Western powers calling for a conference in Warsaw or Prague within two months to conclude a German peace treaty and to discuss the Berlin question are intended to demonstrate Soviet desire to negotiate. The USSR wishes to appear responsive to Western objections to discussing Berlin except within the wider framework of Germany and European security. Soviet leaders apparently expect that the proposal to hold a peace conference will place the Soviet Union in a position to exploit growing pressures within the Western powers—especially West Germany and Britain—for a general policy review of problems relating to German reunification.

The draft peace treaty appended to the notes elaborates the 11 "basic provisions" for a treaty set forth in the aide-memoire Mikoyan delivered to Secretary Dulles on 5 January. It is essentially a formula for a neutral Germany, with the central theme that Western recognition of two Germanys is necessary to any progress on a German settlement. It provides for participation by both Germanys in the negotiation and signing of a treaty. If a German confederation should then exist, it would also be represented.

The draft also provides for the withdrawal of foreign troops from Germany, a ban on German possession and production of nuclear weapons and other instruments of mass destruction as well as bombers and submarines, and a prohibition on German participation in military alliances directed against any of the signatory powers. It would bind "Germany" to suppress any Nazi organizations and activities as well as any organizations, including those of refugees, hostile to any of the Allied powers. A demilitarized "free city" of Berlin would be established pending the reunification of Germany.

The notes warned again that Western refusal to negotiate will not prevent the USSR from "renouncing its functions in Berlin" and transferring control over Allied access to Berlin to the East Germans, but failed to mention again the six-month deadline. Moscow is in a position to be able to hand over its quadripartite functions in Berlin to the East German regime at any time.

Moscow probably does not expect a conference to take place now on these terms. Soviet leaders apparently hope, however, that constant pressure will eventually produce a break in the Western position on Germany and European security or at least will lead to greater popular acceptance of the Soviet view that rapprochement between the two German states is the only solution to the reunification problem.

West European Reaction

Chancellor Adenauer called for outright rejection of the

SECRET

CURRENT INTELLIGENCE WEEKLY SUMMARY

15 January 1959

Soviet draft treaty, and the West German press backed up this demand with sharp criticism of the treaty as demanding a "second surrender" of Germans. On the question of future negotiations, there was less unanimity in Bonn than elsewhere. Most papers saw a high-level meeting on Germany taking place within the next few months. The pro-Social Democratic (SPD) press and some independent papers called for negotiations in the hope of inducing the Soviet Union to modify its "maximum demands." SPD Deputy Chairman Wehner warned against flatly rejecting the Soviet proposals.

Chancellor Adenauer has taken steps to assess world opinion on Berlin. West Berlin Mayor Brandt will undertake a tour of the Far East and hold talks with Nehru. Press Chief von Eckardt will sound out opinion in the UN on a possible UN trusteeship for Berlin, with Western troops acting as UN executors. A top Foreign Ministry official, Herbert Dittmann, has also made a hurried trip to Washington on Adenauer's instructions.

An analysis of Mikoyan's ████-memoire stressed that the 10 January note makes clear the Soviet aim of neutralizing Germany without reunification. Some of the French press, however, noted a more conciliatory language, which was felt to indicate Moscow's desire for negotiations.

The British press with near unanimity continues to argue for "less negative" Western re-

sponses and discussions of the revised Rapacki plan. The Manchester Guardian observed that "an unconstructive Russian approach is not justification for an unconstructive Western reply."

East Germany – Berlin

Strongly echoing Moscow's claim that East Germany is a fully sovereign state, the Ulbricht regime now appears to be laying the groundwork for an eventual claim that it is the only legitimate German state. Its note of 7 January to Moscow reiterated that West Berlin belongs to East Germany. The note further declared that the East Berlin municipal authorities are the "sole rightful organs" for the whole city. Premier Grotewohl's tour of the Middle East is also designed to underline East German claims to sovereignty. Following Grotewohl's minor successes in Cairo and Baghdad, he saw Nehru, but apparently failed to change India's policy of nonrecognition of East Germany.

Soviet authorities in Berlin are continuing to insist that American authorities must now deal with East Germany on all questions concerning American military personnel in East Germany and East Berlin.

While the Soviet Kommandatura in East Berlin continues its normal activities at Karlshorst, a Soviet pamphlet, commenting on the Soviet note of 27 November, explicitly stated that the Kommandatura would be closed down and the guard troops attached to it withdrawn from the city as part of the Soviet handover of its functions to East Germans. American officials note that the USSR is reported to be closing down

SECRET

401

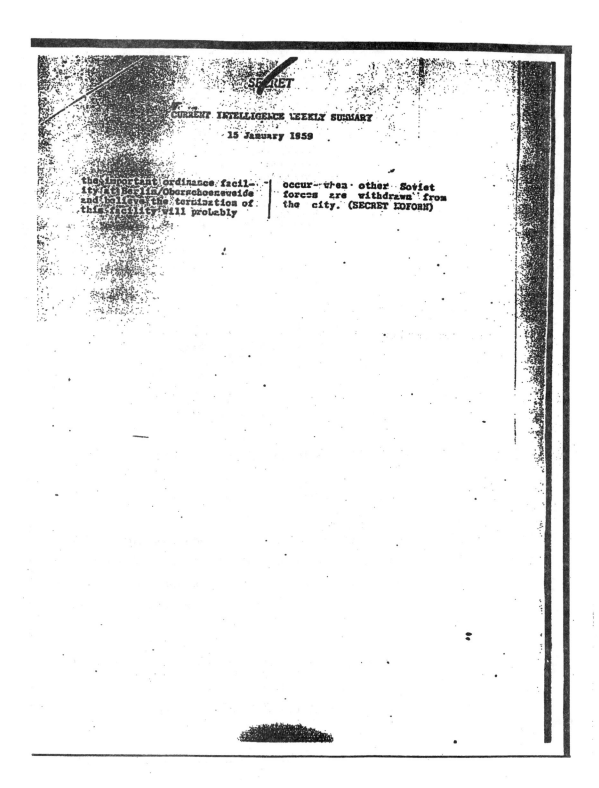

SECRET

CURRENT INTELLIGENCE WEEKLY SUMMARY

15 January 1959

the important ordinance facility at Berlin/Oberschoeneweide and believe the termination of this facility will probably

occur when other Soviet forces are withdrawn from the city. (SECRET NOFORN)

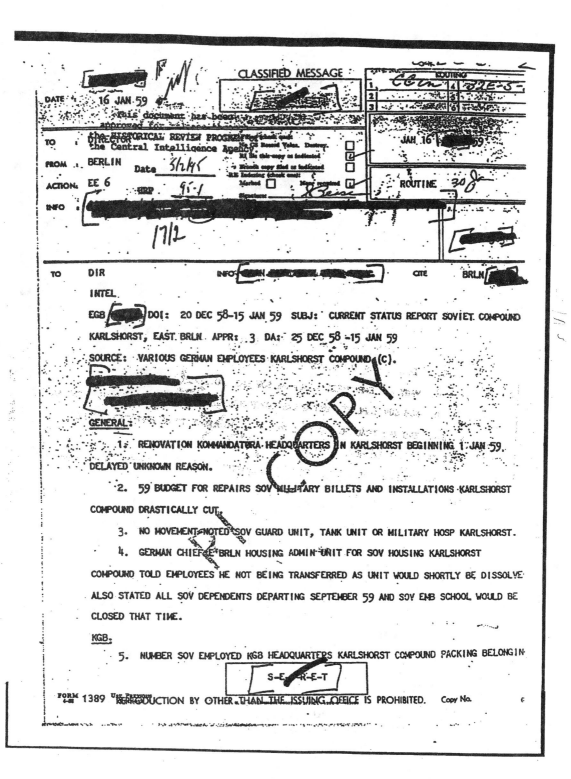

CLASSIFIED MESSAGE

DATE 16 JAN 59

This document has been approved for release through the HISTORICAL REVIEW PROGRAM of the Central Intelligence Agency.

Date 3/2/95

TO

FROM BERLIN

ACTION EE 6   95-1

INFO

17/2

ROUTINE 30

TO   DIR   INFO   CITE   BRLN

INTEL

EGB   DOI: 20 DEC 58-15 JAN 59   SUBJ: CURRENT STATUS REPORT SOVIET COMPOUND

KARLSHORST, EAST BRLN APPR: 3 DA: 25 DEC 58 -15 JAN 59

SOURCE: VARIOUS GERMAN EMPLOYEES KARLSHORST COMPOUND (C).

GENERAL:

1. RENOVATION KOMMANDATURA HEADQUARTERS IN KARLSHORST BEGINNING 1 JAN 59

DELAYED UNKNOWN REASON.

2. 59 BUDGET FOR REPAIRS SOV MILITARY BILLETS AND INSTALLATIONS KARLSHORST

COMPOUND DRASTICALLY CUT.

3. NO MOVEMENT NOTED SOV GUARD UNIT, TANK UNIT OR MILITARY HOSP KARLSHORST.

4. GERMAN CHIEF E BRLN HOUSING ADMIN UNIT FOR SOV HOUSING KARLSHORST

COMPOUND TOLD EMPLOYEES HE NOT BEING TRANSFERRED AS UNIT WOULD SHORTLY BE DISSOLVE

ALSO STATED ALL SOV DEPENDENTS DEPARTING SEPTEMBER 59 AND SOV EMB SCHOOL WOULD BE

CLOSED THAT TIME.

KGB:

5. NUMBER SOV EMPLOYED KGB HEADQUARTERS KARLSHORST COMPOUND PACKING BELONGIN

S-E-C-R-E-T

CLASSIFIED MESSAGE

S-E-C-R-E-T

DATE :

TO :

FROM :

ACTION:

INFO :

RE Filing (check one):
No OB Record Value. Destroy.
RE file this copy as indicated
Branch copy filed as indicated
RE Indexing (check one):
Marked ☐   None required ☐
Signature:

ROUTING

PAGE 2   BRLN
IN

INFO   CITE

6. RUMOR AMONG GERMAN KGB MAINTENANCE EMPLOYEES IF KGB LEAVES KARLSHORST WILL BE REESTABLISHED VICINITY BRLN.

7. KGB PLANS RELEASE HEADQUARTERS BUILDING (ST ANTONIOUS HOSP, KARLSHORST COMPOUND) DELAYED AS BUILDINGS IN STRAUSBERG NOT YET READY.

8. MANY KGB EMPLOYEES ASSUMING SOV EMB AND TRADE DELEG COVER.

9. KGB SOV EMPLOYEE USING EMB COVER STATED ONLY MILITARY PERSONS VACATING E BRLN. EMB AND TRADE DELEG WILL REMAIN. THIS MOVE TO BE EFFECTED WHETHER AMERICANS LEAVE OR NOT.

10. BETWEEN 25 AND 31 DEC 58 HEADQUARTERS OF MFS ADMIN SECTION RESPONSIBLE KGB ADVISOR BILLETS KARLSHORST VACATED.

11. KARLSHORST HEADQUARTERS MVD ADVISORS TO E GER SECURITY FORCES VACATED SHORTLY BEFORE CHRISTMAS. GERMAN JANITOR THIS HEADQUARTERS REPORTED UNIT POSSIBLY MOVING STRAUSBERG.

RU:

12. IN CONNECTION SOV MILITARY WITHDRAWAL RU STRATEGIC INTELLIGENCE UNIT LOCATED GODESBERGER AND WESELERSTR KARLSHORST COMPOUND PLACING SOME PERSONNEL UNDER COVER OFFICE MILATT SOV EMB REMAINDER REASSIGNED HEADQUARTERS GSFG WUENSDORF

13. FIELD COMMENT: ABOVE AND PREVIOUS REPORTS INDICATE DEFINITE PLANNING

S-E-C-R-E-T

CLASSIFIED MESSAGE

S-E-C-R-E-T

ROUTING

PAGE 3   BRLN 1731

IN 48343

TO   INFO   CITE

FOR EVACUATION ALL SOV MILITARY UNITS KARLSHORST AREA AND PROBABLE REESTABLISHMENT IN SOV ZONE VICINITY BRLN, SOME IN STRAUSBERG. BULK RU BEING TRANSFERRED GSFG, SOV CIVILIAN UNITS SUCH AS EMB AND TRADE DELG WILL REMAIN E BRLN. KGB SUPPORT UNITS WILL PROBABLY BE MOVED INTO ZONE VICINITY BRLN WITH OPERATIONAL TYPES REMAINING E BRLN UTILIZING EMB, TRADE DELG OR OTHER CIVILIAN AGENCY COVER. ON CONJUNCTION EVACUATION MILITARY EXPECT CONSOLIDATION KARLSHORST COMPOUND WITH LARGE PORTION RELEASED TO GERMANS. REPORT EVACUATION SOVIET DEPENDENTS NOT YET CONFIRMED.

DISSEM: USCOB AND USBER.

RELEASE 161130Z.

END OF MESSAGE

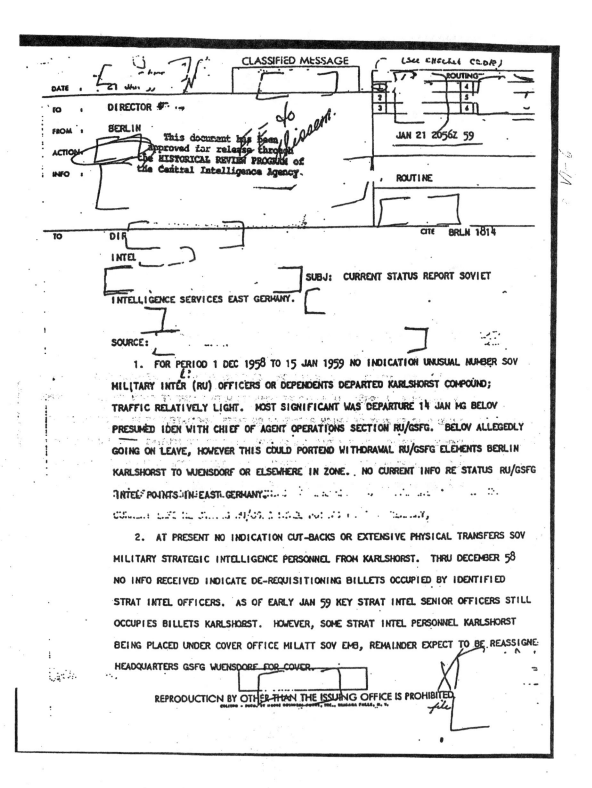

CLASSIFIED MESSAGE

DATE : 21 JAN

TO : DIRECTOR

FROM : BERLIN

ACTION :

INFO :

This document has been approved for release through the HISTORICAL REVIEW PROGRAM of the Central Intelligence Agency.

JAN 21 2056Z 59

ROUTINE

TO   DIR

INTEL

CITE   BRLN 1814

SUBJ: CURRENT STATUS REPORT SOVIET INTELLIGENCE SERVICES EAST GERMANY.

SOURCE:

1. FOR PERIOD 1 DEC 1958 TO 15 JAN 1959 NO INDICATION UNUSUAL NUMBER SOV MILITARY INTER (RU) OFFICERS OR DEPENDENTS DEPARTED KARLSHORST COMPOUND; TRAFFIC RELATIVELY LIGHT. MOST SIGNIFICANT WAS DEPARTURE 14 JAN MG BELOV PRESUMED IDEN WITH CHIEF OF AGENT OPERATIONS SECTION RU/GSFG. BELOV ALLEGEDLY GOING ON LEAVE, HOWEVER THIS COULD PORTEND WITHDRAWAL RU/GSFG ELEMENTS BERLIN KARLSHORST TO WUENSDORF OR ELSEWHERE IN ZONE. NO CURRENT INFO RE STATUS RU/GSFG INTEL POINTS IN EAST GERMANY.

2. AT PRESENT NO INDICATION CUT-BACKS OR EXTENSIVE PHYSICAL TRANSFERS SOV MILITARY STRATEGIC INTELLIGENCE PERSONNEL FROM KARLSHORST. THRU DECEMBER 58 NO INFO RECEIVED INDICATE DE-REQUISITIONING BILLETS OCCUPIED BY IDENTIFIED STRAT INTEL OFFICERS. AS OF EARLY JAN 59 KEY STRAT INTEL SENIOR OFFICERS STILL OCCUPIES BILLETS KARLSHORST. HOWEVER, SOME STRAT INTEL PERSONNEL KARLSHORST BEING PLACED UNDER COVER OFFICE MILATT SOV EMB, REMAINDER EXPECT TO BE REASSIGNE. HEADQUARTERS GSFG WUENSDORF FOR COVER.

REPRODUCTION BY OTHER THAN THE ISSUING OFFICE IS PROHIBITED

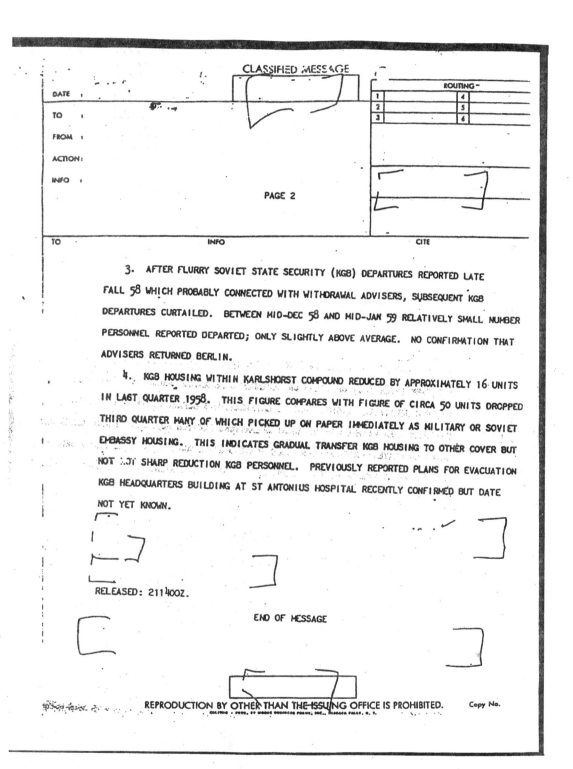

CLASSIFIED MESSAGE

DATE :

TO :

FROM :

ACTION:

INFO :

PAGE 2

ROUTING

	1		4	
	2		5	
	3		6	

TO   INFO   CITE

3. AFTER FLURRY SOVIET STATE SECURITY (KGB) DEPARTURES REPORTED LATE FALL 58 WHICH PROBABLY CONNECTED WITH WITHDRAWAL ADVISERS, SUBSEQUENT KGB DEPARTURES CURTAILED. BETWEEN MID-DEC 58 AND MID-JAN 59 RELATIVELY SMALL NUMBER PERSONNEL REPORTED DEPARTED; ONLY SLIGHTLY ABOVE AVERAGE. NO CONFIRMATION THAT ADVISERS RETURNED BERLIN.

4. KGB HOUSING WITHIN KARLSHORST COMPOUND REDUCED BY APPROXIMATELY 16 UNITS IN LAST QUARTER 1958. THIS FIGURE COMPARES WITH FIGURE OF CIRCA 50 UNITS DROPPED THIRD QUARTER MANY OF WHICH PICKED UP ON PAPER IMMEDIATELY AS MILITARY OR SOVIET EMBASSY HOUSING. THIS INDICATES GRADUAL TRANSFER KGB HOUSING TO OTHER COVER BUT NOT ..JT SHARP REDUCTION KGB PERSONNEL. PREVIOUSLY REPORTED PLANS FOR EVACUATION KGB HEADQUARTERS BUILDING AT ST ANTONIUS HOSPITAL RECENTLY CONFIRMED BUT DATE NOT YET KNOWN.

RELEASED: 211400Z.

END OF MESSAGE

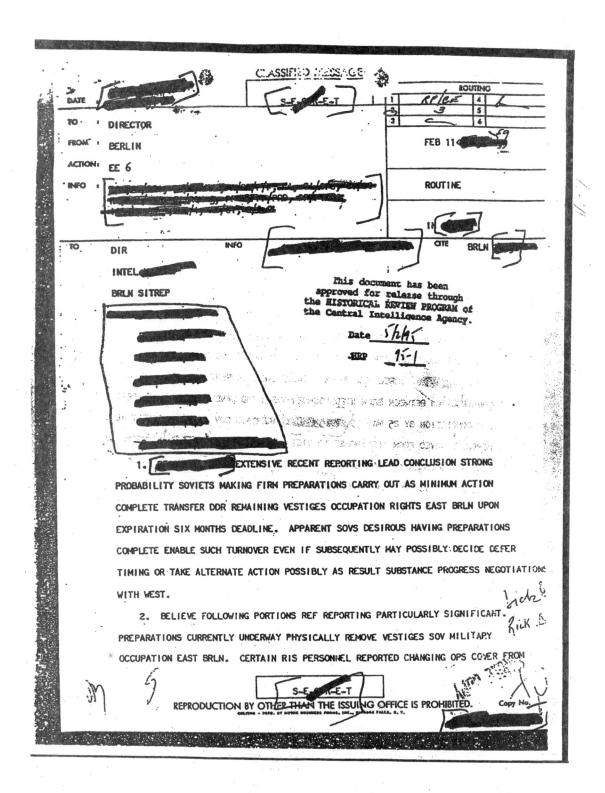

CLASSIFIED MESSAGE

S-E-C-R-E-T

DATE

TO : DIRECTOR

FROM : BERLIN

ACTION: EE 6

INFO :

ROUTING

FEB 11

ROUTINE

CITE   BRLN

TO   DIR

INFO

INTEL

BRLN SITREP

This document has been
approved for release through
the HISTORICAL REVIEW PROGRAM of
the Central Intelligence Agency.

Date 5/2/95

HRP 95-1

1. EXTENSIVE RECENT REPORTING LEAD CONCLUSION STRONG
PROBABILITY SOVIETS MAKING FIRM PREPARATIONS CARRY OUT AS MINIMUM ACTION
COMPLETE TRANSFER DDR REMAINING VESTIGES OCCUPATION RIGHTS EAST BRLN UPON
EXPIRATION SIX MONTHS DEADLINE. APPARENT SOVS DESIROUS HAVING PREPARATIONS
COMPLETE ENABLE SUCH TURNOVER EVEN IF SUBSEQUENTLY MAY POSSIBLY DECIDE DEFER
TIMING OR TAKE ALTERNATE ACTION POSSIBLY AS RESULT SUBSTANCE PROGRESS NEGOTIATIONS
WITH WEST.

2. BELIEVE FOLLOWING PORTIONS REF REPORTING PARTICULARLY SIGNIFICANT.
PREPARATIONS CURRENTLY UNDERWAY PHYSICALLY REMOVE VESTIGES SOV MILITARY
OCCUPATION EAST BRLN. CERTAIN RIS PERSONNEL REPORTED CHANGING OPS COVER FROM

S-E-C-R-E-T

REPRODUCTION BY OTHER THAN THE ISSUING OFFICE IS PROHIBITED.   Copy No.

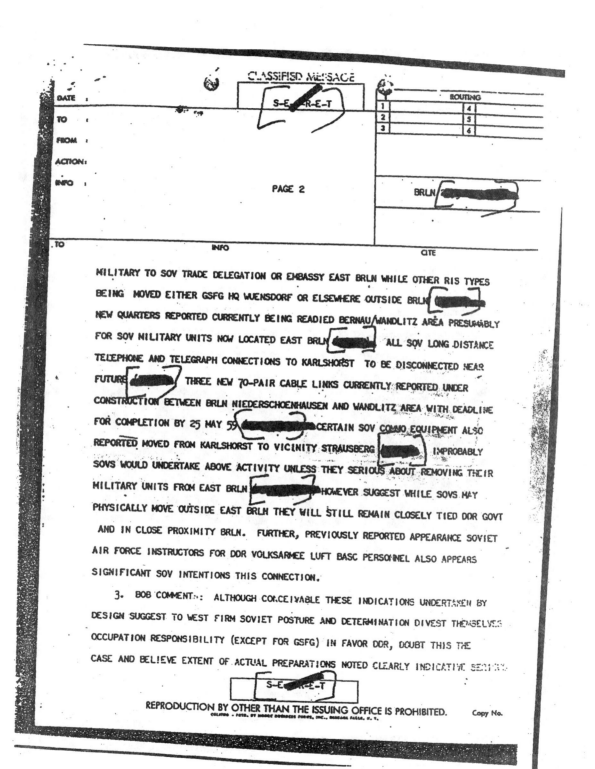

CLASSIFIED MESSAGE

S-E—R-E-T

DATE :

TO :

FROM :

ACTION:

INFO :

PAGE 2

ROUTING

1		4	
2		5	
3		6	

BRLN

TO   INFO   CITE

MILITARY TO SOV TRADE DELEGATION OR EMBASSY EAST BRLN WHILE OTHER RIS TYPES BEING MOVED EITHER GSFG HQ WUENSDORF OR ELSEWHERE OUTSIDE BRLN NEW QUARTERS REPORTED CURRENTLY BEING READIED BERNAU/WANDLITZ AREA PRESUMABLY FOR SOV MILITARY UNITS NOW LOCATED EAST BRLN ALL SOV LONG DISTANCE TELEPHONE AND TELEGRAPH CONNECTIONS TO KARLSHORST TO BE DISCONNECTED NEAR FUTURE THREE NEW 70-PAIR CABLE LINKS CURRENTLY REPORTED UNDER CONSTRUCTION BETWEEN BRLN NIEDERSCHOENHAUSEN AND WANDLITZ AREA WITH DEADLINE FOR COMPLETION BY 25 MAY 59 CERTAIN SOV COMMO EQUIPMENT ALSO REPORTED MOVED FROM KARLSHORST TO VICINITY STRAUSBERG IMPROBABLY SOVS WOULD UNDERTAKE ABOVE ACTIVITY UNLESS THEY SERIOUS ABOUT REMOVING THEIR MILITARY UNITS FROM EAST BRLN HOWEVER SUGGEST WHILE SOVS MAY PHYSICALLY MOVE OUTSIDE EAST BRLN THEY WILL STILL REMAIN CLOSELY TIED DDR GOVT AND IN CLOSE PROXIMITY BRLN. FURTHER, PREVIOUSLY REPORTED APPEARANCE SOVIET AIR FORCE INSTRUCTORS FOR DDR VOLKSARMEE LUFT BASC PERSONNEL ALSO APPEARS SIGNIFICANT SOV INTENTIONS THIS CONNECTION.

3. BOB COMMENT: ALTHOUGH CONCEIVABLE THESE INDICATIONS UNDERTAKEN BY DESIGN SUGGEST TO WEST FIRM SOVIET POSTURE AND DETERMINATION DIVEST THEMSELVES OCCUPATION RESPONSIBILITY (EXCEPT FOR GSFG) IN FAVOR DDR, DOUBT THIS THE CASE AND BELIEVE EXTENT OF ACTUAL PREPARATIONS NOTED CLEARLY INDICATIVE SERIOUS

S-E—R-E-T

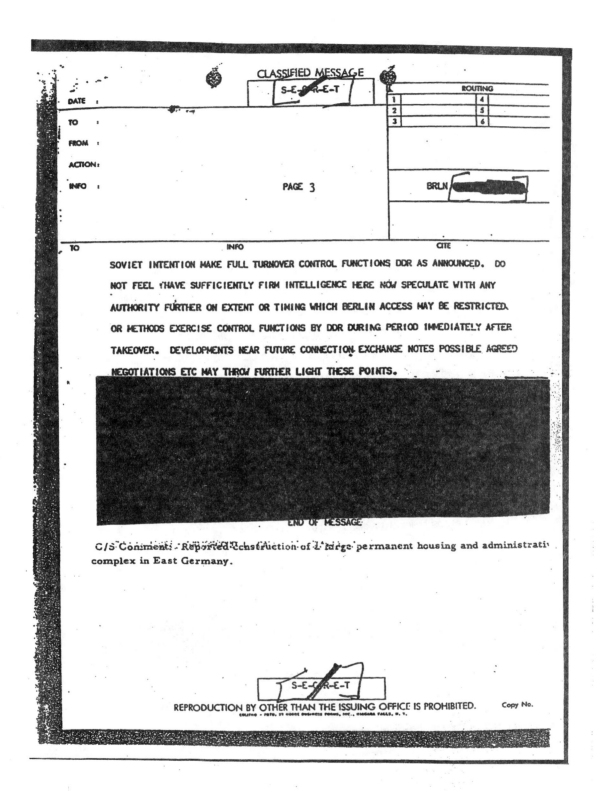

CLASSIFIED MESSAGE

S-E-C-R-E-T

DATE :

TO :

FROM :

ACTION:

INFO : PAGE 3

	ROUTING	
1		4
2		5
3		6

BRLN

TO   INFO   CITE

SOVIET INTENTION MAKE FULL TURNOVER CONTROL FUNCTIONS DDR AS ANNOUNCED. DO

NOT FEEL HAVE SUFFICIENTLY FIRM INTELLIGENCE HERE NOW SPECULATE WITH ANY

AUTHORITY FURTHER ON EXTENT OR TIMING WHICH BERLIN ACCESS MAY BE RESTRICTED.

OR METHODS EXERCISE CONTROL FUNCTIONS BY DDR DURING PERIOD IMMEDIATELY AFTER

TAKEOVER. DEVELOPMENTS NEAR FUTURE CONNECTION EXCHANGE NOTES POSSIBLE AGREED

NEGOTIATIONS ETC MAY THROW FURTHER LIGHT THESE POINTS.

END OF MESSAGE

C/S Comments - Reported Construction of a large permanent housing and administrativ
complex in East Germany.

S-E-C-R-E-T

REPRODUCTION BY OTHER THAN THE ISSUING OFFICE IS PROHIBITED.   Copy No.

OCI NO. 0487/59

5 February 1959

CURRENT INTELLIGENCE WEEKLY SUMMARY

CENTRAL INTELLIGENCE AGENCY
OFFICE OF CURRENT INTELLIGENCE

CONFIDENTIAL

CONFIDENTIAL

CURRENT INTELLIGENCE WEEKLY SUMMARY

5 February 1959

PART III

PATTERNS AND PERSPECTIVES

COMMUNIST TACTICS AGAINST WEST BERLIN

The vulnerabilities inherent in West Berlin's isolated position and dependence on Western aid and protection will be exploited by the Communists in their long-term campaign designed to weaken Western determination to maintain Allied rights in West Berlin, force the West to deal with East Germany, exclude Western influences from the city, and undercut its political and economic strength. The Communists hope to undermine the will of the population to resist and thus bring West Berlin under complete Communist control, either as a "free city" or in some other manner.

Character of Communist Threat

Berlin is a trump card in Moscow's strategy to gain recognition for East Germany. In its note of 27 November 1958 to the Western Allies, the Kremlin asserted that "the most correct and natural solution" to the Berlin problem would be to unify the city and incorporate it into East Germany. As a "concession," however, the Soviet Union offered to underwrite the creation of a demilitarized "free city" of West Berlin from which all Western "subversive" activities would be eliminated.

Moscow asserted its intention of turning over to the East Germans those remaining occupation functions it now exercises, if its proposals should be unacceptable to the Western powers. The USSR added, however, that no changes would be made in present controls over Allied military transport for six months

PART III   PATTERNS AND PERSPECTIVES   Page 1 of 12

CURRENT INTELLIGENCE WEEKLY SUMMARY

5 February 1959

provided the Western governments did not seek "complications."

During this period the Kremlin can try to exploit divergent Western estimates of the importance of maintaining a position in West Berlin by force and of continuing to refuse recognition to East Germany, and continue its war of nerves against West Berlin citizens.

Allied Military Position

The Allied garrison in West Berlin consists of only 6,626 combat troops and some 2,500 service personnel; there are also some 14,000 West German police there. In East Berlin, on the other hand—apart from Soviet personnel attached to the Kommandatura at Karlshorst—there is an East German force of some 18,000 security police of various types, backed by a 10,000-man workers' militia. Within ten miles of the city there are some 30,000 Soviet and 16,000 East German soldiers, as well as 6,450 security police.

Allied military forces in West Berlin are almost completely dependent on external sources of supply. Their line of communications extends across East German territory and is subject to Communist interference at any time.

Moscow has already made certain moves toward turning over access control to East German authorities and appears to have actually transferred

its function of dealing with Allied personnel in East Berlin. It is also preparing to move its Berlin Kommandatura from Karlshorst to some nearby point outside the city. East German personnel have appeared alongside Soviet officials checking Allied documentation at the railroad and highway checkpoints and others are reportedly being trained to take over access

COMMUNICATION ROUTES BETWEEN WEST GERMANY AND BERLIN

control duties. When controls are turned over, the East Germans may be phased into their new duties in order to test Western determination at each stage of the transfer.

Interference with Allied surface and air access need not be overt. Railroad access is particularly vulnerable, since all rail facilities are East German and all locomotives and train crews of Allied military

SECRET

CURRENT INTELLIGENCE WEEKLY SUMMARY

5 February 1959

trains are supplied by the Ulbricht regime. There are many means of harassment, some outwardly minuscule but nonetheless effective, that could interfere with access but which would not lend themselves to effective Western retaliation or protest.

East Germany has already challenged the Allied right to use the air corridors and is likely to reiterate its demands for control. Without resorting to direct use of force, the Communists could make Allied flights to Berlin a hazardous proposition by means of electronic interference or by crowding the air corridors with planes.

Harassment of Civilian Supply

West German traffic has been highly vulnerable to harassment, and Bonn has heretofore been reluctant to resort to reprisals. West Berlin is almost entirely dependent on Western sources of supply for its population of 2,200,000 and for its booming industry. In 1957 approximately 39 percent of freight from the West to the city, including 65 percent of its foodstuffs, was carried by truck, mainly on the Helmstedt autobahn; 61 percent of outgoing freight went by truck. Railroads carried approximately 34 percent of incoming shipments and hauled out some 15 percent, while canal barges accounted for a corresponding 26 and 23 percent. Only a small proportion of West Berlin's supplies come from East Germany, notably brown-coal briquettes for heating, some construction materials, and certain perishable foodstuffs.

Civilian travelers and freight move along the autobahn and three other designated highways. The Berlin-Helmstedt railroad line carries the greatest number of passengers and the bulk of the freight transported by rail. Barges move through the Mittelland Canal and Havel River system or via the Elbe-Havel route.

Civilian traffic, other than by air, is completely under East German control. West German nationals en route to or from Berlin must present passports or identity cards but have not yet been required to obtain visas. West Berliners show their identity cards.

Civilian traffic could be subjected to a large variety of harassments, including physical interference, delays, taxation, or requirements for more documents. Generally, there would be nothing the West could do to prevent these harassments or to retaliate in an effective way. West German economic sanctions could be used but would not be sufficient to stop a determined Communist initiative.

Civilian Air Access

Three Western civil airlines (Pan American, British European Airways, and Air France) use the air corridors under safety guarantees from the Berlin Air Safety Center (BASC), with West Berlin's Tempelhof airport serving as the terminal. East Germany has already claimed that such aircraft have no right to fly through the corridors without its permission and have charged that they often carry illegal goods. If the Kremlin removes its representatives from the BASC, these airlines would have to operate without air safety guarantees or deal directly with the East Germans, which would mean further demands such as the right to inspect manifests.

East German interference with civilian flights to West Berlin would be designed, among other objectives, to put an end to the transportation of refugees,

SECRET

CURRENT INTELLIGENCE WEEKLY SUMMARY

5 February 1959

a long-sought objective. Such a step would seriously interfere with the use of West Berlin as an asylum for East Germans. More than half of all refugees from East Germany make their escape through Berlin. The percentage rose to 64 percent during June, July, and August 1958.

Harassment of West Berlin

Current Soviet tactics in the war of nerves against West Berlin have emphasized a "soft" approach, advertising the prospect of closer and "more natural" economic relations with East Germany. The USSR and East Germany have declared they are ready to place orders for industrial goods with the city's enterprises and undertake deliveries of raw materials and foodstuffs. These orders would be designed to lay the groundwork for West Berlin's eventual economic assimilation.

The Communists could stop the shipment of East German goods to West Berlin, although this measure alone would have only a limited effect.

In connection with the West Berlin election of 7 December, in which the Communists received less than 2 percent of the vote, East Germans threatened certain West Berliners with reprisals if they did not support the Socialist Unity (Communist) party's electoral campaign. German employees of Allied missions were warned they would be blacklisted or worse if East Germany took over the whole city.

The East Germans have already taken steps to separate their transport system from West Berlin's and to eliminate their remaining dependence on transportation facilities in the Western sectors. The Communist ability to harass transportation to and within West

Berlin will increase as improvements are made in the railroad and canal bypass rings.

Measures to isolate West Berlin from the transport nets, although they would entail adverse economic consequences for East Germany, would be designed to limit travel from East Germany to the Western sectors, thereby sharply restricting the flight of refugees, and making it more difficult for the weary East Germans to view the West's "show window." East German authorities have already instituted measures to bar access and, if internal tensions increase, further controls are likely to be imposed. Restrictions are being put into effect to halt East German attendance at the "Green Week" agricultural fair in West Berlin, which in the past has been attended by more than 100,000 of Ulbricht's subjects.

It would be extremely difficult for the East Germans to seal off the Western sectors completely. The border passes through streets, squares, woodlands, fields, and lakes, and along canals. There are also several Western enclaves in East Zone territory. The East German police, border guards, and workers' militiamen could be posted at strategic points, but it would be impossible to seal the dividing line effectively. Instead, the Communists are likely to continue their tactics of intimidation, infiltration, and harassment.

Western Retaliation

The West has limited capability, short of force, to prevent continued Communist encroachments. There are no longer opportunities to retaliate against East German traffic passing through West Berlin. West Berlin must count on the Federal Republic for support, and Bonn has been highly

SECRET

415

SECRET

CURRENT INTELLIGENCE WEEKLY SUMMARY

5 February 1959.

reluctant to take steps necessary to deter Communist harassment. Apart from cutting off steel and coke shipments, these steps could include severing East German shipments through Hamburg--a step which would arouse vigorous resistance from West German business circles.

American officials in Berlin report a "steadfast" public confidence in the Western powers, particularly the United States. Recalling their 1948 experiences, Berliners feel that a firm Western reaction will be sufficient to cause Moscow to reconsider any blockade plans.

████████████ indications of ████████ have been revealed in West Berlin business circles, and there has been some movement of valuables and belongings out of West Berlin.

As this uncertainty concerning the future continues, the economic situation in West Berlin is likely to show progressive deterioration. Any substantial decline in orders for West Berlin firms would result in an increase in unemployment and a weakening of the West Berlin economy. 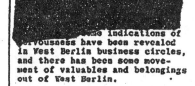 (Concurred in by

CONFIDENTIAL

OCI NO. 0488/59

12 February 1959

CURRENT
INTELLIGENCE
WEEKLY
SUMMARY

CENTRAL INTELLIGENCE AGENCY

OFFICE OF CURRENT INTELLIGENCE

CONFIDENTIAL

Approved for Release
Date   SEP 1993

SECRET

CURRENT INTELLIGENCE WEEKLY SUMMARY

13 February 1959

PART II (continued)

..... Page 4

NR

FLIGHT OF REFUGEES FROM EAST GERMANY . . . . Page 5,

Defections from East Germany, although down 22 percent from 1957, continued at a high rate throughout 1958,
when over 204,000 persons fled, most of them to West
Berlin, in reaction to the increasingly repressive policies of the Ulbricht regime. The total number of escapees
from East Germany has reached approximately 2,350,000
since 1949. In addition to the loss of skilled workers,
technicians, and managers, a very large increase in the
defection of doctors, scientists, and teachers has created
serious problems.

. . . . Page 7

NR

SECRET

iii

SECRET

CURRENT INTELLIGENCE WEEKLY SUMMARY

18 February 1959

(FLIGHT OF REFUGEES FROM EAST GERMANY)

Defections from East Germany although down 32 percent from 1957 continued at a high rate throughout 1958, when over 204,000 persons fled in reaction to the increasingly repressive policies of the Ulbricht regime. The total number of escapees from East Germany to West Berlin and West Germany has reached approximately 2,- 350,000 since 1949; this loss of personnel makes unlikely any rapid increase in economic development. In addition to the loss of skilled workers, technicians, and managers, a very large increase in the defections of doctors, scientists, and teachers has created serious problems.

SECRET

PART II   NOTES AND COMMENTS   Page 5 of 18

SECRET

CURRENT INTELLIGENCE WEEKLY SUMMARY

12 February 1959

By increasing internal controls, the regime succeeded in early 1958 in reducing the number of refugees. The exodus, nevertheless, rose last summer to a high figure, including a large number of intellectuals, forcing the regime to make certain concessions, notably to doctors and small shopkeepers.

The authorities in Bonn estimate that there is but one doctor per 1,700 persons in East Germany, compared with one per 750 in West Germany; 1,242 doctors, dentists, and veterinarians fled in 1958, an increase of almost 300 percent over 1957. It is reported that doctors from other satellites may be called in to help staff some East German institutions. To alleviate the shortage of teachers, the call has gone out to

ers and farm workers, 360,000 skilled workers and craftsmen, 32,000 persons in the technical professions, and more than 350,000 children have fled. The majority of the refugees are under 45, a

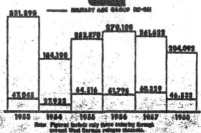

EAST GERMAN REFUGEES TO WEST GERMANY

high percentage of them of military age (18-35).

References to shortages of agricultural labor have appeared in numerous reports, and East Zone publications are urging women to work a few hours daily on the farm or in the factory. Almost 10,000 farmers fled last year, largely because of the intensification of pressures on the private peasant.

The loss of some 11,000 engineers in the last five years, including 2,345 in 1958, has also had an adverse effect on the regime's ambitious plans. The chairman of the party economic commission, dismayed at the flight of the intelligentsia, expressed anxiety that the loss of technical and scientific personnel would hinder the chemical industry, which is designed to become one of the pillars of the East German economy.

BREAKDOWN OF EAST GERMAN REFUGEES BY OCCUPATION

young workers and housewives to volunteer for training to replace some of the elementary-school teachers who fled in 1958.

The flight of personnel has also had a deleterious effect on some sectors of the economy. During the 1949-58 period, more than 133,000 far-

SECRET

PART II

SECRET

PROBABLE SOVIET COURSES OF ACTION REGARDING
BERLIN AND GERMANY[1]

THE PROBLEM

To estimate Soviet objectives and tactics with respect to negotiation over Berlin and Germany, the likelihood of Soviet turnover of access controls to the East German regime, and Bloc reactions to certain Western responses to this action.

THE ESTIMATE

I. SOVIET OBJECTIVES AND TACTICS IN NEGOTIATION

1. We continue to believe that Moscow has raised the Berlin issue at this time because of a variety of related factors, some bearing on the consolidation of the Communist position in Eastern Europe, others on weakening the Western Alliance. Specifically, we believe that Soviet objectives include the reduction and eventual elimination of the disruptive influence which West Berlin and the presence there of Western troops exerts on the East German regime (GDR), the raising of the internal and international prestige of that regime, the fostering of discord among the NATO Allies, the limitation of West German armament and the prevention of a West German nuclear capability, an early summit meeting, and the eventual neutralization of West Germany as an effective member of the Western Alliance. Whatever may be the order of priority among these objectives, it is clear that the Soviet leaders have now committed themselves on the issue of Berlin in an unprecedented manner.

2. As their repeated statements imply, the Soviet leaders probably have a genuine interest in negotiating with the West on the subject of Berlin, and indeed on the broader German problem. Their attitude reflects the high confidence they have in their bargaining position. While the Soviets wish to avoid general war, they almost certainly consider Soviet advances in nuclear capabilities as having brought about such an improvement in Soviet military strength that the West will hesitate increasingly before taking any action involving substantial risk of general war. The Soviets probably also hope that they can play upon differences of view among the Western Powers as to the extent of the risk that should be assumed in regard to Berlin. To pose a choice between actions risking war and actions tending to erode the Western position in Berlin must therefore be likely, in Soviet eyes, to make it more difficult for the Western Allies to maintain a united front.

[1] This estimate was prepared in response to a series of questions posed by the Department of State and therefore represents a specialized supplement to SNIE 100-13-58, "Soviet Objectives in the Berlin Crisis," 23 December 1958.

SECRET

1

2

3. Furthermore, the Soviet leaders almost certainly view the Western position in Berlin itself as overextended. They see West Berlin as a remote enclave within Bloc territory, the supply of whose civilian population is already subject to East German controls, and they view the Western garrisons as token forces whose right of land access is not specifically defined in any legal or political instrument. The Soviets probably believe that the facts of the access situation are such that, in the event of a turnover, the Allies would be obliged to acquiesce, to resort to a garrison airlift, or to initiate the use of force.

4. While we believe, as stated above, that the Soviets have high confidence in the bargaining position and their military posture in the Berlin situation, we also believe that the Soviets wish to avoid serious risk of general war. Hence, they will consider their military strength primarily as a factor increasing the likelihood of their obtaining advantages by political means, i.e., by negotiation. The Soviets will, in our opinion, continue to take an intransigent position and to believe that they can achieve important gains without making significant concessions. Nevertheless, we believe that they would prefer to avoid an actual confrontation of forces over the issue of access to Berlin lest events get out of control. On the other hand, they view the risk involved in confrontation as at least equally alarming to the Western side, and they will, until late in the game, play upon this risk, and the Western fear of it, as a principal counter in their maneuvering.

5. The Soviets probably also feel that in a negotiated settlement they could reduce some of the disadvantages to the Bloc which are inherent in the present situation. Any agreement which prejudiced the Western position in West Berlin and which tended to confirm the division of Germany and Europe would discourage the forces of discontent in the GDR and elsewhere in Eastern Europe and impart greater stability to the Satellite regimes. Quite apart from the substance of any agreement that might be reached, the mere participation of the East Germans in any negotiations would enhance the status of the Pankow regime. An agreement which forbade nuclear arms to West Germany would lessen the Soviet fear of the impact of a resurgent Germany, particularly on the Soviet position in Eastern Europe.

6. Finally it is possible, though on the whole we do not believe it likely, that the Soviet initiative on the Berlin issue reflects a desire to explore the possibilities of changing the situation in Central Europe on the basis of concessions on both sides. The Soviets have not offered concessions from their previous positions on Eastern Europe, German reunification or Berlin and prior to negotiations they would not be likely to indicate what concessions they might make. Their tactics in any negotiations on such a broad scale would vary according to the moves and reactions of the West.

7. In negotiating on Berlin, the Soviets would press for acceptance of their "free city" proposal and might introduce modifications in this scheme in the hope of securing Western acceptance for it. The minimum terms on which the Kremlin would be willing to call off the planned transfer of access controls to the GDR would probably be the establishment of official dealings between the GDR and the West, together with restrictions on propaganda and intelligence activities in West Berlin, and the flow of refugees through that city. The Soviets would estimate that any modification in Berlin's status and any other arrangements tending to imply Western recognition of the GDR would provide a precedent for further attacks upon the Western position in Berlin and a vital step toward achieving their larger objectives in Germany.

8. In negotiations on the broader German problem, the proposal for a peace treaty with a divided Germany would form the core of the Soviet position. In addition, the Soviets might propose that the Four Powers endorse direct negotiations between the "two Germanies" on the Communist-"confederation" plan. While Moscow probably would not expect to gain Western acceptance of these pro-

posals, they would hope in negotiations to push the West in this direction with the particular view of extracting some concessions which would enhance the international standing of the GDR. Moreover, they would probably hope to engage the West in serious negotiations on certain features of the peace treaty proposal, in particular the establishment of a nuclear-free zone and the limitation of forces in Germany. But whatever their proposals, the Soviets would almost certainly continue to adhere to certain key positions. They would seek the substance of the conditions regarding Berlin mentioned above. In addition, the Soviets would almost certainly maintain their long-standing position that the problem of German reunification can only be solved by the "two Germanies," that this problem cannot be negotiated by the four former occupying powers, and that, at most, Four Power talks should seek to facilitate negotiations between the "two Germanies." They would insist that free elections on the territory of the GDR were not an acceptable means of achieving a unified German state and that a reunited Germany would not be free to join NATO.

9. While the Soviets have formally rejected the linking of Berlin and Germany with discussions of European security, they would probably enter such a negotiation, provided they were given parity of representation. They would be prepared to discuss disengagement and arms limitation, particularly in the nuclear and missile fields. To the extent that such discussion touched on Berlin and Germany, they would probably insist on the substance of the conditions mentioned in the foregoing paragraphs, and on the participation of the "two Germanies" in some appropriate form.

10. Whatever the scope of the negotiations which the Western Powers were willing to entertain, it is likely that the Soviets would at some stage attempt to make their proposals more attractive by modifying some of the positions they have heretofore taken. For example, they might offer to place a "free

city" of West Berlin under UN administration. They might agree to UN guarantee of the access routes. It is within the realm of possibility that they might agree to the inclusion of East Berlin in the "free city" arrangement in some fashion, but we believe this to be extremely unlikely.

11. There will hang over all negotiations the threat that control of the access to West Berlin will be handed over to the East Germans if some agreement satisfactory to Moscow is not reached. We do not believe that a turnover will be undertaken prior to 27 May, or that it would take place at a later date if negotiations were under way or impending, unless the Soviets came to believe that progress through negotiation was not possible. The Kremlin probably conceives of itself as able to confront the Western Powers with an unpleasant but inescapable alternative, either to agree to or acquiesce in changes in the present situation which would lead to an erosion of the Western position in Berlin and West Germany, or to face substantial risk of war in order to maintain what would appear to the public at large as minor procedural arrangements at the frontiers.

II. THE QUESTION OF TURNOVER

12. The question arises of whether, if talks fail to materialize or veer toward a stalemate or collapse, there exist any means by which the Western Powers could deter the Soviet Union from turning over access controls, or persuade it to make the turnover in form but not in fact. It is our view that if negotiations failed to produce results acceptable to the USSR, only a conviction that the West intended to use force would cause the Soviets to reconsider turning over access controls to the East Germans. A principal factor would be the Soviet assessment of Western, particularly US, intentions. The Soviets might believe that the West would use force to probe their intentions, but be uncertain as to how far the West would go in the use of force. Or they might believe that the West would use whatever force proved necessary, even if such use of force led to general war.

13. In the event that the Soviets were convinced that the West intended to use force to probe Soviet intentions, but were uncertain as to how far the West would go in the use of force, we believe that the odds are about even that the USSR would not turn over to the GDR complete control of land, water, and air access to Berlin. On the one hand, they would fear that local clashes would lead to such an involvement of prestige and emotions that the situation could get out of control and result in grave risk of general war. On the other hand, they would realize that they had local military superiority. They would doubt that Western leaders would press the use of force to the point of seriously risking general war. Moreover, it would be difficult to convince Moscow that the Allied governments were united in their determination to use any force, or that they had the support of Western public opinion.

14. The USSR would almost certainly back away from a full turnover of access controls if it were convinced that the Western Powers were determined to use whatever degree of force was necessary to maintain access to Berlin free of GDR controls, even if such use of force led to general war. But it would be most difficult to convince the Soviet leadership that this was so. In the absence of manifest preparations for war on an extended scale they would doubt the intent of Western leaders to take such risks. Even in the face of specific warnings and military preparations the Soviets would probably remain skeptical of the ability of Western leaders to obtain public support for resort to general war, particularly if the Soviets could make the issue appear to be merely one of whether Soviet or East German authorities were to check Allied credentials at the access points.

15. If they decided to avoid a showdown over the question of access controls, the Soviet leaders would still seek to avoid the appearance of retreat. They might withdraw their garrisons and officials from East Berlin amid great fanfare without relinquishing their responsibilities over the access routes to West Berlin. Or, while making formal announcement of the turnover, they might in fact retain Soviet personnel at the check points to deal with Western military movements.

16. If the Soviets turned over all access controls, they would probably seek to head off an abrupt Western reaction by prior assurance that free access to West Berlin would be maintained by the GDR and might intimate that the East Germans would not interfere with Allied military movements despite the refusal of convoy commanders to show their credentials.

III. SOVIET REACTIONS TO VARIOUS WESTERN COURSES OF ACTION

Western Acquiescence

17. Should the Allies elect to acquiesce in the turnover of controls, the East Germans initially would probably be correct and unprovocative in the operation of the checkpoints. This would be true whether or not the West asserted the "agent" theory of continuing Soviet responsibility for free access.

18. However, once the Western Powers were firmly committed to dealing with the East Germans on the access issue, Bloc authorities would make political capital of that fact. Particularly for the benefit of the West Germans, they would stress the contention that Western acquiescence constituted *de facto* recognition of the East German regime and acceptance of the "two Germanies" concept. Sooner or later; perhaps in connection with the tenth anniversary of the GDR in October 1959, propaganda pressures would probably be augmented by harassing moves aimed at inducing the withdrawal of Western garrisons, expanding the area of dealings with the GDR, and at persuading the West Berliners that their safety and livelihood depended on reaching an understanding with the GDR. Such harassment might be minor at first, but in due course the Western Powers would be forced to choose between accepting the progressive erosion of their position in Berlin or taking a strong stand on the basis of a legal position weaker than it is now.

A Garrison Airlift

19. Should the Western Powers decide, after the turnover had taken place, to supply their small garrisons entirely by air, Soviet and East German authorities would probably not initially interfere with force. Given the small tonnages involved, a garrison airlift could almost certainly be carried out by visual flight methods and the Communists would be unable to effectively hamper Western military air traffic by jamming controls and communications. Extensive physical harassment of such an airlift in its early stages probably would be considered politically inadvisable, and the Communists would instead concentrate on making the Western Powers appear ridiculous for using an expensive airlift merely to avoid dealing with GDR officials. The Communists would sooner or later probably commence direct physical harassment of the garrison airlift. Such harassment might include flying their own aircraft in the corridors, firing antiaircraft weapons in the corridors, attempting to force down aircraft alleged to be engaged in intelligence activities, and the like.

20. It is also likely that the Soviets would formally withdraw the guarantee of safety of Western civilian flights through the air corridors to Berlin. They would justify this act on the ground that sovereignty over these corridors resided in the GDR. In its turn Pankow could refuse to assume responsibility for the safety of these flights unless the Western Powers accepted an East German representative in the Berlin Air Safety Center. Without adequate guarantees the Western airlines would probably refuse to fly to Berlin and if the air connection to Berlin, including the evacuation of refugees, were to be maintained, Western military aviation would have to assume this responsibility.

21. If these pressures failed to induce the West to negotiate on Berlin, the Soviets would probably undertake some harassment of civilian surface access from the West to West Berlin. By such means as raising tolls and introducing arbitrary procedures they could make it difficult for the West Berlin economy to function. They would probably expect that such low key tactics would in time produce growing pressure in West Berlin and West Germany for an accommodation. They would probably not initially impose a total blockade for fear of the impact on world public opinion.

Economic Sanctions

22. An embargo of all trade between the NATO Powers and the GDR would create an important dislocation both of the East German economy and of East German-Bloc trade. The total commodity trade between the GDR and the NATO countries is on the order of $580 million a year, about two-thirds of which is between West Germany and the GDR. This trade is about 17 percent of the GDR's total commodity trade. This dislocation would be greater if the NATO countries refused to charter ships to the Bloc and if the use of water routes through West Germany to East Germany were denied. Initially, the application of sanctions would lead either to a considerable increase in unemployment in East Germany and a general failure of the GDR to meet its export commitments to the Bloc, or to a Soviet crash aid program in behalf of the GDR together with some local disorganization of Bloc production and trade.

23. Economic sanctions to be effective would have to be applied by the NATO countries principally involved, particularly West Germany. Sanctions would be considerably weakened if other free world countries filled the gap or if free world trade with the GDR were rerouted through other Bloc countries. It is doubtful that unity of action among all the countries concerned could be achieved. As indicated, economic sanctions would injure the GDR and the Bloc. We do not believe, however, that the threat of such sanctions alone would prevent the Soviets from proceeding with turnover, or that their imposition after turnover would cause the Soviets to reverse themselves. They could be an important factor if associated with other means of pressure.

The Use of Force to Maintain Access[2]

24. If, after the Soviets had turned over access controls, they were actually confronted with a Western effort to maintain road access to Berlin by force, Soviet and East German authorities would almost certainly feel compelled to react vigorously. The nature of the reaction would doubtless depend, to some degree, on the way the situation had developed by the time the issue was faced. As a general proposition, however, we believe that if confronted with a convoy escorted by a token force, the Soviets, probably through the use of East Germans, would almost certainly try to bar its passage by means short of active combat, i.e., by road obstructions, demolitions, a show of force, etc. If, however, these means

were not successful we believe they would resort to active combat. It is conceivable, however, that Bloc authorities would allow one or more such convoys to get through while an effort was made to convoke a high level conference.

25. If a heavily armed and sizable task force had entered the GDR, the East Germans and Soviets would probably first demand the immediate withdrawal of the force and a peaceful settlement. But if this demand were not complied with, we believe the Soviets would commit the forces they considered necessary to defeat and drive out the Allied units in a minimum of time. The Communist leaders would probably believe it imperative to demonstrate effectively the inviolability of Bloc territory because of the danger that even limited and temporary Western success on East German soil might lead to defections among GDR troops, or to widespread civil disturbances in the GDR and elsewhere in Eastern Europe, not to mention the blow dealt by such successes to Soviet prestige throughout the world. The Soviet leaders would thus have strong incentives to defeat the Western effort and they undoubtedly would possess high confidence that they could do so with locally available Soviet forces. They would recognize that engagement of a Western task force would involve substantial risk of widened hostilities, but they would probably not have allowed the situation to get to this point if they had been convinced that it would result in general war.

26. Throughout any military crisis over ground access to Berlin, particularly if a confrontation of forces was imminent or had occurred, the USSR would almost certainly conduct an energetic diplomatic and propaganda offensive designed to limit the area and character of the conflict and to bring about a negotiated settlement. If it could not achieve a settlement, the USSR might end the crisis in a manner involving some loss of face on its part, lest matters get out of hand, but the greater likelihood is that it would take all necessary action to force the withdrawal of any Western forces which had entered the GDR. In these circumstances, there would be great danger of an expansion of the conflict.

---

[2] The Assistant Chief of Staff, Intelligence, USAF, believes that the reasoning presented in paragraphs 24, 25, and 26 is valid only insofar as the Soviets are convinced that the actions they take will not gravely risk general war. He further believes that the Soviets will estimate that any active combat between Western and Soviet or GDR forces will gravely risk general war; and, therefore, they will not permit the situation to develop to the point where active armed combat occurs.

In support of this, he cites the following from NIE 11-4-58, "Main Trends in Soviet Capabilities and Policies, 1958-1963," ". . . we believe that the Soviets would seek to prevent any crisis from developing in such a way as to leave themselves only a choice between accepting a serious reverse and taking action which would substantially increase the likelihood of general war." (Paragraph 105, page 29)

In order to establish the perspective of the above, the Assistant Chief of Staff, Intelligence, USAF, would introduce paragraphs 24, 25, and 26 with a lead-in paragraph substantially as follows:

"As we have said in paragraphs 12-14 above, the Soviets would be skeptical of Western intentions to use force or of Western ability to obtain public support for a resort to general war. However, we believe that the Soviets, realizing the risk of general war, would be extremely unlikely to allow the situation to develop where active combat between Western and Soviet or GDR forces was on the verge of becoming an actuality. Rather we believe that they would almost certainly accept a reverse before they would run the grave risk which could result from actual armed engagement. Paragraphs 24, 25, and 26 below discuss the situation under which the Soviets have decided to accept this grave risk."

CONFIDENTIAL

Current
Intelligence
Weekly
Summary

CENTRAL INTELLIGENCE AGENCY

OFFICE OF CURRENT INTELLIGENCE

CONFIDENTIAL

CONFIDENTIAL

CURRENT INTELLIGENCE WEEKLY SUMMARY

5 March 1959

T H E   W E E K   I N   B R I E F

PART I

OF IMMEDIATE INTEREST

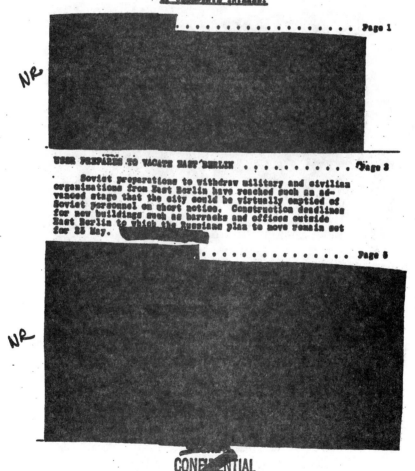

NR

. . . . Page 1

USSR PREPARES TO VACATE EAST BERLIN . . . . Page 3

Soviet preparations to withdraw military and civilian organizations from East Berlin have reached such an advanced stage that the city could be virtually emptied of Soviet personnel on short notice. Construction deadlines for new buildings such as barracks and offices outside East Berlin to which the Russians plan to move remain set for 25 May.

. . . . Page 5

NR

CONFIDENTIAL

SECRET

CURRENT INTELLIGENCE WEEKLY SUMMARY

5 March 1959

NR

USSR PREPARES TO VACATE EAST BERLIN

Soviet preparations to withdraw military and civilian organizations from East Berlin have reached an advanced stage. There are extensive packing activities in the compound at Karlshorst, and a new headquarters is being built between Bernau and Wandlitz See, a few miles north of Berlin.

SECRET

SECRET

CURRENT INTELLIGENCE WEEKLY SUMMARY

5 March 1959

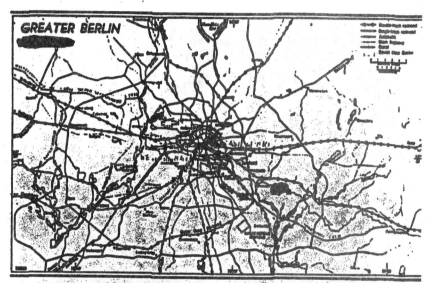

GREATER BERLIN

to move have been noted principally in the Soviet State Security (KGB) units in Karlshorst, which is the largest organization in the compound. In addition, the principal Soviet hospital in East Berlin has been almost vacated, and preparations are being made to close the school, trade mission, and other installations.

The advanced preparations indicate that the Russians could be ready in a very short time to evacuate virtually all their personnel from the city. Construction deadlines for new buildings outside East Berlin, to which the Russians plan to move, such as barracks and offices, remain set at around 25 May.

In addition to the KGB, other Soviet organizations which are believed to exercise close control over the East Germans are involved. Since these organizations will probably be quartered at Bernau, Strausberg, or Fuerstenwalde--all of which are near East Berlin--Soviet officials will be able to continue close observance of East German activities.

One report indicated that the Karlshorst compound would be used by the East German Army in the future. Such a move would be symbolic of the increased authority of the East German regime.

If control over East Berlin is transferred to East Germany,

SECRET

CURRENT INTELLIGENCE WEEKLY SUMMARY

5 March 1959

the sector border between East and West Berlin will for all practical purposes become an international frontier, and Allied access rights to the entire city, spelled out in a quadripartite agreement, will be retained only through East German sufferance. East Germany would probably assume access controls at the same time, leaving West Berlin subject to being cut off completely. Refugees would find it more difficult to go to West Berlin, and, if the already stringent security controls were tightened further, the refugee flight through the city would for all practical purposes be stopped.

SECRET

PART I   OF IMMEDIATE INTEREST   Page 5 of 11

FILE MR Case No. _93-550_

Document No. _1_

~~TOP SECRET~~

TS# 141931b

CENTRAL INTELLIGENCE AGENCY

27 March 1959

MEMORANDUM

SUBJECT: Soviet and Other Reactions to Various US Courses of
Action in the Berlin Crisis

THE PROBLEM

To estimate Soviet and other reactions to four US courses
of action in the event of failure of negotiations in the Berlin
crisis and Soviet interference with Western access. The courses
of action are: (a) a substantial effort to reopen ground access
to West Berlin by local action; (b) a substantial effort to reopen
air access; (c) reprisals against the Communists in other areas;
and (d) preparations for general war.

INTRODUCTION

1. The consequences of any US course of action on the
international scene will always depend on the context of events

~~TOP SECRET~~

APPROVED FOR RELEASE
APRIL 1994

TOP SECRET

within which the US makes its move, and on the manner, style, and timing of the action. In the present Berlin crisis there has already been extensive maneuver on both sides. The issues at stake have been defined in various ways, ranging from the relatively narrow question of Berlin's status to the wider problem of European and even of world security. Propaganda and diplomacy are continuously active. Neither side has finally defined its own position, while it tests as far as it may the strength and resolution of the adversary. Given the importance and dangers implicit in the whole complex of issues surrounding the Berlin problem, the mood and even the intentions of the protagonists may shift as the crisis is prolonged.

2. This being the situation, an estimate of the consequences of certain US courses of action in the Berlin crisis presents peculiar difficulties. It is impossible to predict the particular context of events within which these actions might be taken, and we think it important to point out that an estimate made without knowledge of this context might be seriously misleading. A US move made at a particular juncture of events, or executed

- 2 -

TOP SECRET

in a particular manner, might have consequences altogether
different from the same move made under different circumstances,
or in a different manner. We have therefore not tried to make
a detailed estimate, but instead have attempted to describe, in
a general way, some of the limits within which we believe the
consequences of US action would be likely to fall, and to explain
some of the factors which would be likely to determine these
consequences.

3. In particular, Soviet and free world reactions to the
Western measures listed above would be influences by the
manner in which negotiations had failed as well as by the underlying
reasons for this outcome. Much would depend upon whether the
Soviet or Western side seemed to be responsible for the final
breaking off of negotiations. If the whole chain of negotiations
had been run through, and the breakdown occurred at the summit,
international tension would be markedly greater than if it came at
the ministerial level or lower. Incidents arising from harassment or interference with Allied traffic by Soviet or GDR authorities

- 3 -

~~TOP SECRET~~

might have heightened tensions and influenced world opinion for or against one side or the other. Similar effects would result if either side had begun military preparations. Also, the skill with which the Western measures were justified to the world would influence both Soviet behavior and free world opinion.

    4. It is clear that the whole array of circumstances prevailing when the courses of action under discussion are put into play cannot be known in advance. However, in order to narrow the range of uncertainty the following general factors, applying to all four cases, are assumed to be operative:

    (a) At the time when negotiations break down the Western Powers will have made statements indicating that they intend to maintain their rights of unhampered access to Berlin by force if necessary. Their public posture will be such that resort to force will be clearly implicit as a next step. Some preparation/manifesting readiness for war will have been undertaken.

- 4 -

~~TOP SECRET~~

TOP ~~SECRET~~

(b) It is recognized that the Soviets and GDR will almost certainly not deny access to Berlin outright. Instead, they will simply be making access subject to certain conditions, beginning presumably with replacement of Soviet GDR controllers at checkpoints. Thus, the Western justification for resort to force will have to rest on the West's own determination that one or another requirement governing access is in effect a denial of access.

COURSE A: A substantial effort to reopen ground access by local action* -- defined as the dispatch of a reinforced US battalion, with forces up to a reinforced division with tactical air support in readiness if required. The force will proceed toward the opposite end of the autobahn taking over control points as required. The force will not fire unless fired upon but will deploy off the autobahn if necessary to meet the situation.

---

* See SNIE 100-2-59, especially Paragraphs 25 and 26, for an estimate of the Soviet reaction in this case.

- 5 -

TOP ~~SECRET~~

5. Once the Soviets were actually confronted with such a task force, they might estimate that to oppose it with force would set off a train of events which would end in general war. If they so concluded they would either seek the advantages of surprise and the initiative by launching a pre-emptive nuclear attack on North America, or they would decide not to oppose the Western force at all and, while appealing to world opinion and the UN, would abandon for the time being their effort to impose the conditions on access which had led to the Western action. We do not believe, however, that the appearance of a US force on the autobahn, without very extensive additional military and psychological preparations, would lead the Soviets to the conclusion that the US was willing to proceed to general war.

6. Instead, Moscow would probably estimate that the US lacked the military means to deal effectively on a local basis with the Soviet forces in the GDR, and that the US, rather than increase the scale of military involvement up to and including general war, would prefer to make concessions to the Soviet-demands

- 6 -

TOPSECRET

on Berlin. We believe, therefore, that the most likely Soviet response would be to resist the US division with force. Soviet resistance would be aimed at driving the invader from GDR soil while minimizing the risk of expanding hostilities.

7. In this action Moscow could limit itself to use of the East German Army. This would have the advantage of avoiding a direct confrontation between Soviet and Western forces, and it would lend plausibility to the claim of the GDR to sovereignty and independence. On the other hand, there would be definite risks in the use of East German forces. The political reliability of some of these troops may be regarded by the Soviets as uncertain and they might fear the possibility of defection among them. If the East Germans suffered a defeat or a large-scale defection, there might be flash risings in the GDR and the possibility of these spreading to Poland or Hungary, or both. We believe that the Soviets might attempt initially to use East German forces for setting up road blocks and other obstructive action, but that once fighting had broken out they would feel obliged to use their own forces along with East Germans.

- 7 -

TOP SECRET

8. In the greater part of the non-Communist world there would almost certainly be a strongly adverse reaction to a substantial Western effort to reopen ground access to Berlin by local action. This reaction would stem primarily from fear of war, and from disapproval of the Western resort to armed force. In the more important countries of NATO, public reaction would probably be mixed, and would depend to some degree on how far Soviet obstructive actions appeared designed merely to enforce technical requirements for GDR supervision of Western access to Berlin, rather than to isolate Berlin from the West and communize the city. If the latter case were established there would be considerable public support for the Western countermove. Should the Western troops succeed in opening the road without violating adjacent GDR territory, the action would probably be generally approved, but should there be fighting in which Western troops deployed widely, many even in Western countries would believe that the West had initiated aggression.

9. We believe that most of the NATO governments would support the US move, providing they were convinced that the issue

- 8 -

at stake clearly exceeded a mere technicality. Most other
governments, however, and especially those of neutralist
countries, would oppose. The matter would almost certainly
be raised in the UN. Once in the UN General Assembly (assuming
that the Security Council could not act), a resolution might be
passed calling for a withdrawal of forces. This might have the
effect of conceding nominal East German control of Western
access to Berlin.

COURSE B: <u>A substantial effort to reopen air access</u> -- Western
action would be graduated depending upon the degree of Soviet
and GDR interference. If there is harassment (e.g., barrage
balloons) which endangers the safety of Western aircraft peaceably
transiting the corridor, Western combat aircraft will enter the
corridors to come to their assistance.

10. We believe that the USSR would probably refrain from
attacks on Western aircraft with fighters and antiaircraft fire,
inasmuch as the USSR would thereby appear before the world as the
initiator of hostilities which could lead to general war. The Soviets

- 9 -

might attempt to interfere with Western aircraft by less direct.
means: "accidents" might occur and there would probably be
ECM interference. Western aircraft might be fired on, however,
if they flew outside of the air corridors. The main Soviet reaction
would be directed to political exploitation of this situation,
especially in the UN. The Soviets would calculate that the
Western action could not be sustained for a long period without
seriously adverse political effects, even in the Western countries.

11. The extent to which the protection of Western air
traffic would be condemned or approved by free world opinion
would depend in large part on what provocation the USSR had
given, that is, on how specific its threats to air traffic had been.
Also, far wider approval would be found for this action if the
Communists were simultaneously attempting to deny all
ground access. Even so, the fact that the US had resorted to
military action would tend to alienate some sections of world public
opinion.

- 10 -

COURSE C: <u>Reprisals against the Communists in the form of</u>

<u>tripartite naval controls on Soviet Bloc merchant shipping</u> --

Delays will be imposed for inspection of documents, cargo and

health conditions, or search for illegally carried personnel. This

will be done in parts and on the high seas. Execution will be

by US, British, and French naval forces. Collaboration of other

countries in their ports and national waters will be sought.

    12. The Soviets would reason that the effects of such an

interruption on the Bloc economy would not be immediate,

and that these need not therefore determine their short-term

actions in the Berlin crisis. They would probably not therefore

desist immediately from whatever interference they had imposed

on access to Berlin. They would seek to make maximum prop -

aganda capital out of the Western action, warning that it had

brought international tension to a new height and was, in fact,

virtually an act of war. They would undertake whatever legal

recourse was open to them in international forums including the

UN. They would probably take similar reprisals against the

shipping of the three powers in Bloc ports and national waters,

- 11 -

enlisting the collaboration of other states if they could. They might also attempt to detain or take custody of merchant shipping on the high seas near to their own coasts and ports. Finally, they might declare certain waters, such as the Black and Baltic seas, closed to ships of the three powers.

           to
13. Free world reaction/such restrictions on Bloc trade would probably be generally adverse. Such measures would be viewed as exclusively retaliatory actions which did not contribute to negotiation and settlement of the questions at issue, although they would probably win far wider support if they came at a time when West Berlin was under full blockade. Those NATO powers which carry on substantial seaborne trade with the Bloc would be most reluctant to accept the sacrifices entailed in the interruption of that trade. Free world opinion generally would be inclined to regard such reprisals as leading to a further deterioration of East-West relations.

- 12 -

~~TOP SECRET~~

COURSE D: <u>Preparations for general war</u>.--Measures of
partial mobilization to be taken would include unit deployments,
increased emphasis on readiness of units, on increased
alert posture, and heightened civil defense activity. Public
awareness of these activities is assumed.

14. The extent to which these measures were effective
in convincing the Soviet leaders that the West was determined
to go to war over interference with its rights of access to Berlin
would depend less on these measures themselves than on what was
said concerning them. The Soviets would probably be convinced
of the Western intention actually to go to war only if the measures
were explained to the Western publics as having that meaning.
If the USSR was convinced that the West was prepared to wage
general war rather than permit the loss of its rights in Berlin,
the Soviet leaders would almostcertainly reach a negotiated
settlement which respected basic Western interests. They would
still come to this, however, only by a series of steps in negotiation,
hoping that the gradual easing of their position would weaken Western
resolve and unity and permit the USSR to avoid the appearance of
backing down abruptly.

- 13 -

~~TOP SECRET~~

15. If the military preparations indicated were accompanied by credible statements by the highest leaders that the Western Powers intended to go to general war over the Berlin issue, there would probably be widespread alarm and dismay among the people of the Atlantic community and profound disapproval in most of the rest of the world. There would be demands in the UN for action to halt the trend toward war. Yet these would not necessarily be the permanent or decisive reactions. To the extent to which NATO countries recognized that the issue posed over Berlin really involved the defense of the free world, we believe that public opinion would accept the Western measures with firmness and resignation. This would be especially true if it were widely believed that large-scale military preparations held good promise of maintaining the essential Western position without actual resort to war. We cannot judge at this time whether such reactions would be likely to ouweigh those of fear and opposition.

16. If military preparations and declarations of intent to go to general war had not produced a shift in the Soviet

- 14 -

position and the Western Powers then issued an ultimatum

demanding a redress of grievances, say within 24 hours,

it seems to us impossible to predict the Soviet response

with assurance. Confronted with such a public, clear-cut,

and uncompromising challenge, the USSR would consider its

prestige as a great power with its prestige at stake and would

surely find it very difficult to back down. If the Soviet leaders

considered their forces to be in an adequate state of readiness

they might unleash a pre-emptive attack. Alternatively,

they might make the concessions demanded. We consider the

latter course the more likely, but we do not believe that the

Western Powers could act with confidence on this assumption.

17/3

CENTRAL INTELLIGENCE AGENCY
TELETYPED INFORMATION REPORT

This material contains information affecting the National Defense of the United States within the meaning of the Espionage Laws, Title 18, U.S.C. Secs. 793 and 794, the transmission or revelation of which in any manner to an unauthorized person is prohibited by law.

CLASSIFICATION	DISSEMINATION CONTROLS
C-O-N-F-I-D-E-N-T-I-A-L	NOFORN

TDCS	DATE DISTR.		PRECEDENCE
		6 April 1959	X ROUTINE

COUNTRY
USSR/Germany

PLACE ACQUIRED
Germany, Berlin

This document has been (in part) released through the HISTORICAL REVIEW PROGRAM of the Central Intelligence Agency.

SUBJECT
Soviet Official's Comments on the Berlin Situation

DATE OF INFORMATION
Late March 1959

REFERENCES

APPRAISAL OF CONTENT (TENTATIVE)
3 and Opinion

SOURCE (EVALUATION DEFINITIVE)

A fairly reliable East German Communist source (C), from a Soviet official in Berlin whom source has been on intimate terms with for some time.

A Soviet official stated that it is inconceivable and out of the question that the Berlin crisis would deteriorate to the point of war, because both sides possess the means to annihilate the other side. He did not rule out the possibility of localized conflicts, even in Germany. He alleged that the Soviets are considering, among other measures, an intermittent blockade of Berlin as a harassment measure. The Karlshorst compound is in the process of almost complete turnover to the Germans.

Field Distribution: None.

End of Message

DISSEMINATION CONTROLS	CLASSIFICATION
NOFORN	CONFIDENTIAL C-O-N-F-I-D-E-N-T-I-A-L

TO: ACSL, AF, NAVY, JCS, OSD, STATE, NSA, ONE, OCI, OCR, DD/I, OCI, CRR

CONFIDENTIAL
~~SECRET~~

OCI NO. 1685/5

30 April 1u5

CURRENT INTELLIGENCE WEEKLY SUMMARY

CENTRAL INTELLIGENCE AGENCY
OFFICE OF CURRENT INTELLIGENCE

CONFIDENTIAL
~~SECRET~~

Approved for Release
Date   SEP 199

③

SECRET

CURRENT INTELLIGENCE WEEKLY SUMMARY

30 April 1959

PART III

PATTERNS AND PERSPECTIVES

The Soviet Union has exploited the absence of a clear-cut agreement on access to Berlin to establish mechanisms which enable it to harass all forms of surface transportation to the city. East Germany has come to play a considerable role in the regulation of surface traffic, particularly West German. The Communists could readily block all surface routes by destroying bridges, overpasses, and canal locks. An airlift could supply Allied garrisons, even if Communist electronic measures against air navigational systems made all but visual flights impossible, but the West Berlin civilian population could not be sustained by such a limited airlift.

SECRET

vi

450

SECRET

CONFIDENTIAL

CURRENT INTELLIGENCE WEEKLY SUMMARY

30 April 1955

PART III

PATTERNS AND PERSPECTIVES

THE PROBLEM OF WESTERN ACCESS TO BERLIN

The Western powers' rights of access to Berlin derive from their participation in the defeat of Germany in World War II and the agreements reached with the USSR concerning the postwar occupation. These are embodied in a number of documents including a London agreement of September 1944 and an exchange of letters between President Truman and Stalin, and a verbal agreement between General Clay and Marshal Zhukov during the summer of 1945. The Paris Agreement of 1949 terminating the Berlin blockade is also relevant. There is, however, no single document signed by all four powers providing for unrestricted access to the city by surface and air. Allied rights are based on precedent and usage.

At the time of the Soviet-East German treaty of 1955 which granted "sovereignty" to East Germany, there was an exchange of letters between East German Foreign Minister Bolz and Soviet Deputy Foreign Minister Zorin in which the USSR stated that it would "temporarily" retain control of Allied access to Berlin pending the conclusion of further agreements with the Allies. It is the Soviet contention that the USSR's planned peace treaty with East Germany will invalidate all Allied occupation agreements, including those governing control of access to West Berlin. This control

would then pass to the "sovereign" East German regime.

Road and Rail Access

The West's right to ground access to Berlin was established during a June 1945 meeting between General Clay, Marshal Zhukov, and a British representative. The memorandum of conver-

sation resulting from this meeting was never authenticated, however. The agreement has, in practice, been interpreted to mean that the Allies would submit to Soviet traffic regulations and document checks but not to inspection of vehicles or cargo. Zhukov stated at the

SECRET

CONFIDENTIAL

CURRENT INTELLIGENCE WEEKLY SUMMARY

30 April 1959

meeting that he did not deny the right of Allied access, but that the Soviet Union would not "give a corridor." The agreement is vague enough to be open to honest differences of opinion by both sides and has given the USSR manifold opportunities to harass traffic.

All Allied road traffic must travel via the Helmstedt-Berlin autobahn. There are three other routes open to non-Allied nationals, but 80 percent of all road traffic goes via Helmstedt. Some 37 percent of Berlin's imports and 57 percent of its exports by tonnage go by road. Of military interest is the fact that the 105-mile stretch in East Germany includes 47 bridges (the Elbe bridge is over 1,200 yards long, including 160 yards over water) and 81 overpasses. There are Allied, West German, Soviet, and East German barriers or checkpoints at each end.

After passing the Western checkpoints, Allied vehicles come to a barrier manned by East Germans which normally is raised automatically. Then comes the Soviet checkpoint, where the movement order—issued unilaterally by Allied military authorities—is stamped, but the delay is generally longer than would seem necessary. The Allied vehicle driver or convoy commander is given a small white form when he leaves the Soviet checkpoint. This is surrendered at another East German barrier—some 75 yards farther inside East Germany—which normally is raised without question.

The form appears to be no more than permission from the Russians to the East Germans to permit the vehicle to proceed. This procedure for passing through an East German - manned barrier gives the East Germans a foot in the door toward full control of access. When Allied vehicles leave East Germany going east or west, the East Germans merely raise the barriers and no white form is involved. The Russians do, however, check the travel documents at their checkpoint.

All Allied rail traffic and all rail freight goes via the Marienborn-Berlin rail line, which roughly parallels the Helmstedt autobahn. There are five other interzonal rail lines in use. Some 35 percent of West Berlin's imports and 21 percent of its exports, by tonnage, as well as 90 percent of Allied freight to the Berlin garrisons, are handled by rail. Allied trains while in East Germany are hauled by East German locomotives with East German crews.

The Allies operate 34 regularly scheduled trains per week, with the arrangements being made between West and East German railway officials. There are a considerable number of similar low-level trade and commercial agreements between the two railroad systems. There is only one checkpoint on the rail line, four miles from the zonal border at Marienborn. Allied trains have no contact with East German officials; processing is handled by the Russians.

Air Access

The question of air access is the only one governed by a properly authenticated document. This was approved by the Allied Control Council in 1945 and updated in 1946. There are a number of points, however, which are not entirely clear: one is whether the Allies have exclusive or priority rights to the three air corridors. Thus far the Russians have, in general, appeared to recognize that the Allies have exclusive rights, since they have seldom used the corridors themselves.

The most pressing question is that of minimum and maximum

SECRET

CURRENT INTELLIGENCE WEEKLY SUMMARY

30 April 1959

altitudes. A maximum altitude of 10,000 feet was mentioned in a draft of the 1945 agreement, but did not appear in the final document. There is a 10,000-foot altitude limit within 20 miles of Berlin.

The air space around Berlin, known as the Berlin Control Zone, is administered by one of the two remaining quadripartite bodies: the Berlin Air Safety Center (BASC). The group administering Spandau Prison is the other such body. The BASC, located in West Berlin, coordinates traffic in and out of the three airfields in West Berlin and the one airfield just outside East Berlin but within the Berlin Control Zone. This does not mean, however, that the Soviet Union actually submits its flight plans to the BASC, as the Allies do; the USSR schedules its flights so as not to conflict with Allied flights.

In addition to military traffic, three civil air lines from the three Allies regularly operate to and from West Berlin. None of the navigational aids, such as beacons or radars, servicing the three corridors are in East Germany.

Air travel to Berlin is the only means of travel which is not subject to Communist control. This freedom made

possible the Berlin airlift; it also enables the Allies to transport East German refugees from West Berlin to West Germany.

The Allied garrisons could be supplied almost indefinitely by airlift if a surface blockade were enforced--even if the Communists jammed Allied air navigational aids, making all but visual flights impossible. An airlift could not, however, sustain the West Berlin civil population if surface access were denied.

Canal Traffic

Barge traffic via the extensive canal and river system is of considerable importance to West Berlin, although not to the Allies. Some 2,600 West German barges are licensed for interzonal movement, and last year they carried some 35 percent of all freight in and out of West Berlin. All canals and locks in East Germany are controlled by the East Germans. As in the case of rail access, arrangements for barge traffic are made at a technical level between West and East German authorities. The canals were closed during the Berlin blockade, and since then the East Germans have from time to time harassed traffic by closing the locks "for repairs."

NR

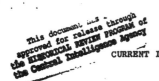

CURRENT INTELLIGENCE WEEKLY SUMMARY

21 May 1959

PART I

OF IMMEDIATE INTEREST

FOREIGN MINISTERS' TALKS

Soviet moves in the second week of the Geneva foreign ministers' conference were designed to break up the West's package plan and to induce the Western ministers to discuss the Soviet peace treaty and Berlin proposals separately on terms most favorable to the USSR.

Foreign Minister Gromyko, in his speech on 18 May, developed the line used by Khrushchev in his speech two days earlier, accepting the Lenin Peace Prize. Gromyko said the Western package was "clearly unacceptable," but indicated willingness to discuss those parts dealing with European security and disarmament if they are separated from the "negative and unrealistic" proposals on Berlin and German reunification. He made it clear, however, that debate on a peace treaty and Berlin must precede consideration of all other questions.

The Soviet leaders probably hope their moves to detach the questions of European security and an arms-limitation zone from the Western package will tend to divide Britain from the United States and France in view of Prime Minister Macmillan's commitment, at the end of his Moscow visit, to discuss these questions separate from German reunification.

Gromyko has also attempted to probe for dissension among the Western powers by floating hints of readiness to discuss a separate or interim agreement on Berlin. After rejecting the Western proposals on Berlin "from beginning to end," he urged the West to display a "sounder and more businesslike approach" and said the USSR is ready to work out a solution "together with the governments of the states concerned." He emphasized Moscow's readiness to consider Berlin and European security as separate and independent subjects for negotiation.

On the day following the widely publicized reports that the United States might consider an interim Berlin settlement if the USSR rejects the Western package plan, Gromyko, in a private talk with British Foreign Secretary Selwyn Lloyd, renewed the USSR's previous offers of three alternative solutions: (1) complete withdrawal of Western forces from West Berlin; (2) addition of token Soviet forces to the Western garrisons; or (3) replacement of Western troops by neutral forces under United Nations authority.

Two high-ranking members of the Soviet delegation, in a private talk with an American official on 14 May, had suggested that token Soviet forces could be stationed in West Berlin along with Western troops. This idea was first advanced publicly by Khrushchev in his speech in East Berlin on 9 March.

Moscow's maneuvers to exploit any differences between Britain and the other Western powers were also reflected in Soviet propaganda. Pravda claimed on 17 May that the circulation by Reuters of a version of the West's package plan a day before it was formally

SECRET

CURRENT INTELLIGENCE WEEKLY SUMMARY

21 May 1959

introduced was an attempt by the British to "stress that they have some ideas of their own on settling international problems which do not coincide with US and French viewpoints."

Khrushchev's conciliatory letters of 15 May to President Eisenhower and Prime Minister Macmillan highlighted Soviet efforts to manipulate the nuclear test cessation issue as a device for exploiting Anglo-American differences and for creating an impression of progress toward agreement which could be used to justify a summit meeting. Khrushchev welcomed the President's readiness to study Macmillan's proposal, endorsed earlier by Khrushchev, for a predetermined number of annual on-site inspections of suspected nuclear explosions. He asserted that agreement on this proposal "would pave the way for the conclusion of an agreement to end all kinds of tests" and portrayed the President as agreeing to the Soviet thesis that "such inspections should not be numerous."

The Soviet premier's warm note to Macmillan referring to the "closeness of our positions on your idea" was calculated to place London under increasing domestic pressure to conclude an agreement.

While Khrushchev's letter to the President accepted in part the Western proposal for further technical discussions on condition they are limited to a study of high-altitude detection, the USSR continues to insist that the fixing of the number of annual inspections is essentially a matter for high-level political decision.

Khrushchev contended in his letter that there is little need for a "special study of criteria for settling so simple and clear a question" as the number of inspections. He warned that debates on criteria might be endless and implied that the United States might prolong them as a means of forestalling an agreement.

Khrushchev has reaffirmed the Soviet position that unanimity of the three nuclear powers would not be required to dispatch inspection teams if the number of inspections is agreed upon in advance.

The Soviet leaders probably hope that the British Government will be inclined to favor their thesis that an inspection quota should be established on a high political level and that any differences between London and Washington on this issue can be exploited to advance Soviet objectives on other questions under negotiation at the foreign ministers' conference and a possible summit meeting.

Western Reactions

The plan of Reuters news agency to open an office in East Berlin gave rise to renewed French and German charges of British "softness." In a tripartite meeting in Bonn, the French minister called the move most unfortunate at this time in view of its undesirable political aspects. The British Government appears not to have been consulted on the move, nor to have advised Reuters of any possible repercussions. The Federation of British Industries has denied a report that it, too, planned to open an office in East Berlin.

SECRET

SECRET

CURRENT INTELLIGENCE WEEKLY SUMMARY

21 May 1959

The Western European press has adopted a generally pessimistic tone on the prospects for serious negotiations on the German question. The British press for the most part is agreed that the West's package proposal contains several items which might tempt Moscow, but that the items will have to be discussed separately. The Communist-inspired press in France has been emphasizing the possibility of agreement on nuclear test cessation.

Leading papers in France and Britain have admitted that the question of Berlin may have to be considered separately from the German question or face the risk of breaking off the talks. Several German papers pointed to Berlin as the central question. One prominent progovernment paper in West Germany stated that neither side had made an effort toward serious negotiations. (SECRET NOFORN) (Concurred in by OSI)

MIDDLE EAST HIGHLIGHTS

Iraq

Iraqi Prime Minister Qasim has reiterated his opposition to a renewal of activity by political parties in the face of local Communist pressure, and he apparently is still refusing to admit Communists to the cabinet as party representatives. Foreign Minister Jawad, a non-Communist, said again this week that the general political situation in Iraq is "improving." Jawad, who claims to know Qasim's thinking, believes the prime minister will gradually take steps to check pressures which tend to "alter Iraq's neutrality."

The National Democratic party (NDP) of which Jawad is a member, has announced suspension of its own activities in what appears to be an effort to support Qasim's stand. This move, the NDP leaders argue, demonstrates their party's obedience to Qasim's wishes and leaves the Communists isolated. It may have the effect of also leaving the field of mass political

activity even more open to the Communists.

Since 16 May Cairo's press attacks on the Iraqi Communists have been sharpened with charges that the party intends to "go underground" to prepare an uprising.

Economically, Iraq is still suffering from administrative chaos, growing labor unrest, and a general exodus of Western businessmen and technicians; there is a distinct possibility that a new round of wage demands, spurred by Communist elements in the labor unions, will produce inflationary pressures which would in turn provide further opportunities for Communist agitation. Lack of coordination between Iraqi Government departments has resulted in such situations as the boycott--for doing business with Israel--of a petroleum firm which supplies the bulk of the Iraqi Air Force's jet fuel. The "purge committees" which have demoralized government offices are being extended to private enterprise.

SECRET

C E N T R A L   I N T E L L I G E N C E

Date 7/9/93

HRP 93-3

11 June 1959

SUBJECT: SNIE 100-7-59:   SOVIET TACTICS ON BERLIN

THE PROBLEM

To estimate likely Soviet tactics on the Berlin issue,
assuming that the Geneva Conference terminates without result
and without agreement to a summit meeting.

QUESTIONS POSED BY THE PROBLEM

1. If the Soviets allow the Geneva meeting to end in
stalemate, they will presumably do so on the calculation that
a period of additional pressure on the Berlin problem will
finally induce the Western Powers to make substantial concessions. The Soviets might anticipate creating a situation in
which the Western Powers under pressure of a deepening crisis
would be forced to come to the summit, and would be prepared
there to accept a settlement more favorable to the USSR than
any they have so far contemplated. The main questions posed by
this assumed Soviet course are: What degree of pressure
would the Soviets think appropriate to achieve the result

SECRET

sought? What would be the measures they might undertake to apply this pressure?

COURSE I -- THE ALTERNATIVE OF EXTREME PRESSURE AT AN EARLY DATE

2. As an extreme degree of pressure the Soviets might proceed forthwith to conclude a separate peace treaty with the GDR and simultaneously turn over Berlin access controls to the GDR. The latter could then begin, possibly after a brief interval, to apply restrictions or conditions to access intended to test the determination of the Western Powers and to raise tensions still further. The USSR could repeat its warnings that any resort to force by the Western Powers would cause the USSR to invoke its obligations under the Warsaw Pact. The Soviets would recognize that this degree of pressure would probably provoke a major crisis, and they would not so act unless they estimated that the West would not resort to force and would finally accept in substance the Soviet demands for a revision of the status of Berlin.

3. There are a number of reasons why the course of extreme pressure described in the preceding paragraph is probably not the one which the Soviets would adopt at this time. We believe that, as the Berlin crisis developed, the Soviets may have become less certain that they could count

- 2 -

SECRET

SECRET

on the West not to react with force. They apparently concluded at some point after they initiated the crisis last
November that, unless they were willing to run grave risks
of war, they would have to achieve their aims by negotiation.
Moreover, to provoke such risks now would further compromise
the "peaceloving" image which Soviet policy is trying to present, especially in Asia and Africa. Even if the Soviets believed that the Western Powers could be forced out of Berlin
without hostilities, they would recognize that many of the post-
crisis effects would be highly undesirable from the Soviet
point of view. The Western Powers would probably be stimulated to close ranks and to increase their military effort. This
latter would probably take the form of accelerated growth of
the missile-nuclear threat to the Bloc in Western Europe,
which the USSR has been trying hard to check. The outlook
would be for an intensified period of cold war tensions.
The net effects of all this on the Bloc's current domestic
and foreign policies would probably be seen by them as adverse.
These considerations persuade us that a course of extreme
pressure in the wake of a Geneva stalemate is not one the
Soviets would be likely to pursue. Even if they did pursue
it, however, we believe that they would not do so beyond a
point which they estimated would be likely to lead to war.

- 3 -

SECRET

COURSE II -- THE ALTERNATIVE OF GRADUATED, PROTRACTED PRESSURE TO OBTAIN RENEWED NEGOTIATIONS

4. The more likely alternative for the Soviets to adopt would be to increase pressures on the Berlin issue gradually and only in such degree as in their opinion would tend to induce the Western Powers to resume negotiations later, preferably at the summit, this time on terms more favorable to the Soviet positions. There would have to be a nice degree of calculation in this course. The measures taken to implement it would have to be of a kind which the West would not see as mere verbal threats. On the other hand, they should not be of a kind to present the West with a _fait accompli_ in Berlin which would provoke a showdown prematurely. These measures would be intended to convince the West that the Soviets were prepared to take unilateral action, but that some time and room remained for negotiations to avoid a showdown, and perhaps to salvage something of Western interests. Inducements would be provided in the form of Soviet statements of readiness to resume negotiations at any time. We think steps of this kind would be open to the Soviets to take, and that their course of action after Geneva would probably be of this character.

5. Such a Soviet campaign to build up pressure gradually accompanied by demands to resume negotiations, would probably

- 4 -

SECRET

begin with propaganda blaming the Western Powers' rigidity
for the breakdown at Geneva. There would be warnings that
the danger of a clash over Berlin was increasing, and announce-
ments that the USSR was still determined to achieve its demands in Berlin. Such propaganda could be orchestrated with
harsher notes issuing from East Germany. A plausible next
step would relate to the negotiation of a separate peace
treaty with the GDR, with intervals of time between the successive phases -- setting of a date for negotiations, then a
negotiating conference and initialling, and finally ratifi-
cation. Once this latter stage had been reached, full implementation would not need to be undertaken at once. The Soviets
might first withdraw their forces from East Berlin as an
earnest of their intentions, and only later and by degrees
turn over access controls to the GDR. Even when this process
was complete the GDR might still not attempt to interfere
with Western access, and might even announce that it would
not do so for a certain period. At this stage the Soviets
would probably estimate that the Western Powers would still
believe that they had room for negotiation since they have
already agreed to accept GDR access control under some
formulation of the agent theory. The aim at all stages
would be to convince the Western Powers, or at least one or

- 5 -

more of them, that the possibility of negotiation remained open but was constantly narrowing.

6. The Soviets would probably recognize that such gradually mounting pressure might fail in its purpose of inducing the Western Powers to resume negotiations on terms more favorable to the Soviets. But the Soviets would nevertheless see several advantages in it. They would believe:

(a) That the steps taken would have advanced the Soviets toward a unilateral achievement of their aims in Berlin or would have prepared the basis for direct harassment or closure of access to Berlin along the lines discussed in Paragraph 2.

(b) That, even if they wished to resort to such extreme pressure finally, the protracted tension over the Berlin issue would have sowed sufficient alarm and disarray in the West so that it would be unable to confront an eventual showdown with unity and firmness.

(c) Finally, that even if the course of graduated pressure did fail the Soviets would not be obliged to pass over to the more extreme course described in Paragraph 2. They could always decide to settle for a "compromise" which

- 6 -

SECRET

would leave the GDR and the USSR in a better position than they had before raising the Berlin issue last November.

7. The carrying out of each Soviet move outlined in COURSE II would be influenced by the firmness and unity with which the West met each successive step.

- 7 -

SECRET

FILE OCR Copy No. *81-229*

Document No. *3*

CIA MEMORANDUM   13 July 1959

U. S. Negotiating Position on Berlin - 1959-62

1. The Joint Chiefs of Staff memorandum states a US view of the probable alteration of the balance of military power between the present and 1961/62. The West's ability to maintain its position in Berlin after a moratorium would depend on many nonmilitary factors and also upon interim developments which cannot now be foreseen. Among these will be the view the Soviets will then take of their over-all power position vis-a-vis the West, since this will determine the degree of pressure they will think it feasible to apply. They may, for example, take a different view of the military trends discussed above. Likewise, the view taken generally in the West of the relative power position will bear heavily on the outcome of a new trial of strength over the city.

2. In our view, the probable course of developments between now and 1961/62 will lead both the Soviets and the West to conclude that the relative power position of the USSR has substantially improved, and that the position of the West in Berlin is more untenable than it is now. The most important and the most predictable of these is the Soviets' relative gain in nuclear delivery capabilities referred to above. Their increased ability to inflict catastrophic damage on the West, and particularly on the US, is likely to convince them that they can apply still greater pressure on positions like Berlin without assuming increased risks. Awareness of these Soviet gains may reduce the inclination in the West to take a firm and united stand for an exposed position like Berlin. In Western Europe in particular, realization that the US has become more vulnerable to Soviet nuclear attack may sap the conviction that the USSR would in a showdown really be deterred by US retaliatory capability. Any decline of confidence in US power would also have some erosive effect on the firmness of the resistance spirit in West Berlin.

APPROVED : RELEASE
DATE 2 6 JAN 1989

Copy 2 of 4 Copies (INR)
INR-14765, Att. #3

-2-

3. Other developments over the next few years are likely to reinforce an impression in both the Bloc and the West that the Bloc is growing stronger relative to the West. The outlook is for a period of political stability within the Bloc under the firm leadership of Khrushchev. Bloc economic growth is likely to continue at a rate more rapid than that of the West. New Soviet scientific achievements are likely to further enhance Soviet world prestige. At the same time, NATO seems likely to be in for a rough passage, in part over issues unrelated to the confrontation with the USSR, and this will probably add to an impression of declining strength in the West relative to the USSR.

4. A number of developments are possible by 1961/62 which may counterbalance the impression that the USSR is in a stronger position to contest an issue like Berlin. It is possible, for example, that Khrushchev will no longer be on hand to giv. Soviet policy its present quality of exhuberant and confident brinkmanship. After his departure from the scene other Soviet leaders, especially in the early succession phase, might play a more cautious game. There may be political or economic difficulties and setbacks within some Bloc state, or in relations between members of the Bloc, which would diminish the impression of growing Soviet power. Depending on wholly unpredictable political developments in the principal Western states, the West may react to the sense of a growing Soviet threat by increasing its unity and determination.

5. Taken together, all the above considerations point in the direction of making the Berlin position more difficult to defend at a later date. Nevertheless, the tendency is not in our view so highly probable or so weighty that we must take this as a foregone conclusion. The importance of factors which cannot now be foreseen is likely to be as great as those which can now be tentatively estimated. It is also possible that the Soviets will estimate that their over-all world position in 1961/62 offers such favorable prospects of important gains without serious risks that they will not wish to provoke a sharp new crisis over Berlin which would jeopardize such gains. Moreover, the West has open to it actions and policies which could have the effect of improving the outlook.

3.

6. Even if the relative Soviet power position improves in fact and in the world's view of it, we believe that the USSR will still be under considerable constraint, in 1961/62, in seeking to enforce its will on a key issue like Berlin. The Soviets' relative gain in nuclear capabilities will not enable them to conclude that they can surely defeat the West in a general nuclear war at a cost that they would regard as acceptable, except in the highly unlikely event that they were able to achieve complete strategic surprise. They will still be deterred from bringing maximum pressure to bear because they will still wish to avoid nuclear war and they will still be uncertain that the West would allow itself to be expelled from Berlin without going to war. The fact that there will continue to be a considerable degree of deterrence imposed on Soviet actions will mean that, in 1961/62 as at present, they will be led to seek their aims by negotiation. Their negotiating position will probably be stronger but it will not be so decisively strong as to compel the West to accept their demands.

7. All of these imponderables bearing on the situation following a moratorium period would be profoundly affected by the actual terms of the moratorium. Most damaging to the strength of the Western position in 1961/62 would be any implication in those terms that at the end of the moratorium a fundamental change in the status of the city was a foregone conclusion. On the other hand, if the West agreed merely to resume negotiations later, without prejudice to its present rights and clearly with the intention to continue to uphold them and with them the freedom of the city, this fact would offset other factors acting to weaken the Western position. The terms of the moratorium would probably be the singly most important factor affecting the attitude of the population and political leadership of West Berlin in particular. Likewise any so-called peripheral concessions attending the moratorium, in particular any reduction of Western troop strength in Berlin, could seriously weaken the will of the city to maintain resistance. Without this, as the Soviets clearly recognize by their attempts to obtain drastic peripheral concessions, the position in West Berlin would in fact become indefensible.

CONFIDENTIAL

SECRET

OCI NO. ~~~

27 August ~~

CURRENT
INTELLIGENCE
WEEKLY
SUMMARY

CENTRAL INTELLIGENCE AGENCY
OFFICE OF CURRENT INTELLIGENCE

SECRET

Approved for Release
Date   S.P ~~~

CONFIDENTIAL

CURRENT INTELLIGENCE WEEKLY SUMMARY

27 August 1959

PART II (continued)

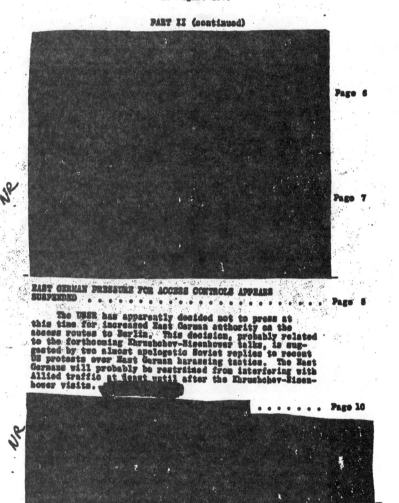

NR

. . . . Page 6

. . . . Page 7

EAST GERMAN PRESSURE FOR ACCESS CONTROLS APPEARS
SUSPENDED . . . . Page 8

    The USSR has apparently decided not to press at
this time for increased East German authority on the
access routes to Berlin. This decision, probably related
to the forthcoming Khrushchev-Eisenhower talks, is suggested by two almost apologetic Soviet replies to recent
US protests over East German harassing tactics. The East
Germans will probably be restrained from interfering with
Allied traffic at least until after the Khrushchev-Eisenhower visits.

. . . . Page 10

NR

THE WEEK IN BRIEF

CURRENT INTELLIGENCE WEEKLY SUMMARY

27 August 1959

NR

EAST GERMAN PRESSURE FOR ACCESS CONTROLS APPEARS SUSPENDED

The USSR, in a move probably related to the upcoming Khrushchev-Eisenhower talks, has apparently reversed a June decision which appeared to forecast increased East German harassing tactics against Allied traffic to Berlin and has decided not to press at this time for more East German authority on the access routes.

General Zakharov, the Soviet commandant in Berlin,

PART II   NOTES AND COMMENTS   Page 8 of 23

CURRENT INTELLIGENCE WEEKLY SUMMARY

27 August 1959

replying, on 23 August to his American counterpart's protest over East German interference with official American travelers on the autobahn, said these harassments "seemed unnecessary" and that he would look into the matter. Having just returned from a two-month absence, Zakharov seemed surprised to learn of the matter. The acting Soviet commandant on 30 July had replied in a similar conciliatory vein to an American protest over East German interference with a US military train.

These two almost apologetic replies follow sporadic efforts during the Berlin crisis to assert East German authority on the autobahn. On 22 June the acting Soviet commandant had stated in a letter to the US commandant that, while the USSR accepted the responsibility to control Allied traffic at the checkpoints, the autobahn itself was beyond the Soviet "sphere of influence." The effort to impose East German control has mainly been on the autobahn, with only a few minor attempts to include East Germans in the checking procedure on the railroads. Moscow evidently considered the heavily traveled autobahn route most susceptible to East German encroachment.

This apparent Soviet decision not to press for East German authority on the access

COMMUNICATION ROUTES BETWEEN WEST GERMANY AND BERLIN

routes probably does not please the East Berlin leaders, who are sensitive on the sovereignty issue and would like to push ahead to improve their regime's status wherever possible. Concern over this issue may be one reason party boss Ulbricht is presently conferring with Khrushchev on the Black Sea coast.

According to Albert Norden, East German party politburo member, Ulbricht intends "to stay as close as possible" to Khrushchev in order to make sure the Soviet leader does not waver in his resolve to abide by previously agreed positions on the German and Berlin questions. Ulbricht may fear that Khrushchev, in his coming talks with President Eisenhower, may make

SECRET

471

SEC̶RET

CURRENT INTELLIGENCE WEEKLY SUMMARY

27 August 1959

some concession at the expense of East German aspirations for sovereignty.

While an agreement that would bar East Germany permanently from trying to assert its sovereignty over the ac-

cess routes is unlikely to result from the Khrushchev-Eisenhower exchange, the East Germans will probably be restrained from interfering with Allied traffic at least until after the visits.

NR

SECRET

SNIE 100-5-60
22 March 1960

SECRET

SPECIAL
NATIONAL INTELLIGENCE ESTIMATE
NUMBER 100-5-60

THE SOVIET ATTITUDE AND TACTICS
ON THE BERLIN PROBLEM

THE SOVIET ATTITUDE AND TACTICS ON THE BERLIN PROBLEM

THE PROBLEM

To estimate the current Soviet attitude on the Berlin problem and the manner in which Soviet tactics may develop over the next several months.

THE ESTIMATE

The Current Soviet Approach To the Berlin Issue

1. The issue of West Berlin probably seems to the Soviets to be a key one in the May Summit meeting. Although they have subordinated it, at least in a formal sense, to the other agenda items of disarmament and a peace treaty for Germany, they probably do not expect any very far-reaching results at this first Summit on these latter problems. They probably think that there is a fair chance that the Western Powers will take some step toward accommodation on the Berlin issue if the Soviet case is pressed hard and skillfully.

2. Their hope for a success of some sort on Berlin in the Summit negotiations evidently rests on a genuine confidence in the strength of the Soviet position. Khrushchev undoubtedly hopes that the Western Powers will be disposed to make concessions because they recognize that the USSR is capable of and intends unilateral actions which, if reacted against with force, would involve them in greater risks than they are willing to take. Apparently contributing also to Soviet confidence is a continuing belief, which was manifest during the Geneva Foreign Ministers meetings, that the Western Powers may not be able to maintain a united front against Soviet demands.

3. Reflecting this appraisal of the situation, as well as an attempt to build up a strong bargaining position in advance of the Summit, there has been a noticeable hardening of Soviet public statements on the Berlin question in recent months. The threat of a separate peace treaty with East Germany has become more insistent and innuendoes about the consequences of this act for the Western position in Berlin more ominous. In thus attempting to build up pressure Khrushchev has come as close as possible to repudiating his pledges against issuing an ultimatum without actually doing so. The Soviets are probably aware that a too obvious and excessive use of pressure could have the effect of compromising the move for detente which they claim to want, or possibly even prejudice Western attendance at the Summit Conference. But their dilemma is that they realize that, without pressure at least in the background, the Western Powers have no incentive to consider the Soviet demands on Berlin seriously at all.

4. There is a sense, we believe, in which the Soviets do genuinely want a detente. In many respects, Khrushchev's internal policies and his plans for competing against Western influence in uncommitted areas would be

474

favored by some degree of cold war truce. Nevertheless, the Soviets' understanding of what constitutes detente continues to be defined in terms of Western concessions or, as they put it, "abandonment by the West of cold war positions." This is not all hypocrisy; Khrushchev probably really believes that the West should see the Soviet gains in power as a reason for finally accepting the status quo in Eastern Europe, adjusting the "abnormal" situation in Berlin, and giving at least de facto recognition to East Germany. While Khrushchev spoke on 31 October of "mutual concessions," this note has not been sustained, and there is currently no sign that the Soviets intend to approach the Berlin problem in a spirit of what the West would consider mutual accommodation.

5. We do not believe that the Soviets' desire for a relaxation of tensions is urgent enough to exclude tactics of very severe pressure on the West in pursuit of their objectives in Berlin. While the language of relaxation and peaceful coexistence is the same as that which has been employed by Soviet policy on other occasions during a negotiating phase, it now clothes a fundamentally different motivation. Negotiation is not now conceived, as so often earlier, as a tactical maneuver to cope with an enemy of superior power, but rather as a procedure to obtain peaceful delivery of the concessions which the Soviets consider their growing power entitles them to expect. This reasoning applies particularly to the case of West Berlin which the Soviets now see as an overextended Western position. In this mood, they will not be willing to accept for long a total rebuff to their demands without an attempt to increase the pressures very substantially.

Tactics at the Summit

6. When the Paris meeting opens the initial Soviet position is likely to be a maximum one—participation of the two German states, a peace treaty or treaties with them on the basis of the Soviet draft, and the Free City arrangement for West Berlin. We do not believe that Khrushchev will allow the issue of German participation to endanger the conference, and even the Soviet peace treaty draft is likely to

be pushed only pro forma. As for Berlin itself, the Soviets already are on record as being willing to approach their objectives by stages, or through an interim agreement limited in time. Therefore, in negotiations concerning Berlin, the hard bargaining areas for the Soviets will be: (a) whether in principle the "abnormal" situation in Berlin should be altered (this will exclude explicit acceptance of the West's principle that its rights continue until Germany is unified); and (b) what first steps should be taken toward altering the "occupation regime" in West Berlin in the direction of a new status. Since the Summit conference will be of too brief duration to permit any intricate or prolonged maneuvers in developing a negotiating position, we expect that these essentials of the Soviet position will appear fairly promptly.

7. This approach probably excludes any Soviet design for a major tension-producing showdown in the Summit itself. It means that the Soviets will not insist upon achieving their full Free City plan at once. We believe that they would be satisfied to obtain undertakings which would mark Western consent to *begin* changing the situation in West Berlin. The Soviets may even be willing to accept a certain ambiguity about the meaning of the steps taken. They recognize that the ability of the West to maintain its position in Berlin depends, to a critical degree, on a belief on the part of the West Berlin population in the will and power of the West to preserve the freedom of the city. If the steps taken were viewed in Berlin as likely to lead ultimately to Western withdrawal, a major loss of confidence in the intentions of the Western Powers would result, and could undermine the situation politically and cause severe economic disruption. Unfavorable reactions in West Germany also would probably further contribute to the political and economic weakening of the situation in Berlin. In such an atmosphere, the Soviets would expect to move still more rapidly toward the outcome they seek.

8. Consequently, the steps for which they are most likely to press in order to give the impression of Western retreat will probably include: a reduction in Western troop strengths;

3

removal of West German political and administrative activities from the city; a formal repudiation by the Western Powers of any constitutional link between West Berlin and the Federal Republic; Soviet (and if possible East German) participation in a supervisory commission to control "subversive activities" and otherwise to "reduce tensions" in West Berlin during an interim phase of limited duration. We are unable to judge whether such steps, or which of them, would constitute the minimum Soviet position. It is possible that the real minimum would be simply an agreement to resume negotiations on Berlin with terms of reference which the Soviets could interpret as a step toward an eventual outcome favorable to them.

9. It is possible, but we think unlikely, that the Soviets would be willing to postpone their demands on the Berlin issue if they thought there were good prospects for progress on other issues. The disarmament field, taken as a whole, is too large and complex and the positions are too far apart to permit of anything the Soviets would be likely to call progress. It is possible that Western concessions on nuclear tests, or on partial disarmament steps in Germany, including restraints on West Germany, could have the effect of removing the Berlin demands from the center of the stage for the time being. However, any postponement of the Berlin issue achieved in this fashion would probably be of brief duration. The development most likely to lead Khrushchev to hold the Berlin issue in abeyance would be agreement for negotiations by a four-power commission or an all-German committee within a set time limit on the terms of a peace treaty with the "two Germanies."

Soviet Actions Post-Summit

10. If the Summit should result in a complete standoff on Berlin, and the Soviets are convinced that no movement in the Western position will be forthcoming, they would have two broad choices. They could agree to a formula for extending negotiation at some level without any Western commitment in principle to agree to a change in the Berlin situation. Probably they would think that to do this would be tantamount to calling off for the present at least the campaign on the Berlin issue which began in November 1958. They would probably not expect to be able to maintain sufficient psychological momentum or pressure if negotiations could thus appear to be extended indefinitely. Alternatively, they could proceed to make the separate treaty with East Germany. Their commitment to do this has been so explicit and so often repeated that we think it likely they have already resolved, barring a development at the Summit favorable to the Soviet demands, to take the step. They probably have not yet decided upon the timing or upon what "consequences" they should apply to the Western position in and access to Berlin.

11. A separate treaty would probably not be signed immediately after the Summit and a decent interval might also be allowed after the President's visit to the USSR, although an announcement that they were beginning consultations with interested parties for such a treaty might come at any time, even immediately after the Summit. In any case, if no prospect of a break in the stalemate appeared within a few months, it is likely that a separate treaty would actually be signed.

12. In taking this step, the Soviets would probably not intend immediately to put a squeeze on access to Berlin. They might use some technicality to delay transferring access controls for several months. And when the transfer took place, they would probably expect the Western Powers to continue to use the access routes under the "agent" theory, although the Soviets would not themselves concede that the East Germans were present at entry points as their agents. In this new phase their principal lever would be the threat of an unacceptable administration of access controls by the East Germans. We believe that even in this phase the Soviets would still seek to achieve their aim of altering the status of Berlin basically through Western agreement in negotiations. However, at some point, depending on their judgment of Western intentions, they might attempt to deny access or to impose conditions which in the Western view were equivalent to denial of access.

SECRET

CONFIDENTIAL

COPY NO. 71
OCI NO. 3819/60

18 August 1960

CURRENT
INTELLIGENCE
WEEKLY
SUMMARY

DOCUMENT NO. 10
NO CHANGE IN CLASS.
DECLASSIFIED
CLASS. CHANGED TO: TS S C
NEXT REVIEW DATE:
AUTH: HR 70-2
DATE _____ REVIEWER _____

CENTRAL INTELLIGENCE AGENCY
OFFICE OF CURRENT INTELLIGENCE

Approved for Release
Date 27 OCT 1966

CONFIDENTIAL

SECRET

PART III

PATTERNS AND PERSPECTIVES

KHRUSHCHEV'S STRATEGY ON BERLIN

Since the breakdown of the summit conference, Communist tactics on the Berlin issue have been gradually brought into line with the more aggressive posture toward the West adopted by Khrushchev. Following an initial period of reassuring gestures by Moscow, the bloc has mounted an extensive psychological warfare operation apparently designed to focus public attention on the dangerous aspects of the Berlin situation and to dispel any notion in the West that Moscow has retreated from its basic demands on the Berlin and German treaty questions.

The dominant element in this campaign remains the threat to conclude a separate peace treaty with East Germany, followed by East German assumption of access controls to Berlin. Public warnings to this effect by Khrushchev, although still imprecise as to manner and timing, have been buttressed by threats voiced in private to Western officials and by an intensified effort to create a state of anxiety and uncertainty in West Berlin, weaken its ties with Bonn, and generate dissension among the Western allies.

Early Post-Summit Tactics

The violence of Khrushchev's performance in Paris, his offhand comments to the press there about a separate peace treaty with East Germany, and the announcement of a stopover in Berlin caused widespread speculation that he would follow through on his frequent presummit threats to take unilateral action and force a showdown on Berlin.

In the atmosphere of heightened tensions, Khrushchev also probably felt compelled to spell out his position as soon as possible.

To the visible displeasure and astonishment of most of his audience at East Berlin, Khrushchev in his speech there on 20 May counseled patience and forbearance on a separate treaty. Asserting the bloc's "moral right" to proceed without delay, he nevertheless held out hope

ULBRICHT AND KHRUSHCHEV

for a new summit meeting and stated, "In these conditions it makes sense to wait a little and to try, by joint efforts of all the victorious powers, to find a solution to the questions." More categorically, Khrushchev declared that the existing situation would have to be maintained until a new meeting, "which, it should be assumed, will take place in six to eight months."

As a condition to this pledge, however, the Soviet leader added that the Western powers would have to adhere to the same principles and take no unilateral steps which would prevent a meeting of the heads

SECRET

of government. He also warned that neither the USSR nor East Germany would wait forever on a peace treaty.

The East German leaders, who apparently had concluded that the Paris debacle signaled a sharp and immediate shift of position on Berlin and Germany, privately pressed Khrushchev for prompt action.

COMMUNICATION ROUTES BETWEEN WEST GERMANY AND BERLIN

In the foreign policy review which undoubtedly took place in the Kremlin, the Soviet leaders probably realized that agreement to maintain the status quo for six to eight months could deprive Soviet policy of a means of pressure to ensure continuing Western interest in negotiating a Berlin settlement. They may also have been concerned over increasing Western speculation that Khrushchev's torpedoing of the summit was designed to cover a retreat on Berlin.

To counter any such impression, Khrushchev used a press conference on 3 June to warn that the Western powers should not delude themselves into believing that if they delayed a summit meeting, a solution of the Berlin and German questions would be "indefinitely postponed." He stated that at the end of the six- to eight-month period, "we shall meet, discuss, and sign a treaty" giving the East Germans full control over access to Berlin. In effect, Khrushchev attempted to put a new US administration on notice that it must be amenable to negotiations on Berlin or face a new and dangerous crisis.

The New Phase

As the more militant campaign against the United States gained momentum, Communist tactics on the Berlin question were considerably sharpened. The East Germans have used a wide variety of means to create a state of anxiety and uncertainty. The principal targets for harassment have been the Allied Military Liaison Missions in East Germany, whose personnel have been physically assaulted, closely watched,

SECRET

restricted in their travel, and subjected to insulting and irritating incidents. The East Germans have also pointed up the vulnerability of West German access to Berlin by detaining West German trucks and warning against "misuse" of the roads and air corridors.

The new moves have been undertaken against a background of East German claims to sovereignty over West Berlin and repeated assertions that the Allies have forfeited all rights through violation of the Potsdam agreements.

The bloc has also initiated a series of moves on the diplomatic level. Both the Soviet and East German regimes have dispatched notes protesting against alleged recruitment in Berlin of personnel for the West German armed forces and against West German plans to establish a radio station in West Berlin. Warsaw has challenged the NATO powers to explain any commitments given Adenauer on recovering territories beyond the Oder-Neisse line, and the Czechs have generally echoed East German statements and protests.

The East German leaders have reportedly made plans for a wide variety of actions ranging from mass disturbances to an outright coup if the Kremlin decides to force a showdown.

Vague hints

of future action are probably designed to recoup the prestige which the East German leaders have lost and to distract attention from serious internal problems. They may also be trying to bolster the sagging morale of the rank-and-file Communists who had expected more action from Khrushchev after the summit.

Bundestag Meeting in Berlin

The most serious threat of action in the immediate future came from Khrushchev during his visit to Austria. In reply to a planted question in his final press conference on 8 July, Khrushchev warned that if Bonn held its annual session of the Bundestag in Berlin this fall, "perhaps at the same time a peace treaty will be signed with East Germany, and thus all Bundestag deputies will have to obtain visas from (East German Premier) Grotewohl to be able to leave Berlin for Bonn."

Khrushchev probably seized on this issue to test the unity and firmness of Western reaction. Realizing the differences which developed among the Allies, Bonn, and Berlin when a similar situation arose in 1959 over holding the West German presidential elections in Berlin, Khrushchev probably anticipated that the issue would again prove divisive and provide Moscow with some indication of Allied policy in the event of a showdown on a separate treaty. As in the past, however, Khrushchev has been careful to avoid committing himself irrevocably in the event the meeting is held. This issue could be used as a pretext for unilateral action, however, should Moscow decide to seek a showdown rather than await new negotiations.

Should Khrushchev decide that his political and diplomatic campaign is failing to generate sufficient pressure on the West, he could instruct the East Germans to provoke further incidents and serious disturbances to underline his claim that the West Berlin situation could "give rise to dangerous accidents." The East German regime can call on some 6,000 Communists already living in the Western sectors and can rapidly infiltrate, if need be, 12,000 to 16,000 members of the specially trained workers' militia (Kampfgruppen). Last October 1,000 to 5,000 Kampfgruppen members were brought over during the riots over the display of the new East German flag on the Berlin elevated railway, which is controlled by the East Germans.

Outlook

In the current phase of Moscow's policy, Berlin remains the test case of whether the Soviet leaders intend to pass from bullying behavior to actions involving grave risks. Khrushchev's handling of the issue thus far suggests that he continues to realize the danger of resorting to unilateral action to advance his objectives, and that he is in no hurry to implement his threats. Since the opening of the Berlin crisis in November 1958, the Kremlin has consistently employed the threat of a transfer of Berlin access controls as a pressure tactic to force negotiations and extract concessions. Since the lapse of the initial six-month ultimatum, Khrushchev has been careful to avoid committing the USSR to a specific time for a separate treaty.

Khrushchev's long and close personal identification with the issue, however, is a compelling reason for him to crown his two-year campaign on Berlin with some significant advance which would justify his past policies and demonstrate their continuing validity. The achievement of some gain by means of negotiation, preferably at the summit, probably has taken on a new significance for him in the face of continuing Chinese Communist criticism of both his methods and his strategy in dealing with the West.

Post-summit statements by Khrushchev and other Communist leaders suggest that the Kremlin may feel that insufficient effort was devoted to propaganda and agitation to build up pressure prior to the Paris meeting. That the Kremlin does not intend to make a similar error was recently evident in *Pravda's* republication of Italian Communist leader Togliatti's remarks:

"While it appeared before that the leaders of all the Western powers, with the exception of Adenauor's Germany, realized the need for a summit conference, it now suddenly became impossible. Consequently a new struggle is required for creating conditions for convening a summit conference and its effective work. New public pressure upon the governments of main capitalist countries is essential...."

With negotiations temporarily in abeyance, Communist tactics will probably continue to reflect Togliatti's call for struggle and pressure.

Despite Khrushchev's apparent intention to hold open the possibility for new negotiations, a long and bitter anti-Western campaign will have the effect of erecting barriers against an attempt to work back toward the conference table. Khrushchev may well overestimate the ease and speed with which he can shift gears. While Moscow probably continues to prefer a further round of negotiations as a necessary prelude to a separate treaty, the day of decision cannot be postponed indefinitely without a substantial loss of prestige for Khrushchev in the eyes of his bloc and Chinese colleagues.

In anticipation of renewed diplomatic pressure to force negotiations in the spring of 1961, the campaign of harassments, probing actions, and political warfare can be expected to intensify. ████████

SECRET

VII: The Wall

VII: The Wall

The enduring problem of the DDR was its utter inability to engender the loyalty of more than a small minority of its citizens. This was, in part, a self-inflicted wound—the product of repression, mismanagement, and the ruthless Sovietization of the economy—in part a reaction to the clearly collaborative nature of the regime and its abject subordination to Moscow. Then, too, East Germans were confronted daily with the example of the Federal Republic, where a liberal democratic state presided over a burgeoning economy that ultimately combined social responsibility with an unprecedented level of prosperity. Within a few years of the founding of the German Democratic Republic, it was apparent to German Marxists that whatever hopes they might have had that it would become a worker's paradise were misplaced. The East German regime remained unable or unwilling to respond positively to the permanent, widespread disaffection of its citizenry. From at least the summer of 1953 onward, the Communist regime survived only through the institution of increasingly thorough instruments of internal repression.

From the perspective of East German President Ulbricht and the leadership of the SED (*Sozialistische Einheits Partei Deutschland*), the latent popular hostility to the Communist regime was most damaging in the steady hemorrhage of refugees from east to west. Between 1949 and 1961 more than 2.7 million East Germans "voted with their feet," leaving East Germany for the Federal Republic, many of them escaping through West Berlin.[1]

In 1958 Ulbricht appealed to the Soviet Union for help, but this was not a problem that Moscow could solve. The Kremlin had economic difficulties of its own and could not afford the kind of massive, continuing aid demanded by the East German leadership. Moreover, nothing would persuade the millions of disaffected East Germans to remain, so long as it was not only more promising, but easier to simply abandon the poverty and repression of the DDR and decamp for the West. In the end, Ulbricht finally put an end to the mass exodus by sealing off the borders. This happened over the night of 12-13 August 1961, when East German troops halted traffic and strung barbed wire along the border separating East from West Berlin. Over the next few months this barrier was expanded and improved to

---

[1] David Childs, *The GDR: Moscow's German Ally* (2nd Edition, London: Unwin Hyman, 1988), p. 64.

become the Berlin Wall, soon to be the universal symbol of the Cold War and of the Soviet tyranny imposed on Eastern Europe. But from first to last it was an East German project, built and maintained by the DDR.[2]

In West Berlin, the closing of the sector borders was not completely unexpected—although the thoroughness, secrecy, and speed with which the East Germans erected their barrier caught everyone off-balance.[3] Washington's first priority was to calm the situation in West Berlin, where the populace was daily confronting the East German guards in massed demonstrations at the now-closed sector borders. There was, of course, little short of war that the US could do to force the East Berlin government to open its border, but, in response to an urgent request by West Berlin Mayor Willy Brandt, President John F. Kennedy ordered that the West Berlin garrison be augmented. Kennedy also dispatched Vice President Lyndon B. Johnson and former military governor Lucius D. Clay to the scene.[4] With the West Berlin government thus reassured, the tension slowly eased.

The construction of the Berlin Wall came at the end of a season of rising international tension. The new Kennedy administration had been humiliated by the Bay of Pigs fiasco that April. In June, Khrushchev tried to bully the Western powers into abandoning Berlin during his Vienna summit with President Kennedy, and on 3 August—days before the Wall went up—he once again threatened to sign a separate peace treaty with the DDR.[5]

Intelligence concerning the sources of Khrushchev's conduct did not make the situation look any less dire. Midsummer reporting from Col. Oleg Penkovsky, the CIA's agent inside the Soviet General Staff, explained Khrushchev's belligerence as the product of Politburo dissatisfaction over his handing of the Berlin situation in general.[6] Threatened with outright deposition, Khrushchev was engaging in brinkmanship to reassert his credibility as a dynamic leader. Penkovsky followed up his initial report on 20 September, when he met with his CIA contacts in Paris, to warn them of plans to use massively augmented Warsaw Pact military exercises as a cover for mil-

---

[2] Although East German President Walter Ulbricht apparently consulted with Khrushchev during a 3-5 August conference in Moscow, the initiative was his. For a thorough analysis, see Hope M. Harrison, "Ulbricht and the Concrete 'Rose': New Archival Evidence on the Dynamics of Soviet-East German Relations and the Berlin Crisis, 1958-1961," *Cold War International History Project* (Washington, DC: Woodrow Wilson International Center for Scholars, 1993).

[3] Even the KGB had only minimal warning. Oleg Gordievsky, *Next Stop Execution* (London: Macmillan, 1995), pp. 93-96. See also Murphy et al., pp. 378-380. CIA agent Oleg Penkovsky later reported that he had four days' notice of the Wall's construction, but could not get word to his Agency handlers in time. See Document. VII-11, Paragraph 21, below.

[4] David E. Murphy, Sergei Kondrashev, and George Bailey, *Battleground Berlin,* (New Haven CT: Yale University Press, 1997), pp. 379-380.

[5] John W. Young, *Longman Companion to Cold War and Détente, 1941-91* (London and New York: Longman, 1993), p. 44.

[6] See Document VII-5, below.

itary action against the Federal Republic. The signing of a separate peace treaty with the DDR was to be announced at the 22nd Congress of the Soviet Communist Party in October. [7] This last report was examined warily in yet another SNIE considering Soviet tactics regarding Berlin. [8] Western policymakers looked to the coming of autumn with considerable misgivings.

But Ulbricht's construction of the Berlin Wall already had provided the decisive action needed to defuse the situation. Khrushchev did not, in the end, come forward with his proposed peace treaty, but went off on another tangent, using the Party Congress as a forum to denounce the USSR's erstwhile ally, the People's Republic of China! Neither did the anticipated Soviet military exercises occur in East Germany. Instead, tension peaked over 27-29 October with a confrontation between Soviet and US tanks at Checkpoint Charlie. Europe briefly seemed on the brink of war, but after a few days, first the Soviet and then the American tanks slowly withdrew. As the noise of their diesel motors faded, so did Berlin's role as the focal point of the Cold War.

Looking back, the tank confrontation at Checkpoint Charlie seems little more than an anticlimax—at least insofar as the intelligence war was concerned. The construction of the Berlin Wall put an end to the classical period of intelligence activity in Cold War Berlin. With one stroke, Ulbricht's action neutralized the effect of the Western intelligence presence while simultaneously solving the refugee problem and stabilizing the Communist regime. Intelligence activities did not cease with the construction of the Berlin Wall, but with ready access to the East cut off, the value of the city as a base of operations was considerably diminished.

The Wall thus achieved much of what the Soviets and East Germans had been trying to do since the creation of the quadripartite regime in 1945. Khrushchev accordingly claimed a triumph, but, ironically, the Wall was built just as photoreconnaissance satellites and other sophisticated technical means of collection were undercutting Berlin's importance as a strategic intelligence base deep inside Soviet territory. After August 1961 the intelligence activities in the city gradually faded from the limelight, but it is difficult to say whether this happened because the East Germans had eliminated its usefulness as an intelligence base or whether Berlin was simply superseded by more sophisticated and reliable means of collecting strategic intelligence on the Soviet Bloc.

---

[7] See Document VII-11, below.
[8] See Document VII-13, below.

Those most affected by the construction of the Wall were of course the inhabitants of Berlin. The Wall not only stopped the flow of refugees, it cut the economic links between East and West Berlin, depriving thousands of East Germans of their livelihoods. On the other hand, the newly stabilized supply of labor gave the East German economy a needed boost: literally for the first time since World War II, producers in East Germany could be reasonably certain that skilled employees would be in their jobs from one week to the next. By the mid-1960s, East Germany was enjoying a period of relative prosperity.[9]

West Berliners continued to prosper throughout it all, albeit with the aid of considerable support from the Bonn government.[10] Aided by the narrow windows that gradually opened up to the West, East Berliners lived their lives as best they could in the German Communist state. But the Wall remained. Some East Germans at first tried to escape clandestinely, but as the barrier was steadily reinforced with gun towers, dogs, and minefields, escape became riskier and the chances of success faded. Even so, 600 to 700 people continued to make the attempt each year.[11]

VII-1: Memorandum for the DDI: Subject: The Berlin Situation, 1 November 1957 (MORI No. 44001).
This CIA memorandum raised the possibility that the Soviets might abrogate the Quadripartite Agreements and seal the "sector borders" between East and West Berlin as a means of applying pressure on the Western Allies.

VII-2: CIWS: East Germany May Move Against Berlin Sector "Border Crossers" 28 May 1959 (MORI No. 45598).
Before the Wall was built, the economies of East and West Berlin were interwoven, with many East Berliners dependent upon income from jobs in West Berlin's more vibrant economy. The East German regime saw this as a drain on their own struggling economy. The possibility that East Germany (not the Soviet Union) might restrict movement between East and West Berlin thus became an issue in the course of the Berlin crisis.

VII-3: CIWS: Soviet Policy on Berlin and Germany, 11 May 1961 (MORI No. 28202).
This review of Soviet policy regarding Berlin stresses the political importance for Khrushchev of reaching an agreement on Berlin during 1961.

---

[9] Childs, pp. 70-71.
[10] Economic ties to West Germany were re-established in 1970-72, when a new East German President, Erich Honecker, signed a series of economic and political agreements with West German Chancellor Willy Brandt—in 1961 the Governing Mayor of West Berlin.
[11] Childs, p. 64.

VII-4: SNIE 2-61: Soviet and Other Reactions to Various Courses of Action Regarding Berlin, 13 June 1961.

Another in the series of Estimates postulating specific courses of action that might be taken by the US and probable Soviet reactions. This edition for the first time considers the East Germans as actors alongside their Soviet allies.[12]

VII-5: Oleg Penkovsky: Meeting No. 23, 28 July 1961 (MORI No. 12409).[13]

Oleg Penkovsky, the CIA's agent inside Soviet military intelligence and on the General Staff, was privy to information at the highest levels of the Soviet military. In this oral report, delivered on 20 July 1961, he describes the internal tensions undermining Khrushchev's position in the Politburo as they applied to the Berlin situation. Penkovsky did not have the direct access to the Soviet decisionmaking process that this report implies. However, he was very knowledgeable concerning General Staff matters and often was informed about high-level political decisions by his patron, Marshal Sergei Sergeyevich Varentsov. The intelligence he provided to CIA was valued highly.

Penkovsky began spying for the West early in 1961. Over the next 18 months he made several trips to the West, each time meeting clandestinely with his handlers. The following excerpt is from the transcript of one of those meetings. Penkovsky is identified as "S."[14]

VII-6: CIWS: Berlin, 17 August 1961 (MORI No. 28205).

Five days after the Wall went up, this report summarizes developments over 12-17 August.

VII-7: SNIE 11-10-61: Soviet Tactics in the Berlin Crisis, 24 August 1961.

A survey of Soviet policy in light of the changed situation in Berlin and the DDR.

VII-8: CIWS: Berlin, 24 August 1961 (MORI No. 28206).

A more detailed look at developments in Berlin and East Germany.

---

[12] This SNIE updates SNIE 100-6-59, *Soviet and Other Reactions to Various Courses of Action in the Berlin Crisis,* (6 April 1959). Document VI-12 is a version of this Estimate.

[13] This document survives only in the fragmentary form reproduced here.

[14] Penkovsky also provided much documentary material. The standard history of the Penkovsky operation is Jerold L. Schecter and Peter S. Deriabin, *The Spy Who Saved the World* (New York: Charles Scribner's Sons, 1992).

VII-9: CIWS: Berlin, 7 September 1961 (MORI No. 28211).
In the month following the construction of the Berlin Wall, the East German regime initiated a general crackdown to further the "Sovietization" of East Germany and threatened to restrict Western access to Berlin by air.

VII-10: Memorandum for Washington on Berlin, 14 September 1961 (MORI No. 14414).
The construction of the Wall had profound implications for the conduct of intelligence operations in Berlin. These are detailed in a memorandum sent to Washington.

VII-11: Penkovsky, Meeting No. 31, 22th September 1961, paras. 17-25 (MORI No. 12412).
Meeting with his CIA handlers on 20 September 1961, Penkovsky passed important information regarding Khrushchev's contingency plans for military action that Autumn. See Document VII-13, below. "Varentsov" is Marshal Sergei Sergeyevich Varentsov, Penkovsky's patron on the Soviet General Staff. In this transcript, Penkovsky is again identified as "S."

VII-12: Memorandum for the Record: Subject: Conversation with Mr. Helms Re [ ] Report on Large-Scale Soviet Military Preparations, 26 September 1961 (MORI: 12292).

VII-13: SNIE 11-10/1-61: Soviet Tactics in the Berlin Crisis, 5 October 1961.
Upon receipt of Penkovsky's information concerning Khrushchev's plans for the coming fall, the Board of National Estimates prepared a Special National Intelligence Estimate (SNIE) devoted entirely to evaluating his information—a highly unusual procedure. Of particular interest is the nuanced approach to Penkovsky's report.

VII-14: Dispatch: Berlin Since 13 August, 6 November 1961 (MORI No. 14411).
A look at Berlin in the months immediately after the Wall went up.

VII-15: Memorandum for the DCI; Subject: Survivability of West Berlin [in the Event of a Soviet Blockade in Response to the Blockade of Cuba], 23 October 1962 (MORI No. 9409).
The Cuban Missile Crisis raised concerns that the Soviets might retaliate for the blockade of Cuba with a similar action directed against Berlin. Here, the Board of National Estimates reviews West Berlin's ability to withstand another blockade.

SECRET

CENTRAL INTELLIGENCE AGENCY
OFFICE OF CURRENT INTELLIGENCE
1 November 1957

OCI No. 5535/57   Copy No.

TO: Deputy Director (Intelligence)

SUBJECT: The Berlin Situation

There have been several reports in the past week that the Berlin sector borders will be sealed, thus abrogating Berlin's status as a Four-Power city. In this connection, according to the latest information, preparations reportedly have been made which would enable additional trains to operate from Potsdam to East Berlin using the outer ring, bypassing West Berlin.

According to an unconfirmed report East Berlin-Potsdam traffic is to be routed over the Berlin Outer Ring and the wooden S-Bahn stations near the sector border at Baumschulenweg and Friedrichstrasse are to be reactivated. This suggests that S-Bahn traffic through West Berlin is to be greatly restricted to permit customs checks at the wooden stations which were specifically designed for customs checking purposes when built two or three years ago. Steamdriven trains via Baumschulenweg to Potsdam over the Outer Ring could be used to carry passengers to Potsdam. This would restrict, but not eliminate S-Bahn traffic service in West Berlin.

Recent East German harassments have included increased controls over interzonal trains consisting of thorough searches of cargoes, removal of a number of mail cars from trains, and confiscation of parcel post and freight shipments. Highway traffic has been subjected to delays and intensive searches of passengers and cargoes. Threats have been made by the East Germans that they may assume control over the air corridors to Berlin.

SECRET

NO OCB OBJECTION TO DECLASSIFICATION
REQUIRES
DATE

NND 901028-100

SECRET

Soviet interference with Allied traffic has been sporadic and inconsistent. Negotiations on new documentation procedures have been in progress for some time, but the Russians continue to raise objections to Allied procedures on a variety of pretexts.

The East Germans and the Russians have the capability to seal both the zonal and sector borders without prior warning if they should decide to take such a drastic step. An example was the East German regime's 13 October currency conversion with complete secrecy. In connection with the conversion, the regime sealed the Berlin sector borders, and stopped all autobahn traffic between West Germany and Berlin.

This series of harassments of Berlin has been undertaken by the East German regime apparently with the purpose of eroding the Allied position there and establishing East German authority over its zonal territory and East Berlin.

HUNTINGTON D. SHELDON
Assistant Director
Current Intelligence

Orig: GEN DIV
William McCall
ext. 3184

Dist: White House (General Goodpaster)
NSC (Mr. James Lay)
State Dept. (Mr. Hugh S. Cumming, Jr.)
ACSI (Maj. Gen. Robert A Schow)
ACSI (Maj. Gen. Millard Lewis)
ONI (Adm. L. H. Frost)
JCS (Brig. Gen. Richard Collins)
OCB (Mr. Roman Mrozinski)
DCI
DDCI
DDI
DDP
ADNE
ADSI
ADRR

SECRET

901028-101

.33

~~CONFIDENTIAL~~
~~SECRET~~

OCI NO. 2332/59

28 May 1959

CURRENT INTELLIGENCE WEEKLY SUMMARY

CENTRAL INTELLIGENCE AGENCY

OFFICE OF CURRENT INTELLIGENCE

~~CONFIDENTIAL~~
~~SECRET~~

Approved for Release
Date SEP 1993

SECRET

CURRENT INTELLIGENCE WEEKLY SUMMARY

28 May 1959

PART II (continued)

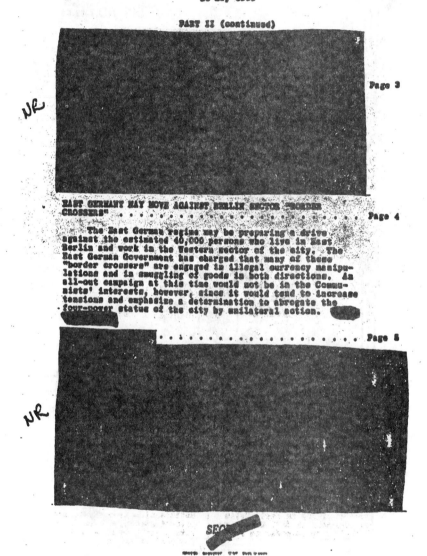

Page 3

Page 4

EAST GERMANY MAY MOVE AGAINST BERLIN SECTOR "BORDER CROSSERS" . . . .

The East German regime may be preparing a drive against the estimated 40,000 persons who live in East Berlin and work in the Western sector of the city. The East German Government has charged that many of these "border crossers" are engaged in illegal currency manipulations and in smuggling of goods in both directions. An all-out campaign at this time would not be in the Communists' interests, however, since it would tend to increase tensions and emphasize a determination to abrogate the four-power status of the city by unilateral action.

. . . . Page 5

SECRET

492

SECRET

CURRENT INTELLIGENCE WEEKLY SUMMARY

28 May 1959

NR

EAST GERMANY MAY MOVE AGAINST BERLIN SECTOR "BORDER CROSSERS"

The East German regime may be preparing a drive against persons who live in East Berlin and work in the Western sector, according to unconfirmed reports from Berlin.

Such a drive against these "border crossers" would have one or more of the following purposes: a) to isolate West Berlin from East Berlin and East Germany; b) to renew pressures on the West Berlin government to negotiate on this issue; c) to force skilled workers living in East Berlin to take jobs in East Berlin or East Germany in order to relieve the serious labor shortage and fill positions opening up in East Germany's expanding industry; and d) to eliminate or reduce the present uncontrolled transactions in East German currency at other than official rates.

The Communists are not likely to undertake an all-out campaign at this time, however, since it would tend to increase tensions and emphasize a determination to abrogate the four-power status of the city by unilateral action. Under Berlin's present status, all residents have a right to move freely to any part of the city.

SECRET

PART II   NOTES AND COMMENTS   Page 4 of 19

CURRENT INTELLIGENCE WEEKLY SUMMARY

28 May 1959

An estimated 40,000 residents of East Berlin or East Germany now work in the Western sector, an increase of some 6,000 since 1957, while during the same period the number of West Berlin residents working in East Berlin declined from approximately 16,000 to about 13,900. The East German Government has charged that many border crossers are engaged in illegal currency manipulation and in smuggling of goods in both directions. Under present arrangements the East-to-West border crossers receive 40 percent of their wages in West marks and the remainder in East marks at a 6-to-1 rate. The West-to-East crossers are permitted to exchange 90 percent of their wages into West marks at the official 1-to-1 rate. Since the present free-market rate of exchange is about 3.8 East marks to 1 West mark, the border crossers can realize a tidy bonus.

In addition to the advantages of the currency situation and the opportunity to shop in both parts of the city, there are other reasons why many residents of East Berlin continue to live there. One of the most important is the continued housing shortage in both parts of the city, despite the vast amount of building in West Berlin. If a person has a house, even in East Berlin, he will try to keep it rather than move to West Berlin through refugee channels and go to the bottom of the long list of people waiting for housing.

The East German regime undertook brief intensive campaigns in 1957 and in 1958 to reduce the number of border crossers. The major result of such campaigns was to induce the border crossers to make a permanent move to West Berlin or West Germany. A new drive at this time probably would have a similar result.

NR

PART II   NOTES AND COMMENTS   Page 6 of 19

~~CONFIDENTIAL~~

~~SECRET~~

COPY NO.

OCI NO. 0279/61

11 May 1961

CURRENT INTELLIGENCE WEEKLY SUMMARY

CENTRAL INTELLIGENCE AGENCY

OFFICE OF CURRENT INTELLIGENCE

Approved for Release
Date 17 OCT 1986

~~SECRET~~

CONFIDENTIAL (9)

CURRENT INTELLIGENCE WEEKLY SUMMARY

SOVIET POLICY ON BERLIN AND GERMANY

The crisis over Berlin precipitated by Khrushchev on 10 November 1958 was the logical extension of the policies developed by the Soviet leaders following the Western decision in 1955 to accord full sovereignty to West Germany and bring it into the NATO alliance. Having failed to block these developments, Moscow adopted a new course aimed at gaining Western acceptance of the concept of two Germanys.

Its initial move in this direction was to establish diplomatic relations with Bonn in September 1955. The USSR then concluded a state treaty with Ulbricht's regime granting it all the attributes of sovereignty except control over Allied access to West Berlin. Next, Molotov at the Geneva foreign ministers' conference in November 1955 rejected reunification of Germany by means of free elections and declared that unification was possible only through a rapprochement between the two German states.

Thereafter the USSR took the position that a peace treaty should be negotiated with and signed by the two German states. Previously, the Soviets had said a treaty would be concluded with a reunified Germany. This new approach still left two significant issues unresolved: the status of Berlin and the conclusion of a final peace settlement. Therefore the final step in this policy was the crisis over Berlin and the Soviet demands for a peace treaty with East and West Germany and a "free city" in West Berlin.

Berlin Crisis: 1958-60

Khrushchev's aim was to confront the Western powers with the apparent dilemma of risking war to maintain their existing rights in Berlin or making concessions which would erode their position not only in Berlin but also on the question of German unification. In addition to using the Berlin threat as a lever for overcoming Western resistance to a summit meeting under conditions favorable to the USSR, Khrushchev's strategy was to manipulate the Berlin issue as a means of wringing concessions from the West which could lead eventually to some form of recognition of the East German regime and to acceptance of the status quo in Eastern Europe.

Since May 1959, when negotiations opened at the Geneva foreign ministers' conference, Khrushchev's fundamental goal has been not to drive Western forces out of Berlin within some brief period but to bring about a basic change in the legal status of the city. Such a change, in Moscow's view, would seriously undermine the Western powers' long-standing insistence that their rights in Berlin--based on the unconditional surrender of Germany--continue until Germany is reunified by four-power agreement.

The Soviet position, therefore, has consisted of two main elements: an offer to negotiate a modification in Berlin's status, and a threat to take unilateral action if no agreement is reached. Moscow's initial demand for the creation of a free city and all subsequent amendments, including a compromise solution for an interim period, have aimed at liquidating Western rights to remain in Berlin without restrictions pending German unification. Since the West has no interest in negotiating away its rights, Moscow has used deadlines, either explicit or implicit, to guarantee continuing Western interest in discussing the issue in order to avoid a crisis.

The breakdown of the summit conference in Paris confronted

SECRET

496

SECRET

CURRENT INTELLIGENCE WEEKLY SUMMARY

Khrushchev with the choice of carrying out his threat against Berlin and accepting the high risks involved or deferring action until a further round of negotiations could be attempted with a new American administration. His choice of the latter course reflected not only his preference for a policy of limited risks but also his confidence that the forces which brought about the Paris meeting were still operative in the West.

Soviet restraint, however, did not preclude attempts by the East Germans to undermine the Western position in Berlin by imposing arbitrary restrictions on the movements of West Germans into East Berlin. In the face of West German economic retaliation, the Communists gradually retreated and accepted a compromise settlement of the issue, partly because of the potential economic disruption which would result from a break in trade but also because of Khrushchev's desire not to jeopardize the chances for an early meeting with the new President.

Khrushchev also used this period between the summit conference and the change of administrations to spell out his future course. He began to lay the groundwork for new high-level negotiations on Berlin in his discussion with Prime Minister Macmillan in New York last fall. He told the prime minister that the heads of government would have to discuss Germany and Berlin and that the Soviet Union would sign a treaty with East Germany if the West refused to reach agreement. He said that, in any case, the question of Germany must be settled during 1961. Khrushchev made this position public on 20 October and informed West German Ambassador Kroll that postponement of a solution beyond the West German elections, scheduled for this September, would be unacceptable.

In a recent conversation with Kroll, Khrushchev modified his earlier timetable. While strongly emphasizing his determination to achieve a solution during 1961, Khrushchev stated that the bloc had set no precise deadlines and would be willing to wait until the West German elections and "possibly" until the Soviet party congress in October before convening a bloc peace conference to sign a separate treaty with East Germany. He said also that the prospects of a showdown over Berlin "need not affect negotiations already begun with the US" and that he was willing to give the President more time.

This line and Khrushchev's repeated assurances in his recent interview with Walter Lippmann that he recognized that the President needed time to consolidate his position suggest that Khrushchev's future course is still closely tied to his desire to hold a high-level meeting on Berlin, either bilaterally with the US or at another four-power summit conference. At the same time, these statements probably reflect the Soviet leaders' awareness that East-West negotiations on Berlin will require considerably more time than Khrushchev anticipated after the summit breakdown and in private conversations last winter.

The Soviet Position

The USSR's maximum demands have remained essentially unaltered since first spelled out in the notes of 27 November 1958 and 10 January 1959; they were most recently restated in Moscow's memorandum to Bonn on 17 February 1961. The USSR proposes to conclude a peace treaty with both German states and to transform West Berlin into a demilitarized free city. This position was modified slightly at the Geneva foreign ministers' conference, when Gromyko proposed that "symbolic" units of the four

SECRET

VII-3: *(Continued)*

powers could be stationed in the free city.

The repeated references to the necessity of confirming the postwar situation in Europe, although designed in part to present Soviet demands in a reasonable light, also reflect the Soviet leaders' preoccupation with firmly establishing the international position of the East European regimes through a treaty freezing the partition of Germany and recognizing the East German boundaries as permanent international frontiers.

Khrushchev is well aware that the growing strength of West Germany poses a serious political, economic, and military challenge to the Ulbricht regime and to the East European governments bordering on Germany. By demanding a peace treaty, a free city, and complete East German control over communications to Berlin, Khrushchev is seeking to deal a decisive blow to Bonn's aspirations for unification and to undermine its confidence in the strength and unity of the Western alliance.

In his talks with Lippmann, however, Khrushchev indicated that he does not hold any great expectations for Western acceptance of a peace treaty with both Germanys. Recent Soviet

statements provide strong evidence that Moscow instead will concentrate on obtaining a temporary or interim solution for Berlin. The memorandum to Bonn stated as much, and Khrushchev told Lippmann that such an interim solution was a Soviet "fallback" position. Khrushchev made it clear, however, that the USSR would press for an agreement abolishing Western occupation rights at the end of the interim period. The revival of the interim concept, well in advance of any negotiations, suggests that Moscow sees this as the only proposal realistic enough to gain Western agreement.

The interim agreement as originally outlined at the Geneva foreign ministers' conference has three main advantages for the USSR: 1) a strictly defined time limit, which would permit Moscow to reopen the question with a stronger legal and political position; 2) the implication that the Western powers remained in Berlin at the sufferance of the USSR; and 3) the link between an interim agreement and the establishment of an all-German negotiating body. In effect, the Soviet leaders hoped to induce the West to accept a revision of Berlin's status in the direction of the free city proposals in return for permission to maintain troops in and to have free access to Berlin for a limited period.

At Geneva, Foreign Minister Gromyko refused to clarify the status of Western rights at the end of this period and proposed only that negotiations be resumed with "due regard" to the situation prevailing at that time. The interim agreement, therefore, was intended as a stage leading toward the ultimate withdrawal of Western forces from Berlin. This position was made clear shortly before the Paris summit meeting, when Moscow proposed in a note to De

498

Gaulle that the interim period last for two years, but that at the end of the period the four powers would be committed to sign a peace treaty and "take measures" to create a free city in West Berlin.

A constant element in all Soviet formulations for a temporary solution of Berlin's status has been the proposal to convene an all-German commission to negotiate on unification and a peace treaty while the interim agreement was in effect. Khrushchev has privately conceded that he realized that such negotiations would probably fail, but the USSR has insisted on this proposal as a means of gaining Western endorsement of the thesis of two sovereign German states and their exclusive right to deal with unification.

The other points of an interim agreement--duration, abolition of propaganda activities, prohibition of nuclear weapons in West Berlin, and reduction of Western troops-- are essentially bargaining counters. East German statements have listed various terms for "normalizing" the situation, including cessation of recruitment in West Berlin for the West German forces, termination of the West German Government's official activities there, and a "progressive reduction" of Western forces. As to the duration, Khrushchev is quoted by Lippmann as mentioning "perhaps two to three years," which could mean an extension of the last formal proposal--before the Paris summit--for a two-year agreement.

Conclusions

Despite Khrushchev's repeated expressions of skepticism

regarding the West's willingness to resort to a nuclear war over Berlin, his actions during the past two and a half years suggest that a margin of doubt exists in his estimate of the Western response in a crisis, and that he still prefers a negotiated solution. Recent Soviet statements stressing the urgency of the German question suggest that a formal demarche to renew negotiations may be made in the relatively near future. Khrushchev probably would contend that the Western powers, after the abortive summit conference, committed themselves to reconvene the meeting and would cite his conversation with Macmillan as proof.

In any negotiations which take place in the next few months, Moscow might reduce some of its demands for an interim settlement rather than allow the talks to collapse. The main purpose of a limited agreement, however, would still be to document the Soviet contention that existing Allied rights are void and to establish the presumption that further steps would be taken to adjust the status of West Berlin.

If the West refused to negotiate, Khrushchev would probably feel compelled to conclude a separate treaty. His long and continuing commitments to take this action probably act as a form of pressure either to demonstrate gains by negotiations or to carry out his repeated pledges to resolve the situation in Berlin by unilateral action. At any rate, Khrushchev has committed himself to a solution during 1961.

SECRET

TOP SECRET

58

TS# 2317
Limited distribution
SNIE 2-61
13 April 1961

SPECIAL NATIONAL INTELLIGENCE ESTIMATE

SOVIET AND OTHER REACTIONS TO VARIOUS COURSES OF ACTION REGARDING BERLIN

WEST BERLIN

** ACCOUNTABLE DOCUMENT **
RETURN TO P/CDI REGISTRY,
Room 7E47 Hqs.

Central Intelligence Agency

Submitted by the

DIRECTOR OF CENTRAL INTELLIGENCE

The following intelligence organizations participated in the preparation of this estimate: The Central Intelligence Agency and the intelligence organizations of the Departments of State, the Army, the Navy, the Air Force, and The Joint Staff.

Concurred in by the

UNITED STATES INTELLIGENCE BOARD

on 13 June 1961* Concurring were the Director of Intelligence and Research, Department of State; the Assistant Chief of Staff for Intelligence, Department of the Army; the Assistant Chief of Naval Operations (Intelligence), Department of the Navy; the Assistant Chief of Staff, Intelligence, USAF; the Director for Intelligence, Joint Staff; the Assistant to the Secretary of Defense, Special Operations; and the Director of the National Security Agency. The Atomic Energy Commission Representative to the USIB and the Assistant Director, Federal Bureau of Investigation, abstained, the subject being outside of their jurisdiction.

*This estimate was approved by the USIB on 13 June 1961, subject to certain further action by USIB representatives, consulting as necessary with their principals (USIB-M-159, item 4). This latter action was completed on 19 June 1961.

~~TOP SECRET~~

CENTRAL INTELLIGENCE AGENCY

13 June 1961.

SUBJECT: SNIE 2-61:   SOVIET AND OTHER REACTIONS TO VARIOUS
COURSES OF ACTION REGARDING BERLIN

THE PROBLEM

To estimate Soviet and other reactions to four courses
of Allied (US, UK, and France) action in the event of an unacceptable degree of Soviet or East German interference with
Western access to West Berlin. The courses of action are:
(a) a substantial effort to maintain ground access to West
Berlin by a limited military action; (b) a substantial effort
to maintain air access; (c) other pressures and reprisals
against the USSR and East Germany; and (d) large-scale preparations for general war.

~~TOP SECRET~~

SCOPE NOTE

This estimate is a revision of SNIE 100-6-59, dated
6 April 1959.[1] The courses of action considered in that
estimate have been altered and expanded in the present paper.

THE ESTIMATE

1. It is now two and one-half years since the USSR projected the Berlin issue into the forefront of East-West contention. During this period the USSR has persisted with great
seriousness in its attempts to bring about a change in the
status of the city. At the same time, the intervening events
have almost certainly caused the Soviet leaders to increase
considerably their estimate of the importance attached by the
US to the Western position in Berlin and of the lengths to
which the US would go to defend it.

2. During this same period, attitudes in France, the
UK, and West Germany have also undergone some change. On
the one hand, the sense of vulnerability in these countries
has grown with advances in Soviet weaponry and corresponding
increases in Soviet confidence and assertiveness. On the

---

[1] SNIE 100-6-59, "Soviet and Other Reactions to Various
Courses of Action in the Berlin Crisis," dated 6 April
1959, TOP SECRET, LIMITED DISTRIBUTION.

- 2 -

other hand, these countries have drawn encouragement from the fact that the Soviets, at least to date, have been unwilling to implement threats which initially seemed to foreshadow immediate encroachments. There has also been time for the Western Powers to explore the Soviet position and to canvass a variety of possible concessions which might accommodate the USSR without jeopardizing the essentials of the Western position. This process has led to a wide measure of agreement that the Soviet purpose is, ultimately, absorption of the city by the GDR rather than some lesser objective.

3. Nevertheless, while much has been clarified, much remains uncertain. In particular, each side finds it difficult to reach a confident judgment of the point at which the other would be willing to run substantial military risks over Berlin. In these circumstances, the USSR will almost certainly continue its efforts to induce the Allies to negotiate their own gradual departure from the city. Throughout these maneuvers, however, the Soviet leaders will be continually reassessing the willingness of the three Western Powers to defend their interests with force. In this appraisal, they will consider the official positions and military dispositions of the Allied governments. But they will also have to make judgments about

- 3 -

intangibles -- the willingness of each government to disregard or be guided by the advice of its partners; the degree
to which each is influenced by domestic public opinion; the
readiness of each, in a moment of crisis, to assume risks
which may run as high as general nuclear war.

4. In deciding when and how to move against Allied access
to Berlin, the Soviet leaders will seek to turn these factors
to their own advantage. They will precede any such move with
diplomatic measures designed to demonstrate that they are resorting to unilateral action only after all other alternatives
have been exhausted. These measures may include another round
of negotiations and, almost certainly, a separate peace treaty
with the GDR intended to provide both another warning and another occasion for the Allies to reconsider their position.

5. Even after these steps have been accomplished, the
USSR and the GDR almost certainly will not explicitly deny
access to Berlin. Instead, they will simply make Allied access
subject to certain new conditions, beginning presumably with
the replacement of Soviet by East German controllers in the
access procedures. They will almost certainly not attempt
at the same time to close off Berlin from West German civilian
access, which is already under East German control. Thus the

- 4 -

TOP SECRET

USSR will hope to make it as difficult as possible for the
Allied governments to conclude that the new situation is a
clear-cut denial of access, to agree among themselves on
strong countermeasures, and to justify these to their populations.

6. In spite of such Soviet efforts, however, there has
been, according to the terms of our problem, an "unacceptable"
degree of interference with Western access to Berlin. It is
assumed that the US, UK, and France have therefore agreed in
undertaking one or more of the stated courses of action.2/
The subsequent course of the crisis would be heavily influenced by the particular context of events at the time when
access was interfered with. Further, the exact nature of
tactical moves, and the manner in which they were made, would
have important effects on the way in which each side assessed
the continuing resolution and intentions of the other. An
added difficulty is that we necessarily treat each course
first in isolation, although we recognize that its effect
might be greater if it were combined with other actions. We
have therefore attempted only to describe the basic factors

2/ It should be stressed that this assumption is by no means
an estimate of British and French willingness to agree to
all of these courses of action.

- 5 -

TOP SECRET

TOP SECRET

underlying Soviet and other reactions to these courses, recognizing that these reactions will also be influenced by specific elements of the situation which cannot now be foreseen.

> COURSE A: A substantial effort to reopen and maintain ground access by a limited military action -- defined as the utilization of up to two reinforced divisions with tactical air support in readiness if required. The force would proceed on the autobahn toward Berlin. If its movement was opposed, it would attempt to overcome resistance and to secure the road.

7. In their advance planning for their introduction of new access procedures, the Soviets would have considered a reaction on this scale as possible but unlikely; if they had judged it to be probable, they almost certainly would have avoided provoking it. They probably would not conclude from this reaction alone that the Allies had taken a firm decision to press all the way to general war if necessary; yet they could not be certain that they would not miscalculate further Western steps as they had the first. They would wish to minimize the risks of general war, and they would be gravely concerned lest large-scale fighting within East Germany create

- 6 -

TOP SECRET

an uncontrollable situation. Yet they would regard their prestige as being heavily engaged, and they would greatly fear that failure to act would undermine Communist authority in East Germany, and perhaps lead to popular uprisings.

8. We believe it virtually certain that the Soviets would not permit Western forces to seize control of the entire autobahn and march unopposed into Berlin. They would probably try first to block the Western forces at or near the zonal border, using forces moved into position as soon as Allied preparations were noted. If this failed, and a substantial penetration occurred, the Soviets would seek at a minimum to halt and neutralize the Western forces and, probably, to force their withdrawal. In general, we think that they would undertake the minimum response necessary to accomplish their objective, recognizing that, the larger the scale of any military engagement, the greater would be the risks of a further expansion of the conflict.

9. In the first stage, it is probable that the USSR would use East German troops, in order to be consistent with the claim of GDR sovereignty and to postpone a Soviet-Western confrontation until it became clear how far the West intended to go in its initial local action. We believe, however, that the USSR would commit its own troops whenever it became clear

- 7 -

that East German forces could not deal with the situation.
The Soviets would not use other Satellite troops.

10.   Throughout, the Soviets would seek to keep the
fighting limited and to bring it quickly to an end, in a
manner which would demonstrate that a Western resort to force
was bound to fail. At the same time, they would mount an intense campaign in support of a call for immediate negotiations,
calculating that this would redound to their credit, generate
pressure on the Allies to desist, and perhaps contribute to
an end to hostilities. They would probably refrain from
molesting West Berlin; we do not believe, however, that they
would immediately offer to restore the former conditions of
access. Their political and psychological activities would
be employed as a supplement to military action rather than a
substitute for it.

As a step subsequent to the above, the commit-
ment of West German troops as reinforcements. [3]

11.   The reinforcement with West German forces would presumably occur only after some fighting had already taken place.
Simply because it was a reinforcement, the Soviets would probably give increased weight to the possibility that the West

[3] We do not here estimate whether or not the Federal
Republic would agree to this course of action.

- 8 -

TOP SECRET

was prepared to go very far and take very great risks in defense of its position in Berlin. The fact that West German
forces were used would probably cause the Soviets also to
fear that the conflict might transform itself into a liberation campaign, involving East German Army defections and popular risings. The Soviets would therefore probably regard
any failure to defeat such a force quickly as highly dangerous
to their position in East Germany in Eastern Europe as a
whole.

12. The possibility that the Soviets might decide to
seize the initiative with a general nuclear attack on the
West would rise with the commitment of West German troops,
even though no more than minimal surprise would be possible
at this point. However, we regard this as very unlikely.
Their most probable response would be an intensification of
political pressure and a major military effort, although
still nonnuclear, to expel the Western forces. We believe
that they would still wish to confine the encounter to East
German territory, because of a fear that to retaliate against
or invade West Germany could lead rapidly to general war.

COURSE B: A substantial effort to maintain
air access -- defined as efforts to continue

- 9 -

TOP SECRET

510

TOP SECRET

flights unilaterally following attempts by the
USSR and the GDR to alter existing flight procedures. If there were interference which en-
dangered the safety of aircraft in the corridors,
Allied combat aircraft would come to their assistance.

13. This contingency is most likely to arise by way of
Soviet withdrawal from the Berlin Air Safety Center and Allied
refusal to accept an East German substitute. In taking such
a step, the USSR would probably have concluded in advance that
the West would react initially by continuing flights to Berlin
without the usual guarantees of safety, and accordingly would
have planned its next step.

14. The Soviets and East Germans would probably employ
means of interference short of firing upon aircraft. If the
Allies felt obliged to employ combat aircraft as escorts, we
do not believe that the Soviets would even then actually fire
upon planes which remained within the corridor, although the
likelihood of their doing so would increase. Actual firing
would cause them to appear before the world as the initiator
of hostilities, and they would probably prefer to limit themselves to electronic countermeasures (ECM), "buzzing," and

- 10 -

TOP SECRET

TOP SECRET

other nonviolent actions. If Allied aircraft opened-fire, however, Bloc aircraft would probably return it.

15. The Soviet and East German capability for electronic countermeasures in the Berlin area and the air corridors is sufficient to limit Western air traffic to that which could be maintained under visual flight conditions. Such limitations would not be serious if ground access to West Berlin remained open for West German civilians and their goods. Even if a complete blockade of ground access were established, ECM alone would not succeed in preventing the movement of essential supplies to the city by visual flights, although Berlin's industry would be seriously disrupted. The use of ECM together with other forms of harassment short of actual combat would reduce the volume of flight traffic still further, but the effectiveness of these tactics would depend on the degree of deprivation which West Berlin was willing to bear; stockpiles in the city are sufficient for a considerable period of time.[4/]

> COURSE C: Other pressures and reprisals --
> e.g., tripartite interference with Soviet
> and East German merchant shipping, Allied and

4/ These stockpiles include basic foods sufficient for at least a year, a 12-month supply of hard coal, and a six-month supply of brown coal briquettes, dry milk, dehydrated vegetables, clothing, and medical supplies. West Berlin has its own utilities, with the exception of sewage disposal.

- 11 -

TOP SECRET

<u>West German economic sanctions, the rupture</u>
<u>of diplomatic relations, and other retaliatory</u>
<u>measures.</u>

16. We believe that such measures are among those that
the Soviet leaders would expect in the way of Allied reactions
to altered conditions of access to Berlin. Taken by themselves,
they would probably have the effect of strengthening the Soviet
judgment that the Allies were unwilling to risk the direct
use of force against any but the most clear-cut challenge to
their position in Berlin.

17. The Soviet response would probably be limited largely
to propaganda, to diplomatic and legal counteraction, and, in
the case of naval controls, to reprisals in the form of detention of Allied shipping in areas of Communist control and
closing of certain waters to Allied vessels. The USSR could
circumvent controls by recourse to ships of other flags and
by overland shipments if it felt obliged to do so. It might
use armed escorts for its shipping where feasible.

18. Allied naval measures and economic sanctions, even
in combination, would have little effect on the Soviet economy.
The repercussions for East Germany of a cutoff of all Western

- 12 -

trade would be substantial, although current attempts to reorient GDR trade away from the West will reduce this vulnerability in the future. East Germany would probably respond with harassments of West German traffic to Berlin, but we doubt that the Communists would wish in the first instance to cut off this traffic entirely, preferring not to raise this additional issue at a time when Allied access was in contention. The USSR would probably calculate that the Allies could not maintain most of these policies effectively over a long period of time. We do not think, therefore, that these courses of action, undertaken in the absence of other moves, would have a significant effect on the Soviet position regarding access. Taken in conjunction with other measures, they would probably reinforce in the Soviet mind the possibility that the Allies were prepared to run substantial risks over Berlin.

> COURSE D: Large-scale preparations for general war -- defined as widespread deployments, preparations to bring the US to full military and civilian readiness, and corresponding official acts such as declaration of a state of emergency, appropriate Congressional resolutions, and consultations within various alliances.

- 13 -

TOP SECRET

19. While US preparations for general war of this scope
and nature probably would not convince the USSR that the US
had firmly decided to proceed if necessary to that extreme,
the Soviet leaders would certainly view the chances of general
war as dangerously increased, particularly if the principal
NATO Allies of the US appeared to be in agreement. We think
that, under these conditions, the Soviets would probably seek
ways to reopen negotiations in order to ease the crisis, hoping
that they could in the subsequent bargaining achieve some change
in the status of Berlin favorable to them. It should be observed, however, that the danger of miscalculation in this
situation would be great. If the NATO Allies clearly were not
in step with the US, we still think it likely that the Soviets
would seek to open negotiations; in this case, however, they
would probably expect the divided policies of their opponents
to assure a favorable diplomatic outcome for themselves.

Reactions to the postulated courses in other areas

20. In the <u>NATO countries</u>, much would depend on the
manner in which the issue was posed. In general, the postulated courses of action would excite widespread public alarm
and dismay in varying degree as they appeared to threaten
general war. To be sure, according to the problem as postulated in this estimate, the British and French Governments

- 14 -

TOP SECRET

would have agreed in advance to the stated courses of action, and presumably they would have done something to prepare their peoples for the crisis. It goes without saying that the other members of NATO would expect to have been consulted. Yet we believe there would be little public support for the more drastic allied responses unless the earlier Soviet (or East German) action could be convincingly portrayed as an attempt to seize control of Berlin rather than merely to introduce changes in access procedures. Even in this case, many Europeans would balk at taking such risks for the sake of Berlin, and public support from some NATO governments would be reluctantly given.

21. In East Germany, there would be a possibility, particularly in connection with Course A, of popular risings, but we think it more likely that the population would not expose itself to retaliation so long as the outcome remained uncertain. The longer the fighting under Course A, the higher the chances of scattered antiregime demonstrations and violence. Both hopes and fears would be aroused among the populations of East Europe, but these would have no great political effect in the short term.

- 15 -

22. In most non-European countries, attention would be focused primarily upon the possibility of general war, and this consideration would probably override views about the rights and wrongs of the access issue. Few countries would cooperate in multilateral indirect reprisals of the type envisaged in Course C. It is almost certain that the situation would be brought to the UN, and that many countries would exert pressure on both the US and the USSR to resume negotiations and ease the crisis.

General Considerations

23. It is important to emphasize again that the courses of action postulated in this estimate have been considered mainly in isolation from each other and from other events, and that such a treatment is to a large degree artificial. Just as the initial Soviet action would have been based on an assessment of numerous indications, tangible and intangible, of probable Western responses, so the Soviet reaction in the second round would be based on a similarly broad assessment of the West's next step, drawn from the entire range of political and military activity. Central to this assessment would be the Soviet leaders' impression of the will and determination of Western leadership to persist in a firm course,

- 16 -

and the ability of that leadership to carry the Western peoples
with them. The Soviet judgment would be taken in a context of
severe international crisis, with many countries making their
weight felt in diplomatic exchanges and, probably, in UN debate. As tensions rose, worldwide demands that the parties
to the dispute take no precipitate action and return to negotiation would grow in intensity, to such a degree that both
sides might feel obliged to weigh seriously the reactions of
world opinion to any further steps.

24. The Soviets would probably consider that the consequences of forcing their policy on Berlin under conditions of
intense and possibly prolonged crisis could be damaging to the
further perspectives of their policy. They might hesitate to
persist in their demands if they believed that the result would
be greatly heightened tensions and an atmosphere of such hostility that nothing could be negotiated for a long time to
come. On the other hand, they would also consider the damage
to Western confidence and unity, and the advantages to their
own cause, that would result from a clear victory on Berlin.

25. We are confident that the Soviet leaders do not
intend to wage general war in order to change the status of
Berlin. At the same time, however, the Soviet leaders have

- 17 -

not yet been persuaded that the US will go to general war in
order to prevent a change in that status. If they were to
become convinced that the US will actually do so, we believe
that they would back off and seek negotiations, providing the
US had left them this recourse. We doubt that they can be
fully convinced that the US will do so, but even if they are
not fully convinced, we believe that one or more of the postulated courses of action, taken together with supporting political and diplomatic action by the US and its allies, might
make the Soviet leaders uncertain of ultimate US intentions,
and persuade them that the West was willing to take actions
of such high risk that the situation would soon get out of
control. Thus the Soviets might be prepared to believe that
the crisis could eventuate in general war even though neither
side originally had intended to go that far. They certainly
desire to avoid such uncontrollable situations, but it is
impossible to estimate at just what point they might be
willing to modify their Berlin policy in order to retrieve
the situation, or when they would consider that the stakes
were already so high that they could not afford to compromise.

- 18 -

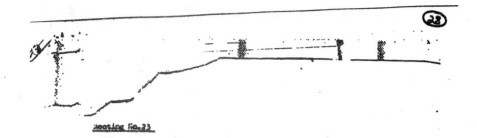

Meeting No.23

1. Subject arrived at 1510 hours on 24th July, 1961

2. Subject opens package and shows KIALTA camera.
S: They have 4 types of cameras: one KIALTA, one cine-camera, a new German one, and two ordinary Soviet ones. I got this from PAVLOV, yesterday, for my trip to STAMFORD. This camera is now loaded with a British made film (ILFORD). I brought this for you to take the number etc. in case operational use is made with this camera in the future – and secondly I'd like to have the photographic instructor to tell me how best to use it. I have an exposure and time chart here which they gave me, and I would like it checked.
G: That is fine, we will do all this before you go on your trip.

3. S: I have one very interesting thing to tell you. I was even thinking of calling you yesterday. SHAPOVALOV came up to me yesterday after I had had my conversation with PAVLOV, and said "Oleg Vladimirovich I would like your advice, you are my former boss, I've some trouble concerning my work". Before that I had read a telegram from SEROV enquiring about his family, a reply has been sent mentioning the £20 loan and the shopping expedition. PAVLOV has already sent off the telegram about ANITA, here in the text: "During the British Industries Fair in MOSCOW, such and such a firm exhibited two prototypes of a portable computer ANITA. At the present time the firm has signed a great number of contracts with certain capitalist countries for the supply of this machine (mentioning October). During the fair our specialists in MOSCOW considered the advisability of acquiring the ANITA computer. The English firm had then replied that they can only sell it on the basis of one thousand at a time. The English specialist who maintains scientific – technical relations with the Committee has promised (Subject's name) to obtain an ANITA machine against cash down and subsequently pass it on to us. The price of the machine is £400. Please reply urgently whether it is advisable to give this sum, via (Subject's name) to the British specialist or there may be the possibility of repayment after delivery of the machine. Let us have your instructions."

4. G: Did you mention the dates of the exhibition? S: No, I gave PAVLOV all the other details orally. He asked me to thank .I?:E and to arrange a meeting with WIGGX at the Embassy at 10 o'clock on Monday. VORONIN came in and told PAVLOV and me that he is leaving LONDON by air on either Saturday or Sunday.

5. S: Then I went with SHAPOVALOV to his office. I have been in five rooms already which are involved with intelligence work, I will draw it up for you later. SHAPOVALOV's trouble consists in the fact that the "Centre" had ordered him to drop his Indian contact as he was suspected of being an "agent-provocateur". The Indian in question is a journalist, a young man, representative of an insignificant Indian paper. I reported this to you in the Spring. His name begins with K, and on the 23rd July he is supposed to have gone on a trip to PNG, as a member of a delegation of journalists

....../invited

(Pages 2-3 missing from the original document)

- 4 -

21. Subject then refers to Van VLIET and how displeased he was by his transfer from MOSCOW. G.Explains that van VLIET was removed because of woman trouble. S. The people in the (Soviet) Ministry of Foreign Trade, who have spoken to me about him, were of a very low opinion as to his abilities. They thought him a fool. Subject then repeats that SMITH, the Ambassador, treats him (Subject) in a very friendly manner.

22. S: Now, about MERRIMAN, I am to ring him? H: Yes.
S: All right. And think about McBRIDE. On the 31st I will take WYNNE to meet PAVLOV. Prior to my departure I need receipts, hotel bills, which WYNNE should obtain for me.

23. Subject mentions the Zenith radio, and George tells him to be silent and look. The radio is shown him. George explains in detail that this radio is being given him to show him we are sympathetic to his wishes as good friends. The gift is from the heart against our better judgement and should show him that money is no problem but security is. Therefore, the tape recorder (personal use) is out since he would be suspect having it and risk a disaster by trying to record VARENTSOV if the latter should visit subject.

24. Furthermore Subject should abide by our advice and decisions in future requests of a security risk nature and minimise his acquisitive desires. Subject was visibly touched and thanked us profusely.

25. S: However I'll have WYNNE take it in, rather than taking it now. (The set was removed from its packing box and Subject was shown its components, operation etc. Its unpacked size permits it to be carried in a normal suitcase easily. Subject reassured us that he can easily legend his having obtained the set in the Commission store. He explained how it is registered, how easily it can go through customs, etc. Since WYNNE had requested to postpone his trip to the USSR till 26th August due to his son's sudden appendectomy, the schedule was reviewed and to permit Subject's leave Janet and husband's leave and WYNNE's arrival to fit in, the 23rd August was decided upon.)

26. G: Regarding the military article you wanted our help to write; it seems that since you are an artillery officer and have been given access to the PTURS data by VARENTSOV, and other artillery studies; you should look over the material in the GRU spetsfond to see what manuals or data there is on the same subject - anti-tank weapons, are from Anglo-American Military material - and give us the bibliography.
S: I'll consider this and I will get a list of subjects and magazines dealing with Anglo-American forces which KORENEVSKI's people hold in the GRU Information Directorate. I will even expand the subject matter, maybe an infantry topic would be O.K. I will also try and send photocopies of my other papers and articles which I can get - through WYNNE.

27. G: Just send us a bibliography. S: I will send you a complete list of what we have on your forces. Then if you can send me the material back I'll work it over properly.

28. G: Now to reassure you that your information is definitely reaching our leaders - here is a report on President KENNEDY's speech. I won't read it to you but I can point out to you that in a number of statements, exactly those thoughts which you suggested were mentioned. (Subject was delighted).

/29. ....

- 5 -

29. S: I reported to you last Spring about the situation at the time of KHRUSHCHEV's coming to power. When he kicked out the opposition - MALENKOV - etc. There was even three days when he was not in power. KHRUSHCHEV is adopting the same technique with the Army he had previously with the Party officials. During his "reign" he has personally promoted approximately 1500 officers to Generals out of a total of 4 - 5000, and also promoted a number of old Generals to higher ranks, up to the rank of Marshal, and even Chief Marshal. He relies on their support. But both in the Praesidium and in the Central Committee there are still a number of people who supported MALENKOV, MOLOTOV, BULGANIN, etc. PERVUKHIN is one of them. There are also unconfirmed rumours that KHRUSHCHEV fights occasionally with MIKOYAN. MIKOYAN is in opposition with regard to some of KHRUSHCHEV's opinions, arrangements etc. KHRUSHCHEV is not popular with the masses. They do not care for his jokes, comments, etc. They blame him for the miserable life they have to live. We know he is a political adventurer.

30. S: Among the leaders (rukovodstvo) there exists a secret opposition, which remains secret because the majority are still KHRUSHCHEV's protegees and the others don't want to lose their jobs. But there could be a distribution of forces and a split as a result of the BERLIN question. All of them who are aware of the weak points, with regard to the economic and military situations, who will say "It is too early to go to war! We've got to wait. What's the point of heating up the situation because of a BERLIN which has existed for the last 16 years." Should this occur, it is possible the KHRUSHCHEV will carry the day and win once again, on the other hand the reverse might happen. We have to take this into consideration. They could either remove KHRUSHCHEV, saying he was ill or else he might resign - as MALENKOV did, or they could say "You go on being the boss, but let's r treat on the BERLIN question, let's think something up." Let's say outright that we are defenders of the peace, the Anglo-Americans have taken the extreme view of our declaration and are preparing for war, we don't want war, there's no hurry, we'll settle the BERLIN question oneday". There are lots of diplomatic words that can be found in order to meet the situation and to fool the people and lie again.

31. The 22nd Congress will decide what action is to be taken. It doesn't appear on the Agenda, but as I have told you before whenever there is one of these big gatherings they have secret sessions, the plenum, the praesidium, and I am positive that this matter will be discussed, it might even be discussed before the official opening of the Congress. So we must keep in mind these three possibilities. (Subject continues on this theme for some time, repeating roughly what he has already said.) - Namely:

1) KHRUSHCHEV may crush all opposition and proceed to sign East German peace treaty, inviting local hostilities and risking general war.

2) KHRUSHCHEV may be forced to compromise and delay signing peace treaty in view of Western opposition and propagandise this more as his desire for peace - still postponing possible action re East Germany and Berlin to a further date.

3) KHRUSHCHEV may be deposed.

/ 32. ......

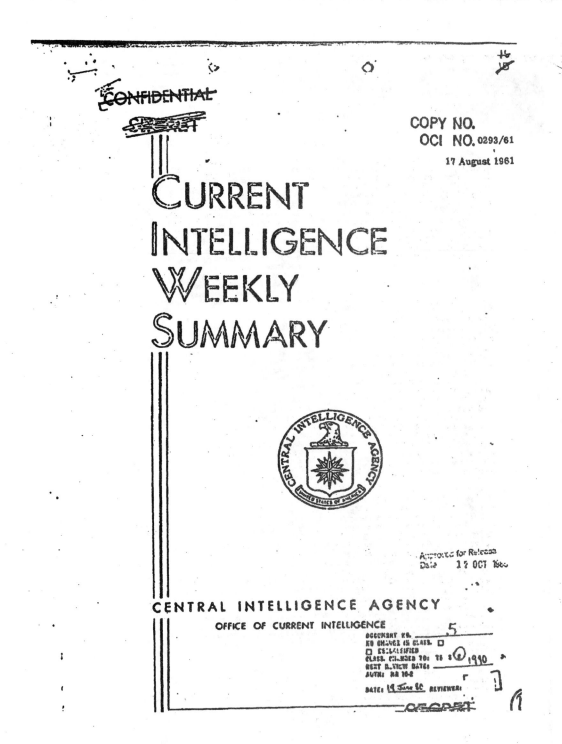

CONFIDENTIAL

~~SECRET~~

COPY NO.
OCI NO. 0293/61

17 August 1961

CURRENT
INTELLIGENCE
WEEKLY
SUMMARY

Approved for Release
Date   1 7 OCT 1960

CENTRAL INTELLIGENCE AGENCY

OFFICE OF CURRENT INTELLIGENCE

DOCUMENT NO. _____5_____
NO CHANGE IS CLASS. ☐
☐ DECLASSIFIED
CLASS. CHANGED TO: TS S ⓒ 1910
NEXT REVIEW DATE: _____
AUTH: HR 70-2
DATE: 19 June 80 REVIEWER:

SECRET

CONFIDENTIAL

CURRENT INTELLIGENCE WEEKLY SUMMARY

WEEKLY REVIEW

BERLIN

In an effort to halt the refugee flow, which reached near-panic proportions last week, the East German regime--purportedly at the behest of the Warsaw Pact countries--moved swiftly and effectively in the early morning hours of 13 August to seal off West Berlin from East Berlin and East Germany. At the same time it announced a series of decrees spelling out its actions.

The New Decrees

All East Germans and East Berliners who wish to go to West Berlin will have to secure special permits from their local police. A veiled warning was issued to East Germans to stay out of East Berlin unless on official business. The number of crossing points on the sector border between East and West Berlin was reduced from 87 to 13. East German army, police, and security forces were brought in to control movement over the sector and zonal borders surrounding West Berlin. It also was decreed that East Berlin and East German "border crossers" who have been working in West Berlin must no longer work there.

The East German Ministry of Transport took steps to cut off elevated railroad (S-Bahn) service between West Berlin and both the Soviet sector and the East Zone. The S-Bahn, operated by the East German regime, has been the main transportation artery in the city and surrounding suburban areas. The S-Bahn service will be continued within West Berlin and, separately, in East Berlin and the zone. Similarly, the subway (U-Bahn) --under Western control except for one line--is permitted to make only one stop on the two lines which run through East Berlin.

On 15 August, the East German Ministry of Interior issued a regulation requiring West Berliners to secure special permits for their cars or motorcycles to enter East Berlin. Thus, for the first time West Berliners are forced to secure permits to enter the Soviet sector. This decree, like those of 13 August, violates the postwar quadripartite agreements providing for Four-Power occupation of all of Berlin as well as the Four-Power Paris agreement of 20 June 1949 which ended the blockade of Berlin.

The East Germans also reduced the number of East - West Berlin sector control points where West Germans may secure passes to visit East Berlin. This move underlines the regime's claim to the right to control West German travel into East Berlin, set forth initially in a decree of 8 September 1960-- also in violation of the Four-Power status of Berlin. This decree was one of the major reasons leading Bonn to abrogate the interzonal trade agreement last September. Bonn rescinded this action only after the East Germans in December agreed, among other concessions, not to give effective enforcement to the 8 September decree.

The regime has announced also that it will be illegal for East Germans to accept identification papers from West Berlin or West Germany. Bonn hitherto had granted such identification to East Germans, on grounds of common German citizenship.

Refugee Flights

Figures on the official registrations of East German refugees at the Marienfelde Refugee Reception Center for 12 through 15 August total 10,-712. The large majority of those escaped before the border closed on 13 August. No reliable count is yet available of those refugees who have since circumvented the new controls. Of the four-day total, 1,656 were border crossers; 994 of these came from East Berlin.

CONFIDENTIAL

CONFIDENTIAL
~~SECRET~~

CURRENT INTELLIGENCE WEEKLY SUMMARY

sanctions might be imposed against the Communist bloc if the Berlin issue could not be settled.

There has, however, been interference with communications linking East Germany, West Berlin, and West Germany. The US Mission in Berlin reported on

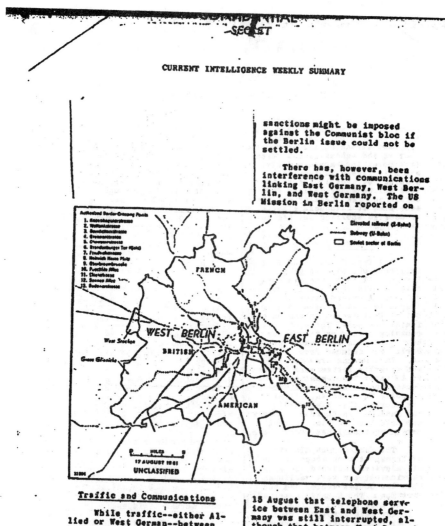

Traffic and Communications

While traffic--either Allied or West German--between West Berlin and West Germany has not yet been affected, the regime has threatened to interfere with West German freight shipments if Bonn resorts to economic countermeasures. Chancellor Adenauer in a speech on 14 August warned that trade

15 August that telephone service between East and West Germany was still interrupted, although that between West Berlin and West Germany was functioning normally. Telex service between East and West Berlin has been cut. These moves probably reflect the regime's attempt to deprive its own population of means to communicate with the West.

CONFIDENTIAL
~~SECRET~~

SECRET

CURRENT INTELLIGENCE WEEKLY SUMMARY

Travel of East Germans to the West appears to have been drastically cut. The press reports that East Germans are being ordered off trains at frontier points between East and West Germany. The Swedish travel bureau says that East Germans are no longer to be allowed to organize travel groups via ferry to Sweden.

Military Moves

Elements of two--and possibly three--Soviet divisions stationed outside Berlin were at the outset deployed in small tank and infantry groups in a circle two to three miles from the city's Outer Ring. These elements had evidently withdrawn or moved into assembly areas by the afternoon of 16 August. The East German army and police units which moved into the Berlin area this past week end are apparently still there.

Popular Reaction

The East German population, cowed by the show of Soviet - East German force, is generally taking a cautious line in commenting on developments and evidently is closely watching for reactions by the Western powers.

Soviet Position

The Soviet decision, apparently taken at the Warsaw Pact conference on 3-5 August, to authorize the controls to halt the refugee flow underscores the dilemma confronting Khrushchev. Since his talks with President Kennedy in Vienna in early June, the Soviet premier has sought to impress the West with his determination to bring the Berlin situation to a head.

before the end of the year. As part of his campaign to force the West into early negotiations on Soviet terms, he had gone to some lengths to create the impression that no Western moves could deflect the bloc from carrying through with its announced intentions. This more aggressive tone, however, was largely instrumental in precipitating the mass flight of East Germans which was an acute embarrassment for Soviet police.

SECRET

TOTAL ANNUAL REFUGEE FLOW INTO WEST BERLIN AND WEST GERMAN

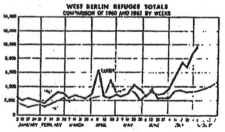
WEST BERLIN REFUGEE TOTALS
COMPARISON OF 1960 AND 1961 BY WEEKS

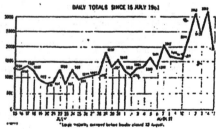
DAILY TOTALS SINCE 15 JULY 1961

CONFIDENTIAL

17 Aug 61

17 Aug 61

WEEKLY REVIEW

SPECIAL ARTICLES

Page 3 of 20

Page 1 of 5

527

(Page 4 missing from the original document)

CURRENT INTELLIGENCE WEEKLY SUMMARY

indicated that the bloc foreign ministers will meet in "late fall" to consider the "results of the preparatory work" on a treaty, while Ulbricht indicated that drafting of a treaty was now in progress.

Khrushchev's speech of 11 August, however, is evidence that the USSR is still holding the door open to negotiations. While giving equal weight to threats against NATO Allies and to appeals for negotiations, Khrushchev sought to display some flexibility on the possibilities for a negotiated settlement. He reaffirmed that the USSR would offer "reliable guarantees" for a free-city status and indicated that there could be several "variations" on the terms of such guarantees. He also claimed that the question of West Berlin was "in itself" not so difficult to solve, provided the issue was not turned into a "trial of strength."

The announcement on 10 August that Marshal Ivan Konev had been appointed commander of Soviet forces in East Germany was probably related to the decision to seal the Berlin sector boundaries and to the general Soviet strategy vis-a-vis the West. Konev's appointment places a highly trusted and close associate of Khrushchev in a key position during a period of greatly increased tensions in Berlin. The advance notice that Konev was in command was probably calculated to impress the East German populace with the extent of Soviet support for the regime and Soviet willingness to use its forces to suppress any popular opposition.

The naming of Konev also served to underscore the seriousness of the measures recently announced by Khrushchev to "make the defensive might of the So-

viet Union even stronger and more dependable." The selection of Konev, commander of the Warsaw Pact for five years and leader of the forces which captured Berlin, is also calculated to sharpen the repeated warning that the bloc will rebuff any resort to force by the West following a separate peace treaty. Khrushchev probably feels that the appointment of a man of Konev's prestige and experience will strengthen his efforts to impress the West with his determination to conclude a separate treaty in the absence of a negotiated settlement.

The 15 August letter of the Soviet commandant in Berlin, rejecting a 3 August Western protest against restrictions at that time on border crossers, previews the general diplomatic line the USSR can be expected to follow in connection with Western protests against the current control measures. The Soviet letter reaffirms Moscow's contention that East Germany has sole legal jurisdiction over East Berlin. Underlining the "exclusive competence" of the Ulbricht regime in East Berlin, it charges the West with using the "occupation regime in West Berlin for intolerable provocations and undermining activities" against East Germany and the bloc.

Reaction in West Germany and West Berlin

CURRENT INTELLIGENCE WEEKLY SUMMARY

West German and West Berlin leaders have urged all Germans to remain calm and patient and avoid "emotional behavior" which would only worsen the situation in East Germany. Defense Minister Strauss, at a campaign rally on 14 August, warned that any explosive reaction by West Germans to East German moves would lead to developments "impossible to control," adding, "If shooting starts, no one knows with what kinds of weapons it will end." Strauss criticized the overeagerness of West German businessmen for trade with the bloc and said that the East German Leipzig Fair, scheduled for 3-10 September, was no place for West German participation.

West Berliners, meanwhile, are becoming increasingly restive over the lack of prompt Western countermeasures.

West Berlin crowds on 15 August criticized Brandt for making "high-sounding statements but failing to take concrete measures." To reduce the chances of incidents, West Berlin police are being kept on "maximum alert" and all demonstrations near the sector borders are forbidden.

At the large demonstration addressed by Mayor Brandt on 16 August, West Berliners waved banners saying "Better dead than Red"; "We demand countermeasures"; "90 hours without doing anything"; and "Betrayed by the West?" Berlin officials scheduled the rally as a means of allowing the restive populace to "let off steam" and restore confidence. Some instances of panic buying have been reported, and city officials have been queried by anxious individuals as to whether they should go ahead with vacation plans or whether they should make preparations for leaving the city. Political leaders are fearful that a "crisis of confidence" may develop as a result of unfulfilled expectations of Western countermeasures.

West Berlin officials maintain that no "serious" trouble is expected from the loss of the 50,000 East Germans who had jobs in West Berlin. Most firms expect only a temporary inconvenience since they were careful to limit the proportion of border crossers working in any one part of their operations. The greatest hardship will be experienced by small firms where the lack of one or two skilled workers can cause serious trouble or where most of the workers were border crossers.

CONFIDENTIAL

17 Aug 61   WEEKLY REVIEW   Page 6 of 20

17 Aug 61   SPECIAL ARTICLES   Page 1 of 5

SNIE 11-10-61
24 August 1961

ACCOUNTABLE DOCUMENT
RETURN TO O/DCI REGISTRY
Room 7E47 Hqs.

SECRET

SPECIAL

NATIONAL INTELLIGENCE ESTIMATE

NUMBER 11-10-61

SOVIET TACTICS IN THE BERLIN CRISIS

Submitted by the
DIRECTOR OF CENTRAL INTELLIGENCE

The following intelligence organizations participated
in the preparation of this estimate: The Central Intelligence Agency
and the intelligence organizations of the Departments
of State, the Army, the Navy, the Air Force, and The Joint Staff.

Concurred in by the
UNITED STATES INTELLIGENCE BOARD

Concurring were: The Director of Intelligence and Research,
Department of State; the Assistant Chief
of Staff for Intelligence, Department of the Army; the Assistant
Chief of Naval Operations (Intelligence), Department of the Navy;
the Assistant Chief of Staff, Intelligence, USAF; the Director for
Intelligence, Joint Staff; the Assistant to the
Secretary of Defense, Special Operations; and the Director of
the National Security Agency. The Atomic Energy
Commission Representative to the USIB, and the Assistant Director,
Federal Bureau of Investigation, abstained, the subject being outside of their jurisdiction.

ACCOUNTABLE DOCUMENT

SECRET   N° 375

SOVIET TACTICS IN THE BERLIN CRISIS

THE PROBLEM

To estimate Soviet tactics in the Berlin crisis over the next few months, with particular reference to the effect on these tactics of possible developments within East Germany.

THE ESTIMATE

1. With the action of 13 August, the Communists have taken a long step toward their objectives in Berlin and have created a new political situation there. The border controls instituted on that date have met East Germany's most pressing need by reducing the refugee flow to tolerable proportions. At the same time, the division of Berlin into two separate cities has been made virtually complete, with the eastern portion all but incorporated into the GDR. Thus the Soviets, induced by the rising tide of refugees, have taken unilateral action to achieve results which they had intended to accomplish at a later date, and by different means.

2. The refugee question, however, was only one aspect of the larger problem of stabilizing the GDR, and the closing of the Berlin escape route may worsen other aspects if it leads to a further buildup of tensions within East Germany. Even apart from this, the stemming of the refugee flow will not change the USSR's view of the necessity to bolster the GDR's claims to sovereignty with a peace treaty and eventually to eject Western influence from Berlin altogether. We do not believe that the USSR has given up its intention to press for a peace treaty and a "free city." The question is whether the Soviet leaders will accelerate their movement towards these objectives, or will moderate their pace after their considerable achievements of 13 August.

3. The action in Berlin has initiated a momentum which the Soviets may wish to sustain. A wide variety of further unilateral measures is available to them. The termination of military liaison missions would be a relatively low-keyed act which might appear to the Soviets as a means of keeping events moving in their favor.[1] Another option would be to deny Allied rights to enter East Berlin, thereby carrying to its conclusion the destruction of the four-power status of that part of the city. More drastically, the East Germans might disrupt or harass civil traffic between West Berlin and the Federal Republic; most dangerous of all, interference with Allied access might begin. Politically, the USSR might choose to accelerate the timing of a peace conference and a separate treaty with the GDR.

4. Another factor which could importantly affect the USSR's timing and tactics is the increasing involvement of Soviet prestige. Khrushchev in recent weeks has reacted to the stiffening US attitude by increasing his commitment to early action. He now asserts that the issue transcends the problems of Germany and Berlin, important as these re-

---

[1] Under the occupation, the US, French, and British forces in West Germany presently have military missions accredited to the Soviet Commander in East Germany, who in turn has missions to the three Allied Commanders.

1

main, and that the West's refusal to conclude a peace treaty represents an attempt to achieve a "strategic breakthrough" against the Bloc. In claiming a challenge to Soviet power and prestige, he wishes to convey to his opponents that the Soviet Union cannot be expected to draw back from crisis situations in which reason and prudence would appear to dictate restraint. He might decide to take new steps on Berlin which would strengthen the image of inflexible resolve.

5. In our recent estimates of the USSR's policy toward Germany and Berlin, we have regularly attributed to the Soviet leaders a confidence that they can move gradually toward their eventual objectives without incurring unacceptable risks. We have pointed to their belief that the West could probably be induced to make negotiated concessions. And we have further estimated that, if these Soviet expectations are not borne out, the USSR will move unilaterally, but still intending to proceed in such a way as to avoid at any stage unduly high risks of war.[2]

6. We believe that Soviet actions in the recent phase of the Berlin crisis do not indicate that the USSR has departed from this general approach and method. Thus we conclude that the Soviets' present intention probably is not to take further drastic action immediately, though they may undertake measures of limited scope. For example, they will probably further restrict German civil and Allied access to East Berlin, and they may embark upon a program of gradual harassments of German civil traffic to West Berlin. But rather than pose a major challenge to West Berlin itself and the Allied position there, we believe that their present preference is to let the effects of the border closure sink in and see whether the Western Powers have

become more inclined to accept Soviet terms of negotiations.

7. In the absence of fairly definite proposals by the West, we think it unlikely that Khrushchev will take the initiative in formally proposing a date and other specifics for East-West negotiations. He clearly wishes to appear as the champion of negotiations, and he may throw out hints, in an effort to encourage a Western proposal, that the USSR could be persuaded to reduce its demands if a conference were arranged. If presented with a Western invitation, he would respond favorably but would undoubtedly attempt to define the task of the conference in a fashion which served Soviet interests. If the negotiations were in train toward the end of the year, he would probably postpone his deadline for a treaty. If negotiations do not materialize, we believe that the next Soviet step will be to issue invitations to their own peace conference, probably accompanied by a revised draft of a treaty applicable to both German states and providing for the declaration of a "free city" status for West Berlin. We think under these circumstances that the chances are still considerably better than even that the treaty would not be signed before the Party Congress which convenes on 17 October.

Effect of Developments in East Germany

8. Soviet tactics will be affected by a large number of factors, including the posture adopted by the West, the movement of opinion in the important uncommitted countries, and domestic developments in East Germany. We have recently examined the possibility that serious unrest might arise in East Germany and have concluded that, under most circumstances, a major eruption is unlikely;[3] here we consider how popular disturbances or an uprising might affect Soviet tactics.

9. The Soviet leaders evidently are confident of their capability for keeping discontent in check and repressing any outbreaks which might occur. If they came to feel that the chances of a general rising were becoming

---

[2] Our principal estimates on Soviet policy with respect to Berlin and Germany are NIE 11-4-60, "Main Trends in Soviet Capabilities and Policies, 1960–1965," dated 1 December 1960, paragraphs 161–164, TOP SECRET; NIE 11-7-61, "Soviet Short-Term Intentions Regarding Berlin and Germany," dated 25 April 1961, SECRET; and SNIE 2-2-61, "Soviet and Other Reactions to Possible US Courses of Action with Respect to Berlin," dated 11 July 1961, TOP SECRET, Limited Distribution.

[3] SNIE 12.4-61, "Stability of East Germany in a Berlin Crisis," dated 15 August 1961, SECRET.

SECRET

substantial, their main domestic efforts would probably be in the direction of menace and intimidation. They would alert and deploy their own forces in East Germany, as well as those of the GDR, and the public would be warned of the regime's determination to react with speed and vigor to hostile manifestations. Additionally, they would probably make available additional supplies of consumer goods in order to relieve economic shortages.

10. Popular dissatisfaction with internal political and economic conditions would be the basic cause of mass unrest. However, the Communist efforts to consolidate the GDR as a separate German state by isolating it from further contact with the West, combined with the international tension generated by Communist pressures against West Berlin, are adding to popular unrest. Thus, there is a relationship between the degree of unrest in East Germany and Moscow's pursuit of its policies aimed at neutralizing West Berlin and fixing the division of Germany, particularly since the 13 August action has deprived the East German regime of a safety valve.

11. Even so, we see little chance that the USSR, if it believed that an East German rising was likely, would respond by altering its principal aims or policies with respect to Berlin. While it is possible that the Soviets might temporarily modify their tactics or extend their timing to reduce the likelihood of a serious German uprising, we think it unlikely that such a Soviet response would be either very significant or lasting. Moreover, we believe that it would be next to impossible to convince the USSR, the GDR, or the East German people that the West intended or had the capability to support widespread anti-regime activities.

12. We believe that the Communists will act speedily and firmly in meeting evidences of public disorder, if these actually develop, in East Germany in the months ahead. If an uprising should occur, they would regard themselves as having no other choice than to put it down, despite the cost to their position and the danger of Western involvement. In the wake of such a repression, the Soviets might accelerate their moves toward a separate peace treaty, believing that it was unprofitable to spend further time in cultivating world opinion or waiting for East-West talks, and that an early treaty would start the process of rebuilding East German sovereignty and authority.

SECRET

BERLIN

Border Controls

The Ulbricht regime has made further moves to strengthen the security of the sector and zonal borders surrounding West Berlin and to reduce and more efficiently control movement between East and West Berlin. New measures over the past week involve controls that might be encountered at a recognized international frontier--including replacement of the barbed-wire barricades along the East-West Berlin sector border on 13 August with concrete barriers, the strengthening of barbed-wire fences along the zonal border adjoining West Berlin on three sides, and various types of personal checks on those desiring to cross the border.

The regime has gradually reduced the number of crossing points on the sector border from the 13 announced on 12 August to 7. The Ministry of Interior on 22 August issued a series of decrees, to go into effect the following day at 0001 hours, regulating access to East Berlin by West Germans, West Berliners, and Western military and diplomatic personnel. The announcement stated that the new regulations--as was the case in the 12 August decrees closing the sector borders--would remain in effect "until the conclusion of a peace treaty."

Foreign nationals (other than West Germans), members of the diplomatic corps, and personnel of the Western occupation forces now may cross the sector border at only one point, Friedrichstrasse. West Germans will be permitted to cross at only two points, Borholmerstrasse and Heinrich Heine Strasse. West Berliners are restricted to four crossing points--Chausseestrasse, Oberbaumbruecke, Sonnen Allee, and Invalidenstrasse-- and, for the first time, they will be required to obtain an East German permit, at the cost of one West German mark, to enter East Berlin.

There has been some actual interference with travel over the sector border by Western Allied personnel. On 22 August, prior to the imposition of the new restrictions, East German police detained a US military patrol--the first incident of this character involving US personnel since the promulgation of the 12 August decrees, although instances of interference have occurred in East Berlin in the past. A British patrol which strayed over the zonal border was detained for three hours last week.

In a test of the new restrictions, a US military patrol crossed into East Berlin on 23 August at the Friedrichstrasse checkpoint. When it sought to return via a street not designated as a checkpoint, it was turned back. It then proceeded to Eisenstrasse, where it found the road blocked. East German guards refused a request to talk with a Soviet officer, but did not prevent the patrol from leaving the area. Finally, the patrol returned to West Berlin via Sonnen Allee.

In and around Berlin, security and police forces are still in evidence. Controls at the sector and zonal border nevertheless appear to have been

CONFIDENTIAL

24 Aug 61
-
24 Aug 61

WEEKLY REVIEW

SPECIAL ARTICLES

Page 1 of 25

Page 1 of 8

CURRENT INTELLIGENCE WEEKLY SUMMARY

exercised somewhat sporadically. Although the number of refugees has been drastically reduced since 13 August, a significant number of East Germans and East Berliners are still escaping. On 22 August, 629 refugees registered at the Marienfelde reception center, of whom 168 had arrived since 13 August; the respective figures for 21 August were 1,202 and 238. No fewer than 13,837 persons regis-

Walter Ulbricht displayed great self-assurance at having successfully completed the difficult problem of sealing off West Berlin. There was, however, a note of concern about the reactions of the East German population. "For some time," he said, "there will continue to exist in the GDR capital and its environs people who have allowed themselves to be influenced and depraved by West Berlin." Ul-

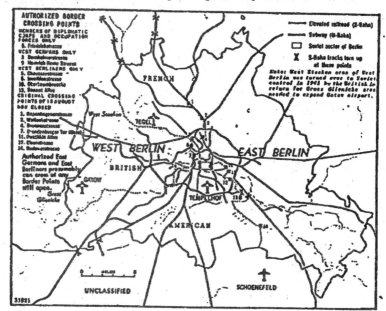

tered between 13 and 22 August, of whom more than 2,000 claimed to have fled after the clampdown.

Popular Attitudes

In a television broadcast on 18 August, East German leader

bricht is due to make another speech on 25 August.

The regime took extreme precautions to prevent any manifestations of public enthusiasm in connection with the move of the US battle group to Berlin on 20 August. People's Police were posted in pairs at frequent intervals along the Auto-bahn.

Party functionaries are organizing a drive to dismantle radio and TV antennae required only to turn in foreign broadcasts. In *Leipzig*, radio repairmen reportedly have "pledged themselves" not to build or install such aerials, and party propagandists are to visit the homes of those people who persist in listening to Western broadcasts.

The regime also has cracked down on Evangelical Church leaders in East Germany who, on 17 August, signed a telegram protesting the 13 August restrictions. East Berlin Mayor Fritz Ebert called Kurt Scharf, chairman of the church's All-German Synod, on 18 August to rebuke him for signing the telegram. Other East German churchmen have also been lectured by local authorities in an effort to make them withdraw their public position against the regime's ban on free travel.

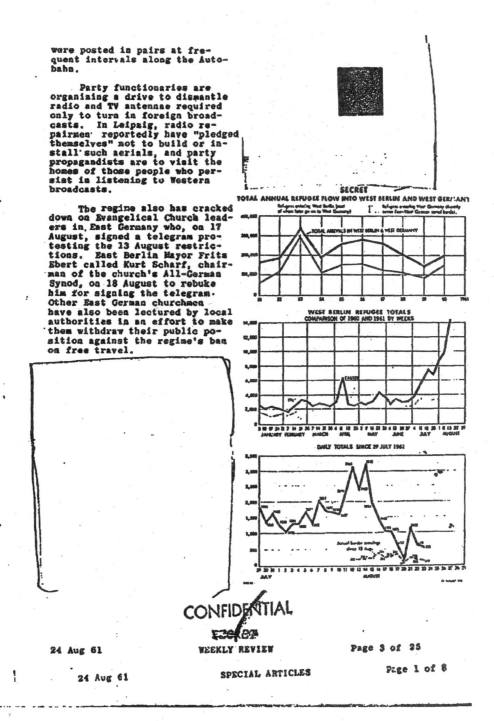

SECRET

TOTAL ANNUAL REFUGEE FLOW INTO WEST BERLIN AND WEST GERMANY

WEST BERLIN REFUGEE TOTALS
COMPARISON OF 1960 AND 1961 BY WEEKS

DAILY TOTALS SINCE 29 JULY 1961

CONFIDENTIAL

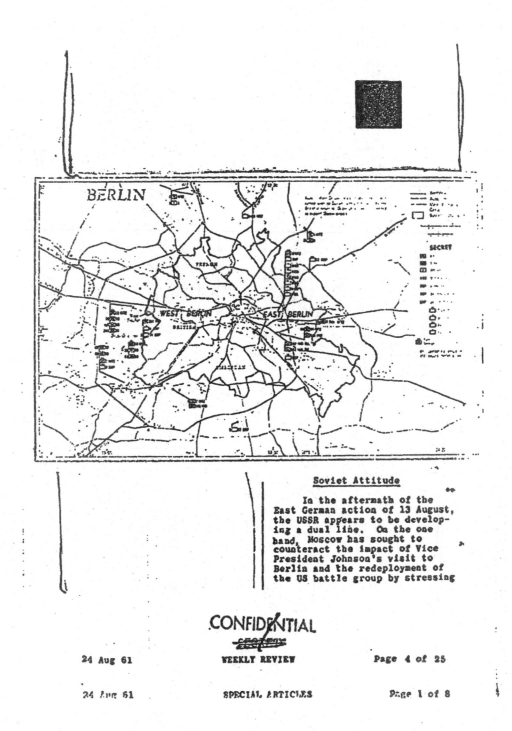

Soviet Attitude

In the aftermath of the East German action of 13 August, the USSR appears to be developing a dual line. On the one hand, Moscow has sought to counteract the impact of Vice President Johnson's visit to Berlin and the redeployment of the US battle group by stressing

CONFIDENTIAL

24 Aug 61	WEEKLY REVIEW	Page 4 of 25
24 Aug 61	SPECIAL ARTICLES	Page 1 of 8

the temporary nature of current access controls. Mikoyan in his public remarks in Japan predicted that a separate treaty would be signed by the end of the year and that access to Berlin for any state would then depend on the conclusion of "special agreements" with the East German regime. This general line was also stressed by the Czech Government, which declared its "irrevocable decision" to conclude a treaty before the end of the year. Khrushchev, in a "letter to American readers" on 21 August asserted that the bloc has reached a firm decision not to postpone a peace conference any longer.

The Soviet protest note of 23 August is consistent with the bloc's broad effort to demonstrate the urgency of a peace treaty before the end of the year. The note, apparently intended as a threatening response to Chancellor Adenauer's visit to West Berlin on 22 August, charges the United States with failure to take measures to suppress "provocative activities" of West German officials in West Berlin. The warning of "possible consequences" of continued West German "interference," together with the demand for immediate measures to terminate "illegal and provocative" actions in Berlin, suggests that Moscow may be preparing the groundwork to justify East German harassment of or restrictions on West German traffic to West Berlin and within Berlin.

In an effort to build a case for continued tightening of East German controls in

Berlin, the note accuses the West of "abusing their situation" in Berlin and flagrantly violating four-power agreements by misusing the air corridors to transport "all kinds of revanchists" to Berlin. On 18 August Moscow had replied to the US protest against East German actions by reiterating its position that the East Germans have legal "sovereignty" over East Berlin and that the four-power status of the Soviet sector had long ceased to exist.

At the same time, Soviet leaders have sought to minimize the prospect of an immediate crisis. The Soviet news agency Novosti transmitted the text of Khrushchev's "letter," which restated the Soviet position on Berlin in a relatively moderate manner and is apparently intended as a sign of reassurance that the bloc will not encroach on Western access to West Berlin pending a peace treaty. He also stressed that the possibility remains of negotiating the terms of continued Western access to and presence in Berlin. However, he ruled out any settlement which would reaffirm Western occupation rights in the city and candidly admitted that the question of East German control over Allied access to Berlin is primarily an issue of "political significance" rather than technical procedure.

Mikoyan dismissed the question of access as a "minor point" and repeatedly asserted that the USSR would accept a four-power or UN guarantee for Berlin.

CONFIDENTIAL

~~SECRET~~

Reaction in West Berlin and West Germany

Vice President Johnson's visit to West Berlin and the movement of additional US troops to the city have succeeded in bolstering the badly shaken morale of the West Berlin populace. According to US officials in Bonn, Chancellor Adenauer's appeal for calm, close association with the Allies, and eventual negotiation with the USSR appears to be closely attuned to the West German public mood. They believe that although Mayor Brandt may have gained increased sympathy and respect from West German voters as a result of the current Berlin crisis, they doubt that this means votes for Brandt's Social Democratic party in the 17 September elections.

West German political figures, despite expressions of wrath and indignation at the sealing off of East Berlin, have generally avoided advocating strong countermeasures and have indicated a feeling of relief that the situation has not gotten out of control. American observers feel that the real impact of the recent events may come only after the elections, when some politician may try to attack the longstanding thesis of Adenauer's Christian Democratic Union that the best chance for ultimate reunification lies in firm ties with the West.

The mission   states there have been no significant movements of workers or businessmen from Berlin and no abnormal change in bank deposits or transfer of funds indicating a loss of confidence in the city's economy. Local industries are compensating for the loss of East Berlin workers by transferring personnel and re-employing retired workers.

Although Bonn is not planning any formal ban on West German travel to the East German Leipzig Trade Fair beginning on 3 September, the German Manufacturers' Association has urged a boycott by both exhibitors and visitors. An official of the Munich Chamber of Commerce stated on 21 August that his organization is having a difficult time persuading businessmen to support the boycott. They feel any orders the Germans let go will merely be taken over by British exporters.

CONFIDENTIAL

~~SECRET~~

#14

CONFIDENTIAL

~~SECRET~~

COPY NO.

OCI NO. 0[illegible]3/61

7 September 1961

CURRENT INTELLIGENCE WEEKLY SUMMARY

CENTRAL INTELLIGENCE AGENCY

OFFICE OF CURRENT INTELLIGENCE

DOCUMENT NO.

NO CHANGE IN CLASS. ☐

☐ DECLASSIFIED

CLASS. CHANGED TO: TS S C

NEXT REVIEW DATE: 1990

AUTH: HR 70-2

DATE: 19 June 80 REVIEWER: [illegible]

~~SECRET~~

CONFIDENTIAL

CURRENT INTELLIGENCE WEEKLY SUMMARY

BERLIN

The Communists have continued their threats against the use of the Berlin air corridors by Western commercial carriers, charging them again with transporting West German "militarists" and "revanchists" to West Berlin. While the campaign was timed to coincide with the 1-3 September Homeland Day celebrations in West Berlin by expellees from former German territories in Poland and Czechoslovakia, recent statements lay the groundwork for future interference with commercial air traffic, in an effort to intimidate the Western carriers to suspend their flights or accept East German authority over the corridors. As in the past, the propaganda is directed against the general target of West Germany's ties with West Berlin and forms part of the bloc's effort to further a sense of isolation and helplessness among West Berliners.

The USSR addressed notes on 2 September to the three Western powers in which it recapitulated the position taken in its earlier notes of 23 August that there is no legal basis for the operation of commercial aircraft in the postwar quadripartite agreements relating to Berlin and that the corridors were set up only to supply the needs of the Allied garrisons in Berlin. The notes warned that the Western Allies will be held responsible for any consequences of "provocative activity" carried out by the West German Government in West Berlin.

On 5 September, the Soviet commandant in Berlin, General Solovyev, visited US Commandant Watson to deliver a reply to the Western protest against the sealing off of the Berlin sector border. Solovyev charged that West Berlin "rowdies" had interfered with Soviet officials on duty in West Berlin, notably Soviet controllers in the Berlin Air Safety Center (BASC). He warned that further such interference might affect BASC operations, implying the Soviets might end their participation. The day before Solovyev met Watson, the East German news agency carried what purported to be the gist of the Soviet commandant's remarks; it was couched in very insulting language and bluntly threatened a walkout from BASC. The US Mission in Berlin reported that Solovyev's remarks followed the broad lines of the East German release but in essentially different tones. Solovyev had no explanation for the premature release of his statement or the insulting character given it.

East German spokesmen have gone out of their way to reaffirm the regime's intention to abide by the terms of the Soviet - East German agreement of 20 September 1955 under which the USSR retained control of Western Allied access to West Berlin. The regime, however, has recently hinted at some qualification of this position.

On 31 August, East Germany delivered two notes, each dated 26 August, to the US Embassy in Prague through the Czechoslovak Foreign Ministry, charging the US with misuse of the air corridors and of its ground access rights between West Germany and West Berlin. The notes in general restate the charges made by Walter Ulbricht in his 25 August speech in which he insisted that the East German regime has a legal right to control non-military traffic over its territory and will eventually demand control over all traffic to Berlin.

The second note specifically protested the reinforcement of the US Berlin garrison on 20 August and declared that the regime would

CURRENT INTELLIGENCE WEEKLY SUMMARY

ALLIED ACCESS ROUTES TO WEST BERLIN

UNCLASSIFIED

ALLIED ACCESS ROUTES TO WEST BERLIN

1. Helmstedt–Berlin autobahn
2. Helmstedt–Berlin railroad
3. Three air corridors

NOTE: Personnel of allied military liaison missions accredited to the commander-in-chief of Soviet forces in East Germany may cross East Germany on other land routes, but all other allied personnel as well as supplies for allied garrisons in West Berlin may use only the routes listed.

SECRET

CURRENT INTELLIGENCE WEEKLY SUMMARY

abide by the terms of the 1955 agreement only as long as these lines of communication are not used for purposes "diametrically opposed" to the postwar agreements. The note charged that the reinforcement of an occupation garrison, "at a time when

crew, presumably summoned by the police, then appeared and took the train through to Berlin. Three days earlier, the US train had been held up when the engineer defected.

On 3 September, however, East German customs police at

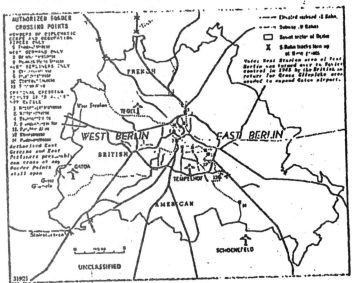

UNCLASSIFIED

it is necessary to abolish occupation regimes," is such a violation.

The East Germans have not yet attempted any serious interference with Western Allied access to West Berlin from West Germany. On 4 September the US military train from Bremerhaven to Berlin was delayed at Brandenburg by East German police, who removed the crew—allegedly for running through a red signal light in the fog. A substitute

the Marienborn checkpoint on the Berlin autobahn attempted, unsuccessfully, to examine the passports of three State Department employees en route to Berlin on official business. On the return trip, the East Germans again attempted to exercise control. This time, a Soviet officer, summoned on the demand of the Americans, waved them on, after commenting that they should have shown their passports to the East Germans.

SECRET

7 Sept 61

WEEKLY REVIEW

Page 5 of 24

7 Sept 61

SPECIAL ARTICLES

CURRENT INTELLIGENCE WEEKLY SUMMARY

East German "Frontiers"

The regime has taken a further step to convert the sector border between East and West Berlin into a state frontier: by establishing a central customs control station at the Friedrichstrasse crossing point. A West German press service reports that East Germany has quietly introduced a customs duty on all parcels from West Berlin and West Germany to East Germany. No duty had been levied on such articles in the past.

On 2 and 3 September, East German police built a barbed-wire fence along both sides of the road leading through East Germany from West Berlin to Steinstuecken, an exclave of the US sector of Berlin. While the measures may have been taken simply to cut off refugee escapes through Steinstuecken to the Western sectors, it may be a further step toward the absorption of the exclave into the surrounding East German territory or, alternatively, in East Berlin. West Berlin police have reported that two Steinstuecken residents were arrested for helping refugees reach West Berlin.

In an effort to improve security along the East-West German frontier, the regime has resorted to frequent helicopter surveillance. US military officials report that there has been a marked increase in border violations by Soviet-type helicopters along the frontier. There were seven such violations on 28 August, ten on 29 August, and four between 1 and 3 September.

Pressures on East Germans

The Ulbricht regime, confident of its control over the population, is resorting to hard-line domestic policies in an effort to silence opposition and increase production. Industrial workers clearly will no longer be handled with the great care previously accorded them. A top planning official--politburo member Bruno Leuschner--recently revealed that the party politburo has sharply criticized the trade union leadership for slackness toward "the class enemy," neglect of the struggle against work slowdowns, and general political and economic weakness. This suggests that harsher provisions for payment and work hours may soon be introduced in an effort to overcome, as far as possible, manpower losses stemming from the refugee flow prior to the sealing off of West Berlin. West German statistics show that more than 184,000 persons fled from East Germany during the first eight months of 1961, compared with just under 200,000 in the whole of 1960.

Leuschner revealed that industrial production during the first six months of 1961 had slumped slightly below the comparable period in 1960, although there was wide variation from sector to sector. Steel and coal apparently came close to plan fulfillment, while the production plan for chemicals was overfulfilled. Shortfalls were chiefly in the key machinery and equipment industries and in construction. Leuschner did not specify what measures are being planned to strengthen controls over labor and management, but he noted that industrial wages paid in the first six months had amounted to 49 percent of the annual plan figure, whereas production had been only 45 percent of plan. The regime probably will put into effect some changes in the work norms and the wage structure; such measures are already authorized by the labor code, which went into effect on 1 July.

VII-9: *(Continued)*

CURRENT INTELLIGENCE WEEKLY SUMMARY

Leuschner also noted that the Economic Council is drawing up specific proposals to eliminate weakness in the union organization. This suggests that Alfred Neumann, who was appointed to head this council in early July, and Karl Mewis, named chief of the State Planning Commission at the same time, may have clashed with long-time trade union chairman Herbert Warnke on the feasibility of speed-up measures to overcome production problems. Widespread shake-ups throughout the union structures are probably in prospect.

Under these pressures, the East German population appears to be tense and uneasy. At the Hennigsdorf locomotive plant north of Berlin, the regime reportedly has arrested at least six engineers after a succession of incidents beginning in early June. Potsdam District party leaders are reported to have been censured for permitting unrest in the plant. A show trial intended to connect worker unrest and alleged American activities in West Berlin is said to be in the making.

The Church

The regime has made new moves to split the Evangelical Church in East Germany from its leaders in West Berlin and West Germany. On 30 August, the East Berlin police president ordered Dr. Kurt Scharf, chairman of the All-German Evangelical Church synod and a resident of East Berlin, to cancel a synod meeting scheduled for the following day. At the same time, East German churchmen were forbidden to attend a synod meeting in West Berlin.

The regime followed up with a move to expel Dr. Scharf from East Berlin, on grounds that he had retained his West Berlin identity card, had protested against the sealing off

of West Berlin, and belonged to "an organization inimical to peace." The regime also refused to permit the provincial Berlin-Brandenburg synod to meet on 2 September to elect a successor to Bishop Otto Dibelius.

By these moves, the regime has effectively split the church into Eastern and Western halves. It may soon attempt to institute an East German "national" Evangelical Church.

West Berlin and West Germany

The US Mission characterizes the feelings of West Berliners as a combination of grim resolve to hang on and nervousness over where the next blow will fall. They find it especially difficult to adjust to the loss of the city's long-standing "special mission" in the East-West struggle—i.e., its role of "escape hatch," show window to the East, and meeting place of Germans from East and West. As alternatives, West Berlin leaders have already begun to stress further economic progress and development of West Berlin as a center of science and education. The mission doubts, however, whether in the long run any of the younger West Berliners will be able to resist the appeal of a "less complicated" life in West Germany.

CURRENT INTELLIGENCE WEEKLY SUMMARY

The Homeland Day rally was uneventful, with no interference from the East German regime. East Germany used similar meetings a year ago as a pretext for imposing restrictions on West German civilian access to West Berlin. West German Transport Minister Seebohm visited West Berlin and returned to Bonn on 2 September without incident, despite East German threats of "demonstrations" against his flight into Berlin on a Western commercial aircraft.

According to the West German newspaper Die Welt, only 300 West German firms have exhibits at the East German Leipzig Trade Fair from 3 to 10 September, as compared with 815 last year. Many large West German firms which had been represented for many years are conspicuously absent.

SECRET

COPY C I

21/19

This document has been
approved for release through
the HISTORICAL REVIEW PROGRAM of
the Central Intelligence Agency.

14 September 1961

Washington

Dear [ ]

I am writing my part of the answer to your letter [ ] while
here [ ] to discuss the programs with which your letter is concerned. While I may not follow your letter point by point in this response, I believe all items requested of me will be covered in the following categories into which this letter is organized:

a. The Intelligence Scene in Berlin

b. CA Programs in Berlin

c. Reorientation of the Berlin Base to Meet New Situation
   and Tasks

I. The Intelligence Scene in Berlin

The border between East and West Berlin has been converted into a
Communist-style international border across which traffic in either direction is rigidly controlled. The unique asset of Berlin is, therefore, a
thing of the past. But it is essential to bear two points in mind:
traffic is still crossing the border in both directions, including West
Berliners, West Germans, East Berliners, and almost any nationality you
wish to name. Crossings number hundreds—total East and West; counting a
round trip as two crossings—daily; and the unique nature of the Sector
Border prior to 13 August means that there is no substitute for it in West
Germany (or elsewhere) as a means of achieving access to East Germany.
The border between the Federal Republic and East Germany is tightened up as
part of the measures launched 13 August to (in our assessment) accomplish
the division of Germany, and in another week or so a restricted zone will
have been established along the entire FedRep-East German border to a depth
of perhaps 25 to 35 miles, in addition to the erection of physical barriers
at points judged by the East most vulnerable to black crossings.

While the border between West Berlin and East Germany is being converted into a plowed strip - barbed wire - watch towers - patrolled border,
the border between East Berlin and East Germany is now virtually uncontrolled - a change of the past few days. In short: A West Berliner can
visit East Berlin, with appropriate excuse (this varies but East-West
traders, newsmen, students, and a few compassionate travelers are getting
passes). Once in East Berlin, a suitably outfitted agent can presumably
cache his West documents, and on East German documentation and suitable
cover story travel into East Germany. We have been waiting for just such
pattern to emerge from the chaotic and unpredictable administration of

-2-

border controls which has obtained until very recently, and will now begin to test in practice this presumed operational potential.

Refugees are still reaching West Berlin at a rate in excess of 30 or 40 a day. By contrast, only a little over 100 reached Bavaria in the period 13 to 31 August.

While not denying that there is a role for the agent to play in collection of imminence indicators, I believe we should not overemphasize this.

So the intelligence problem is still very much one of gathering political intelligence showing intentions too. This by way of lead-in to my conception of the intelligence collection missions of BOB:

a. Reactivate agents now out of touch with us. This involves courier missions to some agents; courier missions to deaddrop communications material and instructions; resupply missions to agents with S/W commo and pads. Our more than 100 agents in East Berlin and East Germany are probably a greater asset than anything we will ever be able to build up inside East Germany through new recruitments. They must be preserved, recontacted securely, in some cases reoriented (many, especially two of the ⌐   ⌐ may have great potential as U/W assets if we can get radios to them). Some of our West Berlin assets may be usable for resupply missions, and we will need to recruit support agents in West Berlin for contact, caching, and observation missions.

b. Recruit new sources for East German coverage. Opportunities appear to lie in East-West traders in touch with East German officials; in the contacts of West Berlin students with East Berlin students (taking due note of inherent political dangers and existing prohibitions on student operations); in non-Germans, especially nationals of the developing areas

549

-3-

(who may be recruited in West Berlin and elsewhere) for their contacts with East Berliners (they currently have fairly easy access to East Berlin) or even as long-term agents for legal infiltration into East Germany probably as studdnts; recruitment of East Berliners who visit West Berlin (at the moment a small and pretty hopeless category largely party faithful and railroaders but one which may expand); and CE operations (Chief of LfV Berlin told me 12 September his double agent operations are proceeding unhindered by the border changes.

c. Support ⌐   ⌐ operations by providing leads, case officers for recruitments, and commd support from Berlin to recruits who return to East Germany.

d. Greatly expand our contacts among West Berlin newspaper, business, and professional circles for (a) reports on West Berlin morale and suggestions for possible CA operations to counteract bad morale; (b) leads to persons having contacts in the East; and (c) for their own eastern contacts. A few sources on West Berlin morale—we won't overdo it—will not bring us into conflict with State, and will provide us coverage now not available; the principal purpose of West Berlin contacts, though, will be as avenues to sources in the East.

While the above is doubtless not exhaustive, it represents a fair scale of operational opportunity remaining in Berlin, which will continue until and unless eastern authorities completely seal the border and prevent any contact between East and West Berlin.

II. CA programs in Berlin.

I have had some reservations about various types of CA programs in Berlin which I have explained pretty fully t⌐   ⌐ Let me say by way of introduction that I do believe there is a field for CA operations, but that we must eschew the "gimmick" type operation for which we became so famous - via our groups - in years past. I would see three basic types of CA operations:

a. Operations to harass the East German regime;

b. Operations to dramatize the Berlin issue worldwide;

c. Operations to bolster or maintain West Berlin morale.

In the category of harassment of the East German regime I include operations to deter the East German border guards from shooting fleeing refugees; operations encouraging defection of border guards; operations to bring factual news to the East Germans and otherwise undermine the control of the regime over the populace. ⌐   ⌐and I have discussed the possibilities of

-4-

erecting billboards at the Sector border; of painting signs on buildings facing the East; and of setting up mobile projectors to project slogans and straight news (including facsimilies of West Berlin papers), on various types of screens. Screens may be buildings, or under some conditions the low cloud cover not unusual for Berlin at this time of year. I am having [   ] get information on projectors and plastic screen materials with the idea of building mobile projection trucks with the capability of projecting slides on a translucent plastic screen forming the side or back of the truck; such trucks would include a generator, and projection equipment to project on building sides, clouds, or billboards as well, and also could perhaps carry loudspeaker equipment. They could be used all around the border, including the West Berlin-East Germany border. The theme (other than straight news) most appealing to me at the moment is Willy Brandt's "Lass dich nicht zum Lumpen machen" as a message to the guards on the border, likely to be the only audience shortly after the truck arrives, since the authorities would certainly clear away any crowds in sight of such moving signs. Still, the border guards are a good target for campaigns such as the current one offering 10,000 marks for the identity of the murderer of the refugee who tried to swim the Teltow Canal. This program would be done by the Senat, as we see it, with our support.

The idea of a second TV channel [   ] is a good one, too. TV will reach East Berlin, because no special aerial will be needed at such close range.

More news signs like the one at Potsdamer Platz would be good, too, but will take a long time to construct and will probably be seen by very few East Berliners, since the Eastern authorities will clear out the people in range.

A somewhat minor point, but worth doing I think, would be transmitting some straight news and music program (perhaps VOA has one suitable) over AFN Berlin from 0100 (when AFN signs off) until 0300 or even until 0600 when AFN comes on again. State has recommended this recently, to counteract the current "pirating" of the frequency by Radio Moscow English language programs, which come in loud and clear on the AFN Berlin frequency as the "Star Spangled Banner" fades away. I suspect Radio Moscow is aiming at East German listeners to AFN as much as anything, and feel we should deprive them of this free ride.

-5-

Operations dramatizing the Berlin issue world-wide will show an upturn shortly, I hope, partly through greater concentration of . . on the Berlin theme (and expansion of its normal production) to include one to three pictures a day, two picture features a week, all to an expanded mailing list which will shortly include journalists who have visited Berlin under any one of the several past and current programs stimulating such visits.   is clearly interested in using his facilities to produce and spread Berlin items, which we will encourage. I think we can indeed do much more in this direction, and do think we should not discount the possibilities of worldwide interest in the variety of dramatic events characteristic of the current Berlin situation. Pictures are the big thing, I believe, and I feel ___   can (and shortly will) do much, much more in this line.

The plans for making Berlin a cultural center, for building up specialized industries, and even for establishing one or more technical commissions of the UN in Berlin (I would suggest the ECE, perhaps UNESCO, perhaps WHO) are all of great importance, although our own role as KUBARK in these may in some instances not be particularly large. Willy Brandt, partly for election impact and partly because it is needed has started a program asking for still further tax advantages to Berlin residents (among other provisions) to help induce people from the FedRep to move to West Berlin. The city will need to stop the previous outflow of approximately 20,000 to 25,000 annually of its working force (up to now replenished by refugees), and achieved an inflow resulting in a net gain in working force annually, to maintain vitality. Moreover, right now West Berlin critically needs over 20,000 workers to replace the East-West Grenzgaenger of whose services the city was suddenly deprived on 13 August. Thus the economic proposals face some formidable initial problems, but should be pursued. Mayor Brandt's plans include proposals startlingly similar to your Long Range Plan, which we shall certainly encourage. Perhaps now would be a good time to lay out the proposal to Shep Stone and ask him to pursue it with the Senat, keeping us informed and hollering for help if it were needed.

The above is by no means an exhaustive catalogue of actions most, if not all, of which would appear already to have policy approval. Let me urge, therefore, that[   ]indeed be sent to Berlin, because I cannot possibly run the base and a large CA program without [   ]and without any CA officer. [   ]is already well on his way to entrenching himself in Berlin, and will be just what we need there.

III. Reorientation of Berlin Base: [   ] and I have spent all our spare
moments on the dual questions of reorienting the BOB effort and selecting
officers for assignment elsewhere in Germany. Morale is, as you note, admirably
high in Berlin Base, and most (or all) the officers currently want to stay there.
But I doubt that there will be enough opportunities to justify the current number
of officers, nor that the best talents of many of the officers now on hand will
be utilized under the current conditions. The result, in the near future, will
be a drop in morale, I think, if some officers do not soon get new assignments.
There is the usual aura of uncertainty hanging over the base, and I want to
announce as soon as possible the nature of the tasks BOB will do, and the nature
of other programs being established in light of the threatening situation, to
which BOB officers will be assigned. Every sign gives me reason to think that
all officers selected for the proposed "Task Force" will be enthusiastic about it.
           of course, has the respect of every officer on the base, and beyond this
the officers in Berlin Base now want to do something about the threat to Berlin,
which this proposed assignment will provide them every opportunity of doing.
Sending eight officers on TDY in the next week or so will avoid the occurrence of
any stagnant period at the base (which, believe me, there has as yet not been)
between the time of activating alternate communications with agents, the initial
phase of which is now largely completed, and the decisions on further activities
in Berlin and elsewhere.

     I am thinking in terms of a base of about 75 people in Berlin. This will
permit diversion of more than 20 case officers to other assignments, principally
to the paramilitary and perhaps the black radio operations. Some officers will
definitely be transferred from Berlin   ), while others
will tackle the "Task Force" in TDY status at least initially. Some officers
will definitely be selected for transfer out of Berlin; others can only be
selected after decisions are made with respect to the plans [   ] is carrying
back, and criteria can be established for selecting the officers.

     My present plans also call for a simplification of Base structure. While
tentative, plans now call for a CA branch of six or seven officers under
[   ] a positive intelligence branch under [   ] (who will also be Deputy
Chief of Base if [   ] leaves), and a CE Branch under [   ] Firm
recommendations will be along in a matter of days. A small Coordination and
Liaison Branch under   , and an expanded Intelligence Support Staff under
[   ] to exploit the numerous sources of useful information on Berlin aside
from BOB agents, are the other main operational components. A case officer
strength of around 30 can be achieved with the total strength figure of 75.
Obviously, some personnel shifts are going to take a little diplomacy, but the
urgency of the situation will obviate serious problems, I believe. I agree completely with [   ] comment that the necessity of change will be recognized.

Finally to close what has become a rather long letter, let me state
that all of us in Berlin, West Berliners, U.S. Army, and State Department
alike, feel most strongly that no amount of propaganda, no clever deception
operations, can make any real difference to the Berlin situation. Our
policy stance will provide us the support of the West Berliners and the
West Germans, or lose it. What is crucially important now is firm and
unfaltering response. We must maintain uncontrolled air access. And
unquestionably the greatest factor in maintaining West Berlin morale beyond
the uncompromising maintenace of access is the presence of American troops
in numbers sufficient to ensure that any attempt to take West Berlin by
force, conventional or unconventional, must reckon with meeting and sub-
duing American troops, with all the implications that entails. I do not
think we have enough troops in Berlin yet; we cannot keep a very extensive
level of patroling going with the forces at hand. I have suggested to
General Watson every time he asks me (which is once a week at least) what
more we can do in Berlin that the troops should be at the border, and more
troops should be here. It's way out of my field, but I would suggest the
Army rotate a combat group to Berlin every three weeks or so, and I do mean
by road. That way an additional group would be in Berlin, and the soldiers
would get valuable training. I suggest the Air Force, too, increase the
flight of military aircraft to Berlin, even if they don't need to carry
anything in or out just now. Increased flights would afford pilot training
for Air Force officers who may soon be flying the route regularly, and would
sound a note with the Berliners, valuable psychologically, of our determination — a determination backed up by readiness.

#31

- 7 -

17. S.: Now I will relate to you the report which I have prepared and
which you should immediately report to your superiors. VARENTsOV's birthday
party was celebrated not on the 15th but on Saturday 16th in order to permit
more time. On the 15th September at 0900 hours I met VARENTsOV at the
Leningrad Railroad station where he had just arrived from LENINGRAD.
After having left you I had given him his razor but on the 15th at the
railroad station I brought him a package containing the cognac, about which
I will tell you in a moment, and which has great significance, as well as
the rocket-shaped lighter and the cigarette box with inscriptions thereon.
He kissed me as he greeted me at the station. He was also met there by
General Lieut. VOZNESENSKIY and General Lieut. NIKOLAYEV. VARENTsOV had
been in LENINGRAD because a Party conference was held there and he was elected
as the delegate to the 22nd Party Congress, and very probably VARENTsOV at
this 22nd Party Congress will be elected a member of the Central Committee
of the CPSU. He will be elected as a candidate or a member of the CC, in
other words he will receive a promotion along the Party line. Having given
him the packages I went to the Committee, whose car I had at my disposal,
while he went to his Directorate where he was greeted and where a ceremony
took place in which he was awarded the Order of Lenin. He told me to be
sure to come on the 16th at 16.00 hours together with my entire family,
including my daughter and mother, to his dacha. He said that he had invited
many people but many would not be there because they were out of town concerned
with military matters. Who and with what military matters I will relate in
a moment.

18. S.: He said that the Minister MALINOVSKIY would be there and CHURAYEV
Viktor Mikhailovich, who is a member of the Central Committee and the Head
of the Party organisation of the RFSFR - one of KHRUSHCHEV's right hand men.
Gen. Polk. FOMIN will be there, Gen. Polk. SAMSONOV, Gen. Pol. G.S. KARIOFILLI,
RYABCHIKOV, a Professor of Chemistry and Lieut. Gen. SEMENOV, who was
VARENTsOV's Deputy on the First Ukrainian Front. Incidentally one of
VARENTsOV's two present deputies, the one who replaced GOFFE is also Gen.
Lieut. SEMENOV, that is a namesake of the other. In a moment I will tell

....you the details

#31

- 8 -

you the details of the party.   Since I left you in England I have had the
opportunity of speaking with VARENTsOV, ZASORIN, BUZINOV and many others.
This is what I must relate to you at once.

(19.)   S.:   In the beginning of October this year there will begin extensive
general (vse-obshchiye) manoeuvres.   There were never such manoeuvres in
the history of the Soviet Army.   This is because all headquarters of all
military districts will participate and also all headquarters of groups of
forces.   Even all rear services in the military districts will participate
in these manoeuvres.   In other words every Army formation will execute its
assigned mission in these manoeuvres just as they would be called upon to do
in case there was a war.   In addition all headquarters of all countries of
People's Democracies will also take part in these manoeuvres.   These
strategic manoeuvres will begin in early October and will take place
throughout the entire USSR and throughout all of the countries of People's
Democracies all based on combatting a hypothetical enemy in the direction
of Germany.

(20.)   S.:   I will now try to explain to you in detail why these manoeuvres
will take place and what their objective is.   Later I will tell you who,
why and when gave me this information.   These manoeuvres are called strategic
because they involve very great territorial depth and all military districts
and all groups of forces will participate as well as all the headquarters of
the countries of the People's Democracies.   These manoeuvres will continue
for a period of one month.   The objective of these manoeuvres is to examine
everything as a whole and to determine what units have specific capabilities.
They will examine who can best fulfil offensive missions shock action,
defensive operations and to examine the state of training and combat
readiness of all units, as well as their joint action.   Through these
manoeuvres deficiencies in training can be corrected and experience in joint
operations gained.   But this is only one purpose, the second purpose is to
have these huge forces in a state of combat readiness exactly at the time
that the Peace Treaty with East Germany will be signed, so that if any
difficulties occur immediately after the signing of this Treaty; they would
be in a position to strike a heavy blow.   In other words what KHRUSHCHEV
wants to do is to backstop with actual large-scale military preparations

....../camouflaged

* which will be signed right after the
Congress.

#31

- 9 -

camouflaged as manoeuvres his signing of the Peace Treaty with East Germany.

21. S.: KHRUSHCHEV considers that if NATO swallows the second pill and he considers that the first pill, which was the closing of the borders of East and West Berlin, has already been swallowed, - that is the action of 13th August - incidentally, I know about this closing four days before the fact and I wanted to pass this information on to you but had no means for doing this, since the phone call arrangement was only good for Monday and this took place on a different day. I did not want to risk putting the information into the dead drop and calling by chance. We will have to work out a system that will permit me to pass critical information to you quickly in future.

22. S.: KHRUSHCHEV, his Central Committee and his government plan to do this - on the 17th October to open the 22nd Party Congress. This conference we should call Conference "Aggressive". That is because a very aggressive attitude will be prevalent, all sorts of propaganda speeches are being prepared asking decisive action against imperialism and colonialism. And by firing up the Congress with such speeches KHRUSHCHEV hopes to untie his hands for aggressive action by placing the responsibility for the decisions which support KHRUSHCHEV and his government's position on the Congress. Even if a war takes place after the Congress, KHRUSHCHEV can refer to this situation as a decision of the Congress. For Bolsheviks the Congress represents their programme for the immediate future. All secretaries of Central Committees will be present at this congress as well as secretaries of the Parties of other People's Democracies and Communist Parties from capitalist countries as well, many of the latter will come secretly. It will be of interest to see how the Communist leaders throughout the world react to the concept of military action at this time as proposed by the leading Communist Party, namely that of the Soviet Union. I suggest for your consideration and that of our leaders how advantageous it would be to introduce some sort of split in views at this congress. It is important that there be no unanimity of views between all of the Communist leaders of the various countries.

23. S.: Already there have been orders issued that during the month of

..../October no

- 10 -

October no foreigners should be admitted to the Soviet Union. All MOSCOW
hotels are now being retained for the use of Central Committee members and
Party delegates. They are even fumigating the rooms to be sure that
foreigners previously living there have not left bacteriological contamination.
Even in our Committee we have turned down all requests for foreign visitors
during the month of October by saying there is no room, and that they will be
busy with the Party Congress. This will continue until the 15th November
since many Party delegates will stay after the Congress to attend the
celebration and parade of 7th November. In addition they are now preparing
to set up very strict counter intelligence procedures in MOSCOW and the Moscow
oblast during this time. Therefore, I request you to have all of our agent
operations in MOSCOW suspend activity during this period. It will be very
difficult to work in MOSCOW during this time and the KGB from other cities
have also been called in.

24. S.: Let me review. Immediately after the Party Conference
KHRUSHCHEV wants to sign the Peace Treaty; at the time of the signing he
wants to have all possible military units in a state of combat readiness.
If necessary he will strike. If it is only a local attack by us then it
will be parried, but of course if a larger conflict develops that is why
combat readiness is needed. KHRUSHCHEV, our General Staff and the GRU know
prefectly well that secret preparations in modern times are not possible due
to intelligence techniques. But under the guise of manoeuvres, concerning
which he will insist that they are only manoeuvres, their extent and duration
can easily be extended. If the allies swallow the second pill and say
"very well since you have signed a treaty with East Germany we will deal with
East Germany", then the strain will be relieved and the manoeuvres will
terminate and the result of these will still serve as a valuable training
exercise for joint operations. If not the powder is still dry and military
action can be employed. This is the dual purpose for which these manoeuvres
are planned for the early days of October.

25. S.: Right now MOSCOW is boiling with all kinds of representatives
from the headquarters of the countries of People's Democracies, both in

...../military and

- 11 -

military and civilian dress. I have seen them everywhere and anyone can spot them. Secondly, all prominent military commanders are in the field with troops, for example, at VARENTsOV's birthday party his deputy PYRSKIY was not present.

26. S.: There are two deputies, PYRSKIY and SEMENOV, who replaced GOFFE. PYRSKIY is now at NOVAYA ZEMLYA where they are experimenting with atomic detonations. There is a large base there on which are rockets with atomic warheads, the details of which I will give you shortly. The other deputy SELENOV is now attending the atomic bomb tests in Central Asia. Here is how I found this out. At VARENTsOV's party, Viktor Mikhailovich CHURAYEV asked VARENTsOV - where is PYRSKIY? and MALINOVSKY said that PYRSKIY is doing a fine job in running the tests and the training programme at NOVAYA ZEMLYA.

27. S.: I can now report to you about the atomic tests being conducted now since KHRUSHCHEV felt that it was impossible for him not to run these tests. These tests have two phases; in the past years the first phase consisted of testing the individual TNT equivalent weapons. They were raised on towers, from masts and dropped from aircraft. But now KHRUSHCHEV and his military commanders are testing nuclear detonations delivered by rockets. This is phase II. These tests are conducted by means of firing a rocket with a conventional charge against the selected target and then assembling an atomic warhead and firing it against the same target. Both MALINOVSKY and VARENTsOV answered CHURAYEV that Gen. Polk. PYRSKIY is now at NOVAYA ZEMLYA running the tests and will continue to remain there because there will be additional tests.

28. S.: There is a huge rocket launching base at NOVAYA ZEMLYA which is equipped to fire the R-12 and the R-14 rockets. There are no R-11s there; this was all told to me by BUZINOV. Now with respect to these rockets the R-12 is already adopted and is being serially produced. Its range is two and a half thousand kilometres. The R-14 is now being prepared for serial production but it has not yet been produced in quantity. The range of the R-14 is four and a half thousand kilometres. Both ranges I have given are those for these rockets carrying an atomic warhead. Of course the ranges are greater with conventional warheads. ......G.: Approximately?

26 September 1961

C-48

(75)

1.3(a)(4)

MEMORANDUM FOR THE RECORD:

SUBJECT : Conversation with Mr. Helms Re
▓▓▓▓▓▓ Report on Large-Scale
Soviet Military Preparations

1.3(a)(4

1. When Mr. Osborn and I were discussing the above report with Mr. Helms, upon its receipt yesterday afternoon, I told Mr. Helms we should expect renewed consumer questions about the possibility of deception. I pointed out that the ▓▓▓▓▓ material had not only been accepted by most of our consumers, but that the material was: a) extremely costly in terms of Soviet security; and b) apparently inconsistent with any discernible Soviet policy purposes. However, I said we must face up to the fact that ▓▓▓▓▓ was now in a key position to give us information vitally affecting our own reaction to recent Soviet moves. For example, ▓▓▓▓ could assure us that all the preparations we would be seeing over the next few weeks were, indeed, part of the maneuvers already described, in which case the Soviets would be able to take aggressive military action without alerting our indications mechanism. On the other hand, at some critical juncture, ▓▓▓▓ might tell us that the Soviets were now ready to strike unless we made significant concessions, even though, in fact, the entire Soviet effort was bluff.

1.3(a)(4)

2. Mr. Helms agreed that such questions would probably arise, but that we should take the position that the consumers themselves would have to make up their minds as to the answer. He said all we could vouch for was that, from strictly an operational standpoint, we had been unable to fault ▓▓▓▓▓ and could see nothing in the operational and CE aspects of the case which would cause us to question the validity of the information being supplied.

1.3(a)(4)

APPROVED FOR RELEASE
3 1 MAR 1992

JOHN M MAURY
Chief, SR Division

JJM/r

1.3(a)(4)

560

TOP SECRET

TS 1-9597-61
Limited distribution
SNIE 11-10/1-61
5 October 1961

SPECIAL NATIONAL INTELLIGENCE ESTIMATE

SOVIET TACTICS IN THE BERLIN CRISIS

Supplement to SNIE 11-10-61

○ Partially Clearly Partially Legible
○ Action Review Management

NOTE: This is the final version of the estimate and additional distribution is circulated

Central Intelligence Agency

TOP SECRET

TOP SECRET
LIMITED DISTRIBUTION

TS # 142397-c

CENTRAL INTELLIGENCE AGENCY

This document has been approved for release through the HISTORICAL REVIEW PROGRAM of the Central Intelligence Agency.

5 October 1961   Date 2/18/94

HRP 94-3

SUBJECT: SNIE 11-10/1-61: SOVIET TACTICS IN THE BERLIN CRISIS

THE PROBLEM

To estimate Soviet tactics in the Berlin crisis over the next few months, with particular reference to reported Soviet intentions to take radical unilateral action during this period.

BACKGROUND

A recent report from a source, judged at this time to be reliable, states that Soviet and Satellite forces will be brought to a high state of combat readiness in exercises "of unprecedented scope" beginning in early October and lasting for one month. This source supplies many details supporting this theme, citing personal observation and the remarks of senior officials, mostly military officers. He reports learning from a senior commander that Khrushchev's present policy is to hold back, putting the brakes on international tensions until the Party Congress, at which time he will abruptly go over to a highly

TOP SECRET
LIMITED DISTRIBUTION

TOP SECRET
LIMITED DISTRIBUTION

militant line. According to this story, a separate peace treaty
with East Germany will then be signed immediately after the
Congress. Without specifically so stating, the report implies
that a challenge to Allied access will follow promptly upon the
signing of the treaty. It is thought that perhaps the West will
"swallow the second pill" (the first having been the border
closure in Berlin); if not, Bloc forces, already at a high state
of readiness, will "strike first if the situation warrants."[*]

THE ESTIMATE

1. The fourth quarter is normally the peak of the annual
military training cycle in the USSR and Eastern Europe. In
addition, there is an unusual stress on readiness at the present
time, and the 25 September announcement of exercises by the
Warsaw Pact forces suggests that these will be on a larger scale
than on any previous occasion. Such preparations are clearly
intended to convince the West of Communist military strength,
readiness, and determination in the Berlin crisis and to increase
pressure on the West either to make concessions or to acquiesce

---

[*] We have examined closely the possibility that the source could
be, wittingly or unwittingly, a channel for deception material.
Our present judgment, based mainly on the sensitivity and
volume of the material he is providing, is that this is
unlikely.

- 2 -

TOP SECRET
LIMITED DISTRIBUTION

TOP SECRET
LIMITED DISTRIBUTION

in Communist encroachments. They are also aimed at strengthening the USSR's military posture for the period of crisis and uncertainty which the Soviets foresee. But the preparations of which we are at present aware from all sources of information are not of such a scope and nature as to support a conclusion that the USSR is "peaking" all its forces for general war in the near future.

2. On the basis of his previous reporting and independent confirmation of portions of this report, we accept the source's statements concerning measures of military preparedness as correct in many although not in all respects. He is not in a position, however, to report reliably or completely on deliberations and decisions of the highest military and political bodies in Moscow. His statements concerning a decision to sign a separate treaty in October and, if conditions warrant, to strike an initial military blow, appear to us to fall into the category of speculation arising from knowledge he has acquired about contingency military planning.

3. It is evident that the Soviets must have contingency plans for the next phases of the Berlin crisis, but we doubt strongly that the USSR has made any irrevocable decisions

- 3 -

TOP SECRET
LIMITED DISTRIBUTION

concerning the timing of a separate treaty and of unilateral
steps thereafter against the status quo in Berlin. We continue
to believe that the USSR regards negotiations as the least
risky method of advancing toward its objectives, and also that
Khrushchev still hopes that the threat of unilateral action
will force the Allies to make at least some concessions to his
demands. And, if these hopes fail to materialize, he has at his
disposal a wide range of unilateral actions, each of which, he
believes, is limited enough to create only a minimal risk of
forceful Western response, yet each of which can bring the USSR
a step closer to its aims.

4. Currently the USSR is seeking to display a more positive
attitude toward negotiations; it has ceased to reiterate deadlines
for a separate treaty and has indicated some flexibility in its
approach to negotiations. These maneuvers are designed in part
to appear responsive to the calls for peaceful compromise
emanating from the Belgrade Conference and the General Assembly.
They are also intended to encourage those sectors of opinion
which are urging the Allies to consider concessions to Soviet
demands. Perhaps most important, they are intended to probe the
Allied position in order to determine whether negotiations are

- 4 -

likely to bring some progress toward their objectives. We continue to believe that the Soviets prefer to enter negotiations
before undertaking major unilateral steps or signing a separate
treaty with the GDR.

5. Along with this, however, Khrushchev has several
times voiced concern that the Allies would use negotiations
merely as a device for stalling. He recognizes that, once
formal talks are under way, any move on his part to break them
off and turn to unilateral measures might solidify NATO unity
and forfeit the support for his Berlin policy which he has tried
to develop among the non-aligned nations. However, he would
feel it necessary to respond positively to a formal Allied
tender of negotiations. But he would also attempt to assure
himself in preliminary discussions that some advance toward his
objectives would result from such a conference. If he felt that
the prospects for this were poor, he would probably proceed at
some point with a separate peace treaty, in part as a means of
bringing the Allies under greater pressure to talk on Soviet terms.

6. If the Soviets decide to make a major unilateral move
against Allied rights in Berlin, they would clearly wish to be
in a state of maximum military readiness at the time, both to

- 5 -

deter the Allies from a forceful reaction and to be prepared
for any eventuality should deterrence fail. They recognize
the dangers of a situation in which the West would feel itself
confronted with the alternatives of deep humiliation or a military showdown, because they realize that such a situation might
escape their control. They have deliberately left unclear the
question of whether they would, immediately after a peace treaty
back up with force their demands for new access procedures.
The source's references to "striking first" are ambiguous and
could mean any level of military action, possibly undertaken
only after a judgment was reached that the West was about to
resort to force locally. We think it very unlikely, however,
that the Soviets would "strike first" in the sense of launching
a major military offensive, unless they were convinced that a
large-scale Western attack was inevitable and imminent.

7. In conclusion, we believe that the course of action
outlined in the present report -- signature of a separate peace
treaty in late October followed by a prompt challenge to Allied
access -- has been construed by the source and others from their
knowledge of military preparations. We do not believe that firm
decisions of this kind have been taken by the top Soviet

- 6 -

leadership. But the considerations outlined above do suggest that the higher state of military readiness to be achieved in October/November will make this a favorable period, from the Soviet standpoint, for limited unilateral moves against Western rights in Berlin, if their prospects for advancing toward their objectives at that time via negotiations appear dim.

- 7 -

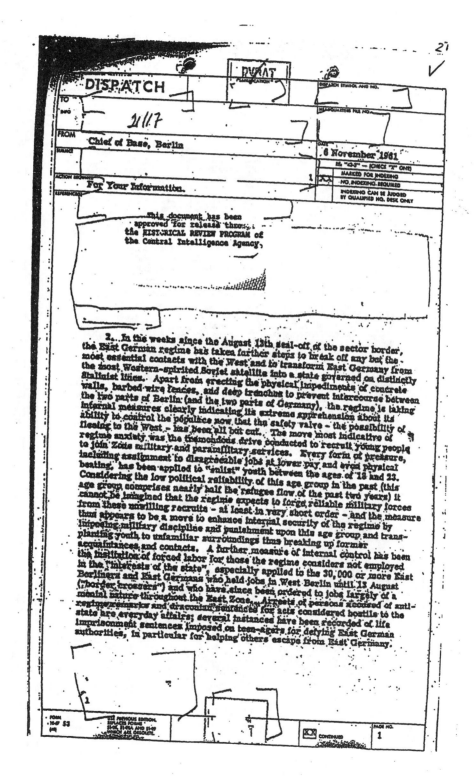

DISPATCH

TO

FROM
Chief of Base, Berlin

SUBJECT

For Your Information.

This document has been approved for release thro... the HISTORICAL REVIEW PROGRAM of the Central Intelligence Agency.

6 November 1961

2. In the weeks since the August 13th seal-off of the sector border, the East German regime has taken further steps to break off any but the most essential contacts with the West and to transform East Germany from the most Western-spirited Soviet satellite into a state governed on distinctly Stalinist lines. Apart from erecting the physical impediments of concrete walls, barbed-wire fences, and deep trenches to prevent intercourse between the two parts of Berlin (and the two parts of Germany), the regime is taking internal measures clearly indicating its extreme apprehension about its ability to control the populace now that the safety valve - the possibility of fleeing to the West - has been all but cut. The move most indicative of regime anxiety was the tremendous drive conducted to recruit young people to join Zone military and paramilitary services. Every form of pressure, including assignment to disagreeable jobs at lower pay, and even physical beating, has been applied to "enlist" youth between the ages of 18 and 23. Considering the low political reliability of this age group in the past (this age group comprises nearly half the refugee flow of the past two years) it cannot be imagined that the regime expects to forge reliable military forces from these unwilling recruits - at least in very short order - and the measure thus appears to be a move to enhance internal security of the regime by imposing military discipline and punishment upon this age group, and transplanting youth to unfamiliar surroundings thus breaking up former acquaintances and contacts. A further measure of internal control has been the institution of forced labor for those the regime considers not employed in the "interests of the state", especially applied to the 30,000 or more East Berliners and East Germans who held jobs in West Berlin until 13 August ("border crossers") and who have since been ordered to jobs largely of a menial nature throughout the East Zone. Arrests of persons accused of anti-regime remarks and draconian sentences for acts considered hostile to the state are everyday affairs; several instances have been recorded of life imprisonment sentences imposed on teen-agers for defying East German authorities, in particular for helping others escape from East Germany.

CONTINUED   PAGE NO. 1

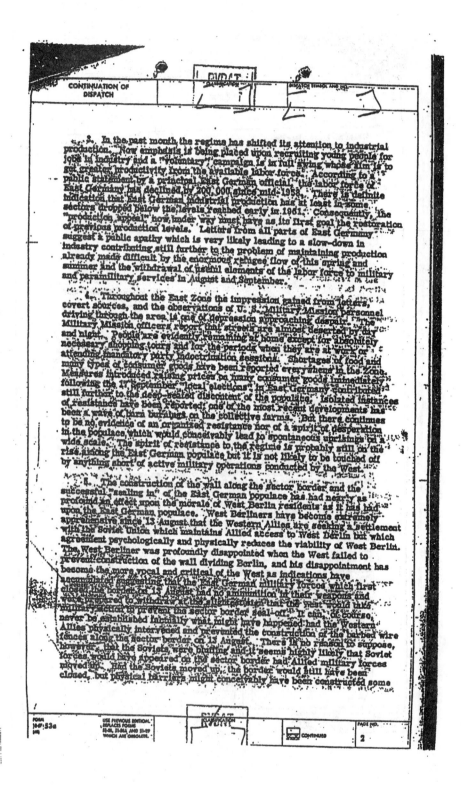

3. In the past month, the regime has shifted its attention to industrial production. New emphasis is being placed upon recruiting young people for jobs in industry and a "voluntary" campaign is in full swing whose aim is to get greater productivity from the available labor force. According to a public statement by a principal East German official, the labor force of East Germany has declined by 200,000 since mid-1958. There is definite indication that East German industrial production has at least in some sectors dropped below the levels reached early in 1961. Consequently, the "production appeal" now under way must have as its first goal the restoration of previous production levels. Letters from all parts of East Germany suggest a public apathy which is very likely leading to a slow-down in industry contributing still further to the problem of maintaining production already made difficult by the enormous refugee flow of this spring and summer and the withdrawal of useful elements of the labor force to military and paramilitary services in August and September.

4. Throughout the East Zone the impression gained from letters, covert sources, and the observations of U. S. Military Mission personnel driving through the area is one of depression approaching despair. The Military Mission officers report that streets are almost deserted by day and night. People are evidently remaining at home except for absolutely necessary shopping tours and for the periods when they are at work or attending mandatory party indoctrination sessions. Shortages of food and many types of consumer goods have been reported everywhere in the Zone. Measures introduced raising prices on many consumer goods immediately following the 17 September "local elections" in East Germany contributed still further to the deep-seated discontent of the populace. Isolated instances of resistance have been reported, one of the most recent developments has been a wave of barn burning on the collective farms. But there continues to be no evidence of an organized resistance nor of a spirit of desperation in the populace, which would conceivably lead to spontaneous uprisings on a wide scale. The spirit of resistance to the regime is probably still on the rise among the East German populace but it is not likely to be touched off by anything short of active military operations conducted by the West.

5. The construction of the wall along the sector border, and the successful "sealing in" of the East German populace has had nearly as profound an effect upon the morale of West Berlin residents as it has had upon the East German populace. West Berliners have become extremely apprehensive since 13 August that the Western Allies are seeking a settlement with the Soviet Union which maintains Allied access to West Berlin but which agreement psychologically and physically reduces the viability of West Berlin. The West Berliner was profoundly disappointed when the West failed to prevent construction of the wall dividing Berlin, and his disappointment has become the more vocal and critical of the West as indications have accumulated suggesting that the East German military forces which first closed the border on 13 August had no ammunition in their weapons and were prepared to withdraw at the slightest sign that the West would take military action to prevent the sector border seal-off. It can, of course, never be established initially what might have happened had the Western Allies physically intervened and prevented the construction of the barbed wire fences along the sector border on 13 August. There is no reason to suppose, however, that the Soviets were bluffing and it seems highly likely that Soviet forces would have appeared on the sector border had Allied military forces moved up. Had the Soviets moved up, the border would still have been closed, but physical barriers might conceivably have been constructed some

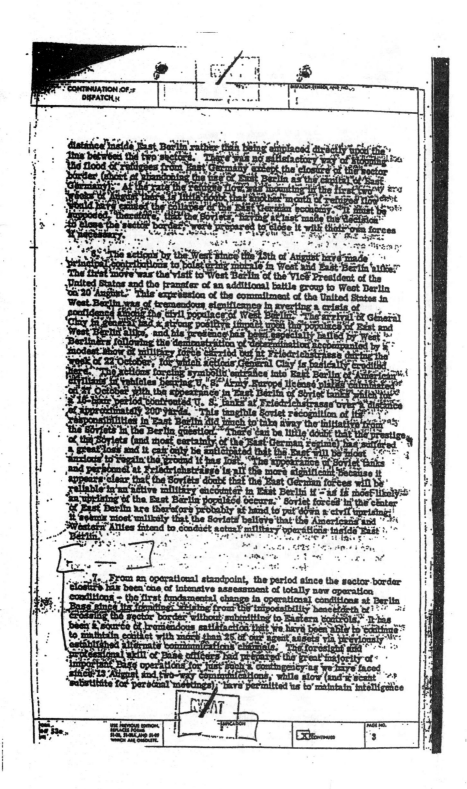

distance inside East Berlin rather than being emplaced directly upon the line between the two sectors. There was no satisfactory way of stopping the flood of refugees from East Germany except the closure of the sector border (short of abandoning the use of East Berlin as the capital of East Germany). At the rate the refugee flow was mounting in the first half of the weeks of August there is little doubt that another month of refugee flow would have ended the collapse of the East German economy. It must be supposed, therefore, that the Soviets, having at last made the decision to close the sector border, were prepared to close it with their own forces if necessary.

6. The actions by the West since the 13th of August have made principal contributions to bolster the morale in West and East Berlin alike. The first move was the visit to West Berlin of the Vice President of the United States and the transfer of an additional battle group to West Berlin on 20 August. This expression of the commitment of the United States in West Berlin was of tremendous significance in averting a crisis of confidence among the civil populace of West Berlin. The arrival of General Clay in general had a strong positive impact upon the populace of East and West Berlin alike, and his presence has been especially hailed by West Berliners following the demonstration of determination accompanied by a modest show of military force carried out at Friedrichstrasse during the week of 22 October, for which actions General Clay is basically credited here. The actions forcing symbolic entrance into East Berlin of American civilians in vehicles bearing U. S. Army Europe license plates culminated on 27 October with the appearance in East Berlin of Soviet tanks which for a 16-hour period confronted U. S. tanks at Friedrichstrasse over a distance of approximately 200 yards. This tangible Soviet recognition of its responsibilities in East Berlin did much to take away the initiative from the Soviets in the Berlin question. There can be little doubt that the prestige of the Soviets (and most certainly of the East German regime) has suffered a great loss and it can only be anticipated that the East will be most anxious to regain the ground it has lost. The appearance of Soviet tanks and personnel at Friedrichstrasse is all the more significant because it appears clear that the Soviets doubt that the East German forces will be reliable in an active military encounter in East Berlin if – as is most likely – an uprising of the East Berlin populace occurs. Soviet forces in the center of East Berlin are therefore probably at hand to put down a civil uprising; it seems most unlikely that the Soviets believe that the Americans and Western Allies intend to conduct actual military operations inside East Berlin.

7. From an operational standpoint, the period since the sector border closure has been one of intensive assessment of totally new operation conditions – the first fundamental change in operational conditions at Berlin Base since its founding. Arising from the impossibility henceforth of crossing the sector border without submitting to Eastern controls, it has been a source of tremendous satisfaction that we have been able to continue to maintain contact with more than 25 of our agent assets via previously established alternate communications channels. The foresight and professional skill of Base officers had prepared the great majority of important Base operations for just such a contingency as we have faced since 13 August and two-way communications, while slow (and a scant substitute for personal meetings), have permitted us to maintain intelligence

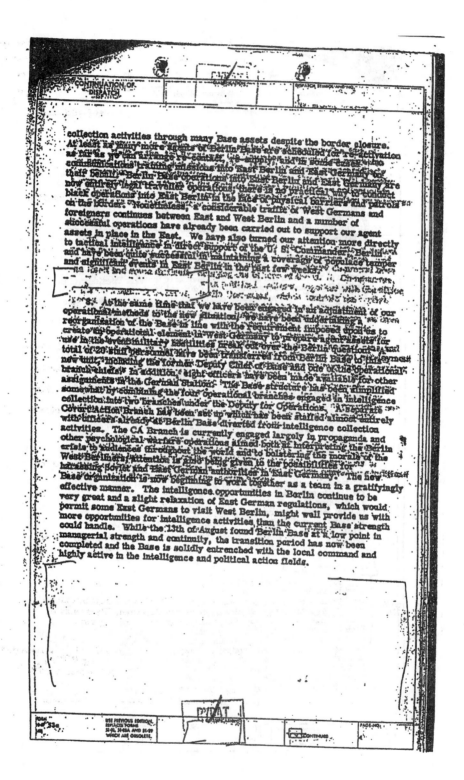

collection activities through many Base assets despite the border closure. At least as many more agents of Berlin Base are scheduled for re-activation as far as we can arrange. To counter the supply, and in some cases also communications, training missions into East Berlin and East Germany for their benefit. Berlin Base operations into East Berlin and East Germany are now entirely legal traveler operations, there is no practical way to conduct black operations into East Berlin in the face of physical barriers and patrols on the border. Nonetheless, a considerable traffic of West Germans and foreigners continues between East and West Berlin and a number of successful operations have already been carried out to support our agent assets in place in the East. We have also turned our attention more directly to tactical intelligence in direct support of the U. S. Commander, Berlin, and have been quite successful in maintaining a coverage of populace temper and significant events in East Berlin in the past few weeks.

As the same time that we have been engaged in readjustment of our operational methods to the new situation, we have been undertaking a reorganization of the Base in line with the requirement imposed upon us to create an operational element in West Germany to prepare agent assets for use in the event military hostilities break out over the Berlin question. A total of 20 staff personnel have been transferred from Berlin Base to this new unit, including the former Deputy Chief of Base and one of the operational branch chiefs. In addition, eight officers have been made available for other assignments in the German Station. The Base structure has been simplified somewhat by combining the four operational branches engaged in intelligence collection into two branches under the Deputy for Operations. A separate Covert Action Branch has been set up which has been staffed almost entirely with officers already at Berlin Base diverted from intelligence collection activities. The CA Branch is currently engaged largely in propaganda and other psychological warfare operations aimed both at interpreting the Berlin crisis to audiences throughout the world and to bolstering the morale of the West Berliners. Attention is also being given to the possibilities for harassing Soviet and East German authorities in East Germany. The new Base organization is now beginning to work together as a team in a gratifyingly effective manner. The intelligence opportunities in Berlin continue to be very great and a slight relaxation of East German regulations, which would permit some East Germans to visit West Berlin, might well provide us with more opportunities for intelligence activities than the current Base strength could handle. While the 13th of August found Berlin Base at a low point in managerial strength and continuity, the transition period has now been completed and the Base is solidly entrenched with the local command and highly active in the intelligence and political action fields.

ULK-77-1035 #9

TS# 185467-a

CENTRAL INTELLIGENCE AGENCY

OFFICE OF NATIONAL ESTIMATES

23 October 1962

MEMORANDUM FOR THE DIRECTOR

SUBJECT: Survivability of West Berlin*

ASSUMPTION: SOVIET BLOCKADE OF WEST BERLIN IN
RETALIATION FOR US ACTIONS IN CUBA

1. West Berlin is economically prepared for a total blockade. We estimate that existing stocks of critical items are sufficient to maintain the physical well-being of the West Berlin population for at least six months. With respect to particular categories of critical supplies, we estimate:

FOOD: At least six months (with selective rationing)

FUEL: About 1 year
(Coal)

MEDICINES: Six months

INDUSTRIAL MATERIAL: Sufficient to maintain employment for 4-5 months.

* This memorandum has been coordinated with the representative of the Director of Intelligence and Research, Department of State, and the Director, Defense Intelligence Agency.

GROUP 1

Excluded from automatic
downgrading and
declassification

Declassified by 953775
Date 6 APR 1978

2. The critical factor, however, is not physical or economic but psychological. Everything would depend on the context of the Soviet move, and how quickly and forcefully the US reacted. A total and uncontested blockade would cause the West Berliners to lose all hope in a matter of weeks. A blockade contested by a successful airlift would probably relieve initial apprehension and sustain morale for a few months. Over a longer period, however, morale would deteriorate rapidly in the absence of a reasonable expectation that the US would break the blockade. The West Berliner's would become extraordinarily sensitive to, and suspicious of any indication from either side that the Cuban crisis might produce an accommodation at their expense.

ABBOT SMITH
Acting Chairman

- 2 -

Glossary of Abbreviations

BOB . . . . Berlin Operations Base
BRD . . . . Bundesrepublik Deutschland (Federal Republic of Germany, West Germany)
CIA . . . . Central Intelligence Agency
CIG . . . . Central Intelligence Group
CSI . . . . Center for the Study of Intelligence
DCI . . . . Director of Central Intelligence
DDCI . . . . . . Deputy Director of Central Intelligence
DDP . . . . Directorate of Plans
DDR . . . . Deutsche Demokratische Republik (German Democratic Republic, East Germany)
GRU . . . . Soviet military intelligence
HVA . . . . Hauptverwaltung Aufklärung (East German foreign intelligence)
IAB . . . . US Intelligence Advisory Board
IAC . . . . US Intelligence Advisory Committee
IWF . . . . Institut für Wirtschaftswissenschaftliche Forschung (cover name for the HVA)
JCS . . . . US Joint Chiefs of Staff
KGB . . . . Committee for State Security (Soviet foreign intelligence since 1954)
KI . . . . Committee of Information, (Soviet foreign intelligence, 1947-48)
MfS . . . . Ministerium für Staatssicherheit (East German Security and Intelligence)
MGB . . . . Soviet Ministry for State Security (Soviet foreign intelligence, 1946-47)
MVD . . . . Soviet Ministry of the Interior
NIE . . . . National Intelligence Estimate
NKGB . . . . . . People's Commissariat for State Security (Soviet foreign intelligence, 1943-46)
NKVD . . . . . People's Commissariat for Internal Affairs (Soviet intelligence and security, until 1943)
OCI . . . . Office of Current Intelligence
ONE . . . . Office of National Estimates
OPC . . . . Office of Policy Coordination
ORE . . . . Office of Reports and Estimates
ORR . . . . Office of Research and Reports
OSO . . . . Office of Special Operations
OSS . . . . Office of Strategic Services
R&A . . . . Research and Analysis Branch of OSS
SED . . . . Sozialistische Einheitspartei Deutschlands (East German Communist Party)
SI . . . . Secret Intelligence Branch of SSU
SIS . . . . British Secret Intelligence Service
SMERSH . . . Smert Shpionam (Death to Spies!) Soviet counter-espionage unit
SNIE . . . . Special National Intelligence Estimates
SSU . . . . US Strategic Services Unit
USIB . . . . US Intelligence Board
X-2 . . . . Counterintelligence Branch of SSU

The African Dream

The African Dream

Visions of Love and Sorrow: The Art of John Muafangejo

ORDE LEVINSON

FOREWORD BY NELSON MANDELA

162 illustrations

THAMES AND HUDSON

'My themes, I do dreams....'

First published in the United States in 1992
by Thames and Hudson Inc.,
500 Fifth Avenue, New York, New York 10110

Library of Congress Catalog Card Number 92-70865

Printed and bound in Slovenia

Contents

Foreword

John Muafangejo's prints are dazzling. He has gone beyond literal interpretation of ideas and takes the viewer into the realm of symbolism and dream. The message which each work conveys is illuminated by a mesmerising repetition of line, mark or pattern which course and flow in rhythm. This in combination with the simple contrast of black and white shape would be enough to hold one's attention. But there is more: the subject matter in each picture is detailed, beckoning the intellect; a story is being told. The works, besides being picturesque, are records of his traditions, his day-to-day life and the life of the peoples of South Africa.

A second dimension has been added to this documentary aspect of his work by the introduction of written words which are incorporated into almost all of his pictures. In this purely visual form of communication and expression, the use of written illustration emphasizes, highlights and adds to the content and subject matter of the works. He has chosen the use of the English language, leading one to believe his aims are twofold: to preserve his memories, and at the same time, to transmit, reach out and impart this experience to the world.

In a society familiar with the alienation and isolation of its people, John Muafangejo was therefore also a teacher, functioning as one who unites people.

Muafangejo is no longer with us, but his art manifests his continuance.

Nelson Mandela, January 1992

Introduction

The linocuts of John Ndevasia Muafangejo are world famous, and his work has received praise and recognition accorded to no other contemporary African artist. Although cut short by his early death on 27 November 1987, his unique life gave rise to a very distinctive, open and autobiographical style. He is now considered among the best exponents of the linocut in the twentieth century, and his work gives cause for a re-evaluation of the importance of contemporary African art to a western audience.

He was born Ndevasia ya Muafangejo (Ndevasia son of Muafangejo – his father's first name), but changed his name to John Muafangejo when he converted to Christianity at the age of fourteen, and then again in 1981 to John Ndevasia Muafangejo. His parents were both Kwanyamas – the largest of the eight Owambo tribes whose territory now forms part of southern Angola and northern Namibia.

His birth date is uncertain. In keeping with the Kwanyama tradition of relating time to the seasons he initially said of it: 'I not sure between winter and summer with the trees bearing new leaves. I choose date'; but he later adapted to western tradition by fixing upon 5 October 1943. While this date is generally accepted it may be inaccurate, for in the work *Muafangejo's Kraal*, created in 1979, he refers to himself as 'John has 38 years old' which would imply a birth date in 1941.

Muafangejo was born in Etunda lo Nghadi in southern Angola, about forty miles from the border with Namibia, and when he was five his family's *Eumbo* or homestead *(above)* was moved a few miles deeper into Angola to Ombala Muandi, where he lived until 1956. His father was probably one of approximately three thousand headmen with their own homesteads, while his mother, Petelena Hamupolo (pl. 103), was the eighth wife of his father, and the second in seniority because she was 'the keeper of the corn'. As well as Muafangejo she had six daughters and another son. None of the rest of the family clan could read or write, for in 1985 Muafangejo recounts: 'I am the only educated one, so the responsibility is mostly mine. I cannot go overseas anymore, there is no money.'

Muafangejo's artistic roots lie partly in his cultural background within the Kwanyama tribe and partly in tuition he received from an uncle, Stephen Paulus; then later, between 1967 and 1969, he received technical training at the Evangelical Lutheran Church Art and Craft Centre (ELC), part of the Swedish Oskarberg Mission Station at Rorke's Drift in Natal.

Kwanyama tribal life is particularly rich and sophisticated in its cultural ceremonies and games, and these undoubtedly influenced and were echoed in Muafangejo's approach to art. Kwanyama children from a very early age participate

fully in the clan's social life. Each morning Muafangejo would have received a greeting from his father – a traditional sign of respect accorded daily to all members of the *Eumbo*, including the children. Then, along with the other young boys, he would have spent the day tending the cattle. In the evening the entire clan would gather around the sacred fire to converse freely and recount stories: for example, a

herdboy might tell of his escape from lions (pls. 35, 36), or the gathering would be told of Kwanyama warriors (pl. 14). Everyone present would also participate in symbolic dancing and play communal games of reciting prose-poetry, exchanging proverbs and metaphors and guessing riddles. These activities were quite everyday, and to the children they would have been as ordinary yet exciting as sport to many western children.

The strong philosophical and moral content of these absorbing 'literary' games was woven into Muafangejo's way of thinking and clearly influenced his development as an artist and the subject matter of his work. Thus, the eulogising of King Mandume in many of his works probably stemmed from his hearing and participating in traditional songs of praise (*okulitanga*). Proverbs (*omise*) are used (or 'thrown' – *okuumba omuse*) frequently in everyday Kwanyama life – for example, *Ounyuni wokambia, wai p'ombada, wai p'osi* ('the world is like a full pot of sorghum grain, now up, now down') – a reference to a pot that is swung up and down between two sticks (*below*, and in *A Woman is cooking Food*, pl. 10).

Proverbs abound in Muafangejo's work, and two are beautifully illustrated by moving linocuts: 'The love is approaching but too much of anything is very dangerous' (pl. 117) and 'Hope and optimism in spite of present difficulties' (p. 6).

Exchanging riddles (*onambula-mo*, literally: 'that which is taken from within') is a game played by two lines of people. One side challenges the other with a riddle. If it is correctly answered then the right to ask a riddle passes to the other team. One such double riddle could have a reference to *A Sad People* (pl. 116): the clue, 'A wild fig has ripe fruit on one side, on the other the leaves are beginning to open ', is answered: 'People: on the one hand some are dying, on the other some are being born...'

Thus from a very early age, Muafangejo *(below)* was encouraged in free and open self-expression. Those who met him as a man remark on his complete openness and his 'booming voice and friendly manner'.

Apart from the influence of these oral traditions, Muafangejo was also surrounded by many other forms of art. Kwanyama men are hunters and providers, but are also expected to be creative and make the wooden domestic utensils, drums, leather garments, pottery, baskets and crafted weapons. Design elements are added in poker-work *(left)*, or pyrography as it is sometimes called, and the children imitate this by carving names and images in the bark of the omupapa trees, which turns from white to yellow when incised.

Recently another important influence on Muafangejo's artistic development has come to light, namely his association with the catechist at Epinga, Stephen Paulus, apparently an uncle or close member of the family. In 1955 Muafangejo's father died and his mother, who according to tradition inherited nothing and was destitute, moved to Epinga in 1956, where she converted to Christianity. Muafangejo must have been terribly unhappy at her departure for he left his late father's homestead within a year, on foot and by himself, to find her. They stayed at Epinga until 1963, whereupon they all moved to the Holy Cross Mission station on the border at Onamunama, and then in 1964 to St Mary's Mission at Odibo *(opposite page)* where Father (now Bishop) Mallory was in charge. Muafangejo remained in Odibo until his acceptance by the ELC Art and Craft Centre in 1967.

In 1967 Paulus' *Epukululo Lovawambo* ('Setting things straight of the Ovambos') was published, containing 'pictures by the writer and John Muafangejo'. This book, which is a unique mixture of Christian subject matter and traditional African lore, and contains a page devoted to Kwanyama proverbs, shows the earliest development of Muafangejo's art. The drawings of Paulus are decorative illustrations

with little artistic merit, but Muafangejo's pencil-drawings *(p. 8 and left)* are accomplished, with a distinctive style and depth of feeling. Some of the images he later repeated in linocuts: for example *Ehamba Doukwanyama* (The Kings of Oukwanyama) becomes *Kuanjama Kings, Manduma has Assagai* (pl. 15), and *Okuteleka Oikulia* (cooking food) becomes *A Woman is cooking Food* (pl. 10). As a teacher Paulus encouraged Muafangejo to see and record scenes from everyday life and to develop his own individual approach and style.

These years were also significant because Muafangejo learned to read and write. Throughout his life he wanted to further his education at the same time as trying to persuade others of the benefits of literacy. In an interview in March 1987 he refers to two of his students (who were also his nephews) saying: 'They are already good weavers and they show potential at lino-cutting. However to cut well you have to be able to read English and they can't.' Although Muafangejo was aware of the importance of education, he was not academic, and by the age of twenty-four he had completed only his primary education, possibly because he was too absorbed in his work as an artist. Sally Kauluma who was a teacher at Odibo during John's stay describes him as 'a dreamy type', and 'not too concerned with his studies, and very protective of his art work.'

The illustrations in *Epukululo Lovawambo* as well as Muafangejo's desire to continue his art studies must have impressed people at Odibo, for in February 1967 Shanon Mallory began a process of application to the Government for permission for Muafangejo to leave Namibia to further his artistic education at the ELC Art and Craft Centre.

This art school was one of the very few in Southern Africa that admitted black Africans interested in art but without academic qualifications. Muafangejo was the first Owambo to follow a fine art course, and so far as I know he was the first black Namibian. At the time of his arrival in 1967 the emphasis within the school was practical – to explore arts and crafts as a means of providing income for the students. Courses were conducted on a relatively informal basis, and Muafangejo would have received much of his tuition – instruction in the basic techniques of weaving, etching and cutting lino – from teachers who were themselves senior students. There was no study of the history of art, no art library, and at no stage were diplomas or any form of

11

certificates awarded. This tuition was somewhat similar to that of Paulus, in allowing Muafangejo to develop in his own way, rather than demanding that he follow the teacher's style or aesthetic viewpoint.

Muafangejo's aesthetic style, the open and autobiographical content of his work, the rhythm and metaphors in his images, coupled with his highly unusual use of words and phrases deviated from the approach traditionally associated with the ELC Art and Craft Centre, of geometric patterns and designs, orientated towards sales to tourists and whites. This 'deviation', which has been praised by critics and historians, has been seen as something unique to Muafangejo, and is generally attributed to his early childhood memories. Muafangejo agreed, in interviews, that his early years as a herd-boy, hunter and tiller of the soil furnished him with the themes for many of his images; but his Kwanyama upbringing gave him more than material subject matter. It surrounded him from birth with a richly poetic and allegorical approach to art and culture. Consider, for example, the anthropomorphism of works like *Elephant with its Baby Elephant* (pl. 42) where the baby elephant is being carried around on his mother's back as Kwanyama mothers carry their infants. As a child in Africa Muafangejo would have observed the trees, the stars, stones, warriors, insects – all stood equal to him, to be combined and recombined – animals are shown to us as men, men as animals, stars as stones, stones as foliage, clouds trees.

As for his idiosyncratic grammar and spelling, while much of this was because English was his third language, after Kwanyama and Afrikaans, there is also a strong poetic content to his choice of words, and his use of repetition and non-standard upper and lower casing.

During Muafangejo's time at Rorke's Drift *(left)* important features of his character developed – on one side his sense of isolation, but also his desire as an artist to learn and to teach. Princess Ngcobo, a staff member at the time of Muafangejo's arrival and now Administrator of the ELC Art and Craft Centre, recalls:

He was very isolated. He was neither Sotho or Zulu and spoke little English and thus could not converse with his class which numbered about six – mostly women – or most people at the school. He seldom talked and was known to do 'funny things' like running naked up and down the Shiyane Mountain shouting and singing.

Muafangejo was hospitalized a number of times, and suffered his first mental breakdown in 1968, shortly after he heard of the death of Stephen Paulus and the deportation from Namibia of some of his Anglican friends. He was admitted to the Madedeni Mental Hospital and classified a 'manic depressive'. During his lifetime his

12

treatment for mental illness ranged from being put into chains in the early seventies (see pl. 94, in which he writes: 'They were talking lie to say I was mad man') by some members of the Anglican church who could not tolerate his erratic behaviour, such as ringing the bells of the church at all hours, to being given medication of lithium in the late seventies as an out-patient of the State Mental Hospital in Windhoek. Stories abound of the volatility of his moods, though none of them contains any mention of his being violent. He was at times irrational and excessive, and was a compulsive spender of money – buying a car when he could not drive, buying suits which he then did not wear, drinking vast quantities of coca-cola and smoking incessantly. And loneliness gripped him deeply at times.

Muafangejo developed a great pride in being an artist, and was always keen to learn and to pass on his knowledge to others. Often he would sign himself 'Yours faithfully/lovingly/sincerely artist, John Muafangejo'. When he returned to Odibo at the end of 1969 Sally Kauluma recalls that he was far more self-confident, and enjoyed being an artist and the sense of importance it brought him. He tried to introduce the teaching of art at the Mission school but this was not successful. In 1971 he applied to study art at the Michaelis School of Art, University of Cape Town, was interviewed and rejected (see pl. 97). Notwithstanding these rejections, he applied to Rorke's Drift for a refresher course in 1974 and was awarded a scholarship as 'artist in residence'.

After his return to Odibo in 1974 he applied himself to teaching, and had a rubber stamp made with the words 'John Muafangejo, Anglican Art School, St Mary's Mission, Odibo' which he on occasion stamped on to his prints. In a letter of 27 April 1976 to the present author, he gives as his biography:

I am an artist of S.W. Africa. The Anglican Artist Who is very interesting in Art Work for My or his life. I am always doing Art in defferent things. I Can Say, I like to Study Art More again until I get Diploma or Degree in Art. e g. I am take International Correspondence School, P. O. Box 19 C. [ape] Town. I can say that John is born Art. because every Year I am developing New defference pictures neither I am not in school just to my own will.

A year later on 26 October 1977 he drew up his Will, leaving twenty per cent of his estate '... to train an artist from Namibia', the balance to his mother. Furthermore in correspondence to friends he wrote of how he taught art in the mornings and did his own work in the afternoons, and continually asked them for money or materials for an art school. However, today no school survives, and there are no known students of his still practising art in any form.

Muafangejo's preferred medium of expression was graphics, and in particular the linocut. At Rorke's Drift he did weave a number of tapestries on tribal, animal and family themes, completing about fifteen up until 1975. In total, about one hundred tapestries exist, but most of these are from a period after 1975 when two nephews who were assisting him designed the images, choosing to use more geometric patterns. Muafangejo also created six oil paintings, three of which survive today – their themes reflecting those of his graphic work. The only other known creative works of his were a church altar at Isandlwala near Rorke's Drift and a large mural of St Thomas at St Thomas's Church in Oshikati, Owambo, of which only the latter survives. In view of the above, it is as a graphic artist that Muafangejo is generally spoken of today.

From 1968 to 1987 Muafangejo created 262 known and a further 31 untraceable graphics, the latter being referred to in invoices, or the journal that he kept of his transactions from 1 February 1973 to 12 August 1987. The journal indicated the quantity, edition number, title and price of each work sold, and is an invaluable source of information. Of the 262 works, 31 are etchings and 12 are woodcuts, including two which were printed in three colour variants; the remaining 221 works were linocuts. Colour other than black was used in only 12 different images, and was either blue, red or yellow.

Muafangejo printed and published all his own work, but did not have a printing press or a purpose-built studio. Even when he built his own house in Katatura in 1987, his studio was still a detached garage. His tools *(above)* were very basic. He printed, not by the traditional method, using the back of a spoon to impress the image, but rather with one of three rollers – simply rolling over the paper once it had been placed on the inked block.

Although the printing was by hand, and therefore no two graphics are alike, the degree of variation was also due to loose wool from nearby weaving looms, and to dust within the garage which would have settled on the blocks or image after inking. Very few of Muafangejo's images are perfectly pulled, and he seemed unconcerned with a need to be uniform in printing or to destroy works that were not perfectly printed. When this was queried, his response was, 'but it is still my work'.

He would print from five to ten prints of each image, and these would be stored until he received an order. Only then would he pencil in signature, number and date (even if the block had been carved years earlier). Printing to order meant that his linoblocks were stored for later re-use, and when he died 161 linoblocks, 1 etching plate and 2 woodblocks were found. The very basic storage of the blocks, without any protection, affected the clarity of image in subsequent reprinting; on two occasions sections of blocks were eaten by mice, but Muafangejo clearly felt that this alteration did not destroy the work as he subsequently pulled, signed, numbered, and sold prints from these altered blocks.

Muafangejo's linocuts and woodcuts up to 1979 were marked as printed in editions of 20, 50, 80 and 100, and thereafter 100, 150 or sometimes 200, while his etchings were always marked out of 50. Except for a few very popular works such as *Adam and Eva* and *The Love Is Approaching*, the journal shows that very few editions were printed in full. For example, there are only nine copies of *A beautiful Ovamboland* although it was editioned to 150, and a number of images exist only in one copy. From the journal one can calculate that Muafangejo produced in total about 5,800 individual graphics, of which no more than 2,200 survive today.

On 7 May 1987 Muafangejo demonstrated the creation of a linocut at the art school of the Academy in Windhoek. He said little, simply setting to work according to his usual practice. He would sketch the image and text, always in reverse, in pencil on to the linoblock (though sometimes he would draw on paper first). He would then gouge out the image, working either on his lap (pl. 92) or on a table, but not necessarily directly following the pencil lines, as can be seen from unpublished works and lightly inked blocks.

What inspired him to create certain images is described by him in terms of an inner need: 'something is pressing, pressing to come out. See this work *Arch* [sic] *of Noah*? (pl. 56). When it came out I was relieved.' In one of his last interviews, given about October 1987, Muafangejo said: 'My themes, I do dreams, look around me, and read the newspaper ... when I dream I dream something [in particular] and then in the morning I begin immediately before I forget. That is what I mean – I dream some pictures.' When pressed in an interview of April of the same year on the question: 'What gives you the idea?', he replied: 'Sometimes, I'm naturally self-copying – just I use mostly – ah – imagination. Ya. When I see you like that and I want to draw you, I will add the more – things – to make it more story, more power story.' It would seem that his work is not only autobiographical, but deeper in the sense of coming from an inner dream and containing a personal vision. When asked where he appears in the work *Three Bishops of Damaraland*, he replied: 'Maybe I am inside!'

In another interview Muafangejo refuses to indicate which artists he likes, simply saying: 'I like anybody ... Yes, because is still art. They say something you see.

Only the mind is a teaching line, because you can see it – what's going on – and then the children can see it and follow it.' There is almost a religious fervour in his desire for expression, and in the same interview he says about his own work: 'I'm preaching. I'm passing a message – to the owner of that picture, to whom we are going to sell it to, to buy it, there is a message in it.'

The people who responded to his work, the early collectors, were members of the Anglican Church and their friends, as well as a handful of dealers and collectors, most notably the late Olga Levinson, a historian who championed Muafangejo and his work. Moreover as a result of the Church's identification with the struggle against Apartheid and with Namibian Independence, many of the international support groups acquired his work for sale to raise funds.

JOY   THE PREGNANT MARIA   SELF-PORTRAIT

Although Muafangejo began to receive prizes for his work as early as 1970, it was only in the 1980s that his work achieved international recognition, with the exhibition of his work at the Commonwealth Institute, London. The critic Edward Lucie-Smith saw his linocuts as 'consistently the best of all the modern African masters', and compared the work to the best of the German expressionist masters of the woodcut. Similar opinions were expressed by other historians, with the result that Muafangejo's work was brought to the attention of the international art world, and an ever-growing list of exhibitions and articles followed (see pp. 116-18). The most important of these exhibitions were the two travelling retrospective museum shows held after his death, which for the first time showed in one exhibition the range and mastery of his work.

While the critical acclaim was unanimous, Muafangejo's wide artistic vision has resulted in varying interpretations. He has been described as a great expressionist, or in some works seen as cubist, his religious works have been compared to Romanesque art, especially the frescoes of Saint-Savin, and his candour to the early works of David Hockney. His works have been viewed allegorically, as a focus for the current political turmoil in Southern Africa, while his socio-political commentary has

16

been compared to Hogarth, Goya and Daumier. He has also been likened to the Douanier Rousseau, not for his naive style, but for his vitality, rhythm and attention to detail. His depiction of the clergymen who helped Namibia in its struggle for independence has been compared to the role played by Michelangelo for the Catholic popes, while his image of the handshake of love and co-operation has been accorded the universality of Picasso's *Doves*.

Muafangejo breaks free from the traditions of African art, which are non-individualistic, and instead displays a strong autobiographical element and personal openness, while his use of text as part of the image was unique. Unlike any other Namibian or African artist that I know of, Muafangejo shows us for the first time the beauty of everyday life. The art is unquestionably African, but the style and technique can hold their own among the best of contemporary western art – in this he breaks the traditional view of the 'affinity relationship' between primitive and modern art, and has gained the right to be evaluated as a modern artist.

 Above all, Muafangejo was a man of searching honesty, whose art draws us into reflection. What is it to be an artist? What vision do we have of humanity? What dreams?

 Muafangejo was an artist for whom despair fed the burning fire of hope. What makes him so vital and so distinguished today is certainly the purity, honesty and accomplishment in his work, but more importantly, his moral nobility.

 I predict that his importance for the future will be that of a guide, for the history of art is integrated, both as seed and as flower, into the history of the human spirit.

Tribal Life

John Muafangejo's childhood until the age of fourteen was spent participating in the life and ancient customs of his Kwanyama tribe. His linocuts reveal his awareness of the intricacies of tribal life, the social duties, the all-pervasive system of social relationships, the system of divine kingship with its rules of succession, and royal marriages and coronation ceremonies which could last for months and involve the entire clan.

The Royal Wedding (pl. 2) is a depiction of one such ceremony. The image is imbued with a sense of wholeness and the sanctity of love, symbolized by the ring – the couple are ringed by their arms, they are enclosed in a circle, there are two swirling rings within the congregation and even the heads of the guests are portrayed as round.

The strict social structure of the clan is reflected in the layout of the Kwanyama *Kraal*, or homestead, where wives, girls, boys, even the sacred cattle, would have separate quarters, and each member of the family would be expected to perform certain duties (*Two Girls Are Stamping The Corn*, pl. 6). The mud-and-grass huts, the sacred fire, weapons for hunting, the cattle and the individual allotments for the children and other members of the family are depicted by Muafangejo in two linocuts of his father's homestead (*Muafangejo's Kraal*, pls.4, 5), both made from memory during the 1970s. The earlier version is a more gentle, distant memory of the Kraal, with fine lines and sparse text, while the later version is more boldly drawn and has a more detailed commentary.

The traditional Kwanyama dress, warriors, drinking of calabashes of beer, drums and dancing are themes to which Muafangejo returns in many works. Although the images are often simplified, like *A Woman is cooking Food* (pl. 10), nevertheless they manage to capture the essential atmosphere of events. The double eyebrows and jagged teeth of the audience in *A Which Doctor dancing* (pl. 13), for instance, are enough to capture the sense of fear and awe.

Music and dance were certainly an important part of the Kwanyama tribal life. In the first of two images of the *Kuanyama Wedding* (pl. 3) the drummer's hands seem to flow gently to the beat, arms curved and elongated to emphasize the rhythm, while behind the drummer, as if moved by the music, foliage sways. In the second version (pl. 1) the drummer appears as if inset, feet tapping away, his hands now on the drum – a more frenzied depiction, emphasized by the curved lines around the body. *Drummer* (pl. 8) shows the man literally moulded by and at one with his drum.

A Man Is Hunting An Eland In Forest And Skinning It (pl. 12) allows Muafangejo to contrast the fear of the eland, head bowed and urinating with fear, with the dominance of the hunter, alert and upright, while the panel below shows a sequence of events: the sucessful hunter, with knife poised and one hand holding the trophy's legs, then the eland cut up and tied to the pack animals. Here Muafangejo uses the leaves alone to give the sense of a forest. By contrast, in *Shooter Birds* (pl. 7) there are no leaves – just the bird and the man, whose right hand merges with the arrow's shaft and feathers.

In *He is Killing an ox to Collect the corn* (pl. 11) Muafangejo depicts an incident of bartering of food. When you needed corn you slaughtered an ox, and those who wanted meat would bring corn in exchange.

Finally, in the simple portrayal of faces in *Kuanjama Kings. Manduma has Assagai* (pl. 15), Mandume, Muafangejo's favourite king, is shown in profile, linking the past kings to the present.

The Old Fashion in Okuanjama (pl. 9) is a more direct portrayal of traditional dress, while *A beautiful Ovamboland* (pl. 16) – cattle and corn (*engobe noila*), a home and friendliness – is a simple and eloquent rendering of the peaceful life of any tribe, with which the artist identifies.

A kuanjama Wedding. The two brides hold a fan made of hairly Part of horse's tail While they dance. They wear the tanned hides and blets with decorated ivorys. The two bride grooms hold their hats while watching their brides dancing and waving their fans. The Well training men Play the drums while the dancing goes on.

20

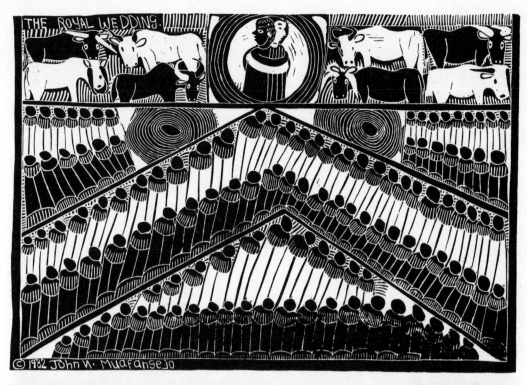

1 A KUANJAMA WEDDING. THE TWO BRIDES *(opposite)*, 1972

2 THE ROYAL WEDDING, 1982   3 KUANYAMA WEDDING, 1970

Muafangejo's Kraal. He had 8 wives, 9 sons. 8 daughters and bushman stayed with us. He had 200 hard of cattle. He got enough corn. He died 1955 while John was 12 years old and John was att end his Fathers Funeral. John was not attend his mothers Funeral in Angola in 5.11.1979 But Johns Father was died also in ANGOLA. John has 38 years old.

4 MUAFANGEJO'S KRAAL, 1979

5 MUAFANGEJO'S KRAAL, 1970

6. TWO GIRLS ARE STAMPING THE CORN, 1975

7 SHOOTER BIRDS, 1980

8 DRUMMER, *c.*1970

9 THE OLD FASHION IN OKUANJAMA, 1984

10 A WOMAN IS COOKING FOOD, 1983

He is killing an ox to collect the corn

©1981 John N. MUAFANGEJO

11 HE IS KILLING AN OX TO COLLECT THE CORN *(opposite)*, 1987

12 A MAN IS HUNTING AN ELAND, 1974

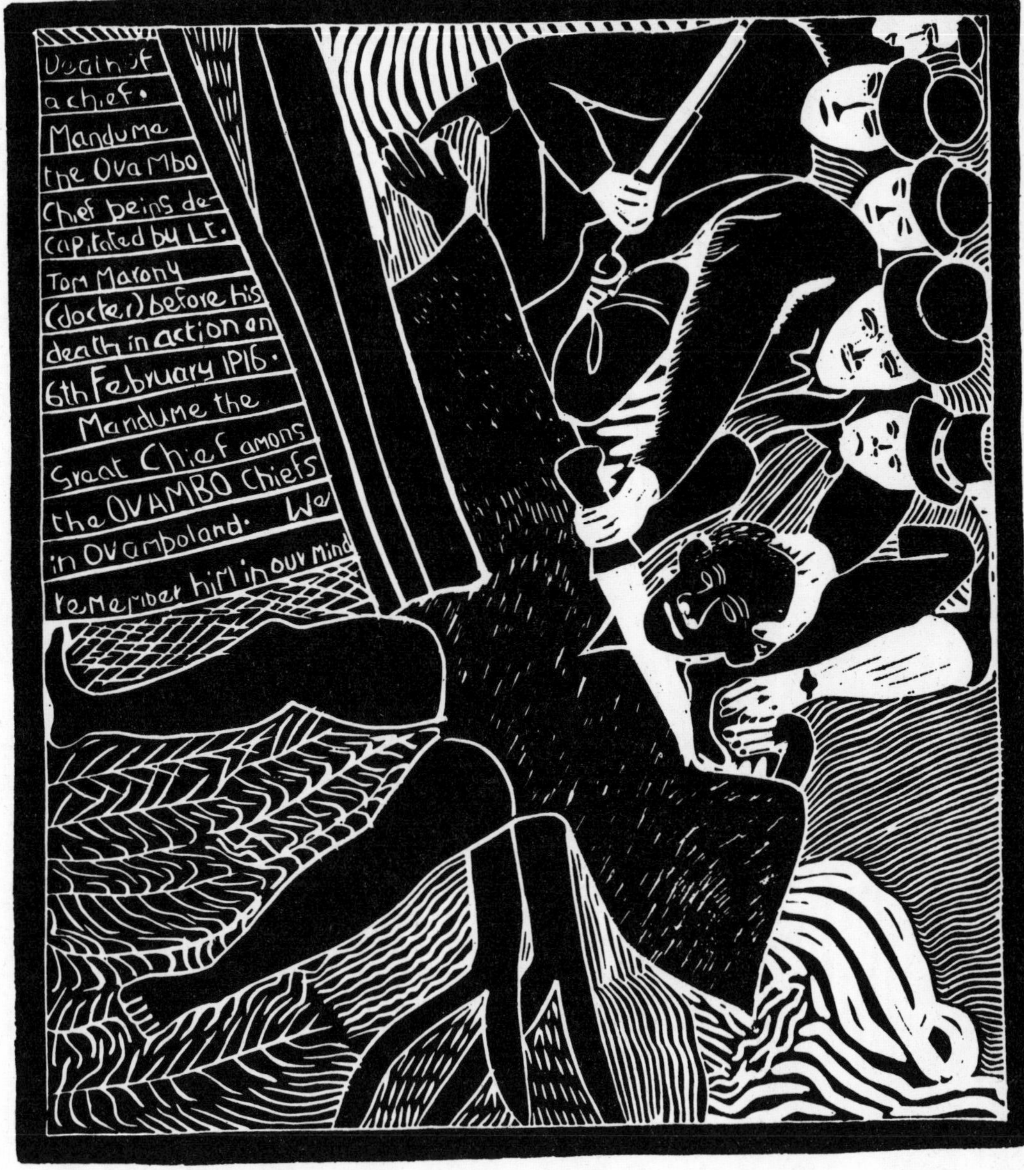
Death of
a chief.
Manduma
the OvaMbo
Chief being de-
capitated by Lt.
Tom Marony
(docter) before his
death in action on
6th February 1P16.
Mandume the
Great Chief among
the OVAMBO Chiefs
in Ovamboland. We
remember him in our Mind

13 A WHICH DOCTOR DANCING *(opposite)*, 1979

14 DEATH OF A CHIEF. MANDUME, 1971

Kuanjama Kings, Manduma has Assagai

© 1983 JOHN N. MUAFANGEJO.

15 KUANJAMA KINGS. MANDUMA HAS ASSAGAI *(opposite)*, 1983

16 A BEAUTIFUL OVAMBOLAND, 1984

Social View

John Muafangejo's linocuts draw on a rich variety of day-to-day scenes. Through a combination of direct words and image he conveys his vision of African life as he experienced it.

While some works are simple and static, like *A Good Family* (pl. 21), others have a more complex and dynamic message, like *The Ancient People* (pl. 24), where Muafangejo is not just making a statement about changing hair-fashions over time but is commenting on the general development of his people: the tranquillity and wisdom of the 'ancients' – the drinking and weapons of the people of the 'middle ages'; the desire for friendship and the role of the Church in the lives of people today.

The importance of cattle to the community is often emphasized. For the Kwanyamas their ownership is synonymous with wealth. In *A Rich Man* (pl. 25), however, Muafangejo seems to be making a more subtle observation. The image is of a mass of disorderly cattle: some are pictured front-on, some in profile, some even from above. Indeed there are strong elements of the cubist technique of overlapping planes which allows us to see the same object from all sides, showing what one knows of an object rather than what one sees at a single glance. The 'pile' of cattle seems to say something about how the rich man must not only amass, but continually take care of his possessions. In contrast, *A Rich Woman* (pl. 27) depicts goats in an orderly pattern, conveying a sense of continuity, even stability. In the contrast between the two works. Muafangejo seems to be pointing to the different approaches of men and women in society.

In *A Jealousy Man* (pl. 30) there is no mention in the text of wealth, but it is evident that one man is seated at his ease beside a tree laden with fruit, while the other is standing stiffly, viewing the herd of cattle, literally boxed off in a corner. Their eyes are similar, but their postures and the way each holds his spear are different. The idea of jealousy is conveyed not only by the visual barrier, but by the outstretched and grasping hand.

Muafangejo often divides his works into sections in order to portray a social circumstance from different angles. *The Thief Who Is In Chain* (pl. 31) reveals the aggressive and superior attitudes of the police, shown above, one of whose raised legs lies on the bar of the words 'the thief', like a trophy hunter with his foot on the animal, and the smugness of the stout judge/jailor, sitting superciliously with an open book and flourished hat, below. The hatless policeman's hands are rubbed together and his face displays an unyielding eye and a mouth shaped as if hurling taunts and insults. Contrasted is the sufferings of the thief, standing chained to the pole, resigned and humiliated, with bowed head, even stripped of his trousers.

Old man (pl. 20) conveys the dignity and frailty of age with particular tenderness – the change in background-pattern draws attention to the hand gently perched on the stick. The facial expression suggests no regrets – the ears are broad, as if to imply that he is willing to listen. Nothing inessential is portrayed. Again, in the etching *Lunch* (pl. 29) one senses a feeling of concern, as in the painting of *The Potato Eaters* by Van Gogh – the child is unnoticed by the adults who are watching each other. The empty plates are surrounded by hands which dominate the table along with the untouched knives and forks, while the child's hands *are* a knife and fork – he is hungry.

Cattle in Farmer (pl. 23) illustrates the basics of Owambo life: the cattle, water and corn which together assure health. In *They are meeting again at home* (pl. 18) the words give a clue to the work's significance. The faces, turned aside, together with the embrace, give a sense of sadness, for they are meeting *again* at home, after an absence, and perhaps looking over their shoulders in fear of a renewed separation.

17 MEN ARE WORKING IN TOWN, 1981

18 THEY ARE MEETING AGAIN AT HOME, 1982   19 BLIND MAN AND CREEP MAN, 1983

20 OLD MAN, 1983   21 A GOOD FEMILY IN OVAMBO, 1985

22 WINDHOEK PEOPLE PRAY FOR PEACE AND LOVE, 1977

23 CATTLE IN FARMER, 1981   24 THE ANCIENT PEOPLE *(opposite)*, 1973

25 A RICH MAN, 1985

26 THEY ARE GOING TO HOSPITAL, 1985   27 A RICH WOMAN 1985

28 SAD BOY, 1985

29 LUNCH, 1974

30 A JEALOUSY MAN, 1976

31 THE THIEF WHO IS IN CHAIN, 1975

Animal Life

Muafangejo looked after cattle in his early years and was therefore very well aware of both the beauty and the dangers of wild animals, especially the lion.

The interrelationship of man and animal is depicted in three panels in one of Muafangejo's important early works: *A Shepard* of 1969 (pl. 33). In contrast to the disorderly cattle in *A Rich Man* (pl. 25), the impression of a herd is achieved here simply by repeating the heads of cattle in a downward spiral. This rendering suggests grazing and tranquillity, reinforced by the protective nature of the dog and the heavily armed shepherd boy. The second panel shows the confrontation with the lion, the ox looking on helplessly; and the third, the kill. Man has changed from protector of animals to aggressor – 'He is Hunterman'. The dog is at first half hidden, but then reaches towards the dying lion, showing Muafangejo's acute observation of the behaviour of animals.

The confrontation of man and lion occurs frequently throughout Muafangejo's works. In two linocuts lions are depicted stalking boys in trees. *Lion wants a boy* (pl. 36) shows a stylized boy in a tree with a reclining, perhaps even laughing, lion. In *Lions are Wanting the two boys up the tree* (pl. 35) both boys appear rigid with fear, but are also trying to hide by blending into the shape of the tree, their limbs like branches. The position of the lion's paws is very peculiar and can be compared to the curved position of the man's feet and body in *Shooter*

Birds (pl. 7). This 'distortion' is clearly not accidental as Muafangejo was a very able draftsman, thus we can assume that Muafangejo intends a parallel between the lion and man: a hunter is a hunter, be it man or animal, the hunted always fearful. The association of human and animal, even to the extent of giving animals almost human features and characteristics, is continued in much of his work. *Elephant with its baby Elephant* (pl. 42) has the baby carried piggy-back in the African tradition. Furthermore, the very concept of motherhood is displayed in these two animals: the weight of responsibility suggested by the almost buckling front legs of the mother, the contrast of the two pairs of eyes, one innocent and pure, the other fuller and wiser; their bond expressed by their gently intertwined trunks. *Strong Man is Strangling the African Lion* (pl. 32, *facing page*) is an altogether more ruthless work, but it too suggests the link of man and animal, their the matching strengths conveyed by the angular lines of their entwined bodies. Paired symmetrical forms express the bond between animals in works like *Giraffe* (pl. 43) and *Kudu friends* (pl. 38). The bodies of the two giraffes are so entwined that they seem almost one, while the attachment between the kudus is suggested not only by the symmetry of the composition and the sharing of fruit, but also by the harmonious design and the reaching out of the tree-branches. In studies of individual animals, too, we notice Muafangejo's keen observation of their characteristics: the pride of a lion (pl. 44) and the ponderous solidity of an elephant (pl. 45). Captions are superfluous.

Elephant Is Killing A Lion In Funny Way (pl. 37) can be interpreted in various ways. There is undoubtedly a degree of humour in the portrayal of the docile lion with its legs gently crossed. However, a analogy with the liberation struggle in Southern Africa has been read into the image by critics: '... the elephant represents the Namibian people and the lion the South African Army'. A work like *Etosha Pan Wild Life* (pl. 40) depicts the animals of Namibia's (and one of the world's) largest game reserves. There is a sense of the taming of wildlife, of animals in a zoo. All the heads are turned to face the intrusion, and there is deep sadness in their expressions.

In portraying animals Muafangejo shows both tenderness and respect, but above all he leaves us with a feeling that animal and human life are not so different in Africa – life is life, only the shapes differ.

A BOY IS LOOKING AFTER THE HERD OF CATTLE IN FOREST

HE IS HITTING THE LION WHILE IT IS KILLING THE OX

HE IS KILLING A LION WITH BOW, ARROWS AND ASSESAI. HE IS HUNTER MAN

33 A SHEPARD *(opposite)*, 1969

34 THEY ARE FIGHTING WITH LION IN OLD DAYS, 1985

35 LIONS ARE WANTING THE TWO BOYS UP THE TREE. 1985

36 LION WANTS A BOY *(opposite)*. 1974

49

50

37 ELEPHANT IS KILLING A LION IN FUNNY WAY *(opposite)*, 1975

38 KUDU FRIENDS, 1979   39 CAMELS ARE IN DESERT, 1984

40 ETOSHA PAN WILD LIFE, 1982   41 A MAN IS SHOOTING DEER IN ETOSHA PAN, 1982
42 ELEPHANT WITH ITS BABY ELEPHANT *(opposite)*, 1979

Elephant with its baby
Elephant in 1979.

43 GIRAFFE *(opposite)*, 1979

44 AFRICAN LION, 1976   45 ELEPHANT, 1976

Church View

Almost all Muafangejo's images of the church are portrayals of friends, or of services that held special significance for him. He saw the church in a fatherly role – comanding respect and reverence. Certain of its members (for example, Bishop Mallory) guided him towards his artistic development, arranged for his studies at Rorke's Drift, looked after him when he was ill, promoted his work and gave him a home and studio to work in, but, above all, were his closest friends.

Remembrance and presence are strongly felt in *The death of Rev. Gabriel H. Namueja* (pl. 48). This is one of only two works where the text covers most of the block (the other being *Zimbabwe House*, pl. 94). Apart from the historical data it gives, this work recalls the importance of the role of the Church and her priests to the Kwanyamas. The Holy Spirit is portrayed as the bird ascending, simple in shape and with strong beating wings. The priest has a background of fine lines and a pair of simple candlesticks at either side. *The Bishop Rt C. S. Mallory* (pl. 52) reveals the deep gratitude Muafangejo felt for the Bishop, but perhaps even further, the open book and outstretched key are symbolic of the world of art which had been opened to him. This work also makes references to Matthew 5: 1-12, the Sermon on the Mount, which was a favourite theme in Muafangejo's work (see also pl. 51).

Cathedral Church of St George (pl. 51) is a striking work commemorating the enthronement of Bishop Kauluma. It is one of the rare occasions when Muafangejo writes in Kwanyama. Here he refers to the two girls playing the trumpets and the two angels holding the bishop's mitre, one black and one white. He also writes that 'God has looked, God has brought his eyes back to us today', and we see in the left corner what appears to be representations of the all-seeing eye (a symbol used by Picasso in *Guernica*). At bottom right is the beginning of the theme of the handshake between black and white which he would develop further in works like *Hope and Optimism* (p.6) and *New Archbishop Desmond Tu Tu Enthroned* (pl. 49).

In *New Archbishop Desmond Tu Tu Enthroned* Jesus is strongly drawn half in black, half in white, like the adjacent large hands, gently cupped in prayer. Tutu points to the cross in a gesture that says: 'do not forget this'. The Archbishop as seen as an intermediary: the Holy Spirit as a dove passes through him and into an abstract form beyond him, on the side with the crucifixion. The text sums up Muafangejo's views on churchmen.

The detailed image of *Our Church at Rorke's Drift* (pl. 47) was created during Muafangejo' first year as an apprentice at the school at Rorke's Drift, in 1968. At the top right, almost in the rafters, Muafangejo writes of the Art School. Perhaps Muafangejo, an Anglican, was feeling insecure in the Evangelical Lutheran Church and felt a need to assert his tribal identity, for he refers to himself as 'J. Ndevasia Muafangejo'. By contrast, on his second visit to Rorke's Drift in 1974, *Evangelical Lutheran Church Womens Meeting* (pl. 55) is a masterpiece of design and technique, with the fine patterning of the brickwork in contrast to the bold black-and-white of the women. The rear section of the church is shown in profile, the cross hovers, and a window becomes a face.

In *How God loves his People* (pl. 53), the divine love is expressed in an all-encompassing embrace for mankind, who, in deep faith, have their hands tenderly placed over their hearts.

The etching *Choir* (pl. 54) is a wonderful encapsulation of the force of the spirit. The book is open to the audience in a welcoming manner, while the choir is given a spiritual quality by floating above the ground. The force of the spirit is evoked, too, by the windswept hair, wide singing mouths, and the single ear of each head, open to the word.

The life is very expansive indeed in the whole world.

47 OUR CHURCH AT RORKE'S DRIFT *(opposite)*, 1968

48 THE DEATH OF REV. GABRIEL H. NAMUEJA, 1974

Text within the artwork:

New ARCHBISHOP DESMOND TU TU EN throned AT →

St. Georges Cathedral C. Town in 7-9-1986. →
OUR NaMibia → We was Praying and Plodding for OUR
New ARCHBishoP DESMOND TUTU of CaPe Town
Father hear our Prayers. Bless him and Keep him in
our mind, Hope, and Be Strong, Peaceful, Kindness
ARCHBishoP in defficlt time but God will help him.
© 1986 John N. MUAFANGEJO

49 NEW ARCHBISHOP DESMOND TU TU ENTHRONED, 1986

50 ST MICHAEL CHURCH IN WINDHOEK *(opposite)*, 1985

60

St. Michael Church in Windhoek.

©1985 John N. Muafangejo.

51 CATHEDRAL CHURCH OF ST GEORGE, 1981

The Bishop Rt.C.S.Mallory
Was the Director of St.
Mary's Odibo from 1961 to
1969. He Was the Anglican
Artist J.N.Muafangejos Apli
:ant for art course training
in 1967 to 1969 and he Was
Paid for 3 years Namibian
Artist is   thanks Very much
for his helpfull Bishop.
John remembers Bishop
in his pray and he
Loves you. He more
help for we younger
         AMEN
Mat.5:1-11
© 1981 John   N.Muafangejo.

52 THE BISHOP RT C.S. MALLORY, 1981

64

53 HOW GOD LOVES HIS PEOPLE ALL OVER THE WORLD *(opposite)*, 1974
54 CHOIR, 1974   55 EVANGELICAL LUTHERAN CHURCH WOMENS MEETING, 1974

Biblical Life

The strong oral tradition among the Kwanyamas made Muafangejo very receptive to biblical stories, and the majority of his themes derived either from the Bible or tribal life. Holiness is the theme of works like *The Birth Of Christ* (pl. 65), while others depict good and evil in various ways.

The first graphic Muafangejo carved was *Adam and Eva* (pl. 57, 1968, reworked 1985), a vivid interpretation of the Temptation in the Garden of Eden. Adam is depicted as smaller than Eve, for Muafangejo felt that his innocence in the face of deception made him childlike and small. The Garden is circular, suggesting wholeness, while God is portrayed overlooking the earth with his hands of creation on either side. The Devil, however, is depicted in a wedge jutting into the world, the point of the wedge in line with the apple. It is interesting to note that Muafangejo makes only slight differences between the appearance of God and the Devil. God is stern but has a look of concentrated involvement and concern, while the Devil's face is mask-like, hiding his true intentions. God has a circular hair-do (reminiscent of Kwanyama tribal hairstyles) with three circles (signifying holiness) around his neck. The Devil is bald, and has rather peaked eyebrows.

As the serpent leers (pl. 58) is divided into two sections – Adam receiving the apple, above, and the Expulsion, below. Adam is now portrayed as an old man, almost reaching out for the apple, as opposed to recoiling as in *Adam and Eva*. We can observe several metaphors and rhymes in this work. Eve's two fingers and

66

the serpent's forked tongue are both coiled around apples; similarly the coil of the snake is echoed in the swirling wings of the Cherubim. The whole bottom panel illustrates Genesis 3: 24: 'So He drove out the man; and He placed at the east of the garden of Eden Cherubims and a flaming sword which turned every way, to keep the way of the tree of life.'

Judas Iscariot betrayed our Lord Jesus for R3.00 (pl. 59) shows Judas entwined around Jesus as the snake coiled around Eve (pl. 58). The halo around Jesus is now a cross since he is being betrayed; the spirituality of the disciples is reflected in their windswept hair (see *Choir,* pl. 54), and even the pattern on Judas' robe resembles a serpent's coils. To contemporize the image Muafangejo introduces the rand currency, and the comment: 'You people be careful of money, because it is the root of Sin.'

Images conveying compassion and holiness are generally accompanied by very little text. *A Good Shepherd* (pl. 60) expresses the depth of caring by the left hand placed over the heart and a halo around the staff, and also by the general tranquility of the scene: The shepherd is not intervening to guide the flock – he appears a guarding rather than guiding figure. Similarly, *Way to Bethlehem* (pl. 62) expresses peace and love through the embrace of Joseph, Mary and Jesus. In *Israel, Jews, Christians, Heathen* (pl. 70) God and Jesus are embracing all the peoples of the world, including 'heathens'. In *The Baptised of Christ* (pl. 64) the sense of spiritual upliftment is shown by the hands and garments of the onlookers, raised in unison with the wings of the bird and God's cloak and arms. By making God's cloak featherlike and placing the Dove centrally, feathers and God's cloak are beautifully and symbollically intermingled.

Many of the biblical images contain complex abstract patterns, usually as backgrounds, as in *The Birth of Christ,* (pl. 65) and *Jesus Meeting with Zaccheus* (pl. 67), but more importantly, Muafangejo was clearly inspired by the stories. He did not portray evil in a grotesque or alarming manner, or apportion blame (in later works the name 'Master Nobody' is given to destructive persons). Remorse is a more usual sentiment, for example *Simson* (pl. 61) shows no gloating self-satisfaction, despite the broken animal. For Muafangejo the Bible was a source of strength that reinforced his vision of the potential goodness of all living creatures.

56 AN ARK NOAH, 1979

57 ADAM AND EVA, 1968   58 AS THE SERPENT LEERS, EVE HANDS, 1973

59 JUDAS ISCARIOT BETRAYED OUR LORD JESUS FOR R3.00, 1973

60 A GOOD SHEPHERD, 1974

61 SIMSON *(opposite)*, 1983

71

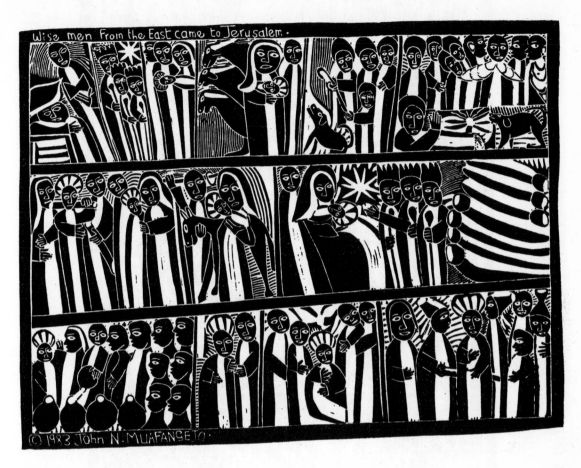

62 WAY TO BETHLEHEM *(opposite)*, 1984

63 WISE MEN FROM THE EAST CAME TO JERUSALEM, 1983

64 THE BAPTISED OF CHRIST, 1968

65 THE BIRTH OF CHRIST, 1977   66 THREE KINGS, *c.*1983

67 JESUS MEETING WITH ZACCHEUS, 1981   68 THE LAST SUPPER, 1978

69 CRUCIFIXION, 1984

70 ISRAEL, JEWS, CHRISTIANS, HEATHEN   OUR GOD FOR ALL PEOPLE, 1981

Places

The opportunity to travel and experience new places is limited for many Africans by cost and the relatively rudimentary nature of the transport systems. By comparison Muafangejo was quite fortunate. He had a good knowledge of Ovamboland, he worked and studied at Rorke's Drift in Natal, and he travelled on a number of occasions to Europe and Scandinavia.

Wherever he was, he usually depicted something of his experiences in his works, keenly observing the life and the people around him. *The Rorke's Drift School* (pl. 74) is a very early linocut that depicts life in the village. The artist is at the heart of the work, looking mischievous and 'going to cut the linocut in wood'. Around him are depicted numerous events of the busy life at Rorke's Drift, but almost all the people seem to be expecting something to happen. They look towards the viewer as if in anticipation of the soon-to-be-created linocut.

Shiyane Home (pl. 76) gives a similar sense of the bustle of village life, but is a more structured composition. The inhabitants are not in any state of anticipation, but are talking to each other and carrying on with their lives: a dog is held on a leash, another begs for food, a child clings to its mother, others play, minute houses contain people engaged in all sorts of activities: arguing, staring out, washing; a man preaches to a polite but uninterested audience; a weaver sits and weaves; the corn grows, people wave. *Angola and South West Africa* (pl. 75) is both a schematic representation of Muafangejo's life, where places stand for events, and a pictorial plan of the area, not to scale but generally accurate, and brought to life with drawings of elephants, trees, corn, broad rivers, a depiction of the church at Odibo and people, as well as remarks like 'Kwanyama means meat eater'. Muafangejo makes no distinction between the historically important features and personal associations. The place where Chief Mandume lived, for instance, appears as significant as the border gate – or that SWA is 'from where we get diamonds'. (Almost all the migrant labour used in the diamond mines is Owambo, and the Kwanyamas is an Owambo tribe.) The 'artificial boundary' is a reference to the arbitrary splitting of the Kwanyama clan, some of whom afterwards lived in Angola and some in South West Africa (Namibia). In the vibrant *Zulu Land* (pl. 82), on the other hand, Muafangejo chiefly conveys the broad river and lush vegetation of the area.

Sometimes a place is represented by its most striking element, as after Muafangejo's visit to Finland, when he carved *Snow was making Artist Fall down* (pl. 78). Here he quite brilliantly limits the scene with the upright trees and overhanging branches, and leaves us with no vanishing point, just the flat white background everywhere. Like the cubists who also eliminated vanishing points, Muafangejo concentrates attention on the subject of the work, in this case, snow.

It was the queues of people and long lines of beds which struck him about his stay in *Madadeni Mental Hospital* (pl. 81). In *Orange Farm* (pl. 71) he shows the striking orange trees and fruit-pickers, but also records the interesting events of the day: the barbecue with friends, and an incident, shown in cameo form in the middle of the river, where a white man saved a black man who had fallen into the water and was unable to swim. Similarly in *Ongwediva House* (pl. 79) he does not wish to record the structure of the house, or its design, but indicates its association for him in labelling it: 'John's Bed'.

Muafangejo visited Britain on a number of occasions to accompany exhibitions of his works, and although no images exist to record these trips, *British Airways* (pl. 72) records his impression of the journey.

Perhaps we can say that for Muafangejo the importance of a place was in the feeling it generated for him, and in the people and events that give places their attraction and meaning.

71 ORANGE FARM, 1974

72 BRITISH AIRWAYS, 1983   73 HOLIDAY, 1983

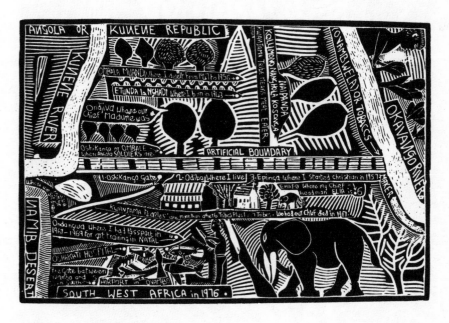

74 THE RORKES DRIFT SCHOOL, 1968

75 ANGOLA AND SOUTH WEST AFRICA, 1976   76 SHIYANE HOME *(overleaf)* , 1969

79

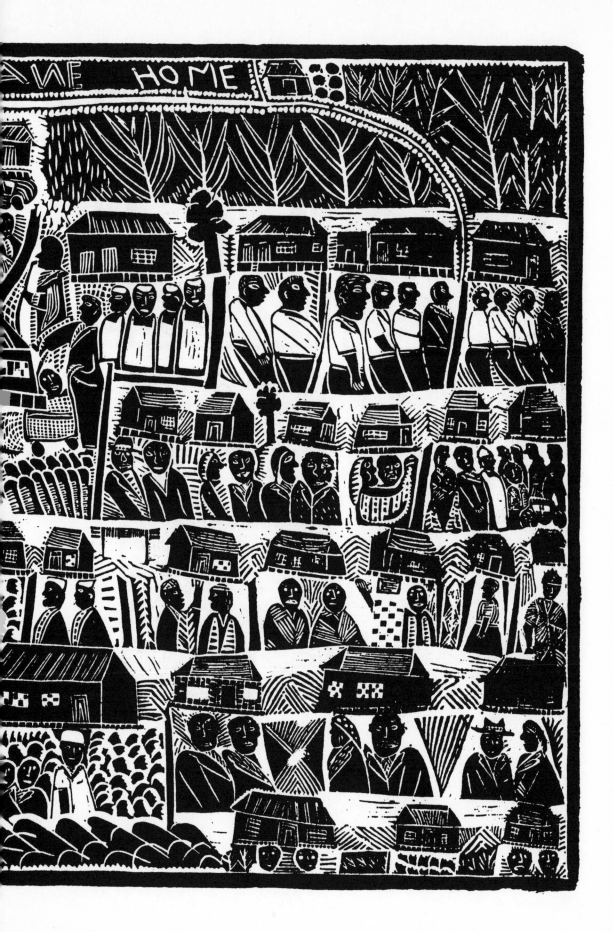

77 FROM FINLAND: A SMALL SHIP, 1981 78 SNOW WAS MAKING ARTIST FALL DOWN, 1981

79 ONGWEDIVA HOUSE, 1986 80 BLUIDING AT MALA COMBER, 1979

81 MADADENI MENTAL HOSPITAL WHICH HAS MANY PEOPLE, 1969

82 ZULU LAND, 1974

Symbolism and Design

All Muafangejo's works contain symbolism, and their composition invariably contains elements of pattern and other design motifs. Consequently the works chosen for this chapter could just as well be included under other headings. However they are gathered here because of their strongly symbolic imagery and powerful use of design elements.

In *The First Bishop Of Doicese Of Namibia* (pl. 90) Muafangejo is remembering Bishop Winter who was deported. The artist has placed himself in the picture, depicting his own body in the shape of a heart. Moreover he refers to John 14:3, which ends with the words: '... that where I am, *there* ye may be also'. Perhaps the artist has chosen this text in reference to himself, and 'John' refers both to the Evangelist and to his own name. Both figures in the work are holding books, the Bible as a common factor, and there is a very tender link of friendship with their touching hands forming a triangle, which suggests the symbolic number of the Trinity. A seemingly secular work like *Judge Man* (pl. 88) is given religious connotations with its three circular symbols, again suggesting the Trinity and therefore God as Judge. There is fine draughtmanship – the stern face, threatening eyes and hard jaw evoke an unsympathetic but knowledgeable character. The Judge is not writing but turning back the pages of the book as if looking back at the deeds of the wrongdoer on Judgment Day. The heavy book may be symbolic of the weight of the law.

A more abstract work, *Design* (pl. 84), is decorative and has a repeat pattern. On looking closely, however, one sees that no two birds or leaves are identical – sterile geometric patterns are avoided. The unity of the composition is achieved by the almost circular shape of the tree and the inward-growing branches. In the woodcut *Self Defence* (pl. 89), Muafangejo blends the gun into the shapes of the surrounding foliage, and, in keeping with the title, the gun is held out in front of the soldier, more like a shield than an offensive weapon.

Live Tree (pl. 87), presumably a reference to the Tree of Life, was used as the theme for the Independence Celebrations of Namibia in March 1990, and appeared on official invitations. The stem of the tree seems to join a human neck, and the rounded tree-top to be part of a person's head. Furthermore one hand can be seen reaching out from the human body and the other from the tree.

Dry Gardens (pl. 86) captures the essence of a parched land with a scattering of shapes that are not recognizable – perhaps they are dried-out leaves, but whatever they are, they appear dead. Indeed, by making the shapes non-specific, Muafangejo symbolizes drought, rather than merely depicting its effects, and this is reinforced by the human response – the man's hands are rigid, his expression empty, as if there is nothing he can do.

Although Muafangejo never visited the seaside resort of *Swakopmund* (pl. 85), he saw a photograph of it in a newspaper, and created his own version. This work is probably the most abstract of all Muafangejo's works. It beautifully conveys the 'lightness' of the seaside air and the essentials we associate with seaside holidays.

A more simple abstract work, *Unite is Strengeth* (pl. 83, *facing page*), may be seen as a symbolic cup or drum, perhaps signifying the need for unity in a divided society. However the cup/drum is very much a tribal cup/drum, and the unity intended may be psychological – the need to avoid fragmentation caused by fame or people or fortune, and to concentrate on work; or, it may refer to the importance of structure in the work of art – its unifying power.

In his next and final work (pl. 102) Muafangejo would write: 'too many people were with him', and refer repeatedly to the importance of his work.

84 DESIGN, 1980

85 SWAKOPMUND, 1986   86 DRY GARDENS, 1985   87 LIVE TREE, 1978

88 JUDGE MAN. 1969

89 SELF DEFENCE, 1976

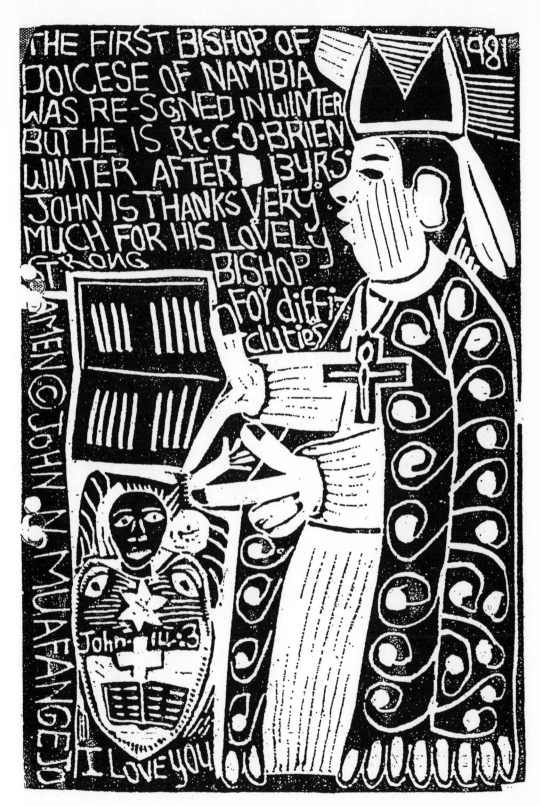

90 THE FIRST BISHOP OF DOICESE OF NAMIBIA, 1981

Personal Life

Muafangejo was not just a master of the linocut, he was also a truly great artist in the contemporary sense of being autobiographical. We can learn a lot about Muafangejo himself and also his philosophy of life from the many 'naturally self-copying' works, as he expresses it, where recurring themes are those of loneliness, hard work and his life as an artist.

John Muafangejo was a lonely man, and sometimes he saw this as a result of being an artist (*Lonely Man, Man of Man*, pl. 99). In the moving *No Way to Go What Can I Do?* (pl. 95), his loneliness is expressed not only in words, but also in the apparent isolation of the figure, perched on the edge of a large, single chair. Muafangejo enjoyed playing the guitar and singing, and took solace in it in times of depression or sadness.

Muafangejo was unmarried when he died, and we do not know of any lasting intimate relationships with either men or women. Given his very open nature, we can conclude that he had not formed any, rather than that he kept them secret. In *Forcible Love* (pl. 92) he shows a degree of indifference to a woman who has distracted him from his work. Expressive details are the eyes – his are narrow and determined, hers wide and fearful. Furthermore Muafangejo clasps his linoblock close to his heart as if to prevent her intrusion.

Muafangejo made a number of self-portraits, like *Self*, where he sees himself as a priest, but more often he depicts himself in a broader context. He was not accepted by the university, and *An Interview of Cape Town University* (pl. 97) clearly made a vivid impression on him. We are shown a wall of white interviewers' faces, their pens poised like knives. They are earnest and academic looking, but ignore the artist, who is seated to one side with his hands hidden.

Material and personal losses are related candidly, as when in *The Ford 250* (pl. 93) he recounts how he was duped when buying his first car. *Well come Back At St Mary's Mission* (pl. 91, *facing page*) tells of his return to the mission station complete with transistor radio, a status symbol. In *John Mother was died* (pl. 103) Muafangejo movingly writes of her funeral: '...the war stops me to go to one I love'.

Zimbabwe House: This is St Mary's Mission (pl. 94) is a touching account of himself as 'the Anglican first famous artist...', and includes his views on his madness, on finance, on love and on 'human need'. The text records his humility, and gratitude to all those who assisted him. He recalls his depressive states and gives the reason for them as '...they were just worried me too much and I was talking too much most reading bible, singing and praying because I was lonelyness'. In another section he tells of his financial problems: 'I have no work and no money salary. I do care because I am not born with work or money.' He writes how he works daily at his art, and how there are just two human needs: 'Light on the Mystery of life and Life for the Mastery of life'.

In his last work, *Bishop R. H. Mize* (pl. 102), Muafangejo mentions his work with 'love in it', and hopes for peace.

In *He is thinking about Art?* (pl. 98), a man sits beneath a fruit-bearing tree, his chair tilting forwards towards the heavily laden branches. One hand reaches out, the other rests on his head. The word 'art' is in capitals letters, and a question mark hangs after it. Is he dreaming, an African dreaming about life, about his ancestors, his art? Muafangejo said of himself that he paints his dreams.

John Muafangejo, a man who felt deeply to the point of madness, opened his life for all to see. His art is without shame or apprehension, and without artistic self-consciousness.

92 FORCIBLE LOVE, 1974   93 THE FORD 250, 1973

94 ZIMBABWE HOUSE: THIS IS ST MARY'S MISSION *(opposite)*, 1975

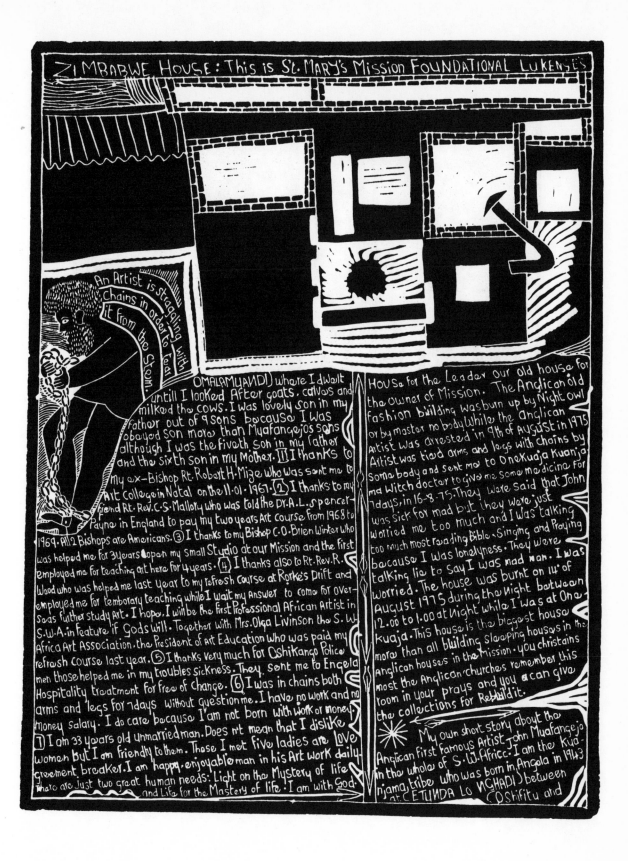

95 NO WAY TO GO   WHAT CAN I DO? 1973   96 THE LUCKY ARTIST, 1974

97 AN INTERVIEW OF CAPE TOWN UNIVERSITY, 1971   98 HE IS THINKING ABOUT ART?, 1974

99 LONELY MAN, MAN OF MAN, 1974

100 MUAFANGEJO'S FEMILY, 1985   101 JOHN'S NEW HOUSE IN KATUTURA, 1987

102 BISHOP R.H. MIZE WAS WELL COME BACK TO NAMIBIA, 1987

103 JOHN MOTHER WAS DIED, 1980

Historical Events

Muafangejo records a number of historical events in his linocuts, often accurately detailing facts in the text. One of the historical subjects done in two versions is *The Battle Of Rorke's Drift* (pls. 105, 106). Technically both are strong images. In both, the English are depicted lined up in an orderly fashion, strung out behind a protective barrier represented by a box. By contrast the Zulus are depicted in a disorderly arrangement with their dead piled high. Muafangejo gives no reason for the battle; indeed in the second image the text in Zulu simply translates: 'They fought – The English and the Zulus fought 1879'. Possibly his interest was stirred by the fact that the battle was fought at Rorke's Drift where he studied, and that the history of the war and this particular battle, now famous, was that there the largest number of VC's at any one battle were awarded.

Chief Mandume (*c.*1890 -1917) was the one historical figure who clearly caught Muafangejo's attention and admiration. He devoted six works, including *Death of a Chief. Mandume* (pl. 14), *Kuanyama Chief Mandume* (pl. 107) and *Mandume was a last chief of Kuanjama tribe* (pl. 108), to portraying aspects of the chief's life and his death. The historical importance of Mandume was not just that he was the last Kwanyama chief, but that he was the one chief who united the Kwanyamas, and later opposed the forces of colonialism. He was someone important whom Muafangejo could admire as part of his tribal heritage, and

Muafangejo passes on a historical message, signalled by the deliberate way he sets out the text, as in *Death of a Chief. Mandume* (pl. 14).

When Muafangejo's interest is more direct and personal the images are usually accompanied by detailed text, for instance in the works depicting the deportation of churchmen. The *7th Bishop of Damaraland Rt. Rev. Colin Winter* (pl. 110) and *1 Bishop R. H. Mize Left Windheok in 1968* (pl. 109) are statements of the various deportations. However the importance lies not so much in the historical fact as in the sense of loss of those left behind. In the former work Muafangejo records their sadness, as well as the courage of those deported.

Although Muafangejo was very aware of the power struggles occurring in the whole region, he nevertheless refrained from political emphasis when depicting historical events. In *Oniipa New Printing Press* (pl. 112), so far from interesting himself in who has caused the destruction, Muafangejo refers to the culprit as 'Master Nobody'. However, the text does make clear that he feels this wanton destruction of an educational facility is an act of betrayal, and compares it to that of Judas Iscariot.

'Master Nobody' is again referred to in *Anglican Seminary Blown Up* (pl. 113). In this work Muafangejo introduces the all-seeing eye again, as well as the dove of reconciliation, but his primary concern is that people should donate money for the rebuilding. 'Master Nobody' also figures in the work *The Death of Chief Phillimon Elifas* (pl. 104). Historically Chief Elifas was considered by the SWAPO fighters to be a stooge of the South African Government, but for Muafangejo he was the murdered chieftain, to be mourned. Muafangejo introduces both the clenched fist and soldiers into the image – symbollically placed under the moon and sun respectively. The coffin is being carried away in one direction by a small bearer and in another by a figure facing the opposite way (or perhaps waving goodbye). The woman adjacent the figure holds a tree of peace in her right hand.

In his portrayal of historical events Muafangejo offers neither arguments nor empty historical facts – the events live for him, and sadness at the destructiveness of Master Nobody is always closely followed by hope and optimism for the future.

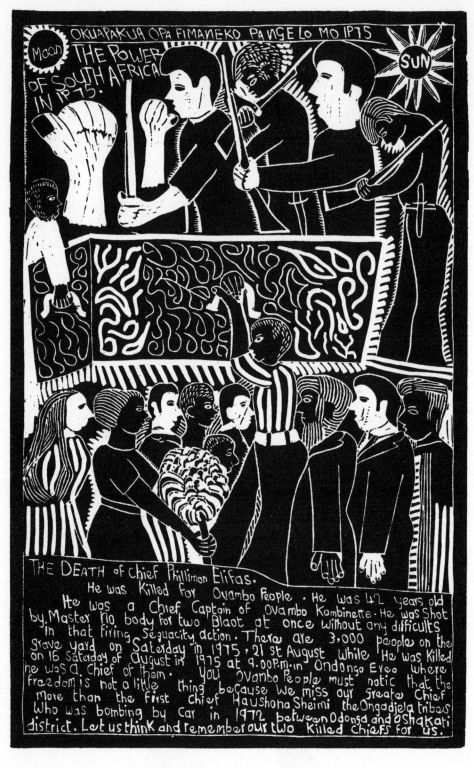

104 THE DEATH OF CHIEF PHILLIMON ELIFAS, 1975

100

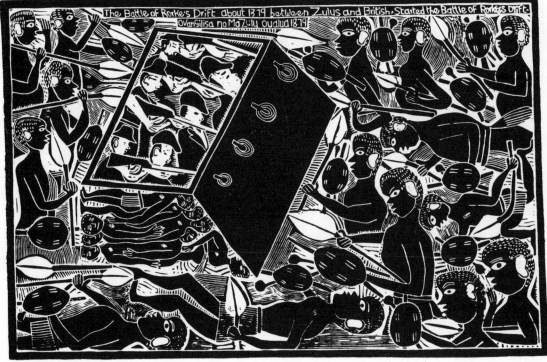

105 THE BATTLE OF RORKES DRIFT, 1969

106 THE BATTLE OF RORKE'S DRIFT ABOUT 1879 BETWEEN ZULUS AND BRITISH, 1981

107 KUANYAMA CHIEF MANDUME, 1971

108 MANDUME WAS A LAST CHIEF OF KUANJAMA TRIBE, 1981

109 1. BISHOP R. H. MIZE LEFT WINDHOEK, 1978

110 7TH BISHOP OF DAMARALAND RT REV. COLIN WINTER, 1972

St. Marys Mission High School Students are very thirsty and hungry for Education. We need qualified teachers here at St. Marys Odibo. Here Many Students willing to study but we are short of qualified teachers. John Muafangejo is the Anglican Artist who is asking for help from University and College Students and to think about their brothers and sisters at Odibo in Ovamboland. They are trying to study in their best.

111 ST MARYS MISSION HIGH SCHOOL STUDENTS ARE VERY THIRSTY, 1973

Oniipa New Printing Press and Book Depot on 11 May 1975 · The old printing Press and Book Depot
was burnt down on 11 May 1973 by Master
no body · He Master nobody bombing it during the night on Same day. Why Master no body was
Willing to burn up the old Printing Press? Just to destroy every things in it like Printing Machines
Books and building in order to be no More Printing Matters to seen by Ovambo People. We
Ovambo People believe in God who is King of Kings and greatest of all on earth and also in
heaven · One Who burnt up the printing press did like Judas Iscariot betrayed our Lord Jesus for
R3 without asking himself what will happen to him in feature ! What was his aim to do that? Did he
gain anything from destroying it?
The New ones were built in modest building and new expensive
Printing Presses more than the old ones · The service was opening by Bishop L·Auala together with his clergy 9.45.
When African Bishop was preaching the Sermon his face was so bright and Shinning telling us that he was very glad
and Proud for God who lot People made the collection to build the New printing press · There were 10.000 people · Wonderful choirs came from all parts of Ovambokavango Churches · On that day there were so many people from all parts
S.W.A. and out side countries except the Anglican Church Bishop R·Wood · The young Anglican Artist was very
ashamed of himself there without his Bishop · Why am I eventing this Picture? is to tell my Bishop what was
happening there · God is light of us all and in him there is no darkeness at all ·

112 ONIIPA NEW PRINTING PRESS AND BOOK DEPOT ON 11 MAY, 1975

113 ANGLICAN SEMINARY BLOWN UP, 1981

World View

In all his works Muafangejo displays an understanding that allows us to relate to them instantly, while some works achieve a visionary intensity. Their subjects range from the poetically gentle *He is thinking about Art?* (pl. 98) to the now world-famous image of *Hope and Optimism* (p. 6).

A vision of what it is to lose a loved one is portrayed in *A Sad People* (pl. 116); the upper section reverberates with loss, but the dead child is not shown, rather the pain, memories and sadness are suggested through the empty faces and the hands covering the heads. It is a portrayal of the thoughts of sadness, contrasted with the more external elements of the joys of life in the bottom panel. Here we are shown a tree, heavily laden with fruit, the relaxed posture of the contented, almost smug father and mother, absorbed in the newborn baby, the attention and devotion directed to the child, and the smiling onlookers.

Muafangejo was concerned not only with the powers of love to bring fulfillment, but also with its destructive nature: jealousy and broken marriages, and prostitution, which he calls 'the love money'. *A Love* (pl. 120) shows (at the right) a young couple standing together. Muafangejo expresses their mutual love through the identical patterns of lines on their faces and hands, as well as around their feet. They jointly hold a tree which seems to be uprooted, as if to indicate that they have uprooted their present existence and will place roots down as a couple in due course. In contrast 'the jealous one' on the left of the picture has her

106

back turned, and Muafangejo warns about the impossibility of 'forcing the love'.

Man and Lady (pl. 115) contrasts 'natural love' and 'the money love'. Muafangejo's concern is not just that he feels prostitution is 'wrong', but for the unwanted children of prostitutes. He focuses his attention on the 'parentless' child, naming him and wishing him well. *The Love Is Approaching But too much of anything is Very dangerous* (pl. 117) is a beautifully designed and balanced work, with contentment and tranquility emanating from the full, rounded figures and rhythmic foliage pattern. The hands and feet do not quite touch, as if there is a nervous tenderness in opening up one's heart.

Muafangejo was clearly in sympathy with romantic love and motherly love. Motherly love is conveyed in many works, and especially in a number devoted simply but strongly to a mother and child. One image (pl. 114) is reminiscent of Henry Moore's *Mother and Child* series. The sentinel-like mother looks ahead for any danger, holding one hand just above the young child's head, while the the other guards her unborn child.

Life Is Very Interesting (pl. 121) is a complex woodcut image, printed in different colour versions, suggesting it was important to Muafangejo. The man on the left fingers the woman's heart-shaped necklace ornament, while her right hand appears to touch his head and her left his heart. At the same time, it is hard to distinguish their bodies, and they may even be in camouflage, hiding their inner feelings. Her heart-shaped necklace ornament could be an apple, with its connotations of betrayal – she is larger than he is, and seems to be tempting him. He looks anxious; neither of them is looking at the other. Life is indeed interesting.

In *Disadvantage Of Fighting For Men* (pl. 122) the opposite of love, war, is presented in a simple way. The attacker is shown with the clenched fist of power, but it is the victim, kneeling and wounded, who attracts our attention and sympathy. Muafangejo does not include names or dates in the text; it does not matter who is fighting, there is always a loss, a death.

Muafangejo undoubtedly yearned for a peaceful world: he was never confrontational, but always optimistic that the good qualities of humankind could win through. His recurrent image of a black-and-white handshake (see p. 6) is symbolic not only of his own personal struggle, but of his vision of love and peace for his people, and for all the peoples of the world.

114 MOTHER AND CHILD, 1983

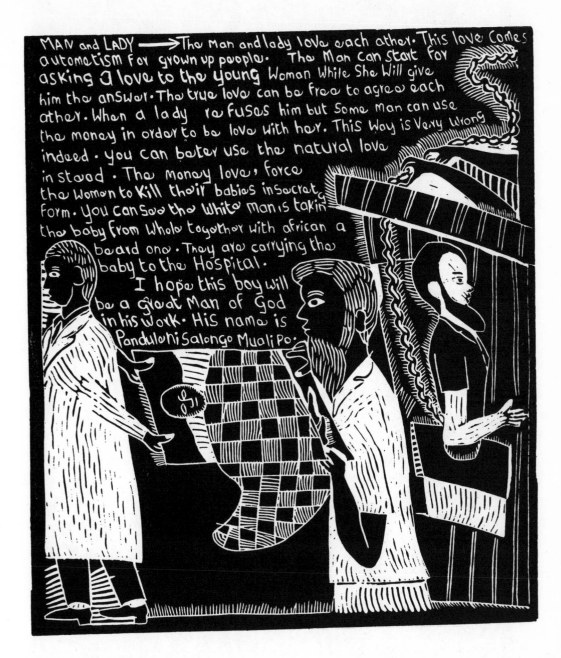

The text within the image reads:

MAN and LADY ——→ The man and lady love each other. This love comes automatism for grown up people. The Man can start for asking a love to the young Woman While She will give him the answer. The true love can be free to agree each other. When a lady refuses him but some man can use the money in order to be love with her. This way is very wrong indeed. you can beter use the natural love instead. The money love, force the women to kill their babies in secret form. You can see the white man is taking the baby from whole together with african a beard one. They are carrying the baby to the Hospital.

I hope this boy will be a great Man of God in his work. His name is Panduleni Salongo Muali Po.

115 MAN AND LADY 1973

116 A SAD PEOPLE, 1970

117 THE LOVE IS APPROACHING BUT TOO MUCH OF ANYTHING IS VERY DANGEROUS, 1974   118 THINKING MAN, 1986

119 A POOR WOMAN WITHOUT HUSBAND, CHILDREN, 1986   120 A LOVE, 1972

121 LIFE IS VERY INTERESTING *(opposite)*, 1974
122 DISADVANTAGE OF FIGHTING FOR MEN, 1974

123 MOTHER AND CHILD, 1979

124 I WISH YOU WELL ON YOUR WAY, 1986

ACKNOWLEDGMENTS

The aim of this book is to present the work of John Muafangejo to as wide an audience as possible, and for this purpose I have found it most useful to divide his work into themes. My choice of themes is a personal one, and naturally does not preclude other interpretations.

In describing the culture of the Kwanyama I have made use, where applicable, of the 'ethnographic present' even though some of the ceremonies mentioned in the essays are no longer current.

A number of people have been generous with their time and have assisted me with information and material. I should like to thank Lisa Eveleigh, Monica Frans, Margrit Hoffman, Sally Kauluma, Debbie Lauterpacht, Gill Marcus and Tobie Openshaw.

Very special thanks are due to those who read and discussed the manuscript, offering valuable and incisive comments and suggestions: Sarah Cannon, Duncan Large and Paul Turner, and in particular Guy Burnell, who also gave me his unstinting support in this publication.

Thames and Hudson have displayed a generosity of spirit and an understanding of the work of John Muafangejo and of this publication which makes my late delivery of the manuscript even more regrettable. My gratitude and respect are due to all the Thames and Hudson staff that I had the pleasure of meeting, and to those I did not, but who also worked on this publication.

Finally I would also like to offer my appreciation to Nelson Mandela who, in spite of all the present demands being placed on him, responded instantly and positively to the suggestion of writing a Foreword.

Oxford, January 1992 O. L.

CHRONOLOGIES

I Life of John Muafangejo

c. 1943 Birth at Etunda lo Nghadi, Angola.

c. 1948 Family moved to Ombala Muandi, Angola.

1955 His father dies.

1956 His mother, Petelena Hamupolo, moves across the border to Epinga in Namibia.

1957 Muafangejo joins his mother at the Mission Station, Epinga. Attends Mission school.

1963 Muafangejo moves with his mother to Onamunama, Namibia. Attends school at Holy Cross Mission school.

1964 Muafangejo moves with his mother to St Mary's Mission, Odibo, Namibia. Attends St Mary's Anglican Mission school. Stephen Paulus gives him art lessons.

1966 Archdeacon Mallory applies to Peder Gowenius for Muafangejo's admission to the ELC Art And Craft Centre at Rorke's Drift, Natal.

1967 Publication of *Epukululo Lovawambo* (see Bibliography). Bantu Administration grants permission for Muafangejo to travel to Rorke's Drift.

1968 Death of Stephen Paulus. Muafangejo twice admitted to Madedeni Mental Hospital

1970 Lives at St Mary's Mission, Odibo. Seeks to raise money to establish an art school at Odibo.

1971 Represents South Africa (one of five artists) at the São Paulo Biennale. Special award for *The Battle Of Rorkes Drift*.

1972 Behnsen award, Windhoek. Founds St Mary's Art School at Odibo. Muafangejo the only teacher, offering weaving, linocutting and wood sculpting.

1973 Begins a journal of all his sales.

1974 Represents South Africa (one of four artists), *Contemporary African Art*, Museum of African Art, Washington, D C. Awarded 'artist in residence' at Rorke's Drift.

1977 Moves to Windhoek. Owambo a war zone and under curfew.

1980 First prize, Graphic Arts exhibition, Helsinki.

1981 Joint Winner of Award for Graphics, 2nd Republic Festival Exhibition, Durban, South Africa. Adopts name John Ndevesia Maufangejo. Visits Finland.

1983 Receives one of ten medals awarded (for *Wise men From the East came to Jerusalem*) at 7 *Internationale Grafik Triennale*, Frechen, Germany. Visits the UK.

1985 Best Graphic Artist award, STANSWA Biennale, Windhoek, June-July.

1986 Commences building a house in Katatura township near Windhoek (5481 Gregormendel Street). Overall Best Artist award, STANSWA Biennale, Windhoek.

1987 Moves to his house in Katutura. Third quarter joint prize winner, Johannesburg Art Gallery. 27 November: Died in his sleep at his home in Katutura, probably of heart failure.

1988 Second Guest Artist Award, Standard Bank National Arts Festival, Grahamstown.

1989 Public auction of the estate of Muafangejo.

1990 Registration of the John Muafangejo Foundation.

II Historical Events

c. 1720 Founding of the Kwanyama kingship (the Kwanyama are a group of the Owambo peoples, who have been living in the area known as Northern Namibia since the fifteenth century AD.

1878 Portugese expeditionary force repulsed by Owambos.

1883 The Region proclaimed a German protectorate (Deutsche Südwest Afrika).

1884-5 Berlin conference draws the Namibian and Angolan border through the middle of the territory of the Kwanyama.

1892 First Missionaries (Finnish) arrive in Ovamboland.

1911 Mandume assumes the Kwanyama kingship.

1915 German forces surrender to South Africa.

1917 Mandume killed by combined South African and British forces (some sources allege he committed suicide rather than be taken prisoner). End of kingship of the Kwanyamas, Government of Owambo now assumed by a council of eight Headmen.

1919 Versailles Peace Conference awards mandate to govern Namibia to the Republic of South Africa.

1924 First Anglican Mission Station in Owambo.

1949 National Party of South Africa amends the South West African constitution disenfranchising all but the whites.

1950-71 Various International Court of Justice decisions on Namibia.

1954-5 Mass demonstrations in Ovamboland against the contract labour system.

1956 South African Government assumes direct responsibility for 'Native Affairs' in Namibia.

1958 First Namibian 'non-white' political party, Ovambo People's Congress, formed.

1960 South West African People's Organization (SWAPO) formed (currently the governing party of the Republic of Namibia).

1966 SWAPO proclaims the armed struggle and military engagements take place. General Assembly of the UN revokes the mandate, assumes sovereignty over Namibia.

1968 First homeland inaugurated in Owambo with its own legislative council.

1969 UN resolution uses the name Namibia for the first time, and the Security Council revokes the South African mandate.

1975 Assassination of Chief Elifas in Owambo. Invasion of Angola by South African and South West African territorial forces. Internal Constitutional Conference for Independence (Turnhalle Conference) begins.

1978 Kassinga Massacre. The 'Big Five' Initiative. Appointment of a Secretary-General's Special Representative for Namibia, and a period of continued UN political activity.

1989 UN peace-keeping and independence forces arrive in Namibia.

1990 Independence of Namibia (21 March).

SELECT EXHIBITIONS

1968 Muafangejo's first exhibition: Art and Craft from Rorke's Drift, Durban Art Gallery, Durban.

1969 Participates in the Annual Exhibition of Contemporary African Art, AJD Meiring Gallery, University of Fort Hare, Alice, Eastern Cape (and in subsequent years). Contemporary African Art, Camden Arts Centre, London.

1969-70 [African Art], Touring Exhibition, Canada.

1970 First church exhibition: [John Muafangejo], Church of St John the Divine, Houston,Texas. National Art Gallery, Stockholm. National Art Museum, Helsinki. Pretoria Art Museum, Pretoria.

1971 Johannesburg Art Gallery, Johannesburg. First exhibition in Windhoek: Kunstkabinett.

1972 Nijmegen, Holland. Sixth Biennale, Art of South Africa Today, Durban.

1973 John Muafangejo, Africa Centre, London.

1974 Contemporary African Art, Museum of African Art, Washington, DC.

1976 Arte Fiere, 76 Bologna. Bradford Biennale, Bradford.

1979 First selection as an artist from Africa, rather than SWA/Namibia: Moderne Kunst aus Afrika, Staatliche Kunsthalle, Berlin. [Modern Art from Africa], Commonwealth Institute, London.

1980 Passion in Südafrika, Evangelical Church of Hessen and Nassau, Germany.

1981 John Muafangejo, Arts Association of SWA/Namibia, Windhoek. Graphic Creativa '81, Third International Exhibition of Graphic Art, Alvar Aalto Museum,

Jyväskylä. 1982 John Muafangejo - Linocuts, Moira Kelly Fine Art, London. Seventh British International Print Biennale, Bradford. John Muafangejo, Ongwediva Training Centre, Ongwediva.

1983 Prints by John Muafangejo, Commonwealth Institute, London.

1983-4 World Print Four. An International Survey. Travelling exhibition beginning at the San Francisco Museum of Modern Art.

1984 Neue Kunst Aus Afrika, Hamburg.

1985 Woodcuts by John Muafangejo, University of Exeter, Exeter. STANSWA Biennale, Windhoek. [John Muafangejo - Linoprints], Dowse Art Museum, Lower Hull, New Zealand.

1985-6 Prints by John Muafangejo, Graves Art Gallery, Sheffield.

1986 John Muafangejo, Gallery 21, Johannesburg.

1987 John Muafangejo - Linoprints, Quay Arts Centre, Isle of Wight. Intergrafik '87, Union of Visual Artists of the German Democratic Republic, East Berlin. Salisbury Arts Centre, Salisbury, Wiltshire. Museum für Völkerkunde, Frankfurt a. M. Prints by John Muafangejo, Royal Festival Hall, London. John Muafangejo Linoprints, Wave Gallery, New Haven.

1988 [John Muafangejo], Yale University, New Haven. Uhuru: African and American Art Against Apartheid, New Jersey State Council on the Arts, New Jersey. [African Contemporary Art], Institute for Foreign Affairs and West German Foreign Ministry Cultural Division, Bonn.

1988-9 Major travelling retrospective: Standard Bank National Arts Festival. John Muafangejo - Linocuts, Plymouth City Museum and Art Gallery, Plymouth. Ter cera bienal de la Habana '89, Havana.

1990 John Muafangejo, Alte Feste, Windhoek. John Muafangejo and an Exhibition of Namibian Artists, Heynitz Castle.

1990-1 Second major travelling retrospective: UK museums organized by the Museum of Modern Art, Oxford. [Mbatha und Muafangejo], Bildungshaus Salzburg, Salzburg.

1991 First permanent hanging collection Heynitz Castle Art Centre and Studios of Namibia, Windhoek. John Muafangejo, Museum für Völkerkunde, Frankfurt a. M.

1991-2 Neue Kunst aus Afrika, Völkerkunde, Frankfurt a.M.

SELECT BIBLIOGRAPHY

The chronological listing below includes TV programmes and interviews on Muafangejo. A complete bibliography and all the interviews appear in *I Was Lonelyness - The Complete Graphic Works of John Muafangejo - A Catalogue Raisonné 1968 -1987*, Struik Winchester, Cape Town, 1992. For the reader interested in Namibia and the Kwanyamas a short list of books is given at the end.

I Muafangejo

Epukululo Lovawambo, Stephen W. Paulus, Ovamboland Anglican Church, Odibo, 1967.
Art South Africa Today, Durban Art Gallery, Durban, 3-28 July, 1968.
Journal, unpublished, estate of John Muafangejo, entries from 1 February 1973-10 August 1987.
Contemporary African Art in South Africa, E. J. de Jager, C. Struik, Cape Town.

Contemporary African Art, Museum of African Art, Washington, DC, February, 1974.

Black /South Africa /Contemporary Graphics and Tapestries, Brooklyn Museum and Brooklyn Public Library, New York, 25 March-16 May, 1976.

[Interviews with John Muafangejo], Olga Levinson, August and September 1977, August 1980, May and September 1987.

John Muafangejo - Linocuts, Woodcuts and Etchings, Bruce Arnott, C. Struik, Cape Town and Johannesburg, 1977.

Mustan Afrikan viisautta ['Black African Wisdom'], edited by Matti Kuusi, Werner Söderström, Porvoo, Helsinki and Juva, 1979.

'Onnellinen mies', Finnish TV 2 documentary, with Raili Seppälä, Helsinki, December, 1980.

Passion in Südafrika, Beratungsstelle für Gestaltung, Frankfurt a.M., 1980.

'The life and art of John Muafangejo - The Moving Story of an Artist in Troubled Times', Olga Levinson, SWA Annual/Jahrbuch/Jaarboek, Windhoek, 1981, pp.107-10.

'John Muafangejo', *Art and Artists*, London, vol.186, no.2, March 1982, p.2.

'John Muafangejo', *Art International*, Zurich, vol.25, May-June 1982, pp.53-54.

'John Muafangejo', Edward Lucie-Smith, *Prints by John Muafangejo*, Bhownagree Gallery, Commonwealth Institute, London, 4-29 May 1983.

'Muafangejo', Waldemar Januszczak, *The Guardian*, London, 17 May 1983.

Art and Artists of South Africa, Esmé Berman, A.A. Balkema, Cape Town and Rotterdam, 1983, pp. 196, 201, 293.

Christliche Kunst in Afrika, J.F. Thiel and H. Held, Dietrich Reimer, Berlin, 1984, pp. 263-65.

'In the Eye of the Sun - John Muafangejo - Namibian Printmaker', Dowse Art Museum, Lower Hutt, New Zealand, *c*. December 1985.

[Interview with John Muafangejo], Hans Blum, Windhoek, 7 August 1985.

The Levinson Collection - Being the Olga and Jack Levinson Collection of S.W.A./Namibian Art, edited by Ute Scholz, compiled by Heilwig and Peter Andreae, University of Pretoria, Pretoria, 1985.

'John Muafangejo - Linoprints', Quay Arts Centre, Newport, Isle of Wight, *c*. January 1987.

[Interview with John Muafangejo], Pedro [A.] Vorster, Windhoek, April 1987.

[*From South Africa*], edited by David Bunn and Jane Taylor, *TriQuarterly*, Northwestern University, Evanston, Spring/Summer 1987.

'John Muafangejo, Künstler aus Namibia', Monika Stötzel, Museum für Völkerkunde, Frankfurt a.M., 15 June-15 July 1987, pp.88-103.

'Namibian Art - An Academic File Databank Report', Natalie Warren-Green, *Academic File*, London, 12-18 Sept., 1987.

'A First and Final Interview', Philip Todres, 22, 24 November 1987.

Schwarze Kunst - John Muafangejo und Peter Clarke - Namibia, Institut für Auslandsbeziehungen, IfA Galerie, Bonn, 3-31 December 1987.

'John Muafangejo - A message of Peace', Nana Wagner, ADA, Cape Town, no.4 1987, pp.4, 11-16.

'Ein Künstler in Namibia', 'Aspekte', Director: Klaus Figge, ZDF, Mainz, Germany, 11 March 1988.

'Four Namibian Artists', Amy Schoeman, *Rössing*, Windhoek, April 1988, pp.6-11.

John Ndevasia Muafangejo (1943-1987), Second Guest Artist Award 1988, Standard Bank National Arts Festival, Broederstroom Press, Johannesburg, c. June 1988.

The Sasol Art Collection, Rand Afrikaans University, Johannesburg, 1 August-3 September 1988. .

The Neglected Tradition - Towards a New History of South African Art (1930-1988), Johannesburg Art Gallery, Johannesburg, 23 November 1988-8 January 1989.

Free Nelson Mandela - Festival Concert Book, text by Mary Benson and Liz Nickson, Penguin Books, Harmondsworth, 1988.

'John Muafangejo' *Art of the South African Townships*, Gavin Younge, Thames and Hudson, London, 1988.

'An artist is Struggling with Chains', From South Africa: New Writing, Photographs, and Art, edited by David Bunn *et al.*, University of Chicago Press, Chicago, 1988.

The Dictionary of South African Painters and Sculptors, Grania Ogilvie, Everard Read, Johannesburg, 1988.

John Muafangejo - Linocuts, Plymouth City Museum and Art Gallery, Plymouth, 10 June-8 July 1989.

African Art in Southern Africa - From Tradition to Township, ed. by Anitra Nettleton and David Hammond-Tooke, Ad. Donker, Johannesburg, 1989.

'John Muafangejo', Sue Williamson in *Resistance Art in South Africa*, David Philip, Cape Town and Johannesburg, 1989.

'Aspects of Twentieth Century Black South African Art - Up to 1980', Amanda Anne Jephson, unpublished M A Dissertation, University of Cape Town, Cape Town, 1989.

'Prominent Artists of Namibia: John Muafangejo', Amy Schoeman, *Flamingo*, Windhoek, vol.2, no.8, February 1989, pp.18-21.

'Namibian artist John Muafangejo (1948 [sic]-1987)', E. J. de Jager, *Africa Insight*, Pretoria, vol.20, no.1, March 1990.

'John Muafangejo', *Nelson Mandela - An International Tribute for a Free South Africa*, Special Wembley Stadium Commemorative Edition, Wembley Stadium, 16 April 1990.

Art of Conflict - South African and Namibian Conflict Images, Michael Morris, Research Associates, London 1990.

'Outside Influences on Traditional and Contemporary Art in Nigeria and South Africa', Jennifer M. Hunter, unpublished 4th year dissertation, Glasgow School of Art, 1990.

'John Muafangejo', Tony Warner, *Arts Review*, London, 8 March 1991, pp.121-22.

'John Ndevasia Muafangejo', *Zeitzeichen. Neue Kunst aus Afrika*, Museum für Völkerkunde, Frankfurt a.M., 24 April 1991- *c*.April 1992.

'My name is Loneliness', director: Laurie Flynn, Channel 4, London, 7 May 1991.

John Ndevasia Muafangejo - Hoffnung für Namibia, Theo Sundermeier, Luther Verlag, Bielefeld, 1991.

II Namibia and the Kwanyamas

Estermann, Carlos. *The Ethnography of Southwestern Angola - I The Non-Bantu Peoples - The Ambo-Ethnic Group*, Africana Publishing Co., New York and London, 1976 (translated from the Portuguese publication of 1957)

Goldblatt, I. *History of South West Africa - from the beginning of the nineteenth century*, Juta and Co., Cape Town, Wynberg and Johannesburg, 1971.

Katjavivi, Peter H. *A History of Resistance in Namibia*, James Currey, London and OAU, Addis Ababa and UNESCO, Paris, 1988.

Leistner, Erich and Peter Esterhuysen (editors). *Namibia 1990 - An Africa Institute Country Survey*, Africa Institute of South Africa, Pretoria, 1990.

Levinson, Olga. *Story of Namibia*, Tafelberg, Cape Town, 1978.

Loeb, Edwin M. *In Feudal Africa*, University of Indiana, Research Center in Anthropology, Folklore, and Linguistics, Bloomington, Publication no. 23, July 1962.

Williams, Frieda-Nela. *Precolonial Communities of Southwestern Africa - A History of the Owambo Kingdoms 1600-1920*, National Archives of Namibia, Windhoek, Archeia, no. 16, 1991.

Wood, Brian (editor). *Namibia 1884 - 1984: Readings on Namibia's History and Society*, Namibia Support Committee, London and United Nations Institute for Namibia, Lusaka, 1985.

38 *Kudu friends 1979* [138], 1979, 29.8 x 45.7 (11 3/4 x 18). JMF, PPAC.
39 *Camels are in Desert.* [213], 1984, 29.2 x 52.3 (11 1/2 x 20 5/8). JMF.
40 *Etosha Pan Wild Life.* [183], 1982, 44 x 69.6 (17 1/4 x 27 3/8). ANG, HCAC, JMF, MV, PPAC, UAG, UB.
41 *A Man is shooting deer in Etosha Pan.* [185], 1982, 70.7 x 56.1 (27 3/4 x 22 1/8). PPAC, UAG.
42 *Elephant With its baby Elephant in 1979.* [133], 1979, 46 x 36.4 (18 1/8 x 14 3/8). JMF, MV, PPAC, TAG, UB.
43 *Giraffe in 1979* [139], 1979, 46.1 x 29.9 (18 3/16 x 11 3/4). JMF, MV, PPAC, SCAG, UAG.
44 *African Lion* [118], 1976, 27.9 x 29.6 (11 x 11 5/8). JMF.
45 *Elephant* [119], 1976, W, 33 x 29.4 (13 x 11 1/2). MV, PPAC, UAG.
46 *Confirmation* [162], 1980, 16 x 10.5 (6 1/4 x 4 1/8).
47 *Our Church at Rorke's Drift* [3], 1968 , 84.2 x 48 (33 1/8. x 18 7/8). ELC, JMF.
48 *The death of Rev. Gabriel H. Namueja.* [96], 1974, 49.9 x 46.1 (19 5/8 x 18 1/8). JMF.
49 *New Archbishop Desmond Tu Tu Enthroned At* [243], 1986, 59.8 x 42.2 (23 1/2 x 16 5/8). ANG, JMF, PPAC, SC.
50 *St. Michael Church in Windhoek.* [218], 1985, 66.1 x 39.2 (26 x 15 3/8). AAN, JMF, MV, UCT.
51 *Cathedral Church of St. George. Windhoek 1981* [178], 1981, 50.2 x 38 (19 3/4 x 15). AAN, HCAC, JMF, TAG, UFH.
52 *The Bishop Rt. C. S. Mallory* [180], 1981, 29.7 x 21.1 (11 3/4 x 8 1/4). AAN, JMF.
53 *How God loves his People all over the World* [83], 1974, E & A, 34.2 x 26.1 (13 1/2 x 10 1/4). JMF.
54 *Choir*, (89), 1974, E, 22.6 x 28.1 (8 7/8 x 11).
55 *Evangelical Lutheran Church Womens Meeting* [62], 1974, 51.5 x 45.5 (20 1/4 x 17 7/8). ANG, JMF, PPAC.
56 *An Ark Noah* [137], 1979, 61.7 x 47 (24 1/4 x 18 1/2). JAG, JMF.V&A.
57 *Adam and Eva* [1], 1968, 63.2 x 52.7 (24 7/8 x 20 3/4). ANG, HCAC, JMF, PAM, SCAG, SANG, UFH, UNISA.
58 *As the Serpent leers, Eve hands* [51], 1973, 46.2 x 34.1 (18 1/8 x 13 7/8). ANG, ELC, JMF, MV.
59 *Judas Iscariot betrayed our Lord Jesus for R3.00* [50], 1973, 33.8 x 45 (13 1/4 x 17 3/4). AAN, JMF, MV, PPAC, SC.
60 *A Good Shepherd* [70], 1974, 42.4 x 61.8 (16 3/4 x 24 3/8). AAN, HCAC, JMF, TAG.
61 *Simson.* [200], 1983, 30 x 21 (11 3/4 x 8 1/4). AAN, JMF, TAG.
62 *Way to Bethlehem.* [207], 1984, 60.6 x 47.6 (23 7/8 x 18 3/4). JMF, PPAC.
63 *Wise Men From the East came to Jerusalem.* [195], 1983, 45.6 x 60.9 (18 x 24). ANG, JMF, PPAC, SAC.
64 *The Baptised of Christ* [9], 1968, W, 55.6 x 30 (21 7/8 x 11 3/4). SANG, UNISA.
65 *The Birth Of Christ In 1977.* [123], 1977, 28.7 x 27.5 (11 1/4 x 10 3/4). JAG, JMF, PPAC.
66 Three Kings [2U3], *c.* 1983, 13.7 x 10.2 (5 3/8 x 4). JMF.
67 *Jesus Meeting With Zaccheus 1981.* [164], 1981, 33.1 x 31.3 (13 x 11 7/8). MV.
68 *The Last Supper* (1978) [126], 1978, 30.6 x 30.6 (12 x 12). JMF, MV, PPAC, UFH.
69 *Crucifixion* [208], 1984, 50.5 x 49.5 (19 7/8 x 19 1/2). PPAC.
70 *Israel, Jews, Christians, Heathen Our God For All People* [165], 1981, 35.2 x 33.1 (13 7/8 x 13). JMF, MV.
71 *Orange Farm* [65], 1974, 45 x 52.2 (17 3/4 x 20 1/4). AAN, ELC, HCAC, JAG, JMF, PPAC.
72 *British Airways.* [194], 1983, 73.4 x 47.6 (28 7/8 x 18 3/4). JMF.
73 *Holiday* [192], 1983, 60.8 x 40.5 (24 x 16). JMF, PPAC, UAG.
74 *The Rorkes Drift School* [2], 1968, 53.1 x 88 (20 7/8 x 34 5/8). ELC, JMF.
75 *Angola and South West Africa* [115], 1976, 45.7 x 68.6 (18 x 27). HCAC, JAG, JMF, SC, SCAG.
76 *Shiyane Home* [25], 1969, 55.3 x 85.3 (21 3/4 x 33 5/8). JMF, KG.
77 *From Finland: A small ship was* [171], 1981, 35.8 x 27.6 (14 1/8 x 10 7/8). JMF, MV, PPAC.
78 *Snow was making Artist Fall down* [166], 1981, 34.2 x 33.1 (13 1/2 x 13). JMF, PPAC.
79 *Ongwediva House* [241], 1986, 42.2 x 28 (16 5/8 x 11). JMF, MV.
80 *Bluiding at Mala Comber* [135], 1979, 45.7 x 30 (18 x 11 3/4). JMF.
81 *Madadeni Mental Hospital Which Has Many People* [24], 1969, 45.5 x 76.6 (17 7/8 x 30 1/8). ELC, UNISA.
82 *Zulu Land* [63], 1974, 46 x 68.3 (18 1/8 x 26 7/8). ANG, ELC, JAG, JMF, PPAC, SC, UAG, UB, WHAG.
83 *Unite Is Strengeth* [260], 1987, 21.3 x 22 (8 3/8 x 8 5/8). JMF.
84 *Design 1980* [160], 1980, 35 x 26.9 (13 3/4 x 10 5/8). JMF, MV.
85 *Swakopmund* [244], 1986, 42.4 x 59.6 (16 3/4 x 23 1/2). AAN, JMF, PPAC.
86 *Dry Gardens* [238], 1985, 23 x 18.1 (9 x 7 1/8). JMF, PPAC.
87 *Live Tree* [130], 1978, 11.4 x 7.6 (4 1/2 x 3).
88 *Judge Man* [16], 1969, 28.5 x 20 (11 1/4 x 7 7/8). ABAG, ELC, JMF, MV, PPAC, UAG, UB, UFH, UNISA.
89 *Self Defence in 1976* [117], 1976, W40.4 x 30.4 (15 7/8 x 12). JMF, MV.
90 *The First Bishop Of Doicese Of Namibia* [170], 1981, 29.9 x 21.1 (11 3/4 x 8 1/4). JMF, MV.
91 *Well Come Back At St. Mary's Mission in 1975* [111], 1975, 33.2 x 30.3 (13 x 11 7/8). AAN, ELC, JMF, MV.
92 *Forcible Love: Here there is a beautiful Girl Who is* [76], 1974, 39.2 x 50.7 (15 3/8 x 20). ELC, JMF.
93 *The Ford 250* [46], 1973, 25.8 x 33 (10 1/8 x 13). ELC, MV, PPAC, UAG, UB.
94 *Zimbabwe House: This is St. Mary's Mission Foundational Lukenge's* [107], 1975, 61.4 x 47 (24 1/8 x 18 1/2). HCAC, JAG, JMF, PPAC, UB, UNISA.
95 *No Way To Go What Can I Do?* [52], 1973, 30.6 x 25.5 (12 x 10). JMF.
96 *The Lucky Artist.* [61], 1974, 40 x 33 (15 3/4 x 13). ELC, JMF.
97 *An interview of Cape Town University in 1971.* [38], 1971, 33.9 x 40.1 (13 3/8 x 15 3/4). JMF.
98 *He is thinking about Art?* [84],1974, 40.1 x 33.2 (15 7/8 x 13). ANG, JMF.
99 *Lonely Man, Man of Man* [69], 1974, 47.9 x 45.4 (18 7/8 x 17 7/8). ELC, JAG, JMF, SCAG.
100 *Muafangejos Family* [220], 1985, 50.9 x 51.7 (20 x 20 3/8). PPAC, UAG.
101 *John's New House in Katutura at Windhoek* [253], 1987, 73.8 x 41.5 (29 x16 1/4). JMF, PPAC.
102 *Bishop R. H. Mize was well come back to Namibia* [261], 1987, 61.6 x 46.2 (24 1/4 x 18 1/8). ANG, JMF.
103 *John Mother was died* [152], 1980, 42.3 x 34.3 (16 5/8 x 13 1/2). JMF, PPAC, UAG.
104 *The Death of Chief Phillimon Elifas. [black]* [109], 1975, 60.6 x 39 (23 7/8 x 15 3/8). ANG, JMF.
105 *The Battle of Rorkes Drift* [23], 1969, 51.5 x 78 (20 1/4 x 30 3/4). ELC, UNISA.
106 *The Battle of Rorke's Drift about 1879 between Zulus and British.* [174], 1981, 44.5 x 69.2 (17 1/2 x 27 1/4). AAN, ANG, CC, HCAC, JAG, JMF, PPAC, SC, SCAG, TAG, UAG.
107 *Kuanyama Chief Mandume* [37], 1971, 25.4 x 30.5 (10 x 12). ELC.
108 *Mandume was a last chief of Kuanjama tribe* [173], 1981, 27.8 x 31.8 (10 7/8 x 12 1/2). JMF, MV.
109 *1. Bishop R. H. Mize Left Windhoek In 1968.* [131], 1978, 30.5 x 32 (12 x 12 1/2).JMF.
110 *7th Bishop of Damaraland Rt. Rev. Colin Winter, who has been* [43], 1972, 25.5 x 30.5 (10 x 12). JMF.
111 *St. Marys Mission High School Students are very thirsty* [49], 1973, 39.6 x 33.7 (15 1/2 x 13 1/4). UFH.
112 *Oniipa New Printing Press and Book Depot on 11 May 1975 [black]* [114], 1975, 63 x 47 (24 3/4 x 18 1/2). DAG, JMF, UFH.
113 *Anglican Seminary Blown Up* [177], 1981, 59.1 x 41.7 (23 1/4 x 16 3/4). JAG, JMF, SC, SCAG, TAG, UAG, UCT.
114 *Mother and Child.* [196], 1983, 48.4 x 40 (19 x 15 3/4). AAN, JMF, MV, PPAC.
115 *Man and Lady* [53], 1973, 40.6 x 35.5 (16 x 14).
116 *A Sad People* [35], 1970, 51.6 x 34 (20 1/4 x 13 3/8). AAN, ANG, ELC, JMF, JMF, MV, PPAC, UFH.
117 *The Love Is Approaching But too much of anything is Very dangerous.* [66], 1974, 39.4 x 39 (15 1/2 x 15 3/8). AAN, ANG, ELC, JMF, PPAC, UB.
118 *Thinking Man* [252], 1986, 43.8 x 28.2 (17 1/4 x 11 1/8). JMF, PPAC.
119 *A Poor Woman Without husband, children* [242], 1986, 51.6 x 34.6 (20 1/4 x 13 5/8). JMF. MV, PPAC.
120 *A Love* [40], 1972, 34.2 x 33.5 (13 1/2 x 13 1/4). ELC, JMF.
121 *Life Is Very Interesting* [orange and black] [71], 1974, W, 51.2 x 30 (20 1/8 x 11 3/4). JMF.
122 *Disadvantage Of Fighting For Men.* [95] 1974, W, 30.9 x 38.8 (12 1/16 x 15 1/4). JMF.
123 *Mother and Child 1979.* [134], 1979, 46 x 30 (18 1/8 x 11 3/4). JMF, MV, PPAC.
124 *I Wish You Well on your Way* [240], 1986, 64.8 x 26.5 (25 1/2 x 10 3/8). JMF, PPAC.

Muafangejo